Praise for Chuck Eddy's

Stairway to HELL

"In *Stairway to Hell*, heavy metal isn't just a *sound*, it's an adventure. . . . [Eddy's] exuberant metaphor-slinging and contentious spirit well suit the music he celebrates."
—**David Fricke**, *Rolling Stone*

"*Stairway's* intro alone is the most cohesive, impassioned and savvy state-of-the-art address anyone has delivered in nearly a decade. . . . A breath of hot air that provides a glimmer of hope for genuine discourse." —**Deborah Frost**, *LA Weekly*

"*Stairway to Hell* catalogues the 500 best heavy-metal albums in the universe with such droll wit that the titles and the bands hardly matter. They're simply fodder for the 100-m.p.h. spewing of Eddy, who makes the topic interesting. Essential . . . for the attitude." —*The Philadelphia Inquirer*

"Brushing aside notions of rock as civic forum or cultural subversion, Eddy cranks his prose up to warp 11 and breaks on through to a universe where ageless troglodytes and Spandex-draped satyrs stomp their hands and clap their feet to airy strains of noxious guitar ooze."
—**Howard Hampton**, *Minneapolis City Pages*

"Eddy writes with a humor and irreverence that's more fitting to rock and roll than most straight-faced critical diatribes."
—**Mike Rubin**, *Newsday*

Stairway to HELL

THE 500 BEST HEAVY METAL ALBUMS IN THE UNIVERSE

Updated Edition

by Chuck Eddy

DA CAPO PRESS • NEW YORK

First Da Capo Press Edition 1998

This Da Capo Press paperback edition of *Stairway to Hell* is an updated edition of the one first published in New York in 1991, with a new introductory essay and one hundred additional reviews. It is reprinted by arrangement with the author.

Published by Da Capo Press, Inc., A Subsidiary of Plenum Publishing Corporation, 233 Spring Street, New York, N.Y. 10013

All Rights Reserved

Manufactured in the United States of America

Designed by Nancy Kenmore

Library of Congress Cataloging-in-Publication Data

Eddy, Chuck.
    Stairway to hell: the 500 best heavy metal albums in the universe / by Chuck Eddy.—Updated ed.
        p.   cxm.
    First published 1991.
    Includes index.
    ISBN 0-306-80817-X (alk. paper)
    1. Heavy metal (Music)—Discography. 2. Heavy metal (Music)—History and criticism. 3. Rock groups. I. Title.
ML156.4.R6E3   1998
781.66—dc21   97-47312
                                                           CIP
                                                            MN

For Martina, Linus,
and Cordelia
. . . .

CONTENTS

An OVERVIEW of OVERKILL

The turbulence that calls itself "heavy metal," or the best of it anyway, is a triumph of vulgarity, velocity, verbal directness, violent apathy, conceptual simplicity, pissed-off punkitude, adolescent overeating. Once upon a time, for years and years and years, it was the one place financially and familially and fornicatively frustrated post-pube brats (musically inclined or otherwise) could turn to vent their drunken distress or hear others approximate the same. (Misery loves company.) Best of all, metallic heaviosity had NO REDEEMING SOCIAL VALUE, and it was real *loud* about it and funny too, and sometimes (once in a while) it still is. Metal bands, when their riffs and wails hit the target, are true independent voices, oblivious to trends, unconcerned with what the intelligentsia thinks about 'em, rocking 'cause it'll help 'em get rich or famous or laid, mutating and innovating with nobody taking notes.

Until recently, rock criticism always fostered a kind of elitism against this common man's fanfare, rejecting it as mere stylized pseudorebellion, nothing but plodding volume. Supposedly the music has no subtlety or melody or movement, hurts people's ears, exhibits delusions of grandeur, and says mean things about women. All of which are true on occasion, and some of which even make a difference now and then, but none of which apply across the board. Like people who criticize any genre as a genre, people who criticize metal as a genre are mostly people who've never really listened to the stuff. It really *doesn't* "all sound the same"—running the gamut from robust to emaciated, fast to slow, raw to slick, stiff to polyrhythmic, pop to free-form, transcendent to useless, by now it's more varied than any other white-rock genre. Music can accomplish stuff it doesn't set out to accomplish; it succeeds best on a level that's more subconscious than self-conscious. So crass intentions help blockheads on the make leak humanity, because crass intentions give the people what they want and what they want is what they need, and only a blind man would deny that metal's blessed with a mother lode of crass. "Flair for language" is what rock 'n' roll rebelled *against*, and it's more honest to admit your IQ's no eighth-wonder-of-the-world than to pretend you've got something new or poetic to say when really you don't. This is just common sense.

The metal I love most strikes me as pretty darn smart, but quite a bit of the okay stuff's always made something of a virtue out of its dumbness. At a time when rock criticism was being born of the milieu that proclaimed *Sgt. Pepper* a masterpiece, metal was rising from the humble ashes of mid-sixties garage-rock; it was the hippies' little brothers' music, and it flew in the face of every hypocrisy the

1

Summer of Love had established. Born in automobile factories, emphasizing technological tentacles over the human voice, produced above football stadium Astroturf by wah-wah pedals and fuzzboxes and stacks of amps, mass-produced by seedy businessmen in ivory towers, reproducing itself in eternal reverb and redundancy as solos and leads looped into feedback and pushed songs past the seven-minute mark, feeding faceless and presumably mindless hordes of acned and sopored parking-lot youths, metal was the music of industry, a capitalist con-job that repudiated the ecological flower-child dream. It was sexist, fascist, decadent, pompous, superstitious, amoral, puerile, and tuneless. Ugliest of all, it made sixties snobs feel old.

Me, I'm a seventies snob, married with two kids, and I'm beginning to understand how those sixties snobs felt. But I'm not so old that I'd start disparaging metal as "juvenile." The charge is absurd, unless you're one of those schmucks who denigrates cream-of-the-crop Archies or Abba or A Flock of Seagulls as "too commercial," in which case you'd best get your long-haired butt off this bus while you've still got one to sit on. Teens (mostly working-class Anglo-Saxon teen males) have always been metal's bread and butter, and the style's greatest contribution has come from capturing the antics and dilemmas of this consumer demographic on vinyl—in "I'm Eighteen," "Rock and Roll All Nite," "Surrender," "Dance the Night Away," Metallica's "Fade to Black." Metal's preoccupation with doing the wild thing stems from the biological fact that postpube males are so single-mindedly interested in getting laid. And in the eighties, a decade when even the Top 40 kept threatening to succumb to the tired tastes of ladder-climbing baby-boomers with plenty dinero to keep the advertisers hopping, the presence of an explicitly immature sound like metal (just like rap and post-Madonna bubblesalsa) was hardly something to lament.

HM's long been chastised for its misogynous and/or authoritarian lyrical slant; this slant used to bug me a lot, but now I wonder how I could ever have taken the shit so seriously. To be offended, you've gotta put the stuff on some pedestal where it neither deserves nor asks to be put. The one thing I've learned from Tipper Gore (and Axl Rose, and Public Enemy!) is that it makes no sense to judge popular entertainment against some kind of ethical litmus test, by which I mean left-wing "political correctness" no less than right-wing "moral propriety." What matters aesthetically is not whether Ted Nugent's "Wang Dang Sweet Poontang" or AC/DC's "What Do You Do for Money Honey" reveal a certain dehumanization of women, but whether they do so with some kind of fearless conviction. When since Leadbelly's time *hasn't* great rock 'n' roll expressed repulsive ideas? It's part of the game, man.

It helps to be born with a sense of humor, I guess. If dominance and submission are what inspired Blue Öyster Cult and Accept to craft superlative sludge, who am I to knock it? The stinkeroo comes when bands hyperbolize their womanhate to the point of camp (as with Tipper's fave raves the Mentors), or when the nihilism gets completely rote and ritualistic (as with Judas Priest, not to mention morbid multitudes of bandwagon thrash-Satanists). But the pissant me-against-the-world "Republicans-suck" protests of countless hardcore-crossover brats are no less reprehensible. It ain't so much what the music says that matters, in other words; it's *how* it says it. And as idiotic as metal gets sometimes, it's no more guilty of feigning passions than any other genus of hootenanny.

Which brings us to the authenticity question—a red herring if ever there was one—and more importantly, to the question of pretension. Obviously, the Moog organ and *The Lord of the Rings* and the God of Dry Ice begat a heap of medieval melodrama and sci-fi schmaltz in metal in the seventies; most of this noble nonsense deserves no apology. But Led Zeppelin and Metallica have used grand-scale flourishes to add anthemic weight to Brontosauran crunch, and when used as a metaphorical language, Arthurian archaisms are not inherently meaningless; to my ears, Metallica's mystical teen-violence epics "Welcome Home (Sanitarium)" and "Fade to Black" communicate more unforced human feeling, and are therefore *less* pretentious, than any narcissistic/ironic grad-school poesy you're liable to hear from the Pixies or 10,000 Maniacs in this lifetime, not to mention any simulated granola-bar innocence the alleged authenticians in the Cowboy Junkies or Robert Cray Band might toss your way. Not all metal tries to loom so large, though, or even to show off musicianly "technique"—in the eighties, you'd've been hard-pressed to find a rock act less gaudy than those riffin' minimalists in AC/DC.

But enough excuses. If you agreed with the liars, you wouldn't be reading the book, wouldja? So let's talk history, and first let's get one thing straight: None of this junk would exist if it weren't for music by black people. The tools of the HM trade—distortion, feedback, amplification (electrical energy in general, in fact), guitars as penis-extensions, sympathy for the devil, barks at the moon, so on and so forth—were harnessed by African Americans like T-Bone Walker and Robert Johnson and Charlie Christian and Howlin' Wolf and Screamin' Jay Hawkins and Ike Turner and Johnny Guitar Watson and Otis Rush and Bo Diddley back when most every white boy 'cept Link Wray (an American Indian, anyhow) sang like Eddie Fisher. You won't read much about these combatants in this book 'cause blues devoid of suburbanite sequins do nothing for me, but it's important you know the names in case anybody asks. Before heavy metal was called heavy metal, it was called "white blues." The people who called it that were primarily white bluesmen.

In the mid-sixties, such British and American garage-band singles as the Who's "My Generation" and the Kinks' "All Day and All of the Night" and the Sonics' "Cinderella" and the Count Five's "Psychotic Reaction" funneled all that hot primeval R&B guitarwork in a direction Clapton/Page/Beck would pick up on in famous classic-rock-station-destined superhypes like Cream, the Yardbirds, and Led Zeppelin. Jimi

Hendrix happened in here somewhere too, as did such din-busters as Blue Cheer and the Velvet Underground and the entire population of metro Detroit; in a sense, HM peaked "artistically" (ha ha) before it even existed.

Giants walked the earth in those days. 1970–73 were the Years of Sludge, the years you could open your copy of *CREEM* or *Phonograph Record Magazine* and read future Angry Samoan Mike Saunders or future Delinquent Lester Bangs (or somebody else!) sing the praises of Alice Cooper's *Killer* or *Love It to Death*, Black Sabbath's *Paranoid* or *Master of Reality*, Zep's *III* or *Zoso*, Deep Purple's *Fireball* or *Machine Head*, Uriah Heep's *Look at Yourself* or *Demons and Wizards*, BÖC's *Blue Öyster Cult* or *Tyranny and Mutation*, Grand Funk Railroad's *Closer to Home* or *Live Album*, Mountain's *Climbing* or *Nantucket Sleighride*. Not to mention obscure stuff by Atomic Rooster and UFO, Bang and Budgie and Black Pearl and Bull Angus, Head over Heels and Highway Robbery and Nitzinger and Sir Lord Baltimore and Dust, all of which would disappear off the edge of the horizon before Donald Duck could count up to Jack Robinson. This was a time of snowplow quagmires and speed-freak excesses, with major labels snatching up every trio of un-haircut degenerates whose stink they could sniff out, only to see most of 'em never graduate from their respective close-to-home club scenes to the hockey rinks of Valhalla. Nitzinger had about as much chance of being Cream as the Shadows of Knight had of being the Stones, and they sold even less vinyl (but the message was familiar: mainly, "Fuck off and die"). By the time I entered high school in late '73, metal was kinda sorta already *over*.

And it was kinda sorta not, at least from a salability standpoint. Because what the starched shirts in the record industry's penthouses learned quickly, and it is a lesson they take heed of to this very day, is that once one headbang generation has had its fill, another generation is just sitting down to the table. And since that new generation will probably not wanna eat exactly what their older siblings ate, and because the cycle is eternal, marketing strategists can revitalize and/or redundify the headbang appetite (preferably in watered-down form) almost annually merely by stamping labels like "New!" and "Improved!" on the cereal box.

Which is not as awful as it sounds, because in rock 'n' roll, trumped-up newness and improvedness is where real newness and improvedness sprouts its seeds. Once heavy metal finally took its name (to distinguish itself from "hard rock," which at the time anyway was more blues-oriented rather than orchestra-oriented, plus its clothes were more normal, or at least that's how the theory went), there were *rules*, like f'rinstance no more timbales or letter sweaters. But rules are made to be eaten so they'll turn into bile and bullshit and big bucks, and the years between Nixon and Reagan produced any number of acts worth recalling for distinctions major and minor.

Like for example: Aerosmith (funky), the New York Dolls (campy), Mott the Hoople (literate), Kiss (made-up), Heart (female), Boston (squeaky-clean and systematic), Ted Nugent (carnivorous and manually dexterous), Queen (homoerotically symphonic), Bachman-Turner Overdrive (fat, workman-like Canucks), ZZ Top (fat, bearded Texans), Cheap Trick (well-dressed Chicago comedians), Black Oak Arkansas (hillbillies with washboards), Thin Lizzy (black Irish Springsteenesque singer), Foreigner (Junior Walker on sax), et cetera. This was the era of David Bowie and Bobby Riggs, so some of these combos chose to dress up like girls (thus inducing much concern amidst the adult populace). But most of 'em (even the girls) opted instead to establish an image as "just regular guys," and the band who proved most able at said task was some jokers called Foghat, whose primary distinction derives from the fact that they were so damn, well, *Foghat-like*. If you were there, you know what I'm talking about.

Truth be told, several of these seventies heroes and heroines really had nothing to do with heavy metal, but then, as girlie-disco theorist Frank Kogan has astutely pointed out, "*heavy metal* has nothing to do with heavy metal." After you've heard *Paranoid*, everything else seems more like prog-rock or glam-rock or powerpop or boogie or punk rock or boho noise or AOR jizz, right? In October 1979, with young phenoms like Starz and Angel floundering at the box office, Richard Johnson declared in *CREEM* that heavy metal had run its course and would no longer prosper as we had come to know it.

In October 1980, Richard Johnson declared in *CREEM* that heavy metal had pulled a Jesus Christ and was back in the saddle again. Seems those fickle Brits had traded in their porkpie hats for leather and chains, and there was suddenly this "New Wave" of metal overseas, all these bands (Saxon, Sampson, Marseille, Girl, Diamondhead) that everybody forgot about real quick, plus Iron Maiden and Def Leppard, who either inexplicably or explicably (depends on your point of view) would thrive forever. The eighties got pretty weird after that—everything kept going back and forth, and punk rock (which from its Ramones/Pistols gitgo was just ninety percent speeded-up metal anyway) had a lot to do with it. As did MTV, a song-oriented visual medium that meant a return to energetic young faces (more appealing than sleepy old ones) and tighter song structures than HM had ever known. In shorthand: Glam again.

Quiet Riot and Britny Fox covered Slade, Shrapnel and Joan Jett covered Gary Glitter, Krokus covered The Sweet, Mötley Crüe covered Brownsville Station, Great White covered Ian Hunter. Crüe and Twisted Sister and Hanoi Rocks borrowed cosmetic tips from Alice Cooper and the New York Dolls and football shouts from Slade, and ex-Runaways returned in droves. Ratt did a video with Milton Berle, who useta wear women's clothes. None of these bands gave a shit about *Paranoid;* in a sense, none of 'em gave a shit about heavy metal. In 1973, none of 'em would've even been considered a heavy metal band. In the eighties they defined the term.

By 1984, music calling itself heavy metal was dominating a major portion of the airwaves, and it was so "unmetal" that top guns Van Halen could cross over to disco stations with it. You could savor the fact that at least Def Lep's "Rock of Ages" wasn't the adult-contemporary-with-guitars-instead-of-violins that REO Speedwagon and Prism had topped the AOR charts with in '82. Or you could complain that, as with all subcultures wild and ragged, metal was being tamed by the profit-makers, falling prey first to twenty-four-track engineering and chainsaw codpieces, then finally degenerating into a neutered self-love sham perpetrated by prancing poodles in Bozo the Clown eyeliner. You started to figure Poison and Cinderella took time out from their accountant meetings and pouting lessons only to add an audience-loathing idea or two to their *packaging*. Mass showbiz, fashion without substance, who needed it? Stryper, your average streetgang of born-agains in shags; this was the last straw.

Only not exactly. "Real" metal riffs had been plundered all decade long by post punk hardcore and artcore auteurs in Manhattan and Manchester and the Midwest and on California's SST Records, among other places, and by '84 a genuine indie-label metal "underground," with fanzines and bands named Acid and Anthrax and Armored Saint and Bitch and Venom, was getting along just fine thank you beyond FM's confines. As several AC/DC and Motörhead LPs attest, punk and metal had been swapping genes approximately forever. Graph their time lines, you'll end up with a double helix. But the subterranean speedmetal/thrash craze had 'em ending their petty cold war once and for all, and before you knew it, Slayer and Megadeth were ascending *Billboard*'s album chart in the wake of an '86 hat trick that saw three simultaneous Metallica records scoring top-200 spots. Rejected by more mainstream hairspray-fans, speedmetal split the metal congregation into two very distinct denominations; resurrecting the stamina of garage-era metal, speeding it past comprehension, discarding flash, and incorporating Ü-turns-at-ninety learned from old Mahavishnu LPs, it fostered a democratic sort of insurrection that refused to fade into the background behind the CD player and sushi bar. By 1987, over-the-top HM seemed more plentiful and revolutionary than at anytime since 1972.

But it, too, grew old. Blueslessly celibate to begin with, loaded with blood and guts but no flesh, thrash proved scared of its own shadow, so afraid to "compromise" its pittance's worth of "integrity" that it shut out the rest of the world and turned into a perfectly predictable self-parody in record time. Hooks and beats and prose weren't permitted unless they were constricted to arbitrary specifications believed to be connected to a single personality trait (you know, "anger") that rock 'n' roll had once upon a time allowed to emerge of its own accord, and it all turned into a bogus pseudoprogressive symphony-parody (like W.A.S.P. or Europe, only faster), and the Manhattan/Midwest/SST undergrounds followed suit, or (worse) they all descended into two-bit performance-art professionalism. Which, oddly enough, left room for the fake stuff.

Throughout a significant portion of 1987, half of the Top 10 pop LP chart was clogged up by

Poison and Mötley Crüe and Bon Jovi and Def Leppard and Whitesnake, "false metal" bands all. Yet another generation of normal, disaffected, not-quite-wealthy white kids selected yet more troubadors to pass down a more-diminished-than-ever version of the mass-entertainment myth billing itself as the rock 'n' roll life and cynically masquerading as disobedience to dumb authority. Or something like that. False metal demonstrated that, as the outcome of two decades of research and development, it's got good points (tight catchy snagability, not much screechy histrionics, no Moogs, not much wankeroo) to counter its bad points (drums without beats, indenti-kit hooks, no noise, not much wankeroo). Derivative and unspontaneous, the groups stole from Foreigner, Elton John, T. Rex, the Sex Pistols, everybody. The words tended toward penis envy and ain't-we-dangerous, and the musicians mostly concerned themselves with how they *looked*. But if a consenting man wants to go out in public wearing a consenting woman's spandex, that's his business.

The next couple years saw big labels peddling a profusion of funk-based hard rock groups (most notably Living Coloür), tattooed seventies-boogie revivalists (most notably the Cult), and, in the Beastie Boys' megabuck wake, thrash-rappers (Anthrax's *I'm the Man* went gold, spawning a bunch of self-contained whiteboy bands with full-time rappers instead of singers). Guns N' Roses, by any measure the biggest and best of the new breed, unleashed an astounding debut that owes more to Janis Joplin and Bo Diddley than to Deep Purple. "Metal" 's where record stores filed it.

In 1988, our nation's humble rock critics placed a world-record four metal LPs, three of 'em (by Jane's Addiction, Living Coloür, Metallica) barely above average, in the *Village Voice* Pazz and Jop Top 40, hinting that HM's respectability quotient was flying higher than it ever had at precisely the moment when high-volume riffs were feeling more comatose than they'd felt for a whole quarter-century. Has-beens like David Bowie and Queen and ex–Sex Pistol Steve Jones started busting metal-wise moves, and post-metal continued to fission like an amoeba, awaiting the day when it would simply fizz into oblivion like an Alka Seltzer.

Loud rock's self-cautious arty/progressive wing, which suddenly was being taken way too seriously by people who apparently figured it was better than nothing, commenced to subdivide into a conceptualist faction (Queensrÿche, Savatage, Riot, Metallica) and an eclectic faction (King's X, Jane's Addiction, Faith No More, 24-7 Spyz). Distinctions mainly appeared to be ones of influence (Pink Floyd/late Styx vs. P-Funk/early Genesis) and irony (the eclectics had it, the conceptualists didn't); anointed artistes like Living Coloür and newly bombastic "cyberpunk" faves Voivod straddled both camps, punk grandkids from Vertigo to Ministry to Last Exit jockeyed around the fringes, just about everybody worshiped at the altars of paradiddle and songlength and character development. And not one of these new eggheadbangers had half as much to say or a fifth as much fun as Def Leppard or Kix.

It wouldn't be all that surprising if loud guitar-band rock never successfully communicates perturbed self-affirmation or self-destruction again. I've got my great white hopes (Extreme, Love/Hate, Electric Angels), you've no doubt got yours, but the bottom line suggests that, by now, all this rage comes way too easy; we take it for granted. Then again, if he hasn't already, Axl Rose could turn out to be the new Bob Dylan, which might even turn out to be a good thing. ("Many people hate Bob Dylan because they hate being fooled"—Ellen Willis, 1967.)

The candy kisses Axl mailed to the girls of America on *Appetite for Destruction* and *Lies* were permission for male hard rockers to start sounding enticing and vulnerable, and as the eighties took their curtain call, hearing lonely ballads like White Lion's "When the Children Cry" and Bon Jovi's "I'll Be There for You" and Cinderella's "Coming Home," you felt the singers' relief as they finally inhaled air they'd been walled off from, as they released ether that'd too long been trapped. Churchy vocals and sustained flutters and instinctual hooks surged from a couple miles back, and the confused perspective made the compassion larger than life, raw enough for cats but dreamy enough for chicks, the summer of '42 or '69 and the fair's just come to town. The formula comes from the Eagles, or Boston, or maybe Peter Frampton. With other metal bands learning lessons from hip-hop and using all sorts of music that metal bands aren't supposed to use, everything from string sections (Electric Angels, L.A. Guns) to found-sound jackhammer-and-national-anthem musique concrète (Slaughter's amazing "Up All Night"), can disco-metal be far behind? (See page 216.)

BEWARE *of the* DOG

Okay, here's where I explain to you how I decided to include what I included, what qualified and what didn't. Genre-naming equals corporate categorization equals a shortcut to false order, so for your benefit and my sanity the standard I've used in defining "heavy metal" was necessarily open-minded. Basically, I include all (decent) loud-guitar squashing-ears-like-bugs brain-damage that could *conceivably* (theoretically) appeal to a heavy metal audience, not just observers-of-arbitrary-dress-code already accepted by said crowd. Everybody else's definition changes annually, I decided, so the only sensible way to handle the predicament was to make eligible for *Stairway to Hell* all extant wax that would've been considered metal at any time in HM's elongated life span, *whether said wax was considered metal at the time of release or not*. The only exception was the Rolling Stones, who cannot be heavy metal because, well, they're the Rolling Stones. And so are the Clash.

So we've got a mid-eighties Bad Brains album that would've been called heavy in 1969, early seventies New York Dolls albums that would've been called heavy in 1988, a Teena Marie album that'd be accepted with open arms by all headbangers in the perfect universe of my imagination (which exists in metal's life span because *I* do!), all sorts of surprises. When dealing with acts with a mere tangential relationship to metal (Neil Young, Prince, Miles Davis, Lynyrd Skynyrd, Hüsker Dü, et cetera), I accept only records where at least half the songs *sound* sufficiently metallic (which is to say these might not necessarily be said acts' best discs, only their loudest, though o'course the two do overlap as often as not); when dealing with guys and gals "normally" classified as metal (Led Zep, Guns N' Roses, Manowar, et cetera), I accept everything, whether it sounds "metal" to me or not, as long as it's good enough. (It should be noted here that several bands considered "metal" by nonmetallers—Bon Jovi, Rush, Living Coloür—are considered "nonmetal" by metallers. I usually give 'em the benefit of the doubt. It's only fair.)

Since the stuff's still available in used stores and cut-out bins and specialty racks if you hunt around for it (what with this CD baloney, old vinyl's a buyer's market), and since if there's justice in the world it'll all be reissued soon on CD or otherwise anyway, I include out-of-print LPs and imports as well as in-print domestics, cassette-only releases, and twelve-inch EPs as well as LPs. You don't have to be a star to be in my show—better great obscurities than half-assed commonplaces, right? (CD-only releases were eligible, too, but none of 'em were good enough. The fact that I didn't own a CD player when I wrote most of this volume had nothing to do with it, I swear.) Entries list the earliest known label of release and year of issue, plus the year(s) of recording for reissues, plus the configuration-type for any recording that's not an LP. EPs are defined as any record with three or more songs but less than twenty-five minutes of music, cassettes as anything that'll fit more comfortably in a tape player than on a turntable. Seven-inch EPs weren't eligible, 'cause I had to draw the line somewhere, but they're included with seven-inch and twelve-inch singles in a list on page 212.

To avoid redundancy, as much as feasible I left out albums (e.g., Aerosmith's *Get Your Wings*) whose worthy tracks are already included on preferable albums otherwise listed (in *Get Your Wing*'s case, on *Gems* and *Aerosmith's Greatest Hits*.) Records released after August 1, 1990, missed my deadline. And as for the sounds that survived the final cut, they're listed in order of merit, from top to bottom. But you would've figured that out on your own, I bet.

Stairway to
HELL

1. LED ZEPPELIN

Zoso Atlantic, 1971

This music holds nothing back. The angriest punk rock was never as balls-out as "Rock and Roll" or "When the Levee Breaks," the most idyllic doo-wop never as sweet as "Going to California" or "Stairway to Heaven." *Zoso* expresses the full range of human emotion; you cannot feel ambivalent about it; you cannot like it "just a little." It's got finesse and weirdness and newness and noise and funk, it makes you sweat and makes you groove, it's the same as sex, it stops time and history and seems to last hours, it's what the blues could never be. So it makes people uneasy: Ten-years-plus after the Sex Pistols, almost everyone who ever liked punk rock "likes" Led Zeppelin, but almost nobody likes "Stairway to Heaven." The band's other music they can stay detached from; they can like it as camp, as something stupid and cute and quaint and naive. "Stairway" doesn't give them that luxury.

Zoso demonstrates Zep's willingness, unparalleled in the rock annals, to fool around with form-as-form: "Black Dog" is a rope-burning shipwreck of rut-in-search-of-estrus, "Misty Mountain Hop" an angular depiction of a country boy's acid-altered awe on his first trip to San Francisco, "Four Sticks" the treadmill at the end of the rainbow, and though any of the three would leave your head spinning anywhere else, here they're overshadowed by monstrous myths and lissome legends that deserve credit for inspiring Prince and Sonic Youth far more than they deserve blame for encouraging Kingdom Come and Whitesnake. This band got away with murder—only Parliament-Funkadelic, who fell on their faces far more often, owns an oeuvre of comparable scope and variety. But where for years P-Funk's audience wasn't much more than a cult, Led Zeppelin was the most popular rock band in the world.

Some people despised the way Zep bleached the blues white and pocketed starving black men's royalties all the way to the bank. Others hated Robert Plant's voice, said he sang like a Martian or a guitar or an anorexic fop. Their shows were supposedly "impersonal" fascist indoctrination sessions, or something

like that, and it's well documented that they did disgusting things with sharks and black magic. But I'd argue that Zep's modus operandi was basically honest; eschewing the easy-way-out purist regurgitation of Britain's late-sixties blues revival, they sounded white because they *were* white, and I doubt anybody without a conflict of interest would deny that their "When the Levee Breaks" makes mincemeat of Memphis Minnie's version (from '29, available on *Roots of Rock* on Yazoo Records if you wanna compare). Zep's zillions of fraudulent imitators, just like P-Funk's or the Velvet Underground's, only confirm their greatness. Yet the splendiferous immediacy of the sound has never been matched, and never will be.

The fundamentalists are right: This music, by any biblical standard, should be illegal. It is a golden calf. If you have a heart, a brain, a soul, an ass, a set of gonads, it will change your life. In "Rock and Roll," Robert Plant sings *about* rock 'n' roll, alluding to "Book of Love" and the stroll, but that's subsidiary; the sound *is* rock 'n' roll, it rewrites the dictionary, curses anyone who won't accept the new way. While John Bonham's thunderbolts and Jimmy Page's cloudbursts of guitar-storm cascade from above, you cannot care about any other music, any other people, any better life you might be living, any better world you might help make. *Zoso* is a jealous god, it will accept no competition, it demands that you devote your life to it. "Open your arms, open your arms, open your arms," Plant screams; next, in "The Battle of Evermore," he's crooning about the "prince of peace," and the sound's gorgeous; it's a mass, a place of worship. With Sandy Denny from Fairport Convention at his side, Robert takes up the offering ("ohnow ohnow ohnow ohnow bringit bringit bringit"), which adds up to billions.

Then comes Holy Communion. "Stairway to Heaven" might be a song about a rich woman buying clothes at Bloomingdale's, who knows, who cares. Everybody I know has been sick of this epic warhorse for years; Robert Plant himself, when I talked to him—like Irving Berlin disowning "Alexander's Ragtime Band" as a funeral march in 1925—called it "that bloody wedding song." Me, I can't stomach the live "does anyone remember laughter" version, but the studio "Stairway" was the most famous song in Western Civilization in the seventies because it was the *best* song in Western Civilization in the seventies, or real close. It's constructed *as* a stairway, with four steps; on every subsequent one, the music gets louder, and you can either turn the volume higher or turn the radio off. If you vote "yeah," to reach the top step, the altar, you will do anything.

If "Stairway to Heaven" is how you get there, "When the Levee Breaks" is how you get back. It, too, is a procession, a stairway with hundreds of steps (someday I'll count 'em), and they're the most massive drumbeats the world will ever know. "Cryin' won't help ya, prayin' won't do ya no good," you're told; it's too fucking late, you've cast your ballot, you should've thought about that before we left home. "Goin' down, goin' *down* now, goin' down, goin' *down* now," the cantor intones over and over: "When the Levee Breaks" is the Stairway to hell.

2. GUNS N' ROSES
. . . .
Appetite for Destruction Geffen, 1987

Sick and sexist Robert Williams's rape-by-robots scene was on the uncensored (and now very expensive) original sleeve, so boycotting puritans predictably shivered behind their high horses, but then when I say this scraggly-as-sin (and interracial?) funkmetal five-some smoke movingly and unboundingly, I'm not saying I'd want 'em to eat dinner at my house (I'd sooner invite Suzanne Vega—she'd probably eat less!). Not only don't they cover their tattoos and needle tracks with mommy's panty hose, they've got the world's most hondo (and, real often, most gorgeous) whiskey-river twin-ax attack, and, wonder of wonders, they *can actually keep a beat*—one that swings harder than Bobby Brown and Big Daddy Kane and Jody Watley combined.

Though "Out ta Get Me," "You're Crazy," and "Anything Goes" are more or less crap, "Welcome to the Jungle," "Nightrain," "Mr. Brownstone," "Think About You," and "Rocket Queen" (hard rock's an-

swer to Donna Summer's "Love to Love You Baby") burn first and crash later. And as "Sweet Child o' Mine" proved throughout the summer of '88 as its valentine verses fluttered down with more nail-tough beauty than in any Stones or 'Smith ballad ever, GnR attained *both* emotional extremes (not just the nasty one). Way-sloppy zero-perimeter long-song Delta doo-dah that takes *Exile* Stones to a sonic realm where dance-rock equals Aerosmith plus Skynyrd (and supposedly Zep, though I don't hear it) minus gray matter, sometimes *Appetite* needs an editor, and initially I figured Axl's screech killed Steve Marriot/Janis Joplin by overdoing it. But watching him drop inhibitions and shake groove-thang on stage like no white man since before disco sucked, watching him show Terence Trent D'Arby what a hardened slut with happy feet and a soulful heart really looks like, watching him vibrate outrageous and obscene, he reminded me what live rock 'n' roll could be, and his overdoing it made everyone else seem insignificant. When you're high you never ever wanna come down.

More and more, especially now that 1990's "Civil War" has made its stake as the "A Hard Rain's A-Gonna Fall" of the Iraq Age, encapsulating a point in history almost by accident, melding ambiguity and sensationalism and corny social concern into a gigantic nihilist/antinihilist metaphor, I can't help thinking of Bob Dylan. Axl in 1987, as much and maybe more than Dylan in 1963, came from an unexpected place, pushing further and gambling more than anybody else, so much that at first you just wanted him to go away. You hated his voice at first, and you couldn't separate the sweetness from the apocalypse, and even the nastiness seemed like a joke, and if every song was its own animal, which it was, what difference did it make? But Axl made his presence felt, maybe even in our dreams. He mind-fucked in lyrics and in interviews and in concert, did flip-flops that made similar moves by Neil Young and Prince seem timid, put good and bad ideas in people's heads. He suggested possibilities that, in hard rock, at least, nobody had ever considered, or everybody had forgotten about, or given up hope for. Ambitious garage bands thirsty for more than mere campus respectability picked up on certain of Guns N' Roses' ideas, turning heavy metal back into rock 'n' roll, or at least pointing it in the right direction. So GnR are the '65 Stones too. Obviously.

Cynics might argue that this band would be better if Axl could learn to write more literate lyrics, but that's only to say he's artless—he knows the overall atmosphere is what matters most, but he's also coined and radio-tested more archetypal every-man-for-himself/the world-is-a-trap proverbs than any antisocialist evangelist his age, and his incidental side-disses on *A for D* surpass David Johansen's on the New York Dolls' debut album, no small accomplishment. Sometimes it seems that all the guy really wants is to get back to the womb he started from. Then again, what with a libretto that details ugly uses for turned-around bitches with panties at knees and rumps in debris, what with collective lawbreak records longer than Slash's third leg, it's no wonder sensitive souls who confuse ethics with aesthetics find the stardom of such ill-mannered pelvis-weapon dumbshits reprehensible. Myself, all I can say is it's about fucking time, and I hope the dumbshits don't stop now.

3. ALICE COOPER
Greatest Hits Warner Bros., 1974; rec. 1971–74

What's documented here is Alice's great hard-rock mean, as represented by "Is It My Body" 's transactional analysis gibberish and "Elected" 's Watergate maneuver and "Muscle of Love" 's Sabbath sleaze. What's not documented are his/their extremes, and I don't miss the psychotronic symphonies of *Killer* and *Love It to Death* half as much as I miss the eventual Muppet Show trilogy ("Only Women Bleed"/"I Never Cry"/"You And Me"). Nonetheless, this is the most hook-intensive collection of hammerhead rock you'll ever hear. By any stretch of the imagination, these smasheroos were what normal Nixon-era tykes who needed Stones-type aggression opted for, and two big reasons, of course, are the unanimously lauded *pièces de résistance*. One of which ("School's Out") makes more sense than anything ever has, or could,

from June till August ("We got no class/We got no principles/We got no innocence/Can't even think of a word that rhymes" seemed Mensa-worthy about five different ways back at Our Lady of Refuge), the other of which ("I'm Eighteen") does the same from September till May.

In a sense, Alice's most important contribution may have been to demonstrate (again) that rock 'n' roll's got origins that stretch way beyond country and blues into supposedly more respectable regions of electronic media and vaudeville variety, a notion that apparently offends purist pundits more because it's blasphemy than because it's false. Here, reducing the rockola to showbiz schmaltz (lotsa movie stars on the cover) proves more amusing than annoying, and good taste would just gum up the works. Without those corny cinematic orchestrations, "Desperado" would fall off its horse. Anybody who's not humored by "Billion Dollar Babies" should've been aborted, "Teenage Lament '74" tosses awkward doo-wop at growing pains as accurately as anything by Dion, and the blatant insincerity of "Under My Wheels" and "Be My Lover" is so fetching Detroit saw fit to adopt the chump after all. If he never caught up with punk, at least Alice cut "No More Mr. Nice Guy," autobiographical self-pity that plays mozzarella to "Public Image" 's sharp cheddar. Mainly, though, if cynical scams can't be considered capital-A Art in oligopoly capitalism, what can?

4. AEROSMITH
. . . .
Toys in the Attic Columbia, 1975

Five skinny guys speed off New England's streets with the sleaziest and sassiest set of sex-swagger ever assembled, hauling in almost a million dollars a month in the process. From the startgate the frustration and fury dash so dang fast; after this, punk couldn't possibly have mattered, no way. Usually when people call music "haunting" they mean it's already dead (like a ghost, I guess), but "Toys in the Attic," the opening cut, haunts like something *within* you, your Catholic upbringing making your heart race amphetaminesque as you're prone in bed at three A.M. after watching *Rosemary's Baby* on the late flick, and reason flew out the window at midnight. Two tracks later, original sin: "back when Cain was able, way before the stable," Eve eats Adam's apple, it's "love at first bite." Steve Tyler's snake, like Bull Moose Jackson's before, is a big ten-inch, but when some wisenheimer in my tenth-grade Oral (har har) Communications class record-pantomimed that his was just as long, he flunked.

"Walk This Way" gets high school right: an outrageous defjam boast-toast of psychosexual discovery, a zitkid eyeing three skimpy skirts in a gym locker room then swapping spit with the skirt next door. As Steve Tyler relates said soliloquy, the only other sounds you hear are a herky-jerky bass line, its congruent rhythm guitar line, and some proto-gogo cowbells; afterward, Joe Perry lays into one of his trademark greasy Strat riffs, depicting said kiss. In "Sweet Emotion," the rabbit dies; in "No More No More," you live at night; everywhere, clothes make the man. James Brownian thrusts get harnessed into call-and-response rhythmetal, into folksongs and tokesongs for basement-bound bong-blowers. "Round and Round" drops the Godzilla-rock neutron bomb, destroys your dad, but leaves the stadium standing. In the end, Tyler, on laryngitis and on bloodstained baby grand, takes a generation under his wing, crying.

5. KIX
. . . .
Kix Atlantic, 1981

Thoroughly indoctrinated with every last four-minute hack-riffed ripsnorter ever to weasel its way onto Baltimore AOR in the late seventies, these five rug rats emerged from the woodwork dressed like Ramones yet scratching a sort of adolescent itch that outsiders immediately identified as "metal." I have no idea what their intention was, but legend has it they covered AC/DC songs back-to-back with Clash ones in their shows, and that makes 'em ahead of their time by six years at least. None of which really explains why this record is so undeniable. Let's just say Donnie Purnell's puns are as corny as the cereal his band's named after, and the guitars are even funnier (e.g., "Heartache" 's bounce welds "Batman" to some forgotten Cars standard to the Knack's immortal "My Sharona"). And above all there's Steve Whiteman's screech, which I'd define as the aural equivalent of unexpectedly finding chewed-up gum rotting beneath your desk top—yum yum yum!

They've got gal problems: They wait to hear atomic bombs when they're between the sheets, they look for a love that's 6.5 on the Richter scale from their "one-two-three-four pretty girlfriends," they stay away from the chicks mom warns 'em about. They open "The Itch" with a tormented hangover-mood that'd make Axl Rose gloat, they try to imagine how Cheap Trick's parents might've answered "Surrender" with "The Kid," they run a nursery rhyme through "Walk the Dog" then through Neil Diamond or Starz or somebody in "Contrary Mary," they state their reason for existence in "Kix Are for Kids." They clap their hands as if they've been doing it for sixteen years minimum, they've got ants in their pants and they wanna dance. And though their tendency is to keep the songs real short, especially by 1981-metal standards, they end with seven minutes of "Yeah, Yeah, Yeah," and during those minutes Whiteman pays tribute to the Beatles and Stones, requests permission to pull some babe's hair, and imitates Elmer Fudd even better than rap woman Roxanne Shante would in "Wack It" in 1988. Then, after all that stuff, he cruises into this post–Peter Wolf/proto–Sam Kinison monologue where his date (who has the nerve not to sleep with him *despite* the fact that he bathes sometimes and has two arms) drinks all his beer and whiskey, swallows one of his 'ludes, then barfs all over his bedroom floor. Give or take the three Kix albums that came later, there is no other eighties "rock" that can approach the joy in this music.

6. NEW YORK DOLLS
New York Dolls Mercury, 1973

They wore lipstick and high heels and pouted like brazen tarts, that's the main thing, and the tarts they wanted to be were bad girls, probably the Ronettes. But not even Phil Spector himself ever heard a girl group who fought back this ferociously, this flamboyantly: Johnny Thunders lets go brickbats of fuzz that the Sex Pistols would steal first and Poison would steal second. Then David Johansen, who's got more Jagger-slime in him than even Steve Tyler does, glides down some ivory through smoke into the reptile-strewn sewer or subway. If you're him, you'll do anything to make people notice you. In Lower Manhattan you've got no choice, that's why you came, you've got a personality crisis. You'll even let a rock 'n' roll nurse put a spike in your rock 'n' roll nerves, you'll even "make it" with Frankenstein, but like Frank (Sinatra) says, if you can "make it" here you can "make it" anywhere.

Everything stops... "AND YOU'RE A PRIMA BALLERINA ON A SPRING AFTERNOON." Huh? The singer loves himself, he's peeking at his pocket mirror, lets you see his nipple, knows how to turn his ankle to catch a man. When Johansen starts vowing to "shout about it bitch about it scream about it shout about it" (but he already *is*!), "Holiday in the Sun" by the Sex Pistols isn't far off, yet there's less *Never Mind the Bollocks* here than *Dirty Mind,* less Iggy than Madonna, it's that kind of *épater les bourgeois:* the sex kind, not the violence kind. Which is to say that though punk-rockers listened in, punks would never

have this kind of intestinal fortitude. And needless to say, neither did hippies: Not only do these tunes have Vietnam and nukes in 'em; they've got "I've Been Workin' on the Railroad," not to mention succulent sax-sap and Del Shannon—very unabashed, not even close to what you'd call humble.

7. LYNYRD SKYNYRD
Second Helping MCA, 1974

These Wild Turkey–primed good ol' boys embodied piss and grime and wisdom and wit (not to mention barbiturates, bongs, and brazen broads in flimsy white tank tops) till their '77 plane crash (numero-uno death-tragedy in rock history); the greatest and most underrated of rock's R&B-bred populists, on both sonic and lyric terms they leave Springsteen easily, and even Fogerty/Seger/Mellencamp, in the dust. Segments of the boogie competition may have rocked louder, but not a single one rocked harder or smarter. Here, where their two Gibsons and one Fender grind at a career-cresting clip, Skynyrd follow up rock's most unshirkable direct command ever ("turn it up") with the music's best-ever fuck-you to a fellow performer ("Sweet Home Alabama," a reply to Neil Young's liberal hypocrisy in "Southern Man"), best-ever fuck-you to rock critics ("Don't Ask Me No Questions," which gets the nod over Sonic Youth's "I Killed Christgau," Nick Lowe's "They Called It Rock," or "Don't Believe the Hype" by Public Enemy), and best-ever fuck-you to a record label ("Workin' for MCA," which I'll take over the Sex Pistols' "EMI" or the Clash's "Complete Control" or Graham Parker's "Mercury Poisoning"). What they think about George Wallace is "boo! boo! boo!" what they think about Watergate is that it was business as usual. "The Ballad of Curtis Loew" is their rejoinder to Merle Haggard's "Uncle Lem"; "The Needle and the Spoon" is their rejoinder to Neil's "The Needle and the Damage Done," but with a colossal beat that connects the Stooges' "I Wanna Be Your Dog" to the Pistols' "Submission." In "Call Me the Breeze," with guitars chomping like gators and Professor Billy Powell racing his pinetop through green lights and red alike, they dadburn near make up for the Civil War.

8. NEIL YOUNG AND CRAZY HORSE
. . . .
Rust Never Sleeps Reprise, 1979

First side's quiet folk music commencing with the world's second-greatest r'n'r un-eulogy, second side's loud folk music ending with the world's *greatest* r'n'r un-eulogy, and both sides gobble your heart. On the quiet half, Neil's on the road, dissatisfied and displaced, stuck like a dinosaur in a time he didn't make, so he just keeps following the North Star with his frankincense and myrrh. Rambling toward his messiah, he conjures up reams of crazy, surreal images. He remembers the Grand Canyon from TV, passes the Astrodome with Marlon Brando, meets herb-toting Martians, ponders the scavenging of the scavenger as vultures collide into asphalt, crosses more geography, never stays long in one place—a nomad, a wandering Jew, though "Pocahontas" could be about Palestine.

The album's loud half opens with a locked cell called "Powderfinger," and violence is Neil's escape hatch: The seer raises his rifle to his eye, but mostly the violence is in the sound. "Powderfinger" 's drone is eclipsed by the silly "Welfare Mothers"; "Welfare Mothers" 's feedback, by the urgent pusher-anthem "Sedan Delivery," which climaxes on a guitar squeal that solders your zipper shut like a lightning bolt; "Sedan Delivery" 's screech by "Hey Hey My My (Into the Black)," a horrific distortion-dirge for the smoldering souls of Elvis and Sid, even though the Sex Pistol who's mentioned by name is Johnny.

By refusing to cater to the coke spoon narcissism of La-La Land popstrum, Young stayed viable longer than any of his thumbsucking peers, and his technophobia and preference for noisy blur made him a natural to outlive the blitz of '77, but the naive primitivism he finds here is so unschooled and unshackled it makes punk seem slick.

9. TEENA MARIE
. . . .
Emerald City Epic, 1986

If listing this manifesto of freethink in a metal-guide weren't so perverse I'd probably list it even higher, so call me gutless, but don't deny it belongs. Side One is the hardest rock any woman's ever made, and it may well be the only legitimately "psychedelic" music of the eighties. Onetime Rick James protégé Teena is a true feminist who cannot be pigeonholed into any womanly role outlined by Phyllis Schlafly or Helen Reddy or their moms; she's an open-souled soul who drinks in the whole world and refuses value judgments and omits nothing. A white person who's spent her adult life entertaining blacks, a miracle offspring of Patti Smith and James Brown and Robert Plant (c. "Fool in the Rain") and Minnie Ripperton who's been known to toboggan down moonbeams and visit Atlantis and Neptune, she's got a batch of LPs on Motown and Epic, most of 'em rather guitarless. Here, she hits Shangri-la and Oz and the southern tip of Spain, lustily stretching and snapping and bending her voice, tasting life into words for all they're worth, slipping into trances, exploding into jive asides and spit-in-your-eye taunts.

She works her scats gymnastic as a Hendrix solo, her soul leaves her body, she breaks syllables into subatomic particles like she's just learning to talk. Which she is. The lyrics are too silly, too ingeniously ingenuous, to believe: "to live inside the major not the minor chord/and forget how we made love in a '57 Ford." One song's metaphors are almost all edible—candy-coated kisses, heavenly Milky Ways, ice cream "sammiches," Beaujolais. Guests include Branford Marsalis and Stanley Clarke, the first voice you hear belongs to Bootsy Collins, the excitement takes a couple minutes to get started, and it calms down sooner than it should, with Brazilian bossa novas and lush torch-lullabies. "The rhythms used on *Emerald City* are called Sha Sha a La Fum," says the sleeve, which also features instrument-credit hieroglyphics as crazily cryptic as any runes Zeppelin ever devised. A whole new language.

So it's hard to figure out who plays what, but I think the guitars, fuzzers that roar toward internal-combustion culminations like Hawkwind helping out Funkadelic, belong to Teena and to Nikki Slick. (Teena's ax on the cover has aquamarine paisleys, the brand doesn't matter.) "Once Is Not Enough," "Lips to Find You," and "You So Heavy" are frantically bongoed salsa-metal; the latter, an instructively named ripchord-ripper dedicated to Rick James, concludes with what sounds like frets being sawed in half before the feedback's disappeared. Since Teena hates no music, and absorbs everything she likes, the sounds hint at possibilities no one else has even considered. None of it's art, and all of it is, and no other eighties rock 'n' roll derives so much pleasure out of its singing and dancing and bombast. Nobody else is so cosmic, nobody lets so much hang out—Teena's in her own galaxy, and she cannot be controlled.

10. THE JIMMY CASTOR BUNCH
. . . .
Phase Two RCA, 1972

Between taking over for Frankie Lymon in the Teenagers and suing the Beastie Boys for copyright infringement, Jimmy Castor released a whole bunch of albums on a whole bunch of labels, practicing an incidentally nonexclusionary novelty/toss-off policy not unsimilar to the ones employed in their primes by Louis Prima, Blowfly, Elton John, and Kix. Nobody ever accused him of being "eclectic" (thank God), but he knew he was: he nicknamed himself "The Everything Man," sang songs called "E-Man Groovin' " and "E-Man Par-Tay," even one called "Everything Is Beautiful to Me." His biggest hit, the oft-sampled 1971 disco-metal prototype "Troglodyte," starring "Big Bertha, Bertha Butt, one of the Butt sisters," was caveman rock in the tradition of "Alley Oop" by the Hollywood Argyles and "Neanderthal Man" by Hotlegs. Jimmy explained how prehistoric studs useta pull their women by the hair, but you can't do that today, 'cause "it might come off!" On *Phase Two*, he tried to repeat "Troglodyte" 's success with "Luther the Anthropoid

(Ape Man.)" In 1975 he took "The Bertha Butt Boogie (Part 1)" to number 16; later, in the wake of *Star Wars,* he even recorded "Big Bertha Encounters Vadar"!

Jimmy generally balanced these groovy anthropology lessons with heaping helpings of goofus sci-fi and parapsychology, not to mention mimicry of and/or homages to Count Dracula and the Archies and Jimmy "Dy-No-Mite" Walker of "Good Times," scary voices demanding you "deny the prince of darkness," frequent timbale-rock taunts at some sad sack named Leroy, and completely serious and heartfelt soulsonications of the sappiest serenades in humankind's history ("Mandy," "You Light Up My Life," like that). *Phase Two,* the most metallicized of the pile of albums I've found, kicks off with demiclassical "fanfare" (twenty-four seconds' worth). Then Jimmy hollers at Leroy that the creature from the black lagoon is his daddy, which introduces a salsa jam where many an unforgettable "Sanford and Son"–era slogan ("when you're hot, you're hot," "try it, you'll like it," "what you see is what you gonh' get"—a belt!—"how'd you like one across the lips") makes way for Harry Jenson's maggot-brained feedback. The noise gets more unholy as Luther the Anthropoid dances the breakdown and asks us to sock it to him and looks through a peep-hole at a naked lady and exclaims "power to the peep-hole!" Finally, Side Uno ends with the friendliest samba-bath you ever soaked toes in, complete with impromptu Portuguese scat-singing.

Side Two's got a twistedly transcendent fallout-guitar protest-funk beast tackling racism and tomato prices and fluid fashion trends and how balancing the budget will "balance some more money outa my checkbook"—Jimmy raps that he "don't want nothin' for free, but I'm not *workin'* for nothin'," wonders about university sit-ins when back in the old days kids couldn't *wait* to remove their butts from school, then climaxes with a ghastly howl that starts all the way down at Screamin' Jay Hawkins's feet. He switches gears, hums a sunshiney hymn to love and paradise, then relaxes into a fragile and saxy "The First Time Ever I Saw Your Face" (sans words). *Then,* after rhapsodizing briefly about why Jimi Hendrix was "a genius of some sort, there's no question about it," he combines "Purple Haze" and "Foxy Lady." Only, it's not a medley—he sings "Lady" while Jenson bangs out "Haze," then vice versa! Or at least that's how it sounds to me! More fanfare, and time's out.

On the LP cover, our main man wears his white webbed silk V-neck, his red suede leisure suit (w/tails), his four-inch white-buck platforms, his Afrosheen. He's jumping higher than Mr. Bojangles, slam-dunking skyscrapers. Jimmy Castor is what George Clinton could've been if George wasn't such an art dweeb.

11. **KIX**
. . . .
Blow My Fuse Atlantic, 1988

This is kind of a sore spot with me right now, seeing how my word processor just devoured an entire microdisc's worth of *Stairway to Hell* entries (as if I'm really in the *mood* to play hide-and-seek in some remote corner of electronic hyperspace) so now I gotta completely rewrite this one and a dozen others, but this LP's underlying point is that it demonstrates how fun it can be for pun-crazed/punk-raised boon-dock boys with a hotshit rhythm section (from Maryland's panhandle in this case) to imagine that they're machines. They call themselves M16s and radars; they ask you to blow their fuse (har har), to overload their circuits. Yet, amazingly enough, *this isn't a concept or comedy album*!

Instead, it's *the only known instance* where main-streamish AORguys (subconsciously!) acknowledge their role as children of the industrial revolution. The band plunders its usual idiosyncratic gamut of play-ground games (Ring Around the Rosie, Red Light Green Light) and big rock sounds (Stones harmonies, Zep changes, Abba hooks), and they whip out a Poison-style Aerobilly bop called "Piece of the Pie" that concerns both the pie-graph variety and the Mom's Apple flavor too, and their thrash (in "Dirty Boys" especially) has Top 40 zeal. Every track should've been a huge hit single. But mainly, Kix comes to terms sonicwise with the digital disco millennium or some approximation thereof. So we get dub-doctored Who synths, and we get a studiofied beaut of a surprise B-side-turned-A-side smash called "Don't Close Your Eyes" that sounds as if Def Leppard suddenly woke up one morning with Die Kreuzen's hygeine problems. Over creepy piano from Super-tramp's "Breakfast in America" and Aerosmith's "Dream On," Steve Whiteman prays the Lord rock 'n' roll's suicidal soul to keep, thus closing the lid on a year's worth of Nerf-metal ballads (Bon Jovi's "I'll Be There for You," Warrant's "Heaven," White Lion's "Little Fighter") that, in their own way, debated whether or not this dying music was still worth believing in. When your microdiscs commit suicide you wanna do the same, and it takes a song as momentous as "Don't Close Your Eyes" to keep you breathing.

"Good love is all you need," Whiteman insists somewhere else, "but you don't wanna know." Yeah, well maybe—you can't always get what you want, but if you try sometimes you'll get laid, right? Nice philosophy, even if it doesn't stop technology from totally spoiling my day sometimes. Regardless, this record is as good-humored as any heavy metal I've ever heard, and maybe the reason I love it so much is 'cause it halfway suggests machines can be benevolent beings. Or maybe I love how it turns our inevitable self-imposed doom into a three-ring circus. Or maybe I just love it because I know all the words by heart.

12. **VAN HALEN**
. . . .
1984 Warner Bros., 1984

It was the reelection year of "When Doves Cry" and "Jam on It" and "Boys of Summer" and "Girls Just Want to Have Fun" and "If I'd Been the One" and "Missing You" and "99 Luftballons" and "Round and Round" and "Foolish Heart" and "Authority Song" and "Borderline," the kind of radio landslide that comes around once in an adolescence if you're lucky, and somehow these hams absorbed the whole fucking zeitgeist, and what they couldn't fit into "Jump," one of the most supersonic singles of any decade, a song so invincible it actually let me love Aztec Camera for five minutes, they fit somewhere else. This was pop cock-rock, it had convertibles with their tops down ("Panama"), it had Betty Boop with her top down ("Drop Dead Legs"), it had self-mocking wide-angle shots ("Hot for Teacher": best sexist rockvid ever, period). It had ostentatious crescendos ("Girl Gone Bad"), it had meaty mung ("House of Pain"), it had space-age symphonics ("1984"), it had "Baba O'Riley" electronics ("Jump"), it had unrooted tributes to roots bands ("Top Jimmy"), it had drum solos that made you think Kenny Aranoff just joined Motörhead ("Hot for Teacher" again), it had indigestion. It was avant-garde vaudeville, it was pure Hollywood, it was a chorus line in bed with the chainsaw massacre, it was

loads of fun, it meant nothing, it meant everything, it was for everybody. Its excruciating eruptions ripped an awesome band apart at the seams, but sometimes you have to roll with the punches to get to what's real.

13. **ADVERTS**
. . . .
Crossing the Red Sea with the Adverts
Bright UK import, 1978

This is Moses-level prophecy from bored teenagers, subterranean vandals, one-chord wonders with Motörhead patches on their jackets, bombsite boys with a woman playing bass, recreating themselves as somebody else because there's no other way out. Punk rock was the token the Adverts used to board the tube, but their sound is poppish sludge like the Sweet used to play it, zooming by lickety-split as if the players know they'll never again be allowed to get away with such stuff. No other punk had so much spunk, so communicated this feeling of scared kids diving headfirst into uncharted waters. The Adverts wonder whether the audience will walk out on them, and if so, who'll be laughing. "I'm ready for whatever happens," T. V. Smith's ragged, pretty, nasal voice, a voice to die for, says somewhere; nobody could even guess. The tunes are so commercial they could've been huge; a 1977 single about Gary Gilmore even got AOR airplay in Detroit. Who knew whether punk rock would take over, or even what it was?

Side Two starts "Life's short, don't make a mess of it/To the end of the earth you look for sense in it," a motto of sorts; the previous cut starts as a tense Pere Ubu dirge, glass crashing everywhere (everything punk would end up doing), then speeds up, "life goes quick and it goes without warning." On *Crossing the Red Sea,* both the first and last sounds you hear are heavy metal feedback, but Smith talks about the frailty of words, about looking for a new church. No music I know so gleefully conveys the day-to-day downhill slide of a people under siege by their own nation. In the glee, there's dread.

14. Nuggets, Volume One: The Hits

Rhino, 1984; rec. 1965–68

Here's where it all started. Affluence-age backlashes at teachers and parents and peers ("Pushin' Too Hard," "Talk Talk," "Summertime Blues"), confused recollections of initial substance abuse ("I Had Too Much to Dream Last Night," "Psychotic Reaction," "Journey to the Center of Your Mind"), big fat tales of frustrated women and double-negatives and long-haired sissies (the Barbarians' astounding "Are You a Boy or Are You a Girl," which for some unknown reason mentions female monkeys and swimming stones). There's probably not a band in this book who hasn't (directly or indirectly) stolen something from one of these songs at least once: Off the top of my head, I'm thinking Robert Plant, Foreigner, Uriah Heep, Jimi Hendrix, and the Angry Samoans, not to mention Black Pearl and Head over Heels (who stole musicians) and Def Leppard (whose Rick Allen must bow only to the Barbarians' Moulty, whose left hand was a hook). The Five Americans, Nazz, Blues Magoos, and Balloon Farm pale in this company, but "I Had Too Much to Dream . . ." by the Electric Prunes is a staggering renovation of "Paint It Black" that sounds as if it were recorded beneath Puget Sound. Former Mouseketeers and phys-ed flunkers from the sticks skyrocket to the top of the world, only to crawl right back through the slime (unless their surnames are Nugent or Rundgren) just months later. These are the basics, the classics, the canon, feedback and runny noses in nascent backyard unyippiediluted form.

15. MOTT THE HOOPLE

Mott Columbia, 1973

A heroic and hostile meditation on the uselessness of playing music for a living in a world and an era where nothing else could conceivably be so useful, and why usefulness, as D. H. Lawrence points out in the gatefold poem, is a stupid yardstick in the first place. In Ian Hunter's songs, "spades" say all rockers look alike while pool sharks shack up with the spawn of punks and drunks. Elvis shows up in one tune and Chuck Berry in the next, but the quiet spans are how rock 'n' roll might've sounded if it'd happened a half-century earlier, before C&W was C&W and R&B was R&B, and the loud spans evoke either a circus where no trapezist's got a safety net or a church where God might not be dead after all. In "Whizz Kid," Hunter gets all teary-eyed, then pulls the rug from under himself, and you're the one who crashes; in "Violence," over vindictive violinclimb and lisping lulu and mind-numbing Mick Ralphs guitarnoise, he foresees an England like Germany in '33, where dropouts lash out at the old and the lame, who deserve it. Self-consciousness keeps threatening to push the theatrics off a precipice, but the delusions of grandeur stay checked and balanced like in no other rock, and not until the six-minute flamenco-metal interlude does everything fall to pieces. After that comes "I Wish I Was Your Mother," with piano that for a couple seconds seems as if it could assuage the injury, patch everything up, but from Ian's mouth pours nothing but spite and scorn, and we're left with nothing to believe in, and it stings like salt in an open wound.

16. Vision Quest

Geffen, 1985

Twenty-first-century musicologists interested in the Golden Age of Mid-American AOR (yes, there really was such a moment, though it was hard to know it at the time) are directed here, even though AOR was never really this good, because AOR never played Madonna (this soundtrack, the most eternally listenable flick-vinyl of the eighties, does twice). This is semimetal, mostly, post-Boston high-clarity swoops helping superb mall-blues voices like Steve Perry and John Waite and Don Henley set a generation of romantic high school horizons on distant lands beyond the municipal limits of Jefferson City and Grand Rapids and Terre Haute. No less than half of the tracks—Waite's "Change," Journey's "Only The Young," Madonna's shivery and dusky "Crazy For You,"

Foreigner's testosteronic "Hot Blooded," Red Rider's surprisingly paranoid "Lunatic Fringe" (most mind-blowing Bryan Adams surrogate ever!)—can hold their own against just about any anthem broadcast on the commercial wireless in the decade after punk swallowed its tail. In "She's on the Zoom," Henley hires two Go-Gos and puts over a flashdance-riffer lauding a Home Ec major who wants more out of life, and if the other leftovers seem too glued to their respective MOR disco (Style Council, Madonna's "Gambler") and MOR metal (Dio, Sammy Hagar) niches, at least they do their part to educate stragglers across the stylistic fence. For the record, Dio plunders "Baba O'Riley" riffs and bridges the gap between the Godz and Queensrÿche while Sammy answers Dionne Warwick's "I'll Never Fall in Love Again." And even *those* two putzes pass the test.

17. **AEROSMITH**
. . . .
Gems Columbia, 1988; rec. 1973–82

Way-altruistic as cash-ins devised by corporate bigwigs go, this mishmash joins just two nonhits from these lipfarmers' best regular-issue LP (*Toys in the Attic*) and just three from their second-best (*Rocks*) to seven wonderfully durable oddments from six records that weren't quite so hot, thus enabling the consumer to both save mucho bucks and procure an object that can actually be listened to. A lot. Because not only does Side One slyly start with their all-time most mercurial protospeedmetal ("Rats in the Cellar") and Side Two with their all-time heaviest postLed-metals ("Nobody's Fault," "Round and Round"), but both sides get their *Rocks/Toys* redundancies out of the way right away, thereby leaving room for "Chip Away at the Stone" (obsessive country-Stones that kicks cowpies like Jason and the Scorchers would've if they'd been as punk as everybody pretended), "Mama Kin" (real famous in the age of Axl), "Lord of the Thighs" (with title and beats L. L. Cool J's gotta envy), "Train Kept a Rollin'" (Yardbirds who?), "No Surprize" (junkie autobiography worthy of Mott the Hoople, with Max's Kansas City in it, plus *NME*, BMI,

"Too Much Monkey Business," and a *Duck Soup* reference where asses get vaccinated by phonograph needles!), and more. Everything but their Rufus Thomas remake (installment number one in the Aerosmith Dog Trilogy), but corporate options have gotta remain open, right?

18. **THE DICTATORS**
. . . .
Go Girl Crazy! Epic, 1975

Nearly nobody got the joke at the time, but these herculean Hebes bridged the gal-slurping-Jewligan gap between Lieber and Stoller and the Beasties. With a future Twisted Sister and a future Manowar and a singing wrestling roadie who filled bathtubs like William Howard Taft and a singing bass-playing songwriter who criticked for fanzines when fanzines still mattered, they were the first *CREEM*-inspired rockband, maybe—stinky, sweaty, graceless, tasteless, booger-eating, stash-smoking, sopor-swallowing teen-generates reveling in something they knew gosh-darn well was absurd. Punks a whole year early, on this debut they trash Lou Reed, spurn the gasoline shortage, destroy your house, beat up foreign exchange students, rhyme "growing up" with "throwing up." (The last of which Bruce Springsteen had already done on *his* debut two years earlier, but who's counting?) Eons before Paul Westerberg and Steve Albini took the piss out of such gimmicks, they retool

Sonny and Cher and surf-frugables like prodigal sons of Bette Midler and follow up "Back to Africa"'s calypso-metal ooga-chucka with a friendly ditty called "Master Race Rock." In "California Sun," they invent the excellent word "shicktapoobah"; in "Next Big Thing," they pass as goyim in Dallas and yearn for the cover of *TV Guide*. And though the provocative photos on the back hide the guitarists' weenies behind pink elephant trunks and hot dog grills, riffs somewhere between youthful Blue Öyster Cult and youthful Motörhead letcha know they're boys.

19. DEF LEPPARD
. . . .
Hysteria Mercury, 1987

Rick Allen, the drummer, lost his left arm in a car accident on New Year's Eve, 1984, and though you wanted to give these tax exiles the benefit of the doubt, at first nothing here seemed to grunt as gleefully as the keepers on *Pyromania* and *On Through the Night*; the blast-off booms and laser-wars all glimmered like mere audiophilic stargazing for the baby boomlet's junior techie Trekkies. The first four words ("In the big inning") are the same ones that prove the Old Testament's about baseball, but the first two singles ("Women" and "Animal") were technometal devoid of personality, and they distorted the rest of this hour-plus montage into something more hollow than it really is. The next thirty-or-so hits were just fine, shameless nicks from "Rock & Roll, Part II" ("Rocket"), "We Will Rock You" ("Pour Some Sugar on Me"), "Bang a Gong" ("Armageddon It"). The last's got the slyest phrase-turn ("Are you gettin' it? Armageddon it!" Get it?), but "Sugar," a ridiculously giddy Aerorap formulated during a coffee break, has one throat-lumping moment where the operator knocks upon your door-or-or.

The title hymn's this profoundly desperate thing of unadulterated beauty: A subtly eloquent guitar-glaze, five wistful notes repeated unto perfection with winter-breeze briskness for something like six minutes, comes out of early Boston (the group) while near ambient harmonies, pining lovelorn over some tenderoni, come out of heaven somewhere, via Badfinger I thought at first but the way Joe Elliot croons "tonight" eventually convinced me it's the Easybeats. Almost two years and ten million sales after *Hysteria*'s nativity, by the time the Sheffield horde mindfucked MTV with "Rocket," their homage to seventies transvestite-rock, trading in the jeansy "natural look" that'd earned 'em acclaim since their teen debut for the Max Factor all their peers had discarded in Guns N' Roses' wake, all this World's-Most-Popular-Rock-Band bizwiz started to seem like good news: You learn to groove along with Side Two's throwaways, and you commence to get off on how the cinematic Pac-Man potpourri incorporates hip-hop and dub and Burundi and AC/DC chunks and lewd gasps and (in "Gods of War") what seems like cyberpunk anti-Reaganism without acting like any of the above are a big deal where the listener's supposed to go "Wow!" An aural antecedent of Joe Dante's gopher-borogue improvisation in *Gremlins 2*—this is the nineties, I hope.

20. BLACK SABBATH
. . . .
Sabotage Warner Bros., 1975

They were never so listenable as in this last gasp, and never so eccentric: strange cut-up pastiches inside stranger cut-up pastiches, a harbinger of Queensrÿche's *Operation: Mindcrime,* or maybe a throwback to the Firesign Theatre, or William Burroughs. Everything—concise solos, voices chanting "opcit, opsist, obsessed . . . ," evil laughs, seven seconds from some ancient jugband 78, choruses grunting "suck me!"—jumps out from nowhere. Like in a great hip-hop mix, every sound disorients you, surprises you, but somehow every sound fits so perfectly that you couldn't imagine it anywhere else. (It's the Miles Davis effect, in other words, but the sounds themselves are the *least* Miles-like the group had ever come up with.) Monster riff-tumbles like "Hole in the Sky" and "Symptom of the Universe" are linked together by all these tango-turns and solemn chamber-strings and Aquinan chants like Ozzy'd been listening hard to the White Album or *Over Under Sideways·Down* or something, but he's suggesting a direction prog-rock never had the fortitude to follow. Nothing comes to complete stop; it's all segued together. And Ozzy's howl, which inhabits this insane dimension of rent-free apartments and flying unicorns and undying love and sold souls, then signs off with a deranged appeal to fans or critics or demons or taxmen or *somebody,* never misses a beat. Just don't ask me to explain Geezer Butler's disco duds, okay?

21. MC5
Babes in Arms R.O.I.R. cassette, 1983; rec. 1966–70

These Cong-rockin' Michigan commiesymps came real close three times, but they never quite earned the completely-satisfying-album cigar. They tended toward messes, and the cleanup didn't work perfect either. This is the most useful document you'll find, 'cause not only does it collect a whole range of their shrewdest wordclots ("Shaking Street," "American Ruse," "Sister Ann," and "Gotta Keep Moving," all in takes you'll unearth nowhere else, "Kick Out the Jams" with the censored "motherfucker" left in, "Looking at You" the mutinous way John Sinclair produced it for A-Squared Recs sometime circa the riots or World Series downtown), ballsiest soundclots ("Skunk" hornier than ever, "Poison" so you can understand Mike Davis's self-actualization speech, "Future Now" so you can hardly understand anything) and inspired homages (to Little Richard and Van Morrison), it's got obscurities only anal-retentive fanbelt-belt record-collectors ever heard of before, most notably the shape-of-jizz-to-cum dry runs "Gold" and "I Just Don't Know." The sum total's still no stogie, but the fantastic thing about the Five is their shrewdness was ballsier than most anybody else's idiocy, and their ballsiness was shrewder than most anybody else's wimpitude. As were their haircuts.

22. FUNKADELIC
Maggot Brain Westbound, 1971

A woman's head is surrounded with mud on one side of the cover; on the other, only her skull's left. "Mother Earth is pregnant for the third time for y'all have knocked her up," this deep groan intones, then we're heaved into ten weaving and swelling minutes of Hendrix/Crazy Horse disorder that may well express the saddest emotion I've ever heard wrenched from a mere musical instrument. Next comes "Can You Get to That"'s dizzyingly finger-snappable multilevel bubblegospel sermon, the message of which is something along the lines of neither a borrower or a lender be when it comes to love or life. Then several misshapen slabs of diddybop harmony and Dixieland hornhoot fortressed by a riff-fortified funk so brown, viscous and fathomless you could lose a shoe in it, climaxing with the *Agharta*-like coda "Wars of Armageddon," a metalish title comprising all sorts of flatulence, telephone, moocow, time bomb, cuckoo clock, wildcat, and heartbeat effects. By 1989, when Sabbathoid midwestern garage bands finally dug up "Super Stupid," a boogie so enormous it makes Leslie West seem like Ollie North, history was as far removed from this album as this album was from "The Stars Get in Your Eyes" by Perry Como.

23. SLADE
Sladest Reprise, 1973; rec. 1971–73

The sharpest dressers in the gang-district, these chimney sweeps wore platform boots and rolled plaid trousers, spelled like guys who cheat at Scrabble, and were gonna be the next Beatles. In England, where everything here hit at least number 16 and five shouts hit number 1, they came close. So condemning 'em for spawning Quiet Riot and Twisted Sister just doesn't make sense. Dickensian rowdy rudies chortling blue jokes about quidpence and kippers, chasing good-time gals around Leicester Square, sending their pre-neo-Hitlerite fandom pissed on firewater back to the tube so they could roll bums around or whatever, they tossed maniacal tararaboomderay off the Oxford Music Hall roof like no one since 1914. Noddy Holder boasts that his off-key throat and ineptness at orthography will make him rich, yells out a transvestite-rock smash so you still think the he's a she, makes every last gumbo-beat rally of the troops romp like roughage, and makes half of 'em ("Gudbuy t' Jane," "Cum On Feel the Noize," "Skweeze Me Pleeze Me," "Mama Weer All Crazee Now," "My Friend Stan") last forever. Seems like a real fine chap, too—kind of guy who'd help your jalopy out of a ditch before you even asked him. Salt o' the bloomin' earth.

24. AC/DC
High Voltage Atlantic, 1976

The first year of punk, they surpassed it, with more threatening bile and a better beat. In "Rock 'n' Roll Singer" Bon Scott tells you where to stick your moral standards, nine-to-five drudgery, "and all the other *shit* they teach the kids at school." His parents wanted him to be a doctor or lawyer, but he can make more money playing music. He's honest about his motives, and certain flashes make me shiver: the acidic way he draws out the phrase "*Ahhh . . . ain't . . . no . . . fool,*" the exasperated way he screams "I ain't foolin, *can'tchoo tell?*" using his lethal wrath to lambaste the social order, to demand respect for values too foreign for any counterculture, punk or otherwise, to comprehend.

But that's only part of the game: Most of it's bowlegged brothelsong and lumpenprole lampoon, juicy dicehall crotchgrind. Years before any American could translate such jolly exclamations, the gang shouts "Oi! Oi! Oi!" again and again. "Can I Sit Next to You Girl" is off-color Shadows of Knight movie-theater salaciousness; in "Little Lover" a nymphet in the front row stands up, and all Bon can see is the wet spot; he carries a poker/syphilis double entendre all the way through "The Jack" with a straight (aces high) face; "She's Got Balls" may or may not be about sex with a

man. The third-funniest piece of correspondence on the back cover comes from the Young brothers' headmaster, re "obscene gestures and obstreperousness" (!) at school; second-funniest is a love note to Bon, where a girl quotes her dad the mayor's pledge to "erase your tattoos by pulling off your arms." Funniest is to Phil Rudd: "Enclosed please find the remains of the drumsticks you broke over my daughter's head last Friday night. Or was it a billiard cue?" Beat that.

25. AEROSMITH
Rocks Columbia, 1976

Atop this shiny and sleek shotgun broncobuck blues, suburban cowboys long for the ghetto or the plough, the nitty-gritty, the holy land, anything more exciting than the bum hand they've been dealt. Their verbose, detailed, raunchy language comes across like *Ulysses,* the Hombres' "Let It All Hang Out," Cab Calloway's "Jumpin' Jive," and *Narrative Poetry from the Black Oral Tradition,* all tossed together into a classified-document shredder, then burned in a hash pipe; in a mere three lines, they tackle homesickness, syphilis, "hottail poontang sweetheart sweat," and creative uses for J. Paul Getty's auditory canal, and they make it *rhyme.* You spin the disc for the thousandth time, and Steve Tyler's throatburn in "Back in the Saddle" still gives you a hotfoot, the yodels and sirens and mortuary ivory still confound your expectations, that "you really ain't that young" line still makes your breath skip as it did when you were sixteen. Their feral flash suggesting an unironic *Tyranny and Mutation* more than it does an ill-remembered *High Tide and Green Grass,* these Boston hoodlums play their sweet sassafrassies off, kicking "Lick and a Promise" into gear like it's "Subterranean Homesick Blues." Tyler calls himself the last child, just a punk, and in retrospect the moniker fits him more than it fit most anyone who emerged from New York or London with it only months later.

26. THE STOOGES

Funhouse Elektra, 1970

When they were noticed at all (radio wouldn't touch 'em, except maybe in Detroit), the Stooges were generally considered the worst band in the world, but that's just 'cause everybody was scared to touch 'em. All the revelers are naked at this party; their flesh is in your face, you smell it, it stinks. On the cover the band's bathing in hot orange flames. Inside, they're savages, perspiring, playing some kind of deathjazz, and the center will not hold. My lawyer friend Rob says that if a devil exists, and if he's ever visited a recording studio, he's on this record. *Something's* inside Iggy Pop—this voice keeps bursting out, the one that groans "uh, look *out*..." at the start of "Loose," "LAAAAAAAWD" at the start of "T.V. Eye," and the voice is not Iggy's. The band isn't controlling the music—the music is controlling the band.

Drummer Scott Asheton's Diddleyfied tribalbeat tomfoolery tries its damnedest to keep the mania in tow. But Scott's guitaring brother Ron bends and twists collision-shop fuzzriffs every which way until like Gumbys their wires pop out, while a convulsing Iggy bends and twists belched phrases ("Do you *feel* it I feel al*right* takin it *down* lemme *in*"), always in the opposite direction. Steve MacKay's tenor sax, a couple years earlier it could've been Albert Ayler blowing for the Islam Nation, works to dissolve all structure from the inside. The singer calls himself dirt, says he's been hurt, but doesn't care.

Another Saturday night and he ain't got nobody, looking for love in all the wrong exhaust pipes, his O-mind tuned to the Red Alert setting, Iggy peers at pretty things out his third-story window, ready to dump his chamber pot on 'em if they won't look back; when they look back, he tries to shield his vision from their glare. The energy slows to entropy, then turns into a trance, then a primeval rite in the wilderness, until at last in "L.A. Blues," an expressionist exorcism so unhinged it'd sound pretentious anywhere else on the album, either saxist or Satan triumphs, and the evidence is all over your rec room floor, and you have to hire domestic help to clean it up.

27. BLACK SABBATH

Paranoid Warner Bros., 1970

The dirges we all sing in the dark the day the music dies in "American Pie" probably come from this bold stroke of personal and public nuclear and narcotic Armageddon, a dense dissertation with howling hooks and a beat as sure and rage as searing as "Living for the City" or *What's Going On.* The long loops of reverb and repetition have less to do with rock 'n' roll than with some immolating dance-in-ruins mood that probably dates from before the Enlightenment, and where heaviness-qua-heaviness is concerned, there's no competition anywhere. Ozzy Osbourne's some kind of mythical bird, this ungodly gargoyle, this saint. In the first cut, with silencing concentration, his voice switches back and forth between giant grunge-punctuation, relating this nightmare of politicians planning apocalypse, plotting destruction; in the title track, trapped in the world's most claustrophobic speeding boxcar, he tries and tries to let happiness in, but can't find a window.

The rhythms compress circular zero-chops wah-wah wank over steady tomroll marches, with secondary beat-apparatus from powerchord pulverizations constructed into pseudosymphonic forceswing headbang progressions; you can locate the embryo of not just Metallica and Voivod, but electric Miles, solo Eno, Pere Ubu, Joy Division. I'll never know what "Fairies with Boots" means, but only "Rat Salad" sinks into overconfident mastery of instruments, and only "Iron Man" into kitsch, and even then only for a few seconds, after which it's become an allegory of technology striking back or, more likely, God striking back at a race that gives technology free rein. Extremely religious, extremely moral, *Paranoid* ranks with pop's most persuasive politics ever: The rumble articulates what no rhetoric could.

28. THE SEX PISTOLS
. . . .
Never Mind the Bollocks, Here's the Sex Pistols Warner Bros., 1977

No other disc in all rock, except maybe "That's All Right"/"Blue Moon of Kentucky," has ever so devastatingly divided time into a "before" and "after." For that alone this deserves its place in the annals, and though it took me forever to realize it, the division owes almost as much to the band's music as to their hairdos. At my high school, from where I stood, with *Love Gun* just out (a sex pistol = a love gun, get it?), these guys seemed like the next Kiss, not a bad novelty, but hardly a great one either. I always felt "No Feelings" 's nihilism, which at least didn't seem playacted, more deeply than anything else here; the "Liar"/"Problems"/"Pretty Vacant"/"Seventeen"/"New York"/"EMI" filler's all good fun, but it's not much more earthshaking than any Sham 69 or Megadeth Sid's bad habits would inspire. The music, much of it banned by Parliament (which makes it as dangerous as Barry McGuire or Frankie Goes to Hollywood!) is mainly Dollsmetal with R&B ripped out, its rhythm stuck in 1965—"Submission," a Doors-like lust-dirge that made Public Image Ltd. inevitable, has the only throb that feels much like great rock 'n' roll. And why would a girl who just abandoned her unborn child live in a tree, anyway?

But I now understand why the revolution was an aesthetic one after all, not just a sociological one, and mostly the reason is Johnny Rotten. His Johansen mimickry in "New York" is a nice in-joke, but I'm talking about how he sings maybe three songs as if he's a witch at Salem or a Jew at Dachau or a condemned man in the execution room or Edward Woodward in the final scene of 1973's *The Wicker Man* (though he looks more like Christopher Lee, who's in charge of the burning), how Paul Cook and Sid Vicious have this knack for nudging his corpus delicti toward the frying pan. My conscience wants me to believe the Rotten of "Anarchy in the U.K." is an animal; I can't allow myself to think a human being could sound like that. "God Save the Queen" reads more apocalyptically than it sounds, but when that string of "fuck"s follows the dead stop in "Bodies," more than just birth control and sex and language are at stake. There are unplanned outbursts, for instance at the end of "Bodies," when Rotten's voice collapses into insane, babbling convulsions.

Above all, if the renowned way Rotten keeps jerking you inch by inch toward then over then under then around the Berlin Wall in "Holidays in the Sun" doesn't constitute one of the most courageously inescapable antifascist decrees in all history, and it might, it almost certainly constitutes twentieth-century popular music's most frightening few seconds, seconds during which you can almost imagine someone dreading and demanding a new Sex Pistols for the same reason Rotten dreads and demands a new Belsen: If you can find the terror, you can stamp it out; if not, you've got blood on your hands. Either way, it's a gas.

29. TED NUGENT
. . . .
The Best of Ted Nugent: Great Gonzos Epic, 1981; rec. 1975–81

Ted Nugent loves animals. He loves to shoot them, loves to wear them, loves to eat them. If "Cat Scratch Fever" is meant to be taken literally, he loves to fuck them, at least if they leave nail marks on his back. (Flashback to high school, in the 'burbs: Mike Murphy explains that women *really do that,* not that he would've known or anything.) Someday, if we're lucky, Ted will record an answer to *Animal Liberation,* the lamest vinyl released in 1987, which featured harebrained hacks such as Lene Lovich, Nina Hagen, and Howard Jones whinnying about why only naughty boys eat dogmeat. Ted starts two titles here with derivations of the noun "wang" ("a molar, a grinder [Obs.]"), but his two most dangerous lock-and-load mixtures of riff and rave are the one wherein he whips "it" out then jerks it around a little, thereby inventing the Beastie Boys, and the one wherein he goes around flipping over police cars and starting a riot amid the long hot summer of '67 not 'cause he's sick of long lines at the welfare office but just 'cause he's Ted Jesus Christ Nugent and he motherfucking feels like it, that's why, asshole. In Ted Nugent's world, "Dog Eat Dog" is a political statement, and the way Ted sees it anything that hangs around that close to a fire hydrant and gets it wet *must* be a dog. He has trouble putting two and two together sometimes. So call him a moron, call him a bigot, call him a throwback to an age when men were men and girls were free and drummers drummed, call him a traitor who sold his nation's secrets to "Miami Vice." Just don't call him late for poontang. He might swallow you whole.

30. BEASTIE BOYS
Licensed to Ill Def Jam, 1986

Fueled by alcohol and junk food and angel dust, three white Brooklyn Heights and Manhattan smartasses, let loose in their wildest and most diseased daydreams, piss all over the sober face of socially acceptable adult

decorum. Reveling in orgiastic fantasies of next-big-thing rock stardom, they pillage with hammer-of-the-gods riffs burglarized from Tony Iommi and Jimmy Page, all atop Bronxzilla beats enormous enough to turn skateboards into rocket ships. Laying claim to the collective bravado of Bill Haley and Bobby Fuller and Brownsville Station and Johnny Rotten, demanding a riot of its own like the reggae-enamored early Clash, this suburban saturnalia hoards the irreverent cool of black and white kid-rebellion, cross-ethnically merging

symbols of American adolescence like nobody before or since.

Ad-Rock, Mike D, and MCA inhabit a teenage wasteland of swirlies and Wiffleball bats and ripped-off ten-speeds, Colonel Sanders and Rice-a-Roni, Ed Norton and Phyllis Diller, Old Crow and Budweiser and Thunderbird wine; their signifying monkey is the Brass kind. They do the wild thing with "ladies of the eighties" and "classy hos," dance the smurf and freak and Popeye and Jerry Lewis, hang perfume pines from rearview mirrors so their Lincoln Continentals won't smell, get ill eyein' homehards shootin' jive turkeys in the back. They turn Richard Pryor's *Bicentennial Nigger* inside out.

Rick Rubin plunders the hard-rock past like nobody's business: massive skins from "When the Levee Breaks," crude jolts from "Sweet Leaf," snippets from "The Ocean" and War's "Low Rider" and Creedence and Barry White and Mr. Ed here, verbals from "Fly Like an Eagle" and "Take the Money and Run" and "No More No More" there. All these salvaged shards are used to make connections, to outline youthcult perimeters. And when the brattiness falls together into a delerious delinquent anthem like "Fight for Your Right (to Party)," or an enormous excess-imbibing raveup like "No Sleep 'til Brooklyn" (phrase from Motörhead, glaciated guitar from Slayer's Kerry King), or a google-eyed ghetto-gangster brag like "The New Style," I can't figure why even a black supremacist would resist.

31. SEX PISTOLS
Flogging a Dead Horse Virgin UK import, 1980; rec. 1976–78

It could be argued, though not necessarily by me, that the filler surrounding "Holidays in the Sun" and "God Save the Queen" and "Anarchy in the U.K." on this singles anthology is smarter and harder than the filler surrounding the same on *Never Mind the Bullocks*. In a lot of ways, few of 'em having anything to do with "historical importance," this is the more entertaining document. "No One Is Innocent," about fascists running free and punks wearing dirty clothes, might be where the Mekons found their sound; "Silly Thing" feels happier than you'd ever guess, upgrading Bowie's "Oh You Pretty Things" into Buzzcocks Land. Lots of the words are about how you can't always get what you want, and if the frustration in the Stooges and Monkees remakes isn't nearly as fun as the frustration in the Eddie Cochran remakes, that's probably the point. "Do You No Wrong" (which starts with Pink Floyd cash-register effects!) smashes rock-hypocritic Smith-Coronas against subway walls (by comparison, Public Enemy only threatened to grab notepads); "Great Rock 'n' Roll Swindle" is a big fat final fuck-you to everybody dumb enough to have believed. And Sid's *hara-kari* demolition of "My Way," which *New York Times* writer John Rockwell used to open his 1974 Sinatra biography, *An American Classic,* has the imminent corpse hanging kittens from rafters and puking his guts out because there's nothing fucking else to do.

32. ELECTRIC ANGELS
. . . .
Electric Angels Atlantic, 1990

This quartet straddles mascara and Mad Dog camps like the Stones and 'Smith once did, like Guns N' Roses still do. They're wimps at heart, craftsmen who offset sweet spirit with poison puns: "While we were makin' out you were makin' out my will"; "She became Kryptonite and left me paralyzed"; "There's a hole in my head where the pain gets in." Electric Angels act like their idea of classic boogie is Elton John's *Rock of the Westies,* and though Tony Visconti's production (especially the bottom end) could afford to be more dense, and though I wish the combo would update their garage with a few Kix/Lep-style synths, they use the history of pop like the New York Dolls did on their first LP, like Death of Samantha does on *Where the Women Wear the Glory and the Men Wear the Pants.* It's not smug enough for "postmodernism," thank God; suffice it to say that the disc's littered with allusions (to "Baba O'Riley," "You Shook Me All Night Long," "Every

Rose Has Its Thorn," the Pistols' "Submission," 999's "Homicide," U2, the Drifters, Judy Garland, Robert DeNiro, Marilyn Monroe, Mona Lisa), and they feel like apparitions. In "I Live for the City," Cheap Trick rewrite "One in a Million" minus Axl's bile; in "The Drinking Song," the '83 Replacements come back from the dead, drunk off their rears.

Though eventually displaced when GnR debuted "Civil War" at Farm Aid IV, "Cars Crash" and "True Love and Other Fairy Tales" were the first best rock songs of the nineties. The former wraps a sadistic Mott the Hoople fuzztone around a crackling voice who hears a siren and worries his sweetheart is hurt, and from there acoustic ripples and ascending harmonies take him to a place too perfect for words, except maybe the somersaultingly sardonic words here: "Can't say I wish you were dead/Some things are better left unsaid." And "True Love" 's a majestic five-minute epic, a distant descendant of Dylan's "Desolation Row." The carpet's got holes in it, Jill's on the pill, so Jack ditches her then hitches up with Little Boy Blue (that's the "fairy" part). There's five violins, two violas, and two cellos, and when I hear 'em I pump up the thermostat.

33. PAUL REVERE AND THE RAIDERS
. . . .
Greatest Hits Columbia, 1967; rec. 1965–67

Ages before Subpop Records made the Great Northwest famous again, this Portland bunch rocked with more guts and gusto than Soundgarden or Mudhoney ever would, dressing up in Revolutionary War outfits like real live British invaders, clowning around Monkees-style in gypsy and gangster and British bobby drag in the deluxe booklet inside, ripping off drugginess from the Yardbirds and hillbilly drawls from the Stones and harmonies from the Beach Boys and chaos from Bob Dylan, protesting against drugs and (sort of) labor strife, slopping "Louie, Louie" all over the frat-house walls, making all manner of explosions with their guitars, but most of all doing it all as if it were just business as usual, dude.

In 1965 they were on TV every day, on "Where the Action Is"; six years later, in 1971, the Raiders (sans Paul) even topped the charts with a save-the-Cherokee editorial ("Indian Reservation"), thus insuring their heavy metal credentials once and for all. "Melody for an Unknown Girl"'s melody ended up being borrowed for a girl named Jean in the 1969 movie *The Prime of Miss Jean Brodie*, but here it starts and ends with a terrific sappy oratory about how "most songs have words"; "Kicks" is an answer record to Steppenwolf's "Magic Carpet Ride" two years before Steppenwolf even *did* "Magic Carpet Ride"; "Legend of Paul Revere" is a mariachi autobiography and on-our-knees plea for airplay, complete with cryptic references to Dick Clark and somebody's "bunboy." Mark Lindsay preps himself for a straitjacket in "Just Like Me" and belligerently waits through mail call for a Dear John letter (having "left town because of Uncle Sam's deal") in "Steppin' Out." And as if all that stuff's not wild enough, the editor of *16 Magazine* wrote the liner notes!

34. KIX
. . . .
Cool Kids Atlantic, 1983

On their sophomore set, Hagerstown's hottest hunks make some excursions into faceless arena rock (what with that Lou Gramm grunt and those metalbilly riffs lifted from "Women," "Burning Love" could be a parody of Foreigner's disgust with the opposite sex) and some other excursions into what I will always call "new wave" (the staccato vocals and synthesized rhythms in "Body Talk" and the gloriously hooky "Loco-Emotion" could've come from Lene Lovich's little brother). The other major touchpoints are mod-era Who (lines from "The Kids Are Alright," licks from "Can't Explain") and Bon-era AC/DC. But "For Shame" is the suburban sort of blues ballad most dentheads wouldn't master until 1989 at least, and when Whiteman's falsetto dives up and touches the sunroof of his girlfriend's new (little red?) Corvette in the title cut, he leaves no doubt that he's just found the skeleton key to the secret of the universe, or at

least of his neighborhood.

Then there's "Get Your Monkeys Out," where Kix achieves what's likely metal's only fusion of power-chords with "Monkey Man"/"Sympathy for the Devil" jungle-rhythms ever. Extending the not-always-crypto-racist tradition of whiteface monkey-minstrelsy (see: Hoagy Carmichael's "Monkey Song," Nervous Norvus's "Ape Call," the Kinks' "Ape Man," J. Geils's "Monkey Island," Starz's "Monkey Business," Beastie Boys' "Brass Monkey," George Michael's "Monkey," Rapeman's "Marmoset"), they foretell the country-cousin-visits-the-city nightmare of "Welcome to the Jungle," only this time the dream's a good one. And the one time their tempos race toward hardcore-punk levels, it's to give Steve Whiteman a chance to praise a ninety-pound smalltown weakling who grows up poor and withdrawn until he learns the power of his trap—"Mighty Mouth" oughta be the anthem of every debate-team alumnus everywhere. For all we know, given his less sanguine rebuttal in the Smiths' 1986 "Bigmouth Strikes Again," Morrissey himself might have been listening in.

35. POISON
. . . .
Open Up and Say . . . Ahh! Enigma, 1988

The artwork's even uglier than what Prince wrapped *Lovesexy* in, but with Tom Werman's production providing this raucous recombinant-pop feel and riff-banger C. C. DeVille sliding through the dust like a teenage Luis Aparicio, the outcome's less top-heavy than Poison's debut, more immediate. Bret Michaels's larynx has been hitting the Nautilus, his extrovert-chutzpah's long surpassed Dave Roth's, he snaps vowels like towels, and you have no idea whether he's being ridiculous on purpose or by accident: For cover material he perversely picks Loggins and Messina's "Your Mama Don't Dance," the most decrepit smash hit ever to exploit rock 'n' roll's good name. "Nothin' But a Good Time," real rousing as working-for-the-weekend anthems go, bites the Raspberries' "Go All the Way"; "Back to the Rocking Horse" quotes "Humpty Dumpty," bucks like "Back in the Saddle," and features a teenager begging the gods for a second childhood. "Every Rose Has Its Thorn," which could be the prettiest Troggs ballad since "Love Is All Around," is heartbreak-overload from some land beyond the soul's edge, beyond everything. C.C. strums steel strings that well up at the most impactful second available; Bret pretends he's a cowboy (a hot Nerf-metal topic, somehow), cries over spilt Milk Duds, kicks himself for some fuckup. "Fallen Angel" is good-girl-gone-bad fill-the-gap powerschmaltz, closer to a TV theme than a rock 'n' roll song, but when Bret muffles his mouth through his nose to duet with himself, it flies like an eagle. These hermaphrodressers have their hearts in the right place, and their simple-minded non sequiturs prove the common touch will prevail. Dumb escapism doesn't come any smarter: "We don't make art," drummer Rikki Rockett insisted. "We make hamburgers."

36. PRECIOUS METAL
. . . .
Right Here Right Now Mercury, 1985

Wonderful suburb-in-summertime cheeriness from Vancouver-and-Nebraska-and-otherwise-born California-girls-turning-women neither too shy nor too full of themselves to give you Technicolor rock 'n' roll to dance to, this is the most irresistible kind of anomaly available this late in the game, like a sixties garage band playing eighties radio music, or like Tiffany joining Fanny after a steady diet of Raspberries, Shadows of Knight, Eddie Money, Mud, and Judds

Photograph by Richie Aaron

singles. These sultry short-skirt shouts of heartache and abandon and femme-bonding friendship are all hook, powerchorded raw by Mara Fox and Janet Robin, semidrawled at the top of Leslie Knauer's untamed lungs, all on top of Carol M. Control's semipolyrhythmic twixt-'65-and-disco Burundi-slam. This glow-in-the-dark quintet of one-room-schoolhouse grads, Randy Rhoads disciples, *Hard Rock Zombies* extras, and former Eurobubble chirpers outkicks most any male mob on the globe without even trying, and their lusciously gasped grunge-tease "Cheesecake," with a beat too big for its britches, is the distaff "Wild Thing" (or the metal "Push Push in the Bush"?) the world's waited years for—mean enough to eat.

37. MC5
. . . .
Back in the USA Atlantic, 1970

The original punk-rock retreat-to-roots, an attempt (like the Clash's *London Calling* a decade later) to return hard smoke to its beginnings in Chuck Berry's nifty fifties (a long time ago, in my book), the Five's sophomore waxing also constituted rock's first conscious attempt (fifty-seven years after Randolph Bourne's *Youth and Life* thesis, twenty-one after Isadore Isou's *Treatise on Nuclear Economy: Youth Uprising*) to initiate an adolescent community-of-rebellion (and, hence, revolution!) amid Amerika's sizzling burgers and terminal stasis. Mainly, these White Panthers were out to change the world so's they could get laid more often by politically correct chicks. Jamkickers found Jon Landau's overcontrolled knobturns too slick, and in retrospect the punchiness does feel kinda half-formed. I wish they raved-up nervous-breakdown-style more often, like they do in "Human Being Lawnmower" and the ruthless "Looking at You"; almost all the songs are over too quick, and the one that isn't is balladic semensmarm that can't hold a candle to James Taylor's "Fire and Rain."

Still, I love how the LP situates its sis-boom-bah cuddlechoruses (as symbolized by the *Tiger Beat*–ready pix on the back) behind gonads full of tanked-up lust (as symbolized by the beastly perspiration on the front), and for sure it has the crew's best protests, warm and knowing and ready to kill: My favorite's "American Ruse," complete with "The Battle Hymn of the Republic" quotes, plus complaints re crummy guitars and (Detroit-built!) cars, not to forget the draft. The Pledge of Allegiance line should've been revived everywhere during the Bush/Dukakis presidential run, and why 136 albums were selling more copies when this thing peaked in *Billboard* will forever elude my comprehension.

38. THE JIMI HENDRIX EXPERIENCE
. . . .
Smash Hits Reprise, 1969; rec. 1967–69

Token Negro demigod to any number of racist ofay hairwaggers, Hendrix was a humorless blowhard as given to onanistic showboat puke as any of his metallic heirs, and by knowing a million chords and insisting on displaying every last one of 'em to mooncalves too stoned to get up and walk the other way, he initiated rock's cult of virtuosity for its own sake, turning a once-vernacular music into something it was never meant to be. His "poetry" is guilty of ditto. I'm told he was fun to watch (lit his eyelashes on fire or something—I can't remember), but that doesn't help his vinyl much, and since unlike most of his disciples he really *was* a virtuoso, his overapplauded "taste" and "imagination" precluded him from resorting to mere workable grooves. None of which has much to do with the dozen famous ditties gathered here, all concise enough for radio play, and a couple ("Crosstown Traffic" and "Purple Haze" especially) with housequakingly hard beats the kids on "Soul Train" can do the funky chicken to. For once, you can forget about being impressed by the playing, get off instead on the silly period lingo and wild percussive underpinnings. *Smash Hits* is living proof that corporate constrictions and market research can be our friends, and why any sane person would play any other Hendrix LP for the pleasure of it is one mystery I'll never figure out.

39. THE STOOGES
. . . .
The Stooges Elektra, 1969

Industrial youth reborn in the jungle, like *Tarzan* or something, bored. The words are sort of like haiku: "Last year I was twennyone, didn't have alotta fun." You're wondering how many more years it'll take before the bush burns, or before the singer's dick's up Cheetah's butt. Iggy Stooge spurts so much virility through his vas deferens it makes the sidewalk sticky. You can dismiss his bestiality as a metaphor, you can say it's no more meaningful than the broken glass and peanut butter he smeared his torso with on stage. You can call this an art record, and you'd be right, but only partly. Supposedly what Jimmy Osterberg really wanted to be wasn't a canine but the new Jimmy Morrison, and when his gang resorts to Krishna consciousness in the hour-long horse-latitude lullaby "We Will Fall" (and maybe in "Ann" and "Not Right" too), he's a maudlin joke, Gilbert O'Sullivan minus high

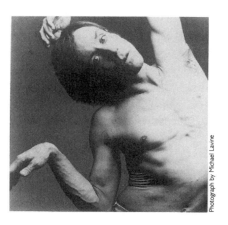

IQ. But in "1969," "I Wanna Be Your Dog," "No Fun," "Little Doll," he has no choice but to do what he's doing. He really wants to murder or rape somebody, probably himself. It couldn't have come about anywhere or anytime else, but this music is nothing so simple as a reaction to a time or place, certainly not a reaction to any other music; it's a reaction to a life. It is not music you can build a "community" on, which is where Ig's punkly descendants screwed up. The emotions have more to do with asthma medicine or humidifiers than with the newts who frequent rock 'n' roll clubs. Which of course isn't to suggest that the drummer and wah-wah pedaler wouldn't liven one up.

40. FUNKADELIC
Standing on the Verge of Getting It On
Westbound, 1974

A scatological slumdung vision of a universe gone berserk, masterminded in some secret singularity linking River Rouge to the Sea of Tranquility: On Pedro Bell's cover cartoon, a sea monster/penis/submarine-warrior battles the world; inside the gatefold, posse-participants are disguised as lost-in-space aliens, werewolves, sphinxes, and more penises, while two Richard Nixons fight for space with Bruce Lee, Sammy Davis, Jr., King Kong, a pimpmobile, and about three thousand orange and gray maggots. The opening monologue, a 45 played at 78 RPM first, then at

33, derives its primary inspiration from a Parkay commercial; in two different songs, the vocalist suggests we urinate on him as if he were a tree and we were dogs. Setting Sly's *There's a Riot Goin' On* to "Purple Haze" redux, the nasty groove's psilocybin-infested-sweet-potato-pie metalsoul bonds an ode to a sheet-staining switch-hitter with twelve minutes of heartrending antideterminist Eddie Hazel doozak-ethera plus a non-LP Parliament B-side that originally suggested ZZ Top playing Howlin' Wolf's "Tail Dragger" in Mammoth Cave cleaned up so now they're merely in an abandoned warehouse. Ray Davis is featured on "stinky finger," Calvin Simon on "suave personality," Gary Shider on "sinister grin," Tiki Fulwood on "stereo armpits," George Clinton on "behavior illegal in several states." Ron Brykowski's the "token white devil."

41. LOVE/HATE
Blackout in the Red Room Columbia, 1990

These LA dirtbags aim for the all-encompassing scope they set forth in their chosen monicker, and there are intervals where you're convinced they've hit the snail on the head. We're talking multi-switcheroo prog-minimalist decadence and cut-rate insanity delivered in an any-way-you-want-it vomit a few blocks to the west of Axl Rose's, maybe how Guns N' Roses would sound if somebody stripped 'em of their proud African-American heritage, or maybe how Die Kreuzen would sound if they grew up near film studios instead of near cheese factories (or maybe this CD is to *Appetite for Destruction* as Die Kreuzen is to *Ride the Lightning*). In their back-cover photo, Love/Hate even squat on the floor like GnR on the back of *A for D*. And one guy's named Jizzy instead of Izzy and one's named Skid instead of Slash (or maybe instead of Sid—same tradition, right?).

As you'd figure, and as the extremely groovy (inspired by "Paint It Black"?) LP title indicates, more than a few L/H tales concern euphoric substances—"Why Do You Think They Call It Dope?" "Fuel to Run," "Mary Jane," "One More Round." "Slutsy Tipsy" is an absolute undisguised rip of the Stones' "Little T.A." and "Hell, CA., Pop. 4" starts like the Beach Boys getting revenge on the Jesus and Mary Chain; mostly, the arrangements are the work of hip-hopped hop-heads, brain-rushed Rush fans, remote-controlled speedfreaks, suburbrats with abnormally short attention spans. Three minutes is a long time for these wildboys, and by then they've changed channels twelve times already. None of it exactly computes, and any one track would probably make more sense on FM or on a party tape than surrounded by stuff as like-minded as what we've got here. But I like the harmonies (straddling gaps between power-balladry and oi-revivalism and hippie-jangle) and I like the spirit and I like how the beat rolls (when it does, which isn't always). And I like when Jizzy sings about a girl who's trying to have a good time even though these are bad times. Weird, colorful, moving, painful, dopey in more ways than one—the future of punk rock?

42. The Great Glam Rock Explosion!
Biff! UK import, c. 1984; rec. 1971–74

Bands as smart as the Angry Samoans have been known to do songs making fun of humans who useta have blue hair in 1972, but the truth is that, attitudinally if not musically, glam rock accomplished just about everything both punk and disco accomplished later in the seventies. (Face it: At least compared to disco, punk accomplished *nothing* musically.) Like punk, glam set out to shock people; like disco, glam said that people should do whatever feels good (as long as they do it with good color sense). Virgin Records' 1989 *Glam Rock* videotape is a mandatory purchase for anybody with even the slightest interest in the fashion foibles of the second half of the twentieth century, but this obscurity here is the only *vinyl* glitter retrospective I've ever chanced upon. Jukebox stompolas like Mud's "Dynamite" and Suzi Quatro's invincible "Devil Gate Drive" conjure visions of young men and women racing out of the garage en route to the discotheque, oblivious to any artificial distinctions that might eventually arise between the

two habitats, shouting their teenlife love above Mike Chapman's ageless Diddley-daddied Bow Wow Wow bump—what the stiff-shirted art-punk band X would one day dumbly dismiss as "all that noble savage drum drum drum."

(But this book's about *metal,* right? Well, the record starts with "Metal Guru" by T. Rex and ends with Slade's "Far Far Away." Plus, "Touch Too Much" by the Arrows might well have inspired the song of the same name on AC/DC's *Highway to Hell.* So there.)

The tendencies toward rockarolla nostalgia can be hard to take if your stomach's (even) weaker than mine—There's flamencofied teen idol tripe from Barry Blue, proto-Rollers wimpabilly from Kenny, brassy diddybop-schmaltz from Wizzard, cockney calypso feyness from Steve Harley. But Gary Glitter's "Sidewalk Sinner" and Chris Spedding's "Motor Bikin' " tie for the Heavy Metal (or Punk, whatever) Award for their snarls and riffs, and David Bowie (alias Arnold Corns here, don't ask me why) earns the Cyberpunk Award for freaking out in his moonage daydream-oh-yeah. The Disco Award goes to Hello, not so much for their prescient electropop in "Hi Ho Silver Lining" as for how "New York Groove," later taken to number 13 on Casey Kasem's countdown as a rock/dance crossover by Ace Frehley in 1978, wiggles bass and synth that lead directly (either backwards or forwards) to Bohannon's "Disco Stomp" (though not to his "East Coast Groove," oddly enough). And the Teezers get the New Wave Award for dressing and singing just like Bananarama—They even cover a girlie-oldie! (Whaddaya mean you "don't care"?)

43. M C 5
Kick Out the Jams Elektra, 1968

Not merely the only live debut album that's ever mattered (damn few have ever even *not mattered*!), this is one of the livest *anythings* ever (Grande Ballroom, Zenta New Year, Halloween '68), a toast to civilization and its discontents, pinkos-in-training defending armed love atop insurrectionarily inflamed

National Guard jeeps on Murder City's East Side, dredging up hoodoo demons from the darkness, from "the dance from which all dances come," a euphoric state where pinning pendants on your bare chest doesn't hurt a bit. The MC5 were as American as apple pie, red-bleeding white-skinned blues-belters no matter how black they wanted to be, and "Ramblin' Rose" and "Kick Out the Jams" are the loudest, loosest freak-rock ever, a roar to end all roars, with falsettos to end all falsettos. On the lighter side, there's all these hilariously redundant "thank you thank you thank you"s and "right now right now right now"s, there's "brothers and sisters" hiding "motherfuckers" (unless you're lucky), there's Rob Tyner shouting "resounds and bizounce off the ceiling" like he's either imitating Ben Harney's turn-of-the-century ragtime routine or inventing Double Dutch, there's Brother J. C. Crawford introducing the band with a phrase that perfectly mirrors the Wizard of Oz's testimonial-presentation to Hugo Ball–lookalike the Tin Woodsman. And there's Sonic Smith's and Wayne Kramer's riffs dueling their way into the spontaneous simplicity of a Sun Ra cover where everything unravels in unropable freedback-jazz and where every last little honky sings and every last little honky plays whatever he motherfucking feels. Like wow man, it's anarchy.

44. JOAN JETT AND THE BLACKHEARTS
Album Epic, 1983

Generically titled long before John Lydon turned the same idea into a gimmick worthy of Kim Fowley, this tract's one of a kind, and not just 'cause the doo-wop echoes of "A Hundred Feet Away" and the remade Sly Stone desegregation plea are so charmingly clumsy. Ms. Jett's uninhibited defiance puts over this preprocreative desire that's usually (in the eighties anyhow) only conceivable with any credibility at all in the guise of discothrob (Exposé's "Point of No Return," Sweet Sensation's "Take It While It's Hot," et cetera). Where this occurs is severalfold: "Handyman" (where Joan moonbays re stark-nakedness and how

she's "sick and tired of masturbatin'" then begs her "too hard" beau to "come" as fast as he can), "Tossin' and Turnin'" (Bobby Lewis was never this explicit about *why* he couldn't sleep at all last night), "The French Song" (a bilingual and perhaps bisexual ménage à trois that hooks you real friendly-like). The one duff cut, "I Love Playin' with Fire," gets the words okay, but not the passion, so I'm not just talking songwriting; I'm talking intensity-of-delivery, unashamed steam-the-windows stuff, like the singer's alone in her room with a picture of a very handsome fella. Maybe, I dunno, Geddy Lee or somebody.

But something's going on. In "Secret Love," Joan bares more than mere naughty bits, and "Why Can't We Be Happy" is a celebrity spousal-shred as disquieting as Springsteen's "One Step Up" or Womack & Womack's "Night Rider." You hope the marriage will last, but you doubt it. "Fake Friends" is one long run-on sentence about toadies who stab you as soon as your back is turned, "Coney Island Whitefish" 's obscenities liken some loser to a used condom, then Joan ends it all like no rockwoman you can name, gobbing Johnny Rotten's venom all over said scumbag in "Had Enough." Somebody's shaken her up bad, discolored and shrunk her leather at the laundromat or something. As we eavesdrop we hear revenge, a life-style falling apart in Status-Symbol Land, the walls of the nuclear home crumbling.

45. LED ZEPPELIN
Houses of the Holy Atlantic, 1973

Devotees of Zep's lead mode apparently have little use for this (it's got Bob's most effete singing ever), and indulgers in "intricacy" consider the funk and reggae tossoffs gaffes, but I like it a bunch. Since (like the Byrds in the sixties and college radio in the eighties) they forfeit hookage for janglage so's even frequent crash-reverberations hardly help, such technically ace attention-getters as "The Song Remains the Same" and "No Quarter" never quite click, but "The Rain Song" is my kinda new age, and "Over the Hills and Far Away" is magnificent once Jimmy kicks it into gear, and that's only the strum-stuff. The fun stuff's better: "The Crunge" is backwards James Brown with a lost bridge, "Dancing Days" is just right at seven P.M. when you're sunning on your back porch on the first hot day in May, "D'Yer Maker" is the island where Kingston's located and the natives sing "Angel Baby" and Bonzo gives great steel drum. "The Ocean"'s riff is so cocksmanlike that Rick Rubin stole it for the Beasties' "She's Crafty," which makes sense 'cause it starts with this invisible Cockney raplet that's only audible if you turn your volume way up high. Plant winds up falling in love with a three-year-old (hence outscoring Chuck Berry in "Memphis" by thirty-six months), and somewhere else there's a pet tadpole. Not to mention Thor.

46. FUNKADELIC
Funkadelic Westbound, 1970

"If you will suck my soul, I will lick your funky emotions," it starts, but it could be Sanskrit and you'd still know something was up. Gumbo-voodoo echodub bubbles back from Dr. John's *Gris-Gris*: sustained earth-bass, mind-alteringly spare snare tortured with bones on a dark dark night, funeral-wake organ, unnerving beats stripped to the inquisition-stake essentials, percussive combustibles suggesting territory Miles and Marvin would occupy for the next couple jai-alai seasons, where Lee Perry and Burning Spear would end up a few years later, the Beastie Boys on *Paul's Boutique* and Bam Bam in "Where's Your Child" a decade after that. Eddie Hazel's dense blues-wah works like one long aphid-rock solo, winding through the whole record, slashing your skin open like a rusty tire iron in "I'll Bet You" and "Qualify and Satisfy." Fuzzy Haskins recollects leaving North Carolina, escaping the funk history laid on him as heritage, slicking his hair back in New York, then deciding the old way was better after all. So in "Music for My Mother" he heads back south, and his car speakers cough up a sound he's never heard before. He names it "way back yonder funk"; you'd guess he was talking blues (says he's in Mississippi), but he's playing some

primitive Nyabinghi reggae chant. In 1970, reggae barely existed even in Jamaica, where Desmond Decker had only just initiated his international pop-patop smash "Israelites." But back east on the alluvial plains between the Tigris and Euphrates, this chitterling foo-yung might hark back five millenniums, at least.

47. BOSTON
Don't Look Back Epic, 1978

Very much a plea for youth-unity at a time when no youth-unity was thinkable, Boston's triple-platinum followup flop lacks the epistemological oomph of their octuple-platinum debut, but its unsullied zoom, brawnier and less orchestrated, is immensely more successful at demonstrating their studio-as-arena horse sense. Since nobody in their right mind would listen to Boston for muscle, their barely believable attempts at Ledboogie machismo (visible in mere tropes like "party" and "rock 'n' roll music") defeat their wimpy reason-for-existence, and too often I hear *Third Stage*'s deflated fluff on the way. But Tom Scholz's real roots remain entrenched in the cleancut Brian Wilson proto-yup of "When I Grow Up"/"In My Room"/"Wouldn't It Be Nice"/"Wendy," and this disc's lonely-but-optimistic parts ("Used to Be Bad News," "A Man I'll Never Be," the slowdown in "It's Easy" where Brad Delp insists on "taking it day by day," and above all the chilling chimes and surf-harmonies in the title track, an eternally uplifting abandonment of subpar suburban youth whose vagueness only makes the song's passion more intense) are proof for scoffers that, in a high-tech age, high-tech precision may well be the most potent medium for communicating coming-of-age neuroses. At least if the high-tech gadgets are in the hands of a burble-brained mellowed-out animal-welfare-concerned health-food-eating engineering major.

48. GETTOVETTS
Missionaries Moving Island, 1988

Rammellzee, the Queens graffiti auteur best known for his *Stranger than Paradise* cameo and his beatnik jazzoetry on Sly and Robbie's *Rhythm Killers*, ends this rapmetal round with an attack on right reason and classical order where he illustrates how the supposed fifteenth-century catacombic invention of the vocoder (we're talking potential *Ripley's Believe It or Not* stuff here) set the scene for hip-hop's eventual displacement of Western Civilization, the two-millennium reign of which he figures was pretty well completed by Michelangelo's time anyhow. Joined by a gaggle of celebrity guests (including Nicky Skopelitis on distorted dementia), Ram whips triple-Dutch word repetition, top-of-the-head hog-Latin, and mystifying mojo-humor into a mock-messianic vision he calls Ikonoklast Panzerism, grand-scale gothic-cybernetic atonalism with comic-book war-death everywhere. Raveups inside the syncopation yield oodles of ornate wandering, especially in "Go Down! Now Take Your Balls!", corny cartoon-classical pomposity recommended to Rush partisans who feel cheated by their pet trio's recent Devo fixation. But in "Death Command," rambunctious Sahara-licks undulate across mountain ranges as multiple rhythms accelerate like coitus toward a Rammellzee climax where he harangues at auctioneer pace about overlords and overeducation and overdoses, as sonic a boom as your booty can handle.

49. CHEAP TRICK
Heaven Tonight Epic, 1978

In middlest America, ersatz Kiss riffs meet ersatz Raspberries harmonies on training wheels, Rick Nielsen's bowtie and flipped-up capbill forecasting Pee Wee Herman, Bun E. Carlos's pinstripes and granny-rims setting a standard for algebra-teacher outrageousness that'll likely remain untouched forever, Robin Zander's and Tom Peterson's looks and locks wowing the chickadees, who wooed back. The deejay rap, ELO handclapper, and Eau Claire pun barely save Side Two from sinking beneath its own bluster, but no other powerpop's ever trucked as surely as Side One, where "On Top of the World" 's like "Jack and Diane" with a wicked smirk ("she was dark she was fair"— make up your mind already!), "California Man" 's midsong silence erases the Move's original from memory, and "Auf Wiedersehen" (which should've ended Side Two instead) flirts with "All Around the Watchtower" as it divides "goodbye"'s like loaves and fishes amongst the world's populace. Before everything else, there's "Surrender," the finest parent/kid sociology modernism has known. Ma and Pa smoke your stash, spin your copy of *Destroyer*, get frisky on the couch; all you can think about are WACs with VD, your copy of *Revolver*, and never giving yourself away. Tragically, in their dealings with corporate America, the group didn't take its own advice; within a decade, they might as well've been Firefall.

50. SHAKIN' STREET
Shakin' Street Columbia, 1980

As "Whole Lotta Shakin' Going On," "All Shook Up," "Shakin' All Over," "Shake," "Shake Your Hips," "Shake Your Booty," "You Shook Me All Night Long," Eddie Money's "Shakin'," and Debbie Gibson's "Shake Your Love" demonstrate, to "shake," in r'n'r lingo, does not mean to clasp hands as a greeting, and these unjustly forgotten French metal-wavers, christened in honor of an MC5 anthem, don't. Overmadeup Gallic dominatrix Fabienne Shine no speaks English too good ("I feerll rllike a rllevorllution"—that's funny, you don't *look like* one!), but her awe-inspiring accent, which mainly consists of distended yelps and quivering cries of pure joy, nonetheless captures the complex exuberance of graduating into womanhood, learning the ropes, rebelling against a familial older generation she still loves, and just generally taking on the world, all in a way that the overwhelming majority of Americans her age would already be far too jaded to put over.

Silly, sturdy, vivaciously straightforward, you'd have to be a clod not to care about her.

With Sandy Pearlman producing and an ex-Dictator spraying tense Yardbirdchord overkill behind her, Fabienne sings to all the girls in the world, tells 'em to get their backs ready and make their eyes pretty and come up with an even better rock 'n' roll song than this one. She transmits anticipatory adolescent lust by gradually, maybe unconsciously, transforming her "I'm sixteen now" mantra to "I'm sexteen." There's a mangily fingersnappable homage to Generation X and the Who, an enigmatic Nugeknocker called "I Want to Box You" (as in "box you in," "bang your box," Boxing Day, Tyson/Givens, or what?), a side-opener named for an Aleister Crowley commandment, whizzbang Eurosyncopation toward the end of "Soul Dealer" for no apparent reason ('cept why not?), and a throat-lumping beauty of moody lushness named after the 1960 movie *The World of Suzie Wong* and dedicated to a Hong Kong prostitute who travels too much. Shakin' Street's almost as generous as San Francisco disco's great Stacey Q, almost as naive as Japan bubblepunk's great Shonen Knife—but leaner, meaner, with higher stakes.

51. DEF LEPPARD
Pyromania Mercury, 1983

With *Flashdance* and *Synchronicity*, it was one of the most profitable sub-*Thriller*s the biz came up with in Michael's year, and more than anything else, what these Mexican-chidin' spondoozles' coming-of-age LP (they were twenty-one) instigated was an indelible market strategy, eventually refined by Bon Jovi on *Slippery When Wet* and the Leps themselves on *Hysteria*: Ace hooksmanship, post–Springsteen/Maiden melodramatic condescension ("Die Hard the Hunter," "Billy's Got a Gun"—the titles tell all), butch banality, Journeyesque love-gush, put it all together and it spells "money." Which is fine, because no matter *what* Billy Bragg says, corporate capitalism's done more to help rock 'n' roll than to hurt it, because the primary impetus for good music-making has

always been *hunger,* for fame and dames and bread. The best parts ("Rock of Ages," "Photograph," "Rock! Rock! Till You Drop") are semiinflated powerpop AC/DC, simple romps junior goodwrenches can pump fists to while their girlfriends wish and hope. "Photograph" keeps switching back and forth between naive longing and he-man get-outta-here; as "Rock of Ages" begins, *der kaiser* from *das Vaterland* counts backward or something, in German. It's a hoot. You opened your car window, cranked it at the stiffs, and it was hard to hate, hard to "feel" *anyway whatsoever* about, in fact. That's what made it so profitable, Billy Bragg might explain. But he'd be wrong.

52. AEROSMITH
Greatest Hits Columbia, 1980; rec. 1974–80

Contrary to prevalent illuminati propaganda, they really weren't a singles band, and there's at least three discs more convincing than this one to show you why (one of which is an LP-track anthology, but what the hey). Four of these ten songs are also on one of those three discs. The great ones that aren't: "Dream On," a poison-ivy piano-dirge, closer to what Die Kreuzen became than to anything Zep had ever been, about the past coming back to give you the creeps as you get on in years; "Same Old Song and Dance," with "coincidental moida" and "old hurdy-gurdy" and reams of wah; "Draw the Line," Steve Tyler beating redneck girls at chess and craps then singing cowboy songs (see Bon Jovi, Poison) then screeching like a scorched salamander on some strange astral plane during Indian summer. "Kings and Queens" is a castle-pomp legend (or parody?) that I suppose furthers "Draw the Line" 's checkmate motif, and the awful Beatles and okay Shangri-Las covers are sixties tributes, who cares. Then, available elsewhere, sure, but not in this order, there's "Sweet Emotion," "Walk This Way," "Last Child," and "Back in the Saddle": Some kinda unique freaky-deke riff-rock, catchily fast and gluteusly maximal despite the sleazy/teasy AOR time-changes, seasoned with rhythm lines and maracas and cowbells, all from a time when hard guitars were something you were supposed to throw cherry bombs at instead of dance to. The bluesfunk blackness was never a "move," and the screamer up front wore colorful scarves.

53. THE THREE JOHNS
. . . .
Atom Drum Bop Abstract UK import, 1984

England's premier posteverything power trio was pissed about all the right stuff: jungle imperialism, emotional fascism, screwed-over mineworkers, the works. But they were smart enough to be mixed-up enough to know that they really didn't know what the heck was going on. And they realized that no way are our lives gonna be saved by rock 'n' roll, so they flushed the fashion and forewent the pop charts and reveled in hard stuff, tendencies that made them seem like cynics in the Philanthropic Pop Age, though really they were more metapop than antipop. They could sound like Cream with no instrumental training or the Gang of Four with a sense of humor or the Moody Blues with male gonads, but mostly they did for the Stooges what the Stooges did for Bo Diddley, and they did it with a goddamn drum machine. On their least meek (and only indispensable) album, alone

and left to rot in a dead-wrong world that doesn't really want them, they find affinity with the wandering cowhands and oppressed true believers of American myth, incorporating sample-like snippets of Hank Williams, Jimmie Rodgers, the Swingin' Medallions, the Golden Gate Quartet, and Bobby Vee, amidst which touchstones these feedback-funkers falsetto, growl, refuse to tune up, and swing like thumpasauri caught in crosstown traffic. These court jesters may fuck around, but at the outset anyway, they didn't fuck around.

54. Michigan Rocks
. . . .
Seeds and Stems, 1977; rec. 1965–70

In which draft-aged offspring of autoworkers and autoexecs, from Detroit and Ann Arbor and Flint, ingest the amateur passion of Seattle garage punk, the excess of Britain's blues revival, the honking big-beat of Motown's lefternmost wing (Junior Walker, say, or the Contours), and the chaos of Saturn free jazz, and cough it up as one massive momporker of a blue-collar guitar-army teenage-lust death-trip of a real cool time. Bob Seger, the MC5, the Stooges, Mitch Ryder, and Nugent's Dukes are remembered; Frost, SRC, Rationals, and Third Power (who sound like the best of the couldabeens) aren't. Ryder's Detroit do the Velvets, SRC do Cream, Scott Morgan's Rationals do Aretha, but they *all* do sex (Rob Tyner goes "uh huh, uh huh, uh huh," Seger goes "goin' in now, goin' in now, c'mon with me babe, goin' deep-uh, *deep*-uh, woaah! woaah!"), and they all do boredom, escape, seduction, destruction. Nothing in recorded sound has matched the integrity and brute force of the best of what came out of this place at this time—Seger's early local hits ("East Side Story," "2 + 2 = ?," "Back in '72," et cetera) might someday be compiled into one of the most desert-islandable LPs ever. And though a couple tracks here are just curios and a couple are in better company elsewhere, "Heavy Music" and "1969" and "Journey to the Center of Your Mind" and "Kick Out the Jams" (w/"motherfucker") *need to be heard. By you.* Period.

55. PERE UBU

Terminal Tower: An Archival Collection
Twin/Tone, 1985; rec. 1975–80

Side One's got the coolest cold wave ever to blow out of Cleveland, this dark, odd-shaped, pressingly poetic rhythm-rock, riveting Velvet/Hawkwind/Blue Cheer atonal eruptives from sometime rockcrit Peter Laughner ("30 Seconds over Tokyo" is basically Sabbath's "Electric Funeral" with new words) pushing druggy heartland-teen dissatisfaction over the top. Lead fatty Crocus Behemoth, who physically resembles the farcical late nineteenth-century Alfred Jarry villain for whom the band's named, spews the convulsingest declamations you'll ever love, vinegar iconography and hallucinogenic hardy-har-har re alien lands and strange gods, mushroom clouds and evolutionary theories. One rant's named for a '44 WW II flick, another for the Joseph Conrad book that inspired *Apocalypse Now;* the best, "Final Solution," could've been named for Hitler's grand scheme, but the band denied it. Ubu's later stuff, represented on Side Two, is happy-faced musique concrète noise-scaping, dada in the face of factory overload and Laughner's death, from bohemians slowly succumbing to their own solipsistic shtick. The singer changes his name, pledges his soul to Jehovah, starts liking birdies too much, reverts to his crib; the sea chanteys and cellos sink into the demiclassical void. By the end, it might not have *sounded* like Jethro Tull, but it sure did feel like it.

56. ZZ TOP

The Best of ZZ Top London, 1977; rec. 1973–77

Billy Gibbons's grungiest slideriffs ever, and maybe everybody's, so unholy they give you a heartburn that keeps bubbling back from your bowels toward your breath all day (Rolaids won't help), so fevered you could fry an emu egg on 'em, boot into action taut chugalugged Delta-to-desert and border-to-barrio "tall tales" where the son of God (in "Jesus Just Left Chicago") stands in line for hours (in "Waitin' for the Bus") with his paycheck (in "Just Got Paid") and his brown bag full of Lone Star (in "Beer Drinkers and Hell Raisers"), then takes the Greyhound to Brownsville and does the hat dance to Mexican outlaw-kilohertz (in "Heard it on the X") and ogles the stone-washed sacroiliacs (in "Blue Jean Blues") of thirteen-year-old Jewish American Princesses (in "Tush"). The way that mumbled rap and those windswept maraca-spiced strums and that grunted "ungh haw haw haw haw" lure me into "La Grange" 's moosemeat-rock always makes my pores ooze Tabasco.

57. *Nuggets, Volume 2: Punk*

Rhino, 1984; rec. 1965–69

Love's "My Little Red Book," the Shadows of Knight's "Gloria" and "I'm Gonna Make You Mine," the Music Machine's "Double Yellow Line" and "The Eagle Never Hunts the Fly," the Chocolate Watchband's "Are You Gonna Be There (At the Love-in)?" the Standells' petition for interracial harmony, "Sometimes Good Guys Don't Wear White," and above all the Sonics' "Strychnine" are the sort of world-class raunch that made heaviness and metalness conceivable (most of 'em are detailed in long-form elsewhere in this volume), and every last one of 'em's more palatable here than on the single-band reissues where you'll also find 'em, so go for it already. Equally notable on this collection of teenaged TV-watchers (that's where said garageoids learned their stuff, y'know) are New York's Vagrants, guitared by callow fatsby Leslie West. But my personal faves are the mysterious Elastik Band (not to be confused with Bootsy's Rubber Band), who might've come from anywhere, who change genres about ten times in two minutes, and whose singer has serious problems forming words with his mouth. The number's entitled "Spazz," and it deserves to be.

58. THE VIBRATORS
Pure Mania Epic, 1978

These Limey goof-offs dressed up as punk-rockers (wore leopardskin pants!), but they were lying. Really they were squeaky-clean and politically incorrect *old* guys (who even reminisced about the days they were twenty-two!), which means they didn't give a shit and just wanted to raid your wallet, which of course makes 'em neat 'cause it makes 'em plastic and proud. They're Velvets fans (they quote "Here She Comes Now" in this absurd ditty called "Whips and Furs," which is actually about *dancing*), so they pretend to know about drugs and sadomasochism, but in truth they probably know less about either than I do, which is zilch. The phylum's Plain Old Corny Powerchorded 'n' Uncooked Lovestuff, prone to redundant titles ("Baby Baby," "Yeah Yeah Yeah," "Sweet Sweet Heart"), with an unscrupulous forward motion that gets you sprinting in circles around your abode. Singer/guitarer John Ellis is always threatening his girlfriend, but he's so wimpy and clutzy a misogynist she'll probably kick his butt. 'Cept for "Whips and Furs" (same song as Van Halen's "Dance the Night Away," more or less), my pick hits are the one where London girls get him and his Beatlemaniac buddies down and the one where he rhymes "bitch," "feminine itch," and "she's gonna put you in a ditch and you're gonna blow your brains out."

59. AMON DÜÜL II
Dance of the Lemmings United Artists, 1971

This comes from Germany (where, though I've never seen it documented in print, such probable Red Army/Green Party cronies as Düül, Can, and Faust constituted a veritable astro-punk underground in the early seventies), and the scope and vision suggest Captain Beefheart's *Trout Mask Replica* without Beefheart's histrionics, and like *Trout Mask* this'd be a smart item to pack in your desert island kit if only 'cause its four sides would take forever to figure out. Yet unlike Van Vliet's acclaimed twofer, this one's got sounds headbangers of human descent can connect with and care about. Like, for starters, a groove: repetitive identifiable-riff hypnorhythms electronically charged like a fifty-kw power generator spitting petrol; hopped-up textures yanked into Teutonic time structures that detour toward Algeria and the Congo or try to steal away via close encounters of the third kind. With Beach Boys harmonies on top.

Snatches of tasty glissando forecast these semimetal oddballs' eventual prog-rock downfall, and might even remind you of ELP if they weren't caked in so much distorted percussion; who knows, maybe this is even supposed to be a "song cycle." The subject, though, is anybody's guess: Side One's entire sixteen minutes are dedicated to the "Roaring Seventies," and Side Three's set aside for "The Marilyn Monroe Memorial Church." So the sources of Düül's strange kind of wit apparently could've developed even if rock 'n' roll hadn't. The titles (and subtitles) are magically funny ("Dehypnotised Toothpaste," "A Short Stop at the Transylvanian Brain-surgery," "H. G. Wells Takes Off," "Chewinggum Telegram," "Stumbling over Melted Moonlight"), but the jejune jabber's bleared into whispers and glottal cracks and rrribbits and squeaks, not to mention all this uppercrustedly erudite try-to-phrase-every-syllable-just-right-but-get-it-wrong unnaturalness that somehow ends up sounding conversational. Y'see, that's how Germans *talk*. I spent three years there.

60. MOTT THE HOOPLE
Brain Capers Atlantic, 1972

"**D**eath, May Be Your Santa Claus," Ian Hunter calls the first number, and the last one's "The Wheel of Quivering Meat Conception," but despite the goofy titles, Mott's most metal album (dedicated to James Dean) is dead serious. On the first side, especially, there's no way out of the gloom: "howlong 'fore you realize you stink?" the text commences, bitter in-your-face splatter above whistle-stop percussives, this cat in shades and Afro getting off on his own esotericism, not giving a fuck what anybody thinks. Ian covers Dion's brittle "Your Own Back Yard," a '70 single as candid and unapologetic as any junk-rehabilitation homily ever, so briskly you'll need another sweater. He covers the Youngbloods' "Darkness, Darkness" as a gigantic dirge, the world imploding into Buffin Griffin's drum set. Then "The Journey" 's eight minutes build to repetitive bloody-boned chord-hysteria so you can barely figure out what's happening, just that somebody's following somebody somewhere, and he's leaving something behind. The way out amid Side Two's heavified *Blonde on Blonde* crescendo-rock is Ian's habitual cheat (nice women who'll munch his jelly roll), but then he turns around and directs "The Moon Upstairs" at his audience ("We're not bleeding you, we're feeding you, but you're too fucking slow"). He ends the number with a sarcastic sort of laugh that'd lay dormant until Minor Threat's "Out of Step" over a decade later, and you know for sure he's not gonna do himself in, though his band's future was another question entirely. It took David Bowie's pleading to get them back together.

61. MC5
High Time Atlantic, 1971

From what I can see, especially judging from the "before" (clean-cut), "after" (hairy and naked), and "after/after" (crippled) photo opportunities inside, this is where these Motorboys forfeited their Children's Crusade and settled down to make music qua music, seasoning *Kick Out the Jams*–type skronkjazz stretches with *Back in the USA*–type high school hooks. Like one cut's tipsy gypsy, the results wander all over the street: "Gotta Keep Moving" (where Vietnam and atom bombs induce human growth) and "Over and Over" (*Who's Next*/"2 + 2 = ?"–brand antiextremist cynicism) are the closest it gets to agit-rah-rah, "Miss X" (with Sonic Smith on sandpaper) is supposedly intolerably antiwoman but I've never deciphered Rob Tyner's mumblification, "Future/Now" features Dennis Thompson on "Acme scraper," and they even follow a fancy tarot-cards-on-Mars spaghetti western with some dippy EST poetry.

The opener and closer are best: "Skunk (Sonically Speaking)" (with Bob Seger, Scott Morgan, and other neighbors on an oil refinery's worth of drums) is surfbeat hornmetal you can dance to, and "Sister Anne," which has gotta be the most whimsical ode ever dedicated to a nun (she saves souls but didn't save Tyner's, and the cleverest line suggests she's either an antievolution creationist or an antirevolution reactionary), ends with some Dixieland theme apparently called "Freedom Now" squawked off-key by a tuba and trombone from Ann Arbor's Salvation Army (a proletarian version of Fleetwood Mac's USC Marching Band collaboration). As an object, *High Time* sacrifices some of the categorical imperative of its more celebrated predecessors (you could say it plays cover-all-the-bases *Sign o' the Times* to *Kick Out*'s renegade *Dirty Mind* and *Back in the USA*'s mass-market *Purple Rain*), but the sounds strike a happy compromise for the band's biggest *visceral* wallop. Still, though I play it as often as or more than the MC5's other two official outings, I'd be lying if I claimed to get as much out of it.

62. BLUE CHEER
Outsideinside Philips, 1968

In Frisco just months after the Summer of Love, truths about human nature rear their ugly noggins. Acid-wrecked Allosauri eat alive tiny tie-dyed evolutionary mammals with flowers in their hair, a broken-down Gibson curdles like extra-large-curd curds-and-whey, famous songs by the Stones and Booker T get torn to pieces like Coltrane having a go at Rodgers and Hammerstein. "Satisfaction" predicts the Stooges' "Not Right" for a couple seconds, and Babylon is established for the entertainment of not merely the Dolls, not merely Faster Pussycat and Rock City Angels, but also Pajama Party and Boney M and everybody else who sang about the place. Abe Kesh sculpts *Vincebus Eruptum*'s preposterous mob rule into a turbulence that actually halfway approximates "music" ("Magnolia Caboose Babyfinger" is expeditious concentric repetitious braindrain instrometal that demonstrates how Johnny & the Hurricanes connect to Slayer, and "Gypsy Ball" 's "maze of liquid smoke" is escorted by an honest-to-Zeus *hook*!), but purists needn't fret 'cause the atonal Altamont that concludes "Just a Little Bit" is unequivocally impossible. Who was this band's audience, I wonder?

63. THE VELVET UNDERGROUND
· · · · · · · · · · · · · · · · · · ·
White Light/White Heat Verve, 1968

Vocals designed to make you check your speaker-chord hookups are juxtaposed with motionless feedback free-for-alls in a manner that Actually Makes You Want to Go Out and Mess Up Your Head and Your Life and Your Family's Lives with Drugs, so be real careful, okay? It's like a loaded gun, and Metal Mike Saunders of the Angry Samoans has pointed out that if the primary instigator (a minor New York folksinger known as Lou Reed) could go back in Mr. Peabody's way-back machine and point such a weapon to his head upon completion of said artwork and thereupon proceed to release the hammer, "that'd really unclog a lot of back product on those shelves," and I'd be inclined to agree. Once upon a time rock critics had a habit of checking each others' copies for wear and tear in much the same way German metal bands check each others' penises for same (made 'em feel like "men," y'see), but budding youngsters are advised

(starting right now) to act As If the Velvet Underground Never Happened, which in a certain sense they never did. (The next time you get your oil filter changed, ask the mechanic if he's ever heard of 'em. I bet not.)

WL/WH is the Velvet Underground's noisiest album, and as such it has several well-known underground "hits," one of which ("Sister Ray") lasts over seventeen minutes and apparently concerns lollipops and dirty carpets or perhaps barn doors, and another of which ("The Gift") is a performance-art piece detailing one poor chap's devious attempt to get the better of the U.S. Postal Service and simultaneously save on airline tickets by boxing himself up as a party favor for his object of affection who probably oughta purchase a crowbar next time. The rest of the record is rather comforting if you're sick with the flu. Of the two songs with feminine pronouns in their titles, one ("Here She Comes Now") has almost the same title as "There She Goes Again," a song on the Velvet Underground LP from the previous year. It gets real confusing after a while.

64. BAD RELIGION
· · · · · · · · · · · · · · · · · · ·
Into the Unknown Epitaph, 1983

Supersonic bombast that builds to incredible mighty climaxes, fully awash with track upon track of uplifting-as-all-get-out piano and organ and synth and guitar, this sounds like Hawkwind but feels way less exotic, more like how the prairie art-schlockers in Kansas and Styx always *tried* to feel. Teen angst for a post-Tang generation where everybody loves an anthem, the songs are little parables about bad things old people do and how young people should keep from becoming bad like their elders: A man walks out on the good life; a woman kills herself when marital bliss turns out not to be so blissful after all; a regular guy blows up his car, loses his mind to dope and worms, and just generally goes bonkers to a tune lifted from Steve Miller. The fables break down to your life-sucks-when-you're-young-but-not-enough-to-do-that numbers and your grownups-really-fouled-up-the-ecology numbers. Can't figure out which endangered species they're trying to save (I'm hoping Tasmanian wolf but betting pronghorn antelope), and "Time and Disregard" 's 6:50 of Zep-to-Tull grandiloquence would be real annoying if it wasn't so catchy it gives me goose pimples, but the first and last cuts are inconceivably inspirational: When you haven't a friend in the world, and you turn to light and all you get is darkness, and you're lost in space, and your life's in the garbage, it's only over when you give up. If I knew a kid who was considering suicide, I'd spin him these songs, and he'd start a band instead. That's what music is for, right?

65. PINK FAIRIES

Pink Fairies Polydor UK import, 1976; rec. 1970–73

Smart Brits originally headed by widely published social-criticker Mick Farren (who'd skedaddled by the time their first LP came out), the Fairies useta bang their beanies for no charge outside the gates of big-moneyed rock festivals, the notes say, a protopunk sort of subversion-strategy for sure. This cheapo comp adds to their bluesbelch-burlesque saga the overboard phallusbilly fuzzwiggle surf-clangor of "The Snake" and the ZZ-just-left-Chicago goobaloo of "Well, Well, Well." The remainder consists of the first four tracks from their confused *Never Never Land*, the side-openers and one side-closer from their streetbound *Kings of Oblivion*, and three noncovers from their airheaded (as in "headed toward the air") *What a Bunch of Sweeties*. The very best stuff from the latter two LPs is left off, the inclusion of the jagged Optimist's Club rallying cry "Do It" from *NNL* renders said slab irrelevant, and you'll never find any of 'em anyhow so what difference does it make? "Pigs of Uranus," which almost enables me to forgive the Fugs, does not concern a planet.

Photograph by Dean Freeman © 1989

66.6. THE OSMONDS

Crazy Horses MGM, 1972

Institutionalize my butt at your own peril, but a couple of their singles ("Yo-Yo," "Down by the Lazy River") are epitomes of Sweetdom where Donny goes completely mad, his siblings think they're on Motown, and tuff little riffs keep walking the dog. "My Drum," on 1971's *Phase III*, could be Cactus-doing-Funkadelic, and this scabrous slab here delves even further into the den of iniquity: Marie's and Little Jim's big bros open with a cannibalistic "Immigrant Song" rip called "Hold Me Tight" and keep up to date with rebellious teen trends by dressing up like drug-crazed "Electric Company" rejects. The title track's got the most apocalyptic Book of Revelation imagery this side of Dylan/Osbourne, and I swear to Joseph Smith its demented kicks and whinnies were stolen *outright* by Aerosmith in "Back in the Saddle" (you always thought Mick taught Steve to sing, but really it was Don) and eventually by Poison (the new Osmonds?) in "Back to the Rocking Horse," which is of course a song about wanting to be a toddler again, which is only appropriate. Plus there's soulful booglegum about taxiing back to the Land of the Mormon and tossing a hash-bash, irresistibly tape-doctored toetap ragpop ("Girl" beats Redd Kross's *Neurotica* by fifteen years and fifteen miles!), and parroted Bee Gees-circa-*Idea* ambrosia. The eighteen-second "Big Finish" is a self-parodic reprise of their fruity fave "One Bad Apple," still the most effective Michael Jackson genesplice of all time. And the horn charts all over the place make no sense whatsoever, but then neither does bigamy.

67. BILLY SQUIER
Don't Say No Capitol, 1981

Showered 'n' shaved schoolboy sex, Plant and Page in the land of white picket fences and eavestroughs, a beastly boom from drums and drum machine on up, one of the Cash Decade's lewdest grooves, the farthest thing from broomstick-up-the-butt AOR formalism, yet somehow it fit right in. "You Know What I Like" ties "Immigrant Song" into granny knots, and hearing "Lonely Is the Night" for the first time in Dunkin' Donuts once, I assumed it *was* Zep, but "My Kinda Lover"'s itchy dancetrance bassplay is three recurrent notes direct from Chic, and "The Stroke" ranks with the sleaziest, sassiest, strangest, slyest hit singles of the eighties—punkfunk for real (not a satire like Zep's "The Crunge"), with words that equate greed with a handjob with the newest dance craze. Squier's metaphors are droll and bent, all these firm handshakes and big breaks and charitable contributions out of Wall Street's tax-sheltered ivory towers of brokerage; he says "business" a lot. And just when his frustration with the opposite gender starts to get the best of him (and hence starts to get intolerable) in "Whadda You Want From Me," he goes pop, cries on his baby's shoulder, and adds purty harmonies. He dedicates a feathery fluffed slow one "to the life of John Lennon," and its tune would've sounded fine on *Double Fantasy*—this is something Teena Marie would do. Damn near makes you forgive the rest of the second side for feeling kinda nondescript.

68. ANGRY SAMOANS
Back from Samoa Bad Trip EP, 1982

Rudely mutilated, emotionally stunted, impervious-to-criticism menace-riff fear-and-loathing praying at the altars of '65 and '71, as pop as the Go-Go's, as big-hearted as David Lee Roth, and as Hollywood as either: Almost every toilet-water screed ends up turning back on itself, and in screeds so short they're almost over before they start; it's a wonder they have time to turn *anywhere*. Angry as the Samoan hulks in Tom Wolfe's *Mau-Mauing the Flak Catchers* (who make "Bubba Smith of the Colts look like a shrimp"), friendless and frustrated white middle-class teendorks who haven't been teens for years end up stuck with their heads on the bedboard or asses in the gas chamber or ears on the blasting car radio, not knowing for sure whether they're gays or Nazis, just happy they're not social types. Not half as distanced as it pretends to be, this is truly deranged dry-rot about not belonging anywhere, sung deadpan by Metal Mike Saunders as if he's used to it—"My Old Man's a Fatso" is the closest anybody in the eighties came to "Yakety Yak." The fourteen righteous goofus hookchunks fly past in eighteen minutes, and though I've listened literally hundreds of times, I've yet to absorb even half of 'em.

69. THE WHO

Meaty Beaty Big & Bouncy Decca, 1971; rec. 1965–70

The first sound you hear—"I Can't Explain"'s primally clipped riff—is also the first sound you hear on *The Clash*. Pete Townshend was inventing something called "teenager." (Well, the Jazz Age invented it first, then WW II, then Dion DiMucci. But you get the idea.) He wrote songs about jacking yourself off to sleep, hanging out with your homeboys, experimenting with your chemical set, being born with less money than rich people, believing for a couple minutes you might end up on top someday. They were little songs, but there was more sense in them than in any of the big songs he would write later, and more feedback too. (This is all a matter of public record by now, obviously.) The sounds in "The Kids Are Alright" and "Substitute" didn't fit a context again till the late seventies, not when punk happened but when powerpop did; the voice in "I Can See for Miles" eventually found a context in pop-calypso star Johnny Nash, of all people. "Boris the Spider" and "I'm a Boy" probably helped instigate Alice Cooper and David Bowie. The feedback found a home in garage rock and metal and punk, of course, as did the journalism. Wasn't hardly ever so articulate after this, though.

Likewise, you could make a pile of every "rock opera" Townshend has ever waxed verbose in, and you still couldn't say half as much about angry young men approaching adulthood as the tied tongues in "I Can't Explain" or the stammers in "My Generation" do.

70. LED ZEPPELIN

3 Atlantic, 1971

Starting, ending, and centering itself on punkfunk devastations of Odin's Norse rovers and the singer's women—"Immigrant Song," "Celebration Day," and the very underpraised "Out on the Tiles"—the first side belongs to John Paul Jones. Side Two seeps up from the Everglades or Appalachians, or over from the Salisbury Plain in Wiltshire or the Snowdonia peaks in Wales, with bondage-free bluegrass, backside-first blues, and blue-eyed bathos for men on death row and scared hippie heroes. Robert Plant's sinuses vibrate like an elastic G-string, like a crazed canary trying to warble its way through the rusty third rail, and though as usual his blues matters least, for once it at least matters: "Since I've Been Loving You"'s stately keyboard arpeggios could be Alan Price or Gary Brooker or even Felix Cavalierre, and "Hats Off to (Roy) Harper"'s 78 RPM mix would've sounded timely in Mississippi in '31 or Manhattan a half-century later.

71. CHEAP TRICK

In Color and in Black and White Epic, 1977

Neither gushy nor hot-doggy in the riff department, this is krafty kookiness all down the line, starting with the cover's bikes vs. motorbikes. The sing-alongs are sing-alongable, Bell Telephone determines the opening notes of "Clock Strikes Ten" (a better refashioning of "Rock Around the Clock" than even the Honkers on "Sesame Street" have managed), and "You're All Talk" boogies with disco-inspired flair. Slackjawed awestruck sap like "I Want You to Want Me" and "Oh

Caroline" and "Southern Girls" works better still, "Downed" 's teary-eyed ethics-dilemma best of all— "Too many people wanna save the world/Another problem is a boy or girl," plus we're asked to choose between suicide, Christianity, and Australian mountain ranges. For a while this pile brought hushaby harmony-hooks back to midwestern airwaves, and if so much of it weren't as hollow as it expects your head to be (in one ear out the other, y'know), it might be the most delectable metalpop anywhere.

72. MOTÖRHEAD
Orgasmatron GWR/Profile, 1986

Produced to the hilt by a guy who usually works with Herbie Hancock or Mick Jagger or Afrika Bambaataa, released on a label that usually works with Run-D.M.C., fortressed by an explicitly disco-influenced backbeat, centerpieced by slow songs with "rapped" vocals, named for a device in an old Woody Allen movie, this disque in no way caters to the technology-shunning speedmetal subgenre Motörhead almost singlehandedly inspired. The most commercial music the band ever made and at the same time the riskiest, *Orgasmatron*'s got knob-watcher Bill Laswell accentuating the foursome's violent thundersquall by pushing the bottom all the way forward: Each side begins with a gargantuan syncopation-rock "dance" tune, breaks down to a couple familiarly rebellious rapid-fire detonations, then climaxes with a claustrophobic nightmare framed in no-wave white noise.

The midside crunch-formalities chew like raw prime beef, as lustful as post-Detroit gunk gets, with screams, sex-moans, and handclaps as supplementary hooks so subtle you barely notice Laswell put 'em there. Where he's most visible is on the brick walls of sound that frame the thing. In "Deaf Forever," he drops whiplash drums behind an immense Lemmy bassline and a lyric that uses Valhallas and Vikings (a medievalist first for this combo) to suggest that war is not only hell, but noisy as hell, too; "Mean Machine," a midnight black bash that shares its title with a sharp single Laswell produced for proto-rappers the Last Poets in '84, addresses AIDS years before any alleged agit-rockers thought to. In "Built for Speed," Lemmy defends rock against the church, admits he's getting old, then decides it's too late to call it quits.

But the LP-concluding title-track is nothing less than the most ominous and dead-on reworking of the "Sympathy for the Devil" evil-talks-to-us motif ever to slither down Pluto's pike. In a lowing drone that makes his usual husky shout seem like Dionne Warwick's, over experimentally caved-in groove-tension that owes as much to Lemmy's old art-rockers Hawkwind as it does to Laswell's old art-funkers Material, the singer plays "religion," then "the politician," then "Mars, the god of war," mocking how this triumvirate's always turned history into a lie, civilization into barbarism, bones into palaces. Don't expect they'll call it quits any time soon either.

73. PRINCE AND THE REVOLUTION
Purple Rain Warner Bros., 1984

Not the Purple People Eater's best album, but close, and (though his most roof-tearing thump, "Bambi," dates back to before his well-hyped "conversion" to hard rock) certainly his most "metal" (not to mention his most profitable): Hi-volume Page/Hendrix/Hazel wah-blankets pop out of the pop everywhere, most blatantly at the beginning and end of both sides, in "Let's Go Crazy" (sex 'n' God), "Darling Nikki" (bump 'n' grind that starts to stop like Laurie Anderson's "O

Superman" starts), "When Doves Cry" (slay the father, lay the mother, strip your beat till it bridges Sly's *There's a Riot Goin' On* and Chip E.'s Windy City parking-lot blues), "Purple Rain" (cosmic John Lennon nuke-Armageddon). Select lightweight passages forecast the 3-D/sitar/quiet-storm/new-age-psychology/smiley-face/fuck-patter beezwax we wanted to strangle him for circa *Around the World in a Day* and *Lovesexy*. Although sometimes he's lazy and lispy and devoid of the gospel-to–Gamble/Huff hooks he puts in his slow ones when he doesn't suck, "Take Me with U"'s crispy and flaky as a tasty pastry, "The Beautiful Ones" has a suicidal wail out of Funkadelic's "Into You," "I Would Die 4 U"'s a prayer, and "Baby I'm a Star"'s tough Sylvester-disco hears Deep House on the way. Unlike most everybody else in the eighties, Prince's strangeness was no fake: His "message" was totally wrongheaded or at the very least contradictory, and he knew it, but like any true rock 'n' roller, he didn't give a shit. Always, when he's being really strange, he kicks my ass, and when he's just being a little strange, I want to kick his; here, soaked in soulful Farfisoid zaniness that goes as many different routes toward the same goal as an ace choir, he's mostly the former. He left "Erotic City," which just might've been the best track, off.

74. ANGRY SAMOANS
Inside My Brain PVC, 1987; rec. 1978–80

Aside from holes drilled in your head, laughably naked (soon-to-be-ex-) girlfriends, mentally handicapped pedagogues, and two-tub turkeys who pick their noses, deep-seated psychological problems are perhaps the most prominently abused topic on this turn-of-the-presidency "work" by two erstwhile *CREEM* scribes and three other nitwits under the combined tutelage of Nitzinger (early seventies hardcore), Unrelated Segments (sixties speedmetal), Dion and the Belmonts (fifties punk rock), and other such combos whose hot-dog riffing and/or (smelly)-sock-hop hooks get under your skin like body odor. Their idols the Dictators cared about "Cars and Girls"; the

Samoans care about "Carson Girls," ones so cute they deserved to get kissed ("in the . . . face!"). Fresh from their legendary sanitarium gig, assorted loners and Mudhen fans send the second-meanest rockjoke ever ("You Stupid Asshole," as in "baby I'm one too") sliding directly into the first-meanest ("Get Off the Air," which is also the least crapulous antiradio kvetch ever, mainly 'cause it's anti-"*alternative*" radio, namely KROQ's Rodney Bingenheimer, "jerking off in Joan Jett's hair"). Then they go home.

75. SUZI QUATRO
Suzi Quatro Bell, 1974

Hey, they let her play Fonzie's pal Leather Tuscadero on "Happy Days" (after playing a go-go dancer named Suzi Soul somewhere!), and her back made the front page of *Rolling Stone* (1/2/75, three years after her debut 45 "Rolling Stone"!), so Quatro must've been doing something right, right? I mean, I don't care about mummy and daddy's annual income *or* what instrument her brother wound up making a fool of himself on, "48 Crash" and "Can the Can" hit you with screaming meaninglessness that feels like a kiss, "Primitive Love" is as immodest as it is crypto-racist (plus its production has foreknowledge of acid-house!), glitterstomps about fat aging groupies banging on the backstage door are a hoot by definition, and there's even a song with the nonword "suburbian" in the title!

The rest is Burundi 'n' roll revivalism no more respectable than Sha Na Na, but when Suzi conjugates the erotic rockverb "to shake" with every protodisco thigh-quiver at her disposal in her covers of Elvis's "All Shook Up" and Johnny Kidd's "Shakin' All Over," and when she shows Joan Jett how one bends one's gender in her ace redo of Lennon/McCartney's "I Wanna Be Your Man," she clearly paves the way for how her real-life niece Sherilyn Fenn knotted that cherry stem in her mouth on "Twin Peaks." I mean, in "All Shook Up" Suzi's friends call her "queer as a bug," and it's still a *girl* whose lips are volcano top–like! And "Shine My Machine" may well be the least machismo-burdened tune ever writ about that timeworn subject "growing up in Detroit" (as if anybody who brags about said experience, myself included, really *did*!). Anyhow, Kim McAuliffe of Girlschool calls Suzi an inspiration, and so do I, and so should Madonna. Phonies rule the world, you know.

76. BLUE CHEER
The Best of Blue Cheer: Louder Than God
Rhino, 1986; rec. 1968–69

These Golden Gate lunatics not only predated heavy metal (big deal—so did your mom!), but rather anticipated the *entire history* (well, the first half-decade or so) of the genre, from the Mississippi insane asylum (documented with *Vincebus Eruptum*'s degenerate Delta Force sludge-annihilation in February '68) to the Detroit Ford Factory (with *Outsideinside*'s stonecarved grunge-eclecticism in September '68) to the Sistine Chapel (with *New! Improved!*'s slight artification in April '69) to Mrs. O'Leary's cow (with *Blue Cheer*'s considerable mellowfication in December '69), and this comely compilation tallies all phases. Three of the twelve songs were originally released prior to Robert Kennedy's assassination, five more prior to National Turn In Your Draft Card Day, two more prior to Neil Armstrong's giant leap for man-

kind, and two more prior to the Chicago Seven conviction. "Come and Get It" is where Sir Lord Baltimore learned to speed, "Peace of Mind" is where Led Zep learned to druid, "Fruit and Icebergs" is where Black Sabbath learned to thud, the Delaney & Bonnie cover (!) talks about county jails and Greyhounds and po-boy sandwiches, and I omit the rest not 'cause they're filler but 'cause they're beyond concise verbal elucidation and analysis, 'cept perhaps in Jeff "Vox Pop" Dahl's swell liner info, which you can read in the store if I've been too sketchy.

77. NEIL YOUNG AND CRAZY HORSE
Live Rust Reprise, 1979

Drifter-rock on the cusp of the metadecade, lonely vays, lovely almost always, too reassuring too often, formless and ungraspable except when it's amped up, dirty rotten mayhem when it is. I don't particularly care for the gauzy parts where Neil's chemicals and sacred roots confuse him into believing that optimistic relatin' can change the weather or that he's a little kid way more sugary and innocent than any kid would ever wanna be (though I respect his sincerity even then), but the first time he honors Johnny Rotten, his tone's almost as chilling as his words. When he admits there's "more to the picture than meets the eye," you wonder if he's being self-serving, if his audience (who, in 1979, probably dreaded disco more than anything, and who get most excited when their hero endorses "gettin' high," which tells you how much Bruce Berry taught 'em) understand what he means, if he understands himself. But sides three and four, with "Powderfinger" and "Cinnamon Girl" and "Like a Hurricane" and "Hey Hey My My," are where his roadies earn their druid costumes, where the buckshot meets your pants. Neil's kaboomeration convinces you he'll never fade away, but of course it's a trick: After a while, the smile on his face would turn to plaster. And once he's gone, he can't come back.

78. VOIVOD
Killing Technology Noise International, 1987

Burrowing at a churn-punk pace toward the echo at Earth's core, these ever-dependable hockey pucks take their apocalyptic "concept" (their word, not mine) into the space age, lyrically (lasers and jailships) and musically (the sputtering meat-grinder ear-hurt gets some automaton assistance, especially in the title track) and visually (drummer Away's typically ingenious cover-scribble depicts a many-tentacled creature looking out his rocket windows at some moons, and the calligraphy's real hard to read). Axman Piggy doesn't so much just glop his grindings down (like on the previous *Rrröööaaarrr*) as spread 'em out like hunks of animal lard, and Snake's screeching actually begins to make some sense (particularly in "This Is Not an Exercise," an over-the-starboard nuke-aftermath oink). There's Star Wars and China Syndromes, too, quite extraterrestrially janitorial. Voivod's named after a tribe of medieval Norsemen who useta jab swords through people and slurp up their O-positive; the members' personal monickers are nearly as silly (Piggy's so-called due to his roly-polyness, nothing to do with *Lord of the Flies*), their doofus sci-fi folderol more so. But their bile-flushing, hemoglobin-rushing, ribcage-crushing, neighbor-hushing coagulation. hails from a little Quebec town that houses North America's biggest aluminum factory, and here, they *sound* like North America's biggest aluminum factory.

79. BEASTIE BOYS
Rock Hard Def Jam EP, 1985

The mightiest rap record of its year, an inept, idiotic, sniveling, parodic, brutish, grating circus-of-fleas backed by AC/DC's "Back in Black" and Zep's "Black Dog" (note fixation on nonwhite hue), with technoburban cultural referents galore: TV test patterns, cumulus clouds on the Weather Channel, B-boys too dumb to play their own instruments, big tools of reproduction doing the Alamo. The full-throttle tempo in "Beastie Groove" originates from Treacherous Three's "The New Rap Language," but the attitudes-at-large conjure an image largely comprising two hairy palms protecting future film star Ad-Rock's urinary plumbing, where he deserves to get kicked silly.

80. KIX
Midnite Dynamite Atlantic, 1985

Steve Whiteman better not put that stick of TNT in his mouth—looks as if he's mistaking it for a microphone, but it's bound to blow his face out. Anyhow, this is the closest Kix has come so far to making a conventional pop-metal album, and it's not very conventional. Kip Winger contributes a brainbang with Castaways and AC/DC quotes, the title cut's heavensent harmonic chomp beats Def Lep at their own game (either soccer or golf!), staggering etherea introduces a slow psychedelicatessen where the singer considers telling his love interest he's a doctor or lawyer, a chorus of kiddies repeatedly chant "yeah-no-stop-go" at varying degrees of intensity as Whiteman peels rubber into a raver about drag-racing. Side Two gets more and more Zeppy for the first four tracks, the first of which ("Scarlet Fever") is apparently a tribute to *Gone with the Wind* (says here Scarlet's "Rhett-hot night and day," or at least that's what it sounds like), the second of which ("Cry Baby") might well have persuaded Kix's Maryland homeboy John Waters to make a movie of the same name a half-decade later, and the third of which ("Cold Shower") is a not-yet-metally-fashionable rap reporting on either blue balls or energy conservation. Last and best is "Sex," an unabashed dance floor–filler where panting hip-hop beatboxes inititate discussion of how lustful mating rituals in an adjacent room tend to induce insomnia at night. (Only other statement of *that* theme I can think of offhand is Ray Parker, Jr.'s "The People Next Door.") What makes Kix an exceptional band is that they always give you a little something you'd never expect.

81. BRYAN ADAMS
Reckless A&M, 1984

This military-brat Canuck leaves no romantic-martyr/beautiful-loser cliché unturned, and as a white soulster trying to come off heartfelt, he mainly comes off as a white soulster trying to come off heartfelt. From videos where nothing ever happens to LP covers dreary and gray to a forced-blues bark so repressed you swear he needs more fiber in his diet, the antiimage Adams peddles is Mr. Average, an original idea by no means, but with him you buy it 'cause who else but Joe Normal could get away with being so *drab*? Damn if he don't have a way with those tasty two-riff turbo-rockers, though: Nowhere near as embarrassing as the war-torn—empire set of vague-statement chime he followed it up with when his Protestant work ethic got the best of him, *Reckless* burns barns like *Scarecrow* with a monkey on its back and a skewer through its navel. Yeah, I have trouble telling the songs apart, and it's idiotic how "She's Only Happy When She's Dancing"'s dainty disco kiss-up contradicts "Kids Wanna Rock"'s brutal antidisco gang-shout, and only "Summer of '69"'s hamletburg oral-sex nostalgia is anything like immortal (even the Tina Turner duet and "Run to You"'s ozone moan sink like suet on the radio). To fully comprehend the relevance of it all, you're urged to track down Nik Cohn's justification of Eddie Cochran's generic faceless meat in *Rock from the Beginning* (figure Bry is to Bruce as Eddie was to Elvis), then to realize that Keith Scott pounds as concisely and conclusively in his own way as prime Angus Young. Less "substance," maybe, but Side Two's trashy climb toward "Ain't Gonna Cry"'s savage musique concrète Dumpster-solo (!) packs as mindless a wallop as any string of strut in recent memory.

82. MEAT LOAF
Bat Out of Hell Epic, 1977

It looks more metal than it sounds and feels more metal than it looks, and Todd Rundgren's "motorcycle guitar" and the lead lardo's former partnerships with Ted Nugent and Rocky Horror are only an ounce of what's good about it. What's good about it, mainly, is what's ridiculous about it, namely that Jim Steinman takes "Leader of the Pack"/*Born to Run* to their natural Götterdämmerung conclusion, beyond unctuousness, beyond anything any sane person could take at face value, like if Bruce had punctuated "Thunder Road"'s first sentence with a *real* screen door. So bloatedness signifies nothing other than bloatedness $(X = X)$, and we can get off on the bloatedness because bloatedness (not "art") is the reason for being. In the spectacular nine-minute title cut, you barely even listen to the dumb words, just treat it like a Glen Branca composition, pound your fists as the three-keyb surges summon Thor's wrath, crack up when Todd's chords quote "Born to Run," cheer Mr. Loaf's pacing at the peaks (like he's been chugging brake-fluid chasers after all those high-calorie chocolate shakes). He insists he'll be "gone, gone, *gone*," when any fool can see he's been gone for years. "Paradise by the Dashboard Light," partly an eternal annoyance and partly kin to Alec Costandinos's classic discodelic symphonies, tastelessly soups up salsoid piano runs and creepily cutesy puns with marital strife and foreplay-by-play from Yankee shortstop Phil Rizzuto. And though the slower schlock mainly makes me retch with morning sickness, if you think there's ever been a more bittersweet ballad with a Cracker Jack box in it than "Two Out of Three Ain't Bad," you didn't drive your car to many malls in '78.

83. NEW YORK DOLLS
In Too Much Too Soon Mercury, 1974

Max-Factored junk on his face tells you David Johansen's from Babylon, as do his pouts and stylish pumps, as does Marilyn Monroe on the album cover. And with all this campful "decadence" everywhere (the way Dave brings up Berlin '33, uses terms like "divine," imitates your average slavering Negro gee-zer), you can tell he's a showman, that his brashness is where the camaraderie comes from, that he's got a heart in him, that he likes singing (though unlike, say, Axl Rose, I never get the idea he *needs* to sing). No doubt he would've been rapture to watch live.

Right away when needle hits groove you can tell the band can't play for shit, which in '74 must've seemed like quite an accomplishment. But of course we now realize that incompetence is not a virtue in and of itself, right? Here, the ineptitude moves too slowly, and despite occasional mock-Africanisms the beat's incredibly clunky compared to Aerosmith's, as are the words. Only "It's Too Late" 's Delta-to-Velvets horseplay indicates why Johnny Thunders's chainsaw might've been a big deal. His fracas ain't bad per se, but it doesn't *do* anything. Knobsman Shadow Morton's firearms are funnier.

On the other hand, the best stuff (not usually even entire songs, 'cept maybe "Mystery Girls") *is* kinda carnal (in the bitchy way you'd expect), and there's daffiness too. Everybody from Cyndi Lauper to Celtic Frost has *something* rooted here. Dave's record-collector rape-and-pillage of rock 'n' roll's past (not just the remakes of the Cadets and Sonny Boy Williamson and Archie Bell and whoever, but such

sneakiness as the "Surf City" allusions mid-original) portends semiironic postmodern/post-mortem scavenger-hunting of the Cramps/Beasties/David Lee Roth/(and for that matter Buster Poindexter) ilk, and if the Dolls aren't necessarily more "audacious" at it than their descendants, arriving first has gotta count for something even when the party's a lame one. In "Human Being," their sign-off, the boys nearly get their obscene arrogance right, but though the ditty's riffs eventually graduated to "Anarchy in the U.K.," Johnny Rotten got his ardency from somewhere else.

84. SONNY SHARROCK
Guitar Enemy, 1987

The voluptuousness and violence clustered on this forty-seven-year-old guitarist's one-man album sound secreted, never constructed; it's as if these passions from on high were passing *through* him, or maybe all the sorrow and scorn had been building up inside him, lying latent through the decade-long break he took from free jazz to work with psychologically disturbed kids. Too intimate to fixate on "chops," Sharrock's discord muscles through like spontaneous combustion: blues-fiber climbing toward a rugged screech in "Blind Willie," creek-bottom–scraping fatback splat in "Black Bottom," caterwauling whacks in "Kula Mae" that switch into the Bo Diddley riffing that helped get Sonny started in the biz, then switch back into deranged spurts. Eruptions circle around mountaintops like storm clouds, nanoseconds of echo trailing every note, notes hunching together like orgiastic sardines. For "Princess Sonata," the suite that ends the record, you'll need a tissue box: random incendiary shrieks against a bed of either flowers or nails, bouncing off the ceiling, relaxing into an immaculate sadness that whistles like the mandolin wind and reminds me of Eddie Hazel's anguished flailing throughout Funkadelic's "Maggot Brain." And the way Sharrock counters a gravelly high-pitched hum in "Broken Toys" with this nursery-rhymingly simple melody feels like a lullaby, as well it should—he wrote it for his nine-year-old daughter.

85. FOREIGNER

Records Atlantic, 1982; rec. 1977–82

Melodramatic pansy-metal and chauvinist hunk-rock from one of the postpunk era's finest 45-RPM bands, this junk almost justifies AOR. Obviously the hit package should've been postponed till after their genius gospel-move "I Want to Know What Love Is" (one of the eighties' most awe-inspiring songs by any sane standard), and I wish it had "Women" 's Duane "Cool Last Name" Eddy metalbilly rip and the studio version of "Hot Blooded" instead of "Feels Like the First Time" 's rancid cardiac arrest and the overlong live version of "Hot Blooded." But jerks who lumped Foreigner into Syx/Toto/Journey limbo are jerks who miss the point, 'cause even if Lou Gramm was no Steve "Pipes" Perry, Foreigner had twice the oomph and thrice the imagination of those other brand-name boobs. "Cold as Ice" is a not-bad *Who's Next* steal, "Waiting for a Girl Like You" drips precisely the same prissy kindness as the Stones' "Waiting on a Friend," "Jukebox Hero" is some grass-roots life-saved-by-rock wafflestomp, "Urgent" 's mutant funk has Junior Walker squawking sax, "Hot Blooded" 's as phallus-proud as dumb drooling Bad Company cynicism gets. And in '79's "Dirty White Boy," Foreigner one-upped punk rock with a concise fleet-footed nugget that merges the Standells' "Dirty Water" and "Sometimes Good Guys Don't Wear White" both texturally and textually. How darn with-it can you get?

86. VOIVOD

Dimension Hatross Noise International, 1988

Snake Voivod's Zamboni-driver diction, at last shriek-less enough to be all-the-way decipherable, comes out of nowhere like God's prophet: "Go for it, we need it. . . . We'll turn it upside down." The revolution will not be televised, or else we'll know it's revolution 'cause there won't be no commercials. Spooked by current events, tormented by monsters they're real-izing aren't entirely of their own making, Voivod

learned to cope by channeling their trapped varmint impulses into a gigantic mutation stripped back to a nervous, finger-on-the-button twitch. The aural equiv-alent of a Survival Research Laboratories' spike-roller, this sounds like nothing ever: Too rounded to be thrash, too economy-of-scale technostructured to be boogie, the bombardment's more akin to something neoclassically atonal than to anything alloyed. Imagine *Confusion Is Sex* as done by the MC5, or *Metal Box* as done by the Sex Pistols.

First this thick gunk races back and forth at the speed of light 'tween your speakers; after that, a million billion rhythm breaks get juxtaposed and returned to, but there's no melody, no fancy-schmancy bushwa, no crescendi. Air and dead space help gravity-eluding drones dodge Piggy Voivod's riff-permutations as he hangs ten through whatever long thin wire he can find, as quasi-tribal clatterdrums curl into the fetal position, as all this sound closes in on itself. The woodwork squeaks and out comes Baby Godzilla, who's been stuck there for centuries. This human voice, phrased like Iggy Stooge's, goes, "There is no freedom/No satisfaction/I want some action"; cyborg cuts in, informs us that "everything is over." Snake despairs at corporate capitalism's reliance on chaos, on a world built up to be torn down. Megatons of ideas slip out; he sounds bitter (my kinda guy).

Matter collides with antimatter, converting energy to mass (which is just latent energy anyhow) like an inside-out nuke, and a bionic Steve Austin type trucks into some perpendicular miniature meson galaxy. Or so we're told, but guffaw at your own peril, 'cause this is NO JOKE; really, it's an Old Testament fall-from-grace allegory about what it's like to live in an epoch where the only sensible responses are dread and disbelief and other such diffuse dissatisfactions. And with their high-activity-level blitzkrieg defying Newton's laws of motion, Voivod may well be the first rock ensemble in the annals of our particular four-dimensional space-time continuum to take quantum physics into account.

87. EXTREME
. . . .
Pornograffitti A&M, 1990

Extreme aim to make hard rock boys and girls can dance to (in *pairs,* even!), and frequently on their second album (in "It's a Monster," maybe the title cut, maybe "Get the Funk Out") they *actually seem to be*

Photograph by William Hames

stretching the groove. If I'm not mistaken, there's genuine instrumental interplay being attempted here, with horn charts, and it's not confined to a real teensy closet! So they wanna be the Bar-Kays, let's say—gosh, that only puts 'em fifteen groove-years behind where house music was before it killed itself by reverting into genteel soul-revival swill. Yet I'll cut 'em slack, seeing how they're from Boston (home of one-time rhythmetal princes Aerosmith) and seeing how Nuno Bettencourt (whose solos don't bore me!) guitared on a Janet Jackson record once, and seeing how *Pornograffitti* also has genre-expanding falsettos and offhand noises and even a gallant attempt at antimisogyny. Not to mention a piano ballad to balance the prog-blues power ballads, a rap about running for president, and a supply of loud Van Halen-circa–*Fair Warning* screechers with zany names. Though such sounds might never blow me away on their own, it oughta be obvious why "When I First Kissed You" 's angelic candlelight waltz-schmaltz can stick out in Metal Land in a way that, say, "Over My Head" (same kinda lounge-lizardry) never could on Aztec Camera's 1990 *Stray* LP. And if some necrophilic Wax Trax perverts opened with a track called "Decadence Dance" I wouldn't think twice, but here that title *means* something (plus I dig the words). In a game of inches, context counts for a lot.

88. IAN HUNTER
. . . .
You're Never Alone with a Schizophrenic Chrysalis, 1979

An AOR breakthrough but also a professorial analysis of the death of Saturday night and life after death, this longtime cutout starts with three Jerry Lee–shaped four-square punts about looking for kicks in an age when boots are going out of style, on the Atlantic seaboard ("Wild East"), in the land of Alan Freed ("Cleveland Rocks"), and elsewhere ("Just Another Night"). And then it gets mean: "Ships" is built on a cliché so pukey Barry Manilow wound up weaseling a top 10 hit out of it, but then again it's the spooky melody that got him the hit; Side Two, with Roy

Bittan's holy sustained Moog-worship gushing geyser-like out of Mick Ronson's filthy bee-stung funk-mulch, is an apocalyptically atmospheric shitstorm. Max "E Street" Weinberg slams skins, John Cale adds ARP. Ian imagines corpses swept across clouds, refuses to trade with the fate of the New York Dolls, rejects disco, ogles chicks with crimson lips, promises not to touch you if you let him spend the night, remembers the rock 'n' roll his grandpa boogied to during World War II. This is his most rambunctious solo job, yet in 1979, compared to punk or Mott the Hoople, it seemed somehow slight; a decade-plus later, it still kinda does. But years from now, every last martyred minute is guaranteed to still hold up.

89. AC/DC
Who Made Who Atlantic, 1986; rec. 1976–86

This Stephen King soundtrack isn't quite the perfect AC/DC retrospective—not enough Bon-era stuff (no "Highway to Hell," even), one of the new cuts is an instrumental, and so on. But so what? Nobody's ever accused these dynamos of being perfectionists. And if you're dumb enough to only have room for one AC/DC slab, this might as well be it: Nowhere else will you find swingin' gutpunches like "You Shook Me All

Night Long," "Sink the Pink" ("about" shooting snooker the same way "The Jack" is "about" playing five-card draw), "Shake Your Foundations," and "For Those About to Rock" all in one place. Count as a bonus "Ride On," the only Bon-spot here, an actual no-lie drained-bottle blooze *ballad* (wherein he asserts, "I'm just another empty head"!). And figure the title track, which gets its initial synth-hook from Michael Jackson's "Billie Jean," and where guitar-sibling Malcolm Young complexifies his literary muse by advancing full-blown into the Late Cenozoic with sundry ontological quandaries concerning taxes and one-night stands and substandard video-game play and the creation of the universe, as one of the most cherished musical moments of my postcourtship years. AC/DC's lewdness embodies the orgy Lester Bangs once claimed for the Troggs: They never expend so much energy on Not Being Pretentious that their "sincerity" turns "important."

90. VAN HALEN
Van Halen Warner Bros., 1978

"Runnin' with the Devil," the first cut on this, our first peek at these gypsies, opens with the same synthonic swoop that opens Side Two of Elvis Costello's *This Year's Model*, the year's most critically acclaimed record. Critics didn't like Van Halen much at the time, and you can understand why: The guitarist makes loud, crazy noises that only he can find, to no end except to potential imitators' amazement and everybody else's utter boredom; the singer makes louder, crazier noises, to the same effect. He destroys a Kinks' hit; scatting and screaming and ice-creaming, he seems like a minstrel showman. "I live my life like there's no tomorrow," David Lee Roth starts, and though you couldn't quite tell whether he was lying or not, within a couple years he'd earned his "not." I liked Costello, my older brother liked Roth, and the trains wouldn't meet, even though Dave called one squeal "Atomic Punk," even though "I'm the One" outsprinted punk and castigated the music biz (like "Radio Radio") and stopped dead for a strange diddybop break, as if this were a close-harmony group, not a heavy metal band. Two songs deserve gold medals: "Ain't Talkin' 'Bout Love," maybe rock's most-forceful-ever macho-man self-condemnation, and "Jamie's Cryin'," Spectorish compassion that shows up nearly all coexisting powerpop as both soulless and brainless. The remainder is silver or bronze or worse, but the singer and guitarist kept improving, and within a couple years Elvis Costello was a has been.

91. PRECIOUS METAL
That Kind of Girl Chameleon, 1988

The two guitarists' gear-shifts and rumblegum-riffs provide stamina, but what's most special are the tricky off-key harmonies of Leslie Knauer, whose sudden asides and across-the-great-divide exclamations switch from tough to tender and sweet to sarcastic in an earthy way that makes even Chrissie Hynde seem pretentious. Leslie's phone's disconnected, her TV's been stolen, her sink's full of dirty dishes, her mom wants her to get married but won't let her go out at night, she cooks eggs over easy but it's not easy getting over her guy; when she sighs, you hear jealousy, affirmation, apathy, frustration, restlessness, desire, determination, déjà vu. (Even sociobiology: "I can see there's something in your genes that I want.") "Seven Minutes to Midnight" starts 360 seconds before Blondie's "11:59," but it's the same night. When curfew comes everybody goes home, so we've only got a short time left to pursue happiness; when the clock strikes twelve the social order topples, and we'll be the ones to blame or credit. "Stand Up and Shout"'s peppered with extracts from the Crystals' "Then He Kissed Me"; "Push" and "All Fall Down" are good-time pick-me-ups like nobody makes anymore. And in "That Kind of Girl," if you don't swoon the second Knauer confesses her undying faith in fairy tales and a one-boy world, your batteries need a recharge, bro.

92. GUNS N' ROSES
Lies Geffen, 1988

The "G Side" generously eliminates your desire to quench your commodity-fetish and thereby affirm your (I-consume-therefore-I-am) existence by owning their '86 indie bar-band object *Live ?!@ Like a Suicide,* a nice move seeing how hundreds of dollars is probably too much to pay for by-the-numbers Aerosmith and Rose Tattoo speedboogie reconstructions and a couple ballsy-but-inconsequential speedboogie originals. (Bootleggers can still make hundreds of dollars off the balladboogie reconstruction "Knockin' on Heaven's Door" and the balladboogie original "Shadow of Your Love," 'cause they're not here and they're better than what is.) The "R Side," where every second counts, is what you listen to, and "Patience" is the main reason: the way Izzy's hard strums work sweet pain out of his acoustic, the way Axl's whistling (coolest since Michael Jackson's in "Rock with You") works sweeter pain out of his piercing rasp. The lyrics are the side's simplest (Steve Perry could sing 'em, and maybe he has); the music's not merely the side's best, but damn near the era's, maybe (time will tell). Midway through, the guitar turns into "Lola," downstrokes run your blood cold, Axl's fire alarm saves the world from burning. "Used to Love Her" is a David Allen Coe goof that's a stunner at first and thereafter just catchy; "You're Crazy" was a drag before Axl subjected it to his mushmouth, and his my-week-beats-your-year scats and Izzy's Hendrixity help a little but not much. "One in a Million" is sad and sumptuous, equal parts "Ballad of Dwight Fry" and "Every Picture Tells a Story," and (to me anyway) its overpublicized xenohomonegrophobia is too LA-punk-'81 to be funny or shocking anymore; it's just *there*. Which is fine—in a way, "One in a Million" is a lot like Spike Lee's *Do The Right Thing*—same fear of foreigners, same local color, same ability to stir things up. Take it or leave it.

93. FLIPPER

Sex Bomb Baby! Subterranean, 1988; rec. 1981–82

These aquatic anarchists were really big on your fish lingo, so howzabout I opine that "we really got a live one here"? Not as live as their (two) live LPs, maybe, but certainly more *lively*, and "Get Away" is so live (at some "Eastern Front Festival") it's got Bruce Lose chewing out tall fans for roughing up short ones. Back in the prehistoric dogfish days of '81, inhabitants of punk-rockdom didn't dare admit their debt to the metallic textures they obviously grew up on, but these porpoiseoid perspirators came along with "Ha Ha Ha"'s suburbanly consumerist gushy wetness that read like the Pet Shop Boys would (eventually) but sounded more like either Blue Cheer or *White Light/White Heat* or one fat drone, and after that things were never the same (as they had previously been). The catch-of-the-day is their greatest-flops collection, whereon epistemological dislocated-outcast sentiments outnumber unlistenable sludge. Two bassists anchor Ted Falconi's ax to the ocean floor; the sound of said ancient mariner screeching his

way surfaceward through lusty looniness and maximal minimalism and antibourgie propaganda is a humane disarray; there's two songs about teensy invertebrates (one of which gets swallowed by an old lady, who tops it off with a minister and a rhino); and "Sex Bomb" has so much explosive speaking-in-tongues you gotta wonder whether Will Shatter's estate oughtn't be earning royalties for Tiffany's "Drop That Bomb" as well.

94. THE SWEET

Desolation Boulevard Capitol, 1975

The most deliberately effeminate intro ever ("alright, fellath...") unveils a cheerful rattlefuzz hop called "Ballroom Blitz" where you dream a party girl wants to "ball you" (only it says "tell you" on the lyric sheet), and stomping my hands and clapping my feet to it in ninth grade, I *knew* it was the future of the world. (I was right too: Fourteen years later, after the Ramones led off their allegedly insurrectionary debut by changing the words a little, after the Damned and Krokus did more literal remakes, it wound up as background sound in a Molson Canadian commercial.) The Sweet married the undeniable power of the hard-rock riff with the undeniable power of the pop-rock hook, an inevitable reaction to a world where heavy metal is just kiddie music anyway, a world where pregnant fourteen-year-olds with twelve-year-old mates make any distinctions between "childhood" and "adolescence" beside the point. Other toons here have been revived by the likes of Benatar and Girlschool (a tribute to said shuffles' healthy freedom from insecure pseudomacho hangups!); there's Who rips and Alice rips and Gary Glitter rips and Zep rips and hound-maul protothrash and bisexual girlfriends and teens leaving the sixties behind. And there's "Fox on the Run" (note quaint Britsport-metaphor), the stickiness of which will crack its gum as long as there's still a world around to crack gum in.

95. LED ZEPPELIN

In Through the Out Door Swan Song, 1979

You'll note that new-wave nostalgia hasn't caught up with this swan song yet, but that's only 'cause new-wave nostalgia hasn't caught up with new wave, which apparently inspired Zep simply by virtue of the fearless four's keeping their ears open, as did disco. Which is to say they absorbed both but didn't change their hairdressers, which is one reason they fare best on Side One, where they don't take themselves so seriously: "Southbound Suarez" 's cheesy sha-la-las and radiating-88s barrelhouse backbone (not unlike Jerry Jeff Walker's "Mr. Bojangles" or George Michael's "freedom 90" or maybe Robert Ashley's "The Bar"), "Hot Dog" 's bluegrassabilly do-si-do and blue dungarees, and especially "Fool in the Rain" 's counterrhythmic Dr. Buzzard conga-line rimshots and Donna Summer toot-beep whistles are too frivolous to resist. (The latter's an idea Guns N' Roses oughta build on.) Side Two's sophisticated blues-symphonies are stodgier and hence more troublesome, but "All of My Love" 's crass AOR hooks make up for "In the Evening" 's album-opening superannuated wheelchair-fodder, and though "Carouselambra" snoozes through seven minutes or so of hollow high-art bed-wetting, once the synth goes Enodisco, you can get up and boogie if you can. All in all, real idiosyncratic but not shapeless, as gracious a bow as a fan could ask for. There's even some noisy guitar parts!

96. DUST

Hard Attack Kama Sutra, 1972

Taking their cue from the three battling Vikings in the cover cartoon, this reckless-crazy power trio chronicled death in the Age of Westmoreland with impeccably cathedralesque prettiness paradiddling tensely toward Homeric fuzz-epics of biblically millenarian woe. Rapture turns rabid; fancy acoustica and mythological penwork ("Amethyst and lace, broken women and their dossier . . .") make way for pygmy-

hippos-doing-the-bump-in-the-rain-forest sludgeparades like the scary "Learning to Die," where Richie Wise, with his hoarse voice, serves as spiritual granddaddy to James Hetfield in Metallica's "One." Side Two commences with canine barks and riffs the Stooges might've embezzled a year later in "Search and Destroy," and there's a magnificent point in the vengeful "Pull Away/So Many Times" where the bombast breaks down to just voice and frontiersman folkstrum. The gang's final testament is a tombstone called "Suicide," and they commit it five different ways—including standing in the rain with their instruments plugged in to ensure the stardom they never won.

97. BILLY IDOL

Vital Idol Chrysalis UK import, 1985; rec. 1980–85

The blueprint for this remix retrospective is "Wild Dub," off the first Generation X album, from back when Billy could still pass as a punk; ergo, the idea is to unite guitarpop stench with ganjafied echo techniques, not so much in Fugazi's or Blind Idiot God's museumized way as in a manner somehow conducive to happy nightclub-wiggling. Unfortunately, Steve Stevens's ax isn't quite as loquacious as it tends to be on Idol's more trad plats, and the lead sneerer's thespianism is (as usual) far too forced to induce unfettered dance-fever. It would've been nice if Keith Forsey had restructured "Rebel Yell" and "Eyes Without a Face" instead of some of Bill's less entertaining earlier stuff, and "Dancing with Myself" is probably worth owning in its original Gen X configuration if it's worth owning at all. Still, MTVacuousness about shotgun weddings and epidermal exploitation and masturbation in front of a mirror (and that's just Side One!) ain't the sort of cheese I can get myself worked up to complain about, and between his pornwise additives in "Flesh for Fantasy" and how his rubbadub carries "Love Calling" into some alternate space-time zip code, neither is Forsey's production. "Hot in the City" 's Exterminator Mix gets words from Nick

Gilder's "Hot Child in the City" and music from Rod Niangandoumou's "Shake It Up (Do the Boogaloo)," and the track before the Tommy James cover broadcasts the selfsame electroblips Tiffany later used to kick open "I Think We're Alone Now." It's almost enough to make me believe in déjà vu.

98. MOTÖRHEAD
No Remorse Bronze, 1984; rec. 1979–84

Even more than their Sab-potency-meets-Ramones-velocity noise-factor, what's always kept the Brit-hits, B-sides, EP tracks, and extras on this two-LP best-and-the-rest off Yank airwaves is their stark pathology: Too far overboard to be passed off as a pose or moneymaking venture, Motörhead lives up to rock's promise to offend, incite, and scare the daylights out of people. What gives 'em their sonic impact isn't merely their speed so much as the way they observe the hook aesthetic, fortifying bass with riffs that swing. Neither ahistorical nor sonically stagnant, they borrow ax-lines from "Cat Scratch Fever," "Dirty White Boy," even "Layla," pinch the Coasters' and Chuck Berry's words, cover the Kingsmen and Holland-Dozier-Holland. Where his competition mainly rides with the Valkyries, Lemmy's content to stay on the highway or in a truck stop or at a pub: Dope fiends, lonesome fugitives, bikers, gamblers, and speed freaks race headlong with the law, just like on Merle Haggard's *Songs I'll Always Sing*. Iron Maiden and the Scorpions worship the idea of power 'cause they're dumb enough to think they'll eventually get some, but Motörhead's got more sense than that, so "Stone Dead Forever" and "Dancing on Your Grave" threaten violent death, very specifically, to rich people, and *No Remorse*'s four newest nontunes reference all the old death-at-dark archetypes—crawling king snakes, nightstalkers, mystery trains, lone wolves. Like Iggy, Lemmy uses military jargon as a metaphor for our own mortality. And when he growls that it doesn't matter anyway 'cause his head is in the noose, he convinces you he's as aware of where this planet's heading as any millenarian mofo anywhere.

99. PARLIAMENT
Osmium Invictus, 1970

More a Funkadelic chunk than a Parliament one, this heartburn hell of ghetto gumbo has raw garage punkateering ("I Call My Baby Pussycat," with every dirty feline pun Tom Jones hadn't already plundered in "What's New, Pussycat?"), brownbear bebop progressing into ditchfuls of dingy distortion ("Put Love in Your Life"), and fast feedback-farts in Frigid Pink's face ("Nothing Before Me but Thang"). Plus Brownian "good gawds," a resplendent gospel choir praying for civil rights, motorized doo-wop with a pinch of the Dixie Hummingbirds' "Christian Automobile" in it, yodels stolen two decades later by prog-rap posse De La Soul, C&W even funnier than Lionel Richie's, stitched-on Bach transforming into bitched-on schlock, a sweet painted lady with lotsa kids bribing a judge fleshwise, and a woman who smells so bad all the roaches leave. And though it makes for far less durable styluses than diamond or sapphire, the metal element for which the LP's cunningly named has the world's heaviest atomic weight—190.2.

100. BLUE ÖYSTER CULT
Agents of Fortune Columbia, 1976

Sinister everywhere, and so pretty in so many places (f'rinstance "True Confessions"'s doo-wop metal) you wonder how their tongues ever escaped their cheeks, BÖC's crowning achievement is so pretty in so many *other* places it'll scare you to death. "Don't Fear the Reaper," which gathers up its Byrdsy tremoloes and layered harmonies then swoops with classical crescendi like Icarus toward the sun, literally did just that: Hot off the presses, it reportedly initiated a nationwide high school fad (and you gotta admit this is more notable than any phone booth–stuffing vogue Chubby Checker or whoever ever induced) where class couples would romantically cap off prom nights by driving off cliffs together so they'd be joined forever Romeo-and-Juliet-style, a real surprise since prior to said hit no Juliet anywhere had any use for the band. "This Ain't the Summer of Love" has lynch mob imagery that lays Timothy Leary's peace sign to rest so blatantly that, once punk-rockers finally figured the song out a good decade later, they couldn't get enough of it. And (speaking of punk-rockers) asking Patti Smith to kick off "Revenge of Vera Gemini" with a dippy reptile one-liner was a real inspired move. That's Side One. Side Two's got what appear to be she-devils, pigeons, Chinese breakfasts, final exams, fake Philip Glass, special edition headlines, and another Patti Smith poem, all of which almost make up for the lack of hooks, but not quite.

101. AMON DÜÜL II
Lemmingmania United Artists UK import, 1974; rec. 1970–74

Eurorock eccentrics making this intense, alarming sound, in their "II" period they got way too rococo, and on later albums, especially, nothing held up. Early on, they were total wiseacres, hiding high-imagination-factor naif-pop (the lieder-roster here includes "Arch-angel's Thunderbird," "Green Bubble Raincoated Man," "Rattlesnakeplumcake," "Jailhouse Rfog," "Soap Shop Rock") and spectral supernaturalness beneath beefier riff-repetition than any baubledom to emerge from Frisco. Gargling Autobahn operatics, alternately male and female, are interrupted by animal squawks, atonal piano, folds of feedback ferocity that fall to your room from the moon. The fraulein doing most of the singing shrieks like Yoko Ono, impossibly high-pitched, knotting up her shrillness then suddenly turning real pure, having fun. The words are in English, bad poetry probably, and I don't so much ignore it as not hear it; it vanishes before it gets to me. You open up your mailbox and water falls on the floor. Given no reference point to make sense of the wacky alien beauty, I keep wondering where it originated: Zeppelin, Zappa, the Velvets, Stockhausen, Brecht/Eisler, the Berlin Dada Club of 1918, mid-thirties German cabaret, the AMM Group improvising electronics near the roof of the London School of Economics in the

summer of '66? To me, the music's closer to heavy metal Kurt Weill than to rock 'n' roll, and a major attraction is that the connection might all be in my head.

102. VAN HALEN
Fair Warning Warner Bros., 1981

Their art record (Eddie's, really), as crammed full of dense suspense as its Kurelek cover, and inspired, for all I know, by labelmates the Gang of Four. Diamond Dave's searching for the hippest new kicks amongst the living dead on Fat City's Mean Street, envisioning "Welcome to the Jungle"'s mood as he peers back at the blackness of the Stooges' "Down on the Street" and Zep's "How Many More Times." Homecoming queens fall like dominoes, lushes leer at their legs, carburetors clog, cars keel over, the bassist and drummer get out and push. The rhythm section slows the Commodores (or Undisputed Truth?) down to the tempo of Sly's "Thank You for Talkin' to Me Africa," stretches the singer's soul, compresses it, rolls it into two hairy little balls, squashes it into a mudpie. Valerie Bertinelli's husband plays and plays and plays, unchained.

103. QUEEN
A Night at the Opera Elektra, 1975

Fred Mercury's aristocratic Sweet Adeline yoo-hoo generally goes over like the proverbial bicycle-built-for-two in a motocross race. Here, though, "Lazing on a Sunday Afternoon"'s suburb-dandy bachelorhood grasps more of Ray Davies's gaslight than you'd guess, "I'm in Love with My Car"'s macho-joke would've fit fine on *Goodbye Yellow Brick Road,* "Seaside Rendezvous" has a charming Charleston beat plus kazoos, and, heck, even "You're My Best Friend"'s got too much heart to argue with. Kinda dig Brian May's chord changes in "Sweet Lady" and "The Prophet's Song" too (though spelling "Prophet" "Profit" would've been more honest), so not till the center of Side Two do we sink toward the usual pablum-puke. Then Fred looks back at that ludicrous Groucho-Marxist LP title, hits us with "Bohemian Rhapsody," and man, it's all over: solipsism, suicide, Beelzebub, body aches, Italian lingo like "Galileo" and "Mama mia" and "Scaramouch." Then somewhere around the third aria, an avowal of identity, then surrender. A year before "no future," we got "nothing really matters," and if you were a lonely teen at the time, it meant just as much, and you could laugh at it.

104. IGGY AND THE STOOGES
. . . .
Raw Power Columbia, 1973

The sides fall apart after revving up with "Search and Destroy" (Vietkid confusion: "street-walkin' cheetah witta hide fulla napalm," et cetera) and "Raw Power" (best burp since the Soul Survivors), and then what're you supposed to do? (Start punk rock or something? "Concentrate" on the former guitarist's bass, or note the new guitarist's manly metal leads? Fat chance!) First two hundred times or so it's like you're getting run over by the Panzer Division, and after that you listen close, and at least if you've listened to the debut and follow-up just as much, something clicks: This is the Stooges album *musicians* like best. It's got well-crafted heaviness and love songs ("Penetration,"

gimme a break) and method-acted nihilism; Iggy gives himself top billing, sings "like" a coyote, but he's *lying.* The sound quality's infamous: The drums seem disconnected, everything's too skinny, David Bowie dropped the tapes in the ocean or something, but if you hear it enough the muffledness starts to seem normal. Iggy tries to sound black, gets real poetic, stuns with tossed-off quasirhyme verbiage and slice-and-dice phrasing, dances his husky alleywise whoopalong like hypnotized chickens, and the crooned drone even sounds handsome sometimes, like Sinatra maybe. "Gimme Danger" and "I Need Somebody," howls in the wide-bodied mode of the Elektra LPs, don't half stand up to the '65-vintage frat-frug "Shake Appeal." Which is almost as good as "Keep on Dancing" by the Gentrys!

105. AC/DC
. . . .
If You Want Blood You've Got It Atlantic, 1978

From Down-Under-bred schoolboys-in-disgrace in the most honest and one of the funniest bands ever to make a good living playing rock 'n' roll, here's the crudest and hungriest sounding live album I own, with Bon Scott slobbering his phlegm all over James-Brownishly-stretched Chuck Berry riffage fried in a high-voltage electric chair. Angus Young is belligerently fast and furious, always impatient to get to his next thrill-solo even though it's probably the same as his last one. This is impalement-rock, aimed at Jezebels who bring out the devil in ya: The dirty little bitch calls herself a virgin, Bon gives her a finger and she bites off his hand. So it's "misogynous," yeah, no shit Sherlock, yet so happy-spirited it comes off as mere bawdy bile from old salts in favor of barrel-housing all night long with big dicks and bigger tits, like the forty-two-inchers on Whole Lotta Rosie. The primary contention's that we've gotta get our kicks someway and we better take the chance while we still got the choice, 'cause we've already died and gone to hell, and we'd be fools not to make the worst of the burn.

106. ROCK CITY ANGELS
Young Man's Blues Geffen, 1988

Beats me why he followed up with such a two-bit promo-blitz, but initially Dave Geffen was so hot on these backdoor boyos he let 'em debut with a double album (or, really, a single-and-a-half, since Side Four's a disco remix!). The dual-exhaust hoots come from *Sticky Fingers,* "South of the Border"'s structure comes from *Love It to Death,* and the suicide-ballad that tumbles its tonnage like Dust's "Pull Away/So Many Times" comes from nauseating "21 Jump Street" mod-squadder Johnny Depp, a fallen Angel. Friends of ZZ and Jerry Lee lent hands at Sun Studios, and with "La Grange" grunge, Tiffany odes, Tex-Mex turns, go-cat-gos, and juvenile-delinquent myths, these Confederates tell it like it useta be, so you can trace the mystery train of straying and stability and salvation and sin and stuff back to Son House and William Faulkner if you want. Gruff as if he inhales three packs a day, Bobby Durango slides into this sneakily risqué falsetto for a word or two; in lush laments like "Rough 'n' Tumble," lassoing leads rope you in. Waltz-like spans recall silly outfits who once tried to make mohawk-rock for Aggies, there's too much Idol/Morrison drama, and twentyish honkies should never touch Otis Redding. But "Hush Child" catches the mood of the Eagles' "Already Gone," and Durango wants that *Star Hits* cover so bad his torn tonsils keep contradicting his pose with compassionate nonearthtone colors, so when he's not playing with rats or taking on the world in his '66 Chevy there's adolescent romance tearing up the charts deep inside his heart. If his penned-at-sixteen "Wild Tiger" isn't quite as wholesome as Bobby Rydell's "Wild One" or Fabian's "Tiger," it's at least as showbiz.

107. FAITH NO MORE
The Real Thing Slash, 1989

In which some college-radio-stuck white-rap wannabes nobody had any right whatsoever to pay attention to unite with the singer from an alleged Frisco "funk" fraternity named Mr. Bungle and decide to, um, "get progressive"—like, excuse me if I was too cynical to "get into" this record for so long, but these are not exactly what one would call "promising" credentials, not in *my* book (i.e., the one you're reading!) anyway. But wonders never cease: There are those who have been known to kvetch about how Mike Patton winds his whines as if his nose had never been introduced to Kleenex or a handkerchief, and while I'll admit I'm a wee bit annoyed by his tendency to flap his lips real minstrellike during the rap jams, overall I'd say his techniques are rather *endearing.* The real problem, inasmuch as there is one, is that the "speedcore" tossoffs (what a dumb term—you mean, there's "core" that *isn't* "speedy" somewhere?) are your usual orthodox rut. But they're few and far between, and they do contribute a necessary sense of "balance," I guess one might call it.

"Epic," the surprise MTV/CHR hit, is exactly what its title claims it is—On the air at the time, that "you want it all but you can't have it" line juxtaposed with Young MC's "you want it you got it" (in "Bust a Move") to create a real profound late-capitalist philosophical discourse. (Note, too, that Young MC has an *economics* degree—he's the John Kenneth Galbraith of hip-hop, as it were. So these statements weren't accidents, I don't think. They should've called in Neil Tennant of the famed econo-disco duo the Pet Shop Boys to referee the debate.) Not to mention that, to some Iowa fourteen-year-old, "it's in your face but you can't grab it" must've evoked *plenty*—girls, grass, good grades, gasoline, most any precious commodity you can name.

Elsewise, while an innocent bystander might think it merely arty how FNM offsets Jim Martin's Sabbish wrench with Bill Gould's dubbish time warps (in "The Real Thing" and "Underwater Love," mainly) and Roddy Bottum's Gabriel-era-Genesis keyb-pomp, it's also quite *beautiful,* in its own way. Which is what really matters, right? These wiseguys have figured out how to use their talent at making disillusionment seem fun to turn their rhythm section's inability to swing worth beans into a *strength.* Golly!

108. CELTIC FROST
. . . .
Into the Pandemonium Combat, 1987

These Swiss misters were already the heaviest bunch in the galaxy, but for them that wasn't enough, so they digressed in zillions of degenerate directions that likely left your typical headbang-brat gasping for further explanation. There's tracks where sodomite orgasmoan-breaks prep us for Tom G. Warrior altering his patented human-beatbox gutpunch-grunt into a sort of Bela Lugosi whine ("Mesmerized," "Sorrows of the Moon"), a weird semiclassical demi-atmospheric thingamajig ("Oriental Masquerade"), a bizarre nuke-sleaze cover (of—get this—Wall of Voodoo's "Mexican Radio"). Avant-gardy opportunists who evidently latched onto the now-moot speed-metal hype to pay a few bills, the Celts obviously realize that the infinitely repetitive nature of disco's and heavy metal's respective percussion elements in fact makes the phyla kissing cousins, so here they "go disco" before there's even a disco (revival) to go. Rhythm moves include a pared-to-bass-line astronaut-talkover ("One in Their Pride") that I can only compare to Adrian Sherwood's Tackhead and Keith Leblanc productions, a unique thrash/strobelight concession (ironically called "I Won't Dance"), and a dub/riff mixture ("Rex Irae") that's at least up there with Chain Gang or Ruts DC or A. R. Kane even though it's got some dainty dame yodeling French

opera tra-la-la who should've stayed back at the perfumery. These undertakings don't always work, but as far as I'm concerned it's cool they're even *attempted*. On top of it all, to satisfy the mosh section, the slab's got plenty of these Norse gods' patented Stygian goreplod, which is pretty bent in its own right.

109. PINK FAIRIES
. . . .
Kings of Oblivion Polydor UK import, 1973

More than Mott the Hoople even, this British cult act anticipated what punk rock would sound like, what it would say, what it would it do. Almost as if to beg the question, they start here with something called "City Kids," end with something called "Street Urchin," even quote Jean Cocteau on the sleeve. In between, there's a tribute to a woman who cleans hotel rooms and copulates doggie-style, a riveting speedrock instrumental called "Raceway," and more. "I Wish I Was a Girl," a seven-minute-to-crescendo fuzzpump "We Shall Overcome" for sissies, pansies, and pink fairies everywhere, has a kid who's no sports fan leaving a fight early 'cause he faints at the sight of blood. (Hence, chicken-rock; see also: "Rats Revenge" by the Rats, *Back from the Grave, Volume One.*) Elsewhere, chromium plating hides the not-quite-enunciated words, but not the bored consumerist tension. Speed up the tempo of "When's the Fun Begin," retain the diction and structure and mood and message, which apparently concerns a country gone to seed so now it's time to inhale nail-polish remover, and you've got the Adverts, whom riffsman Larry Wallis would one day produce.

110. BOSTON
. . . .
Boston Epic, 1976

Better an engineering-school art-rocker than an art-school art-rocker, I'd say—unlike allegedly "avant" *Time* cover-bore David Byrne, who's never penned a hymn half as everlasting as "More Than a Feeling" and never fucking will, Tom Scholz does not pretend to be something he's not, and does not go through motions. He once spent seven years constructing an album, even endured a twenty-million-buck CBS lawsuit filed in response to his taking so long, all because he wanted to make sure he did it *right* (which for him means a technologically blemish-free recording that eschews electronic percussion, ignores transitory trends, and sells eight million copies). His whole purpose in life is stated right here in the liner notes of this, his first vinylized demo tape: "The use of technology as an instrument."

And if you can't "relate," you'll never comprehend how Tom's music applies its science into transcendent special-effect guitars zooming across the heavens and intertwining with the grandiose pipe organ and choir blasting out of an isolated chamber in some Renaissance monastery, all to show just how important the romantic despair and escapist impulses and utopian idealism of one normal American white-bread-fed twerp can be. Supposedly R.E.M. later used their wide-eyed posthippie nothing-groove to convey much the same feelings, but Boston's wide-eyed posthippie nothing-groove is catchier and more original. And says more, too: "I woke up this morning and the sun was gone," "I hide in my music, forget the day." Like Zen, but way more anthemic. Though I'm told Brad Delp sings "some people have to make believe they're living," to me sounds like "some people have to make a legal living," which makes more sense, especially when you listen to the second side, which should've been outlawed years ago.

111. Nuggets, Volume Six: Punk, Part 2
Rhino, 1985; rec. 1964–69

The midwesternmost muck on this anthology most likely gave the Igster of Stooge some bright ideas, to some extent sonically (e.g., hopped-bass cryptothreat riffthumps by Mo-City "U" bands the Underdogs and Unrelated Segments), but more importantly attitudinally (e.g., the way Chicago's Shadows of Knight slither stinking drunk and greaseballish through your back door babbling "I *love* her, I *love* her, I *love* her . . ."). As for protometal, We the People drool like dogs till they get flattened by drumboom and axcrash alike, the Electric Prunes' lunar bluster in their humongously hyperactive "Get Me to the World on Time" makes Hawkwind and maybe even Public Enemy both inevitable and inconsequential, Don Van Vliet's Blind Blake blooze veers closer to metallicness than his heart of beef ever would again, and future astronomy prof Dave Aguilar instructs his virginal honey to "*sweat, young thing,*" thus helping the Chocolate Watchband's "Sweet Young Thing" set a standard Mudhoney's "Sweet Young Thing Ain't Sweet No More" never had a chance of outsleazing. The Brogues, Seeds, and Nightcrawlers don't live up to their reputations, and Black Pearl's postprotometal fuzzturd funkatelechy forget-me-not lays Steppenwolf's postprotometal fusoid fellatio-foolishness to waste. And in "Public Execution," Mouse and the Traps seize Dylan's Fourth Street in preparation for Seger's "Persecution Smith" and Costello's "Lipstick Vogue." Which is to say they serve up their crucifix with a vinegar sponge.

112. LED ZEPPELIN
Physical Graffiti Swan Song, 1975

It certainly oughta take a tribe of Zep's size and stature to pull off a studio twofer (and Zep was *about* size and stature), and I can only think of two or three clans who've ever really turned the trick. *This* multistylistic grab bag of day-and-night contrast, boundary-stretching, and vulgar overkill works only when it gets delicate or rhythmic, which is fairly often: I like the *Zep III* leftovers ("Bron-yr-Aur" is an acoustic mermaid, "Down by the Sea Side" 's inspired kitsch portends the Honeydrippers' "Sea of Love" remake as it reflects back on "The Twist"); I love how "The Wanton Song" 's twisted funk forecasts Pere Ubu's *New Picnic Time* then "Boogie with Stu" doppelgängs Richie Valens (and "Tutti Frutti") like Los Lobos never would. But the only side I couldn't live without is the one with "Houses of the Holy" 's tie-dyed lovey-dovey keistershake at the devil's doorknob, "Trampled Under Foot" 's propulsive godhead Über-beat aerobics breaking down to an air-conditioned carnival organ, and o' course "Kashmir" 's steppe-climbing proto-Rai wisdom and sacramental orchestrations. The "Custard Pie" side's dullsville despite Bob's toothache and the gruel Jimmy spills all over "In My Time of Dying," and not only do we get twice as many redundant Bukka White rockabyes, regal monuments, ostentatious flute-flights, masculinity tests, Icelandic myths, sepulchred wanderlusts, razzle-dazzle virtuosities, and narcoleptic lurches as normal, but most every balderdash lasts twice too long, and one of 'em's got Bobby begging to "blow" Gabriel's "horn." Then again, sometimes quantity means a lot.

113. PUBLIC IMAGE LTD.
First Issue Virgin UK import, 1978

Second Edition (*Metal Box* if you're rich) has the eighties' most vital white-people rock 'n' roll on it, and '85's laughably Laswellized *Album* was plugged deceitfully as "metal," but in retrospect it's clear that this hodgepodge of trial-and-error was the erstwhile John Rotten's real artZep tribute. The weighty echo underneath pounds the ground like Bonham-gone-dub, and there's streams of formless feedback atop. Our friendly neighborhood Antichrist drone-wails baloney (or nonbaloney, doesn't matter) re loss and realization and suicidal impulses for nine minutes or so in "Theme," and before long it's a bore (though apparently the Swans didn't think so, seeing how they based a whole career on it). "Annalisa" is the same with a gram or three more energy, "Religion" 's non–a cappella version's the same only fleshed out some (though I prefer it as a spoken word thing, an ex-Catholic alone in church yellowing the pews and trying hard not to crack up, kinda like Madonna in her "Like a Prayer" video). Somewhere else John-boy whinesqueaks "we-own-lee-wanted-twobee-loved" for six minutes over defanged disco claptrack, and it's dandy to iron shirts to. But when the disc's over the only thing left in your head is the theme song (best ever), which (ha ha) *isn't* "Theme," but rather "Public Image." It's the man's greatest postpunk homily, and probably pop history's most disillusioned and defoliating denouncement-of-audience rant, like Lydon just woke up one day and suddenly concluded that he'd always had a congregation of simpletons. Not a pleasant feeling at all, so a couple years later he decided if you can't beat 'em, join 'em.

114. LOU REED
Rock n Roll Animal RCA, 1974

He chronicled narcotics when everybody else was chronicling hallucinogens, and though we're supposed to believe that automatically qualifies him for Cooperstown, somehow I've always been skeptical. Which ain't to deny that a couple of his chronicles were pretty awesome, and there are a greater concentration of 'em here at this live Howard Stein's Academy of Music gig than anywhere else. More often than not the expressive steroid-fungus of Motor City Two Steve Hunter and Dick Wagner carries more absinthe and athlete's foot than Reed's and Sterling Morrison's did in the Velvets—"Sweet Jane" 's eight minutes and "Rock 'n' Roll" 's ten show up *Loaded* as second-rate, and the thirteen-minute "Heroin" 's failure to frighten is owed more to the over-the-hill frontman's lukewarm cabaret disinterest (and Ray Colcord's séance-piano) than to fuzz, which abounds. "White Light/White Heat" 's improved beat provides punch, and "Lady Day" at least tells a story, albeit an arch one. Not Lou's loudest or most undead album, maybe, but his loudest and most undead since '68 for sure.

115. DIE KREUZEN
October File Touch and Go, 1986

Dan Kubinski wails straight from his tonsils, gagging on hard consonants, stretching vowels like Steve Tyler screeching "Ah'm baaaaack in the saddle," but the vowels stretch so far they tear, and you can only decipher occasional snatches. His rhythm section

Photograph by F. Fischer

takes Aerosmith's heavy metal hip-hop and acceler-ates it beyond recognition, but so convincingly that Run-D.M.C.'s Profile label once offered the group a deal. Nakedly soulful in a way that cuts deeper every time you play it, but not about how you oughta hate everybody and everything, maybe not about anything, you could call this blues, or maybe jazz, or maybe art-rock from hell. There's some real quiet drawn-out slow parts and some other parts, too; Kubinski sounds as if he's tearing the rubber casing off live wires with his teeth, then suddenly some "Layla"-esque lick comes out of the abyss, then it all degenerates into sonic quicksand and you're sinking, but soon you're racing against the speed of sound, and then the off-kilter beat belches like a spastic elevator or Erik Tunison's drumsticks pop like miniature firecrackers, then Herman Egeness's pickax slashes your throat, and next thing you know Kubinski's screeching and drooling about tunes in his head or the Memphis borough he imagines he was born in. This crew's hyperactive, but darn tight; slide-rule precise and minimalist at any given nanosecond, but all over the place before you know it. Scary as mortal sin, and beyond oft-arbitrary constructs like "meaning."

116. FUNKADELIC
. . . .
Cosmic Slop Westbound, 1973

In the frightful fable that provides the album's name, easily the heaviest and smartest and most multidirec-tional decibel-funk this side of "Crosstown Traffic," a woman sells her soul to the devil to feed her fourteen starving young'uns. "No Compute (Alias Spit Don't Make Babies)"'s ribald ragtime revisionism instructs that "all holes are not a crack"; "Trash a Go-Go" is forcestomping Jimi-meets-Ozzy spuzz with a pimp's persona; "March to the Witchcastle" is a grotesquely deep-voiced Vietnam-readjustment sermon with martial bootsteps, drug addiction, druidic chants, and ghastly dark guitar squigs. Sly-like soul-balladry (George Clinton making fun of string-slick zodiac-ooze, yet coming across more soulful than his target ever did) fronts unanglicized Afro-Caribbean nonsong clickclack duckquack percussion. Again and again, you're mugged by a half-formed mother lode of double-clutchingly spasmodic bass lines and land-locked Deltoid mulch—a creeping, defeated leer.

117. FLIPPER
. . . .
Album Generic Flipper Subterranean, 1982

These saltwater San Franciscans followed up their swell disconant saxmaniac single "Sex Bomb" with what was likely the best debut LP of its particular year of our Lord. They didn't win any Grammy awards, as I recall, but that didn't bother those of us who couldn't afford a TV. After all, this was hubbub that detonated as hubbub ought, hardcore-associated, sure, but way too heavy to be pigeonholed, and also sloppy and grating and artless and artful and constructed in the cruelest manner possible. Yet the clamor-mongering hid an honest-to–Grateful Dead (c. "St. Stephen") soul, by which I mean Flipper displayed warmheart-edness and friendliness in the face of unspeakable dread. Never before had such gloomy humans re-joiced so joyfully in their own nihilistic nausea. They found the elusive Smothers/Sabbath/Sartre connecting rod, and though they were giving in, just like we all have to sooner or later, they were giving in at *full blast*. Except of course *their* full blast was slowed to the gills, or—okay—lungs, seeing how dolphins are mammals not fish, and during the fifty percent of the time that the jokes aren't peaking, the detachment gets in the way of the despair, and the self-deprecation doesn't help much. But let's not be picky: If "life is the only thing worth living for" isn't a slogan to live (or die—it's your choice) by, not only wasn't Tinkers-to-Evers-to-Chance not a great infield (relevant here since Flipper have one of the best "Ever"s ever), but Harry Steinfeldt wasn't their third baseman.

118. JOY DIVISION
Unknown Pleasures Factory, 1979

Apocalyptic heretic-sludge, approximately halfway to the grave Metallica dug in "Fade to Black" (though this cult's chieftain resorted to the noose and Metallica's never did): In a dark basement late at night, still haunted by my Baltimore Catechism, Ian Curtis's willful marination in the stigmata of the King of the Jews had me checking for burnt boogiemen bodies beneath the staircase. He could almost make you want to follow his epileptic footprints toward no-man's-land, but virtually all that survives now is moderately incessant hooks, hesitant Bernard Albrecht spaghetti-metal overtones ("Interzone" clones "Paranoid"), and occasional benedictions reminiscent of the old days. Only the fittest survive, love's a bitch, God's dead, we'll wander aimlessly forever looking for just one honest man, we'll never feel again, the city's walls will topple and with our luck there'll be no doctor in the house. The erstwhile Stiff Kittens' "talent" was for making increasingly austere whirrs and roilings repeat for a long time, no huge deal when you consider how much livelier Sabbath and Kraftwerk and Eno had already done the same thing, and it's not enough to suggest that the analness served as its own Freudian metaphor. Yet no matter how fully Ian's doldrums rest on selective method acting, no matter how dulled the blades of his fellow mommy-lovers' scimitars, the earth still opens for him when he lays it on the line. He's seething with every resource at his command, and you are moved. The promised "Louie Louie" cover never materialized, but with

1989's "Round and Round," the first JD-graduate 45 with a voice to match the synbeats, I finally learned to like New Order.

119. DAG NASTY
Field Day Giant, 1988

Straight talk rejecting smug obliqueness as it seizes control of the disenchanted-white-youth majesty staked out in Hüsker Dü's "Real World," Mott the Hoople's "The Moon Upstairs," and Boston's "Don't Look Back," this DC postcore is a headrush: Barge-guitar hoisted by scaled-down stadium-paradiddles and dramatic humalong hooks, making normal-guy nonart enunciation and a sea of CSNY harmonizing ring truer than true. Maybe half the LP holds up to analytical scrutiny; we're subjected to three split-second toss-off goofs, a too-obvious us-vs.-them anti-skinhead-nationalism tirade, too many weepy and overstatedly "responsible" and "sincere" tendencies. But the opening rips the Adverts, "Ambulance Song" 's ending is keyed on an admonition from Thin Lizzy's "Jailbreak," wise declarations jump out of jangling jumbles of bad drunk poetry and forced flamenco eclecticism. "Under Your Influence" transforms fast from cackling cynicism to true faith to a gargantuan Zep-do–Willie Dixon parody, which annoys you till you notice it's about passing somebody you used to be close to on the avenue, ignoring 'em, then feeling like shit; "Dear Mrs. Touma," about how what seems like a tragedy can destroy agnosticism, sounds like random thoughts passing through my head at certain times in my life. These are young adults rebelling out of "rebellion," feeling guilty about laziness and boredom and brokedom and mixed-up confusion, but learning love's for real, "home" (a word they say a lot) is where the heart is, satisfaction's in security. Peter Cortner closes with sentimental miss-you sap, and you know he knows it's sap, but he's gonna be sappy anyway, 'cause that's how he feels. In this world, that takes balls.

120. BLACK SABBATH
Master of Reality Warner Bros., 1971

An asthmatic cough, a Tony Iommi grungehook that won't stop, then a voice from above: "All*right* now, woncha listen," purple poesy to a marijuana leaf, pretty goofy, right? But then after "Sweet Leaf" ends a *new* Tony Iommi grungehook won't stop, and the Lord's back, wants to know if you still trust him or only your Christ-crucifyin' buddies who'd rather have the Pope on a rope than soap. Church organ, then dumdededum - dededum - dededum - dede*dumdum,* DUMDEDEDUM - DEDEDUM - DEDEDUMDEDE-*DUMDUM.* The same rhythm went to number one a lucky seven years later when Giorgio Moroder stole it for Blondie's "Call Me" on the *American Gigolo* soundtrack (there was even a Spanish version!), so you could say Geezer Butler and Bill Ward are inventing disco but smartass scholars with no imagination will take you too seriously and start bandying around names like Barry White and Bohannon, so instead let's just say it sounds like golfball-sized hailballs hitting your roof, and leave it at that. You couldn't do the bus stop to it, but then it's music for marching, not dancing, and the children of the grave marching to it are the boom-babies of the bomb, the pig in the python, mad as Helga and not gonna take it anymore. Since, unlike the Ig/MC5/Alice HM-wing, Sabbath didn't follow in the Stones' footsteps, culture-burg shunned 'em. A shame, 'cause their grind was punkier than their progressive intentions suggested. But give or take "Into the Void" 's anthropoid ecology, Side Two bogs itself down with bogus Iron Maiden crystal-ball-gazing anyway.

121. GIRLSCHOOL
Nightmare at Maple Cross GWR/Profile, 1987

The giddily flirtatious spunk never goes camp by turning into some stale "concept"—it's got "Leader of the Pack" quotes, "one-two-three-fowah" and cartoon-horn-fanfare kickstarts, fart and storm sounds,

lotsa Cockney joking around, but the corn's all spontaneous. These four gals just kept their slumber party going when Vic Maile started rolling tape. A technologically clarified glam/Burundi beat hyperventilates beneath a well-endowed upside that struts like AC/DC doing the peppermint twist, and when Chris Bonacci solos, she just switches into some tasty beach-blanket distortion for nine seconds, purges the "musicianship" from her system real economic-like, then gets back to the unserious business of riffs as beefed-up bass-hooks. In the side-closers, two guitars and copacetic girl-group backup go all anarchic like everybody's just chiming in (*tunefully*) whenever they want to: "Tiger Feet" 's got Dixie Cups voices, Dave Clark Five backbeats, bass lines that boing like a Duncan yo-yo, a rockabilly follow-through, and a title that rhymes with a magazine that treats rock the way it's meant to be treated. Hidden behind regurgitated platitudes about playing with fire and living in danger there's an ace tribute to the rebellion-value of the volume knob, some you-don't-own-me autonomy, no happy-victim cycle-slut crap. Instead of pretending to be She-Ra, Girlschool simply identify unpatronizingly with the fifteen-year-olds (mainly female, I bet) in their target audience, and rock out as zestily as your wacky kid sister.

122. BILLY SQUIER
The Tale of the Tape Capitol, 1980

He was almost the Anglo-Saxon answer to Prince, and nobody noticed but a few South Bronx B-boys.

What they mainly noticed was "The Big Beat," the title of which tells you everything you need to know. In fact, "The Big Beat"'s tale ended up on so many early hip-hop tapes you've gotta wonder whether Billy heard those rappers' wheels of steel coming. Bobby Chouinard's drums and Bucky Ballard's bass don't let up, but where the Prince comparison comes in is in Billy's hot-to-trot persona—tells ladies he can feel (fill?) 'em inside, gets away with vulnerably semimacho aural ambrosia like the ex-Sidewinder powerpop dude he is ("Who's Your Boyfriend" is pure Raspberries right down to its handhold-and-handclap innocence), imitates Bob Plant just like Prince had in his slop-roaring "Bambi" the year before. This guy's dreamy, sews his sheets real silky and soft, and though (except in the fine zipper-ripper "You Should Be High Love") neither voice nor words quite go all the way with Plant's sultry chutzpah, the sleeve's come-hither centerfold pose (*almost* comparable to *Dirty Mind*'s backside) sure does. If I were a girl, I'd be sliding off my seat.

123. VAN HALEN
. . . .
Women and Children First Warner Bros., 1980

The engine room's at its loudest and most energetic, so smart and harried and vehement and primitive and high-speed you confuse it at times with the Stooges circa '70, but the skipper's at his dumbest, knocked out from too many yo-ho-hos and too many bottles of rum. In "Everybody Wants Some," "Loss of Control," "Romeo and Juliet," and most of all "Fools," Smiling Ed emits these perverse jungle-burps whilst the faceless guys in the background maintain their monstrous rhythm-and-bulk shake for five or six minutes on end, improvising on extremely basic forms, digging dense chordage deeper and deeper with an automachine lack of personality that's downright menacing. David Lee repeatedly sprinkles lustful asides that occasionally entertain but more often sound real gratuitous; he mimics Tarzan, makes fun of Robert Plant, cracks his larynx like a B-girl's gum, does

his jumpin' jive shtick, gives the golden rule a golden shower. Halfway through the generation battle "And the Cradle Will Rock," he shows you Junior's report card, and if you hadn't already figured it out from LPs #1 and #2, you know for sure now that Dave's not content to be a regular Joe. Despite all this, his jabber feels *weak*, somehow. He can't keep up with what his mates are doing; they're already dog-paddling through the River Styx, and he's like he is on the free poster inside, still chained to some wire fence on the outskirts of Pasadena, playing the fool.

124. CHAIN GANG
. . . .
Mondo Manhattan Lost, 1987

Presaging the following year's Tompkins Square police riot, four feral miscreants cooked on Contra crack, disgusted by evil on the block, and bored by the skeletal tenement shell where they've been crashing at night decide to play soldier. Urban America's a war zone already, they figure, so they load up their spray-paint cans with Mace and their Jolt bottles with gasoline and shanghai a cop's shortwave scanner. They keep fucking with the frequency knob, trying to tune it in. At one point they hear a guy using the call sign Dave Clark Five, doling out orders to One-Adam-Three, but usually all they pick up are dead zones, and eventually they settle on just broadcasting through the static. So they jury-rig some microphones and start ranting: "Saw the Virgin Mary making love like a hound, hey hey."

Mondo Manhattan's Cro-Magnon crudity suggests a Folkways document, as if John and Alan Lomax set up their big recording rig amid the cement and manholes of the final vestige of precivilization. The singing's a rough deadpan, often recited without instrumental backing, often pretentious, just a recapitulation of some corny old saw some Gangster heard in some bad B-movie or read in some yellowed pulp novel he found lying in a Gotham gutter. Lots of what's said is obvious, and everything that's said, an inordinate amount of which concerns babies tossed off bridges or out windows, is bleak. Chain Gang can be comical, sarcastic, even compassionate, but mostly they're indecipherable, howling through caterwauling gamelan-honk membrane that hints at a new kind of dub. They lunge at you in cumbersome chunks, molding themselves in "Satan Cut Down" into this unlikely rumbleseat-through-a-blender thump. Larry Gee's guitar flickers like ghettos on fire, crashes with Crazy Horse feedback like TV sets thrown from the top floor, gropes around like silverfish feelers, clearing its throat with staccato chickenscratch throbs halfway between Steve Jones on *Never Mind the Bollocks* and Keith Levene on *Metal Box*. The inner-city horrors go voiced unhysterically, like these rat-slugging hoods take their gentrified environs for granted. Nothing's due to improve in the foreseeable future, so nothing's at stake—any way they look at it, they lose.

125. VAN HALEN
. . . .
Van Halen 2 Warner Bros., 1979

Stripped of dirty sludge and bullshit pomp yet still somehow sterile, this pander-to-Pasadena's-pubs pop-metal pegged the eighties on the head, and you can credit it or you can blame it. In "Dance the Night Away" some freshman looker's inebriated for the first time, in your cellar on booze from your daddy's cabinet, swaying to your merengue collection's Latin lilt, and you're wondering what happens next. "Bottoms Up" throbs its stupid throb like the singer's privates want it real bad, and when the tempos and attitudes dilate toward couch-potato punkdom in "Light Up the Sky" and especially the Stoogebeated "D.O.A." where Davey's mom kicks him onto the streets, the torn denim fits just fine. Eddie pretends he's Steve Howe and/or Mother Nature, so this is sporty stuff for the most part. But they turn Motown into a lie, and damn near all the tunes with dames in 'em are tripe.

126. DEATH OF SAMANTHA
. . . .
Where the Women Wear the Glory and the Men Wear the Pants Homestead, 1988

In the "let's be regular" indie milieu they inhabit, these flaming Lake Erie fashion plates are some kinda godsend. They look like glitter's answer to "The A-Team," and though on one hand they're neither art-rockers, shock-rockers, roots-rockers, or joke-rockers (or maybe I just don't get the jokes), on the other hand they're *all of the above*, which hurts sometimes: Smart campus DJs segue their acoustic-eulogy rewind of Cleveland homey Peter Laughner's "Sylvia Plath" into "Bell Jar" by the Bangles (and when John Petkovic tells his collegiate claque they'll never be so cruel or graceful you know why he's telling *them*). Though "Good Friday"'s only slightly preferable to three hours of silent prayer, in other songs John's vocal shiver can grip you nastily, sometimes as if he's holding back tears—in his ill-reasoned anti-surrogate-mom crusade "Monkey Face," when he starts deriding see-no/hear-no evil like Tom Verlaine on Television's *Marquee Moon*, then twisting "Satisfaction" into just-say-yes, then slamming a Dolls-burglarization through Grateful Dead–descended manglation, he's capturing part of what made late-eighties CNN viewing so inconceivably bizarre. I spot ghosts of "Heroin," "Baba O'Riley," "Monkey Man," "Lucy in the Sky with Diamonds," even "Wanted Dead or Alive," and despite hackneyed poetry that reads like Nick Cave misplacing his Ouija board at a *River's Edge* screening, "Blood Creek" 's epic Berlin-Wall-of-cans groovebuild is one grungemungous furnace of Asheton/Laughner power-wah carnage. These Buckeyes are con men, but their fabricated foppery weighs a lot, and if the guitarguy's fruitboots don't exactly freeze my follicles, his karmachords sure do.

127. SONIC YOUTH

Walls Have Ears Not I UK import, 1986

Some sad sack opens the show whining an anticensorship speech whilst the guitarists pretend to tune up, then these Manhattan art pupils start right in on their cover of "Permanent Green Light" by the Godz (the ESP-Disk ones, not the Casablanca ones). The

record has two discs and about five different names. It might or might not be a crime against the state, might or might not include the final song from every concert the band performed one year, and might or might not sound exactly like *Live Steppenwolf*. When fret-wrecker Thurston Moore threatens to do "a couple Alice Cooper songs" and, later, "a couple Grand Funk Railroad songs" but then never follows through on his promise, you get the idea he views real-world rock (and, by implication, real-world people) as kitsch. Sometimes that's an aesthetic liability, and sometimes it's not. Sonic Youth are children of the Weathermen like hardcore brats were children of the Yippies, and their best songs here embrace their idols: Sean Penn, Susan Denise Atkins, Winston Rod-

ney, Robert Christgau. The band can't tell the difference, and sometimes *that's* an aesthetic liability, because Madonna as Madonna is weirder than Madonna as Manson. The first time they do "Death Valley '69" they call it "Spahn Ranch Dance," and like the filmed car crashes Alfonse's students watch in Don DeLillo's *White Noise,* which probably sound a lot like the music on this record, it's a celebration not of violence, but of tradition. Otherwise, the guitars are generally a bore, the singing's generally okay, and there is an embarrassing dearth of rock 'n' roll. And sometimes that's an aesthetic liability, and sometimes it's not.

128. BUTTHOLE SURFERS

Psychic . . . Powerless . . . Another Mans Sac Touch and Go, 1985

These Texas fart-rock fakirs have shat so much Muzak in their life span that real soon it'll be easy to forget 'em entirely, but on their first full-length they came dangerously close to putting it all together, "it" primarily being lotsa found sounds and roly-poly tribal-fungus and dirty humor and saxblurt, seldom arranged in any sorta logical order. Which is to say that (at least till I stopped paying attention), this outing has the most respectable ratio of good (hard, amusing) snowjobbery to bad (soft, tedious) snowjobbery. (They've done hard tedious snowjobs like "Moving to Florida" and soft amusing snowjobs like "Hey" too, but not here.) "Dum Dum" steals its plunger-bop beat from the Sabs' "Children of the Grave," the toothless bluesbelter in "Lady Sniff" wipes used toilet paper on the walls of his stall, and there's inspirational anecdotes re Negroes and brown heroin and cocksucking. The 'holes aren't yet limiting themselves to the dubwise tape-mixology and fluttering buzzsaw-hum of their senile years, and as "Gary Floyd" indicates, they've yet to lose the natcheral riddims embedded in their Tex-Mex genealogy. Nonetheless, you may not appreciate 'em much without the lighter fluid and live sex they brandished beneath their traveling bigtop. In other words, a snowjob's a snowjob.

129. THE WHO

Who's Next Decca, 1971

In more ways than one, this is the place Pete Townshend's and Roger Daltrey's egos got too haughty to handle, where they staked their claims once and forever as the city-sound's most pompously "mature" morons. For most of my life, I hated it, and lots of it, I still do: "Bargain," "Love Ain't for Keeping," "Getting in Tune"—I've ignored these bloated sonnets of self-pity on AOR for centuries, have no idea why anyone would put up with their oily timidity, and don't care. "My Wife" *might* pass as run-of-the-mill dumbass womanhate boogie if the boogie wasn't so half-assedly mawkish, but I doubt it; "Song Is Over" wears its sappy significance on its sleeve for six minutes, and you can imagine Bono taking notes. The remaining mythic phrasemakers, though, have the kilometers-long reach (not to mention synth-hooks) rock's bigger-is-better phase aspired toward. If "Baba O'Riley" is more "about" the teenage wasteland than of it (its fatal downfall), "Going Mobile" sure sounds good in a car when the sun's out, and the refusal-to-smile portion of "Behind Blue Eyes" and almost every portion of "Won't Get Fooled Again" have this cynical venom that detects punk's distant loom. Though they can't quite get 1977's mood right, Pete's agonized screech eight minutes into "Fooled Again" comes close, and it doesn't hurt that he realizes left-handed bullshit is no less bullshit than right-handed bullshit.

130. ZZ TOP

Deguello Warner Bros., 1979

You can note how their cheap-sunglasses beatnik-move on the inner sleeve presaged Metallica's cheap-sunglasses beatnik-move on . . . *And Justice for All*'s inner sleeve a near decade later (not to mention that Anthrax guy's bandwagon goatee). Though Isaac Hayes's concurrent Roy Hamilton cover ("Don't Let Go") wielded a swarthier scrotal sac than ZZ's Isaac cover here, the lowdown smoked-over-hot-coals raunch is more all-hit-no-miss than ever. Lotsa dirty-old-man comedy re car sex and once-a-week freak scenes and feet fetishes (nylons, stockings, leopardskin tights, et cetera), and especially once you hit the Final Four (cuts), the goosedblues blewjob goo deltagrammatons down enormous as an ocean liner. Robert Johnson's "Terraplane Blues" is metamorphosized into "She Loves My Automobile," his "Phonograph Blues" into "Hi-Fi Mama," his "Dust My Broom" into "Dust My Broom." "I'm Bad I'm Nationwide," later displayed on stage by none other than Bwuce Spwingsteen, is a low-rider epic where the beautician drives and the bluesman gets the backseat, and "Manic Mechanic" 's where ZZ octave-multiply their grunts and hence "go" new-wave (via simultaneous Police lick!) and thus rev engines for their sooncome *El Loco*. In the last song, a woman shoots you with a machine gun.

131. LED ZEPPELIN

Led Zeppelin 2 Atlantic, 1969

These social drinkers' third-most-leaden regular album is for some imcomprehensible reason considered The All-Time Heavy Metal Classic (see *Rolling Stone, Spin*, et cetera), which just goes to show that people who hate hard rock make decisions in this world. "Heartbreaker"/"Living Loving Maid" (one long song, really) swings its misogyny like Hindenburgs doing the Latin hustle in a cow pasture, and despite its dippy jazzschlock clutter "Whole Lotta Love" is of course as spacious and exorbitant a hunk of sonic nightmare as has ever trod the verdant earth (or at least its proto-skronk midsection is), and the singer's fake-orgasm-as-noise move is, like, neato. But the rampage only lasts five or six minutes at the start of each side, after which everybody capsizes from too much sharkflesh except maybe Bobby, who performs some intriguing prestidigitation with legjuice and gallows. The beat's as drab as the brown carboard it's wrapped in, Jimmy showboats more than usual, and he's lethargic. "Ramble On" and "The Lemon Song" and "Thank You" would come off as hollow overregulated clodplotz even on a Savoy Brown LP, and Bonzo's most tepid solo ever renders "Moby Dick" useless. If rockcrits really believe Zep never improved on this ashtray, I suppose I understand now why they think we needed punk rock.

132. THE DICTATORS
. . . .
Manifest Destiny Epic, 1977

On the heels of the debut there's a considerable dropoff in the tuneage department—"Disease"'s bombastic six-minute horror-rock satire hides real feeblemindedness behind the fake kind, and the first two songs have golden harmonies and not much else, a shame since the texts are okay, especially the one where Handsome Dick Manitoba's wife catches him flinging and he considers turning Quaker. "Science Gone Too Far"'s quantum mistake, with that awesome Sir Lord Baltimore screech on the word "haywire," is the only joke that kicks hard enough to support its buffoonery (and Eurodisco maestro Cerrone took the same idea further the same year in a ten-minute syndrum-symphony called "Supernature"). Supposedly all this adds up to a "metal"-move, and it's true the Dics cover "Search and Destroy" instead of "California Sun," dress up like Eric Bloom, and sing about Adny Shernoff's swelling (church) organ once. But the parts that stick are more like a maturity move. Or, okay, maybe a maturity *parody*, yet what saves mostly quiet straightforwardness like "Hey Boys" (copenned by Dick Destiny) and "Steppin' Out" and "Sleepin' with the TV On" (late-night tubeview being a recurrent theme hereon) is that their heartache feels sincere. "Young, Fast and Scientific," where rock 'n' roll makes a man out of a Jewish rookie, is no joke either. Bet the Beastie Boys never grow up this graceful. But is that bad or good?

133. THE TROGGS
. . . .
Best of the Troggs Rhino, 1984; rec. 1966–68

Unfortunately, this ignores their '72 collaboration with Black Sab producer Rodger Bain, and even "Wild Thing" (the definitive antiprogressiveness move wherefrom these cavemen earned their species designation) has decreased in value o'er time, thanx most recently to *Something Wild* and to the simultaneous exploitation by fatties Sam Kinison and Tone-Loc (both of whose "Wild Thing" videos parodied Bob Palmer's "Addicted to Love," a Lincoln/Kennedy–level coincidence for sure). So it's hard to hear 'em as the "Party" Lester Bangs once claimed they represented (now even *Madonna* wants to know "Where's the Party"), yet it's not exactly like Reg Presley seems refined after all these years, either. Though it is true that much of what holds up best is the voluptuous broken-heart lullaby-naivete (and "ba-ba-ba-ba-BA"s) of "With a Girl Like You" and "Any Way You Want Me" and especially "Love Is All Around," plenty of which (Poison take note) use *actual violins*.

But Reg sounds real sleazy when he switches to his fake Mexican accent under the prehistoric gangbang guitars in "From Home" and to his fake gangbang accent under the prehistoric Mexican guitars in "Lover." And "I Can Only Give You Everything" feels like a fanged water rat swimming through muffdive residue on a taxicab's floorboard, and the mere *title* of "Night of the Long Grass" (later reduced by AC/DC to "Night of the Long Knives") oughta send shivers up young minxes' spines or fluid down their thighs, and in "I Can't Control Myself" all Reg sees are low-cut hip-lines. You can tell he wants nothing more than a quick jelly-tight jar of wham-bam-thank-you-ma'am jam, and speaking of Lady Marmalade, "Come Now"'s prurient ungh!-chant ("stronger, it's gettin' *stronger*, longer, it's lastin' *longer*") is certainly the basis of Bob Seger's same in "Heavy Music," but even Rapid Robert himself didn't think to have a saucy Frenchette chirp her morning birdsong in the native, er, tongue. So *bon appétit*.

134. ZZ TOP
· ·
El Loco Warner Bros., 1981

These Yosemite Sams' most underpraised album is also, not surprisingly, their least Gibbons-oriented: delirium-tremens funk, "pure as the driven slush," out of Beefheart ("Ten Foot Pole," all grumblegrunt) and the B-52s ("Party on the Patio," frug-this-mess-around), if that's possible. "Leila" and "It's So Hard" are their career's most soulfully doleful slow ones, and most of the rest ("Tube Snake Boogie," "Pearl Neck-lace," "Groovy Little Hippie Pad," "Heaven, Hell or Houston") are comical hemmorrhages unfathomable if ZZ'd lacked the hemp-derived herbaceous vegetation they're smuggling past that cowboy-philosopher on the cover. On their next album, *Eliminator,* they broke the bank succumbing to recording technology; here, they go for broke fucking with it, and I'll take that option any day.

135. THIN LIZZY
· ·
Jailbreak Mercury, 1976

Irishmen led by a black man, they prophesied metal-to-come as they mimicked R&B–gone-by, and *Jailbreak*'s as terrific as they came, all Catholic imagery and blood at the bar and grill. The complexly stampeding side-closers connect *Led Zep II* to *Master of Puppets,* and "Cowboy Song" 's campfire hymn connects "Red River Valley" and "Cool Water" to "Every Rose Has Its Thorn" and "Wanted Dead or Alive"; I hear the Stones echoed in the cordial "Romeo and the Lonely Girl" and Arthur Lee's Love in "Fight or Fall." "Running Back" is a breathless ballad with archetypal tra-la-la-la-la and now-now-now-now-now tongue-speak trances straight from Phil Lynott's fellow Celtic soul-bro Van Morrison, and the spectacular smash "The Boys Are Back in Town," which might well concern the end of a college semester but we'll never know for sure, carries Van-ism to a mythic realm Bruce Springsteen might reach someday, but I doubt it. This is Lizzy at their most African American: "Hey you, good lookin' female, come heah" and "I am the warrior, I serve the death machine" are purebred Jimi-bravado, Brian Robertson's leads in "Warriors" are pure Eddie Hazel, the searchlight-on-trail chase in "Jailbreak" is pure Robert Johnson-cum–"Riot in Cell Block #9," "Fight or Fall" 's brotherhood spirituality is pure Marvin Gaye. Only thing that bugs me is the lack of pure Thin Lizzy.

136. HEART
Dreamboat Annie Mushroom, 1975

Mysteriously lush and libidinous folk-turning-metal, with the folk and metal coming from the same place, a place where Stevie Nicks and Grace Slick and Sandy Denny and Robert Plant live, a place with a beat like this band's name, a place where sassy young beauties imbibe too much waterpipe and wine on the communal road with masterfully virile magic men, and when they phone mom they pretend everything's all right when they know full well they're in trouble they've never even imagined. Despite momentary boogied competence, the entire second side is one big Tull-lull, but Nancy Wilson's fleet-fingered acoustic strums at the start of "Crazy on You," one of the most ominous pieces of lust-rock I know, reach back centuries, to the very first maypole, then forward twice as far. You feel bombs toppling the roof toward your head, earthquakes tearing the floor from your feet, and your mind empties of everything except everything you've never had the fortitude to do. "Whatcha gonna do when everybody's insane?" this haunting woman taunts, "Whatcha gonna do?" She's remembering last night's dream, how she was a widow (though the libretto says "willow"), how free-flowing desire kept her breathing. But she screams that last as if she's impossibly angry at you, devastated—as if this meeting could never happen again.

137. GLEN BRANCA
The Ascension 99, 1981

The ten axmen credited one after another on the back of this maestrolike mucky-muck's '89 *Symphony No. 6: Devil Choirs at the Gates of Dawn* make for a more hilarious gimmick, but here's where his Orchestra of (five) Air Guitars relights the torch that's lost fire as it has passed from Richard Wagner to Phil Spector to Robert Fripp to Rick Wakeman to whoever. For an artscene that generally takes undue pride in its "minimalism," this is clangor to the max, demonstrating that "classical rock" needn't be an oxymoron after all. Metal's reduced to its war-climax core, sometimes as overpowering as it's overblown, with rake-plucked barbed wire, leaps of faith, mountain kings beckoning rocs and phoenixes (flocks of imaginary Byrds) to reign o'er you. "The Spectacular Commodity" 's like the helicopter scene in *Apocalypse Now*, only with louder sledgehammers-of-the-gods slamming gonglike. The shorter tracks aren't provided quite enough runway space to take off, and the title cut's cold as "Sister Ray" played by preprogrammed refrigerators. Even when it attempts to get "tribal," the rhythm's way too worried about good posture, clunky like your car when it hits speed bumps and chuckholes. But when you're fist-punching overhead oxygen to the cathedralite concentricity that forms "Light Field (in Consonance)" 's superhero hook, who needs to dance?

forgotten" (yeah, right) rock 'n' roll–trash values these spuds supposedly "revived" than said spuds do; no fucking way are their ultraliteral Bobby Freeman and Trashmen covers more audacious than Amii Stewart's ebullient "Knock on Wood" or Santa Esmeralda's vandalistic quarter-hour "Don't Let Me Be Misunderstood." "We're a Happy Family" and "I Wanna Be Well" and "Teenage Lobotomy" are Cabbage Patch dolls, and the wimp-tendencies and fake Peter Noone accents are real reassuring, so there's nothing truly awful here, but since when does rocktrash work *that* way? Since it turned too scared of its shadow for its own good, that's when, and here's who I blame.

138. THE RAMONES
. . . .
Rocket to Russia Sire, 1977

Nobody had ever celebrated the fuckup-at-life disease the way the Ramones do here, and nobody had ever made a bombardment so pure, so free from respite or letup, that the slightest change—a hand clap, a falsetto, an echo, a three-second Farfisa or twenty-second guitar solo—could feel cataclysmic. Nonetheless, their comedy's not as clever as Aerosmith's, and their singer, guitarist, and rhythm section aren't as much fun either; plus, since the effectiveness of rock innocence is inversely proportional to the degree of contrivance, and since AC/DC's never made an *issue* of their smart/dumb simplicity, AC/DC's necessarily more satisfying. It's possible that if I'd been younger and less jaded when I first heard these sedate poseurs, I never would've decided that pretending you're young and not jaded yet is a shtick that gets old too fast and is impossible to recover from. But that doesn't stop "Rockaway Beach" and "Sheena Is a Punk Rocker," the only two songs I prefer to the Euclid Beach Band's small '78 hit "There's No Surf in Cleveland," from sounding like mirror images. (Beach-baby falsettos and three chords chopping down skyscrapers as a way of life: When the going gets tough, the tough improve their tans.)

The disco the bus driver blasts out the radio en route to Rockaway shares lots more with the "long-

139. BLACK SABBATH
. . . .
Vol. 4 Warner Bros., 1972

A bummer from the gitgo, typified by a vomitous disaster called "Snowblind" and coke-addled clues in the notes, this is where some early apologists decided to jump ship. Yet I know other people who consider it the best thing the band's ever done, and the reason (for lack of better term) is jazz. There's moments in "Cornucopia" and toward the end of the depressive eight-minute loss-of-innocence requiem "Wheels of Confusion" where you wish the beat-section's trancy mesh of thump would never end; spin the astonishing funk-frug "Supernaut" back-to-back with Miles Davis's "Black Satin," and you'll find they're coming from the same place. But though the protodub echoes in the electro-experiment "FX" are related not too distantly to "Time Has Come Today" by the Chambers Brothers, several of the other slowdowns have reams of less interesting noodling that too often succumbs to the Euroschlock accusations of Sab's many detractors. As the disc's winding down, with "St. Vitus' Dance" and "Laguna Sunrise" and "Every Day Comes and Goes," it's stultifying. Then again, condemning these guys for playing Euroschlock, per se, is usually less a valid aesthetic critique than a mere description, a little like condemning the New York Dolls for playing R&B–based rock 'n' roll. And when the Euroschlock's as luxuriously tenderhearted as it is in Ozzy's supple breakup-ballad "Changes," as far as I'm concerned R&B–based rock 'n' roll can go bite the big one.

140. POISON
. . . .
Look What the Cat Dragged In Enigma, 1986

Recorded in a dozen days, twentieth-generation party-hearty rhetoric and Ric Browne's powderpuff production killed most of this Bazooka Joe power-chord modness on contact. AOR completely ignored the group, making them the first (nonrap) AM-only (CHR-only, whatever) hard rockers in ages. But one so-called "teen anthem" addresses the unbelievably delinquent act of borrowing dad's car without per-mission, and the singles are awesome: Ostensibly a love letter back to the fans, "I Won't Forget You" is breathy and bittersweet, an ungooey all-I-have-to-do-is-dream mall-blues yearn. Stripped of his roughboy facade, Bret Michaels is forced to admit he's an innocent, so he stumbles from behind this translucent riff trying hard to be John Waite in "Missing You," then his voice starts cracking, he says something he oughtn't, he holds a note too long, and only a drum-shuffle saves him from plunging like Wile E. Coyote. In "Talk Dirty to Me," guitar lines straight from the Sex Pistols kick Michaels down this roller-

coaster slide into an irresistible pattycake singalong with three chords, no sharp turns, every hook just right. After conjuring drive-ins and your old man's Ford, the chorus links itself irrevocably to b-gum tradition (see Shirley Ellis's "The Name Game" and 1910 Fruitgum Company's "1, 2, 3 Red Light") by rock 'n' rolling a kiddie's rhyme: "down the basement lock the cellar door" from "My Little Playmate." At first I dismissed "Talk Dirty" because, like "Baby Talks Dirty" by the Knack, the words seemed too contemptuous and lewd for the bubble-genre, but then I noticed they only *pretend* to be smutty (and by '87, kids were more knowing than in '67 anyhow). I still don't know which 45 is better—depends on my mood.

141. THE CHAMBERS BROTHERS
. . . .
The Time Has Come CBS, 1967

This Bosstown-based and quite nattily attired five-some (four real-life African American bros and Sigma-Kappa-Pi-ready whiteboy Brian Keenan, whose worried look certainly has a knack for standing out in a crowd) had their souls psychedelicized in the late sixties and ended up putting out LPs with satiric Mothership-type titles like *Chambers Brothers Live on Mars*. On their best-seller, they fiercify a bizarre batch of standards ("People Get Ready," "In the

Midnight Hour," "Uptown," "What the World Needs Now") and do some weird-guitared collard-green R&B that doo-wops enchantingly with sturdy Baptist emotional depth. But their one true masterwork is the eight-or-twelve-or-fifteen-minute monstrosity "Time Has Come Today," probably the most outlandish ball of rock-mucus ever expectorated: voluminous Blue Cheer boomthud quoting "Little Drummer Boy," cuckoo clocks, tick-tocks, 'shroom-groomed cackles, echodrum hypnotics that beat everybody 'cept maybe Dr. John to the dub/acid-house game, plus some of the most despairing anxiety-of-displacement in the American songwrite archives, all about homeless and loveless gap-generation subway-strife. The ditty's been covered by such punksters as the Angry Samoans, Ramones, Circle Jerks, Würm, and My Dad Is Dead, and it oughta be obvious why.

142. BON JOVI
. . . .
Slippery When Wet Mercury, 1986

This is of course the *Frampton Comes Alive* of the eighties, by which I mean it piled platinum upon platinum at least as much via pretty-boy blondness as via competent pseudoblandness. Like Peter Frampton, Jon Bon Jovi deftly merges soft-rock and hard-rock signposts, which at his stage means shuffling Springsteen (really John Cafferty or Corey Hart) postfolk born-to-lose mythmake with Van Halen (really Loverboy or Night Ranger) postmetal bigbeat semistomp, thus elaborating on Meat Loaf's *Bat Out of Hell* attempt to overblow the overblownness of Springsteen's first Phil Spector period into actual "Ride of the Valkyries" territory. But it's Dave Bryan's and Richie Sambora's unfathomable synth-tongues, along with Jon's illusive style changes and unanticipated asides, that make *Slippery* the commendably mediocre work it is.

That "oowa-oowa-oo-oo-oo" that revs up "Livin' on a Prayer" (recalling Officer Toody from "Car 54, Where Are You?" even as it drags us into the "tu-uff, so tu-uff" union-strike fate of dockworker Tommy

and diner-helper Gina) was certainly one of 1987's kilohertz highlights. As were that tremendous a cappella start, that incidental word "dollin'," and above all that mystifying Bermuda Triangle–spawned second "bad name" right after Jon's "bad name" in "You Give Love a Bad Name." The singer defies his boy-next-door image by beginning his timely moral commentary "Social Disease" with the sound of sexual intercourse; he constructs a natural "Free Bird"–style AOR epic out of "Wanted Dead or Alive," which in other hands might have stayed just one more arty country-blues about how being a rock star is as hard as being a fugitive; he resurrects the old concept-move by concluding with two nifty numbers wherein he urges nostalgia for downing six-packs and busting cherries beneath dashboard lights back in Homecoming Week in Anytown. Whether he actually experienced all these spills and chills himself as a little Jovi, or whether he's making it up, is left unanswered; this enigma is part of his charm. And when, in "Livin' on a Prayer," his nihilism gets the best of him and he blurts, "It doesn't make a difference if we make it or not," he's already provided us with the courage and hope that enable us to chirp back, "Sure it does." We owe Jon a lot.

143. ZZ TOP
· ·
Eliminator Warner Bros., 1983

Seventies holdovers who oppose MTV on principle (as if "principles" have ever had anything to do with rock 'n' roll) categorize this under the imaginary taxonomical phylum known as "sellout," and admittedly there's a disconcerting spit-shine feel to (for example) Frank Beard's, um, electrodrum sound; there's also sloshy mush in "I Need You Tonight" and by-the-ratings-book CHR in "Gimme All Your Lovin." In retrospect, in fact, it's not farfetched to blame an entire era of radio blandness on the thing, but not until the hapless *Eliminator Jr.* of '85's *Afterburner* (which contains a good bedroll-hit regardless) would such nitpickles really get in the way. 'Cause *Eliminator*'s got it all: cocaine and art museums, whips and chains, fellatin' and cunnilingin', dirty noses and dirty dogs, blue chicken and twenty-year-old turkey, enchiladas and teriyaki, technofunk and technopop, clean shirts, new shoes, silk suits, black ties, white gloves, fat wallets, gold watches, stickpins, diamond rings, topcoats, top hats, panty hose commercials, stylin' videos, grown men guffawing, deep-fried slide, and a real keen auto now available as a Hot Wheels toy. Every human on earth bought about four copies.

144. MILES DAVIS
· ·
Agharta Columbia, 1976

Both the swingingest and the noisiest of the post–Sly/Jimi/James antifuzak LPs Miles unfurled between the 1970s' initial bat-crack and seventh-inning stretch: his usual freeflowing Latinoid percussion intangibles and irregular drum accents under supermusicianly gtr/organ/horn dogfight-complexities alternate between presyncopative shuffle and rabid red-alert sonics, but for remarkably long-lasting spans (most clamoriferously on sides one and four but to some mournful extent everywhere), Pete Cosey's and Reggie Lucas's ax-spasms simply take over, and the pair just plain cut loose, beating the living shaving cream

out of their strings with this bevy of seriously strange sproinging, screeching, farting, hee-hawing detonations. The bottom's all eternally enveloping buttmotion danceskronk, Ituri dub and horrific grumblebee *Shaft*ness, a back-to-Africa move that wears its third world influences on its anthropological labcoat sleeve yet out-ghettofunks any subsequent harmolodia, and the reeds blow some wicked bossa nova. "Interlude" 's speedjazz start has some of the most unsquare knots this former Cub Scout's ever encountered; Sting stole a Michael Henderson bass line from "Prelude Part II" for the Police's "Voices in My Head," I think, and I'd like to see hip-hop volume-pumpers embezzle a bit too. If Lars Metallica is the Miles-worshipper he claims to be (wanted to shake his hand at the '89 Grammys), I'd suggest he study this pissed-off brew in detail—rocks a few soupçons harder than Yes or Diamondhead, I'd say.

145. THE JIMI HENDRIX EXPERIENCE
· ·
Are You Experienced Reprise, 1967

I'll forever have reservations about this Hendrix kid, but here he's nineteen, and no way is he still a virgin—he rides his long black train through your tunnel like he's about eighty, like he's done *everything*. He's laying the groundwork for what metallic guitaring would always wanna be, and he may well be the most "revolutionary" instrumentalist of our time (not that I give a shit about "revolution" or anything), and his music is about sex and world destruction, and from what I can tell he's in favor of both. Here, he and his paleface understudies proffer stallionesque fuck-funk din ("Foxy Lady," "Can You See Me," "Fire"), stallionesque gloom-funk din ("Love or Confusion," "I Don't Live Today"), sprightly roots-moves ("Remember"), cosmic whatchamacallit ("3rd Stone from the Sun," "Are You Experienced"), and real good Don Ho ("May This Be Love"), not to mention stodgy roots-moves ("Red House") and stodgy gloom-funk din ("Manic Depression"). (My copy doesn't have "Purple Haze" or "Hey Joe" or "The Wind Cries Mary" on it, so maybe it's illegal!) Jimi tells Rover to move over (see "Move It on Over" by Hank Williams) and steals riffs from "Cool Jerk." His instrument sounds like it's eaten too many baked beans, and the stodginess is pretty darn incredible, as stodginess goes.

146. URIAH HEEP
The Best Of Mercury, 1976

"**O**ne of the few rock and roll bands to achieve legendary status in their own time," Toby B. Mamis's notes boast, and if you don't believe him, play "Easy Livin'" side by side with "Talk Talk" by the Music Machine. Elsewhere, as Clint Holmes would say, the enraptured Stonehenge la-la-las and cannonball percussives and chamber/garage-fused magic potions take you to the playground in your mind. Wiggly chains rattle around the attic in "July Morning," "The Wizard"'s got Ozzyesque panache and upward organ-spiral, "Bird of Prey"'s gigantic Frye-boot firecracking has the title character (falcon? kite? osprey? owl? vulture? hawk? buzzard? condor? Nope, an *eagle*) combing the ground for edible rodents with a squawk that returns to harass you in "Look at Yourself." With short sharp shockers on Side One and Frodo-metal epics on the reverse, this comp sums up their initial droppings and does its best to ignore the unpardonable pretension of their adulthood, when they started hiring King Crimson vets. I mean, Ken Hensley was a *Toe Fat* vet!

147. ANTI-NOWHERE LEAGUE
We Are the League WXYZ UK import, 1982

Vulgar, homely, ale-chugging, lawbreaking, drug-snorting, war-mongering, masturbating-on-the-Metro misanthropes who say "fuck" more than Schoolly D and Pussy Galore combined, these blokes made some of history's funniest and fiercest punk, huge, simple, and positively infective with invective, a bowling alley of a sound linking oi's singalong sleaze with biker riffs and leather. Growler Animal's got the world's heftiest codpiece, everybody calls guitarist Magoo shit, they admit their music's bad, they hate stuff they don't understand, they're gonna make you stay at home, and they wipe their ass on rock 'n' roll (just like Schoolly D!) 'cause "the man who made it was big and fat." "(We Will Not) Remember You" and "Nowhere Man" are such effectively gobbed taunts at the gray-flannel life they almost make me glad I skipped law school, but these cheerful urchins never let on that they're no dumbies, at least not until they Motörhead folkie Ralph McTell's bagpeople and derelicts in "Streets of London" into one of the most unforgettable cover versions of the eighties. Penniless but not penisless rowdies who despise themselves only a little less than they despise everybody else, the League tries real hard to hide their hearts and minds, but they can't.

148. TOM ROBINSON BAND
Power in the Darkness 1978, Harvest

Tom Robinson was never really any kind of "new wave," at least when he was good. The agit-propped but plainspoken but unconventional but singalongable pub-yell/bomber-jacket/rusty-bumper/teen-guerrila/music-hall rammalam he started out with was more akin to early Kinks (he was a Ray Davies protégé) or Bruce Springsteen (whom Robinson's eight-track cranks in the wonderful consumer-anthem "Grey Cortina") or, especially, Bachman-Turner Overdrive, with long spans of motorcycle guitar plus occasional roller-rink organ plus even some dashes of mellotron pomp. On *Power in the Darkness,* the only album he made before he commenced to turn into some unconscionable cross between late Joe Jackson and late Peter Gabriel, he flubs an attempt at funk (in the title track, which swings as limp as similar moves by Warren Zevon and the Dead), and sometimes his raised fist (particularly in "Better Decide Which Side You're On") veers too close for comfort to the totalitarianism he's supposedly fighting. But at least half of this double-disc ranks with the most rockingly humane editorial-metal ever: Tom drives cars around, hugs his big brother, joins hands with feminist sisters, punches policemen, watches his friends get knocked out cold by cops and queer-bashers, predicts street-riots in the summer followed by street-beatings in the winter. "Glad to Be Gay," which Tom dedicates to a homophobic World Health Organization, and which my spouse used to blast out the window to piss people off when we lived on an Army base, is recommended to Axl Rose.

149. THE RUNAWAYS
. . . .
The Runaways Mercury, 1976

The original hot childs in the city, and the first punk-rock band I ever heard of (they were competing on *Almost Anything Goes,* I think), the Runaways were puppets busting out all over, and what more should rock 'n' roll be? Well, it could be catchy, I guess: The hooks are okay but not great, the beat's okay but not great ('cept maybe when it goes Heavy Burundi), the Velvets cover is okay but not Mitch Ryder (even). They couldn't *play,* and though that's never made a difference per se, here it sure doesn't help. Still, "Cherry Bomb" 's one of the most wantonly explicit glandular-discovery depictions since "Da Doo Ron Ron," and "Dead End Justice" is a side-splitter, easily the most incompetent "rock opera" ever, with the exact same hook as "Cherry Bomb" and the exact

same story line as *Born Innocent,* brazen rockbabes leaving home for "pills and thrills," getting tossed in juvenile jail, breaking out. Two songs in a row Joan Jett moans metal's youngest fake orgasms ever; once, she supersedes a discussion of her own scream-abandon with "Gosh, what's your name?" So the best is lust and the rest is lackluster, glam/garage-rooted grungegum that meant well but was far too nondescript to *do* well. Seminal, though, and not only did it surpass where Fanny and Birtha had gone before, neither the Go-Gos nor the Bangles has touched it. And "Kiss Me Deadly" or no "Kiss Me Deadly," neither has Lita Ford.

Photograph by Greg Allen

150. THE SONICS

!!!Here Are the Sonics!!! Etiquette, 1965

This carport concrete's the foundation on which every subsequent metalband has staked its ugly guts. Ivory, brass, drums, feedback, Gerry Rosalie's yelps (which mostly go "woooaaaaghghgh!!!")—nothing's in kilter. Long before your daddy tricked your mama into the backseat of his paddywagon, these varsity-sweatered schoolboys shocked chaperones at Washington (state) homecomings, proms, YMCA teen nights, and Sadie Hawkins hops, carousing in spit-shined machines, aiming their lo-fi truck-race bawl at chicks who'd run away with their love (and car, and guitar), not making any conscious attempt to be hard guys, not working hard to destroy anything, just doing it. They even encourage impressionable youngsters to ingest strychnine! These psychos take to the Contours, Chuck Berry, Rufus Thomas, Barret Strong, and Little Richard as if they're glad to be Caucasian, and most of said whitewashings don't quite make it, but it's real democratic and Ornette Coleman–like how everybody plays "Roll Over Beethoven"'s notes whenever they feel up to it, and the rumble below and Gerry's "stomp, shtomp, work-it-on-out" made their "Money" definitive, at least till the Flying Lizards one-upped it by throwing rubber toys at a piano. Side Two, where you'll locate most of the performances I've praised, is as fatally fertile a Jonestown Kool Aid surf party as you'll ever flip your wig to.

151. RED CROSS

Red Cross Posh Boy EP, 1980

As barely-teenaged So-Cal tykes, eight years old or something, Jeff McDonald and his brother Steve plied their hate of school (and jocks, rah-rahs, bookworms, surfers, brains, and other such pricks) and lust for bleached blondes and a post-Mouseketeer-era Annette Funicello (whose biggest hit, "Tall Paul," hit number seven in '59) into punk-pop with metal

moves long before punk-pop with metal moves was such a cool (and, therefore, such an uncool) thing to attempt. They've got speech impediments and Patty Hearst–inspired backup squeals, and their entire debut (six songs) lasts shorter than plenty of individual prog-boogie numbers I know. Side Two's pleasant enough as hardcore goes, but Side One is flawless, one of metal's wildest trilogies this side of *The Lord of the Rings.* They make fun of cover bands who use Marshall Stacks and listen to Kiss (and the Knack!); four years later, on *Teen Babes from Monsanto,* they'd cover "Deuce." All told, an afternoon delight for sure.

152. THE SONICS

Sonics Boom Etiquette, 1965

"Cinderella"'s the kind of song where after you hear it the first time they have to slice your palms off your chair-grips with a surgical knife. Gerry Rosalie, one of the coolest heterosexuals ever born beneath the bluest skies you've ever seen, froths at the mouth as if his throat's been torched by the Statue of Liberty and he's wielding a meat cleaver, then turns around and croons "Don't Be Afraid of the Dark" and "Since I Feel for You" as if he's Wayne Newton. These moonstruck Tacoma fratbrutes have a glass shoe but no princess to put it on, an overloaded underside, and what've gotta be among the first documented cases of both Satan-sludge (in "He's Waitin'," he'll burn your soul for eternity 'cause you stayed out late then lied about it) and oi!-shout (in "Skinny Minny," eleven years ahead of "T.N.T." by AC/DC, though twenty-eight behind the smash musical *Me and My Girl* and Britain's subsequent Lambeth Walk fad). "Louie Louie" cuts Motörhead's and almost Black Flag's, and the screams and distortion make your teeth chatter.

153. DEVIANTS

Ptooff! Sire/London UK import, 1968

Limey far-far-lefty equivalents of either the MC5 or the Mothers of Invention or both, skippered by future essayist-laureate Mick Farren, the Deviants came out of nowhere then went back, and nobody noticed. Here, they turn the Stones' "Goin' Home" into an even more threatening fuzztone odyssey called "I'm Coming Home," and neither Cinderella (the band) nor Jon Voight has much to do with it. We follow Farren's sassy nasal yelp and Sid Bishop's tripwire guitars up the landing, to the door, then inside, to your bed, where it feels alright. There's a slippery John Lee Hooker–cum-Dylan mudslide about a cop-killer; echopercussive acid-blackout spacefiller experiments; a perverted medicine man fondling garbage and selling it to middle-class housewives over Diddleybeat harmonica and raunch; a sitar track that's as breathtakingly lush and decadent a private hell as anything by Love or the Velvet Underground. Inside the pop-art gatefold, we get quotes from Tolkein, Guevara, Kafka, Tolstoy, Emerson, Thoreau, Goethe, Nietzsche, Ginsberg, Burroughs, Townshend, Kupferberg, and other droppable names, most of whom address the union of the visceral and intellectual and emotional in ways that cannot be dismissed as merely "liberal." Always captivating (parts of the nine-minute "Deviation Street" prophesy *Funhouse*) if sometimes insufferably pretentious (other parts predate the Shimmy-Disc label's awful art-rock parodies by two whole decades), this is hippiefied excess maybe, but way smarter and jollier than most. Way more rocking too.

154. THE GODZ
. . . .
Nothing Is Sacred Casablanca, 1979

Leaders of their own pack 'cause nobody else would take 'em, riding their Harleys outta the dry ice and into the sunset, sharing a label with Donna Summer and the Village People but acting as if Travolta never happened, even reverting to fiftiesism for their final submarine race, these stoners plow as if they've got stumps for fingers and write as if they've got stumps for brains, breaking for boogachucka amid dumbass Daltreychord distortion and safari solos that go absolutely nowhere. They spell even worse than Slade ("Gotta Muv," "Festyvul Seasun," "Rock Yer Sox Auf,"

"I'll Bi Yer Luv"), and they name another tune "714," after either the number Rorer put on their 'ludes or Babe Ruth's home run total, I'm not sure which. "My Visa card is charged too high/But that's okay 'cause I'll get by/My passion's growing, it's getting large/Will you please take my Master Charge?" This in a sentimental acoustic passage, directed at a, um, prostitute; it's a joke, right? Don't be so sure. Poor Eric Moore growls like a mealymouthed primate about how his distaff half won't allow no open marriage around here no more (sorta like Springsteen in "Trapped," y'know), his smoochface hotelmates call him a fool, he admits that Godz only knows how to do three things, and the Godz School of Rock is as easy as 1–2–3. Everybody answers "1–2–3!!" and I seriously doubt they could count any higher.

155. HAWKWIND

Hall of the Mountain Grill United Artists, 1974

Like George Clinton (and let us not forget those electronic rappers in Jonzun Crew!), these Anglonauts were probably Sun Ra fans, so naturally the most successful installment in their lengthy trek through the comets contains their usual avant-garage keyb 'n' oboe–driven swoosh-symphonics. But a couple stand out. One's "Lost Johnny," caterwauling proto-Motörhead heroin-addict/boy-prostitute wolfbane-worship with gators in its sewers, and the other's got Lemmy Kilmister chanting thusly: "Sick of politicians, harassment, and laws/All we do is get screwed up by other people's flaws/World turned upside-down now, nothing else to do. . . ." The swirls and tweaks of Dave Brock's twelve-string climb toward higher and higher altitudes, steady over this half-organic/half-synthetic percussion groove, eventually building toward multi-climactic doomsday freefuzz crescendos over and over for seven minutes. "That ain't no joke," Lemmy keeps repeating, as if he knows something we don't, "You could disappear in smoke." The roar's like the Challenger lifting off; at song's end, it explodes.

156. THE SWEET

Biggest Hits RCA German import, 1972; rec. 1971–72

Picking up sunny kindergarten cuteness where "Hanky Panky" by Tommy James and "Indian Giver" by the 1910 Fruitgum Company left off, four goofs masterminded by Mike Chapman and Nicky Chinn name themselves after bubblegum's most distinguishing trait, don headdresses and polka dots, and sell immaculate innocence that might be faked but sure fools me. They mix up Stooges licks, curly-lipped Elvis quivers, sheeplike "bah" backup, tom-toms, shimmy shuffledowns, coconut-calypso syncopation; they repeat syllables ("Funny Funny," "Co-Co," "Chop Chop,"

à la "Sugar Sugar," "Yummy Yummy"). Palefaces watch Minnehaha tell Hiawatha "wig wam bam, bam shamalam," and Alexander Graham Bell invents the phone so he can converse with his girl.

157. BACHMAN-TURNER OVERDRIVE

Best of B.T.O. (So Far) Mercury, 1976; rec. 1973–75

My frosh year at West Bloomfield High School, this quintessential gearhead-rock was all you heard; I think they used to play it over the PA system in the morning, and the rest of the Western Hemisphere was apparently the same. Impregnable in their not-fragile mode and tolerable in their fragile one, these bigger-than-a-bread-truck Canadians pile Who/CCR/Sab riffs into hooks as chunky and clumpy as their torsos, and sing about rock 'n' roll as if it's a job, which it is. They're professionals cracking open the myth of counterculture by reveling in the myth of priv-atization. The operable theme in at least half of these groans is money-changes-everything; another ("Lookin' Out for #1") was apparently prompted by a Robert Ringer slogan, another ("You Ain't Seen Nothing Yet") apparently prompted a Ronald Reagan slogan. But at least two rap acts have covered "Takin' Care of Business," which oughta tell you something about its beat, and "Roll on Down the Highway"'s beat is even bigger.

158. CREAM

Fresh Cream Atco, 1967

The chirps they open with could be the Belmonts, but suddenly there's this towering pyrotechnic plea of self-affirmation, "I Feel Free," then "N.S.U.," an even more titanic plea for more self-affirmation, more respect, more idealism, more wonder, more nothing left to lose. The vocals soar around Eric Clapton's feisty guitar-roar with wings spread like an osprey's, diving again and again into the hollow industrial-size garbage tins Ginger Baker apparently uses for drums. The blues respite in the middle of Side One is so mellow it's somnambulant, and Jack Bruce knows it—his lyrics address sleeping, then dreaming. The B-side gooses Robert Johnson and Muddy Waters and Skip James till the Mississippi blues are eight miles high, spirals and tumbles into hurricanes, rips everything apart to make way for bookshelves worth of descending voices, or for crazed Jack Bruce harmonica-grandeur. Or, in the end, for Ginger's presciently quasiprimal five-minute solo, absurdly entitled "Toad," which (even more absurdly, given its gratuitous excess) somehow feels earned. It's as if words weren't currency anymore, that they could no longer do what civilizations generations ago had invented them to do. As of now, only sound and sound alone could matter.

159. THE YARDBIRDS
Over Under Sideways Down Epic, 1966

They were unconventional boys, hung out in unusual crowds, called Antonioni "Mike." They wanted to be hillbillies, or blacks, yet when Keith Relf sang like he was in church, it wasn't a black or hillbilly one; it was a monastery, or maybe a mosque. This is Stained-Glass Rock, but in "Ever Since the World Began," the protagonist is Satan, not God. "Hot House of Omagarashid," another song's called, and it sounds like the bloops your tropical fish might emit if you'd been spinning too much Bo Diddley. The words go "YAH yah yah, yah yah YAH"; Jeff Beck's country-blues guitar overtures start coiling up thicker, flying over your head, a manic tidal wave, and next thing you know he's playing "London Bridge." Somewhere else, there's something ethnic, from Arabia maybe. You can dance in the gym to it, it's happy music, then this sepulchral plaint starts undulating, pleading "when will it end, when will it end?" The voice would disappear for fourteen years, reappear as Joy Division's Ian Curtis moaned "Day of the Lords." Then it would disappear again, maybe forever.

160. NEIL YOUNG AND CRAZY HORSE
Re-Ac-Tor Warner Bros., 1981

Underrated, though just as easy to overrate, the only obvious metal "move" in Neil's feedback oeuvre, this goof's extremely noisesome for no purpose you can figure, and mildly "funky" in the nonswinging way that's the only way Neil knows, but the Neil Young album it most reminds me of is *Trans,* his computer-cowboy Devo-move, and I like that one a lot too. "Opera Star" 's antipomp complaint is dumber than it oughta be, and "Surfer Joe and Moe the Sleaze" 's duo-ode sounds like half a song, but the four consecutive transportation-mantras—highway, train, domestic car, subway—are better. The tracks you remember, though, are the ones that last forever. "T-Bone" 's vegetarian dinner menu (mashed taters courtesy Dee Dee Sharp!) is one of the silliest Dada-excursions any major pro's gotten away with, and nine minutes' worth is all you can eat. And "Shots," eight minutes of blare so discordant it makes everything else here seem like Graham Nash, is one of this great folkie's most harrowing hunks of agitated augury ever: A voice straining as if it's war-torn, kids who'll never grow up, guns that won't stop. Neil calls his car-mantra "Motor City," but as much as Guns N' Roses' "Welcome to the Jungle" or Eric B. and Rakim's "I Ain't No Joke," "Shots" expresses what Detroit in the Robocop eighties really felt like.

161. THE KINKS
Greatest Hits Rhino, 1989; rec. 1964–66

Back when I didn't know "punk rock" from any other category in the *Free Press* entertainment section (before I had any of this *chronological* stuff sussed too) I heard "All Day and All of the Night" on the FM and knew the phrase fit: It's as if this fat unshaven lunk with a club's got some equally fat unshaven woman by the topknot, telling her she's his mate and that's all there is to it. Latest rumor is that Jimmy Page *didn't* nasty up said track or "You Really Got Me" (which I've never liked much), but you can't tell to hear 'em and that's what's important, and you can imagine he's on "I Need You" too. These artistes' other early output primarily alternated between ye olde time piano-roll softshoe and postblues proto-boogie as polite as their Nehru jackets—passably semicomatose Dylan and James Brown swipes, a Dave Davies semisolo now and then, seminally tuneful niceties that're tough to get excited about. Fans of Peggy Lee, Ravel, Gershwin, Ella Fitzgerald, Streisand, and Bach, their cover-clogged nonanthologies invariably induce me to wonder what the big deal is, and "Stop Your Sobbing" 's gripe at a crybaby spouse was sung sweeter by Dave's future sister-in-law Chrissie Hynde sixteen years later. But "A Well Respected Man," "Dedicated Follower of Fashion," "Sunny Afternoon," and "I'm Not Like Everybody Else"—these four are something more. The words are super, back-looking embracements of joyful nonconformity and the tavern on the green, but the real vigor comes from Ray Davies's sneer, which is way beyond ironic. It's pitiless, unmerciful: a whole 'nother way to hate.

162. THE SENSATIONAL ALEX HARVEY BAND
The Impossible Dream Vertigo, 1974

Deadpan, flamboyantly campy glitter-era Brits, their theatre-boogie's almost as brainy as Mott the Hoople's, almost as brawny as Mountain's, and more proto-postmodern than either, but only when it wants to be. Led by an exotic character who once worked as a lion tamer and later found employment in Dixieland and skiffle troupes, guitared in a real wah-happy way by Zal Cleminson, who decorates his face like Joel Grey in *Cabaret,* the disc opens with a "symphony," and Part One's the tale of a baby-eating monster called "Vambo," no doubt where Wiseblood got the idea for "Stumbo," their 1987 dinosaur-dance

single. Drums quote Sabbath's "Children of the Grave" as a joke, riffs play tag like little kids. Betwixt the *Shaft*-synths and Latin horn charts in "Man in the Jar," the symphony's second act, you hear the origins of both MX-80 Sound's "Man in a Box" and Was (Not Was)'s "Oh, Mr. Friction." In two different numbers, Alex Harvey starts scatting "scoobie-doo-zaba-de-bah" like he's Cab Calloway or David Lee Roth. He does something called "Long Haired Music," and what he claims he can't get enough of turns out to be neither classical nor rock 'n' roll, but rather cunnilingus, so he turns into a lounge-crooner, and some yob pees all over his leg. A cover-medley glides "Money Honey" into "Impossible Dream," then some bagpipe-metal half-evolves toward either the Beastie Boys' "Rhymin & Stealin" or the Pogues' "Billy's Bones." The music-hall irony's eventually a downfall, but everybody sure does have a good time getting there. And when the performance finally ends it's more candid than oblique, a biting seven-minute curse.

163. DICK DESTINY AND THE HIGHWAY KINGS
Arrogance Destination, 1986

First off you see this beardo, not a young guy, with a Harley T-shirt and leather jacket and stogie and motorcycle. A *real* man, no doubt; he's got a Ph.D. in chemistry. His fellow guitarist (Byron Goozeman) digs Captain Beyond and Sir Lord Baltimore, and Dick makes the drummer (Carson Mills Carson) repeat his last name as his first name. Also, there's a bassist, but like everybody except the big cheese, he's just there for show. Right away you hear a lick plagiarized unaltered from BÖC's "The Red and the Black," then suddenly men in blue are pulling over commie freaks who cheat at solitaire, and Dick's rhyming "wimpy college nerd" with "booger-eatin' turd." *Arrogance* was mostly recorded in Mr. Destiny's apartment, using the Tom Scholz—designed Rock Module, and it's got plenty of those kind of ugly riffs that stick to your heels so's you can't even scrape 'em off with a hacksaw, and "Highway Kings" is the only Godz tribute

DICK DESTINY & THE HIGHWAY KINGS

ARROGANCE

disastrous-weather metaphors, "Checkmate" entirely of chess metaphors, and the only rec since that's approached the sound's celestial spirit is Bad Religion's *Into the Unknown*. On the back cover, the whole band's upside down.

165. BLACK HEAT
No Time to Burn Atlantic, 1974

Notwithstanding the extent to which such hypes insisted on connecting themselves to a longstanding tradition of double-reverse crossover, the sheer amount of hoopla surrounding Living Coloür's emergence in 1988 and Frisco's wave of funkless "funk-metal" (from Primus, Psychefunkapus, Fungo Mungo, et cetera) two years later demonstrated that some pundits were actually foolish enough to believe that something *original* was going on. No such luck—acid-funk's thrived in both black and white dialects for decades, and the only thing its revivalists contributed was rigid hipbones. I know nothing about the players in Black Heat, have never seen 'em listed in any reference work or periodical whatsoever, but one look at their album covers hints that they were trouble guys, and the innards to this one confirm said hypothesis—Bradley Owens's attack, especially in "You Should've Listened" and the seven-minute sex-grooved *That Was Then, This Is Now* tribute "M & M's," is diabolically gorgeous Hendrix/Hazel dementia. There's lines about taxes getting higher and jobs getting rarer, falsetto blaxploitation raps, a title cut that denies both burn-baby-burn and "Disco Inferno." But what sets Black Heat above most of those late-eighties wannabes is their *sound*—post-*Shaft*/Stooge wah-wah, good vibes (the instrument, I mean!), voices rooted in the Baptist church, flutes and Latin drums worked in Santana-style without acting as if it's an unnatural thing to do. How's this for a sense of community: "All personnel joined in for percussion breaks, coffee breaks, and during solos."

ever. (The Highway Kings are bike-rockers squarely in the Boyz/Godz/Cigaretz tradition, but they didn't end their name with a "z" 'cause it never occurred to 'em.) "Blues Have Got Me by the Throat" is introduced as a "sad sad song," the redo of Dave Bowie's "Jean Genie" retains the mongeese, and the coda's a superb wall-of-mung instro entitled "Road Kill." Plus, if your copy's got a scratch at the start of "You're No Good" like mine does, you can rap over the drumbeat!

164. SRC
Milestones Capitol, c. 1970

White-hick-on-dope Nehru-whoosh pretending to think deep thoughts in Detroit, these organ-drenched patchquilts of fuzztone get me chuckling every time out. Quackenbush brothers Glenn and Gary segue Grieg into Ravel then switch gears toward blood-thirsty Stooge-savagery, whilst Scott Richardson's nonchalant tongue conjures scads of quasiprofound post-Dylan daytripper details: lonely moonbeams, never-ending shadows, pounding mental clocks, clouds of confusions, earthquakes of issues, cyclones of cold conversations, privacies of pain, surrendering pawns, Cheshire smiles, reflections in peril, angels in forgotten times. "Eye of the Storm"'s made up entirely of

166. METALLICA
. . . .
Master of Puppets Elektra, 1986

A loud, fast, innovative, political-but-not-ideological garage band with a defiant populist message that adds up to "let me be who I am and let me kick out the jams," born of a white urban teen subculture, recording for Elektra, climbing charts despite zero radio play—it was like the MC5 all over again. Obsessed with the survival of the individual in a world where individualism's become a façadè, James Hetfield bellows quasi-archaic metaphors about trying to retain an identity in a timè and place where every structure exists either to control him or to con him that he's still in control. Locked up, maybe in his room by his parents, he convinces himself he's crazy, fantasizes violence. His characters are horrified by the cages in which they're boxed—drugs in the title cut, religion in "Leper Messiah," war in "Disposable Heroes," family in "Welcome Home (Sanitarium)." The LP's name sums up the predicament; the record jacket portrays a graveyard as a marionette's stage, with a steel helmet and dog tags flung over two cross-shaped headstones. Trickily elaborate intro-outro flourishes evaporate into damn-the-torpedoes flailing, dulcet riffs jerking out in trots and knee-kicks, blaring with a steamroller persistence that, like nobody since Zeppelin, keeps the symphonics from drifting off like dust in the Kansas wind. Lars Ulrich and Cliff Burton lay down backbeats that shift hard enough to crack a camel's back, and two guitarists charge from the bush like farmboy infantrymen scared shitless to be in a jungle swamp, laying waste to whatever's stupid enough to wander across their line of fire. Burton's baroque bass licks add mere seconds of solace, only to melt into uncontrollable walls of fatally toxic crud.

167. THE GODZ
. . . .
The Godz Millennium, 1978

These skinny morons on motorbikes ain't got a lot on their minds (they acknowledge), but they've just realized what losers they are, and boy are they bummed. Though this Don Brewer—overwatched job's not quite up to the incomprehensible standard of their self-produced sophomore shot, the chariot of the Godz on the cover's a "smart" touch (and just to make sure you know it's no *accident,* they quote Erich Von Däniken on the back). There's "Happy Days" harmonies, titles (not songs, just titles—see Rod Stewart or Neil Young) from girl groups, time changes from Alice Cooper. Stoner-guitars dive-bomb continually in imperfect circles for ten minutes in what may well be the only non–"Radar Love" Golden Earring cover ever, and the band plays as if they've got petrol on their palms and a lube-job beneath their nails.

More relevant still is Eric Moore's philosophical monologue in "Gotta Keep Runnin'," which'd rank as one of the most sidesplitting soliloquies ever concocted by mere mortals even if it *didn't* wind up as part of some TV movie where Keith Partridge pretended to be a high school undercover narc: "They think we're all junkies, but everybody's *some* kind of junkie," Moore starts. Then he's preaching through his nose, summing up the virtues of life on rock's lost highway (long hair and dope, mainly), says he can't think or hear, then he starts getting these Machiavellian visions: "Can't feel nothin', got no heart and soul, but we're Godz/And someday there'll be thousands of us!" It's perhaps the ultimate conclusion of the gnostic theory that each of us is his own deity. We'll outnumber 'em, he plots, then he turns into a "rock 'n' roll machine" without the capacity for emotion, not merely exemplifying what seventies stadiums had turned rock into, but rejoicing in it, arguing that it's no flaw after all—INVENTING HIS OWN AESTHETIC, if you will.

168. BIG BROTHER AND THE HOLDING COMPANY
· · · · · · · · · · · · · · · · · ·
Cheap Thrills Columbia, 1968

Janis Joplin's vocals aren't much to look at, but she does cool stuff *between* words. Behind an R. Crumb cover you'd expect to see on Yazoo Records (there's even a "darkie"), she lifts earth-mom southern-comfort kozmic-blues bliss and its loose-limbed runa-muck rhythms from the public domain into the present tense. More subdued and not as sloshingly troughlike as Big Brother's posthumous live job, this famous one's more listenable anyhow, and in places, 'specially past Side Two's midpoint (where "Oh, Sweet Mary" is already three-quarters of the way toward Zepdom, and "Ball and Chain" is the perfect metaphor for most HM rhythm sections), it's as atonally freaked as you could want. This might be where Axl Rose learned his stuff: Janis does Gersh-win's "Summertime" (all the way through, not just a couple lines of it like Iggy on *Soldier*), and you can tell from her dramatics that she truly gets off on listening to herself sing, fine by me, and though her dynamically swaying scat-ology ("no-no-nana-nah-nah-nah-nah-nah") in no way compares to Billy Stewart's in his 10/6/65 rendition ("blllllllllot-chucka-chot-chot-chucka-chot-chot"), it's fiery nonetheless. Also, though for feminist elucidation of said shanghai you'll need to consult someone more versed in such areas than myself, she really does take a piece of your heart.

169. LOVE
· · · · · · · · · · · · · · · · · ·
Best of Love Rhino, 1980; rec. 1966–70

There's not much loudness on their unanimously lauded frostpop classic *Forever Changes* (though there's oodles of hilarious titles such as "A House Is Not a Motel" and "Bummer in the Summer" and "The Good Humor Man He Sees Everything Like This" and "Maybe the People Would Be the Times or Between Clark And Hilldale"), but these absurdists started out garagey and ended up kinda funky, and stoned little tunes like "My Little Red Book," "Your Mind and We Belong Together," "Robert Montgomery," and "Stephanie Knows Who" are turbulent thrillers, as is the Nevada atom-bomb blast at the end of "Seven and Seven Is." They recorded a seventeen-minute track way back in '67, and unpredictably cheeb-dazed Hendrix disciple that he was, crooner/fretter Arthur Lee was some fantastic wordsmith, tossing daddy in the fireplace and hypnotizing his dog but not crying about it 'cause his eyes were gone, maybe 'cause they got cut off by accident back when he used to sit in bottles and pretend they were cans.

One of the few post-*Pepper* rockfolks-of-color whose blacktion (if only 'cause if you heard him you couldn't tell it existed) didn't get in the way of Whitey liking him, Arthur sang (like Mick Jagger, who wanted to be black) about a girl who comes in colors, whatever that means, and (like Hendrix, who was) about not being alive, even though he *was* alive at the time (Jimi didn't die till later, see). "Seven and Seven Is" and "Number Fourteen," the first and last titles on this comp's Side Two (not unlike, though perhaps less intentional than, "It's Only Over When . . ." and ". . . You Give Up" on Bad Religion's *Into the Unknown*), join to form a sentence. Also, "Seven and Seven Is" is math-rock in a class with the Pet Shop Boys' "Two Divided by Zero" if not Bob Seger's "2 + 2 = ?," and "Number Fourteen" is perhaps the only Band-style Civil War rebel-nostalgia ever sung by a descendant of slaves. Love can be considered the Pacific Coastal answer to the Velvet Underground for three reasons: (1) gorgeous Gay Nineties Tin Pan Alley melodies (e.g., the additional matched-pair-of-titles "Alone Again Or," which has a bullfight bolero from Herb Alpert's Tijuana Brass, and "Andmoreagain," which feels like "Femme Fatale" and has a string section) that you'll fall asleep to if you're not careful, (2) heroin-purchase explanations, and (3) not too many record sales at the time, but plenty later.

170. DEREK AND THE DOMINOES
Layla and Other Assort ' Love Songs
Atco, 1970

Whatever makes this a milestone has very little to do with Robert Johnson, because if it did I'd like Robert Johnson more. Then again, I suppose I'd take "Love in Vain" or "Me and the Devil Blues" or "Stones in My Passway" over foggily sullen laziness like "Tell the Truth" or "Have You Ever Loved a Woman" or "It's Too Late," but only because, in a certain sense, THIS IS THE SORT OF HOOKLESSLY "AUTHENTIC" BULLSHIT THAT DESTROYED ROCK 'N' ROLL. As for the less indulgent minipeaks, they're like *Blood on the Tracks* or the other "It's Too Late" (on Carole King's *Tapestry*) in that they're a heavenly revenge-tonic if you're going through the same sorrow-drowning breakup business the singer's going through, which must be a good one percent of your life if you're like most of us, but they sound pretty geeky otherwise. Yet I've got no problem with the way Clapton's voice goes faster than "Why Does Love Have to Be So Sad" 's music and higher than "I Looked Away" 's, the way he recovers so fast from throwing up in "I Am Yours," and the way "Key to the Highway" suggests somebody locked it. Sometimes I think this music is where Nerf-blues like Bon Jovi's "I'll Be There for You" and Cinderella's "Coming Home" and White Lion's "Living on the Edge" (where the bell-bottom blues are Levi's 501s!) came from, and these days that means a great deal more than Robert Johnson ever could. As for "Layla" itself, the long maxipeak that tries to sound the way "Funeral for a Friend/Love Lies Bleeding" by Elton John would sound a few years later, Eric really does convince you he'd kill to get that woman back. And as for its "tasty licks," I don't know from art, but I know what I like.

171. MILES DAVIS
Jack Johnson Columbia, 1971

The metal comes from Sonny Sharrock, who goes uncredited, and maybe from John McLaughlin, who doesn't. One or both start out riding this rough-and-tumble semifunk rhythm, for which we can thank Bill Cobham a little and Michael Henderson a lot. Miles starts riding it too; trumpet-riffs and ax-riffs have a conversation, or maybe a boxing match (the album's named for, and dedicated to, an early twentieth-century heavyweight champ, according to Arthur Ashe the most important black athlete ever, who died in a speeding car). Miles takes the first couple rounds, McLaughlin takes one, Miles one, the road gets rougher. Miles fires five quick jabs at John's face, they both run out of steam, everything's quiet and eerie. Sonny (I think it's him) emerges from the bullpen (boxing's a stupid barbarian sport anyhow), or maybe it's a tag-team. He starts dancing around, dance and punch, dance punch *pounce*, dance punch *pounce*, hammer-down vengeance. Blood's streaking out Miles's brass. But suddenly Henderson's doing all the work, and he's only supposed to be the *floormat*! Now *everybody's* dancing—Warren Zevon's favorite fighter Boom Boom Mancini, David Roter's favorite fighter Sonny Liston, Spoonie Gee's favorite fighter Mike Tyson, Johnny Wakelin and the Kinshasa Band's favorite fighter Muhammad Ali. Sharrock wins, spews all over the ring. So on the B-side the whole gang goes out for a relaxing round of mint juleps and levitation tricks, and after a while Sonny starts cracking bottles over heads and rolling barstools around, and Jack Johnson reminds us why we're gathered here.

Photograph by Janette Beckman

172. RUN-D.M.C.
· · · · · · · · · · · · · · · · · ·
Raising Hell Profile, 1986

They didn't just cross over—they broke on through to the other side. "Walk This Way" takes subtle lyrical liberties as if it just don't care, confirms my long-standing contention that the original version was prerap rap, and introduces Steve Tyler and Joe Perry to a brand-new audience; "Raising Hell," where Run and D.M.C. behead Satan then play catch with his skull, is the AC/DC move. Otherwise, the pair stir their trademark emcee-metal and subdub minimalism into L.L. Cool J–type guitarless heaviness, Mantronix-type tick-tock tap-dancing, Trouble Funk–type cow-bell percussion, Slick Rick–type mock-proper enunciation (by '89, hip-hop's ragtime-revival affectations would mirror rock's circa '73), Fat Boys–type human beatburps, eclection galore. The rhymes, not terribly astute, chide groupies, clothes-tearers, "sissy soft suckers," and noncapitalists. Slapping around homechicks who don't wanna get busy, the rhymers further flex their ignorance. Then they quote Martin Luther King and boast about not being white, but it's not exactly as if they had any say in the matter.

173. SIR LORD BALTIMORE
· · · · · · · · · · · · · · · · · ·
Kingdom Come Mercury, 1970

Ritchie Blackmore sneakily appropriated his "My Woman from Tokyo" riff from "Lady of Fire," and except for perhaps Al Green or Sam Cooke, John Garner undoubtedly owns the most wondrous voice in the history of the Victorola, and I won't even try to explain why. I wouldn't know where to start, it's real complicated. As are the guitar and bass and drums, all with enough steroids in 'em to rip New York phone books in half with their hands tied behind their backs (yellow pages and everything!). Three Manhattan boys race the fastblast rapids in a galleon stolen from pirates (Willie Stargell, Roberto Clemente, Honus Wagner, et cetera), Garner slavering his tight-trouser castrato like a beached sperm whale on nitrous oxide (I got it: His larynx pulls a time change *every syllable*, the logic's all his own, he's the Cecil Taylor of the microphone, my Rolling Stone my ice-cream cone my twilight zone my Eva Perón), whilst (most notably in "Hard Rain Fallin'," "Ain't Got Hung on You," and the insurmountable mongoose monsoon "Pumped Up") his cronies whirl like dervishes, or like Tasmanian devils tightening wood-screws up Bob Hope's nostrils. With a Phillips. And he has a cold.

174. THE ACCURSED
· ·
Laughing at You Wreck 'Em UK import, 1984

Eight years into punk's dole-queue reign and five years into Margaret Thatcher's, with British unemployment totaling three million and half a nation left to die, three fed-up spikeheads with no alternatives in sight grab cricket bats and start beating skulls. It's no fun at all. The most despondent song, "Going Down," starts "Standin' on the corner, on the road, in the freezin' freezin' cold"; my commas represent calloused vamps, dead ends that send your circulating blood surging fast toward another artery, which it may never find. You're bombarded by blazeballed clumps of black residue these Oliver Twists have scraped off the walls of the tube station loo with some bag lady's fingernail file. Opening and closing his throat like an automatic car-window, Steve Hall never stops shouting, keeps exploring for the point where the wind will slap your cheek hardest. He can't control his rage, can't channel it, can barely articulate it at all. He calls his songs "Laughing at You," "Listen to Me," "I'm Telling You," "I Didn't Mean It," and with maybe five words in each, oozing over and over with escalating determination, titles is mostly all they are. A brave yawp through a hole in the wall by guys who just want you to know they're here, guys you wouldn't notice on the street until they confronted you, after which it'd be too late, this is so abandoned and dejected a depiction of its wasteland you can scarcely bear to listen.

175. CHEAP TRICK
· ·
Cheap Trick Epic, 1977

The one for the annals, partly a devotion to a girl whose face can stop a clock, is "He's a Whore," with a descending stun-riff scratched repeatedly as Rick Nielsen growls repeatedly that he'll do anything for money, an honest way to initiate a career in his biz for sure. Otherwise, we get hopped-up pop with hard-boiled guitar-tempos out of Aerosmith and BTO, angles out of Marc Bolan, and slick harmonies out of AM radio—Edison Lighthouse or the DeFranco Family, maybe. The Tricksters beg the Beatle Question with a McCartneyesque "any time at all" submerged beneath "He's a Whore"'s lewdness; with a bulky White Album paraphrase called "The Ballad of TV Violence"; with one tune titled "Taxman" and another named for *Sgt. Pepper* that parrots ELO. "School's for fools," they shout in one crime journal, and in the next one, called "Daddy Should Have Stayed in High School," they request spankings. At the end of "Cry Cry Cry," Neilson starts crooning "Heartbreak Hotel."

Every Chicagoan I know claims they'd already seen the band twenty times, but to unsuspecting outsiders, Rockford, Illinois, must've seemed like another planet.

176. ROSE TATTOO
• •
Rose Tattoo Mirage, 1980

Backslappingly cheerful baldie-Aussie prole-dole dropout/outlaw esprit de corps as rooted in the Faces as in AC/DC, made loud to be played loud: The rockmasters in charge have cattle-branded biceptuals and rings in their ears and maybe their rears, and they guard their ashcans like flies. They call themselves "boys" ("Nice Boys" is what they say they're not, "Bad Boy for Love" is what Angry Anderson says he is), their fastest cut lasts 1:57, and their slowest and sweetest is a David Allen Coe kind of calypso where Angry invites some nubile schoolgirl home to "watch TV," then his pet parrot and goldfish die and you can't figure out how come, but next he's rasping rigorously about how she's still wet and his balls are dry. Whatever "Astra Wally" 's about, Angry means it, and "The Butcher and Fast Eddy," a hard-to-follow suburban Stagger Lee story with gangs on the loose and switchblades in the chest, is the best song named for your humble servant the author this side of the biggest hit by Rickie Lee Jones, who looked real stoned at a Grammy ceremony once.

177. THE YARDBIRDS
• •
Greatest Hits, Volume One Rhino, 1986; rec. 1964–66

Razorsliced British pop songs, grounded in R&B but only 'cause everybody's gotta be grounded somewhere, with a foreboding nascent-metal buzz from Eric Clapton first and Jeff Beck second. Blues is where they start: Naomi Neville's "A Certain Girl" with one of the most cloyingly canned call-and-responses ever, Howlin' Wolf's "Smokestack Lightning" echoing as if inside a corn silo, Clarence Carter's "I Ain't Got You" sung like Keith Relf has a cold, later Bo Diddley's "I'm

a Man" with lines that would one day signify "coming of age" on the yuppie nostalgia-show "Almost Grown." Pop is why Clapton quit: "For Your Love" and "Putty (in Your Hands)," composed by a guy who later penned skewed-romance ditties for 10cc, could've been penned for Patty Page in 1950. With manic message-corn named "You're a Better Man Than I," omniscient prognostication called "Shapes of Things," a proto-Doors dirge illogically entitled "Heart Full of Soul," and something called "Still I'm Sad" where voices drone like Franciscan friars' even as the melody plunders Soweto umbaqanga via "The Lion Sleeps Tonight," where the 'birds wound up was electric. And as the singer learned conclusively in 1976, electricity can kill.

178. THE LEATHER NUN
• •
Force of Habit IRS, 1987; rec. 1981–87

This punnily headlined compilation-of-sorts contains most of these lusty Swede sleazies' sludgifyingly supersonic astrofuzz classics: their roadburner "Primemover," plus "Desolation Avenue" and "506," indispensable seven-minute takes on the suicidal phaseback-above-beatwall lonely-drone aesthetic previously explored by Sabbath/Ubu/Velvets and so on. These creatures called humans, they make Jonas Almqvist sick. But Nun's destruction of Abba's "Gimme Gimme Gimme (a Man After Midnight)," where they pile freight-train muck and cowbell-chime atop an art-disco synbeat, is mere "clever" campiness, and you'll also find some mostly-guitarless dancedirges of comparatively recent vintage, most creative of which is an absurd anti-Yank retort to Big Daddy Cougarcamp's "Pink Houses" that suggests this whip-crackin' quintet has perhaps spent too much of their spare time male bonding in the public baths. Then again, "For the Love of Your Eyes" is the Lou-Reediest type of snoozeful heartcracked loveliness, and even *Germans* couldn't get much more blatant than "Have Sex with Me," could they?

179. PINK FAIRIES

What a Bunch of Sweeties Polydor UK import, 1972

Total lightbulbhead sound-effect intangibles refuse to form contours amid the backward-masked rotor-blade feedback-alluvia on the first side, and the anus/Uranus puns may or may not have been "humourous" in England in '72, who can really say? But only Side Two's widetracked ecclesiastic tumultuousness in the form of blindfolded broomstick-knockout joyrides in the form of Ventures and Beatles remakes fuzzed and skingrooved toward X-ray-vision infinity equals the pop-art ethos of the gatefolded cover, which is sorta like *Led Zep III* meets *Magical Mystery Tour* meets De La Soul's *3 Feet High and Rising,* with scads of hippie and hashish paraphernalia, plus Narcotic Breadfruit Comix. Very colorful, and the "I Saw Her Standing There" revival is second only to Tiffany's!

180. SIR LORD BALTIMORE

Sir Lord Baltimore Mercury, 1971

There's no way around it, *anything* with John Garner's mutant mouth would sound superb, and even in the eleven-minute four-(Roman-numeraled)-act baroque-Christer extravaganza-cum-bore "Man from Manhattan" he croaks like the wartiest toadstool-sitter your biology teacher's ever dissected. So though SLB's sophomore thang halfway drowns inside its own godawful guru-mystijism, the million-octave range saves the day. It's like outpatients waiting in a doctor's lobby mistake John's trap for an ashtray, then he cools down swigging anchovy juice, and it goes to his head. In "Chicago Lives" he's watching everybody overload their Visas at the department store, he's simulating Donovan or somebody, he's thumping his Bible. "Woman Tamer" is a sequel to *Kingdom Come*'s "Hell Hound," and "Where Are We Going" is labyrinthoid stinkfunk decibellicosity, but the holocaustal masterpiece is this unbelievable plodclomper where Julius Caesar comes back to life and his centurions toss you into a pit and the Roman chorus shrieks "Hayyyl *See*-zah!!" as the lions chow down. Eventually, reportedly, the bassist wound up wearing a suit for the military-industrial complex, one guitarist was Born Again, the other became a nurse, and Garner ended up fronting a wedding ensemble that I bet induces lotsa quickie divorces. If ninnies like Rob Halford are allowed to remain in the metalbiz, why not smart guys?

181. BLUE CHEER

Vincebus Eruptum Philips, 1967

This notorious harbinger of heavy metal, hard rock, punk rock, no wave, skronk, hardcore, speedmetal, deathmetal, and pigfuck hit number eleven on *Billboard*'s LP charts, and its single, "Summertime Blues," a number so glopped with filthy gloop it convinces you your stylus is digging a trench through the tall brown heap at the side of a septic dump, a composition a zillion times more artistic than anything the Feelies or Dokken or whatever those wankers are calling themselves nowadays will ever dream about, went to number fourteen. Which means that Casey Kasem's '68 equivalent had no choice but to dig up fun facts about it! The forementioned smash ("Well lode ah gotta raze a fuss, ah gotta raze a holl-la") hangs an anvil or ten from Eddie Cochran's turkey neck; "Parchment Farm" ("Lode ah think ah'll be heah fo da ress o' mah life/Ah'll ah deed wuz shoot mah wife") is a two-part got-dam symphony of sorrow; "Out of Focus" wobbles self-descriptively from right speaker to left as if on magic 'shrooms, man. And the idiotically vodka'd soporblooze sludge of "Rock Me Baby"/"Doctor Please"/"Second Time Around" makes "Summertime Blues"/"Parchment Farm"/"Out of Focus" seem almost *craftsmanlike,* imagine that.

182. HUMAN ZOO
. . . .
Human Zoo Hospital EP, 1986

Subprimal idiot-savant one-chord Cincy riverfront-gunk with some Stooges clodhops and some MC5 backfeed and some unexpected but unnauseating acoustically introspective tiptoe-through-the-tulips interludes that build suspense while you catch your breath, this plate plows through the world-up-your-ass ooze in a time-honored rustbelt fashion. Gutter bard Bevo Rusza croaks like a big bullfrog who didn't quite make it across the eight-lane expressway. He may be a psychotic sexmaniac but doesn't make that huge a deal of it, just says "cunt" real often, voyeuristically observes menagerie-mammals makin' bacon, and gets hard ogling punk-rock Lolitas. He also enters into these crooked midsong fits ("a clown a clown a clown a clown") that have nothing to do with anything 'cept mayhap his own self-hate/self-knowledge, plus he unwittingly deals Knothole-League-amateur allusions to the Stones' hearse-song "Paint It, Black" in "Human Zoo," Patti Smith's heaven-song "Ask the Angels" in "Space Angel," and both the Animals' escape-song "We Gotta Get Out of This Place" and the Velvet Underground's Jesus-song "Heroin" in "Signs." Recommended to the Cincinnati Arts Center, and the ACLU.

183. LINK WRAY
. . . .
Early Recordings Ace UK import, c. 1981; rec. 1958–64

Legend has it he was raised near Fort Bragg by timber wolves who collected Mexican movie soundtracks, but whatever his upbringing, Link Wray looked like the kind of punk the Shangri-Las would wanna hide from mom. A one-lunged Shawnee Indian, a hillbilly, a Korean War vet tutored by a bluesman named Hambone, proprietors used to boot him from bars in the forties 'cause he didn't wear the right clothes, and if you're talking evolving rock 'n' roll ("Rumble" first hit in '58), he doesn't fit anywhere.

There's connections to Duane Eddy, Lonnie Mack, the Ventures, even Ennio Morricone, but this ain't pop or blues or even pasta 'n' Western; Link was a loner, and his dirges said so. To get the gangliations right, he punched holes in his speakers, recorded on hotel staircases. In "Run Chicken Run," "I'm Branded," "Jack the Ripper," "Rumble," there's this flesh-starved knife-fight on feedback that nobody would even attempt to touch for years; in Willie Dixon's "Hidden Charms," rabid, strangling on his own spit, sniggering at the moon, you wonder what demon could've possessed a white man to use his voice that way. Incomparably heavy from the first bent note, yet almost wordless once Robin tracks his boss's nuclear Batmobile, this is mainly open-chord distortion and nothing else: Pure, seminal, and very, very loud.

184. GEORGE BRIGMAN AND SPLIT
. . . .
Human Scrawl Vagabond Resonance Dutch import, 1986

This raunchily complex Maryland power-triad's first longplayer after a dozen years in oblivion turned out to be a flamethrower, a post-'lude monument of pedalplay that deserves filing on a frazzled shelf alongside the Stooges' *Funhouse,* Captain Beefheart's *Lick My Decals Off Baby* (note Van Vliet–style title–non sequitur), the Mighty Groundhogs' *Who Will Save the World?* and the first Dust album, not necessarily 'cause it's as good or bad as said plats, but 'cause that's the robust, advanced, intense, unbalanced, and harsher-than-harsh avant-boogie territory from whence it hails. There's a sassification of the Groundhogs' "Status People," a version of Brigman's wicked '75 45 "Blowin' Smoke" (which does just that—in your face), a few warped experiments-in-beat with nary a word in 'em ("Symphony in Effigy," "Animal Dope," "Grunts"), a Miles Davis–like lump of bump ("Clap Trap"), some startling recurrences from George's '85 *Silent Bones* EP where some pederast begs your little sister to yank down her drawers and do the Cambodian bossa nova, and even such breathrobbingly eerie stairways-of-softness as "Lazy Eyes" and "The Truth" and "Spaced." Brigman's a lonely madman with a golden touch and a Nolan Ryan fastball and a backwoods-banshee wail that'll send you hightailing back to the hacienda.

185. DAVID LEE ROTH
Eat 'Em and Smile Warner Bros., 1986

As I'm sure he'll inform you if you ask him, Diamond Dave is *thee* consummate entertainer of our era, a nonconformist wildebeest man, the Rambo of bimbos, a real go-getter. Determined to outdo his ex-co-workers (no sweat) and seemingly challenged into rejuvenation by the South Bronx bravado that's his only eighties rival, he paints his face jungle-style, outblacking his minstrel idols. His jazzbo gigolo-jive ("That's Life," "It's Easy") makes more sense in this context, which takes hard rock's inevitable future as showbiz glitz for granted, than it did in his former band or on his campy solo-EP debut; the suburban whiteboy scat-raps in the big brassy funkers ("Elephant Gun," "Big Trouble," "Ladies' Nite in Buffalo?") show off a stand-up routine that someday will take Lake Tahoe by storm. Jacuzzi-drummed AOR coyness like "Goin' Crazy" hasn't quite recovered from its blending into one of the limpest radio years ever, but overall the attempt at reviving Van Halen '78's lost striptease crotchstomp now seems so valid it's valiant. If there's a post-VH letdown it's that the sound's a wee bit *too* sloppy. Everything from the Statue of Liberty to Steve Vai's dynamite-detonation-as-parody-of-guitar-wank to group groupie-grope to how Dave's diction dives toward high notes is milked for laffs, and the Sinatra and Nashville Teens oldies fit the star's persona to a T.

186. KILLING JOKE
Killing Joke Editions EG, 1980

Pea-brained but surprisingly potent gridlock-plot avant-drone somberness, layers of fuzz over kamikaze electrobongos, from proto-post-everything Brits who've got no doubt some negative Nirvanas at hand any minute now. Jaz Coleman hacks and hectors like a Jewish comedian with prostate and marriage and cigar troubles, but he's not spinning any one-liners. By turns exhilarating and deadeningly sluggish, too slow to get down to, his mates march the children of Ozzy's grave into land mines of dub in the superb wiggle-ritual "Change," argue that language is no retreat, gesture hectically into iceberg-insurgence as their imagined bomb keeps ticking. Metallica ended up covering "The Wait" and I detect Voivod-computers-to-be in "$0.36," but though the sound feels separated three thousand years from its proper time, you can't tell in which direction, forward or back.

187. METALLICA
Ride the Lightning Megaforce, 1984

Two guys ratatattatting headlong six-string solos out mom's station wagon hatch, two other guys making Mahavishnu-metered rhythms peel rubber and twirl donuts across 7-Eleven parking lots, a quartet of average suburban men-to-be give punk predicaments popular pull via populist punch. Cliff Burton's bass daintily conjures the dark ages, then this ruthless charge plows time ahead: Side Two's for thrashaholics only, but Side One's got four toxic-shocking psychodramas with enough noise to wake the dead and enough variety not to put 'em back to sleep. Adolescent anxieties descend through nine circles of nuclear hell only to land ass-down in an electric chair—"For Whom the Bells Toll" (title courtesy Hemingway), maybe the most effective death-march since Zep's demise, makes way for "Fade to Black," as moving a hunk of teen-swallowing-Lysol bombast as the eighties produced. James Hetfield bellows about how life whisks away as you revert to your shell, and where on Metallica's debut he tried to ape Beelzebub, here he's conversational, anonymous, private, candid about his confusion. The band's fervor is pure forward motion, a speeding locomotive with broken brakes, with so much finesse you get the idea the train's on a tightrope. The rope's no straight line, and the choo-

choo could Chattanooga off one side or the other at any second, but it never does.

188. FUNKADELIC
Hardcore Jollies Warner Bros., 1976

Potable Pee-thang be plentifully in profusion, practically platterwide. On the "Osmosis" half, a bombastisophic and larvasaurian Jimi-wah "Comin' Round the Mountain" dances one chitlin circuit of a camel-walk 'round James Brown's jail cell, at least till Mike Hampton stops jacking around and boards his latex Trojan pony and boots future traitor-cum-reverend Fuzzy Haskins out the way, y'all, and just lets his crunchadactyloid fetusmylistic euphocannibidextivism impregnate all over the walls and floor, at which time James would likely slip and fall and start firing angel-dusted ants from his pants at the warden, who would proceed to itch like a she-dog. The oi-forecasting title "Hardcore Jollies" is a testosterolodic toilet of guitar qua guitar and zilch else, of the Manwhichian genus that sends gentlemen named "Yngwie" and "Satriani" waddling weepfully back to their long-lost mentors wondering who fooled who and demanding their tuition fees back. On the "Terribitus" half, Hampton gets to slop cosmically in Ed Hazel's soleful shoes, after which subsequent fu-age doosion becometh barely bearably backgroundable, even. None of which precludes the gatefold from casting putrid cold-lampin' aspersions upon "Grand Fraud Railroad," "Piss," "ZZ Flop," "Belchman-Turnip Overdrive," "Creep Purple," and "Slack Sabbath," amongst other placebos of nondark and nonlight tints alike.

189. BLUE ÖYSTER CULT
Tyranny and Mutation Columbia, 1973

I used to think the Black Side, which has a red label, was the most impeccably produced side of riff in the history of the substance, but in retrospect "O.D.'d on Life Itself" and "7 Screaming Dizbusters" don't near stack up (in swiftness/braininess/crispness/catchiness/glisteningness) to the quizzical riddles about Canadian Mounties and subways, both of which hold pompmetal mythopoeia up to the most convex funhouse mirror in all of Strong Island whilst letting the repercussion from Buck Dharma's leads reverberate in your cranium at least as long as the optically illuding pillars and orbs on the outer cardboard. The Red Side, which has a black label, is more like "O.D.'d on Life Itself" and "7 Screaming Dizbusters": oblique inside jokes that must've cracked up the crowd at Columbia Studios, especially if R. Meltzer and/or Patti Smith were there to help explain 'em. Patti's "Baby Ice Dog" is my favorite, but maybe that's just 'cause it admits it's so cold.

190. 4 SKINS
The Good, the Bad, and the 4 Skins Secret UK import, 1982

On the back, these clean-shaven louts stand together on a dirt mound with their fists clenched, guarding turf. This is oi, camaraderie in the established Slade tradition, all boorish swagger and Cockney diction and paranoid lumpenprole rhetoric, shouting so insularly at its stiff-booted clan that Britain's lefty witch-hunters blamed such deplorable audience enthusiasms as "Paki-bashing" on the music itself. The 4 Skins' territory is the dole queue; they hammer out reportage with a plain-spoken, low-rent, unpretty determination that elevates every coarse screed into an anthem. Gary Hodges's phlegm and burr remind you he's always on the defensive, particularly on the disc's unflinchingly lethal live side, where these blokes chant one soundalike soccer cheer after another about why police and unemployment and ennui and conscription send 'em to quaffing pints of bitters down at the pub and all that rot. No asshole National Front propaganda in sight, but a fine gift idea for that budding young fascist in your family nonetheless.

191. BLACK FLAG

Damaged SST, 1981

Antiparent and anti-most-everything-else too, these are captivating hot-under-the-collar declarations of independence from numbed sweathogs and manic-depressive couch potatoes, looking for life in the land of the dead and death in the land of the lens, emptying brewski upon brewski while "Hill Street Blues" and "The Jeffersons" and "Monday Night Football" and "That's Incredible!" gush electric blue from their boob tube. Henry Rollins aims bared teeth and astute wit at some very specific noses he yearns to bloody, and Greg Ginn's ax, already initiating HC's crossover to HM, spews as loquacious a lexicon of squeals, brays, kachooms, sears, and snorts as anybody's planetwide. "TV Party" calls and responds, "Six Pack" nearly swings, "Room 13" anticipates Big Black; unfortunately, it got tiresome fast. Devolving into a vehicle for macho man Hank's cartoonish gob-spit poses and stunted-in-childhood sloganeering re poor oppressed white kids beating their meager brains on bricks, the band spent the rest of its tenure ripping off Flipper and trying unsuccessfully to rip off Trouble Funk. Taking himself far more seriously than any man should, Rollins hid behind his tattoos. Don't let it happen to you.

192. Oi! The Album

EMI UK import, 1980

"Don't worry about them," the storekeep in the secondhand shop in Portobello Road assured me mate re all those skinhead thugs always acting so tough in their Doc Martens and sta-prests. "They're just a little 'ard 'cause they 'aven't got any 'air." A talentless tribe roaring in unison down at the tube station at midnight, parading Rastafarian styles and R&B basics borrowed from blacks against whom they eventually started riots, oi's dressed-down Huns rank as ludicrous even compared to the rest of England's youth subcultures, which is saying a bunch. But here

they're just klutzy fleabags roaming backstreets and robbing banks and praying she'll take it all off: Standard-bearers the 4 Skins are assaultive as acupuncture, and other good guys include Cock Sparrer (whose "Sunday Stripper" is buttnaked bawd along the lines of AC/DC's "Soul Stripper"), Max Splodge (whose "Isulbeleeeene" is ducky daffiness along the lines of Plastic Bertrand's "Ça Plane Pour Moi"), the Postmen (who brag about their black and blue zits), Pierre et les Babies Test Tube (who ill-advisedly straitjacket themselves into proto-hardcore oompah), and Slaughter and the Dogs (where it started). The Angelic Upstarts are pro-Afghan anti-Soviets, and Barney and the Rubbles aren't so hot, but their name makes me say yabba-dabba-doo. Politics-wise, from what I can see, there's nothing remotely objectionable, no rah-rah nationalism even—just an abundance of motorvating keep on keepin' on, get-off-your-arse-and-do-something raucousness that bruises.

193. ROKY ERICKSON AND THE ALIENS

Tea CBS UK import, 1980

Well, I *guess* that's its name—it's right there on the top of the libretto for no apparent reason otherwise, and the cuddly little pagan runes on the cover mean nothing to me. (The inferior American version, on

415 Records, is called *The Evil One*.) Inside: Eternally delectable armadillo-shell riff-hardness and mentally unhealthy screwballhood 'bout gobblin' goblins that apparently inhabit the singer's attic. Erickson's this hirsute Tex-Mex journeyman, as peyote-wrecked as any homeless Austin benchsleeper, who once spent three years in an insane asylum to avoid a jail stretch for grass possession. He's been scorching deranged blacklight paths ever since the groovy sixties, when his 13th Floor Elevators searched for pure sanity even as they reinterpreted and redefined God (so sayeth their liner notes, anyhow). After the Elevators unplugged their electric jugs for good and Roky emerged from his hospital hibernation, he switched to pounding border-town grunge hooked around horror-flick cloven hooves, and with his quartet's Sabbathoid slabs of pure terror pulling you toward that harrowing werewolf vibrato, *Teo* dispels any doubt that Roky might not actually "believe" his ditties' ghastly apparitions. For him, they're as real as the hair on his face; visit his house, I'm told, and he'll talk about nothing else. But what makes "Two-Headed Dog" and "Don't Shake Me Lucifer" and "Cold Night for Alligators" hover so huge is mainly that you can't get 'em outta your head.

194. RUSH
Permanent Waves Mercury, 1980

On these wild and crazy Canucks' introductory (note title) gnu-wave move, patented Peartbeats and a real catchy "Sweet Jane" lick shuffle you posthaste into this charismatic condemnation of the corporate-capitalist scam (-cum-) refusal to use Moogs as mere marketing tools, wisest-beyond-its-years when the Geddster exposes how all those naughty seller-outers (I quote, with added emphasis) "shatter the *illusion* of integrity," which indicates he *realizes* so-called "integrity" was the industry's biggest lie of all in the first place! The poppish commentary ends with this always-startling Simon and Garfunkel ("Sounds of Silence") allusion that replaces "prophets" with "profits" (but how're you supposed to know unless you read the lyric sheet?), after which Mr. Lee screeches (get ready . . .)

"SAYLES-min!" just like Pee Wee Herman opening his front door for no comprehensible reason but it sure sounds nice.

Next composition's prime social-Darwinist gobbledygook wherein indecision is revealed as decision after all, plus there's helpful pedagogic encouragement to the lazily impoverished: "The cards weren't stacked against them/They weren't born in Lotus Land"!! (No maternity wards there!) Geddy likens lovers to planets, then next thing you know he's catapulted toward hyperspace and he's predicting that the moral men among us will survive nuclear holocaust. Along with his fellow free agents he thanks "M*A*S*H" and NASA and hockey players ("for the sticks"!) and Fred Mertz, and it seems Diane Kurys found "Entre Nous" so humane she named a French femme-bonding flick after it in '83! Steel drums or no, the hooks never catch up with "Spirit of the Radio"/"Free Will"'s sequence-launch, but Bob and Doug McKenzie didn't complain when they did for Geddy in "Take Off" what Jody Watley would later do for Goth-rappers Eric B. and Rakim in "Friends," so why should we complain now?

195. THE LEFT
Last Train to Hagerstown Bona Fide EP, 1985

Instead of addressing fairy tales like devils and wizards and loose women (none of which exist in the *real* world), these rural Maryland snot-swallowers compose jocular-vein crash 'n' burn crud like "The Viet Cong Live Next Door" and "AIDS Alley." Brian Sefsic wails Iggyesque about pretty boys for sale, discusses situations wherein fifty bucks might make particular posterior orifices "quiver," and so on. Dunno if songwriter J. D. Swope sympathizes with his subjects or not, and I'm not sure it really matters—guess he's making fun of prejudice and stupidity like everybody else does, but the Left sure don't act left-wing, so you can't be too certain. The Cong song is likewise ambiguous, with Sefsic growling re VCs "taking over the country," no doubt knowing full well he's got the story backward. There's a tune about how yuppies are the real white trash, one about how life's a bore so teens might as well off themselves and get it over with, one about addiction to Channel Zero's soaps, one about rednecks stomping your head at the 7-Eleven video machine, a Stooges remake about how female human beings have a built-in surveillance monitor that'll keep you in line or else. Drums and bass wallop humongous, six-string spits schizo, and there's no snoozeful serenades to speak of.

196. BLACK OAK ARKANSAS
Raunch'n'Roll Live Atco, 1973

In the studio these hicks played too much like Doobie Brothers raised from birth by psychopathic muskrats in sensible shoes, but here they're as unsinkably funked-up with swelter and offal as any roll in any hay ever. Three razorback-nudging-your-pup-tent guitars, demonic backward-masking ("Natas! Natas! Natas!") ahead of its time, washboard solos that'd make your dear mama cry, numbers entitled "Mutants of the Monster" and "When Electricity Came to Arkansas," not to mention Jim Fucking Dandy Mangrum. A gremlin prone to druidic legends about zombies and the window of death in the House of Karma and positive and negative energy, he slobbers into his microphone's air holes like a lecherous seventy-year-old coot with a clogged-up brain or like someone who just swallowed a deck of marked cards and is waiting for the Heimlich maneuver. He calls his followers "misfits," and he starts the titles of his two best songs, one of which has a bottom as dope as

GnR's "Mr. Brownstone," with the word "Hot." And when Jim tells ya he's got a hot rod, he ain't talkin' 'bout no car.

197. BLUE ÖYSTER CULT
Blue Öyster Cult Columbia, 1972

Supposedly if you fix your pupils long enough on the sleeve then stare into the sun you'll see God, but I'm an agnostic, so I wouldn't know. Anyway, these Stalk Forrest Group/Soft White Underbelly offshoots load up their debut with sleek outlaw-odes for overconceited mechanical engineering majors, alchemizing all sorts of chemical magic: The half of "The Red and the Black" they call "I'm on the Lamb but I Ain't No Sheep," "La Grange" riffs before "La Grange" existed (they come from Slim Harpo, but who's counting?), a couple more riffs bluer than this bluesless Cult would ever find use for again, clap effects direct from Phil Spector (which perhaps explains why BÖC called a later work Spectres). In other words, the Meltzer/ Bouchard/Pearlman rock-crit/Velvet-fan trio partakes in its usual urban-cosmonaut-in-S&M-gear charade. "Then Came the Last Days of May" is like gazing zonked at the stars (man) only prettier, and if you can follow with your attention-payer long enough (I usually can't) you'll hear dopers on the run in the seventies until they reach an open plain whereupon one springs a booby trap on the other three; it's a fine idea, but a couple years earlier in "Timothy" the Buoys had one fellow traveler eating his compatriot, so if you ask me Don Roeser missed the boat. Hooks abound everywhere (catchiest are the fiftieslike ones in "Before the Kiss a Redcap"), though for the most part they could generally be considerably huger, as the three axes here would soon demonstrate. As for "She's as Beautiful as a Foot" and "Redeemed," I will only say that they're not as humdrum as "Screams" or "Workshop of the Telescopes." How come Eric Bloom sings like he's reading cue cards?

198. DIE KREUZEN

Die Kreuzen Touch and Go, 1984

Tons of guitar pressure rest on some forked bass lines and a serious case of strep throat, and though this is a single-minded testament to the unguarded power of pure ultrathrash, it's not unvaried by-the-number roteness by any means. It's more like Metallica's intensity-peaks on *Ride the Lightning* diced and preserved in ice cubes, adrenalized stretch-and-hold-and-snap note-elasticity over a beat that lights fires backwards and sideways. Ancient Aerosmith vinyl gets dumped into the trash compactor, you throw the switch, the plunger plunges down, wine bottles grind into tiny shards, glass and aluminum and black wax twist into half hitches, tomato cans squash then defecate leftover paste, and this tension-and-release kind of amphetamine Anglo-Saxon unfunk is all that remains of "Lord of the Thighs." Every couple seconds, though not in any pattern you can predict, electricity shocks the monkey. The resulting mood's analogous to the cover's skeletal industrial-aftermath dog-dragons, a hideous depiction that reminds me of some hell-dwelling Advent-calendar creatures that terrified me toward insomnia as a wee lad. Flip the sleeve over and there's twenty-three songs listed, but don't try to count 'em: Though the last one on the first side seems to have something to do with a dark, windowless room, I can barely make out another word anywhere. And I like it that way.

199. LOU REED

Metal Machine Music RCA Victor, 1975

Almost undeniably the most dauntless "fuck-you" move/hype/tour de force/sham in the history of history (not counting *The Satanic Verses,* I mean), but that's only to say this is real nice to *own,* not necessarily to *listen* to, unless you're a teacher's pet. The basics you oughta already know, but here goes: Four sides, no "instruments," just amps and preamps and distortors and tremolo units and reverb units and modulators and junk like that, lotsa pretentious/unpretentious quasi-/non-quasi–jokes/non-jokes (on the cover, not in the grooves), lotsa repetition (in the grooves), lotsa boredom (not as much as *New Sensations* or *New York,* but at least as much as *MMM*'s prime inspiration, Lamont Young's "dream music," as exemplified by the five-LP Gramavision Records box *The Well-Tuned Piano,* which I proudly display on the shelf to impress visiting diplomats but of course never put on), "no music" (no shit). Suckers who miss the point say you're s'posed to disconnect a speaker or hook up an extra one for "full effect," but I tried once, and in the immortal words of Lester Bangs (who o'course once called *MMM* "the greatest album ever made" then never explained why) re Blue Cheer's *Vincebus Eruptum* played backwards, "it sounded exactly the same as usual." Kinda relaxing, as new age goes, but back in the Signal Corps I frequently spent all night on forested hilltops near the East German border, lulled to sleep by Volkswagen-sized power generators, and lemme tell ya: They kick this crap's ass from here to kingdom come.

200. ALICE COOPER

Killer Warner Bros., 1971

The peaks are the hits, "Under My Wheels" and "Be My Lover," hooky/cocky Detroit-rock revelry with sick old ladies and magnifying glances and doo-wop and sax-poot and ingenues who'll never understand why the singer's called Alice. He's got his eyes mascaraed *Godspell*-style for this costume ball, which celebrates lace, leather, decay, snakes, guillotines, amputation. It's Halloween hackwork, constructed so the well-bred Eurobuild excess holds up as background wraparound: I love how, in "Desperado," everything stops dead and you're "in the *dust.*" "Halo of Flies" has a western-flick theme, a desert-flick parody, a Rodgers and Hammerstein rip, reams of psychotronic six-string zipzoom-nothingness. "Killer" 's tribaldoom Stoogefusion is no less (palatably) cheesy, and another cut fills a much needed void between the

Beatles' butcher-baby cover and a thousand fifth-grade dead-baby jokes. Inauthenticity and over-wroughtness are the prime attractions.

201. MOTT THE HOOPLE
Live Columbia, 1974

Guitars are more prominent here than on any of these mythmakers' post–*Brain Capers* studio jobs, which isn't to say they don't get in the way, 'cause they do, as do the 'luded-out tempos, at least on the Broadway side, where Ian Hunter sounds like his road life's as shitty as he's always making it out to be. Which isn't to suggest that this ain't still expressively powerful material (though the song list's not near unquibblable), or that it's impossible to get wrapped up in the sheer plumbiferousness of Hunter's rifftone or Ariel Bender's topwank, at least in "Sucker," which ain't about dupes. "Rest in Peace" has Procul Harum organ and Dylan-meets–*Mary Poppins* lyrics that pave the way for "All the Young Dudes," the best urban-nerd revenge-anthem David Bowie ever wrote and the God's honest truth if concrete in your head and suicide on your brain is how acnelescence made you feel (and if it didn't, fuck you). On the Hammersmith side, Mott frames selections from their two best elpees around lotsa healthy anticrowd contempt and theological patter and some slutbaiting male-bonding and an anxiously unhinged rock-history medley that mocks Kinks/Beatles/Jerry Lee/Bowie, but kicks off with two words that suggest maybe the sage at the mike knew even more than he was letting on: "It's over." Billy Fury was just ten years ago, he says; now Mott themselves are more than that long ago plus half again. If any Generation Xs, Def Leppards, or Pet Shop Boys were in those Odeon Theater seats, they've got some explaining to do.

202. MOTÖRHEAD
No Sleep 'til Hammersmith Mercury, 1981

On the cover a bomber soars toward the crowd, ready to drop its morning dump, and that's the fatalism Motörhead elicits. "I don't wanna live forever," Lemmy yells. The whole thing's about a man against the rest of the world, nobody else on his side, old since he was young. The American myth. "I don't *care*, I don't *care*," Lemster exclaims, and "shut *up*, shut *up*." They write their own rules, his denthead heroes do; they're pathfinders on a concrete frontier, Saccos and Vanzettis, Bonnies and Clydes, not just stoned but "*ferociously* stoned." Motörhead make the asphalt open up and the world falls in, takes all sound with it, detonation begets detonation begets detonation.

On this so-noisy-it's-almost-arty live-tour souvenir, everybody charges too fast to stay in sync, and the repertoire's juiced to assaultive earpain proportions. But even when the going gets a little elaborate for a couple minutes at the beginning of "Metropolis" the bass and drums retain a post–R&B bounce with as many BPMs as the fastest Eurodisco. Three years later, in fact, Giorgio Moroder scored the reissue of Fritz Lang's '26 silent-futurism landmark, also called *Metropolis*, where the laborers lash out against the modernist machine. I'll wager Lemmy digs the original flick, at least. And maybe "The Hammer" 's as in ". . . and sickle," and maybe "No Class" yearns for the aftermath of class warfare or something. Don't ask me!

203. RED CROSS
Born Innocent Smoke 7, 1982

A sun-scorched cathode-ray side effect made comprehensible by Blue Cheer, Danny Bonaduce, Venus and the Razorblades, and Josie and the Pussycats, its leadoff cut immortalizes the shower-stall deflowering scene in a graphic 1974 TV movie about a girl's reform school. Longing to fly someday in his own private plane like Ace Frehley, the punch-drunk fourteen-year-old singer constantly trips over his own slobber, and two guitarists slobber at even higher speed into his coiffure, splashing a mudpuddle onto Charles Milles Manson's slacks when they cover "Cease to Exist." Buxotic beat helps kiddiepop harmonies summon a tract-house paradise of white trash and burnouts and cellulite dripping off ears, capturing the monotonous barfability of the half-caste 'tween-age rut with plenty of accuracy and panache and yellow journalism that would doubtlessly make the McDonald brothers' classmates on the school newspaper green with envy and perhaps each others' snot.

204. JAMES BLOOD ULMER
. . . .
Black Rock Columbia, 1982

Like HM's been asked to do ever since the world began, Blood toughens the true blues till close-cropped wailing gruel spews out his frets, digging his Deltabilly roots deeper than the ocean and piling 'em higher than the moon. Amin Ali masturbasses out a martial housequake that cooks like an Upton Sinclair sweatshop at chow time, no theoretical shit, just rude jam-on-it musk-ox-in-briar-patch harmelardcore thump both accessible and asswise, large as Blood's thorax and funky as his dashiki, facing off against scraping hog-butcher counterpoint. Though there's times when J.B.'s sumo-weight headkick leaves so little to the imagination that (just like with most blues) I can't figure out where the tuneglitz is located, this time out there's such soulable salaciousness as "Family Affair" and "Love Have Two Faces," and only wishy-washy worrywarts who'd have the big man water his great growl down to the consistency of Eldra De-Barge wouldn't welcome the thing into their home.

205. SONNY SHARROCK BAND
. . . .
Seize the Rainbow Enemy, 1988

Put to tape with two bench-pressing drummers, nerve-ruffling bassist Melvin Gibbs, and numerous bunched-up time changes, this is as beefily visceral as anything by the Sharrock-guitared Last Exit, but more cohesive, more generous, less merely infuriated. In "J. D. Schaa," "Seize the Rainbow," and the carnivalistic "Fourteen," with Sonny vamping out crooked detective-theme strains that chop sideways across a pistonlike twin-drum gait, and Gibbs moaning primordial lines as the polybeat boosts riff-progressions into higher gear, the quartet mates the Mahavishnu Orchestra with Blood Ulmer's hard-rock funk. In "My Song," Sharrock's understated gentleness keeps refashioning these packed-together notes until they curl into woolly distortion, and on top of such an omnitentacled rhythm, his introspection is a revelation. In "Dick Dogs," which initially busts down *Seize the Rainbow*'s door, and in the two tracks that wrap the proceedings up, the crew boils a funk conflagration hardy enough to dislodge continents, strafing wah-wah over a pugilism that leans forward, punches itself into uncharted wildernesses, overlaps itself like a gerrymandering Venn diagram. And "Zydeco Honey-cup" isn't so much Cajun creole as second-line gumbo, with one drummer waddling down Bourbon Street in a chain reaction off the other guy, like Professor Longhair's right and left hands. This is rent-party music, mutiny on the mamaship, with nary a pinch of the quasicerebral irony avant-lunkheads take for granted. Gasoline on fire.

206. SHAKIN' STREET
. . . .
Vampire Rock CBS French import, 1978

This shakes louder than the record these Gallic goofballs would release two years later in the States, but with way less character. The great Fabienne Shine, on *"chant et harmonica,"* sputters, soars, squeals, and switches gears, gives all she's got in fact, but as of yet that's not quite enough; "Vampire Rock" predates both Teena Marie's "I'm a Sucker for Your Love" and Girlschool's "Love at First Bite," but has fewer teeth than either. The slower schmaltz generally sweats saltier than the speedier Stoogeism—French-accent rock 'n' roll being the contradiction-in-terms it invariably is, Shine's emotion sounds less fabricated that way, somehow. But she manages okay anyway, and speedy exceptions include "Love Song" 's frenzied eruption of eros, an apparently autobiographical cross between "The Immigrant Song" and Essential Logic called "Living with a Dealer," and "No Time to Lose," which races even faster on the American LP. "Blues Is the Same" is the silliest title, the Stones remake is unconventional but unmemorable, and the bassist tries very hard to look like one of the Stooges' Asheton brothers.

207. THE YARDBIRDS
. . . .
Five Live Yardbirds Rhino, 1988; rec. 1964

I've been told something on this album is referred to by Black Sabbath on their second and third albums, but I'm still looking; what I mostly hear is rock degenerating (already!) into "instrumental prowess." Continually upping the stakes, suddenly waking up and exploding like upset carbonation in "Smokestack Lightning," Slowhand Clapton applies fresh coats of paint to already wobbly (a beat-yank every six seconds) proceedings. Spitting on the Marquee Club microphone in search of a shock that'll last, Keith Relf essays several songs by American black men, as was the prevailing fashion at the time. "Respectable" turns into "Humpty Dumpty" (which would later turn into a Poison song), and both "Respectable" 's virgin batsman and "Good Morning Little Schoolgirl" 's soda shop feel punkier than "Here Tis," which invents Sonic Youth. There's no denying the frantic edge or tight looseness (!) of it all, but unless you're a slave or a sharecropper, the blues are just the blues.

208. NAZARETH
. . . .
Loud 'n' Proud A&M, 1973

A decade before Roddy Frame discovered Eddie Van Halen, these kiltless Scottish lads heaved out cigs-and-halitosis coughs that rendered "good" taste

even gooder, stomping Joni Mitchell's "This Flight Tonight" and Little Feat's "Teenage Nervous Breakdown" like funkfuzzed Slade. With mindpound detonation broadcasting a hopelessness Dylan's epic of economic calamity and multiple murder had heretofore only hinted at, they expand "The Ballad of Hollis Brown" into a monolithic eight-minute lawn-mower-grunge death-dirge, timelier than ever in the wake of Richard Speck and Charles Whitman and Lieutenant Calley. The melancholic bandido-ode originals are more literate than you'd expect, conscious of their place in history: In "Not Fakin' It," Dan McCafferty's hoarse outcry, muffled as if you're intercepting it over your ham radio, analyzes Richard Nixon and Edgar Wallace, Jack the Ripper and Billy the Kid, Jesus Christ and Jesse James, Cleopatra and Nostradamus. Next to the deeds all those notables accomplished, Dan laments, singing rock 'n' roll means zilch. But he's wrong.

209. AC/DC
. . . .
Highway to Hell Atlantic, 1978

They once told *Time* magazine that if *they* could sell so many records, rock 'n' roll must really be in horrible shape: One boxing-glove riff and singalong shout and hog-hump rhythm after another, the best-dressed midget in the pop universe (book bag, beanie, bare ass, duckwalk) never aiming to be virtuosic with the verbose vocabulary at his disposal, rather just instinctively selecting some huge globular lick, repeating it, bludgeoning it, pounding it into the concrete, again and again and again. And again. They play nine-ball-in-the-side-pocket rock, shooting their sexist yaps off about vaginal vices they don't have the first clue about. There's lackadaisical moments here and there, but in "Girls Got Rhythm," "Shot Down in Flames," "Touch Too Much," and "Beating Around the Bush," *Highway to Hell*'s got some of the rowdiest heads-into-the-wind funk this side of Eddie Hazel, like a medicine ball chucked toward your solar plexus. The Satanism's too dizzy to be taken seriously by anybody smarter than Tipper Gore, but when Bon

Scott moves down the motorway with his "whole lotta booze," his grunt's got an animalism that suggests he knows of what he speaks. Not too long after (April '80, to be exact), he packed his bags.

210. VOIVOD

Nothingface Mechanic/MCA, 1989

Named after a literary genre where William Gibson and Bruce Sterling and Lewis Shiner lead the way, the musical category already being marketed as "cyberpunk" is the paranoid revenge of grown-up megabyte hackers, and its voice depicts the post-capitalist techno-megalopolitan sprawl as a manly mediaholic void. I'd include Mark Stewart, Helios Creed, Von Lmo, the Sewer Zombies, Sonic Youth, Neil Young's *Trans,* Warren Zevon's *Transverse City.* And this, the fifth LP by Canuck particle-physics-metal hoseheads Voivod: It's got mucho cybernetic jargon on it like "synchrogrease" and "forward feed," and in the immortal words of one W. Axl Rose, it's all Greek to me. Something called "Into My Hypercube" commences with this lonely mood that suggests Roky Erickson ascending the long spiral staircase toward Brian Wilson's room, and in the redo of Pink Floyd's "Astronomy Domine," the newly conversational-like vocals of Snake zoom past Jupiter and Titan.

The bionic Viking who's Voivod's chief protagonist oughta be in the seventh dimension or so now, and I gather that translates to the alternate universe inside one of his brain-atoms. (There's a million more where that came from.) So any and all big-body-beat trappings visible on Voivod's earlier work have been discarded. The twisted structures are commendably spacier, paradiddle-city like on King Crimson's *Red* maybe, though one growl could be Edwin Starr in "War," going "good God, y'all." But as usual, "progressiveness" saps visceral punch, and I'm reminded of percussion-combuster Away's Krung-the-bodyless-brain quote in the press kit: "Flesh and bones are cheap. We should be nothing, psychic entities that think but don't exist." Pretty darn celibate point-of-view for metal, I must say. Can you imagine a future without girls?

211. Back from the Grave, Volume 4

Crypt, 1984; rec. 1963–66

A whole cave's worth of prehistoric cave paintings: Two of the most masculinely *named* bands ever (the Sloths, who heave their fat furry bodies real slowly across some she-sloth's fat furry same, and the Huns, whose Attila-like leader screams slayhem like it's 451 A.D.); Larry and the Bluenotes getting nabbed by a "sadist"; the Huns' North Carolina homeboys the Tamrons intoning "ooga-block-ooga-block-mow-mow-mow" and strumming "Twilight Zone" guitar in tribute to the most erect Pithecanthropus erectus they've ever run into; the Munsters' Mockingbird Lane homeboys the Fabs grumbling about LBJ's daughter's theological quest; not to mention those Seattle super-duperstars the Sonics celebrating Christmas louder than anybody since the Ronettes. Plus frenzied french-fried eyeballs swimming in septic pools of high-pressure blood, from (amongst twerpier twerps) Bunker Hill (backed by Link Wray!), Botumless Pit (sic!), Aztex (whose sludge smells like their hometown Gary of Indiana and hence spells Trouble with a capital T), and the unbelievable Rocky and the Riddlers, who know about *half* a chord, if my math's right. Most everybody wears a suit, or at least matching turtlenecks.

212. BUFFALO

Volcanic Rock Vertigo Australian import, 1973

Long before AC/DC, Rose Tattoo, and even Men at Work, these nondomesticated bovines slashed and burned and spilled their vegemite across the 'roo-plains from Brisbane to Perth. At first you mistake 'em for fairly typical downtempo wankola, but then you notice the noiseblisters are all contorted high-strung tension, sparse, even quiet—not till the closing "Shylock" does smoke blow through the bull's snort-holes. Inside "Freedom"'s skincrawl Zeppisms, there's this completely windswept unyieldingness-of-drum, and you're yanked further and further into the outback by some pissed aborigine whose land you've stolen, and you're passing all these cacti and wombat skulls along the way. This scarred throat praying to the sun god sifts through as if he's wailing from two miles down the dirtpath, or maybe (see title) from deep inside Mount Vesuvius's crater, beneath the magma. You hit "The Prophet," a homage to Moses, and you realize that fifteen years early, these Aussies captured the lethal blues-theology their countrymen of Nick Cave's ilk spent entire careers shooting for and missing.

213. BIG BROTHER AND THE HOLDING COMPANY

Live Rhino, 1984; rec. 1966

Hippies mud-wrestling ancient jugband artifacts—big deal, right? As a matter of fact, it is: Janis Joplin rasps like your grandmother, seems at first to stretch for feeling only when she's "supposed" to (where any bluesperson would), but soon she's reaching heights most anybody else merely aims for, and by "Moanin' at Midnight" she's this insane incubus, increasingly inarticulate until your nerves are edgewise and you can't make out a word (which is just as well), you just feel her sinuses smoldering as all this obscene oink oozes out. The two noise-guitarists have no concern for form, and in "Blow My Mind," especially, David Getz's persistent knuckleball drum-lurch could've come from Mississippi, even Detroit. Like Plastic Ono or some Berlin troupe from a half-decade later, the band enters these terroristic trances not of their own volition, showing up Slayer as overrehearsed simps. The unschooledness gets so unruly it's purely amorphous, but by "Ball and Chain" the singer's absorbed the reincarnated soul of some raped-to-shreds black woman buried a yard deep in some plantation cottonfield, staking blame across the centuries, crying out against injustice, and you're no more vindicated than anybody else.

214. QUEEN

Sheer Heart Attack Elektra, 1974

Very appropriate that they'd use some of the punkiest artwork and typesetting of the pre-Pistols seventies to enclose what's by far their most irascible and least baroque plate, even though it doesn't contain their punkiest song (called, weirdly enough, "Sheer Heart Attack"; see also "Houses of the Holy" and "Almost Blue"). I don't care what anybody thinks, I've loved the Bowiesque herstory lesson "Killer Queen" provides since I was knee-high—always thought "gelatine" was "virginity" and "wanna try" was "whatta drag." ('Cause drag is the kinda queen it's about, right?) "Brighton Rock" drums its Zepness so speedy and with registers so high that you always figure your RPM control's on the blink, "Stone Cold Crazy" just is, and not even "Little Queenie" at the bottom of the first side sequence is anything like gratuitous. Split-second more-10cc-than-Sparks operettimoes jump out of the dark like Fred Mercury's teasing you with his black manicure, but Brian May's bombast is at its most floggingly Pagelike. A true stormtroop body-fluid-swap meet, I swear, and Khrushchev, Kennedy, Al Capone, and Bad Bad Leroy Brown all drop by for a piece of Marie Antoinette's axtion.

215. ALICE COOPER

Love It to Death Straight, 1971

Five Phoenix boys halfway dressed up as Phoenix girls, completely disillusioned but also completely full of shit (and loving it), deliver one record-breakingly brattish coming-of-age brag and a ton of tastelessness, ranging from just-dandy ("Caught in a Dream," "Is It My Body") to awful ("Sun Arise"). If you owned a budding body when you first encountered "I'm Eighteen," life's foam on your face and hands, you had no choice but to hear yourself in the song. Alice is twenty-three, rock's most deliberately bad actor, yet somehow the phoniness of his stance is part of what being eighteen is about. Said thespianism's never helped mock-medieval talismans like "Black Juju" and "Hallowed Be Thy Name" much though, and it's no surprise they're the tarot cards the Pigfuck Nation ended up clasping to its disfigured breast. Ostentatious drum-tedium that marches absolutely nowhere save under the soil (where the worms fall asleep), they're harmless entertainment, contagious in a real convoluted way. Given the histrionics I have to strain real hard, but I can almost imagine some deluded soul with serious psychological disorders being "moved" by "Ballad of Dwight Fry," which has apparently had a profound effect on Guns N' Roses. As for the poses and clotheses, they may well have startled somebody's churchgoing ma or pa, may well have placed some subversive ideas in certain young minds. I was only ten at the time, so I'm not the one to ask.

216. CELTIC FROST
"To Mega Therion" Combat/Noise, 1986

This brutish rassler-stampede (from Switzerland, former stomping ground of Hugo Ball and Kleenex/Lilliput) shares nothing with anything else I've ever heard, save maybe some Butthole Surfers encore. Tom G. Warrior belching and urping like a Viking beatbox while his licking stick spurts grease, Reed St. Mark's gargantuan drums and Dominic Steiner's

boogeyman bass furrowing in corkscrews, this nuke-rock trio bends its clatterjazz terrain back toward the early Cenozoic, the era of the oversized ground sloth for which the album's named. Warrior gurgles indecipherable taunts of devilment over semisymphonic changes far too unwieldy to be pompous, and though sometimes doom-epics like "Dawn of Meggido," "Circle of the Tyrants," and "Necromantical Screams" seem to drag on too long, the creepy operatic backup and chunky fretwork-that-goes-bump-in-the-night serve as actual hooks if you're in the right mood. The no-wave guerrilla instrumental "Tears in a Prophet's Dream," closer to Einstürzende Neubauten's "Schwarz (Muteirt)" or Mars' "Helen Forsdale" than to heavy metal, is the sound of the Strategic Defense Initiative: percussion like twenty-first-century humanoid-constructed paramilitary pterodactyls flapping their light-year-long wings, guitars as supersonic bows flinging atomic warheads instead of arrows, an Oriental gong signifying one-kilometer-to-go till the end of the universe. It's all as disturbingly ugly as H. R. Giger's Jesus-on-slingshot cover-art, and I hope Brian Wilson gets to hear "Eternal Summer" someday.

217. REDD KROSS
Neurotica Big Time, 1987

The best cuts are mostly the ones that sound sort of like the Bay City Rollers and sort of like Led Zeppelin, but not exactly. The headstrong sellout statement "Play That Song" demonstrates why wimpy melodies beat punk-rock ruts, "Love Is You" hiccups away hard times like Buddy Holly in cahoots with Tiny Tim, "Peach Kelli Pop" and "What They Say" are perhaps the world's catchiest anticoke (though not anti-Coke!) ditties, "Gandhi Is Dead" has Page-riffs and a jealous message to a fox-on-the-run who keeps flirting with a transvestite who cakes on too much greasy kid stuff, the title track's got longhaired friends of Jesus Christ Superstar in a chartreuse microbus hijacked from the convoy wherein C. W. McCall crashed the gates doing ninety-eight saying let them truckers roll, ten-four. There's a peck of clever Beatles references on the inner sleeve, and maybe even an Iron Maiden homage somewhere, and it's produced real snazzy by Tommy Ramone. So as camp scams go, if it ain't as peachy-keen as a free trip to Six Flags with Tatum O'Neal and Jodie Foster as your tour guides, I'm Tiffany-twisted with the Mercedes bends and Hotel California's my castle 'cause that's where I dwell. Post-"Maude" credo: "We are not stupid boys but we want to do it wrong."

218. HAWKLORDS
Hawklords Polydor, 1978

Former Hawkwinds lay down cosmic cubism re Euclidean geometry and extrasensory perception within a steadfast sea of radioscope-orchestrated horns/keys/strings and spring-loaded axcrash. Though Bryan Ferry's drama from "Remake/Remodel" and "Virginia Plain" finds refuge in "25 Years," "Flying Doctor" 's grunge somehow prefigures Suicidal Tendencies' "Institutionalized." In the soaring "PSI Power," the teenage narrator reads girls' minds and is forced to pretend he's dumber than his teachers so they won't get suspicious; "(Only) the Dead Dreams of a Cold War Kid" is another pizzicato picnic. These eggheads think like Steely Dan with greener teeth, but all their years as students and poststudents haven't done 'em much good, so gravity pulls 'em ground-ward from building tops, and all the king's horses and all the king's men can't put 'em back together again.

219. RUSH
Moving Pictures Mercury, 1981

Neil Peart's Bonham-goes-hip-hop drums in the first five seconds of "Tom Sawyer," this album's first song, about how modern intellectuals waste away their youth inside video arcades, are as high as these blind mice will ever climb, not counting maybe that pine-superiority thing they did once about those trees refusing to join the labor union (or maybe that one was only a dream). Rush are like finance majors who think they inhaled too much THC in their dorm the night before their Composition 101 final, only it was really just catnip and oregano—"An ounce of perception, a pound of obscure" and "Changes aren't permanent, but change is" are their brand of barracks-lawyer sophomorism for sure. Yet "The Camera Eye" has "Saturday Night's Alright for Fighting" chords and NYC-bashing after King Crimson's heart, the rocklife gripe's therapeutic, the immigrant-policy deserves more votes than Axl Rose's, "Vital Signs" could help out Neil Young's *Trans* or Prince's *Lovesexy,* and in the instrumental "YYZ" (chromosomes, algebra, what?), it's instructive to hear where Voivod and Metallica learned to change tricycle lanes so fast. Peart bangs his sticks on everything in sight—timbales, glockenspiel, bell tree, crotales, cowbells, plywood, doesn't matter. And if Alex Lifeson's too rarefied to riff his way out of a Ziploc, I'll still take an excited Geddy over any Gumby-like chrome-dome Midnight Oil can give me. On the cover, some of the free world's less fortunate wage-earners are literally *moving* pictures, nyuk nyuk nyuk.

220. JAMES BLOOD ULMER
Freelancing Columbia, 1981

This iron-enriched breakfast swings like an expectant mom's moods, shaking sacroiliac with an Ornette-style on-the-wump irregularity that knots your intestines tight, yet it's also the most natural place for metal-flash/guitar-hero aficionados to board Blood's bloodcurdling barge without rocking it too much, which explains why it was granted so much muso-mag ink. Unevolved as a Flintstone, hefty as a trash bag, and thick as St. Nick, Ulmer's some blues-centenarian down at the crossroads, but with an improvisatory intellect even the geekiest jazzbos would be happy to do the bump to in the privacy of their own foyers. Rubber wah-notes, kamikaze slide-runs, and cackling cacophony noogie your skull atop a beat like meat on your feet, and in "Where Did All the Girls Come From?" mournful mouthwork addresses a two-girls-for-every-guy predicament à la Warren Zevon's

"Poor Poor Pitiful Me" or the Eagles' "Take It Easy" or "Three's Company." You should have such problems, right?

221. NAZARETH
Hair of the Dog A&M, 1975

In the extremely funkativic leadoff/title hangover-remedy (which, not incidentally, is also the second-best example of the unheralded seventies "bitch"-rock genre that unified Elton John's "The Bitch Is Back," Rod Stewart's "Ain't Love a Bitch," Charlie Daniels's "The Devil Went Down to Georgia," David Bowie's "Diamond Dogs," Billy Joel's "Big Shot," the Stones' "Bitch," and other expletive-nondeleters), these trachea-charred Scottish Scotchaholics talk jivey re poison ivy, and thus help Aerosmith invent rap music. Otherwise, there's scads of anonymous barleyed bar-band chuckmung so big at the hips it makes "Mississippi Queen" seem like "Kentucky Woman." Exceptions include "Please Don't Judas Me" 's thump-whirling ten-minute antibackstab nightmare and of course the Everly Brothers' bonny lonely-heart Nerf-jam "Love Hurts," in more ways than one the '75 equivalent of '88's Erin-Everly-penned "Sweet Child o' Mine," only not quite as sweet, so rock critics didn't like it as much.

222. RAMONES
Too Tough to Die Sire, 1984

This blueprint for "Bonzo Goes to Bitburg" (their truest toon ever) is an attempt to maintain some sort of humor or sanity or perspective after growing and learning that life's no joke after all, that it's not what it's cracked up to be. Taking aim at Russki and Ami war machines alike, kneeling down to pray in not one song but two, the Ramones dish out gut-level politics with something approaching vengeance. In one organ-driven dirge, they ask whether getting older is really the crime everybody claims; after that, with weight-liftin' hulks, little rich Miss Americas, bag ladies, dope dealers, and basic trainees, they predict the grim realities due after Four More Years of Ronhood, the "death destruction bombs galore" Bush/Quayle might eventually initiate in "Planet Earth 1988." Heavy stuff, way heavier than anything they'd done before, and so's the sound. Ig/Oz gunk (you can trace it back to "I Just Want to Have Something to Do" and "I'm Affected") takes over, mutating into raveups and speedtempo schizophrenia and Ventures-meet–Van Halen doodling. Each side ends with Joey-penned escapist "fun," and there's a swift ride in Eurythmic Dave Stewart's banana boat, but the metallic rammalamma's masterminded by Dee Dee, and it's as if he still wants the airwaves, but he's just realized that his bros have a better shot at AOR than CHR. Next step, inevitably, was the decline into professionalism.

223. HAWKWIND
Quark, Strangeness, and Charm Sire, 1977

Though there's more (nonouter) space here than these planet-rocking Morks' callower Lemmy-period Orkness had, there's also more smarts and hooks. On Side One they stretch out, dust off the violins, dig their fuzz deep, tackle such year-2525 themes as dads grounding teen daughters from eternal-preservation ice, the radioactive demolition of Oklahoma and Tennessee, and how lacking individuality makes cloned androids feel left out. Side One's organ/FX groove admits defeat Mottstyle by mourning Che Guevara and the Age of Refusal in "Days of the Underground," evolves a computerized deathgrip that'd get Leonard Nimoy himself tapping along in "The Forge of Vulcan," and in "Hassan I Sahba" initiates a quasi-Arab desert-chant with recurring world-historic mantras like "hashish hashish," "black September," and "petrodollar." The title number draws causal relationships between researching photon physics and dying a virgin.

224. R. E. O. SPEEDWAGON

R.E.O. T.W.O. Epic, 1972

Slogging their way out of the lower Illinois bar circuit in the early seventies, these perennial AOR whipping boys made for a surprisingly likable borderline-metal quintet. Both Neal Doughty's Mississippi-riverboat piano-frolic and Kevin Cronin's concave Midwestern drawl were uncommonly down-home attractions, and skeptics who doubt these Champaign chumps could ever jump higher than the Doobiefied flash-shuffles and bathetic milktoast (and, okay, occasional fervent sentiment and sumptuous uplift: "Can't Fight This Feeling," "Wherever You're Goin'") of their multiplatinum menopause are directed to the blood-thirsty Cronin/Gary Richrath death-wah jam that serves as backbone and eventually zenith of "Golden Country," a trenchant and treasonous seven-minute anger-anthem where they deconstruct the American infrastructure brick by brick from the bottom up, trampling racial (and hair-length!) segregation, economic inequity, unfair housing practices, and anybody (even mortgage people!) who'd turn their backs to the same, and they mean it, maaan. In "Like You Do" Kev compliments his new flame 'cause she's no bible-thumper or Times Square strumpet, and the balance of their one decent collection has 'em pitting good times ("Flash Tan Queen," "Music Man," the Chuck Berry redo "Little Queenie") with raunch-reeking woe ("How the Story Goes," where they ditch Architecture School once and for all; "Being Kind"), scoring points in both courts. Somebody buy these prairie dogs a blow-dryer!

225. DUST

Dust Kama Sutra, 1971

Speedfreak blues with a future Ramone slamming cans and a future Kiss producer ramrodding riffs and a future Rick Derringer sideman pumping bass and bottleneck, this is some landmark of thrash-before-they-called-it-that, real shacklike and down-to-the-dirt with lotsa clogged-up-and-racing elephant-gun bashboogies about mean mamas who won't let our beerful bashful boys be free, the heftiest of which is this sorta MC5-mimic 45 dubbed "Love Me Hard," complete with swell flamenco break. There's a gradual and rheumatic ten-minute scorch-across-the-Sahara-side called "From a Dry Camel" (three wise men debating the relative coital merits of Bactrians and dromedaries—one hump or two?), a bass-based instrumental scuzzabilly snort (à la Blue Cheer's "Magnolia Caboose Babyfinger") known as "Loose Goose," and an astounding cover shot featuring the mummified remains of some unknown and unburied but nonetheless long-expired Mexican power trio seated aside some smokin' adobe (revived cartoonishly years later to match the attitude on Halo of Flies' *Headburn* EP). Plus plenty more definitive and unfrilly moments, not to be confused with the even-less-heralded work of Pet Shop Boy Neil Tennant's "stoned seventies" high school band of the same name, no kidding.

226. RUDIMENTARY PENI

The EPs of RP: Dirges and Ditties Corpus Christi UK import, 1987; rec. 1981–82

There's Blue Meanie–ish idiot-hieroglyphics on the cover, and inside's this sputtering font of knotty beats and belligerence, twenty-three miniature stabs in the dark with a crude instrument, far-lefty but too abstract to convince you you've heard it before, catchy in a way warped enough for you to start humming along re "cosmic plagues" and "teenage time killers" after a listen or two. The tuneless twists that Nick Blinko pulls his six-string through share a notion or three with how Piggy Voivod does his business, and he's got everything to shriek but no time to shriek it, so his anxiety attacks just inhale and exhale as he catches his breath. Adjusting his sights as he fires, he grinds notes into mulch, and though he probably hasn't learned more than a chord or two, he sounds real complicated. Jon Greville's drums lock into quicktime, or tuck and roll around an off-kilter antimelody, or kick

Blinko's adenoidal grunt up and down the ladder. Grant Mattews springloads his bass lines the way Geezer Butler did on Sabbath's *Master of Reality,* but faster, so much faster that even with a lyric sheet, you can never be sure on which grid-coordinate you're standing. But the oblique savvy nonetheless sabotages repression through the back door, and even as they slither into Gothic caricatures like "Mice Race" and "The Gardener," these Britpunks' prickly hooks and pretzel logic ensure that their hostility stays playful.

227. FLAMIN' GROOVIES

Teenage Head Kama Sutra, 1971

They look more or less like Ernie Douglas, but "Teenage Head," with some of the hardest harmonica and slide anywhere, is one of the great 'tween-kidhood-and-adulthood greaseball-anthems, and "Whiskey Woman" 's got some of the downtrodden mountaintop majesty Guns N' Roses would capture covering "Knockin' on Heaven's Door" live seventeen years later. Appropriately for San Franciscans who dedicate their best record to such moderns as R. Meltzer, Kim Fowley, and Randy Newman (whose "Have You Seen My Baby" they gallantly revive), their profuse Robert Johnson blabberblooze roots-moves undulate up-to-dately as this evening's edition of "Entertainment Tonight," a rare occurrence indeed. Thrice in a row in Side One's middle, they reincarnate the Delta as some stenchful kinda avant-garbage, thus pulling off what numerous post-Kerouac cartoons (Hi Sheriffs of Blue, Gibson Bros., Killdozer, Tav Falco and Panther Burns) would always be too ego-bound to get right. You can bet large sums that if they had any idea how weird they sound, they wouldn't sound half so weird.

228. ROCKET FROM THE TOMBS

A Night of Heavy Music unlabeled cassette, 1975

One of the noisiest combos ever to emerge from any heartland, they were never given the opportunity to record legal wax, at least not until they changed their names to the Dead Boys and Pere Ubu. Here, they're broadcasting through the muffle at Cleveland's Agora direct onto Cleveland's WMMS-FM, returning to the scene after a pack of local taverns banned 'em, joking around on stage, telling kids to skip school and get high, bronzing the Stooges' "Search and Destroy," glorifying a gun-toting woman who wears sunglasses, and just generally making a mess in a nihilistically droneful way that must've seemed like Martian music at the time, yet in retrospect doesn't approach Ubu's eventual indulgence by any stretch. Imminent dope casualty and sometime rockcrit Peter Laughner snatches vengeful riff-roisterousness from the Stones, Sabbath, Blue Cheer, BÖC, Hawkwind, the Velvets, even the Raspberries, then heaps more distortion on top; Crocus Behemoth's voice appears to be changing, but even in the semifamous "Final Solution" and "30 Seconds Over Tokyo" his whine's more stable, less forced, than it ever would be again. Yet when one time out of nowhere he nasalizes something about "a ship out on the vacant sea," for all you know he could already be David Thomas and this could already be the lukewarm burlesque on Ubu's 1988 *The Tenement Year,* hardly an encouraging omen.

229. FUNKADELIC

Free Your Mind . . . and Your Ass Will Follow Westbound, 1970

"The kingdom of heaven is within" is how some mousy mofos complete the title line, then this ten-minute monstrosity commences to spill its guts and spoil your day like the baddest trip since the beginning of drugs: Hocus-pocus Hendrixisms, mau-maus who can't hear their own voices yelling "Burn!" at Mr. Charlie, all bounded by a hard ground-round beat. The rest of Side One, "Friday Night, August 14th," is squirmier and more tumultuous and less pretentious, but still generally don't mean diddly 'cept Mr. Clinton best be laying off those discolored sugar cubes. Side Two's got "Funky Dollar Bill," the long-haired sucker's first great treatise on the rhythm and business that rule us all, plus plenty more economic-overview freakouts. And some weird keyboards.

230. BUDGIE
In for the Kill MCA, 1974

Chasms of soporific sludge swing open and this squeaky voice, angelic as your long-lost cigar-chomping Serbo-Croatian grandpa, tumbles in mouth-first while he's washing the dishes. Kitchen-sink quicksand swallows his entirety as he in turn swallows all the leftover tenderloin drippings he can find, and in "Zoom Club" he just keeps clawing further like a gigantic star-nosed mole, swimming through sewers and underground caves, observing whatever natural wonders one can uncover down there. Halfway through one pudgy Zepgroove the rhythm section changes its mind and tries a different one, then spectral pipe organs and rockets emerge from the overwhelming bluesbang like yesterday never happened. When Metallica's big backside itched, they scratched it with "Crash Course in Brain Surgery" 's knitting needle. It did the job.

231. LED ZEPPELIN
Led Zeppelin Atlantic, 1969

Warped funk ("Good Times Bad Times"), hippie dippiness ("Your Time Is Gonna Come"), sitar satire ("Black Mountain Side"), all-the-way wound-up punk rock ("Communication Breakdown"), and bushel baskets of grotesque Stegosaurus blüüze (everything else, as symbolized by the LP cover's oversized metallic black penis), all sculpted to precision and stupidly strafing the ladies and stomping boisterously all over a counterculture that was pretty silly to begin with, so audacious (a joke?) that when it arrived no grown-up knew what to do with it, but times were different then. The boogiethud crud will be overrated forever by tone-deaf nincompoops who consider "Stairway to Heaven" a "wimp-out," but the surest QED of "Communication Breakdown" 's torpedo-aptitude is the fact that the Sex Pistols, supposedly a revolt against (among other social diseases) every excess Zep stood for, stole its riff in "God Save the Queen." And they *slowed it down.*

232. THE JESUS AND MARY CHAIN
Psychocandy Reprise, 1985

These allegedly insurrectionary imps could've just as well called themselves the Jesus and Matty Chain, after baseball's Alou brothers, but where would that've left Felipe? The singer, Jim Reid, always sounds bored; the bassist and drummer might as well not exist. The self-referential melodies are all that matter. It's lovely how William Reid's much-bruited feedback swells and subsides tidal-wavelike, but he's too static to jar you, so the entertainment's purely formal, meshing airy mumbles with meaningless chords that feel the same regardless of volume. It conjures a "depressive mood," but it's most worthwhile when it's giggling about moles in holes or RIP X-mas trees or drowning fishes or rubber holy baked-bean tins. Like Poison, the JAMC draw from a bottomless pit of not-quite-redundant cotton-candy hooks they camouflage within a hard-guitar coating. They're unabashed plagiarists who constantly recycle ancient texts, singles specialists who pack LPs with pseudo-nonfiller, narcissists who turn adolescent escape-from-frustration into a flimsy fashion statement, mouth-fetishists who expound frequently on oral stimulation. (They eat up scum and get head on their motorbikes; cunnilingus statements include "Taste of Cindy" and "Just Like Honey.") Like Poison, they're as safe as a guitarsquad can be—the preposterousness of their pose is what makes them fun. I prefer *Psychocandy* to *Darklands* not 'cause it's "noisier" (it ain't very, trust me) but 'cause it's less murked down in hokey Camus-dirges that rip off Ian Curtis's freeze-dried Ozzy Osbourne ripoffs— 'cause it's *happier*.

233. MOTÖRHEAD

Ace of Spades Mercury, 1980

Everybody calls this Motörhead's magnum opus, seeing as how it's so "unrelenting" and all, but what's so wonderful about unrelentance is what I wanna know. Are you really supposed to subject yourself to it (and if so, how come?), or are you just supposed to "admire" it? Much as I believe Lemmy and gang make this world halfway livable, I really wish they'd sing a nice sappy ballad once in a while for a change of pace. That said, there's probably as much scabrously hooky Götterdämmerung riffage here as on any document ever compiled by Motörhead or anybody else, the Sergio Leone *Once Upon a Time in the West* motif's a trip, Lemmy Kilmister's molars and incisors are bared and sharpened, and his heart's got blood running through it. "The Chase Is Better Than the Catch," "Love Me Like a Reptile," "Shoot You in the Back," "Bite the Bullet"—these are great titles and real good songs. Punk rock with blues windows, only harder, and that they were permitted to see vinyl at all in 1980 is a miracle. "(We Are) the Road Crew," "Jailbait," and "Ace of Spades" are even smarter, even swifter, even more spiteful, even more likely to hold up your stagecoach. They'd be classic 45s, or maybe they already are. But there's no flow, 'cause they can't hang together, 'cause they all feel the same.

234. BULL ANGUS

Bull Angus Mercury, 1971

Let these cattle loose in yer proverbial china shop and I *guarantee* you'll have nothing left to take home for Christmas presents: ferocious gut-mange boogola, organ-driven just like their Heepful labelmates Uriah,

complete with the usual early-seventies fast-tempo proclivities, though Frankie Previte's flutey recorder is quite the metal innovation, I must say. They're open-minded youngsters as well, seeing as how "Mother's Favorite Lover" offers encouragement for an under-cover lesbian tête-à-tête involving the singer's mom and her milkmaid Margaret, who apparently reap-pears in the rampaging "No Cream for the Maid." "Uncle Duggie's Fun Bus Ride" is both funnier and funkier than "Magic Bus" by the Who, and "Cy and Miss Casey" and "A Time Like Ours" combine for twenty long minutes of goatee-and-beret fusion-wah experimentalizing. And I do mean "mental"!

235. UFO

The Best of UFO Nova German import, 1973; rec. 1971–73

They named themselves after a flying saucer, and Phil Mogg's mouth resembled David Byron's after Lister-ine, but (early on, at least) they didn't lose themselves in space all that much. There are tracks here called "Galactic Love" and "Silver Bird" that're your usual Can/Düül/Hawkwind fuzz-stuck-in-a-groove illogical-ness (which explains why them crazy Krauts dug these harebrains so dearly from day one), but mainly, before Michael Schenker's musicianly prowess emas-culated 'em, UFO poured forth the most raunchful and asylum-defyingly awkward accidental Detroitism since Detroitism meant Smokey, insistent Piltdown-man Diddleybeat under motorific bass-shock and wah-goop. This is most notably evident in "C'mon Everybody" (most depraved Eddie-Cochran-torture this side of Blue Cheer) and "Timothy" (a possible rejoinder to the Buoys' great cannibal-rocker of the same name, suggesting the incredible edible man came out of the sky!). The most ear-opening stuff's from *UFO I*, but the surrounding mud (Paul Butterfield's "Loving Cup" done Dust-style) and voluption ("The Coming of Prince Kajuku," which commences with gunfire) and voluptuous mud ("Prince Kajuku," a different item entirely, wherein Mogg bellows that reliable metal standby "Catch a Falling Star and Put It in Your Pocket") are just as kooky in their own way. As are those giant donuts on the cover!

236. SPIÑAL TAP

This Is Spiñal Tap
Polydor, 1984; rec. 1967–82, but not really

If Public Enemy is rap's answer to the Tap, as an unusually literate *Spin* letter once asserted, that would make this LP metal's answer to *It Takes a Nation of Millions to Make Us Multiplatinum*. Regardless, these movie stars put wimpy harmonies and symphonic keybs in their AC/DC hell-howl, which suggests they don't know what the fuck they're talking about, and "Tonight I'm Gonna Rock You Tonight" 's redundancy is no match for McCartney's "world in which we live in" or even Elvis's "the future looks bright ahead." The book-of-Genesis move (despite ying's search for yang) and acoustipomp-patriotism move (despite Afro sheen) don't cut it either. "Heavy Duty" 's brainkill Weltanschauung is up there with "Megadeth" by John Belushi easy, and "Gimme Some Money" beats "Music For Money" by Nick Lowe, and "Stonehenge" has the world's only stomachable Ian Anderson imitation, and the roots-move and twee-move are adorable. But only when the singer refuses to "leave this behind" in "Big Bottom" does he sound as if he "really means it." Bottom line, I guess, is that I'll take David St. Hubbins and Nigel Tufnel over anybody in Priest or Maiden (or Lenny and the Squigtones even) no problem, but the Godz are funnier anyday. Awesome flick and lyric sheet though.

237. HÜSKER DÜ

New Day Rising SST, 1985

A grab bag of gunk, with all these nice big-hearted handclappers like "Girl Who Lives on Heaven Hell" and "I Apologize," so it's tempting to ignore the back braces the rhythm-guys are wearing, not to mention all the merely comforting muffled vagueness (the stuff college-radio programmers call "pop") that's filling space everywhere, especially past Side Two's midpoint. The Hüskers put all this energy into "emoting," into teaching us all the hard-won wisdom they've learned in their painful-as-the-next-loser's lives, so it's impossible not to feel for (and empathize with) them. Their knack for pow-pow-powerpop hooks has rarely been equaled, and unlike so many of their disciples and contemporaries, they wrote actual *songs,* but I still get the feeling something big's missing. Nonetheless, "Terms of Psychic Warfare" may well be the meanest "Positively Fourth Street" retooling Elvis Costello (or Mouse and the Traps) never wrote, and Hawkwind certainly never mooned as catchily as Dü do in "Books About UFOs." And though what surrounds him is frequently soggy, Bob Mould's guitar never lets up its guard.

238. SONIC YOUTH

Evol SST, 1986

In "Expressway to Yr Skull" (alias "Madonna, Sean and Me," alias "The Crucifixion of Sean Penn"), the nicest number in their whole dang repertoire, they search the entire Pacific coast for "the meaning of feeling good," but only poststructuralist Barthesian geeks from Manhattan would figure "feeling good" *needs* a "meaning," and that's their whole problem. Nonetheless, this is their poppiest set, and it sounds more like a means to an end than an end itself. Not that the end they're aiming for is real clear, natch—the desperate-and-used-to-it wanderlust is pretty surreal. "Expressway" 's postmoral refabricating of Zep's "Going to California" reiterates the hunt for "pleasure" and "truth" they undertake in "Secret Girl" and "In the Kingdom #19" (where the sheet metal burns rubber downhill at one hundred miles per hour and you're exhilarated even as the driver's careening toward his agonizing end); "Starpower," "Tom Violence," and "Shadow of a Doubt" would have us satisfy our lust via our own subconscious. The Youths are saying that to fully experience life and grace you've gotta risk death and sin, that John Fogerty rides the same mystery train as Ron Reagan, that "evol" is just "love" spelled backwards (see circa '66 Chicago garagers Trojans of Evol), corny stuff like that. Slow tranquil dissonance builds over simple drum patterns, or mallet instruments commence to clicking one by one, then everything opens up as cheap guitars doctored with screwdrivers and bowed with drumsticks fire their exploding loads into dullsville. Mr. and Ms. Gordon-Moore talk/croon in these after-midnight conversational tones that eventually get you trusting whatever nonsense they recite, but at best that only makes 'em seem talented, never scary or brave.

239. TED NUGENT AND THE AMBOY DUKES
Call of the Wild Discreet, 1973

Maybe clean-living Theodore really was chemical-free throughout his early journeys to the mind-center in inexhaustible quest of the cosmic cabbage—only his haberdasher knows for sure. But here, the original pigfucker wants a *new* drug, and that drug is called "meat," and his bow and arrow bag a bottomless Zeus-suckling cornucopia full. "There's a ringing in my ear," he chants over and over, and he ain't whistling Dixie: The guitars emit a gigantic frontier roar as if he's four-wheel-driving you gagged and bound at top speed through a Michigan blizzard toward the Upper

Peninsula and dropping you off in the dark in the mud in a dense evergreen timberland with nothing but a hatchet and a compass and you gotta sleep in a tree trunk and your bunk mate's a grizzly and suddenly it's morning and Indian summer melts all two feet of white stuff and you're hacking your way out and for grub you munch some damp beaver ('cause that's what Ted would do) then finally you make it to a ghost-town gas station and pump premium diesel into big deuce-and-a-half rigs for an hour for which some two-bit slob pays you with a map and a key to the restroom where you shatter the mirror then grab a glass-shard and slaughter an Irish setter and make his fur coat yours and hitch back to the Murder Capital where Ted slaps you hard between the shoulder blades then broils you some savory marinated quail and you wash it down with rotgut by the quart. Then you turn the record over.

240. THE NEW YORK ROCK ENSEMBLE
Roll Over Columbia, 1970

Well-behaved young billiards players who weren't above donning tuxes and sprucing up with new-thing cellos and oboes, they could be the non-Meathead college boys Archie'd want Gloria to marry, and with a cultured monicker like theirs, with editorials called

"Law and Order" and "Traditional Order," who knows? They might even be Nixonites. But their swagger packs a wallop, and the Gregorian keyb-and-sigh grandiosity only propels Cliff Nivison's chunky fuzz-snort toward mayhem, most notably in the necrophilic abyss-anthem known as "Gravedigger," during which Mike Kamen wants his baby back so he digs up Cold Ethyl and sticks it in and makes a dead girl walk (the astounding power of a fratboy's prick!). "The King Is Dead" is painful postpunk vacuum-cleaner-fretwork, but the "punk" it's "post" to is the sixties kind. And these Dapper Dans are up on jailhouses, guns, the sea, and long snakes too. And the Venom Fun Club should take note of their devil-goat, who's got a baby devil-goat in his mouth.

241. DICK DESTINY AND THE HIGHWAY KINGS
Brutality Destination, 1987

Prior to this sophomore slobber, Dick booted his old bassist and second-string axman for spinelessness and death-metal tendencies, respectively (also, both of 'em were "antisports"), then replaced 'em with a onetime Captain Beyond roadie and a .450-batter (in the Allentown League) whose sister once fell victim to a pickup attempt by Budgie Casanova Burke Shelly. Dick himself remains a chemist among chemists, and despite flattened sound quality, the fungus-soup he concocts leaves whitewall tracks across your physique and attains both a viscosity level comparable to early Point Blank and a humor level comparable to early Venom. "Strategic Air Command," evidently inspired by the custard-pie fight Stanley Kubrick left out of *Dr. Strangelove,* makes way for a poker-faced reading of AC/DC's "The Jack," following which we're dealt the highest sort of flattery for op-art-era BÖC ("X-Ray Eye"), two thick-headed distorto-boogie in-stros ("Whiplash" and the provocatively titled "Dweezils Ripped My Flesh"), and one quick-headed piece of Nugent-criticism ("Letter to Mr. Ted," which demands auto collisions even as it steals phrases both riffwise and vocalwise from "Hey Baby," "Pony Ex-press," "Wango Tango," and the MC5's "Ramblin' Rose"). Additionally, there's obese sorority debs and big cheeses and horny whores. "Ironwork Blues" is an inspirational social protest that perhaps Dave Marsh will someday quill a best-seller about, and the set closes with a brief concerto likely induced by "The Clap"–period Steve Howe. This is a working-class band to (I hope) end all working-class bands; they sound as if they're from Texas, and they even thanked me on the cover.

242. GRANICUS
Granicus RCA, 1973

A verbose bacchanal of highspeed boogiebulk belch from the burning shores of River Cuyahoga, this has Hottentot drums, peaceable kingdoms of acoustica inside souped-up sludge, incomprehensibly maudlin sagas of siblings in Nam and on the run from the law, the Obligatory Heavy Meddle Indians-Got-Screwed Editorial, the works. The lunatic frontguy, Geddy Lee minus tinkerbell tweedledeedee or Robert Plant with a goat in his throat, repeats syllables a zillion times ("crashing through the sky-yi-yi-yi-yi-yi") as if he doesn't know words are eventually supposed to end. On the noun "downtown," his screech keeps dropping down deeper and deeper, and in "Prayer," one of several epic mountain-scalers, he even admits he's losing his voice and forgetting lyrics. "Let me drop my load on you, America," he squeals through the wank-attack, and "When your insides are comin' out, you don't feel so groovy." Even submits an ode to his "untight, uncool, unheavy, ungroovy, unfunky, unneat, unmellow, unhip" (but still lovely) hometown, Cleve-land, where he complains people frown all the time. Sez he's gettin' out.

243. CELTIC FROST
Cold Lake Noise International, 1988

Speedmetal speds took this lipstick-and-panties mind-fuck as a "sellout" (as if there's a *dumber* audience out there somewhere!), but that only makes me appreciate these Leif Erikssons of Love all the more. Watch-wearer Thomas Gabriel (née Tom G. Warrior) surrounds himself with newfound pouty poofs headed by a bassist whose pubic-hair-and-overalls getup is some obscene hybrid between Prince circa *Dirty Mind* and Jim Dandy Mangrum circa *High on the Hog,* and all the filthy unhealthy sex ("Seduce Me Tonight," "Dance Sleazy," "Cherry Orchards") suggests Tom's turntable oughta lay off the art-disco dreck, but though the production displays some unnecessary housekeeping skills, the beefiest helpings brandish the recurrent riffs and dark density of top-grade BÖC, and the vocabulary's not far off. The Marilyn Monroe hosanna outshines the one on *Goodbye Yellow Brick Road* and has eerily erotic gal-counterpoint that's not unlike Patti Smith on *Agents of Fortune*; the opening rap could pass for first-LP Was (Not Was) if Wayne Kramer had remained true to his old self; "Downtown Hanoi"'s got newsreel footage that teaches less about Southeast Asia than "Still in Saigon" but more than "Vietnamese Baby"; Tom pronounces "velvet" "well wet" and asks "What it is?" a lot. Also, you gotta hand it to any glammers-come-lately who can immediately come up with a Poison retort called "Roses Without Thorns."

244. THREE-MAN ARMY
. . . .
A Third of a Lifetime Kama Sutra, 1971

Unrelenting turbo-reversal he-man vortex-jazz with an emotional span that ranges from premeditated murder to the Lamaze method of natural childbirth, this has gotta come from somewhere near the Alamo, I swear. Riveted rhythm changes plus high-decibel bottleneck-wattage plus mongo drum solos add up to weirdness like "Nice One" and the bisexually bent "See What I Took," which circumventally kick smokin' sawdust around the OK Corral like hybrids of Charlie Brown's "Peanuts" theme and Zeke Tchaikovsky's "March of the Wooden Oxen." "Butter Queen"'s an homage to one of history's more notorious been-with-the-band Betties (dunno if they got their casters plastered), and "Another Day" and "Together" are

hard-drinking/hard-swinging gunshot-guitarspurt Dixieboogie laments 'bout meeting your gal at the station but you never get to see her 'cause you're working days and nights and she always hurts ya anyhow then she goes and finds another man then phaseback obliterates all the unfairness. Plus a cool antiwar lecture about a sixteen-year-old draftee, and a mournful beaut of a string-and-keyb intro with a title, "On [sic?] Third of a Lifetime," like a doctoral thesis—breathless, deathless stuff.

245. NITZINGER
. . . .
Nitzinger Capitol, 1972

Augmented by an uncredited guitar that once churned "Maid of Sugar, Maid of Spice" for Mouse and the Traps, a trio of tequila-guzzling longhaired longhorns, including a pretty one named Linda · Waring who slambangs the cans more like John Bonham than Moe Tucker, dance a Texas two-step on your kneecaps. Military fanatics tell their grandkids about the gooks they've murdered to make nongooks free in "Hero of the War"; religion fanatics try to make you dress nice and shine your loafers in "Witness to the Truth"; hicks from the sticks take sojourns to Hollywood in "L.A. Texas Boy"; and in a terrific boogie-ossification called "Louisiana Cock Fight" (to my knowledge the only English-language lyric ever addressed toward this storied sport that's entranced gambling humans since the days of Persia and Rome and gambling southerners since the days of the American Revolution) perturbed roosters get it on with shaving blades. John Nitzinger doesn't indicate whether the cock fight in question is a single battle, a round robin, or a battle royal, but I suspect Henry VIII and James I would be impressed nonetheless, and I hereby recommend that ESPN add the tune to its stable of theme songs.

246. LYNYRD SKYNYRD
Nuthin' Fancy MCA, 1975

Rebel-rousers damning the National Rifle Association's handguns with a muzzle-loaded Strat/Firebird/Les Paul riff (eventually appropriated by Eddie Money, of all people), "Saturday Night Special" 's gotta be the most violent stop-the-violence PSA ever; in the next song, a country-blues, Ronnie Van Zant threatens to shoot his woman with his pistol. Then suddenly he's a hobo, learning about Jimmie Rodgers like Merle Haggard did, riding rails on the run from the law, looking back in time and geography out the corner of one eye, but fixated mainly on what's ahead. Miles away from Communication Central's concrete, he imagines that life oughta be light, but he works all day for a dime, and the sound's heavy. Every equation he proves, he promptly proves wrong, as if truth is a crock. Side Two starts brutal, with "On the Hunt"; you hunt with bullets. Something called "Made in the Shade," dedicated to a famous bluegrass musician, follows "Am I Losin'," about how when you're famous you sacrifice friends, faith, time, your home. The coda's about why rock 'n' rollers' home is the road, why it makes 'em so happy when they've got no choice but to get drunk. There were times Skynyrd sounded wittier, wiser, even sadder, but on no other record do they feel so bitter, nowhere else do they convince you your life would be in danger if you turned and walked away. On the back cover, the drummer gives you the finger.

247. JUNKYARD
Junkyard Geffen, 1989

Fucked-up GnR-gonnabe boondockers-gone-west featuring former punk-rockers Brian Baker (of Dag Nasty/Minor Threat) and Chris Gates (of the Big Boys, who covered Kool and the Gang back in '82) pop corks and brag in moonshine drawls about drinking and driving. They pillage words from "Welcome to the Jungle" and "Who Do You Love," a song title from Skynyrd's "Simple Man," and an album title from the Birthday Party, and that oughta place 'em. Get a little uneventful when they shoot for speedmetal ("Shot in the Dark") and speedZep ("Hollywood") and Motörhead ("Life Sentence") and the Janitors or whoever (the stodgily stunted "Long Way Home"), but the ZZ riffs in "Hot Rod" and especially "Texas" overflow the skillet at higher temperatures than even Rock City Angels, and apparently nobody told 'em the word "blooze" wasn't their invention. The landlord boots 'em streetward for not paying their rent, and in the last and longest and slowest and silliest and saddest song, over more or less the same Skynyrd licks barrio-disco goddess Sa-Fire used in "Thinking of You," Dave Roach tells his girl to stop choking him after she gamahuches his best friend. It's like Marianne Faithfull's "Why'd Ya Do It" turned on its head, and the Woody Allen monologue takes me by surprise every time.

248. BANG
Bang Capitol, 1971

A blistering bluster from millenarian pulpit-pounders with world-historical intent, this Holy Trinity of a power-trio-fest constitutes the savviest Sabbath-cloning ever, assembly-line chucka-chucka hurling its idiot grungemosis toward masterfully mastodonic

Stoogefunk. Frank Ferrara's Ozzyesque phantasm-screech keeps sniveling about how his wife and whores aren't always pleasing him in times of need, and you just wanna kick his teeth in. But the real issue's social relevance, megacorp capitalism and the superstar syndrome and environmental overload ("tin foil hot dogs by the thousands"!) and ladies of the night and of course the ever-popular genocide of–red man (see: Granicus, Ursa Major, Steppenwolf, Anthrax, Ted Nugent, the Raiders, Lone Star, Iron Maiden's "Run to the Hills") leading us into temptation, down the path of destruction and the Stairway to Hell. Which stairway is actually *pictured* on the back-cover cartoon, and all these sorry sinners are waiting patiently in line to be booted below!

249. FIENDS

We've Come for Your Beer Bemisbrain EP, 1984

First they flush their toilet (an unecological waste of water if they only peed in it), and the IQ of this up-your-nose-with-a-Chemlawn-hose metalcore joke only goes downstream from there; last sound you hear is Ann B. Davis and the Brady Six, preceded by a three-second Mark Farner parody. Still, it *sounds* good, very Dictators, with Scott Morrow snorting muttonheadlike on purpose and pushing chubbier riffs than any Ross the Boss ever stepped in. Like all sensible people, he wants to trade Bob Hope to the underworld for John Belushi. "Sexual Explosion #19" burps its teen-angst bull like Tom G. Warrior, the henpecked "Battle Axe" and rednecked "Packin' a Rod" and cranky "Crankshaft" are more howlable ZZ Top counterfeits than John Hiatt's "The Usual" or Pussy Galore's "Sweet Little Hi-Fi" or anything by Molly Hatchet, and the MC5 cover lasts two minutes flat. "Fun rock" for "party people" customarily makes me gag, but mostly I think I like these particular suds-and-pizza jesters 'cause they remind me of my brother-in-law (not an insult, really).

250. PAT BENATAR

Best Shots Chrysalis UK import, 1987; rec. 1979–85

She's been to diva school, but certainly her full-throated crackle is less sissified than plenty of her male cohorts', and though she's addicted to sharing gender-inverted cry-tough/surrender clichés with Greco-Roman choruses, the puny dame's got control. She operates the great "Heartbreaker" like an aria, but what an overwhelming aria it is, and though as "Heartbreaker"'s go I might not take it over the Stones', I'll take it over Zep's and Warwick's for sure, which says a lot. This comp's one righteously span-dexed AOR-junk watershed, all reductionism-for-reductionism's-sake from "We Live to Love"/"Treat Me Right"'s Blondiedisco to "Invincible"'s rebellious Clashfunk to you-name-it's proto-Jovi Jerseydrama to hubbie Neil Geraldo's Chinnichap bubblechords. The most vivacious rock came early on, when Pat could pass for punk, but though her arrangements grew incrementally more continentally cinematic as Madonna took control of the femme-vocal spotlight, the variety provides a healthy emotional tug here. Then again, she does tend to repeat herself: "Hit Me with Your Best Shot," "Love Is a Battlefield," "You Better Run," and the confused feminist PSA "Sex As a Weapon" all equate romance with violence, and though I'm sure that says something about American family life in the Reagan Age, I'll be damned if I know what.

251. THE RUNAWAYS

Queens of Noise Mercury, 1977

Still slaving under Kim Fowley's thumb, the gals remain committed to the portrayal of groupies-in-reverse, but then again it's by chronicling their own situation that they made their mark. There are those who would claim "Born to Be Bad" should've been their theme song, that they couldn't've stated the opposition's case more clearly unless Kim had titled it

"Born to Bite the Big One." But that tune's got Joan Jett phoning Mom from the coast and telling her she's joined a rock 'n' roll band, and Ma starts "cryin' and weepin' and whimperin' like all mothers do," and how could anyone deny that there's an important truth to be heard here? To me, the "Children of the Grave"–percussioned "Neon Angels on the Road to Ruin" describes a way of life, and its philosophy is reiterated in "California Paradise" and "Hollywood" (which I swear owes some significant debt to "Shirley Wood," a bawdy brothelhaus hootchie-cootchie from 1975 by Disco Tex and His Sex-O-Lettes). And of course this same philosophy was lived out by every pay-to-play tattoo-and-haircut gang to sleaze through the City of Angels in the late eighties, except the Runaways were there first. Otherwise, Cherrie Currie sings power ballads (including a real pretty one called "Heartbeat" that features lonely queens in limousines and still deserves to be a hit for Poison or the Angry Samoans or somebody), Lita Ford devises a marginally original riff or two to counter the Slade and Deep Purple ones she's so fond of shoplifting, and the album ends with seven minutes of mushy quicksand. On the cover, Lita displays the most cleavage, Joan displays the least. Surprised?

252. STRAY DOG
Stray Dog Manticore, 1973

The dainty organ acrobatics that kick it off provide no hint as to what'll happen after the singer commands "fasten your seat belts!" Ten seconds later, while his two Texas homeboys commence to suggesting how "Tush" might sound if ZZ Top bassist Dusty Hill were a Visigoth, he's bragging about the seven fine women at his command, hurling joshful asides, telling himself to shut up. Gregorian backup buzz fights for attention with fugitivebilly white Negro pimpsploitation patter, guitar-din drilling its way free-jazz-style, impossibly viscous and vehement. There's no credits, so as far as I know all *three* of these bow-tied Renaissance men are guitaring—I wouldn't put it past 'em. The heartfelt filigrees are commendably otherworldly, "Speak of

the Devil" shakes its moneymaker like a real versatile and discreet escort-service employee, and the Billy Gibbons-authored "Chevrolet" out-ZZs ZZ. But the high (low?) point's gotta be the curiously-named "Slave," the six-minutes-flat of which are way too high-strung and angular for me to be positive about, but that only makes it more foreboding, 'cause there's a very real possibility that it might make "Sweet Home Alabama" seem like Janis Ian's "Society's Child" or even the Last Poets. Which is to say these backroad Confederate brandy-swiggers might not exactly dig black people much. Gotta be just my imagination, right? Hope so.

253. BIG BLACK
Songs About Fucking Touch and Go, 1987

Most of this fucking hodgepodge is Evanston shock-schlock done better before: Two noiseburgers too dense to decipher, a few that mix sex and sadism with

Photograph by John Bohnen

surf or Sabbath licks, the third Big Black hit-man homage, a Wagner-disco outro called "Bombastic Intro." There's a friendly fleshing-out of "The Model," Kraftwerk's sunnily contrived ode to a cover girl's contrivances, with riffs slashing both ways across popular mechanics, and there's "Kitty Empire," light-hearted semiautobiography about a cat-keeper who plays weird music and jumps around naked in the weeds, disturbing neighbors. But in the three cuts that really matter, like Warren Zevon on *The Envoy* only not as smart, Steve Albini bares more of himself than he'd ever deemed proper before, maybe more than he wants to, and ends up sounding frightened, sensitive, alone. "Bad Penny" could concern an unfaithful squeeze, but its spare nasal drone clues you that it's a retake on John Lydon's "Public Image," a denial of past transgressions and rebuke of an audience that's turned the singer into the kind of idol he's always despised. "Pavement Saw" builds its anthemic grace into an out-of-character love song to a pregnant chain-smoker. Finally Albini, a shrimp who's been billed as a "messiah" by gullible fanzine fools, ends his Big Black career with "Tiny, King of the Jews," an understated dirge that carries you back to Joy Division's first LP. Guitars swoop in parabolas over a beat box; the voice, mixed way back, more tired than angry, promulgates self-loathing. It's self-serving, but you wind up feeling embarrassed for Albini even after all the useless venom and derision he's sprayed. So he started a *new* novelty act, and called it Rapeman. Talk about chickenshit.

254. *Back from the Grave, Volume 2*
Crypt, 1984; rec. 1962–68

The walking dead are roasting an eight-track from '72 and a copy of Metal Queen's elusive *New Perm* (plus a *Village Voice,* a King Crimson LP, a questionably masculine dandy clad in disco threads, and more) on the album cover's hot spit, but where do them cadavers suppose heavy metal *came* from, anyway? Maybe from the scores of insane wildcat's-tail-beneath-your-cleats shrieks in "Scream" by Ralph Nielsen and the Chancellors, five pube-aged Jersey Link Wray fans in shiny suits who mined for gold on Route 1 not far from Princeton in the summer of '62. Maybe from the eye-gouging temperament of Roy Junior's "Victim of Circumstance," where a palooka "raised on knuckle-sandwiches" runs from "the barking hounds of Hades" but nobody understands or cares; maybe from the Brigands' white-trash factory-blues; maybe from the fuzztone ferocity in the

Canadian Rogues' "Keep in Touch" or the Reasons Why's "All I Need Is Love" or the Triumphs' sperm-spurting "Surfside Date." Definitely from the doom-beat in the Unrelated Segments' suicidal "Cry Cry Cry," at least if you're the Stooges, and from how the Outsiders toss their cookies all over "Summertime Blues" and the Mods screw up "Satisfaction" 's words, at least if you're Blue Cheer, and from the wrestling motif in the Novas' "The Crusher," at least if you're the Dictators. Not from the Lyrics or the Hatfields, though—they're too fucking mellow.

255. **KISS**
Kiss Casablanca, 1974

Pared-down urban-burlesque bootstrap yellocution, for teenagers who wanna (mostly male), about teenagers who don't (mostly female). Mostly it's dumb, mostly that's the point, mostly the "point" doesn't make it any better than it already is, mostly it's pretty good despite the point. The hooks are catchy, the riffs are loud, the same hooks and riffs return again and again, and the words mostly stink. The star is Paul Stanley, who plays rhythm guitar. The most dramatic song (lasts a half-hour or so) is "Black Diamond"; the most pointless (an instrumental!), "Love Theme from Kiss"; the most overrated, "Strutter"; the most under-rated, "Let Me Know"; the gooeyest (Archies could've done it easy), "Kissin' Time"; the fiercest (Dolls could've), "Deuce," which shows up Terence Trent D'Arby's subsequent grandma-banishment in "Dance Little Sister" as feeble. The participants, who come from New York and whose name stands for "Kids in Service of Spiro" or something, paint their faces to resemble a cat, a "bat-lizard," something with one black star on one eye, and something with one silver star on each eye. Several sleazy harlots in my high school's Designated Cigarette Area did the same, which perhaps indicates that the group will be extremely popular someday.

256. MILES DAVIS
. . . .
Pangaea CBS/Sony Japanese import, 1975

The only jazz sides I've ever seen that demand you play 'em "at highest possible volume in order to fully appreciate the sound," this pair of jam sessions lasts way too long, but the ensemble's the same one that ground out *Agharta* earlier that same frosty February day, and though real often they sound as if it's about time to hit the hay, sometimes they sound like *Agharta* was just a warm-up. Though Miles himself's real audible, trumpeting eerily elephantine out of a sandstorm somewhere, the commotion's generally directed toward no discernible end save Mtume's and Al Foster's eternally stylin' timbale-slamcopation. Mostly, it's a practice: There's relaxed coffee breaks where everybody catches their breath, and for a while in "Godwana" it's like your tub and both bathroom sinks are all leaking at the same time. After the first ten minutes or so, the real stars are Pete Cosey and Reggie Lucas, unloading this unmatched speedcurdle as if they're Slayer's Kerry King and Motörhead's Fast Eddie Clarke, wasting the world. Long about the third or fourth side they get all rueful and bluesome, but now and again they just churn profuse cram-packed noisegunk and zilch else. Toward the middle of "Zimbabwe," it's as if they've driven all their pals from the room.

257. BLUE ÖYSTER CULT
. . . .
Secret Treaties Columbia, 1974

That's supposed to be some Nazi warplane they've commandeered (with a skeleton's help) on the cover, and they're wry right off ("I will not ... apologize," gosh!) in "Career of Evil." Eric Bloom wants to do it in the road with your daughter, I catch something about the Holocaust, I suspect "ME 262" 's about the jet, and the ocular TVs and cagey cretins enable easy Stooge/Ramone connections, so it's not my inability to decipher the way-subdued brainstorms that bugs me most this time—it's the virtuoso slush Bloom's hidden under, real baroque in the synth-category, tough enough as progressiveness goes, but not even the Chuck Berry riffs stick to your ribs. Regardless, "Dominance and Submission" is fine fluoridated Sabtrudge with this creepy loudspeakered voice doing the polka to Little Eva at Times Square as the calendar's welcoming in '64, and that "joke's on you" refrain in "Flaming Telepaths" will intimidate forever. So I'm stumped.

258. THE CHOCOLATE WATCHBAND
. . . .
The Best Of Rhino, 1983; rec. 1966–68

These urban R&B clods don't sound as much like Alice Cooper as Metal Mike Saunders of the Angry Samoans has occasionally indicated (in fact, they don't sound as much like Alice Cooper as the Angry Samoans do sometimes), but (most conclusively in "I'm Not Like Everybody Else") they do sound pretty darn "metal," even though they'd think you were talking Greek if you told 'em so. Like every other garage group in history, they just wanted to be the Stones or Yardbirds. They're named after a timekeeping appliance with a sweet flavor, and I'd rather eat a chocolate watchband than a strawberry alarm clock 'cause chocolate's better than strawberry (though I don't particularly care for either) and a watchband's smaller than an alarm clock so I could get it over with faster, and if I ate the watchband I'd still be able to tell time with the alarm clock whereas if I ate the alarm clock I wouldn't be able to tell time with the watchband, and it might almost be time for a PBS special about whether Easter Island statues were dragged to the island's edge from the volcano quarry erect or prone, something I've been wondering about for years, so I wouldn't wanna miss it. The Chocolate Watchband comes from San Francisco and from the sixties, which are more or less the same thing, and they follow "Are You Gonna Be There (At the Love-in)" with "Don't Need Your Lovin'," which is an intriguingly homonymic juxtaposition of contradictions but I don't think they did it on purpose, do you?

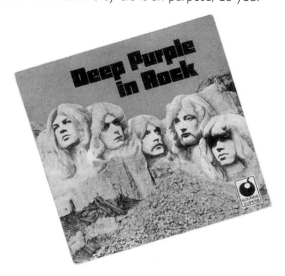

259. DEEP PURPLE
In Rock Warner Bros., 1970

Free-flowing teen-with-job müng-weight that at its most power-hungry ("Flight of the Rat," "Blood-sucker," the terrific "Speed King") darts around corners just like the MC5 (Ritchie Blackmore and Ian Gillan could *be* Rob Tyner and Fred Smith), this landmark helped define metal as a prevailing force in our time. The Purps have given up on London Symphony Orchestra guest-spots and Billy Joe Royal covers for the time being, and they haven't bartered

for Whitesnake's singer yet, so they disguise themselves as Mount Rushmore on the front (a very Spiñal Tap thing to do) and counter Side Two's lacy orchestral-jig midsections with Side One's frantic burghermeister blues and screaming-meemie Little Richard raps. "Child in Time"'s overboard operatics only increase the nastiness of it all, and if the last three cuts spend too much time twirling their conductor's batons (which they do), by the time you get to 'em you almost don't mind.

260. BUDGIE
Budgie MCA, 1971

Nobody can accuse these lovebirds of lacking a sense of humor and/or imagination, as "Nude Disintegrating Parachutist Woman" (title probably courtesy some obscure painter or sculptor somewhere), "Rape of the Locks" (a Sab-alike 'bout how Burke Shelley'd rather not get his hair cut!), "All Night Petrol" (mysterious Ozzyesque millenarianism, how the gas station fits in beats me), and "Homicidal Suicidal" (hot damn!) make clear. "Guts" has all these gradual downbound/downtown *Funhouse* testosterone-swing cycles, then it's straight into an acoustic bolero direct from Madrid's Retiro Park (the stage across from the two bullrings), then just as abruptly we're throbbing inside *Led Zep II* and the Garden of Eden, begging for a bite of Eve's golden delicious. A few Budgie buttbumps quiver too long into crab-nebulous oblivion, and a few others make up for it.

261. THE JIMI HENDRIX EXPERIENCE
Axis: Bold as Love Reprise, 1968

Number two's got the most aimless psychediddling of any of his three "classics," and that's a heap. The most mighty-assed funkmetal is "If Six Was Nine," scary individualist black-out-the-sun apocalypse that turns idiotic when Jimi starts pretending "freaks" are somehow less "plastic" than people who take the bus to work, but concludes with killer Sharrock-rock voluption; best attributes of "Wait Until Tomorrow" are the harmonies and "click-bang, what-a-hang, yo' daddy just shot po' me." The start-line fires fun Clinton/acid-house voice-register-alteration into cycloids that exercise your speakers well, and everything's groovy when the leading man rides his dragonfly and tries to penetrate Cleopatra's brain. Both castle songs are ace and both Beatle-moves are okay, but passably pleasant fairy tales like "Little Wing" have nothing on Blowfly where poetry's concerned, and the new-age bluesjabber would barely impress me if Frank Marino did it. The sleeve looks stupid, and the title tune's bad Prince.

262. SONIC YOUTH
Daydream Nation Enigma, 1988

What we got here, mainly, is two discs of good Hawkwind, with an I Ching groove sleek enough to send your cow jumping over the moon, but most of it's watery wallpaper regardless. "Teenage Riot" isn't—it's obligingly catchable lost-cause pop-optimism, perplexingly naive, like Thurston Moore still believes the punk-rock hoax, even if the only teenage riots conceivable by 1988 would've come from crack-fried neo-Panthers or domehead neo-Nazis. "You're never gonna stop all the teenage leather," he croons, but the leather's already been trampled to death. The song's video came out around the same time as Def Leppard's "Rocket" (weird, 'cause "Teenage Riot"'s followed by "Silver Rocket" here), and both vids are mainly montage-collages of the bands' heroes: SY pick Iggy, the Fall, Henry Rollins; Def Lep pick T. Rex, Mott, Queen. You couldn't see Hawkwind in either, though Lep listed 'em in a newspaper headline. I liked "Rocket" more because of Lep's after-the-fact makeup-move. No texture here can match "Hysteria," no rhythm can match "Pour Some Sugar on Me," and though like *Hysteria, Daydream Nation*'s got startling flashes of light (Kim Gordon's frustrated spoilsport monologue in "The Sprawl," the sad CD signals in "Hey Joni," "Kissability"'s sex, "The Wonder"'s Die Kreuzen mimicry), here they're hidden amid reams of mush and malarkey. SY's malarkey may well tend to be gigglier than DL's, but I have trouble remembering what's giggly about it when I'm not playing it. The most honest review I read recommended that they learn to play their instruments.

263. AMON DÜÜL
Experimente Time Wind German import, c. 1980; rec. c. 1969

Budget-wrapped behind posttechnological dada-art (though other titles in the record's cut-priced sixteen-installment series run toward the meek likes of *Akkordeon Hit-Parade* and Maria Callas's *Norma—Lucia di Lammermoor*), this idiosyncratic item's instrometallic distortion-appliance migraine-wrench performances, six on each of four sides, have no names, only numbers—"Special Track Experience No. 1" through "Special Track Experience No. 24." There are no melodies or rhythms, no way to tell 'em apart. The music's uncompromised and unbounded atonal asteroid-soup, non-new-age rev-up stuff, with cannibal can-rumble, electronically oscillated Hoover-upright effects, a whole *Hofbrauhaus* full of acid-freakback feed and pant-chanted German (or Esperanto?) gibberish. It's rumored Düül were tight with the Baader-Meinhof gang, and it must be true, 'cause who else would've hung out with 'em?

264. RAMONES
Ramones Sire, 1976

The riffbuzz accelerates so compactly at the start, the first syllables are so prewordlike, that it's impossible not to imagine how repulsive this dirt-cheap document must've seemed to the Frampton and Bad Company partisans who likely stormed from record stores upon initial exposure, or how superior that must've made subsequent buyers feel. Cracking your little brother's skull with a Louisville slugger, fearing the one-eyed ghoul in the catacombs, inhaling model-airplane cement, volunteering for the Ice Capades and/or CIA, falling heels over head in crush—this was rock 'n' roll, it *had* to be, right? Well, yeah, at least if you lived in New York. Me, I lived in suburban Detroit, where I read an article about 'em and figured they'd be fifties revivalists, like Sha Na Na. Which they were, sort of: More butcherlike guitars, but big deal. Maybe if when I was hauling around a copy of Barry Goldwater's *Conscience of a Conservative* to rebel against my high school classmates' mindless liberal complacency I'd've realized that the universe's "hippest" r'n'r crew was four nostalgic nonhippies who poked fun at camel-jockeys and employed the American eagle and even more fascist symbols, I might've enjoyed my ROTC scholarship more. As it is, I mainly like the first two cuts, the more blitzful of which the Sweet had already molded into a jollier joke the year before. And a bigger hit too.

265. HAPSHASH AND THE COLOURED COAT
Featuring the Human Host and the Heavy Metal Kids Minit UK import, 1967

They invented metal, because if they didn't, who did? You can't say the Who or Kinks or Link Wray 'cause it didn't have a name then, you can't say Steppenwolf 'cause "Born to Be Wild" didn't exist till a year later, you can't say William Burroughs 'cause he only made spoken-word records. So it was them. Or anyway, they named it, which is the same thing, 'cause it means they were *consciously* originating something. But in a real unconscious way, mind you, 'cause this ranks among the most unthwarted-by-talent improvise-freely-and-babble-Krishna-nonsense-atop-an-obsessive-bongo-groove unidentified-flying-rock (see: Amon Düül, ESP-Disk's Godz, Yoko, Can, Faust, Chambers Bros.) ever constructed, and they didn't even come from *Deutschland*! (They were pop-art pupils from England.) In "H-O-P-P Why?" a man intones the title over and over all the way through, and in "The New Messiah Coming" and "Aoum," he doesn't. The cover's an eye-grabbing Little Bo-Peep sunburst shot,

perfectly symmetrical, though if you find a copy I wouldn't fold it in half and hold it up to a mirror to make sure if I were you. Mostly there's not many electric guitars (though there's some, especially amid the fulminating orgasm that fills Side Two), but so what—heavy metal didn't *have* a lot of guitars yet! And you know it's gotta be heavy metal, 'cause they say so.

266. WHITE WITCH
A Spiritual Greeting Capricorn, 1974

Pseudospade pseudo-star-traveling pseudo-Satanists with polypercussed repeat-a-riffs out of *Master of Reality* amid squishy panty-fusion, these young bucks fell under the charge of the craziest hickmetal throat this side of Mistah Jim Dandy himself. Extremely creative how Ronn Goedert punctuates the first track by drawling "money bags$" (that's how the libretto spells it) every once in a while. In "Slick Witch" he's Ricky Skaggs wanting to be Lene Lovich, and he commences speed-rapping hobo/dada–style (as in Woody Guthrie's "Talking Columbia" and "Talking Dust Blues," Chuck Berry's "Too Much Monkey Business," the Hombres' "Let It All Hang Out," Dylan's "Subterranean Homesick Blues," and Roger Miller's "My Uncle Used to Love Me but She Died") as follows: "workin' for the FBI, hangin' like a shirt-tail, blowin' like a windmill, woopah woopah woopah woopah. . . ." "Crystallize and Realize" 's coloring books and poppycocks and comet tails zygotize Spiñal Tap's "Cups and Cakes" with the Bee Gees' "I Have Decided to Join the Air Force"; "Walk On" 's quite luvverly in a Mantovani sort of heaven-metal way; Goedert dials Rufus's number and it's 666, and in the enormous Nebuchadnezzar-and–Jean Harlow tribute that comes next he's reciting verses from the books of Mark and Revelation. But "Class of 2000" 's Eddie Hazel–meets-Bowie is the shake that takes the cake—ma's got a rooster hairdo, dad's so old-fashioned he still smokes dope, junior's pals get high plugging into laser beams, a kid named Chapes learned 'bout the earth in his history class on Saturn. And the chick from the Uranus Assembly turns out to be a total drag, but ain't that always the way?

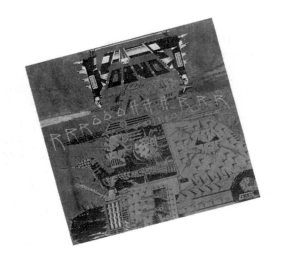

267. VOIVOD

Rrröööaaarrr Combat/Noise, 1986

On this insomnia-inducing regression into Montreal's Pleistocene, an axpicker named after a baby farm ungulate splatters abrasive surf-glop (which indicates parallel evolution with, rather than actual indebtedness to, Link Wray and the Ventures) over rapidly resounding robotic-shuffle herky-jerk skin-skipping, while a vocalist named after a legless reptile snarls like a cat in a hot-tin microwave (which is to say "in heat"). The result's some of the fastest two-chord tractor-pulls ever, and the title's a purely poetic quasipalindrome that sets mucho records in repeated-letter and multiple-umlaut categories alike. Song monickers include "Slaughter in a Grave" (if he's buried already, isn't it too late?), "Korgüll the Exterminator" (about the pesticide man, I'm told), and the self-explanatory "Ripping Headaches." Tush-punting comical excellence oozes from every pore.

268. LAST EXIT

Iron Path Virgin/Venture, 1988

Sick steers in a farm field moo amid a tornado, then Sonny Sharrock's guitar starts yanking the sound back in, restating a warped melody from one of his own records. Ronald Shannon Jackson's traps bulldoze the mess, Peter Brötzmann's sax heads up a battle-charge. A chariot driver cracks his whip, shouts "Hyah! Hyah!" everything speeds up, the horn discombobulates into these horrendous concentric squawks. The bassist, Bill Laswell, rides with the Valkyries, and that's just the first song. In "Sand Dancer," Sharrock, the most seismic axmonster on earth, Einsteins on the bitch, makes your head spin with hirsute swirls; in "Detonator" he plays Tony Iommi, then these electrical shocks fling off at obtuse angles, then Brötzmann, German as a Luger, blows his brains out through his brass. "Cut and Run" grumbles up from Atlantis in the Sargassian depths below, King Neptune's spear slashing through subs and sharks swifter and swifter, popping out and peeping at the sun at the end. "Eye for Eye" is where Piggy from Voivod goes to church in dimension Hatross and the congregation's all mammoths in rut with their fat butts stuck in the pews. They're getting their wool shaved off, Sonny's making wild electronic noise as if he's vacuuming up fur left over from the last Ice Age. The album ends with the drummer repeatedly booting you in the teeth with steel-tipped construction-worker shoes. This is "jazz," by the way.

269. REDD KROSS

Teen Babes from Monsanto Gasatanka EP, 1984

A bubblegunk rosary to the days when Kristy Mc-Nichol had braces, Susan Dey had a smart-ass little brother, Melanie had brand-new roller skates, Linda Blair had pea soup dripping from the mouth at the back of her head, and Squeaky Fromme had a president with poor eye-hand coordination within pistol range, from four wax lip–munching valley guys pretending they don't know any better. By my estimation, the pomp (Stones, Bowie) beats the pop (I think Shangri-Las and Monkees) beats the punk (Stooges, Kiss, Red Cross).

270. FASTER PUSSYCAT

Faster Pussycat Elektra, 1987

These silly Aeroglam fillies fill the netherspace between Guns N' Roses' "rock" and Poison's "pop," and I resisted 'em at first (something to do with eyeliner, studio drums, Taime Down's annoying snot-sneer), but after a year or so I climbed off my high horse and gave in to the fake drawls and cowboy hats. The name's from Russ Meyer, the bassist and singer look like twins, the Dolls/Beastie tribute's got sniffy-snorting flyguys, another fonky thang chews through Tom Waits's frontal lobotomy. The sheen's just shiny enough to emphasize the zesty stolen riff-hooks, the puns just trite enough to make any self-respecting seventh-grade pizzaface spit rum 'n' Coke through his nostrils. Taime digs commercial radio and admits he's gotta resort to public johns and bordellos to get laid, and though his Tyler doesn't near match Axl's, he's no wallflower either—trips over his own tongue in "Cathouse" even though it'll cost him more money. If the galstuff weren't so lethargic, if Side Two's roughneckism weren't so half-cocked and sobersided, and if I were a self-respecting seventh-grade pizzaface, I'd be real happy.

271. WHITE LION

Big Game Atlantic, 1989

This is blues that smokes warm and tuneful because it's not afraid to be corny, because it doesn't say "this is blues." Only the diamond industry would refuse to be moved by "Cry for Freedom"'s antiapartheid worldbeat/Nerf-metal merger, and Mike Tramp's cracked vowel-savoring in "Goin' Home Tonight" curls unblushingly around Vito Bratta's strums exactly like Ferron, the Queen of Lesbian Folksingers. Not long before this album came out, White Lion staked out an uncharted acoustic frontier in their pop-topping "When the Children Cry" single, Mike's bleeding heart offering a naive universalist plaint for "no more presidents," as if he thought he was John

Lennon. He pleaded for little kids to stop fighting, but in real life his own answer song ("When the Children Die"!) was in the can, and he was pledging to get Stryper's lead-preacher laid. Here, he precedes an impossibly infectious Greenpeace ode ("Little Fighter," which could be about Jesus, or Jesse Jackson—the chorus bubbles up with "rise again!" the subtitle's "In Memory of the Rainbow Warrior") and a post-"Luka" anti-kidbeating treatise with some embarrassing Van Hagar cockstrut called "Dirty Woman." After the protests, he mails a yucky "I'll Be There for You"–style mall-valentine with "Tom Sawyer" change-ups, rides into this lush sunset in his beaten 501 Blues, links "Jailbreak" and "The Boys Are Back in Town" (and Mott the Hoople's "Violence," judging from his "no mercy for the old and weak") in "Let's Get Crazy." The rockers, even the antievangelist Metallica-move, couldn't conceivably make a difference to anyone anymore. But the sweetness mostly piles melodies like rappers pile beats—it's a campfire-pop Grand Canyon.

272. THE LEFT

It's the World Bona Fide EP, 1984

A surly King Kong heaves eight midtempo chunks of simmering cancerous filth off the Empire State, and though ones about death and the Army and the like miss (though not so's you can't smell 'em), the tub-tumbling grunge-granite kicks your chest cavity in

just guessing). "Outside Woman Blues" and "Take It Back" and "We're Going Wrong" are no kinda drug but Sominex, and the ragtime-move's camp-crap, so everything's over by the middle of Side Two. But you can drown in the bodies of "Tales of Brave Ulysses"'s sirens and mermaids whenever you feel like it, and the jacket's got several colorful spoonbills and Supermen and African witch doctors and peacocks, even Apollo with a revolving restaurant on his head. Benjamin Disraeli the Earl of Beaconsfield (1804–1881) would be proud, as would Isaac Disraeli, his dad.

274. Less than Zero
Def Jam, 1987

A soundtrack to a lousy flick about rich teens on drugs (named after a lousy novel about the same, named after an Elvis Costello ditty about the National Front). What's supposed to put this set over is producer Rick Rubin's metal/funk/doo-wop adolescent-anomie agenda. What we end up with instead is one truly murderous original from rad-rappin' Public Enemy, a couple cover-reconstructions that update age-old mediocrity, and lotsa filler, mostly annoying. In the smarmy quasielegant ballad-mode, Glen Danzig composes two too-smug-to-stomach ponderosos re death and dying (one sung by the ex-Misfit himself and one by Roy Orbison), L.L. Cool J mumbles pseudomoodily like a rich teen on drugs, and Oran "Juice" Jones (who oughta stick to Trix and cornflakes) and the Black Flames serve up metasoul man/woman mush. In the BPM-past-the-snooze-alarm-but-so-what mode, Poison's wimp-clutz "Rock and Roll A Nite" isn't the Bay City Rollers remake it'd be if Rick Rubin was the genius everybody says he is, Joan Jett demonstrates why she should've hung up her black leather sneakers in '83, and Aerosmith canner Joey Kramer's huge heavy-hop slamming helps his co-horts race through the motions on Huey Smith's "Rocking Pneumonia" as if they've got Guns N' Roses on their tail.

Which leaves three decent tunes. I useta hum Simon and Garfunkel's "Hazy Shade of Winter" to

three times: The time where City Hall gives teenage assholes guns and cop uniforms, the time where your five A.M. alarm clock makes you wanna shoot yourself, the time where hell's where you sweat a lot and everybody hates each other and you're already fucking there. "It's no joke," Brian Sefsic coughs, "I'm not laughing." The war of all against all, Hobbes called it, and fear's the driving force. On the cover, on the North Pole, where Santa's elves oughta be: a big pile of stinking shit.

273. **CREAM**
Disraeli Gears Atco, 1967

Circa the Summer of *Pepper* this must've seemed rather daring, "funky" even. Eric Clapton's not entirely a purist putz so far, and large portions of the aura (such as for instance the Ouija-wisdom re the land of bearded rainbows and trees outside your window that don't belong to anybody else and starfish and purple flounders swimming through your noggin) are I suppose somewhat evocative of the first time you and the newly unwashed blonde next door dropped acid in her basement and sat around fig-leafed on beanbags staring into the drainholes beside the heating apparatus and wondering if they kept going, like, "forever" (an experience I know nothing about—I'm myself on those cold Michigan mornings delivering my paper route many years ago, but the Bangles chirp it in prettier harmony than I ever could ('course, there was only *one* of me), and their folkadelic strum-additives almost turn it into a rock song. Slayer's thrashmanian devils abridge "In-A-Gadda-Da-Vida" so the words make even less sense than before, Kerry King squirting great green gobs of necrophilous free-distortion guaranteed to rid your abode of pesky household pests. Finally, with Chuck D (who probably goes to Raiders games, sees the other team in a huddle, and thinks they're saying racist things about him) whining about rock-crits who can't get enough of him and tough-mindedly if wrong-headedly plugging Anthrax and Farrakhan with bellowed subpoena-envy authority atop a screwily skewered shish-ka-bob sheet of sound, the Bobby Seale of hip-hop starts to demonstrate that he might not have a copy of *Soul on Ice* up his booty after all.

275. THIN LIZZY
Fighting Mercury, 1975

Quintessentially seventies-clothed all the way down to elephant flares and silk shirts and Brian Robertson's killer three-inch heels, they lead with "Rosalie," Bob Seger's incredible lost lust-ode to a woman disc jockey from a Canadian town Detroiters have to drive south to get to, and from there you haven't much reason to fuss. For once, Robertson and Scott Gorham ply the blues for feeling as much as feel, and the vast harshness they get in something like "Wild One" seems as if it's lasted decades. Phil Lynott's bewildered without hope, and though you can tell his alley-mysticizing's headed toward an imminent masterwork, even in the cruel antiboogie boogie "Suicide" his sanctimony won't let him articulate the dread he's got hoarded. When in "Spirit Slips Away" he finally finds the key and opens the door, the room's completely devoid of light, a tomb.

276. URIAH HEEP
Look at Yourself Mercury, 1971

Cover's so clean you can see yourself (it's a *mirror*, stupid, and it's not farfetched to imagine some dope-dazzled Heepie gloating that he'd actually finally *accomplished* something in life seeing as how his photo was now pictured on his heroes' album!), and this be *thee* heap of Heep to seek out if, like so many serious students of sound, you have something against greatest hits records: 'Sgot the widest wide-tracks ("Look at Yourself" and "Tears in My Eyes" over five minutes, "Shadows of Grief" over eight, "July Morning" over ten), and thus gives drums (Ian Clark) and organ-plus-piano (Ken Hensley) space enough to concoct up from the foundation an enchantingly hypnosymphonic groovola whereupon guitar (Mick Box) can spew thick and natty on whicheverupon spot it feels would be most suitably spewtable (and Manfred Mann's Moog helps once too!). The thickness actually shows up more frequently in three-to-four-minute shortcuts such as "I Wanna Be Free" and "Love Machine," whereas the nattiness is evident most everywhere, though (unfortunately!) Dave Byron shrieks less archaeopteryxlike than he'd find fit to in later attempts. Ken resorts to quilling his own liner notes (". . . have continued to add the natural musical progressions that develop within . . ."), but if he would've asked me I would've done 'em, for free!

277. DINOSAUR
You're Living All Over Me SST, 1987

As of this writing, every record by these trans-planted-to-NYC Bostonians sounds exactly the same. *Dinosaur*'s got "Repulsion," the saddest couple minutes I heard in 1986, but not much else: *Bug*'s the snowbank into which your sedan's wheels will spin after about three years if you make re-creating Side Two of *Rust Never Sleeps* your life's goal, at least if you don't have the songs to pull the mission off (which you don't, trust me). So I suppose this one's the

Photograph by Naomi Petersen

Xerox to buy—sounds how I wanted Hüsker Dü to sound at the time, which is to say like Neil and Crazy Horse, but with a more mobile percussive bent and riffs that weigh a ton. The most Zeppish ditties are called "Tarpit" and "Sludgefeast," and live Dinosaur stacked Marshall amps. J. Mascis, like Andrew Gold before him, is a lonely boy. He mumbles in a raw, fractured, pained-but-unfeigned drawl about waiting for someone on a corner: "These guts are killin', but I can't stop now/Gotta connect with you girl, or forget how," then scythe-swaths of his masculinist string-spuzz seep in, and holy fucking shit. The guitars catnap and wake up hungry, the melodies are full and folkish, the vocals more like shadows than monuments, the feelings laid-bare and sensitive and expecting the worst. But there's no self-pity, and though nothing sounds thought-out, nothing sounds sloppy, and the jacket has flowers and smiles. For a while there, it meant something.

278. ZZ TOP

. . . .

Tejas London, 1976

Burrito-rockers, boogie's answer to Sergio Leone, they buried B. B. King in mud, wrote great letdown-laments with beefy hooks and Mississippi harmonica and maraca-spiced polyrhythms, and their thoughtful humor-sense was verbal and vocal and visual all at the same time. Billy Gibbons works the thickest bullroar south of the moon into even the softest songs, and beardless Frank Beard supports it (especially in

"Snappy Kakkie") with tricky drumfunk ready for rap. With "El Diablo," "Ten Dollar Man," "Pan Highway Blues," "Avalon Highway," all bandidos on the gallows pole and crazy lank-legged honeys, this installment's loaded with tumbleweed mythology so whimsically tongue-in-cheek it borders on camp. Even in the mere pedestrian get-off stuff, Billy's dustblown bwa-aangs reverberate in your head ten seconds after he's plucked 'em. "She's a Heartbreaker" 's as funny and felt a drawl-punk beer-cry as any Jason Ringenberg or Tony Kinman uncorked in the Scorchers or Rank and File a decade later, and "Arrested for Driving While Blind" 's hard-charging DWI warning is highly recommended to Vince Neil. I doubt ZZ performed it on the tour Schlitz sponsored.

279. THE REDS

. . . .

The Reds A&M, 1979

Pennsylvania roughnecks who've got a chemistry class and want a piece of your ass, the Reds sometimes button their white collars at the top, yet their riff-and-organ tones are so garbagey that upon initially hearing "Self Reduction" on an AOR station (back when AOR still played such stuff) I thought somebody'd finally knocked some sense into Deep Purple's heads. So how they passed as anorexic-cravat new-wavers beats me. Rick Shaffer spits his bitter banter rapid-fire as often as not, yelping at wrongness everywhere. There's more dronehooks and less supernumerary frills and flurries here than on their later invisible-label follow-ups—"Lookout" 's a seven-minute tower of power that would've made these bombastically pessimist miniaturists the new Iron Butterfly if A&M would've given 'em a real shot; "Whatcha' Doin' to Me" is Jimmy Page pogoing payback on Sid's grave; and the other perturbitude is compressed but complicated, not so much "arty" as just impatient. Sorta like if Joy Division had come from a Philly suburb instead of some stupid factory burg in Blighty.

280. JOAN JETT AND THE BLACKHEARTS
I Love Rock 'n Roll Boardwalk, 1981

Until Axl and Slash came along, the surprise title-blockbuster looked as if it'd wind up as the hardest-rocking number-one "rock" single of the eighties (i.e., "disco" 45s have hit number one that rock harder, get it?), plus it's got a jukebox in it, so it can't be all bad. Classicist-but-unretro slam-glam from a twenty-one-year-old who'd been around for a long time, it certainly felt trashier and more aggressively tuneful than the remnants of rococo rock and powerpap that elsewise clouded the airwaves at the time. "Be Straight" beats like a hambone; "(I'm Gonna) Run Away" gets its portly riff from Randy Bachman; our heroine plates "Little Drummer Boy" in chromium (a barfable carol, as carols go, and if her version is no match for New Kids on the Block's, at least she doesn't serious it up like Bob Seger does); "Nag"'s some obscure Halos oldie that sneers like "Yakety Yak" for grownups. For gold diggers there's Tommy James and Dave Clark Five too. And "Victim of Circumstance" and "Love Is Pain" boohoo into the bozodom you'd expect, but when Joan's up to snuff she can rip relationships in half with fewer lies than anybody. Or at least she could, back then: Ever since *Glorious Results of a Misspent Youth,* a wanky '84 job aimed at the Ratt/Crüe shagmetal fandom, she's usually just seemed ready to go to sleep.

281. RHYS CHATHAM
Die Donnergötter Homestead, 1989; rec. 1977–86

The dissertations on this drastically classical compos(t-heap)er's '82 Kraut import *Factor X* kissed too much brass to matter much in non-artghetto terms, but here he mainly sticks with plugged-in guitars (a half-dozen of 'em sometimes, though not like you can count 'em or anything) and hires drummers who can halfway hold down the fort (no more of this James Lo

dweeb, whose primary claim to fame is defanging Curtis Mayfield's "Pusherman" in the Gentle-Giant-reminiscent cult act Live Skull). Hence, for a change, the mathematical textures do more than just woosh fragilely above your scalp: Amp up the side-long title-epic half as loud as Lamont Young disciple Rhys

does live and suddenly you're out in winter's grayness slowly scaling Mount Olympus with a proton-pack on your back, ringing riffs crisscrossing each other like skinny Greek goddesses playing nude Twister as you reach the summit. "Waterloo, No. 2" is not the Abba sequel you'd hope but rather a formidable fife 'n' drum ceremony; "Guitar Trio"'s nearly a Rocket from the Tombs backing track. And though post–minimal/serial/indeterminal/tonal theoreticalism is a given, the black-tied rehearsedness contributes to the grandeur more than it obliterates it.

282. BLACK PEARL
. . . .
Black Pearl Atlantic, 1969

Lo-fi blooze-machismo featuring two ex-Moultymates from the Barbarians, this has beach bums working hard to earn their place 'tween Lady Soul and Wicked Pickett in Ahmet Ertegun's Atlantic Records fold. They haven't the first clue how, o'course, so instead they manage a slowed-down Stoogedom that smells as if it just slithered out of some ancient spiderwebbed basement trapdoor where years ago you stopped hiding between-meal burgers so mom wouldn't find out. Percussive additives in "Forget It" and "Mr. Soul Satisfaction" and the superlative Temptations-robbery "Climbing Up the Walls" dance the funkiest chicken this side of the San Diego Padres' mascot, and the singer even calls himself "B.B." Chortling toward superspadedom and gargling ectoplasm like Slimer Ghostbuster, he writhes across your floor with corneas a blur, hunting for scraps of bread. When Muslims call him a white devil, he takes it as a compliment.

283. SONIC YOUTH
. . . .
Sister SST, 1987

Select portions would stand fine on a dumbly, pleasurably tuneful level up against "Livin' on a Prayer" or "Head to Toe" or "Battleship Chains," which is to say that given the chance they'd even go over well on midwestern expressways where people have *taste*! First a fat hollow radio-drum sample keypunches itself into an innocuously unforgettable one-instrument-at-a-time melody, and when Thurston Moore's monotone rasp hitches up half an octave in "Stereo Sanctity" and "Tuff Gnarl," damned if I don't hear something like tenderness. But the flaw's more than just straitjack-

eted rhythms and disjointed lyrics and indistinguishable filler—where music this apocalyptic really oughta thrill or excite or at very least disturb, these sawtoothed electrostatics and spacy cyborg pulses and pummeling go-cart-down-a-slippery-slope Venom riffs are mild diversions devoid of emotional effect. The spoken interludes aren't suspenseful, just soggy; the quieter grind-clangs aren't "stark" or "chilling," just lulling. Too colorless, too cold, too jaded, too mannered, never articulating any real anger or scorn, the Youths aren't crazies so much as cracked actors.

Sister refines *Evol*'s bubbleskronk breakthrough with keener pop-formal accommodations; consistent but not revolutionary, it's *Afterburner* to *Evol*'s *Eliminator* (or more to the point, as a friend suggested, *Spectres* to *Evol*'s *Agents of Fortune*). Along with the CHR tributes, we get a pastoral folkboogie interlay in "Pacific Coast Highway," a straightahead 4/4 raveup in the revival of Frisco record-collector idols Crime's "Hot Wire My Heart." Mucho TV movie/pulp fiction trash-horror/sex/God fantasies add up to the usual nothing much, and unless you buy the bull that pretends beatnik pretentiousness is somehow less pretentious than normal pretentiousness, the Summer of Hate iconography eventually hits you as narrow. The cornball way the guitars in the catchier ditties inevitably build toward clatterful acid-rain mayhem even when nothing's otherwise anthemic suggests the band thinks it's cleverer than the popjunk it's so fond of plundering after all. Which makes it patronizing, campy, cynical, and full of shit.

284. TEENAGE JESUS AND THE JERKS
. . . .
Teenage Jesus and the Jerks Lust/Unlust EP, 1978

One more song than *Foghat Live,* but the whole thing's over after 9:06, and it's not as if that's not long enough to get the idea. A bang-the-same-note-till-it-sinks-in power trio led by sometime porn actress Lydia Lunch and produced by sometime somebody Robert Quine, this jerks herkily, with some of the most gnarled, intestine-knotting, soul-inflected slide-massacring in the history of the species; in the essential "Red Alert" and "Orphans" and "Freud in Flop," antimelodies I've almost got memorized by now (great for filling space at the end of party tapes), the CBGB waitress up front shreds your fingers into icicles, squawking like a tone-deaf Sea Scout who's just discovered a wolverine in her rice pudding. (Lester Bangs once drew a connection between "Orphans" and Yoko Ono's 1969 "Don't Worry Kyoko, Mummy's Only Looking for a Hand in the Snow," but an earlier ancestor may well be a cheerful old hillbilly ditty called "The Orphan Girl," which, according to Charles White's liner notes to the Delmore Brothers' *Sand Mountain Blues,* has been traced back as far as 1855. The Delmores called the song "Frozen Girl," and if you haven't figured out the subject matter by now, you're not paying attention.) Anyhow, only the Jerks' "Baby Doll" hints at the bogus graveyard kitsch Dame Lunchbox eventually learned to buffalo New York hepcats with. It lasts ninety-two seconds.

285. LAST EXIT
· ·
The Noise of Trouble Enemy, 1987

Shannon Jackson's cans and Bill Laswell's bass set up this contorted sonic obstacle course; Peter Brötzmann and Sonny Sharrock charge through it alert and avenging as Sergeant Sadler's Green Berets, their respective sax-blat and ax-blat bayonets drawing the goopy kind of mustard-yellow pus that sticks your fingers together. "Jazz" in the sense of the Ornette/Blue Cheer connections in R. Meltzer's *The Aesthetics of Rock* or the Coltrane/Slayer connections on Public Enemy's *It Takes a Nation of Millions,* this is club-emptying smashing-windshields-with-a-sledgehammer arson by men old enough to be your dad, maybe even your grandpa. Kicked into gear by a five-song sequence that alternates chaos and blues boy-girl-boy-girl-style, this live-in-Tokyo date's more listenably balanced than Last Exit's debut, not quite as balls-out. The set-closer's a surprise, an anguished Ayleresque lament called "Help Me I'm Blind," spiced with a pinch

of Brazil from guest Herbie Hancock's keyb-tangoes. But "Bassmetal," as its title implies, is Laswell-heavy crunge, and "Blind Willie," redeveloped from Sharrock's *Guitar* and *Black Woman,* is '75-vintage Led Zep swaggering triumphantly across the parade-fields of Valhalla—to a pachyderm cadence lifted from "Tusk" by Fleetwood Mac!

286. DEEP PURPLE
· · · · · · · · · · · · ·
Machine Head Warner Bros., 1972

The imploding roar of "Highway Star," probably the most exciting thing Ritchie Blackmore ever had anything to do with, makes the Indy 500 look like a Roman chariot race; "Space Truckin'," probably the most intelligent thing Ritchie Blackmore ever had anything to do with, concerns clog-dancing with extremely large feet around Alpha Centauri R. Crumb–style. "Pictures of Home" is a postcard from the land of ice and snow, and "Smoke on the Water" (which my high school marching band useta play real loud in the parking lot every day and we could hear 'em all the way down the block) has an emormous riff that is overshadowed only by Roger Glover's intriguing use of the adjective "stupid" as a noun. The remaining seventeen minutes are showboatingly Moogified coldplod jackboot drabness, as are some of the twenty minutes I've already discussed.

287. ROSE TATTOO
· · · · · · · · · · · · · · · · · · ·
Assault and Battery Mirage, 1981

The sophomore effort by this stout-chuggin' marsupial-metal crew is one more round to bend your elbows and snap your suspenders to: "Sidewalk Sally" 's got nifty see-Spot-run linguistics, "Let It Go" chronicles pack-prowling and backseat sex to an oozebeat whose pretty face is going to hell, "All the Lessons" furthers my Angry Anderson/David Allen Coe analogy by discussing burning bridges like Coe does in "Whiskey & Women"; "Chinese Dunkirk" 's got more feedback than was legal at the time; "Assault and Battery" steals from the rich and gives to the poor; "Magnum Maid"'s a law-and-order plea starring a shapely answer to Dirty Harry; "Manzil Madness" raids alleys like a junkyard dog; "Suicide City" ends it all like Cheap Trick's "Auf Weidersehen," with this kamikaze elasticizing "soo-wah-side" over and over. (Coincidence note: Coe's *Human Emotions* finishes with something called "Suicide," as does Dust's *Hard Attack;* the former even has a "Happy Side" and a "Su-i-side.") Despite a solidity-of-sound courtesy AC/DC think tank Harry Vanda and George Young, Anderson's bald howl sometimes seems it's already sliding downtube, but when he drools "I got the money honey, you got the buns," you know he's got a while to wait before Kylie Minogue lets him score her soap operas. Six years, at least.

288. ACCEPT
Balls to the Wall Portrait, 1984

A midget spark plug clad in battle dress and surrounded by shirtless German gay blades, Udo Dirkschneider wants to "plug a bomb in everyone's arse," and he sings at the tiptop *Luftwaffe* register, as if he's being strangled by someone with very big hands. (And you know what big hands mean, right? Yup, just like Pee Wee Herman said in his first movie—big *gloves!*) From the back, and from a distance, you'd confuse this with AC/DC's *Back in Black,* but real quick you notice all that rough-trade hair on those shapely male thighs—this would be AC/DC if AC/DC were as AC/DC as their name implies, if "She's Got Balls" were metal's answer to "Lola." Though the drums squish like slush and there's specks of baroqueness, mostly these bulging bondage-rockers pitch rapid red bricks, but the best part's the words, like when Cruising Udo stumbles on brutes sucking each other off in a Frankfurt park. Thug gangs yell out "God bless ya" behind him, and in a more helpful advice column than Ted Nugent's mom will ever manage, he recommends you solve all your gal problems by writing a letter. When he's "feeling the power of lust when the guy's passing by," he gets *real excited,* his

leer leaves no doubt. "It would be good to do it the nice way," he slobbers onto his bedmate's navel, "but sorry I ain't got no time."

289. HALF-LIFE
Half-Life Quadruped cassette, 1986

By far the least serene and most bracing of the eleven-or-so mainly instrumental C-30s let loose in the late eighties by graduates of the late-seventies Indiana pack MX-80 Sound, *Half-Life* molds transchordal, near harmolodic gyrations (and flick-themes from suspense-meisters Bernard Herrmann and John Carpenter) into straightforwardly gangliated riff-snorting stomps, taking time out for lovely spots to rend some hearts, but never letting smart-rock resourcefulness dilute hard-rock physicality. A digital machine named S. C. Norman completes Fender-bender Bruce Anderson's and bassman Dale Sophiea's triumvirate (nobody sings), but as with the best rustbelt-reared ax-zowie, these tunelets suggest life amid the manufacturing sector without celebrating industrial despotism. The abrasions gnash and gnarl the dark fantastic, and you don't look gift horsepower in the mouth.

290. SONNY SHARROCK
Black Woman Atco, 1969

Monkey Pockie-Boo's ungraspable anarchy and *Paradise*'s unsavory ivory came later, so of Sonny's three incomparably strident precomeback LPs, this one's easiest to make sense of, and I'll take it over his mostly lackadaisy live-in-Paris '82 trio-date *Dance with Me Montana,* too. It's ghostly blues, with wife Linda caterwauling mystical moans rooted in religion (and X-rated movies) as much as in the chitlin circuit, and in the monastic Middle Ages and even Islam as much as in any strain of Aframerican Protestantism, though she touches every base I've listed. Unfurling with idyllic subtlety in the traditional "Bialero" and in a stripped-bare version of his oft-recorded "Blind

Willy," oozing up like hot lava from the curdling bass-and-drum planetcore in "Peanut," refined holding actions exploding into disconnected-note cluster-thunder as the piano player runs for the hills, Sharrock's squawk simmers. The open-expanse emotionalism's out of John Coltrane and the celestial-omniverse antilogic's out of Cecil Taylor, but the titanic fulminations come from Otis Rush's hell groans, Ike Turner's bashed-in amp, Link Wray's wangbar.

291. POINT BLANK
. . . .
Point Blank Arista, 1976

You stare down a shotgun's two long eyes when you stare at the cardboard this where-the-buffaloes-gore buttmetal's protected by, and that's pretty much how the riffs feel, 'cept maybe the lead's aimed at your spine 'stead of your forehead, and the rebels in charge are what Woody Guthrie once referred to as Vigilante Men. From five guys who look as mangy and musclebound as they sound even though one of 'em only stands as tall as the other four's shoulders, this is state-of-the-fart home-on-the-range-and-the-burner's-on-high I-fought-the-law-and-the-law-ran-away-with-its-tail-through-its-legsmachismo-rock,with a vokist harrumphing as if he's Fat Albert's country cousin. "Wandering" 's a cold-steel-rail symphony that stings like the flight of the bumblebee hives Rimsky heaved at Korsakov, which is sneaky 'cause the very *next* cowpie (there's eight all told) is called "Bad Bees." But there ain't shitfuck hereabouts can touch "Lone Star Fool," where John O'Daniel ponders the asininity of a typically wing-tipped Joe Cool who drives around blasting "psychedelic music for the teenage crowd" and bragging 'bout the city when in truth he ain't nevah once left Texas. As they say in the Ozarks, fucken ay.

292. THE JIMI HENDRIX EXPERIENCE
. . . .
Electric Ladyland Reprise, 1968

He's got lotsa competition, so I suppose it's possible that the gentleman with the cowboy hat isn't the most blatant bore ever to pick up a guitar, and he certainly makes some swell sounds now and then. But he sure has the damnedest time writing songs with *hooks,* y'know? On this overloaded twofer, show-offy stuff like "Little Miss Strange" and "Long Hot Summer Night" and "Electric Ladyland" has a bent lushness to it, and if I concentrate real hard I can appreciate the belladonna din in "Gipsy Eyes" and "And the Gods Made Love" and a couple minutes toward the end of "Moon, Turn the Tides . . . Gently, Gently Away." It's also nice how Jimi starts one side coughing and blowing his nose, but mostly I'm hoping somebody slips him a paraquat mickey. In "Voodoo Chile" he imitates some now-extinct African-American folk-form I forgot the name of, developing an alarmingly unshorn "tone" but often resembling some aged artifact who has trouble keeping his eyes open on stage; hearing the chaotic "Slight Return" version, I think, "Wow, this is really amazing—when does it end?" The cover's got barenekkid breasts bulbous and bronzed, but Jimi just sings about mountain lions and starfish. The only songs with enough life in 'em to keep the car radio tuned to are maybe "House Burning Down" (incendiary for the most part) if you're going real fast, maybe "All Along the Watch-tower" (does for Dylan what the Buggles' "Video

Killed the Radio Star" does for Bruce Wooley!) if it's late at night, and by all means "Crosstown Traffic," which not incidentally is one of the universe's best *dance* songs ever (a *lesson* for all you art 'n' rebellion nitwits). Whatever history claims for the rest amounts to a big fat fib.

293. BUDGIE
Bandolier A&M, 1975

The meanwoman blooze calls itself "Breaking All the House Rules and Learning All the House Rules" (in that order, probably!), and "Napoleon Bona-Part One" is six times as long as "Napoleon Bona-Part Two"! "I can't see my feelings," Burke Shelley complains, but maybe if he banged a hammer on his thumb a few times he wouldn't have that problem! He insists he's "no mountain," when everybody knows Leslie West's in a *different* band! The pot roast smokes thermogenic: Hi-grade Zepboogie progressivism, a rhythm-pair that could empower a hospital's worth of life-support systems, Mahavishnoodled changes, lip-smacking lotusland lullabies, and on voracious voice Burke himself, the France Joli of the predisco era. Even more than on these clowns' first couple plate appearances, the Arthurian acoustica starts to kiss you goodnight after a while, but whaddaya want, a cookie or a chest to pin it on?

294. RUN-D.M.C.
King of Rock Profile, 1985

Though "Rock Box"'s "You Sexy Thing"–gone-Hendrix beatblare on their debut o'course initiated the idea (well, actually, Adventure's "Fantasy Eyeland" had suggested it three years earlier, Lightnin' Rod's "Doriella Du Fontaine" maybe a decade before that, but never mind), sophomore year's when the men in black selected to perpetuate riff-rap as their raison d'être, eventually enabling "much" "cold gettin' paid." (In flyguy-parlance, "rock" *equals* "metal," compre-

hend mah mellow?) In "King of Rock" they reverse the "Rock Box" riff and stake their claim as royalty, in the browner and brawnier "Can You Rock It Like This" they out-headbang most anything on most any Sabbath LP and thereby let the shit hit the fans. And that's about it: "You Talk Too Much" is where Anthrax learned to say "shut up," "You're Blind" 's a sludge-tempoed poke at lazy poor people, Jam Master Jay diddles distortion here and there. The brags and disses are nothing to write yo mama about, and Led Zeppelin's reggae was considerably less flimsy.

295. TRUST
Trust CBS French import, 1979

They are French, and they sing in French, and their songs have French titles such as "Bosser Huit Heures" and "Toujours Pas Une Tune," and you picture 'em carrying long loaves of bread on their shoulders. Bernard Bonvoisin splatters his perfumed patter not unlike Plastic Bertrand smashing end tables after receiving a very large phone bill, Nobert Krief fires up time-trial riffs as if he wishes he was in Motörhead, Jeannot Hanela (on *"batterie et percussions"*) is John Bonham under the influence of Giorgio Moroder, bassist Raymond Manna apparently worships Patrick Olive of Hot Chocolate. Lady soulsters add passionate depth to the remade AC/DC ballad (!), and when the drummer and bassist take solos, they are *disco* solos, syncopated enough for John Travolta to split his seams to under mirrorballs. Then, suddenly, the thrash comes back. If you suspect I'm exaggerating, check out these lyrics: *"Dans ce genre d'endroit t'excelle tellement t'es disco...."* I don't have the slightest what it means, but I get the idea, and it's real noticeable 'cause Bonvoisin chants it unaccompanied. Then without warning he yells "rock and roll!!!!" and it's speed-Sab time again. There's also loungey sax breaks, sickly groans, whorehouse piano, Framptonesque vocodered mouth-wah, police sirens, and castanet-clanked rhumbadelica, all for no reason except no outsider recommended otherwise beforehand. Doesn't appear to be any sort of cheap ironic eclecticism-as-statement, though o'course I could be wrong; either way, these beret-bangers belong in a cuckoo's nest.

296. BO DONALDSON AND THE HEYWOODS
Farther On Capitol, 1976

"Teenage Rampage," originally a Sweet song but so what, is scandalous, an adolescent oration for all times ("at thirteen they'll be learnin', at fourteen they'll be *burnin'*"), swarthy Chinnichap thundergum rebellion that's a note-for-note carbon of Chinnichap's (and Sweet's) "Blockbuster," except Bo's employees try to cackle like Alice Cooper on *Killer* instead, and atonal horn-charts serve no rationale you can figure. Next up's a choir of angels strumming harps and Mellotrons in honor of "our friend upstairs," apparently a cryptic reference to Billy of "Billy, Don't Be a Hero," the classic caveat that a four-year-old Deb Gibson tickled on the family ivories after Bo'd just topped the charts bandleading (but not singing!) it, thus providing him financial leeway for more esoteric ventures like this one. In a nervous quiver, Mike Gibbons sings "This Is Your Captain Calling," a plane-crash escapade that could've been penned by Blue Öyster Cult, and though you might be skeptical about the liner-boast that it took Rick Joswick *two whole Pepsis* to evolve that Billy Gibbons growl in "Shine It On," the proof's in the pudding. When Bo makes his off-key vocal debut in a strange Chuck Berry oldie with French and Yiddish words, it's ragtime wedding-band time till Earl Scott's ravaging Telecaster solo. Sensitive men of style, the Heywoods wear the sharpest duds ever: yard-wide bell-bottoms, skintight painter's pants, bullet necklaces, mile-high platform loafers. *Cheap* ones. They do half of Buddy Holly's "Oh Boy" as otherworldy a cappella, half as crunchy cow-metal, keep switching back and forth, for the heck of it. The program notes indicate they destroyed the song *on purpose,* and not even Tiffany's topped that move yet.

297. CHEAP TRICK
Dream Police Epic, 1979

Submerging its mirth under more boombast than Rick Nielsen's ever stacked before or since, their fresh-from-Budokan heaviness-move entails a simultaneous artiness-move that pegs it like *Billion Dollar Babies-*meets*–ELO's Greatest Hits* only not so clever, a shame 'cause cleverness was why these goombahs were born. But though virtuoso intricacy urges humor and hooks to exit stage left, the latter haven't quite deemed it appropriate to fully comply: The title hit's some mystifying metaphysics where your conscience returns to haunt you, "Gonna Raise Hell" 's ponderousness is halfway justified by the outside chance that Neilsen pillaged the backward mandocello-scratches from Chic's "Le Freak," rockabilly slurs and T. Rex jiggles counter the orchestra pit. "Voices" 's irksome glimpse at the band's bootlicking future exemplifies Side Two's predigested hackwork, and mostly the revelry's too implied to cut it, but with one ditty called "The House Was Rockin' (With Domestic Problems)," you can't exactly accuse 'em of waving the white flag. Yet.

298. THE LEATHER NUN
Alive Wire UK import, 1985

It cruises at you like a snowball made of tar, expanding exponentially as it rolls, and when it hits you want real bad to wash it off, but you can't. Despite exclusion of their four best songs, if you like your power raw-or-not-at-all these concert cuts are probably the best spot to start sullying yourself with Nun's pungent muck. The pretty ballad's dedicated to—surprise!—"a very special *girl,*" but Udo Dirkschneider groupies are welcome: The set refondles both sides of the combo's '81 "Primemover"/"F.F.A." 45, which backed some ugly auto-as-phallus symbolism with the most explicit depiction of getting your hands dirty I hope I'm ever exposed to (the chorus goes "let's fist again, fist and shout," so for Future Farmers of America you'll need to check out Terry

Allen). There's economy-sized crud-punchers like "Fly Angels Fly," "Son of a Good Family," and "On the Road," slimy midtempo sucktoons like "Busted Knee-caps" (complete with Nancy Sinatra reference) and "Lollipop" (no competition for Millie Small). In the fast tracks, bass and drums sway like *E Pluribus* Grand Funk as guitars ejaculate all over the rhythm section's big bottom; in front, Jonas Almqvist displays one of the harshest and deepest Scandinavian accents I've ever heard, as if he's always got a mouthful of some phlegmy substance. His words provide clues as to what that substance might be.

299. METALLICA
Garage Days Re-Revisited Elektra EP, 1987

When this came out, these Cali mosh-marauders were the pube-soundtrack for the post–market-crash recession; the sunny liner letter tells you not to take their bashed-out-in-five-days-in-a-stinky-carport cover songs too seriously, and what with the missed cues, hesitant starts, and 'tween-tune patter, not to mention the shouting contest that opens "Crash Course" and the doo-wop approximation that ends "Green Hell," you won't. With no humping throb to keep it carnal, the delirium gets indulgent, even predictable, when it stretches past five minutes on the A-side's two new-wave-of-pomp-metal remakes, and it's creepy that the most endearing hookline is a brag that the singer just murdered your baby, and it doesn't mean that much to him as long as she's dead. But the B-side's just a gang of malligators ballbusting their fave gooney-tunes: Advancing from preslush tribal-doom innovators Killing Joke to cult-object early-seventies sludge-sockers Budgie to a quick catchy pair from the Misfits (Jem and the Holograms' archenemies!), Metallica bang their collective brain-pans vehemently enough to dislodge cobwebs and knock the 'taters from your ears.

300. PATTI SMITH GROUP
Radio Ethiopia Arista, 1976

The Ronettes had nothing to do with Rimbaud in the first place, and God didn't make little green angels and sphinxes, and Kate Bush and Throwing Muses and the Sugarcubes and Skinbrain O'Connor are all this former BÖC sideperson's fault, and her one metal job's got no fight-for-love-and-glory half as ecstatic as "Gloria" on it, and like always she babbles like too many of the deteriorating hippie creeps I frequently just missed running over as they staggered aimlessly down the center of the left-turn lane during my tenure in Ann Arbor (where there's a bigger fine for drinking beer in public than for smoking dope), but (where was I?) anybody with a bladder can relate to the "Piss Factory" sequel "Pissing in a River," and there's yet more excrement (sex, too, though in '76 Donna Summer had her beat) in "Poppies," and if doing one's dootie ain't the great equalizer, what is? Flipside's where Lenny Kaye takes Patricia's Stooges fixation into a less conjectural realm, and she does the most damage when she's pumping her fist (*on* something?) and heart. The we-are-the-world title-opus constitutes her obligatory eternal-length move (12:01), and doesn't so much "hold up" as just *hold.* The "Beauty will be convulsive or not at all" note had been long-forgot by the time she came back motherly and meaningful in '88, and I bet she shaves her armpits nowadays, too.

301. MEAT PUPPETS
Meat Puppets SST EP, 1982

Though they made HM "moves" later ("Lake of Fire," "Liquefied," "I Just Want to Make Love to You" live, the depressing ZZ Top attempts on *Out My Way* and *Huevos*), here's the only instance where these substance-abused Arizona firecats truly got down and dirty in the mildewed and stalagmited wine cellar of it all. You can already detect how they've maintained

Photograph by Joe Cultice

the wide-awake naivete they were born with, how they've absorbed all that fog and dust and sand and tumbleweed, but mostly what you hear is Curt Kirkwood's prickly Crazy Horse rustic-rust guitar cutting every least-taken path across his brother Cris's hyperfunk bass toward crazed bluegrass-bebop-skronk. Brilliantly titled titles like "Electromud" and "Melons Rising" zero in on the crooked heavycore sprig that droppable names like Die Kreuzen and Prong and Beyond Possession would branch off from. The Kirkwoods stand around staring at things that aren't there, asking questions that have no answers; by ignoring the forest for the trees, they help you notice virtue and strength in a rotten world. And at this early juncture in their journey at least, they're not so cutesy you'll throw up on 'em.

302. RED LORRY YELLOW LORRY

Smashed Hits Red Rhino, 1988; rec. 1982–87

"An MC5 for the eighties" my butt—the MC5 had brains, not to mention balls (not to mention they could *sing,* sort of). But if I can grin and bear sixties and seventies pretension I can grin and bear eighties pretension too, and these crash-happy but otherwise glum Sabbath-night-fever Goths get a surprisingly enticing crawl-groove going from just twang and churn, a fat pulse from primarily electronic machines, a pleasant buzz from pagan drones and tones, medium-energy hooks from the way riffs twist around

bass lines. Moaning their emotionless extreme-unction mantras about masochism and hateful intellectuals and how liquor lays 'em low, they're pasty cadavers who've at least finally seen fit to venture beyond their coffins, which is more than you can say for fellow sadguys Sisters of Mercy, whom Metallica's Kirk Hammet is said to be a big fan of. "Take It All"'s got its "Sister Ray" trance down pat, and when somebody adds a real drum in "Cut Down," the levee breaks.

303. MINISTRY

A Mind Is a Terrible Thing to Taste Sire, 1989

Al Jourgensen and his shifting Chicago slimepool of death-disco-phony cronies attract underage skinheads, artsy-crafties, clubbers, headbangers, everybody; their albums go Top 200, quite an accomplishment. I like the "phony" part—dancey/prancey synth-dweebs since 1982, Ministry perked up some on 1986's Adrian Sherwood–manglated *Twitch,* and soon they were as loud as any noiseboys anywhere. I take 'em about as seriously as if Duran Duran suddenly turned into Motörhead.

On *Thing to Taste,* I can make out nine or ten words, tops: The pointlessly quasidecadent anger-chants are buried beneath too much gunk to induce irritation like Jourgensen's histrionics in Revolting Cocks or Lard or 1000 Homo DJs (I swear I'm not making these up) or whoever. So as far as I can tell the songs make no overt attempt at either message or antimessage. The barked-command samples are as ridiculous as the garbage-dump grunge-riffs, and the doomily dub-mixed synbeats are midnight muzak for people who build bridges all day. If you resign yourself to the inevitability that it's not gonna piss you off or depress you (which I gather is what it *wants* to do), you can give in to the crunch and let it make you feel ridiculous. "I only kill to know I'm alive," some hoarse lamebrain groans. "So what?" somebody answers, which by now is the only answer such a hackneyed lie deserves. If Ministry had intended to concoct a merry parody of eighties noise-punk, *Thing to Taste* no doubt wouldn't work as one. But it does: They should've named this record *Pure Glop for Now People*. One cut quakes and shouts exactly like Big Black, another like Voivod, another like *Another Man's Sac* Butthole Surfers, another like some dime-a-dozen LA hardcore band, others like Killing Joke and Public Image Ltd. before they started (and I stopped) believing their own shticks. I appreciate such music chiefly as nostalgia anymore, and that's how Jourgensen treats it—as a sound to be referred back to. The live EP they put out in 1990 is even better!

304. HÜSKER DÜ
Zen Arcade SST, 1984

Gloss-barrage shouts, two discs worth of 'em, with reams of Bob Mould guitars thick like fluffy blankets knitted by your grandma, freshly laundered, and still warm. Also, a message: Dogma sucks, but that's no reason to kill yourself. Out of twenty-three songs, three are unforgettably anthemic ("Something I Learned Today," "What's Going On," "Turn on the News"), two are dependably defeatist ("Somewhere," "Newest Industry"), three are touchingly sad ("Never Talking to You Again," "Whatever," "Pink Turns to Blue"), three are agreeably pretty ("The Tooth Fairy and the Princess," "One Step at a Time," "Monday Will Never Be the Same"), one might be better if it weren't so hazed-up ("Chartered Trips"), three are psychedelic jackoff ("Dreams Reoccurring," "Standing by the Sea," "Reoccurring Dreams"), four are punk-rock jackoff ("Indecision Time," "Beyond the Threshold," "Pride," "I'll Never Forget You"), three are more or less just there ("Broken Home, Broken Heart," "The Biggest Lie," "Masochism World"), and one sounds like Adam and the Ants ("Hare Krishna"). That's a second-division winning percentage, .478, except really it's much lower, since "Reoccurring Dreams" lasts fourteen minutes and two of the agreeable pretties average less than a minute each. The band is too mindful of its own "integrity," and though sometimes the group therapy pays off, usually it doesn't. Side Three's just fine.

305. MINOR THREAT
Out of Step Dischord EP, 1983

More dynamic and less deluded than their 'core brethren even as seven-inch sticklers ('81's little *In My Eyes* is their real showpiece), DC's band of bald puritans almost certainly could've benefited from a guzzle or toke or three, but there's no denying that Ian MacKaye's straight-edge spit-shout disgorged more than its share of standing-on-the-verge-of-adulthood disillusionment, that Brian Baker's and Lyle Preslar's guitar-blitz never once resorted to the shortest distance between two points. This sign-off's all about friends finding less and less need for each other's company as they reach some major-league age, and if the narrators make more of this private predicament than logic says they ought to (a half-decade later in Fugazi and Dag Nasty, Baker's and MacKaye's scope of discussion hadn't changed much), that's not to suggest they never make sense of it. To me, the thoughts convey the most forlorn sting when they slow down toward the end of each side—in "Look Back and Laugh" and especially in the hidden "Cashing In," a two-part brawn-chorded nonapology from imminent ministars who aren't sure whether they should regret having climbed so high. Ends with this sparkling wash of strings, which to this day burns with self-knowledge, a subculture biting the dust.

306. TED NUGENT
Ted Nugent Epic, 1975

For one thing, it's interesting how Derek St. Holmes howls like Ozzy. Also, here's about the only instance post-Amboy that the Terrible One got away with doing *long* songs. To wit: "Stranglehold," a gradually accelerating eight-minute wrestling metaphor that gets nearly all its hypnotic tension from skinbeater Cliff Davies's automatic-as-the-mechanical-steer-in–*Urban Cowboy* "When the Levee Breaks" routine. Peaking, everything slows down, and Ted begins gnarring his theory that immortality's your choice and yours alone. Though "Just What the Doctor Ordered" and some fusoid others are serious wastes of plastic, you'll garner a purely nihilsmic and annihilistic overdose of arrogant amorality from "Queen of the Forest" (for Mother Nature), "Stormtroopin'" (declaration of war), "Hey Baby" (lustmobile sleaze), "Snakeskin Cowboy" (for Jon Voight or Glen Campbell or somebody), and the fearsome "Motor City Madhouse" (more July '67 than October '68). On Woodward you couldn't drive defensively without 'em. (Unless you're brave, of course.)

307. MOVE
Shazam A&M, 1970

These fine English boys clobbered TV sets on stage, and some of 'em went on to bow big and little violins in the Electric Light Orchestra (thereby transforming *Sgt. Pepper* into the classical bubblegum it should've been all along—see Randy Newman's "Story of a Rock and Roll Band" for complete history), but here they're into a super-reflexive proto-postmodern sort of pop-art flower-metal, often fairly uneventful but sometimes elevated toward noble grandiosity. There's no tunes about extinct reptiles and nothing as delectable as their "Go Now" single, but pansied pinky rings like "Beautiful Daughter" are tinted brightly Brit with absurd chorals, and the 'tween-track person-on-street interviews are daringly darling—some old lady opines that pop muzik's "nice in its own way," but "not when they go naked." "Cherry Blossom Clinic Revisited"'s got catchy quotes from Bach's "Jesu, Joy of Man's Desiring" and other eighteenth-century hits, and the wah-wah sonata penned by an Oklahoma folk-revivalist is eclipsed only by the slow Stooge-plodder penned by a Brill Building team. Those were the days.

308. LORD TRACY
Deaf Gods of Babylon Uni/MCA, 1989

They recorded in Hollywood and their fan club's in New York, which is appropriate, because their groove and demeanor establish some midpoint between quasi-Godz Eastern Seaboard cycleboy bar-boogie and quasi-Crüe Whiskey-a-Go-Go pay-to-play sleaze-rock—good rhythm section, blues and booze base, decent riffage, striped turbans, lotsa sweat. Terrence Lee Glaze has a little more Bruce Dickinson in his vocal cords than any proud American pump-jockey oughta try to get away with (he really has to strain to hit those high notes), and the first six or seven tunes cover yer usual male-bonding/whore-fondling/bitch-dissing/woo-pitching/hard-living terrain in a more or less merely competent manner, though that "no more Amazon underwear" line is pure Dictators and the title "Barney's Wank" is as honest as Spın̈al Tap and "Whatchadoin'" generates the amiable rhythmic-cum-harmonic buzz of early Cheap Trick. But not until the CD's half gone do these degenerates really show what they're made of: In order of occurrence, they line up a Chicago blues moan about being a macho transvestite, some dog-kennel sludge about a cowboy nightstalker who winds up as roadkill, a post-Coasters jungle-minstrel-counterrhythmed rap about a three-headed girlfriend, a one-riffed drawl with sexual nonconformists plus a musique concrète toilet flush in it, "a song about a fish," and some natty tinkling of the ivories on the way out. Genuine eccentrics, and not as dumb as they look, or pretend.

309. THE CELIBATE RIFLES
Quintessentially Yours What Goes On, 1985

These well-read if overprecious Aussies have a couple anti-Falklands scrawls where Britannia rules waves and waives rules (guess they're Budgie fans), and this hodgepodge of early kvetches climaxes with "God Squad," a Sabbathish thud where Damien Lovelock mouths off at Jerry Falwell. But Lovelock's best when he's ranting about the frustration that comes when life goes on after the thrill of living is gone: Nine-to-five tedium in "This Week," fear of not settling down ('cause you're "sick and tired of dad's homosexual jokes") in "Let's Get Married," trying to break free once you do settle down in the great single "Sometimes" (which you'll find somewhere else). Imagine a less loud *Brain Capers* Mott fronted by a more sarcastic prenostalgia Bob Seger—one guitarist plucks acoustically while the other plants three-second H-bombs between verses, or they both push their pedals to the heavy metal. Here, the maelstrom lets up only for "Ice Blue," a silencing Replacements-style arena hymn to a heroin casualty who didn't fear the reaper. Unfortunately, it only took another LP or three for the incessant catchy/political/smashup aura to reveal its true identity as a lack of ingenuity.

310. HARD STUFF
. . . .
Bolex Dementia Phonogram, 1973

Each of the first six cuts kicks harder than the one that preceded it, so though the initial couple opi are mystigogically laid-back fluff making mention of cellos and manatees (which Hard Stuff still believe are "mermen"), before you know it you're getting shoved around by a few Noddy Holder rugby-booters, one ("Roll a Rocket") with blue suede shoes and orangutans, one ("Jumpin Thumpin'") with a "punky little honey just alookin' for some money," one ("Dazzle Dizzy") with a speedrush that knocks you down as guitarlines twist around your bod like the twine of Lilliput. With "Libel"'s David Essex–like clap-beat and the funky bass line "Ragman" shoplifts from "Bad Moon Rising" or "Sweet Mary" or somewhere, Side Two showcases pop tendencies. And the weird vocal slowdowns in the title slugger prove that Voivod didn't invent Neanderthals from Neptune.

311. JEAN-PAUL BOURELLY
. . . .
Jungle Cowboy JMT West German import, 1987

Word-of-mouth dubbed him the "next" Hendrix/ Hazel/Sharrock/Ulmer/Reid heir to T-Bone Walker and Johnny Guitar Watson, which is to say he's black and plays guitar; sometimes if the volume's up, it hurts

your ears. He grumbles in that bluesman-gone-self-conscious tongue-tone (sounds like Dr. John sometimes), compresses and contorts the funk behind him (Julius Hemphill's alto sax helps quite a bit), showboats on the beat, updates Memphis Slim's "Mother Earth." He makes me pay attention when he's galvanizing up a tight-packed racket (in "Tryin' to Get Over," "Jungle Cowboy," "Groove with Me," select parts of "Drifter"), and I wish his burnin' love was always as hunky as it is in "No Time to Share." He's insinuatingly soulful usually, too damn refined almost always, intrusive never, full of himself almost never. I wish he didn't take himself so seriously. His record's pretty much what you'd expect, nothing you'll hate, nothing you'll go gaga over—something you'll pull out of the stacks once in a while, then put back when you're done.

312. METALLICA
. . . .
Kill 'Em All Megaforce, 1983

Before their power got some finesse and they started documenting real life, Metallica were four kids just entering their twenties and looking five years younger. Their adrenaline was "full speed or nothing" (so sez one lyric), with few of the quasi-progressive intricacies it'd adapt later, but that's not to say it was unpretentious. "Blitzkrieg," tacked onto this debut's '87 Elektra reissue, suggests "Hocus Pocus" by Focus played double speed, and much of what's here is old Sabbath played the same way, but with no beat anymore. These are the group's shortest and simplest songs, all composed before Cliff Burton and Kirk Hammett joined, yet with a couple exceptions ("Metal Militia," "Anesthesia"'s dentistry joke, the unbelievably taut speaker-blower "Whiplash"), the smudge-purity lacks pizazz—sung by an actor who constantly sounds like he's throwing up his Sausage McMuffin, the mythological tales of phantom lords and vengeful gods and polka-dot (I wish) steeds belie the comparisons their velocity drew to Motörhead. Which is to say that though the righteous no-frills pyromaniacking was obviously commendable amid an LA metal-scene anchored by Ratt's and Quiet Riot's and Mötley Crüe's makeup kits, it was also kinda bland. And dumb.

313. THE MIGHTY GROUNDHOGS
. . . .
Who Will Save the World? United Artists, 1972

These Limey time-signature athletes knew how much wood a woodchuck would chuck if a woodchuck could chuck wood, and they were so noninfantile in their abstract catwalk-buildup-and-pussyfooted-fade variations of the hillbilly blues that they had a day named after 'em (February 2, which also marks the medieval festival Candlemas, named after some obscure warlock-rockers who're big fans of post-Ozzy Sabbath and the Swedish opera scene). More precise than intense, more tasteful structurally than sonically, the Groundhogs' emphasis on technique entailed a fixation with gadgets that can crack notes like atoms. Read their song and album titles, and you can't help but notice the extraordinary prevalence of the word "split."

On this record, for once, these laffless virtuosos open with some riff-mutations you can actually latch onto, and after that there's real hooks to go with all the space-age equipment you never heard of before. "Earth Is Not Room Enough," the catchiest song here,

has a sneaky Mellotron-loop Gary Numan eventually sequestered on *The Pleasure Principle;* "Death of the Sun" starts just like the Monkees' "I'm a Believer"; and the 'hogs even cover "Amazing Grace." Elsewise, per usual, the complexly rootsy detachment resembles a Hendrix-gravied version of the Hampton Grease Band's *Music to Eat* (which means nothing to you, I know), only not as much fun. Tony McPhee plays real challengingly and grainily and Krishna-like, as if he's been to school, as if he never realized Frank Zappa's a dork. His gruff slowburn slyness could be the work of some nonchalant seventies singer-songwriter non-conformist like maybe Hirth Martinez, but he's absorbed way too much pulpy lit, so his "keen wit" leans toward cyanide in the acid bath and tornado-felled buildings and junkies hoarding blood and soccer fans tossing rubbish out trains, plus the LP cover's a comic book. But when for ten minutes in "The Grey Maze" he shuts his curmudgeonly trap and proceeds to totally kick out the jelly, I start to believe that if he had half a personality I might like him a lot.

314. D.C.3
. . . .
The Good Hex SST, 1986

A reconstruction of the high-watt fuzzoid stampede employed in the early seventies, here's another good eighties idea that got old fast, but nowhere else at the time could you find this brand of astrosludge: Subscribing to the '69–'73 philosophy that says hooks are what count and the bigger the better, the formula slides a modally propulsive bottom (c/o ex-Stains Louie Dufau and Caesar Viscarra) under a simmering strange brew of swirlingly repetitive organ-figures and amateurish fretwork. Very varied, from blustery speed-Purple biltz ("Home Is Where You Hang Your Head") to thrusty G-Funk footstomp ("The Maniac"), and from Hawkwind/Floyd (the real one, not those Syd Barrett jokers)—swoop in the title track to gap-toothed early-ZZ belch in the remembrance of John Lee Hooker's "Bang Bang Bang Bang." Former Black Flagger Dez Cadena can't shriek with the precision of Ozzy or Sir Lord Baltimore's John Garner, but his one-note throat stumbles up and down the scale despite itself. And he delivers no sage words, but then again he doesn't claim to—I'll take a music that admits its dumbness over one that pretends to be smart any day. Rarely has blatant redundancy sounded so original.

315. URSA MAJOR
Ursa Major RCA, 1972

Wank-happy third-generation Detroitlings headed by sometime A. Cooper/L. Reed assistant Dick Wagner, Ursa Major made mood music for counterevolutionary nobodies, mixing massive thundering Dvořákisms with introspective extraterrestrial exhibitionism, just like everybody else. The rockingest pumper's about being born rich, the rockingest ruffler's about a groupie, the second-rockingest protest's called "Back to the Land" (and it ain't even mellow!). In the rockingest pump-ruffling protest, Wagner rallies against injustices against not just black people, but also *dead* people. Not to mention Indians, just like everybody else.

316. BECK, BOGERT AND APPICE
Beck, Bogert & Appice Epic, 1973

The worthiness of this disc derives primarily from the fact that you've got this famous and wealthy technique-master emerging as your dime-a-dozen stupid-trio idiot, admitting for once in his life that the "blues" ain't got beans to do with emotion and/or know-how, that only the size of the sound matters. (A hyperbole, maybe, but a relevant one, you gotta admit.) Most of *BBA* clogs up your living room real hardily, wah-wah-wise like a grain-reaper raping your bookcase like the blues is supposed to, and if the singer comes off rather semirough in "Oh to Love You" and "Sweet Sweet Surrender" and the like (not *necessarily* a liability, changes-of-pace being useful in and of themselves), resulting ickiness is more than made up for in "Superstition" (this being the *second*

LP containing Jeff that also contains a version of said Stevie-classic), whereon the gargantuatude of drums, bass, and guitar alike nearly permit me to forgive the Brit whacking the latter for helping invent "fusion."

317. BLUE ÖYSTER CULT
Spectres Columbia, 1977

Notable primarily for its tuneful leadoff sendup, where Godzilla peeks in windows and yanks high-tension wires and tosses buses around a fine philosophical chorus line, this attains higher speed and stamina scores than students of their later work would figure, and despite frequent drippy sections, even the segment dippily entitled (if Princely initialed) "R U Ready 2 Rock" isn't really all that unstomachable. There's a quasi-Nazi *bier-trinken* lieder, a shivery kitsch-slice called "I Love the Night," an apparent Ian Hunter cowriting credit on something called "Goin' Through the Motions" that unfortunately (on purpose probably, knowing these guys) earns its title. Still, the riffs are dinkier and the smirks more obtuse than ever before, and the aural light-show's only just begun.

318. BELFEGORE
Belfegore Elektra, 1984

All-time heroes of *CREEM*'s late great Triumvirate of Metal Wisdom, these Kaisers teamed up with Zbigniew Rybczynsky for one of the loopiest videos ever—"All That I Wanted" had everybody, even the camera, running away from *something,* we knew not what. The slowcore dirge-disco that produced said tune often devolves into this chic bored hush-hush, most notably in "Wake Up with Sirens" and "Belfegore," the sterile kind of quasi-sinister metronome-gonorrhea Chicago's Wax Trax label started dribbling out a couple years later, where I'd put on rubber gloves just to open the promo packages. But when he feels up to it, Meikel Clauss doesn't so much overdramatize as snap/crackle/pop syllables like Die Kreuzen's Dan Kubinski, and his cutthroat riffwork and throatcut hoatzin-hoot lift these bondaged brutes above their fashion-plate peers. "Love"'s got an intricate grind-tension that holds you off guard, and the astoundingly named "Comic with Rats Now" suggests Hugo Ball at Zurich's Cabaret Voltaire in 1916, reciting "gadji beri bimba glandiri laula lonni caderi" and so on, then Tristan Tzara repeating the word "roar" 147 times. The word juxtaposition frequently makes no sense at all: "Seabird seamoan, little Chinese caves." A deviant sacrificial ritual, a fortune cookie commercial, or both?

319. Back from the Grave, Volume 1
Crypt, 1985; rec. 1964–66

Tim Warren's this Jersey reactionary so tone-deaf he thinks eighties rockabilly bands rocked more lobsters than seventies disco bands, and what the original installment of his mostly nap-inducing nostalgia-series is good for is mainly rodents: First there's Akron's impossibly rude Rats, a junior high bike gang who make several pig noises and foot-solos, threaten to beat your face, and warn that your mom better walk ya home, all 'cause you made their fearless leader look like a fool. ("Super-giant sewer rats are everywhere, hanging from telephone poles. . !.") But when the Pelicans challenge to meet 'em in the local grocery's parking lot, the Rats chicken out, 'cause they don't like to fight! Then there's Pittsburgh's Swamp Rats, who just might have the most unwashed guitarist ever, and he shovels scum atop the Sonics' "Psycho" till Hugh Beaumont's chainsaw's dancing the Aqua Velva with Barbara Billingsley's vacuum cleaner. Additional toons have candy, orange juice, and peanut butter in 'em, but only One Way Streets' "Jack the Ripper" and the Cords' highly flatulent "Ghost Power" ring around your collar. It's all pretty darn inconsequential, and most of it ended up in the historectimic margins for the excellent reason that it's so half-assedly average that nobody outside the hamlets where these g-balls hailed from found any reason to give a darn. Which ain't to deny that there's twits a quarter-century-plus later who pretend to.

320. MX-80 SOUND
Hard Attack Island UK import, 1977

These bookworms rampaged out of a southern Indiana university town spritzing schizoid radiation in fast-forward motion, using improvisatory sax-quackery and photographic memories and clustered pandemonium and Lonnie Mack fan Bruce Anderson's distorted free-for-all to set some eternal noisecore standard. They delivered goods too ruggedly riddled with saber-toothed guitar to be shrugged off as a mere exercise in self-serving quirkiness, and unlike the pseudopsychos who eventually took over MX-80's saber-toothed underground, they offered crackpot humor that cut through their conceptual pretensions. Vokist Rich Stim's amiable chatter, about such bourgeois horrors as ice machines and all-terrain vehicles and CB radios, was purposely mundane, often downright corny: "A horse that lives for a year is a yearling, right?" he asks. "But a horse that lives for a week, is it a weakling?" Yet even on this debut, where their musical highway's less congested than it'd ever be again, Anderson's mulch is still more wash than punch, piling lusciously in "Summer '77" but too often just filling a hole, like Big Black ten years early. Plus, I wish future Spin-crit Stim sang more, like he does in "You're Not Alone," the only time he really yanks my heartstrings—his disengagement can get pretty effete, and if he's bored, why shouldn't I be bored too? I suspect that didn't bother anybody much in 1977, though.

321. FLAMIN' GROOVIES
Super Grease Skydog French import EP, c. 1983; rec. c. 1969

Robust retropunk fuzz-muck with two Chuck Berries and one horrific Stones cover, this tackles some of the territory Billy Gibbons would profit bigtime from a few years later, but there wasn't an audience for it yet. A mushmouthed live (and maybe live-in-studio) powerhouse of rural slide-raunch caked in the impurities that float on the surface of peat bogs, it's like Creedence trying to be the MC5; in the three slimiest tossoffs ("Slow Death," "Dog Meat," "Blues for Phyllis"), Roy Loney's murk-leads never stop thickening. You can't make out the words, but you can't miss the defeated disposition. And as for the mudpie of a sound, which leaves all the livestock in the barnyard either dead or dying, all you can do is dive in.

322. MOTÖRHEAD
No Sleep at All Enigma, 1988

What makes No Sleep 'til Hammersmith definitive is its disintegrated muffler, and there's no way this likewise-live sequel could have the same impact, not just 'cause Lemmy's later racket was more perimetered and percussive than it'd started out, but 'cause by this time we'd grown used to it. So this slab ain't what you'd call new business, and it's somehow pointless—with a repertoire so samey, who needs alternate versions? Lemmy himself calls the song-choice a "faithful reproduction of the current artistic" something-or-other, which stretches the truth: "Orgasmatron" is a more conclusive mid-eighties hitlet than "Eat the Rich" or "Deaf Forever" or "Killed by Death," and it's missing; same goes for "Shine," the only saving grace on '83's dreary Another Perfect Day. Still, with more wankoff than Motörheadheads are accustomed to, No Sleep II salvages and adds needed grime to the few good songs on '87's negligible Rock 'n' Roll, and in the end I think the clue to getting inside lies with the hammer-and-sickle T-shirt somebody's wearing in one of the inner-sleeve shots, maybe also the (ironic?) menorahs and stars of David on the songlist. Which is to say the reasons-to-own are bolshevik propaganda, "Eat the Rich" and the new "Just 'Cos You Got the Power," the latter of which fuzzes with non–wishy-washy exhilaration atop Philthy Animal Taylor's "Stranglehold"/"When the Levee Breaks" secure-the-beachhead groove for seven minutes flat. Both articulate and earned, this is one rare proletarian-struggle move. And it's buffered by

shrewd greeting of a stadium full of Finns: "We're lucky to be here, 'cause we shoulda died a fucking long time ago. But we didn't."

323. KISS
Dressed to Kill Casablanca, 1975

Jagger-'65 swagger to stomp your platforms and snap your mood rings to, even the plodders (for example, "Two Timer") show no mercy, which ain't to deny that they plod. The band struts most rooster-like when there's more harlots to choose from, like when some minuscule jailbait comes up to former schoolteacher Gene Simmons and sucks his dick right when he's about to go to sleep (pretty funny when he runs into her dad). And though the pure-simplistic-brute-force in old yellers like "Getaway" and "Room Service" and "Anything for My Baby" sounds like it came out of a pure-simplistic-brute-force machine, Paul Stanley's rhythm-riffs season "Rock Bottom" and "She" with necessary boogie, and "C'mon and Love Me" 's fanmags and zodiac signs are hepper still. "Rock and Roll All Nite," o'course, is comic-book shout at its dumb body-flattening peak, the most unarguable bubblemetal mixture ever, and as concise a statement of the hedonist worldview that its decade produced. The sum total's more or less a concept LP about kinky sex with groupies. If you're Andrea Dworkin or a

P.M.R.C. pen pal go ahead and be a moralist about it, but not disguising one's vices oughta count for something in this deceitful age, I'd say.

324. AC/DC

'74 Jailbreak Atlantic EP, 1984; rec. 1975–76

The title cut (recorded in '76, so beats me why the cover says '74) is kin to Thin Lizzy's song of the same name and the Coasters' "Riot in Cell Block #9" and Public Enemy's "Black Steel in the Hour of Chaos" as well, 'cept this time the escapee gets shot in the back, which is exactly what these youngsters of grungesterism do to the blues on this record. The pair of eight-to-the-bar barrel-rollers that follow "Jailbreak" are less than super, and though "Soul Stripper"'s badassed butt-naked bawdyism has a temptress rolling Bon in the hay and making him play games he don't wanna play, it'd be even funnier if it was shorter. But in "Baby Please Don't Go," it's like John Bonham's taking a bullwhip off a bed of hot coals and cracking it against your vertebrae. Makes ya hop around like a chihuahua.

325. DRAGONFLY

Dragonfly Megaphone, 1969

He-monkey Copenhagen-mouth blues and quick-time Diddleyfied tubplay marching toward eternity's end zone like a time bomb in your toilet, filling some remote and uncharted tumbleweed-strewn outback somewhere with addled Muddy Waters mojo and stumblebum waltzes and riff dynamics Pete Townshend (and Ron Asheton) wouldn't uncover till a year later and burnt TV dinners ZZ Top wouldn't uncover till 1983, plus deranged echo-chamber epistemology like this: "You can touch the sky with your elastic mind/Don't fall dow-ow-ow-ow-ow-ow-ow-own." The hairwagger in charge starts crying "ohhhhhh, my gawwwd" like all those black cat bones laid him on his

sickbed; from there, you get the idea he wants to be a galaxy when he grows up, or maybe he already is one.

Photograph by Naomi Petersen

326. SAINT VITUS

Born Too Late SST, 1987

Let's admit it right off—these mammals are an unabashed tribute to early Black Sabbath. As tributes to early anythings go, though, they're not all that limited by their backlooking: Blunt lumberjack howlistics (from Wino Weinrich, who don't shriek like Ozzy, which is neat), an able guitarist (Dave Chandler, who convulses all over the place and does these high-pitched Oriental things that make you wonder how), some of the most stunted tempos ever put to wax (especially in "Born Too Late," which always makes me double-check my RPM control), long piercing sobs of grief, wobblin' two-riff narwhal-blubber modalities. Side Two's sorta limp compared to Side One, but there's been no better Sab-plate since *Sabotage* nonetheless. Best factor, believe it or don't, is the words. First lines have organizational nowhere men pointing and cackling at Wino on the dirty boulevard, slandering his long locks and outdated threads, telling him he resembles a zombie with zilch between the earholes and his songs aren't fast enough. Except the way he relates this sad circumstance *rhymes*, so who says rock and poetry can't go hand in hand?

327. **BLACK FLAG**
. . . .
The First Four Years SST, 1988; rec.
1978–81

A good no-way-out to inaugurate Reagan's decade, from self-effacingly enraged LA tantrum-throwers addicted to the paranoid idea that this padded cell of a world's about to do 'em in. Spouses and bosses and cops and blacks are out to get 'em, yeah right, but if they think life is so damn hard for themselves, they oughta talk to some people who *aren't* football-player-shaped Caucasian thugs: "White Minority," an amusing David-Duke-style diatribe paradoxically sung by a Chicano who may or may not have been being facetious, was perhaps the first visible indication that an Aryan youth culture was imminent. Anyhow, this compilation showcases Flag's headlong teeter-totter rush in its larval and pupal stages, inventing hardcore from remnants of the metal that would one day reabsorb it; the pupal stage, with Dez Cadena singing, is best. Greg Ginn, with a post-Brit blur that's all buzz, tells stories with as few notes as any competing ax. The multiple-rendition and radio-commercial excrescence that helps fill four sides of *Everything Went Black* is largely absent, and not only are Keith Morris and Chavo Pederast and Dez not privy to the malaise-laden sham that Henry Rollins would eventually use to exterminate the group, Ginn is the least remedial songwriter the band ever had. "Who needs love when you've got a gun" is the best line any human has sung in any version of "Louie Louie," ever.

328. **HALO OF FLIES**
. . . .
Garbage Rock Twin/Tone EP, 1987

Beat-your-face-in music with what sure seemed like the huskiest drums and most brain-fritzing guitar on God's green earth at the time, this shed my reservations about these Minnesotans, who everybody I knew kept telling me were the second coming of whomever, seeing as how "you never know what they're gonna do next." See, for me, knowing what

they're gonna do next is at least a wee bit important, and while I'd always been theoretically "impressed" by the free-blues scuzz on HOF's previous (and way-rare) singles, I'd never been able to figure out what it was I was supposed to, you know, "grab hold" of—which is I guess to say the stuff lacked hooks. But though by their next EP they were back to square one, and though (not being a junkie) I was still annoyed by its superficially gonzoid verbal claptrap (an Achilles heel), *Garbage Rock* changed my take at least temporarily. The riffs come from U.S. Marine Gunnery Sergeant Tom Hazelmeyer, only I'm not sure if he's a gunnery sergeant or even if that's really a Marine rank 'cause I was only in the Army, but it matters not 'cause it sure sounds like Tom ingested a lot of Tabasco-upgraded chipped beef and beanie-weenie, like he's pouring Prestone antifreeze and Popov vodka into every sensory organ you've got, and he's using a funnel so none spills out (or "oot" as the Voivods say in Canada). Whopper-boogie that switches into *Funhouse* or *Vincebus Eruptum* or *Are You Experienced* for a couple seconds then skids into the garbage can and knocks Oscar the Grouch out to the Sesame gutter where he gets stomped on by Big Bird's big feet—connoisseurs more "with-it" than I insist this is Hazelmeyer's worst record, but I beg to differ.

329. **BIG BLACK**
. . . .
Racer-X Homestead EP, 1985

Stuffing every last fissure full of packed-tight bear-grease, two guitars abrade against each other like steak knives, like tanks in a real narrow ravine; they never manage to swing (at best they just bunch up all their gunk and jerk the "rhythm" with a vengeance), but they sure can kick. All these strings grind up uranium and squeeze out juice, offhand beats or brassy snatches of melodic clang make whole songs change direction, the beatbox pounds out a hammer-like disco-referent march that forces James Brown's "Big Payback" into a bulletproof straitjacket. With brusque bellows learned from Wire, white-trash pride from Skrewdriver, confrontational manner from the Fall's Mark E. Smith, Steve Albini speculates about the ubiquity of evil, about lust for power, about the degradation and even death we're willing to subject one another to out of fear or for entertainment. Here, the little Napoleon's pony-keg of puma piss is at its biggest and blackest, and there's nothing unreal about how he raises self-abuse to a life force in "Sleep!" nothing unconvincing about how his venom reduces seventies Japanese cartoon road hawg Speed Racer's "nip" brother's auto sport to a mere money-making vocation. There's also nothing unusual about how everything else is self-congratulatory Mickey Spillane ice pick–to-the-gonads "irony"—ultimately it's a bankrupt parlor game, an artpunk equivalent of *The Weekly World News.*

330. MX-80 SOUND
Out of the Tunnel Ralph, 1980

The blueslessly unmacho chamber-metal that Mellencamp country's handsome collegiate labcoat-wearers perfected linked to a twentieth-century pop tradition long divorced from rock 'n' roll. Bruce Anderson's schizzily atmospheric feedback-edge owes as much to Lalo Schifrin or Neil Hefti or Henry Mancini soundtracks as to *White Light/White Heat;* the twenty-first-century cathode-ray 3-D trundle underneath, almost Eurodisco in "I Walk Among Them," is automatic enough to pass for a silverware-pressing machine. The enigmatic lingo ("blame it on the bossa nova") is unhysterical, almost emotionless, a misanthropic stream of goofitude and postcapitalist isolation, sitting-alone-with-a-notebook-in-front-of-(B&W)-late-movies stuff. Weird, and worth hearing, but despite flashes of naive sacramental beauty in lipsmackers like "Someday You'll Be King," this crew's so cool and classy they live in a freezer. Not good for the blood flow, needless to say.

331. CHEAP TRICK
One on One Epic, 1982

Their only decent eighties LP is where they temporarily decided they were gonna settle down and be the Beatles once and for all, so as the proud owner of no Beatles albums that weren't purchased for under a buck with lots of scratches on 'em, I probably don't get all the clues. But the tunes are sharp—no overkill to speak of, just straight-shooter pop R&B, a glistening McCartneyesque lament called "If You Want My Love," "yeah yeah yeah"s and yelps and harmonizing and nonsense syllables wherever you turn. Not to mention Link Wray twang, Billy Squier funk, a casting couch, a phone song with triple entendres, and two slant-eyed robot moves. "She's Tight" rocks as hard and weird as anything on their first two albums. But there's no hits, for crissakes. Jon Brant's the odd bassist out, and Rick Nielsen tops his pineapple sweater with Tom Selleck's Tigers cap.

332. RANDY HOLDEN
Population 2 Hobbit, 1970

Super-morose overweight pseudo-Hendrix guitar-lust from a brainiac mercenary, ex of Blue Cheer and before that the Other Half (whose "Mr. Pharmacist" the Fall covered) and the Fender Four, this slab's original configuration is allegedly "worth" hundreds of dollars on the black market (some eighties German reish is rumored), but you're either mad or a millionaire if you pay that much for *any* record. Easy for me to say, o'course, 'cause I've already heard the thing, and it's kinda threatening in a Nipponese B-flick kinda way, real hesitant and gradual like the Three Stooges turning around to see if someone's heaving a cleaver behind their back, with two ax-screecheroos midway through that'll turn your lips lavender and chap 'em simultaneously. In one song ("Between Time," I think) Randy actually gets a moderate groove going that suggests he's ahead of Tony Iommi's game plan, but mostly what he does is look inside his mind and claim he's filling the air with pain, a substance he appears to be in a great deal of himself. His riffroar is quite possibly the most sodden in the history of agriculture, and he babbles like he's dusted in a very serious way, but seeing how he can barely come up with a *tune* worth a damn, I have serious trouble giving a shit. Guitarists and dopefiends would shave off a testicle for this mess, and it'd serve 'em right.

333. THE COUNT BISHOPS
The Count Bishops Chiswick UK import, 1977

Hungry and spunky and unpompous ripped-on-lager lunchbucket-rock by England's first and foremost boogiepunks, pub-dwellers who poured *lots* of gravy on their meat and potatoes, this connects ZZ Top to Ducks Deluxe by roasting Delta and Chitown chestnuts on an open fire just south of 10 Downing Street then urinating all over the prime minister's new oxfords. When Dave Tice changes that "digger in the ditch" line in "Good Guys Don't Wear White" to "nigger" it's a positive liberal statement; as manly a honky as ever held a mike, he bunches up his hoarse grumble in his cheek like snuff, chomps it, dares his buddies to punch it out. When they take him up on the offer, in "Don't Start Crying Now" and "Taste and Try" and "Down in the Bottom" and especially "Shake Your Moneymaker," the resulting battle smokes deadly as a kerosene hotfoot.

334. THE GERMS
(G.I.) Slash, 1979

Unhappy little Bowie scion Darby Crash runs his mouth off, runs his words together, turns his blues into glop. It's like he's been gargling with VapoRub, like he's got a truck hitch strapped to each cheek and the U-Hauls are traveling in opposite directions, tearing his mouth apart; if you cleaned his microphone, you'd probably catch a fatal disease. At the start of the nine-minute sleepwalk/sleeptalk murk-opus "Shut Down," there's a good lisp, and though mostly it's fortunate you can't decipher the snarls, sometimes they jump you from behind: "I waaant out nowww," "another day, another crash," "Gimme gimme this gimme gimme thaaaaayaragh!!" It's a me-vs.-you persecution complex from camera-country, and this economically overadvantaged cretin wants you to believe he's been brutalized all his life, and more 'cause he's a cretin than 'cause he's overadvantaged, you don't buy it for a minute. Pat Smear's choo-choo's worth of staccato mudpie riffage is pretty effective, like he's sawing briefcases in half sometimes, the viscosity metamorphosing into toothsome reverberations in "Richie Dagger's Crime." Joan Runaway produced it all to halfway resemble a rock record, which is good. As is the fact that the singer Chinawhited himself to death the day before John Lennon departed the Dakota.

335. HAWKWIND
Doremi Fasol Latido Liberty, 1972

A concept LP evoking those brief moments when you're not awake anymore but not quite asleep, this protocyberpunk features British Venutians looking to the Orient and refusing to turn android over grooves as gelatinous as the solar system's crevices, and it doesn't feature "Do Re Mi," though Sparks's *A Woofer in Tweeter's Clothing* does (Rodgers and Hammerstein's, not Woody Guthrie's, which John Mellencamp tried once). Anyhow, if these astronomers were ahead of their time, it wasn't in the way they meant to be—"Space is Deep" 's midsection shows where Pere Ubu picked up "Final Solution" 's fuzz; Dave Brock's "dying, dying, dying" mantra was ultimately revivified by R.E.M in "The One I Love" and Hüsker Dü in "Diane." The liner notes are as zany as Teena Marie's or George Clinton's, Lemmy's voyeuristically neurotic ballad "The Watcher" shoots for and surpasses "The End," and "One Change," which lasts less than a minute, has one change. But the sci-fi hasn't yet learned not to take itself so soberly, and though Lemmy's bass and six-string and "Dik Mik" 's "generators and hot electronics" can engulf you when they densify toward Sabness, only two motions are available: soaring and sitting still.

336. THE HEADHUNTERS
Survival of the Fittest Arista, 1975

On moonlight hiatus from Herbie Hancock (whose "Metal Beat" ain't metal at all), these anthropophagously monickered jazzbos devised some beats the Real Roxanne and Salt-N-Pepa plundered only too happily a decade hence, but what earns 'em a plaque on the Black Metal Wall of Fame is the darkly monickered Blackbird McKnight's freely distorted blues-wah in "God Make Me Funky" and "Here and Now" and most notably "If You've Got It You'll Get It." *Bitches Brew* vet Bennie Maupin's freely distended honk-skronk in the same songs doesn't hurt either. And though you'll likely zone out midway through, if you can't shake at least a little leg to Bill Summers's West African gankoquis and agogos, Congolese berimbao, Ba-Benzele Pygmy hindewhu, Brazilian caxixi, Senegalese djembe, and Yoruba shekere, you're a paraplegic and a xenophobe too.

337. SILVERHEAD
16 and Savaged MCA, 1973

Exploitatively sicko (somewhere between *Head Games* and *Appetite for Destruction*) cover (blue-nailed young woman who's just been dragged through the mud frowning mirrorward with clothes torn and nip atwitter) houses shirtless dirtballs (including future Deb Harry understudy Nigel Harrison) who were hyped as the UK's answer to the Dolls (first song: "Hello New York"), which has more to do with their post-Stones structural bent than any truly outlandish attributes. Pre-Bon thorn-throat Michael Des Barres finds his croak tempered by cutieboy Raspberries harmonics, and though such titles as "More Than Your Mouth Can Hold" (as in "I'm a big boy") and "This Ain't a Parody" (as if it had a choice in the matter)

indicate a commendable humor-sense, said talent isn't utilized to any overwhelming extent. "Bright Light" is a demi-effeminate slow-then-fast (Sparks-then-Foghat!) ode to onanism, and the scourge for which the set's named is ace teen-tragic sociologizing, and here and there the antimacho macho's a pleasant change of underwear. But the speediness generally ain't speedy enough, so though most everything comes close, nothing can match the cover.

338. THE DICTATORS
Bloodbrothers Elektra, 1978

"Faster and Louder" doesn't sound too much different from the way "hardcore" (the Angry Samoans, f'rinstance) would eventually sound three-plus years hence, which perhaps explains why certain cognoscenti consider this the Dics' "punk-rock" document. "Baby, Let's Twist" is good Velvet-riffed anti-pseudodecadence (some nose-ringed leather-wench keeps screaming "I'm so strange!") a few years before you'd anticipate such a gripe; "No Tomorrow" is revenge-of-the-nerds nihilism that sounds better on paper than on tape. Working girls get picked up in the Twin Cities red-light district, guitars get picked up (and fingered in hotshit manner) by proud young Americans, a rock-crit in his sports-crit mode gets cannonized. And H. D. Manitoba empowers power-pop with a Johnny Rotten snarl, so maybe *that's* the punk-rock part. Or maybe it's how Side Two starts exactly like "Psycho Killer" by Talking Heads.

339. DIED PRETTY
Free Dirt What Goes On, 1986

Ron Peno's words sound overheard, as if you're eavesdropping on some passerby's depression. Punkzine Dylan-comparisons don't cut it 'cause he's too gravelly and majestic, not nasal enough; I catch snatches where he enunciates by accident, stuff like "the blades of Israel won't cut deep enough to bleed" that suggest he's trying to haul the death of God on his

Photograph by Francine McDougall

I'm not sure) "The Eagle Never Hunts the Fly" and "Double Yellow Line," they were mere organ-drenched hacks, Uriah Heeps ahead of their time. Their bassist invented a kind of fuzzbox, they all wore single black leather gloves years before Michael Jackson, and Sean Bonniwell's sepulchral pensiveness paved the way for Jim Morrison and Arthur Lee and Ozzy Osbourne and maybe me and you, by which I mainly mean he's a weird blowhard begging that his weirdness be respected by nonweirdos, too much to ask in any world. Sean sputters about his sixth sense, agrees with Chicken Little, works hard to sound malevolent. Usually he falls flat on his face, but he always *looks* cool.

shoulders, that he knows how Denny McLain felt. Frank Brunetti's regal keys, caught somewhere in the nether region right of Boston and left of the Electric Prunes, elevate all the post-Reed/Young/Ginn grit from Bret Myers's ax into some lofty realm where contempt only means compassion with more 'nads and knowledge than normal. Side One, waxing incoherent with an outré waltz and climaxing with a half-starved single, is subdued but excitable; Side Two, detonating without respite like toads strung together by Ghoulardi, ups both decibels and proportions. The Aussie fivesome's supplemented by pedal steel, mandolin, and (alternately "Baker Street" and "Funhouse") sax, and on some not entirely theoretical level *Free Dirt*'s what hard rock was always meant to be: Garage grime reinforced by a cerebrum, amped outta sight and tougher than titanium triceratops teeth. Kinda dry though, I gotta admit.

340. THE MUSIC MACHINE

Best Of Rhino, 1984; rec. 1965–67

With the mysterious lines "I got me a complication and it's an only child," five bowl-haired LA boppers in black unveil the encyclopedic minute and fifty-six seconds they call "Talk Talk"; after that, with partial time-out for the extremely metaphysical (about what

341. CAPTAIN BEYOND

Captain Beyond Capricorn, 1972

Seven, count 'em, seven songs with parentheses in the titles, probably some kind of record (can't remember if Ian Dury or even James Brown ever had that many), and it's not as if these are your run-of-the-mill titles either. To wit: "Dancing Madly Backwards (on a Sea of Air)," "Armworth," "Myopic Void" (like me without glasses, 20/400, no kidding!), "Mesmerization Eclipse," "Raging River of Fear," "Thousand Days of Yesterdays (Intro)," "Frozen Over," "Thousand Days of Yesterdays (Time Since Come and Gone)" (these last three headlines perhaps referring to some ice-aged woolly rhino come back to life, and guitarist Rhino is woolly all right!), "I Can't Feel Nothin' (Part I)" (not to be confused with "I Got the Feelin'," by James, which as far as I can remember didn't *have* a "Part I," which for him of course was rare), "As the Moon Speaks (to the Waves of the Sea)," "Astral Lady" (whom singer Rod Evans has probably known for Astral Weeks!), "As the Moon Speaks (Return)," "I Can't Feel Nothin' (Part II)" (which I betcha knew was coming, right?). The music's not quite as rad as what it's called, but it's radder than music "dedicated to the memory of Duane Allman" has any right to be, and though no parentheses-metal here can quite stand up to such parentheses-funk standard-bearers as J.B.'s "I

Don't Want Nobody to Give Me Nothing (Open Up the Door, I'll Get It Myself)" and "Promentalshitback-washpsychosis Enema Squad (the Doodoo Chasers)" by Funkadelic, drum-whacker Bobby Caldwell be clockin' and rockin' nonwackily indeed!

342. LAST EXIT
. . . .
Last Exit Enemy, 1987

Easily the most unyieldingly broad-shouldered ball of Mack motherfucker blues-goo these bohunks've turned out, this debut's so ferocious it's funny, un-thinkable to play often unless you're trying to break your lease: guitars like steam engines, drums excavating asphalt, percussion like teapots boiling over, electric-toothbrush bass, dying-goose sax. I listen to "Pig Freedom" (Sonny Sharrock and Peter Brötzmann defending turf, throwing rocks at each other), "Discharge" (tied to the tracks, you're flattened by the Wabash Cannonball), or "Crackin' " (neighbors in four bordering apartments slamming their fists against walls, telling each other to shut the fuck up), and I wonder why nihilist NYC noise-nitwits of the Live Skull/Missing Foundation–stripe even bother. "Back-water" 's musclebound Delta-funk is the closest this gets to relaxing; otherwise, there's not nearly as much swing as Ronald Shannon Jackson's and Bill Laswell's presence would lead you to expect. There's also not much room to breathe.

343. ROBERT PLANT
. . . .
Shaken 'n' Stirred Es Paranza, 1985

Following his exotic sojourns to the lands of Om Kalthoum (on *Pictures of Eleven*), Ennio Morricone (on *The Principle of Moments*), and moldy oldies (on *The Honeydrippers/Volume One*), and prior to his quite lucrative though mostly lousy reversion to lemondom (*Now and Zen*), Bobby provided us with some of the Teflon Decade's most perpetually abstracted commercially semisuccessful white rock (blows Lou Reed out of the water, easy). The second

side nods to the Human Beinz and Police and contains a creepy hit (about shedding Zeppelin, perhaps) where the smog whisks away so our protagonist can stop suffocating; the first side's got an elegy to times-gone-by called "Easily Lead," but mostly it's got outlandish soundscapes with striking transformations, stutters, skids, and added-and-subtracted tracks. ("Eclecticism," it's called—it's what Def Leppard does by "accident," o'course.) The most expressionist cut is "Too Loud," and had Plant released a twelve-inch hip-hop remix in the South Bronx, I expect it would've sold like Filas. Only sounds I can liken it to are Afrika Bambaataa's "Looking for the Perfect Beat" and certain Mark Stewart obscurities (but considerably more restrained, with the funk frozen to a standstill, not a great thing). Mostly it's like the geezer was making a kind of music that doesn't have a name yet.

344. TED NUGENT'S AMBOY DUKES
. . . .
Tooth Fang & Claw Discreet, 1974

From the Reverend Atrocious Theodosious, a psalm of self-reliance—he can't count on no crystal ball or black magic or rabbit's foot or Lady Luck, on no God or government or you. "I just believe in my own bad self," he spits. Advising us to "beware the public carnivores as they inevitably have a soft-nosed hollow-point Magnum behind every bush," he christens his riffs "Living in the Woods" and "The Great White Buffalo" and "Hibernation." The last's overlong psychedelic gaga, and it ain't alone, but mostly the guitaring ain't what you'd call domesticated. Especially not if it's your job to clean Ted's cage.

345. THE ACCURSED
Up with the Punks Wreck 'Em UK import, 1983

If I had to compare Steve Hall's "Nuclear War" to somebody else's, it'd probably be Sun Ra's. Like everything else here, it's heavy metal, with entropic Stooge-wobble and Hendrix ejaculation and cheapo clumps of waste, only backward. This is dog-attack rock, the *real* underground, about six *feet* under to be exact, or at least that's how it feels. Proglue, prospeed, antilife, Hall's a dole-life prole-threat slang-king. His generation should've elected him spokesman: "Do what you want, do what you will/Get drunk, and take the pill." "People stand around, and they stare/ looking into, into the air." He's looking for a job, for anybody to talk to, he wants out, but it's no go. The way he yodels and retells and changes his mind, I seriously doubt he's ever taken pen to paper. I think he makes this stuff up on the spot.

346. VOID AND FAITH
Void/Faith Dischord, 1982

Two ahead-of-the-game "hardcore" ensembles from the nation's capital subject metalchords to the squeeze play, with Rough Trade bass lines not so much forced as twisted to fit, and in-your-face time shifts guaranteed to electrocute lab-rat neurodendrons. There's a dozen intranslatably fragmentary straight-razor-to-the-wrists rants by each band, and every last brittle one ends before you've even registered its beginning. About the only babble I can make out on Faith's side refers to fake IDs and whoever's in the singer's way; Void's heavier, more henpecked, more hyperactive, with a singer smothered beneath Ted Nugent feedback, plunging breastward from a treetop like an asp dropped by an orangutan. Nobody here plays with a full deck.

347. VON LMO
Future Language Strazar, 1981

Who are these masked men? Their only album's "dedicated to the advancement of the United States space program," and the front informs us that "The Group from the Future Is Here Now! Advance Yourself!" Five terminally out-of-it George Jetsons in tinfoil Devo suits with "international transmitting symbols for universal sound" on their chests, plus adorable red galoshes, claim they're "here to deliver this message to you now: Long live heavy metal!!" The twin-guitar rhythms are borderline-Sabbish, with sci-fryed Hawkwind/Düül gamma-ray effects; the gab is borderline-rappish. As Juno Saturn blurts electronic sax, Von Lmo ("pronounced Von Elmo") ignites white heat and delivers special announcements from the stars, frequently concerning gravity. Was this a joke, or what?

348. LUCIFER'S FRIEND
Lucifer's Friend Billingsgate, 1973

Sort of the unthinking man's Uriah Heep, this pre-progressive Krautplod stacks toxic powerchords and dive-bombing fuzzroar and dizzy trash-key lines atop

a Teutonic bottom that shifts like tectonic earthquake-plates, all inside a cover emblazoned with a midget with a hook for a hand standing in a red pool of plasma. "Ride the Sky," the leadoff boomzoom, crosses "Paranoid" with "The Immigrant Song" (a herd of brassy heffalumps bleat the parts Jim Page might or might not have learned from Shocking Blue), and another cut called "In the Time of Job When Mammon Was a Yippie" would be cool even if it stank (which it doesn't—fits in Mary and Moses too). The Clash once asked whether when they knock on your front door, you're gonna answer with your hands on your scalp or on your trigger; "Baby You're a Liar" opens with the sound of "them" knocking.

349. MOUNTAIN
Nantucket Sleighride Windfall, 1970

"**P**lay this record at high volume for maximum sonority," the notes go, as if we don't have enough sonorities around here already. (Too many *fraternities* too!) The concept's aimed at a land of ice and snow on the hemisphere opposite from Zep's, which explains the old salts on the watch and the old blacks on the porch and maybe even the great train robberies if not the lion-tamers named Beethoven, but then again all I know from Nantucket is a couple dirty

limericks, and Leslie West harpoons himself some massive pork chops of churning funk that'd make an Eskimo smile. As far as Canadian bacon goes, there's no "The Red and the Black" or "Wreck of the Edmund Fitzgerald," no "Stallion Road" (see Mö-törhöme) even, though the title epic comes close: Doubly appropriate, the Great Fatsby's serenading a sperm whale, and the riff's as big as it better be. Leslie knows what's important in this world—the way he chaws his words, it's as if he's munching a drumstick between lines. Singing for his supper like Little Tommy Tucker, he's a hulk among hulks, yet "Taunta" and "Tired Angels" prove he can be as gentle as Eddie's father.

350. URIAH HEEP
Uriah Heep Mercury, 1970

The ghastily Jabberwockesque millipede apparition on the outside sets the stage for what's not, namely ominoso bodies-rolling-down-the-stairs thumpola that anticipates a myriad mid-to-late-eighties gothic groovesters. The Heepcats named themselves after a clerk in *David Copperfield;* they call one song "Dreammare." Only "Bird of Prey" has much punklike testosterone, and even there it's balanced by a generous dose of estrogen, but that's no problem, 'cause what matters most is the way Ken Hensley's setting-sail-for-the-sun organ and Mick Box's witches'-brew fuzz mesh with each other and weird out all the time. Dave Byron's moronic theatricality is just icing; the monk-faced Pearly-Gates-in-peril backup chorales are tastier than what's up front. You either like this morose mole-music or you hate it, but either way, if you take it seriously, you miss the fun.

351. BAD BRAINS
Bad Brains ROIR cassette, 1982

A jazz-fusion act at first, more musicianly than their punk brethren, these dreadlocked Chocolate City shredders applied their already-honed technical skills

toward the slam-dance genre's most overwhelming rhythmic and melodic onslaught, an obsessive if over-disciplined scree. Branded by microphone-man H.R.'s snakingly nasal Arabian-goatherd wail, the furious shocks of bulb-enlightening sound incorporate metal dynamics, Rastafari dub (for which they'd never again find a pocket as deep as the one here), and reckless R&B polypercussion. The last factor's the one they're rarely given credit for, but the first time I heard their manned collision "Pay to Cum," the only great song they will ever record, I thought it sounded like the Buzzcocks produced by Chic. Only nastier, and noisier.

352. **FOGHAT**
. . . .
Live Bearsville, 1977

Maybe they didn't really do "Take Me to the River" better than Talking Heads (or even Bryan Ferry), but for sure they did "Honey Hush" better than Elvis Costello, and that's the one that's here, along with five-that's-all more clumps as earthy as stadium sod, Thorazined Berryblooze bangshangalang reductio ab-surdum from fools (they said it, I didn't) for the city who ain't no country boys. The studio LPs were pedestrian dryness (frequently with fewer Fu Manchu soup-strainers than the three here), but Foghat's glad to be off the bus tonight, and with false stops and drunken gloop and lickety-split changeups you can tell, for at least the middle two minutes of every six-point-

five available. "Home in My Hand" and "Road Fever" constitute a true ramblin'/gamblin'/travelin'–man saga, and there's plenty more tour memories behind that curious hard-to-file-away-without-screwing-it-up cut-out cover, like f'rinstance the shot of drummer Roger Earl ironing his trousers. It boggles the mind: Can you imagine millions of teenagers paying good money to watch four unemployed gas-station attendants? Can you imagine what short of syphilitic slattern would've lowered herself to be a *Foghat* groupie? Can you imagine if you were a kid, and you had to explain to your class that your dad plays in Foghat for a *living*? Yet by the time Dave Peverett finishes salivating all over "I Just Wanna Make Love to You," there's no question he owns the thing. 'Cause put yourself in Willie Dixon's shoes: You wouldn't want the damn song *back,* would you?

353. **PETER AND THE TEST TUBE BABIES**
. . . .
Peter and the Test Tube Babies Profile, 1987

Nearly a decade after contributing dead-Elvis and bank-robbery ditties to Oi!-Mach-One compilations, warty Brighton hoochaholics have a bit of a knees-up and proceed to start rows with oodles of layers of compellingly swooshbucklin' fuzztones. Not especially fast or fervid or far-out or fully packed, all of which adjectives are nothing more than haircut-equivalents that just get in the way by now anyhow, this is well-put-together straight-rock caged by teensy pinches of reedy bop and stringy symphonics, with ultrasongful gripes about being allergic to life, married tippling-partners so tied down they can't tie one on anymore, and having Keith Moon call you an asshole over the psychic telephone. The "Bonanza" rip reminds me that I've never figured out whether the Bonanza/Ponderosa cowboy-show/steak-restaurant connection is inten-tional, and the sky-reaching music-box saloon-ballad-about-love-ballads crosses Sly's "Dance to the Music," Billy Joel's "Piano Man," and the theme from "The Gary Shandling Show." We're introduced to cute Limey slang such as "bedsit," and the drinks are on Peter.

354. LUL
Inside Little Oral Annie Eksakt Dutch import, 1988

This record is to speedmetal what Wire's *Pink Flag* was to punk rock ten years before, but given the qualitative differences between the respective genres, it oughta be no surprise that it's not nearly as durable as its predecessor—it's a riddle, sort of, a *game*. Four everysophomores from Holland's separatist Frisian Liberation Army reinvent Metallica's formal language like Wire reinvented the Ramones' ditto, demystifying the demystifiers by uncynically transforming short-attention-span microminimalism freed from clinical conceptualization into hard-ax structural advancement freed from hate-thy-neighbor dehumanization. Wire's an influence: eighteen songs, every one of 'em under 2:13, a lot of 'em Fruit-of-the-Loom-drowningly delicate, a few of 'em so cold they burn like frostbite. But on the inner sleeve, Lul claims "fandom" to Anthrax, Slayer, COC, MOD, Venom, and Nuclear Assault (not to mention Sigue Sigue Sputnik, Skrewdriver, MX-80 Sound, Chic, Au Pairs, X-Ray Spex, and so on), and the riffs (which generally slash tires for about twenty seconds, then turn cordial again) are straight off *Reign in Blood* or *Master of Puppets* or the Bad Brains' *I Against I* (or even "Renegade," by Styx!). Along with his speakers who look like beakers and record companies who act like Hoovervilles, Sytse J. Van Essen reels off received leftoid abstractions so standoffish it always seems his life comprises nothing more than one big "aesthetic experience," the last thing we need. Nonetheless, if his band's a brave new whirl, they don't know it, and that's the best kind.

355. HÜSKER DÜ
Land Speed Record New Alliance, 1981

A high-molecule-density pitcher of carb-cleaner packed as tight as an ant's ass, Dü's full-length debut has no melody to speak of, just one microscopic blot after another, with so little time-out space that it's not so much as if there's eighteen real short (mainly under a minute) combustions as two real long ones, one per side. Here and there inside the unrelenting compost you detect word hooks (e.g., the days of the week) or bass hooks, but that's it. As the title's adaptation of ELO's *A New World Record* implies, the resulting tar's motorboated as swiftly as any ever, so it's not especially useful save maybe as a background-clogger, at least till the atypically coherent five-minute secret-service coda. I'm still not sure whether they cover the "Gilligan's Island" theme.

356. PARIS
Paris Capitol, 1976

Ten Eiffel Towers' worth of no-let-up bombastickness, oracle overkill, and rhythm-changes doing the Ali Shuffle, this stopstart badluck Zepnoise earpain-exercise demonstrates that even French-kissing Fleetwood-frogs like Robert Welch get a hair up their butt now and then. "Narrow Gate"'s occidental wavecrashes anticipate the mysteries Bob Plant would tackle in his solo career, Nazarenes replace Plant's presolo tangerines, and additional amulets include Don Juan and sorcerers and blood-colored rain and numerological gods and little black books and the day of the locust and that ol' black magic. Welch probably skimmed through a copy of Aleister Crowley's *Yi King* in a dentist's office once.

357. MOTÖRHEAD
Beer Drinkers Chiswick German import, 1982; rec. 1977–80

Slobby, half-cooked, scar-voiced power-trio tapes, pub-metal fixated on amphetamines and cocaine and marital aids and parole, from when people really believed this was the world's worst band. Before Motörhead did anything spectacular, they boogied: The title comes from the ZZ Top keg-drainer they lead with, "I'm Your Doctor" comes from John Mayall, a good deal of the production comes from Dave

Edmunds. Musicians come from the cosmodelic Hawkwind and the ungovernable Pink Fairies, as do the two best tunes, "Lost Johnny" and "City Kids," neither as hammerdown as in their protogenic interpretations. A smuggle-bust at the border of Yankland and Canuckland booted Lemmy out of Hawkwind, so he rang up Larry Wallis, they shared gigspace with the Damned and the Adverts, and the rest you should already know.

358. GRAND FUNK RAILROAD
On Time Capitol, 1970

The big clock one of 'em's holding on the cover predates Flavor Flav by a good two decades, plus the middle one's stogies and toy train look quite a bit like bombs one would perhaps use to blow up buildings, so maybe they really were conscious leaders of the United Proletarian Youth Uprising Against Bourgeois Dictatorship before anybody thought to say so after all. Music's the passably lurchful sixties-turning-seventies slashburn grungeloopism you'd figure, most palatably in "Anybody's Answer," "Into the Sun," "Can't Be Too Long" ('bout a fugitive), and "Heartbreaker," all five-minutes-plus and demonstrably and undeniably *heavy,* with scads of Swiss-cheesy pianner but zero of the infuriatingly incomprehensible-of-appeal sleepism these Flintniks proffered in big-buck (ten million recs a year!) later days. Also of note are the "Row, Row, Row Your Boat" round in "Ups and Downs," the shifting urban sands of the narcotically titled "High on a Horse," and especially the octo-minute overindulgence of the backwardly titled "T.N.U.C.," complete with interminably dexterously emptily mercurial solo-on-skins by Don Brewer. And of course Mark Farner nonsings about nonstuff, and basically it's all completely worthless, but as worthlessness goes it's not bad.

359. THE LEATHER NUN
Slow Death Criminal Damage UK import EP, 1984

Being nowhere near privy to the lingo of the nonheteromonogamous and/or onanistic psychosexual subculture, I can't be entirely certain, but I've got a queasy feeling that this ménage-à-cinq is as "dangerous" (in a sociological sense) as a sound wave–producing entity can be in this age of lethal body-fluid-transmitted viri. Imagewise they rely on none of the effeminate stereotypes certain of us on the other side of the fence have come to associate with said alternative life-style, and though the electrically funereal torments here may not be as decadent as former Throbbing Gristle and future acid-house imbecile Genesis P-Orridge (who guests on violin) might want 'em to be, they do come close. The insurmountably intense (and often insurmountably boring) quarter-hour version of the title cut fills the whole first side with a digital pulse and increasingly decibeled phaseback guaranteed to alter your way of thinking; as Jonas Almqvist's amyl-nitrated whisper keeps recapitulating that he's got only fifty-five hours to live, guitars chop like machetes harvesting a field of people. The flip's got the petrifying anarchist riot-goader "No Rule," plus other material that alternately resembles Gobots playing with themselves or what would've happened if Motörhead had evolved their architecture toward Hawkwind's aluminum siding instead of the Pink Fairies' bricks. Above all, there's no post-AIDS sell-the-straights fantasy-suppression or gay one-on-one—these Swedes want the meat, all the meat, and they want it now.

360. STARZ
Starz Capitol, 1976

Who they wanted to be, of course, was Kiss, which makes sense, since both squads were birthed by Bill Aucoin Management, and both supposedly found members through *Village Voice* ads (though why members of Kiss or Starz would be reading the *Voice* is beyond me). Less ashamed of their bubbleboogie tendencies than their big siblings were, and also louder, they nonetheless had serious problems putting their best hooks into the same songs as their best riffs, and their audition-punk looks didn't mask the powerschmaltz—"She's Just a Fallen Angel" is plagiarism-evidence for Poison-haters. But Michael Lee Smith screams like a cross between REO's Kevin Cronin and Laraine Newman's "Saturday Night Live" imitation of a stepped-on terrier, and if "Tear It Down"'s like weak CCR, "Boys in Action" and "Now I Can" come closer to the actual down-tearing, as does "Monkey Business," a Jagger sendup with black-turning faces that're only racist if you want 'em to be. The real deal, though, is "Pull the Plug," five confusedly climactic minutes that you might presume deprecate the world's least effective method of birth control if I didn't tell you that they're really about Karen Quinlan and euthanasia. Best line: "You don't look the same in an oxygen tank," sung with utmost sincerity.

361. **NAKED RAYGUN**
Throb Throb Homestead, 1985

These industrial-wasteland dislocation yodels come from pent-up Chitown post-oi!/pre–Mort Downey curmunchkins who oughta wear looser-fitting clothes but nonetheless have a tolerable way with their not-exactly-multifaceted modus operandi, which unites one-syllable words and Muscle Beach chord-chunks into marginally anthemic gang-refrains (less marginal in "I Don't Know"). Their liberal-baiting cynicism suggests they're too humorless to laugh at themselves, their soldier-of-fortune ethics suggest they never outgrew their GI Joe collection, their hyperactive voice-switcheroos suggest they're still trying too hard to impress their high school drama coach. Nice how they open "Leeches" with that *Wizard of Oz* reference though.

362. **DEATH OF SAMANTHA**
Strungout on Jargon Homestead, 1986

Cleveland ax-clamor heirs-apparent show off their dissonant-but-fluid fret-interplay, but John Petkovic whines like a Violent Femme and strings hyperbolized jargon together like an art-school dropout running out of nonexistent ideas; his nonhumble epiglottal quiver matches his mates' visual ornateness, maybe, but his Roxy-from-Tombs kultural küttensplice is old hat. Yet I'll grant him his postmod harlots and whores 'cause I'm sure he wants to be a star and he's just pretending to be pretentious, and what with Doug Gillard's more-than-mere-aping of Ron Asheton riffs and "Simple as That"'s slow-boiling compassion, this stands out as one of the very few late-eighties Amerindierock discs that actually sounded better three years down the line than when it landed in the racks. But as usual in late-eighties Amerindierock, though the band's first gig happened in a restaurant and the titles encircling the three most roarful roars ("Coca Cola & Licorice," "Ham & Eggs 99¢," "Grapeland") deal with food, the sarcastic words don't deal with much of anything, as far as I can tell.

363. **MX-80 SOUND**
Crowd Control Ralph, 1981

Sturdy but dawdlingly stoical, this third (and last vinylized) contestant in these Bloomington boys' Little 500 threatens to reduce 'em to nothing more than modernist tinkerers, Laurie Andersons with chest hair, but that's not to imply it's entirely devoid of diversion. "Promise of Love" and "Obsessive Devotion" are as lovely as anything by, I dunno, the Meadowlarks or Mello-Kings I guess (never heard "Shoot-a-Basket" by Meadowlark Lemon on RSVP Records, sorry); "Cover to Cover"'s the closest David Mahoney ever gets to John Bonham *and* the closest Bruce Anderson ever gets to Jimmy Page; the Pharaoh in "Pharaoh's Sneakers" is presumably the one named Sanders; the theme to

Brian DePalma's homicidal-Siamese-twin thriller *Sisters* is ticklish. When Bruce twists his extreme disdain into a technohorror that helps him reimagine Stan Freberg and Ornette Coleman as brothers of Link Wray, he devours your mind.

364. MOTÖRHEAD
. . . .
Iron Fist Bronze/Mercury, 1982

Despite the rote writing toward the end of Side One, despite what now reads like get-it-over-with volleys into all of Lemmy's established themes (groupie life in "Sex and Outrage," fugitive life in "America," pusher life in "I'm Your Doctor," amphetamine life in "Speed-freak"), I've never fully understood why so many Motörfans consider this revolver such a dud. Even more committed to the hook aesthetic than usual, the aura's not so much clean as just *clear,* clear enough to let some brains show, and to my ears the way it pinpoints their punkish rage ranks in spot-on acuteness with anything this glee club's done; when Philthy Animal Taylor's funkbeats bolt open "Grind Ya Down," this feels like one of the hardest *dance* bands rock's produced, and Lemmy's leer in "I'm Your Doctor" is one of his most debaucherous ever. Most of all, I like how you could take two of the last three head-in-noose phrasemakers, "(Don't Let 'Em) Grind

Ya Down" and "Bang to Rights," and apply 'em to Sandinistas in Nicaragua or blacks in South Africa or miners under Thatcher. And the awesome "Cat Scratch Fever" modification those two frame, "(Don't Need) Religion," oughta be heard by anybody who cares about women's control over their own repro-ductive systems or students' control over their own libraries. Their theorizing grew more articulate as the decade progressed, but it was certainly comforting midway through Reagan's first term to learn that Motörhead politics is a politics of liberation. Then again, comfort ain't all it's cracked up to be.

365. JANE'S ADDICTION
. . . .
Ritual De Lo Habitual Warner Bros., 1990

Garden-variety semi-U2 pomp-grunge, for the most part, especially on Side Two, but at least this time (JA's third try since slithering out of Tinseltown) Perry Farrell stops auditioning for bad B-movies and gets down to some nice amiable drone-mumbling whilst his best boys put their pathetic Led Zep fixation aside and get down to some nice amiable drone-grooving. What Perry's trying to say isn't always related to what we hear—until I read my holy-card insert and found out it's supposedly about learning lessons from your older brother, I thought "Of Course"'s raga was a vegetarian protest arguing that animal-killers deserve slaps in the face, kinda like some old David Byrne ditty. My way's better, but even Perry's way it's the second-best song. The best song, "Been Caught Stealing," is about shoplifting and rings my bell kinda like the Stooges might've if they'd stuck around long enough to "go disco." The other okay tracks (espe-cially "Stop," which stops and starts a lot) snap and crackle kinda like how Die Kreuzen's *Century Days* should've; the other not-okay tracks drag on and on and on. The uncensored version of the album cover, which features naked Native Americans and black children of various sexes plus phallic candles and thus drew the wrath of the law in certain unenlightened quarters, is a remarkable work of art, I'm told. Free lunches include barking dogs and a Rasta-dubbed Ian

Dury imitation. The philosophies are based on intense posthedonist soul-searching. The most interesting words are the French ones.

366. MOUNTAIN
Climbing! Windfall, 1970

The only way I can explain "Mississippi Queen" is to say that it sounds as economy-sized as Leslie West's waistline looks and swings like a wrecking ball smack-dab atop your head and you ain't got no hardhat, but if you wanna know how American art from Twain through Mountain distorts the truth about the Mississippi, which is actually a murderer strewn with sewage, you should read *A Confederacy of Dunces* by John Kennedy Toole, page 138 (paperback edition). "Never in My Life" and "Sittin' on a Rainbow" womanize nearly as whoppingly, which is pretty big, as is Leslie's heart, but not so his hooks, not very often anyhow. The imaginatively titled "Theme from an Imaginary Western" is open-spaces cowboy-mythology; "The Laird" sounds pretty much the same. "For Yasgur's Farm" and "Boys in the Band" sound pretty much the same as "Theme" at first ('cept "Boys" has piano) then get half as big as "Mississippi" later, and I guess "Yasgur's" concerns Woodstock and it's supposedly real inspiring except I don't know to whom. In "To My Friend," former Vagrant Leslie sashays through Segovia in a pleasantly polymelodic way, then speeds up so his sashays aren't pleasant anymore. None of it means shit.

367. NECROS
Tangled Up Restless, 1987

The perpetrators hail from Ann Arbor sometimes and Toledo (or okay, Maumee) some other times, and the title thang simmers with hot-blooded dog-eat-dog gnarl. It was my favorite single of '86, and give or take "West End Girls" by the Pet Shop Boys and "Lips to Find You" by Teena Marie and "Gucci Time" by Schoolly D and a few others, it still is: The

deceit-matrix that chokes you ain't of your own doing, yells Barry Henssler, whose orbicular diameter and orangutan auburnness-of-hair make him resemble one of those trollish Dammit Dolls that useta be real popular at amusement parks back when the FM played stuff like "Cat Scratch Fever" and "Lord of the Thighs." Barry's height-lack's propped up by riff-wars like how the Nuge jammed before he met Don Johnson, and his idea's that suffering for everybody else's balks is a pain in the brain, not just if you're a white Anglo-Saxon mid-American male, but that's got a lot to do with it if you're talking affirmative action or what have you. The 45's punk rock for real punks, floor-scrubbing dropouts in Iron Maiden shirts; the LP's got great big post-seventies gulps "about" girls with guns and the tomb of Al Capone, a Pink Floyd redo, and an extremely artistic eight-minute veggie-rocque suite with pianistics that might be lifted from Elton John's "Funeral for a Friend" or then again might not. Plus a few slamdance quickies to keep the skateboardin' townies happy, but not me.

368. *Tooth and Nail*
Upsetter, 1980

Hardcore so early it doesn't have that name yet, California-style: The Controllers do post-Stooge 'burban boredom 'bout viewing church on TV and suchlike, with nice harmonies, and they get the Diddleybop right. The Flesheaters do a manglated sort of monkey-meat blues, harsher than on their LPs, and you wanna boot the singer smack in his lisping jawbone. UXA imitate the Sex Pistols and a circus, and their frontwoman sounds like she chews up Marines for lunch. Negative Trend contemplate breaking glass, killing for cash, and turning into Flipper; Middle Class run very fast, then run out of breath. The Germs try to do everything everybody else does, all at the same time, with Darby Crash stammering like a man stumbling through the dark in search of his own gravesite, which he found later that year. Collector-scumbags love this stuff. I think it's okay.

369. NITZINGER
One Foot in History Capitol, 1973

These woofer-wrecking Texans' second slab disappointed severely, as second slabs frequently do, but dig that title—do they mean "one foot" as in "foot in the door," as in "twelve inches" (thus space equals time!), or as in "one small step for mankind"? Who knows? Who cares? Dean Parks and Dale Oehler are credited with "orchestral arrangements," so you know right off the debut's septic slop's been coerced into Earth Shoes, but there's still fretwork folly and pile-drive percussives like Brahms never broiled, plus Joplin and "Shortnin' Bread" quotes, and laughs: Gourmands in the ground ("Earth Eater"), bugs in your belfry ("The Cripple Gnat Bounce"), beaches where the blues ain't allowed ("Take a Picture"). Not to mention "God Bless the Pervert," a tribute to tower-sniper Charles Whitman that's second only to Kinky Friedman's. And "Driftwood," a novena to the Northern Star, which *might*'ve been stomachable if Ursa Major had done it (hardy har har), but I wouldn't bet on it.

370. PLASTIC ONO BAND
Live Peace in Toronto 1969 Apple, 1969

John Lennon opens by nostalgiafying for the glory days of Carl Perkins and Barrett Strong and Larry Williams (not to mention the glory days of his old group); Eric Clapton strums reasonably loud in spots, but ten years later the Flying Lizards came around and made all these ancient versions seem quaint by comparison. Lennon ends by grinding out a whole side of proto-harmolodic oozegroove whilst his better (which sometimes I truly believe) half first gargles "don't woolly don't woolly don't woolly" again and again to a small Japanese child whose mom's arm just got severed in half at the wrist in the middle of a snowstorm, then she fantasizes she's having bad sex. Regardless, the most disconcerting section is the second half of Side One, which commences with Yoko's hubbie yowling "yes I'm *lonely*, wanna *die*" under noisier feedback than the LP's start and end combined, then raising the ante with "Cold Turkey" as the little woman's Thanksgivingish background gobbles take said title much too literally, then dropping it some with "Give Peace a Chance," which after all is what they say they were there for. "Well Well Well" or "I Don't Want to Be at Soldier" or "Sisters O Sisters" would've empowered the proceedings a bit, but this ranks high as primitivism anyhow. Dunno if the male lead ever saw the Stooges, but I bet he appreciated the Velvets.

371. TEN YEARS AFTER
Watt Deram, 1970

Fresh from raking in $3,250 at Woodstock and crashing the U.S. Top 20, Alvin Lee's authenticians briefly did something worth caring about. "I Say Yeah" springs then pumps then curdles not unlike "Loose" on *Funhouse* for five whole minutes, and "I'm Coming On"'s roundelay I've-been-kicked-and-I'm-kicking-back doghouse-huzza and "Sweet Little Sixteen"'s live-at-the-Isle-of-Wight Berry-squishing additionally approximate Stoogeness. The remainder mostly doesn't: Lotsa bee-guitars aching to make honey in your honey's hive, lotsa now-I-lay-me-down-to-sleep fusionistic sobbola wept with no feeling whatsoever. So it's real easy to mix up Alvin Lee with Arthur Lee and Ten Years After with Ten Wheel Drive and Ten Wheel Drive with some

BTO album (*Four Wheel Drive*) and a different BTO album (*Not Fragile*) with some Yes album (*Fragile*). Confused? I hope so.

372. THE PRETTY THINGS
Cries from the Midnight Circus Harvest UK import, 1976; rec. 1968–71

R&B–thugs who in the sixties set out to challenge the Stones, they crossed over to psychedelica with not too many original members left, and at first proved too twee to bend brains. Their sea-looking/waves-parting/sand-slipping wooziness was caught in some dunce's time warp between Syd Barrett and Robyn Hitchcock. But Dick Taylor's riffs and Twink's skins steer all five of the semiacoustic '68 tracks here ("Well of Destiny" and "Old Man Going" more than the rest) in an astrobluesjam direction, and despite slight hippie residue, by '70 the spiraling swoop's been abandoned for granite Delta-meltdown and unplannedly amp-blowing Stoogedom. The brats on the backstreets have blood on their shirts in "Cold Stone" and "Cries from the Midnight Circus," and Phil May sneers as hard as he croons.

373. KISS
Alive! Casablanca, 1975

No question that these Kabukied bozos deserved a double-live document more than most anybody ever, not just 'cause the cavernous dimensions of the rally-spot unslicks unfortunate studioficationary confection, but for the mere sociological fact of the participants' relevance in the eternal scheme of mass-consumerist hypestory. (Like, if *tens of thousands* of youngsters my age—I was fourteen at the time, perfect—shelled out shells to see 'em in every city on the planet and I didn't, howcum *I'm* writing this book? For all we know the burnouts on the back turned into Mötley Crüe, right?) "It lookth lahk we gohna half owthelvth a rockaroll pahty two-*nite*! I got dith feelin

twonite gohna be one uh dothe *hot* niteth," the sermon thunders from the mount, then it turns toward tequila and vodka and orange juice and cold gin, then finally "you detherve to give yoe-thelfth uhrounduhuhplawth leth *go!*" The applause is rumored to have been taped off "Monday Night Football." If "100,000 Years" brings to mind "good" Grand Funk for twelve minutes too many and "She"'s stockpiled blueschords are preposterous, "C'mon and Love Me," "Black Diamond," and (o'course) "Rock and Roll All Nite" are rather doggone definitive, I'd say. Lyrics like Kiss's *improve* when you can't understand 'em, and oh, those hookriffs, y'know? I mean, I count at *least* three or four!

374. J. D. BLACKFOOT
The Ultimate Prophecy Mercury, 1970

So this microdot magician halfway between Arthur Brown and Donovan, snorting like Celtic Frost's Tom G. Warrior after a Teenage Mutant Ninja Turtle punch in the erogenous zone, informs you that "this is the ultimate prophecy," then there's tribal drums. Amid incompetent violins and about nine guys battling bongos, his recitation is unbelievable, absolute philosopher-king-of-the-zodiac literature: "Lain out on the dawn of creation/The king hath named it ground/ And he hath given to the earth people/To sit and look profound/But they will be known as love creatures/ BORN TO LIVE ON SOUND!!" This is "Song I," and only timid acousticlike pluck and high-mass chanting separate it from "Song II" (a search for truth), "Song III" (the hills that we climbed are just seasons out of time), "Song IV" (we're all semen in the uterus of the earth), and "Song V" (a prayer to the sun god); midsong, the guitars inevitably transform into a mesmerizing mudgulch. "You will come to realize that death, in its finality, is life"—Leonard Cohen oughta just hang it up, I swear.

375. GODDO

Goddo Fatcat Canadian import, 1977

These scatterbrained skeptics open their platter of burly bowling-night crunge with a primer 'bout how tough it is to drive brats to school in a yellow bus every day and always tell 'em to sit down and shut up, an oddly candid commentary 'cause for once it puts rock 'n' rollers on the side of the generation gap where they belong, plus usually when rockers sing about buses they sing about the Magic and/or Uncle Duggie's Fun and/or Chartreuse Micro varieties (or anyway Chevy vans), thus pretending everything's hunky-dory in the wide world of busdom when really it's not. "Hard Years" (which "ain't no blues") and "Let It Slide" analyze has-been rock stars who end up parking cars and whose fans only wanna see 'em hemorrhage (à la "It's Only Rock 'n' Roll"); "Twelve Days"'s speedboogie has Goddo getting headaches ("real migraine stuff") from their own concerts. Dana Orlando is credited with "heavy breathing" on "Drive Me Crazy"'s fuckboogie, and the next boogie's about not tucking your member back in after you're finished pissing, only not exactly. Word is their elusive double-live set's called *The Best Seat in the House,* and they photographed the backside of the girl with said "seat" for the cover, and here's their parting motto: "If indeed it is lonely at the top, who cares, it's lonely at the bottom too!" (See Rancid Vat's "It's Lonely at the Bottom, Baby," 1985.) Nice for once to come across a band who admit the rock 'n' roll dream's a crock.

376. STEPPENWOLF

16 Greatest Hits Dunhill, 1973; rec. 1968–72

They really didn't have this many "hits," I don't think, and neither do you need such a bountiful batch, especially since most of the superest stuff's from the first album they ever issued. But though heavifying longevity didn't do much for their subsequent high points, it worked "wonders" for their filler, and on consistency/competency/mediocrity terms this proves satisfactorily spinnable, so if I were you it's where I'd start (and probably end). Supposedly there's "politics" somewhere, but maybe you had to be there, unless "Monster"'s deceased Native Americans (a longstanding metal tradition, as you may have already deduced, thanx to Wounded Knee in December 1890 maybe) count. What I hear instead is optimistic advice for devil-may-care dudes on the loose with no shirts, racing bikes, screwing snatch, "eating humble pie" (somebody must've been hot for Steve Marriot), overdosing on cocaine ("a one-way ticket on an airline made of snow"!), losing lamps. "Screaming Night Hog" almost lives up to its title, Jerry Edmonton's beats could bring you to your knees when he felt like it, for an East German the vocalist's quite the cosmic cowboy, and two guitars sweep a major mess under the magic carpet.

377. BUCK DHARMA

Flat Out Portrait, 1982

From Blue Öyster Cult's rabbi, one of the most uncharacteristic "solo" sets I've ever heard, modestly ambitious like Lindsey Buckingham (who's used similar Beach Boys harmonies and summer car-tunes) or Daryl Hall, only more resourceful, more cock-eyed, and of course more boisterous. Middle-aged white-collar love-affair smarm and triumphs of AOR production over talent, a film theme for an Arabian head-of-state, an R. Meltzer doo-wop for the Weather Channel, a seven-minute blessed-are-the-pacemakers heart-transplant operetta with the emergency staff singing along with hospital hardware in the background. My two faves are the sparsest sounds available: The acoustic thunderclap about bondage and discipline and/or eternal procrastination, and the Fleetwoods cover, an even calmer tonic for the heart than Percy Sledge's version. Not kosher by any means.

378. KING'S X
Gretchen Goes to Nebraska Megaforce, 1989

The liner notes are a boring piece of quasi-magic-realist fiction that goes on forever, the most verbose monstrosity of its kind since the one on Genesis's *The Lamb Lies Down on Broadway* (maybe even wordier). The inner sleeve dreams of St. Augustine like Dylan on *John Wesley Harding* (quotes *The Confessions,* to be exact), and the sounds inside try their damnedest to reject the City of the World in favor of the City of God. Yet the free-will proponent this biracial Texas trio seems most willing to emulate isn't good old Saint Augie-Doggie so much as Rush's Neil Peart, and the time-changing melodies hardly ever wield sufficient oomph to carry the weight of singing bassist Doug Pinnick's deep depressive thoughts. Still, there's more here than fancydan para-diddles: "Everybody Knows a Little Bit of Something" works wonders with an ungodly marriage of early Funkadelic and early Yes, and between CSNY hippie-harmonies and Oriental exotica and evangelist-dissing and Ty Tabor's placid acoustic breaks and occasional thick riffs, there are times when, if your mood is temporarily uncynical, you'll convince yourself that King's X mine their pretensions more palatably than any egghead headbangers since *Physical Graffiti.* "Over My Head," an atypical "Dial MTV" smash, is the only time Pinnick completely falls victim to those Nehru Hendrix jackets his African-American heritage lets him get away with wearing; "Pleiades," the best track, has scientists denying the earth's flatness then getting burned at the stake. Their souls survive.

379. VENOM
Welcome to Hell Neat, 1981

Glazed in green goo that slimes from Pleasant Valley lawnmowers on a soggy Sunday, waddled through with Abaddon on "drums and nuclear warheads" and Cronos on "bulldozer bass" that basically sounds like a hatchet chopping a chord of wet lumber with no time off for good behavior, in retrospect this sprintmetal ranks with the most inept ever. Nothing holds any-body down, the shout-when-the-next-Nuge/Stooge-riff-comes-around voke-hooks are never in synch, and the charm's got less to do with the horned-and-bearded goat-hero of the fiery bloodpit than with average adolescent antix, i.e., "We're going wild," "Surf, baby" (??!), venereal disease reception, live fast swallow PCP die ugly, even Psalm 23. We're of course supposed to believe that these village vicars have sold souls Robert Johnson–style to the man in red, but the back cover has 'em wading ankle-deep in what appears to be the Boston Harbor, plus immoderately ignorant typos ("If this is scratched, wapped [*sic*] or defaced in any wat [*sic*] please throw it away and buy a new one"), so let's just say that if Satan *did* procure such simpletons' signatures on the proverbial dotted-line-of-eternity, they got a bum deal comparable to beachfront property along the River Styx itself. If you can't trust devils, who *can* you trust?

380. AC/DC
Back in Black Atlantic, 1980

Confused scholars have deemed this AC/DC's tour de force, but I disagree. It certainly enables a patho-logical fascination. First thing you hear is bells, real soon you discover they're from "hell"; first thing you see is crematorium blackness, one of the first lines is "you're only young but you're gonna die"; plus in "Have a Drink on Me," just months after Bon Scott strangled to death on his own booze-induced barf, Brian Johnson vociferates about why it's *good* to quaff one more pint. But this is the *Led Zep II* of the eighties, drab in the same way. Especially on Side One, most everything's just generic AC/DC qua AC/DC: Good licks, good sound effects even, and it's neat how Brian Johnson's newly discovered mouth rescues the microphone portion, but the production's too shiny, the tempo's thwarted, Phil Rudd's cans don't massacre much moose. On the other hand, Rick Rubin had the Beasties record "Rock Hard" over that "Back in Black" track for a real good reason. And if it ain't poetry when the fast machine with the clean motor knocks you out with her American thighs over the rolled-up "All Right Now" riffage in "You Shook Me All Night Long," poetry's a waste of rhyme.

381. THE JIMI HENDRIX EXPERIENCE
. . . .
Live at Winterland Ryko Analogue, 1988; rec. 1968

This dead guy puts out three or four concert albs every year, it seems, and if you really expect me to stay awake through all of 'em you better convince Harmony to pay me more than just ten grand. What's supposed to be wonderful about this one, say antiquity buffs with nothing more current to worry about, is the "sound," seeing how it's supposed to be a CD (but it's *not!*), but then what's wonderful about *all* wonderful records is the sound, right? (I mean, think about it—what else is there?) The way Jimbo introduces performances with talk of "groovy cats" and "old ladies" and "Jefferson Airplanes" is kinda flighty, but I'm grateful that he forfeits malarkey in favor of moo, occasionally real *loud* moo, 'specially in "Foxy Lady," where his Uzi weighs a ton. "Manic Depression" lasts for a patriotic seventy-six seconds longer than in the studio, "Sunshine of Your Love" won't get heavier till George Clinton releases the rendition he's been promising since '87, "Red House" is a bore, "Killing Floor" almost isn't, "Tax Free" 's "right up there" with "Stone Free" and "Free Ride" and "Slow Ride." Side Four advances from "Hey Joe" to "Purple Haze" to "Wild Thing" (Jimi's patented Vanilla Fudge version), which oughta make it "punk rock," and it even *feels* that way sometimes! Speaking of which, the events documented herein not only happened ten years to the, um, year before the Sex Pistols' final show, but they happened in the same place. And the vinyl's transparent, so if you stare at it real hard it looks like the record's spinning backward. Ever get the feeling you've been cheated?

382. THE CULT
. . . .
Electric Sire, 1987

Big problem here echoes the big problem with Zep's first couple, only more so: ALL THE SONGS SOUND THE SAME. Just monolithic cockblues purism—no wanderlust anthems, none of what's called yer "aural experiments," none of the fucking gorgeous art-druid doohickey that made Zep more than just Cream's glorified afterbirth. Except even "early" Zep's ax/can-boom booms *heavier* than the Cult's boom. (Rick Rubin produced, ha ha.) Also: The Cult all look too pale, and the singer (Ian Astbury, whose left nipple is prominently displayed on the cover) wears a Davy Crockett hat, and those went out in '55! And true metal studs would never write Marc Bolan hippie glitter garbage so la-di-da as "plastic fantastic lobster telephone" (they'd write about manly Vikings instead), 'cause true HM white trash *hated* hippies. (There's even a *tambourine,* for Jughead's sake!) Some yahoo on MTV once compared the previous Cult hypework, *Love,* to Zep, but when I spun my younger sis's postmod roomie's copy it sagged soggy like a porridge of Boston and U2. Yet though *Electric*'s rendition of "Born to Be Wild" is an overenunciated fiasco with overdinky guitar and no "lookin' for my dentures," and though Ian's rolled "r"s on the phrase "rattlesnake racket" in "Memphis Hip Shake" are completely un-called for, the rec throttles like Humble Pie/Mountain/Free, not as good as the *real* Cult circa "Baby Ice Dog," but immediate-impact rough-riff stomp-slop regardless. In "Love Removal Machine," the singer castratos *"baby baby baby"* exactly like Bob Plant, then wails "soul shaker," only it sounds like *"salt* shaker"! A brazen jeans-bulge for sure, at least by '87's standard—too bad they had to go turn into the new Whitesnake.

383. EXTREME
Extreme A&M, 1989

Even the songs with the catchiest chorus-hooks seem sloppily half-formed, devoid of beginnings and middles and ends. "Watching, Waiting" is mushy and soupy enough to pass for a pukey Night Ranger ballad. Yet these swarthy Beantown boys are canny enough to cover Wild Cherry's bicentennial disco classic "Play That Funky Music White Boy" live sometimes, and even at its most rote, their debut ranks not too terribly far behind Kix in the late eighties quasiboogie harmony-plus-rhythm department. There's at least as much accomplishment here as "potential." Nuno Bet-tencourt turns some untrammeled middle ground between Steve Vai and Philip Glass into High-Class Entertainment, the Lollipop Kids (from *Wizard of Oz?*) turn the youth choir from Pink Floyd's "Another Brick in the Wall" into cotton candy, additional rem-nants hail from the Four Seasons' "Big Girls Don't Cry" and Aerosmith's "Adam's Apple." Gary Cherone rebukes classmates with big heads, then tells mom he wants to skip school, then lusts after his teacher's anatomy, then admits he sheds tears when he's sad. The coda's a *Sgt. Pepper's* lullaby; the track before it is called "Flesh 'N' Blood," which title I scoffed at until I noticed that Gary makes "eat your body, eat your body" his mantra and the group goes so far as to thank "Our Lord" on the cover—Eucharist metal is a concept whose time has come, wouldn'tcha say?

384. CACTUS
One Way . . . or Another Atco, 1971

These grease monkeys do the Deltaboy harmonica 'n' vocoder hipshake as if they just ingested one of John Lee Hooker's dirty socks and one of Slim Harpo's, and the footwear's mismatched like Sal Mineo's in *Rebel Without a Cause*. They take Long Tall Sally out back and mug her, and you get to listen to her squeal for a while, collapse real slow, drift through this long warm tunnel of beautiful white light into the darkness, all that stuff. The sonnet where Rusty Day wishes his in-laws were in jail instead of his friends (that's what it sounds like, anyway) is a chuckle, and "Rockout, Whatever . . ." 's title admits that it's simply giving the people what they want. The mud-honey's caked unsanitarily enough, but something's missing—momentum, maybe. Weird when the best thing on a decent boogie LP's the acoustic instrumental named after an astrological sign.

385. DEEP PURPLE
Fireball Warner Bros., 1971

Thanks more to Ritchie Blackmore's sprung leads than to anything else, the title-blaze pounds petulantly as fortitude-fortified speedmetal, and the swaggering epic-of-defeat called "Fools" divides its eight minutes between two chords, just enough. The remainder's adequate-to-needlessly-extravagant midtempo soot, typified by an awful "Maggie's Farm" rejoinder called "Anyone's Daughter" and a pessimistic protest called "No No No" that attempts an it-ain't-gonna-improve statement voiced much more succinctly three years later by Stevie Wonder in "You Haven't Done Nothin'." The organ's like Sir Douglas Quintet gone central European, so at least you can't call it conven-tional.

386. HIGHWAY ROBBERY
For Love or Money RCA, 1972

Underneath dumbbell-looker Michael Stevens's bong-fuls of fuzz, a blond ("high fashion coiffure styled by Helene") prettyboy opera-fop clad in medieval lace mixes sixties slosh ladies' choices ("Bells," pure Lemon Pipers or Association or whoever, "All I Need") with frustrated open-menagerie stampedes ("Lazy Woman," "Ain't Gonna Take No More," and "Fifteen," the latter outscoring Alice Cooper by three whole years, five whole years before Eater thought to). Most debonair spectacle of 'em all has to be the def-drummed one where they beg the promotion department to paste their pictures everywhere and make 'em big stars so they can move to Hollywood Hills. Bassist claims his name's "John Livingston Tunison IV," and the object's manufactured on "warp-resistant Dynaflex," an audio innovation some smart smarty oughta revive, if ya ask me.

387. GOLDEN EARRING
Golden Earring Polydor UK import, 1976; rec. 1969–75

"Candy's Going Bad" 's heavy-pedaled tale of a saucy prep-school hussy whose daddy's gonna break her fingers in half is so hep the Godz covered it, and I think Nintendo borrowed its melody for their Marble Madness game too. "Kill Me" kills (partly in French, with cameo appearances by Jesus of Galilee and the Shah of Iran!), and "Radar Love" is tensed-up thoroughfare-trash at its most mindsplitting, even Bobbie Ann Mason says so. The hooks in the latter have driven me batty (har har) since I was thirteen, the horn charts and Cesar Zuiderwijk's tribalbeats make Fela Kuti seem like Gary Glitter, the Brenda Lee footnote is rock 'n' roll mythology at its David Essex utmost, and when Barry Hay yells out "ONE MORE RAY-DAR LOVER GONE!!" the sky falls but Chicken Little's almost home.

"She Flies on the Strange Wings" is recommended to Zamfir and the Motörhead Pan Flute Orchestra, "Avalanche of Love" has a title Sonic Youth would serial-murder for, and "The Song Is Over" 's title doesn't make sense till the end. These space-age wangbar-twangers evidently spend their entire young lives ingesting tequila from wooden shoes, stealing expensive Link Wray and Soft Machine imports from the corner hashish stand, air-violining to Henry Mancini's *Six Hours Past Sunset,* and planting both their two lips and their tulips wherever they Amster-god-damn pleased! Two-hit wonders (*à la* Janis Ian and Dobie Gray—only people with eons separating their fifteen minutes of fame are eligible), they started (as "the Golden Earrings"!) back before the Beatles, and were still plugging away long after the Knack cracked. They *deserved* to be Holland's biggest group ever, and I was there once and saw a bearded lady walking down the street, so I oughta know.

388. BLOODROCK
Bloodrock 2 Capitol, 1970

The morbid masterstroke, as oldtimers will recall, is "D.O.A.," sirens and riffblast tensing you into this fatal jet-crash color-commentaried via the point of view of a passenger who's just now realizing his bucket's being kicked. Reminds me of some "M*A*S*H" episode Alan Alda directed once, and of all those postderegulation air disasters. Bloodrock's other plowboy scufflegrime could use some prune juice though. The punch increases when the tempo does, but the Mooglike accompaniment and the singer's habit of pronouncing "s" like "sh" distracts when the beats-per-minute drag. Versification in the realm of closet-hiding and forcing your kids to dig "artificial rockout" stands out, so the circumference is bigger than Bloodstone's, but any geology student could've guessed that much.

Photograph by David J. Burrows © 1989

389. **FASTWAY**
Fastway Columbia, 1983

The hulkiest moments here ("All I Need Is Your Love," "Another Day," "Give It All You Got," the stupendously levee-busting bloodclot "Heft!") are history's most "accurate" facsimile of the sound qua sound that made preprog Zep zip, at least in ex–Motörhead Fast Eddie Clarke's guitar department. Golden boy David King's Plantalike screamers have competition, but they're up there (and he plays harmonica; if we're to believe the credits, there's no bassist); ex–Humble Pie Jerry Shirley's traps are hacked with far too much audiophile daintiness to hack it, and the verbal platitudes are sadder still. All of which computes to the following: Billy Squier's funkier, Paris louder, Rush nuttier, Queen more mythic, the Cult more verbose, Kingdom Come and Whitesnake more bankable. Uriah Heep's got a better song called "Easy Livin'," and there's dark-horse odds that I'll someday opt for Jane's Addiction's rhythm section if I ever figure out why they didn't ditch Perry Farrell the last time they toured Idaho. But since hairlines have to count for something, I'll take this over Jimmy Page's *Outrider*, Jason Bonham or no Jason Bonham.

390. **JOHN McLAUGHLIN**
Devotion Douglas, 1970

Of the two compositions named after mythical fire-breathing beasts, only "Dragon Song" earns its dungeon; "Don't Let the Dragon Eat Your Mother" (which should've been named after David Carradine's grasshopper or should've traded titles with "Purpose of When") is some kinda yoga-jam, drifting in and out of the I'm-okay-you're-okay abyss. More often, this is pretty loud as EST exercises go, rolling much nappiness over galactic funk-bumps. Thanks to Larry Young and Buddy Miles (mostly Larry Young), who unintentionally split the difference between Can's Teutonic dronation and John Coltrane's infinite ascension, the groove's too tangible to devolve into onanism. As for McLaughlin, who applies Link Wray/Lonnie Mack distortotronic twangblister hoedowns to a postbop context, he's *stately*, there's no other word for it.

391. **VENOM**
Black Metal Neat, 1982

Your typical ibex-with-an-upside-down-star-on-his-forehead concept album, only sludged to a rottener wormcrawl, and loonier, 'cause they got there first. Dredging up grave-rob archetypes that predate the dawn of Christendom, screaming about countesses bathing in virgin's blood, claiming to swig the puke of priests, stomping bass like third-LP Stooges marching to the gallows' pole but closing with high-flown twaddle that could be "Ride My See-Saw" by the Moody Blues, just generally sanctioning your stereo's loudness contour, these schnooks build their twirly-bird spasmodics into a suspense no more chilling than Michael Jackson's "Thriller" video, but that's probably part of the point. *Black Metal*'s got not quite the hooks of *Welcome to Hell* but it sure as the devil has more than Slayer, at least in its two brimstone milestones: One's "Bloodlust," with barbaric Abaddon war drums rolling around like cannonballs in a nocturnal London

fog, plus grunted poesy that no doubt inspired Celtic Frost; the other's "Teacher's Pet," with blooze-wah and nondemonic concupiscence that doubtfully inspired Van Halen's "Hot for Teacher," but with David Lee you never know, do you?

392. ROSSINGTON-COLLINS BAND
Anytime, Anyplace, Anywhere MCA, 1980

Dale Krantz concocts a dirty and unbashful kind of *Every Picture Tells A Story/Cheap Thrills* screech-grandeur here, and if the shapeless seven-piece Skynyrd-survivor progresso-boogie it's set upon isn't always completely "heavy," devotees of W. Axl Rose oughta be able to rally behind it regardless. Sometimes, it's heavy indeed: Slower moving and more solemnly Brit than anything Skynyrd ever did, with intertwined swirls and angular promenades twisting their sustained time-turns into the Moon Mullican album Rush never made, especially when Dale's keening toward Geddy Lee territory in the highly agitated "Opportunity." She's been used and abused and she's searching for just one honest man, and though the clichés come hither (don't throw stones, tomorrow never comes, misery loves company), piercing pacing makes 'em last. Moral's that the fast lane, in the end, is a speed trap.

393. BRITNY FOX
Britny Fox Columbia, 1988

Hairpiled glamboys from Pennsylvania (the province of mummers), Debbie Gibson thanks 'em on the inner sleeve of *Electric Youth,* so you know they must be doing something right, and I bet Mojo Nixon's real jealous. "Girlschool" 's an incredible streak through the halls of distaff academe with rumps and riffs ablaze Angus-style, plus it shares its name with a great band (as in the MC5's "Shakin' Street," Shakin' Street's "Generation X," Generation X's "Kleenex"). In the song's video, Britny's Village People–circa-*Renaissance* "new romantic" togs are tarty enough to make Poison look male, a bit of one-upmanship to carry with pride; they tell interviewers that if Heart can dress this way, so can they, as if somehow it's never occurred to 'em that Heart are *women.* With a few exceptions like the retroboogie where Mike Smith pretends he's Billy Gibbons from Texas, the LP's surface constitutes a Kiss duplication with every detail in place, but there's dopier details beneath: The lead pouter's named after Dizzy Dean, as hurling a St. Louis Cardinal as Bob Gibson and a real barnstormer to boot, yet though "Wabash Cannonball" would've earned him his name he covers "Gudbuy t'Jane," about a transvestite and therefore equally appropriate. "Save the Weak" ("Take a look at what you have, and the things you own/And thank God that you've grown . . .") is a protest-drip in a class with Spiňal Tap's "Listen to the Flower People" if not White Lion's "When the Children Cry," and "Rock Revolution" ("They rate our music down/They take our words and change them around") and "In America" ("A place we could live, you know of it") aren't far behind. I'm in awe.

394. RANCID VAT

Burger Belsen Brilliancy Prize, 1985

These self-deprecating sickos from the Left Coast excel at see-who'll-finish-first mock-shock-rock, laudably contagious and junky and riffwise, but they manage to steer clear of gratuitous gag-me-with-a-spoonism, except perhaps on the LP jacket, which Kurt Waldheim might find amusing. Rants concern shooting your load before you want to and sleeping around the clock and injecting babies with rabies, but what's swell is that the gross-out's always there to convey a *message*—namely, that people deserve to be despised, and life sucks, but "there's always room for hope with your finger down your throat." Headed by an out-of-breath lush named Phil Irwin who testifies like the scared-poopless lovechild of King Kong Bundy and Al Bundy, their earlier *Rulebreakers Rule* was an all-wrestling-song EP with a rendition of Freddie Blassie's "Pencil Neck Geek," and they don't always mean what they say (like f'rinstance in their infectiously diseased paean to "big Johnny Wad, X-rated god," which deserves its own twelve-inch), but usually they do: "It might be nice if we were brothers, and lived in harmony with one another . . . It might be nice, but it won't happen." Realism triumphs again.

395. EARTHQUAKE

Leveled Beserkely, 1977

True to their schools, the kind of acne-prone California beach-jocks mom'd be overjoyed for you to bring home, Earthquake played their seventies-rock '65-style, for its own sake, as if the revolution had never happened, and though their '76 *8.5* album sounds more like the Dictators or Van Halen, this one sounds more like sentient human beings. At the tail end of Greg Shaw's simpler-things-right-around-the-corner "pop revival" (which only happened on paper), long before skinny ties and lapel pins came into vogue, 'quake did the sugar-metal thing, subjecting hard licks to background oohs and ahs, melding Point Blank and Badfinger (in "Trainride" and "Street Fever"), freshening up with Paul Revere and Hot Chocolate covers about drugs (anti-) and suicide (ambiguous). Turpitude would never sound so unthreatening again, at least not on purpose—they might as well've been playing duck-duck-goose. My pick-to-click's a weeper about aloneness in your personal sanctuary upstairs (the only teen predicament with any real credence anyhow, as Brian Wilson and Martha Reeves knew well), but better still is "Tall Order for a Short Guy" (available on the *Chartbusters: The Best of Beserkley* comp), which is to Randy Newman's "Short People" as "Love Connection" is to "Wheel of Fortune." But then, I'm 5'5".

396. HÜSKER DÜ

Metal Circus SST EP, 1983

It seemed far less held-in-check then than it does now, and it initiated a vast hookcore motorcade that'd turn ooze to snooze by decade's end, but some enthusiasm remains intact in the three good songs—one a smarter eighties equivalent of "Revolution" (which is to say it's anti-) that notwithstanding deserves its own Nike commercial, one a nonspecific but not unanthemic piece of harmonizing about why something-or-other's no longer worth laughing at, one a pseudopederastic proto-pigfuck snuff-story that's not nearly as disturbing as either John Anderson's "July the 12th, 1939" or the Mekons' "Karen" but it's got an amiable chorus anyhoo. Also: a deluge of ceremonial rock-the-boat riff-tilt whine and distrusting suspicion of lefty whatevers. Not that the Düs are dumb enough to consider righty whatevers any more respectable, y'understand.

397. QUEEN
News of the World Elektra, 1977

Back in adolescence I associated "We Will Rock You" with Catholic saints getting stoned to death and atrocities of that ilk, considered it even more noxious than "Dust in the Wind," but by '89 it was embraced not at the Aryan Woodstock in March but at the Pistons' championship series in June, and as Grandmaster Flash and "Pour Some Sugar on Me" had already demonstrated, what it'd really been from the gitgo was pure proto-rap: Just chant and drumclaps, words are for the birds. Here, it leads straight into "We Are the Champions," another one of the three Queentunes ("Another One Bites the Dust" eventually completed the trilogy) that paradoxically endeared these fairy godmothers (who para-paradoxically also sang about bike racing and soccer) to the ESPN crowd. Then "Sheer Heart Attack," proof that Roger Taylor took the Pistols' "God Save the Queen" personally and nonetheless the slyest and least dismissable we-can-do-it-too reply to punk rock any old-wave millionaires made so soon after the fact—a seventeen-year-old ripped on TV and DNA wants to disappear, and the one-chord speed-metal bombardment pretty clearly inspired Prince's "Sister." Save for the horrid early Queenfunk attempts "Get Down Make Love" and "Fight from the Inside," though, the remainder's all limp-wristed chicken-livered yellow-bellied piano lessons. The stuff one classmate my frosh year at U of Detroit was referring to when he said Freddie Mercury wanted to be gay without the responsibility of being homosexual.

398. QUEENSRŸCHE
Operation: Mindcrime EMI America, 1988

"**A**n audio move," the guitarist called it, but also a concept move, meaning move, virtuosity move, dialogue move, sincerity move, rhythm move, and let's-stop-cross-dressing move. Never before had so many pretensions been taken on by so few in so short a time (you can hear U2, Midnight Oil, Iron Maiden, *The*

Wall, Hysteria, Sab's *Sabotage,* Styx's *Kilroy Was Here,* death-disco), but most of the time it doesn't sound pretentious at all, just ambitious. Since they were smart enough to omit a lyric sheet, snatches connect like with such prog-disciples as Die Kreuzen or Belfegore or Voivod (or even Mark Stewart): "We'll burn the White House down," "I'm tired of all this bullshit they've been feeding me about the communist plan." It's naive and cynical as any rock-politix ever (all about, you know, how the state and religion and drugs and dirty sixteen-year-old hookers with herpes thwart the Holy Individual Initiative), but no way is it merely "liberal"—seems they're even explicitly pro-Sandinista. First side's pretty cohesive (Side Two's mostly spongy AOR tripe), and the schizzy anitsludge sonics reward close listening with

writhing beyond-Madonna postcatechism subtexts, so maybe Geoff Tate wears his spitcurl like that 'cause he got raped by a nun once. I've never had much use for the sort of gothic melodramatics these Seattlites deal in, so I'm probably either overrating or under-rating it like crazy, but I know for sure there's more jolts and hooks and ideas here than in any random stack of concurrent pigfuck/bigfoot/hardcore/speed-metal plates. Damn thing goes on forever, natch, but it's a relief to know there's still bozos around who aren't content with being half-assed.

399. .38 SPECIAL

Flashback A&M, 1987; rec. 1977–87

You could call 'em one-dimensionally synthetic, you could label 'em a cross between REO and Alabama. But the bounces in "Hold on Loosely," "Caught Up in You," and "Back Where You Belong" might send you shuffling through your teenybop collection for their source, the six-strings and drawls crunch too gruff to affect classicist fake-Brit cadences, and the Outlaws-style brushfire-jam pinnacles nod toward origins in the saloons of Dixieland. Founded as a chopless boogie-squalor bunch in the mid-seventies and converted to diehard metal-pop romantics in the wake of the Cars and Loverboy, .38 Special are constantly yearning for a love that's just slipped beyond their grasp, never more so than in the obsessive "If I'd Been the One," one of 1984's most remarkable smash singles. Wrangling his way from between tumbleweed-guitar and Zildjian-heavy silver-spurs drums, Ronnie Van Zant's little brother Donnie bangs his head on the front door where his lost love lives, pledging to stay there till eternity, not budging from that porch. He keeps settling down, but then he has second thoughts, and he's back to raging: "It just goes on and on . . . did you think I'd just give up?" Low points are the inevitable three wannabes that never-before-appeared-on-any-.38-Special-LP, but the only leftover from the ensemble's chopless-squalor phase, "Rockin' into the Night," earns its place with jumbo riffs and lyrical dorkitude beyond the call of duty ("Well I ain't no Messiah/But

I'm close enough for rock 'n' roll"). Forget REO/Alabama—.38 Special's more like, er, the Beatles (yeah, that's the ticket!) three or four times removed. Beneath your blankets you'd barely be able to tell the difference.

Photograph by Charles Peterson

400. GREEN RIVER

Dry as a Bone SubPop EP, 1987

Late eighties Seattle's definitive coupling of Cripple Creek and Garageland (there were way too many more where this came from) is surging trudge-bottomed elastic-band smut-revisionism with yowl-tendencies that wind and grind and keep slip-slidin' away like every decent thing mouthpiece Mark Arm's ever wished for in his young dog-day of a life, like either the Stooges' "I Wanna Be Your Dog" or Aerosmith's "Sick as a Dog," but certainly like *some* dog song or other. You're conned into wondering whether the Diddleybeat keeps slowing to a wheeze because they want it to (or else what would they do for a "living"?) or because they have no say in the matter. "Unwind" 's the closest Arm or any of his compatriots will ever come to cohesion, and its sound does what its title tells it to, like a crawling king snake would—coil by coil, no less sinister for its sluggishness. Unbearably antiwoman, maybe, but when you're always being controlled you must think you gotta control *somebody,* right? Thing is, if you think you're always being controlled, are you really paying attention, or are you just copping out?

401. FLAMING LIPS

Flaming Lips LSD EP, 1984

No spokesmen for Ron's War on Drugs, and obviously not from Muskogee, these euphoric Oklahippies never again equaled this initial Yuletide-tinted investment in the Strangeness Savings and Loan, which sounded then and still does like some moonman had accidentally let it slip through his porthole whilst en route to some dimension the Aeronautical Administration's been keeping secret: mile-high ghost-fuzz, Dead Sea Scroll bass-zags, cans slapped like a bustle in Amon Düül's hedgerow, all told one of the trippiest bron-y-aur stomps to emerge from the lava-lamp pits of post-"p" rock. Having a hard time on planet Earth, Wayne Coyne packs up his ying-yang in his old kit bag, heads out with "Marseillaise"/"All You Need Is Love" on his Walkman, slurps up the acid rain, suddenly realizes the edge of the galaxy is farther away than he thought. So in his most impeccable slice of Naugahyde-levitation, deciding once and for all that the sun's third stone's a drag, he requests a new one.

402. LAST EXIT

Cassette Recordings 87 Enemy, 1988

Tour highlights taped off soundboards in Denmark, Holland, and Billy Joel's beloved Allentown, this set's more a showcase for individual ingenuity than any of its Last Exit predecessors, and eventually it wears thin. But Bill Laswell's claimed that any two of the combo's members could gig together alone, and if his and Peter Brötzmann's rampaging '87 *Lowlife* isn't proof enough, *Cassette Recordings* oughta be: A sax-wailed wake-up call (somewhat similar to the kindergarten national anthem "José Can You See All the Bedbugs on Me") opens "Line of Fire," the tiring no-boundary squawk-and-rawk fest that takes up all of Side One, then Ronald Shannon Jackson starts rushing ahead of himself, rumbling increasingly drunk and disorderly as Sonny Sharrock and Peter Brötzmann peer up from the surface and bellow like Loch Ness monsters, only to resubmerge. Sharrock's distortion engulfs the whole works, and by the finish the jam's been transformed into a burial procession. In "Sore Titties," on the less academic Side Two, Brötzmann facetiously twists out his sax-spew as if he's trying to turn the rusted-stuck steering wheel of a big old schooner. The "Your Chin" coda belongs to Sharrock's grinding delerium, and Jackson's tubs (and post–Amiri Baraka/Last Poets rant-rap) are in the foreground for "Big Boss Man," the kind of fat-mama Jimmy Reed cover galoots like Killdozer and Molly Hatchet only wish they could pull off.

403. KING CRIMSON

Starless and Bible Black Atlantic, 1974

The first word-phrase on this royal roundtable of classical gastrointestinitis is "health-food faggots," as if John Wetton should talk. (Who does he think health-food fools *listened* to—Slade?) Bottom line's that Wetton *shouldn't* talk, and neither should anybody else here, 'cause when they don't, a commendably clamorific cut-and-paste edge comes into play. "Fracture" roars toward oblivion for at least six of its eleven minutes, and the middle of Side One and the rampaging "Starless . . ." itself suggest percussionist Bill Bruford's been checking out Miles's *On the Corner*. The star, naturally, is Robert Fripp, who turns his colossal floor-waxer on its side to hit all those hard-to-reach spots. And the goat, naturally, is Wetton, whose histrionics are impossible to follow—something about American soldiers carting consumer artifacts (Brylcreem, Dixieland, figurines of the Virgin Mary) overseas and offending Europe's fine taste. Also impoverished Negro children learning Mellotron licks on their bottlenecks, I think, but don't quote me on that one. (No humility about Greyhounds and switchblades like on later-'74's *Red,* a considerably more persuasive denial of kneejerk egalitarianism, with jazzier reeds but less heft.) When Wetton drones the violins get dainty, and with "The Mincer," the health-food fools get their field day.

404. **THE WHO**
. . . .
Live at Leeds Decca, 1970

Side One looks pretty young but it's just back-dated, with volume galore and trivia from days gone by, a failed attempt to connect postskifflers' misapprehension of early rock 'n' roll (i.e., Johnny Kidd, Eddie Cochran, plus the gloriously blue-collared "Substitute") to the impending metal millennium. The Mose Allison–penned opener diddles aimlessly but provides a name for Rock City Angels' debut; "Summertime Blues" whimpers in Blue Cheer's wake but manages to ape some 13th Floor Elevators electrojug; "Shakin' All Over" forfeits all of its sex and most of its dread for Pete's "Get Back" crap midway through; Roger tries a few Plantian glottal orgasmoans. Side Two's bulkier, subjecting the usually icky "Magic Bus" to Delta-overflow that might well have made Ted Nugent rethink a riff or two, but first expanding "My Generation" into fourteen-plus wildassedly Zeppish free-rock minutes of drama and anguish and protogenic Sonic Youthery. The only serious problem with the smash-the-instruments bit, I guess, is that somebody kept buying 'em new ones. Forever.

405. **MOVING SIDEWALKS**
. . . .
99th Floor Eva French import, c. 1984; rec. 1966–69

Future ZZ Topper Billy Gibbons stirs all sorts of acid-accentuated contraband into this prizewinning Tex-Mex cryptopunk chili: Vanilla-Fudged Beatles, raga gaga, woman-woe protoboogie, the ginchiest love-in-the-elevator song north of Paul Nicholas's "Heaven on the Seventh Floor." There's a Hendrix fan's voodoo–patter/splatter in "Need Me," "Joe Blues," "Reclipse," "You Make Me Shake," and "Pluto Sept. 31," and the cartoon voices and backward mantra and Bach-shocked polybeat in "Eclipse" might well've helped spur George Clinton's Parliaments out of their matching sharkskins. Fate always turns trash-organ drowsy, but when big (beardless!) Bill pulls out the stops he haywires like 13th Floor homey Roky Erickson: "All you gotta do is eat me," he demands once, and next his girl's on his mind but his hand's somewhere else. When the moon blocks the sun, he goes blind, gets scared his mind might melt.

406. Max's Kansas City 1976

Ram, 1976

This is punk rock in its most infantile stage, evolving out of lower Manhattan's glitter/Warhol/homosexual underground, and though Wayne County, who later changed his sex to Jayne County, talked *about* the stars—Dolls, Ramones (who later stole his drummer Marc Bell), Heartbreakers (though not Aerosmith or Madonna or Springsteen for some reason), mostly all you get here are farm teams you never heard of, and for the most part you didn't miss anything by not hearing of 'em. The Fast are fey post-Sparks/Queen proto-powerpop, Harry Toledo is some gloom-pomp link between Van Der Graaf Generator and Sisters of Mercy, Cherry Vanilla and her Staten Island Band are the Vanilla Fudge in cabaret drag, the John Collins Band are Iron Butterfly revivalists—this is *heavy metal,* in other words, but pretty unspectacular about it. Wayne/Jayne's Backstreet Boys rock harder and more fun than the rest, pulling off a hiccuppy thing called "Cream in My Jeans" and a louder one where Wayne tallies all the sleaze and decadence and groupies. And Wayne's pretty hilarious about it too—lisps like a madwoman, reminds you to "bring your masquerade mask and your ego trip," calls Patti Smith "the Stagger Lee of rock 'n' roll," generally seems like he/she's aching to get his/her greedy hands into Lou's and Iggy's trousers.

The two most famous bands close the sides: First Pere Ubu, whose truly fearsome live "Final Solution" explodes as many zits as any pubescent-psychosis epic ever to ride its transportation special out of mid-America (Crocus Behemoth calls himself a "victim of natural selection," which pretty much sums up his bookworm self-deprecation), then Suicide, who probably deserve some of the blame for inventing acid house and definitely deserve some of the blame for inventing Big Black. Imagine ? and the Mysterians produced by a sopored-out Giorgio Morodor, with some geek chanting "doomsday, doomsday" on top—quite a laugh.

407. AC/DC

Blow Up Your Video Atlantic, 1988

The first AC/DC waxing produced by ex-Easybeats (Harry Vanda and Angus and Malcolm's big bro George Young) in a decade moves the fivesome back to the back porch, toward the agglomerated Humble Pie-as-MC5 blooze of *If You Want Blood* and *'74 Jailbreak.* Completely against the CD-era grain, this is the group's scummiest-sounding record of the eighties, so quaint it's almost inconsequential; dunno how Vanda and Young pull it off, but somehow they even get distortion off Brian Johnson's *voice.* Built like a brick greenhouse effect, the typically classic AC/DC sleaze-single "Heatseeker" kicks off with Mississippi-crossroads chickenscratch, then kicks down your shanty's walls and windows one by one with a riff that belongs in the zoo and a mad mongrel bark drooling phallic missile metaphors. From there, there's a ration of grungeful walk-the-dinosaur noggin-nodders ("Nick of Time," "Rough Stuff," "Two's Up"), some Chevy-metal Creedence ("Kissin' Dynamite"), a strange strobe-stomp with a Cliff Williams bass line that criss-crosses Bowie's "Fame" with Sly's "Thank You Falet-tinme Be Mice Elf" in a way that'd make Hamilton Bohannon take notes ("Meanstreak"). Then, closing the flow with Iggy/Lemmy–type battle jargon not far from what set the proceedings in gear, "This Means War," an ultracompressed boner-dangling semi–"Turd on the Run"–rooted thrashboogie that drags Mick Jagger's Grecian-formulated tail, bleeding blue blood, all across the killing floor. They make it look so simple.

408. TONY WILLIAMS LIFETIME

Once in a Lifetime Verve, 1982; rec. 1969–70

Maybe I've just got a stunted attention span, but from what I can tell the fusion-founders here noodle a lot. Ill-defined semifunk with Williams's irregular octopus/offbeat patterns providing an oversubtle found-ation for John McLaughlin's improv (and Larry Young's organ providing more drive than oughta be necessary), this reissue revives all of *Emergency* plus select portions of *Turn It Over* and *Ego,* and though the *Turn It Over* cuts at least approach locomotion, no groove's continuous enough to disgorge any kind of preemptive strike, and the hushed post-Dylan poesy is mystic pizza. But McLaughlin's distort-ups are never trite; his tone turns savage in "Where" and coagulates for a while in "Emergency," and the addition of Jack Bruce helps make "Vuelto Abajo" a jazz "Smoke on the Water" (like, maybe this *started* that fire at Montreux!). My primary objection to the rest, I guess, is that you can't dance to it.

409. AEROSMITH
Done with Mirrors Geffen, 1985

Of all the supposed comebacks professional musicians (e.g., Tina/Aretha/Fogerty/Dylan/"the Clash") made circa '84–'86, only this one seemed uncynical enough to live up to its hype. Back in the saddle and riding real high, 'Smith open with a chaotic showcase from Joe Perry's solo hiatus where his tool blows like a horn section, then head direct into "My Fist Your Face," a brazen Beastie-doppelgänger with an immense riff-beat winding around a hyperbolically misogynous rap about teenybop hookers and Betty Boop and "second-floor checkin' makin' Wall Street out the door." Then a good constipated-grunt AC/DC imitation, some grindbump luring Steve Tyler's falsetto into a Police melody, and a late-ZZ midtempo that rhymes "ladies" with "Hades." Then "Gypsy Boots"'s show-off ending two minutes too late (but they deserve a freebie this time around), then "She's on Fire"'s licks linking the Mississippi's banks to the Nile River valley, then finally "The Hop," Chuck Berry–gone-heavy danceability with howlin' wolves, shopping malls, crazy men shaking their "rattlesnakes," and a nifty harmonica coda. Wealthy twelve-year-vet pros are hardly punks, even if their wet dreams are as stuck in puberty as Aerosmith's are, but this set's more straight-on and stripped-down and do-or-die than the guys had sounded in nigh on a decade, not prissy or glossy like the rest of those aged holdovers. Rocking too hard for AOR, it died on the charts, and the band got scared. Next time out they hired outside writers and Bon Jovi's producer, and sucked, and sold.

410. DAVID ROTER METHOD
Bambo Unknown Tongue, 1987

Once in Germany I accidentally manslaughtered a hedgehog by running him over with my car, but fortunately for me no hedgehog demons ever came back to haunt me like the deer who starts shooting hunters with machine guns and tying them to the hoods of their cars in the title song of this, the most noteworthy Blue Öyster Cult–associated elpee in quite some time, which is produced by ex-BÖC tubswaggler Al Bouchard and features guest appearances by Kenny Aaronson of Dust and Scott "Top Ten" Kempner of the Dictators. Additional tunes biographize Sonny Liston, Marlene Dietrich, Joan Crawford, and Benito Mussolini, and the topper's the one quilled by famed bookwriter Richard Meltzer (who coined the record label's name back in *The Aesthetics of Rock*) where a baby begs to be adopted so he can steal all your cigarettes and maybe someday liberate the Soviets or hit home runs. Though unluckily for us there's nothing about Bill Rohr (whose brother Les pitched for the Mets, plus as a rookie for Boston in—I think—1967 Bill had a perfect game going with two outs in the ninth but then Elston Howard fouled everything up by slugging a double), *Bambo*'s only other problem is the thin sound on three-quarters of it—them guitars need to hit Vic Tanny's and get some meat on their bones. But then again so do I.

411. All Guitars!
Tellus cassette, 1985

Assorted Sonic Youths and Big Blacks and Einstürzende Neubautens and the like evoke the following: Celery in the garbage disposal, beer rusting bedsprings, Chrysler rescued with tax dollars, a cheap picnic in Randy Holden's misery, whatever goes up must come down brown, three minutes to tune up, boil water for the new baby but don't boil the baby (a reminder), Evanston altar boy impaled in jail by Rosey Grier's needlepoint kit, Goetz gets off scot-free at the next stop, pluck pluck has anybody seen the bridge pluck pluck, piped-in background sound introduced to offices in 1938 and into the White House during Ike's administration but replaced in Republican Party HQ by Lee Atwater, when the Russkies invade we'll all be corralled in drive-in-movie lots, stuff like that. Nifty ideas, but you turn 'em off before they're done. At least when *Nazareth* did "The Ballad of Hollis Brown" you could tell it had words!

412. CHROME
Half-Machine Lip Moves Siren, 1979

Reels of crudely swelling Hendrix-concertina riding a mechanized weird-science Stoogebeat, firming into hairballs, plugging Sister Ray's gumwrapper in Geezer Butler's light socket, and bridging the Bering Strait between early-seventies Autobahn-garde and Public Image Ltd.'s first single, this works up a huge Edison bill that Chrome's pair of Frisco beatniks will probably never pay, and it'd be some kind of proto-Voivod revelation if not for the zombie frontman's unlistenably artificial (probably doctored) nasal whimper, which does its laughable worst to ape Iggy and Elvis. What makes the mouth "unlistenable" ain't any lack of imaginary "accessibility," mind you, but rather the way its cabaret-quotient inevitably depletes the feedback's disruptive power, renders it moot. The group's first album was a soundtrack for a live sex show, which somehow figures.

413. SILVER METRE
Silver Metre National General, c. 1971

Thirteen reasons why this record deserves its place in heavy metal history: (1) Leigh Stevens, the guitarist, used to be in Blue Cheer. (2) You can tell he used to be in Blue Cheer just by listening to him. (3) Pete Sears, the bassist, looks exactly like Lemmy from Motörhead. (4) Mick Waller, the drummer, wears granny glasses. (5) Elton John wrote three of the songs. (6) "Country Comfort" is probably the only one of the Elton songs you ever heard before. (7) The other two Elton songs are about being a fugitive and growing old, and the one about growing old is death-crunge almost as nasty as Nazareth's version of "The Ballad of Hollis Brown." (8) The band covers "Superstar" (from *Jesus Christ Superstar*), by Andrew Lloyd Webber, the best-paid popular musician in the world, or at least in England (I can't remember which). (9) The three songs with the best titles ("Gangbang," "Cocklewood Monster," "Dog End") are not cover versions at all. (10) "Gangbang" has nothing to with raping women—it's an instrumental! (11) "Dog End" has nothing to do with that Jethro Tull ditty about "picking up dog ends in the rain," yet it still doesn't explain what "dog ends" are. (12) In "Compromising Situation" the singer asks out a girl but she says she has to wash her hair. (13) The band look as if they haven't washed *their* hair for years.

414. HEART
Little Queen Portrait, 1977

Though Freudian elucidation of the textual content might uncover embarrassing vagina-dentata and unleashed-penis metaphors both (plus you can hear one of these seaside sisters "getting off" toward the end), "Barracuda" 's one nasty "Immigrant Song" piracy ('specially them drums), and myself I still like to imagine it's just good ichthyology. "Kick It Out" 's lady rocker "cranking it out in a school zone" and "Little Queen" 's lithe dandy in checkered tights (he's on the back cover) are more adequately autobiographic subZepfunk; "Say Hello" precedes its "Me and Julio Down by the Schoolyard" refraction with a baseball game that for all I know involves Jim Bouton at Sicks Stadium. Much of what the weight-watchin' Wilsons elsewhere accomplish is depicted not misleadingly by the annual gypsy-fest (which both Cher and Stevie Nicks beat 'em to anyhow) their pet lovegoat's helpin' celebrate in the photo session: mandolin madrigalisms, comely first ("Keep Your Love Alive," "Sylvain Song") then homely later ("Dream of the Archer," "Treat Me Well," "Cry to Me"), no doubt motivated by the save-the-sequoia/Bill Walton/SLA/Grape Nuts environs from which Heart sprang, and which they soon left behind. They followed REO Stationwagon into the wicked wilderness of adult entertainment ("Never," from '85, might be the women's lib "Livin' on a Prayer"), devoted their careers to the pursuit of bareback riders who'd cross-dress in the woods, and all it got 'em was Fat City.

415. ANTISEEN
Honour Among Thieves Bona Fide, 1988

Growl-heaver Jeff Clayton sports one o' them black floppy turkey-shoot hats like get worn in the land of shacks, and in the footsteps of his idol Jim Dandy Mangrum, he plays washboard solos. Then he breaks the board in half, or sets it on fire, or blows it up. All of which makes sense, 'cause this big-beat boondock-slime is the most rightful surviving heir to Jim's long-vacant Satanbilly throne. After the manner of former death-row candidate David Allen Coe himself, Antiseen's long hair just can't cover up their red necks, so these Carolina boys mate MC5 tire-kick with Black Oak can kick, and though they only know one mode, it's good for kicks. Their horror stories concern wife-beaters and tortured souls and mill-toilers and infant-murderers and faces full of teeth and small-town wimmins they've knowed, at least one of whom puts her carousin' hubbie (or herself—hard to tell) in the ground, and another of whom plays the lead role in "Ruby, Ruby, Get Back to the Hills," which sees Kenny Rogers's bid and raises him five. On stage, there's lotsa violence and bloodshed—the participants frequently leave each other in stitches. Literally.

416. MEKANÏK DESTRÜCTÏW KOMANDÖH
Berlin Sixth International EP, 1982

If these Krauts ain't Nazis, how come they close with that goose-stepping bootmarch? Don't ask me, 'cause the only decodable English is when Volker Hauptvogel yells "human being" at the end of "Werwolf" (they spell different over there), and the German's a laugh —gratingly ceremonial tragicomic tongue twisters that for all I know just mean today's Volker's birthday and he's jumpy with good will. He cackles his consonants like a banshee as Georg Keller guitars ditto and saxist Stephan Schwietzke bops freestyle over Uli Radike's syndrums (or some organic substitutes called *schlag-zeug*s that sound like 'em), and the more romantically overwrought it all gets, the better: "Die Babies Von Heute" organ-grinds its rhythm like Kurt Weill, "Der Tag Schlägt Zu" is a dirge that goes boom. If it weren't so foreign, I'd probably donate it to the Salvation Army. But no two ways about it, those monikers kill. Like, I understand why "Uli" 's pronounced "Ul-i" and "Georg" "Gee-orgh" and "Volker" "Woltz-kär," but how come Edgar Domin (on bass) wants us to call him "Zee-tha-i"??

417. METALLICA
...And Justice for All Elektra, 1988

Side Two I'll cherish forever, but mainly this blundered twofer prances like Starcastle on steroids. It does register on the Richter, and after *Master of Puppets*, it's even an "improvement" in relatively worthless ways: Lars Ulrich's learned some hot fusiony drumstuff, so his oatmeal's got more fleshy Sab-lumps. James Hetfield's pulling his holler from deeper torso-parts, so it reverberates all the way up, especially in "One," the intravenous-feeding ballad that's both the most harrowing seven minutes of Top 40 (or otherwise) Wagner-rock ever and the only cut that doesn't drag on. Kirk Hammett strums Nordic acousticlike ambrosia and free-blows wankblues leads like an oddball Steve (of Yes) Howe/Mick (of Uriah Heep) Box hybrid. But though the more I hear all these showy Mount Olympus doomblast-notes the more I get used to 'em, I'll never believe 'em, 'cause though by all accounts these young guns lead lush liquorish lives, all they ever yell about is nuclear winter and bureaucratic suppression. That's what they've been taught young guns "should" do, I know, but agonizing too much about should and shouldn'ts destroys rock 'n' roll. So your usual "nutritious" substance-symbolization (and vague lack of even taste-tempting "image") reveals itself as shtick, flail becomes "flail," and before you know it you're feigning danger like Judas Priest. What with their slowdowns, Metallica put over the trapped-by-society's-machinations thing with far less substratum vacuity than your average nephew of hardcore, but the shoe still fits: Pretending everything stinks helps rad-rockers sprint full-blast until they hit the wall. At which point they just keep running in place, digging into a deeper and deeper rut.

418. LED ZEPPELIN
Presence Swan Song, 1976

Discounting the live one and the outtake one, which you won't find in this book primarily because I didn't feel like it, Zep's only onetime cutout is also the only one I never put on. There's something unswimmably dehydrated about it. The Jimmy-masterminded beast called "Achilles' Last Stand" pokes its massive head and tail through the Pyrenees and groans like a Punjabi who's just charbroiled his cow by mistake, and it's nice that they beat the Meters' meat ("Royal Orleans") and turn *Sun Sessions* into *Sex Machine* ("Candy Store Rock"). But Zepblues by any other name is Zepblues, and if "Nobody's Fault but Mine" is "Hellhound on My Trail," I'm Herman Melville. Extremely creative use of obelisks though.

419. BLACK SABBATH
Black Sabbath Warner Bros., 1970

Certain heathens swear by this coming-out party, which earned BS their undeserved devil-tag and confused Stones fans into dismissing 'em as baroque-revivalists, but I've never found much use for it. The storm-effects are more daft than anything on "Count Duckula," and His Ozness begs for assistance from above as flames tickle his umbilicus, but the production's underweight, the tempos necrophilic, the beat and howl unevolved past the cemetery. Still, "The Wizard" spins like a top, with novel blues-harmonica and big drums sweeping away the icy curling rink for Tony Iommi's forty-four-pound stones of sliding riff, and though the first side's echoed reverb shoots the second's chopless exhibitionism all to Hades, better chopless exhibitionism than the chopful kind, right?

420. GRAND FUNK RAILROAD
E Pluribus Funk Capitol, 1971

The A-side tells you where their "Funk" came from or at least where it's going, and smack-dab in the middle, all wavering wah-wah and earth-mover musculature, "People, Let's Stop the War" tells you where they think the world's going to. If somebody other than Tricky Dick were in the White House, Mark Farner conjectures, nobody'd die anymore, and apparently he's talking not just 'Nam, but everywhere—we'd be *immortal!* The B-side starts with "Save the Land," 'cause you gotta save it once you share it, and the Guess Who had promised to share it the year before (but they only said "maybe"). Farner riffs like a bitch, Don Brewer slams like an ogre, the sleeve's almost as perfectly circular as Public Image Ltd.'s *Metal Box*, everything's too fucking slow, everything's too fucking dumb, and that's all she fucking wrote.

421. THE MORTAL MICRONOTZ

The Mortal Micronotz Fresh Sounds, 1982

The Micronotz are about what it means to grow up in the middle of nowhere, in the land of Dorothy and Eisenhower and cornfields and little pink houses and not much else; recorded when they were mere babes in the backwoods, their first and best disc articulates a uniquely midwestern claustrophobia, a frustration heartlanders feel the first time they realize that the big world outside is prob'ly gonna stay outside, that they'll more than likely be calling the 'burbs or boonies home for the rest of their born days. As country miles of John Harper guitar fight their way around a marching-band Aerostooge backbeat, Dean Lubensky pretends to duet with himself, sings the wrong word on purpose, mashes words together to preserve rhymes, stretches words beyond their breaking point, turning one syllable into five. He makes new meanings by emphasizing new words—"All ri-ight/ALL right/I sed ALL RIGHT!!" then surprising us with "But it's NOT alright/I'm tired/I'm really tired." William Burroughs even wrote one cut, and "Song 16" and "The Police Song" are archetypal Townshend/Cooper adolescent ache, and despite the damnable monochromia of it all, I still say that if we don't have room in our hearts for four bored teens from Kansas, we may not have room for anybody. Or maybe there's just not room for us.

422. LONE STAR

Firing on All Six Columbia, 1977

These tin soldiers come out resembling nobody so much as those long-lost Canadian Texans ZZ Rush, a crossbreed that does not compute whatsoever and hence pretty much rules. John Sloman squeals as if he can't wait to squeeze Bob Plant's lemons, and there's so much pathetic pirouetting-on-a-pinhead it's a wonder they don't credit a florist. But Dixie Lee's got one hype can-kit, and when Sloman decides to push past

the lingerie aisle toward the sporting-goods section amid "Hypnotic Mover"'s hookah toothache and "All of Us to All of You"'s four-in-hand electrician knots, it's monkey time. Nonetheless, this awesomely incompetent proto-rap anti-anti-Injun *Billy Jack Goes to Washington* homage "Ballad of Crafty Jack"'s the joint: "That man he drinkum my whiskey, smokum my weed/Stole my woman and planted his seed."

423. MANOWAR

Fighting the World Atco, 1987

"He who refuses to take part in modern mediocrity will forever stand alone, an outcast," the liner proclaims, and these Masters of the Universe, who take metal's barbarian legend to heights your Priests and Maidens have never dared, are proof. Clad in animal skins and Iron Age accessories and Samsonesque hair and Cro-Magnon muscles, they could be a parody, and with ex-Dictator Ross "the Boss" Funichello on board, you never know: "Violence and Bloodshed," warrior-for-hire praise on a Warren Zevon/John Cale plateau, claims our boys "blew it in 'Nam," a pretty extreme way for even would-be Rambos to put it. Boosted by the first big-label production of their somewhat illustrious career, not to mention Scott Columbus's customized MARC Industries Drums of

Death ("the ultimate drum system in the universe—everytning else is junk"), Manowar emerge here with a sort of mini-*Orgasmatron,* tempering the postdigital white noise and forward-charge of Motörhead's masterwork with "slightly lower intellectual and conceptual sights," I guess you'd say.

The firepower counters speedmetal's (then)-upstart mess with actual musicality in the form of sirens, choppers, grenades, and gang-shouts galore, plus medievalist passages that merely enable Manowar to kick your head in with all the more vengeance when it's time to pick up the pace. Even "Defender" 's passing-the-battle-torch spiel tickles your toes if you let it, and "Drums of Doom" 's eccentric tribal-skronk and the Spiñal-Tappish anti-MTV gore of "Blow Your Speakers" embody true audio pain. Incidentally, Manowar tied with the Beatles for third place (behind Michael Jackson and Pink Floyd) in a 1989 poll asking Soviet rock fans which acts they'd most like to watch on stage. All hail these folklorists' mighty amps!

424. CREAM
Best of Cream Polydor, c. 1980; rec. 1967–69

They're no more economical here than on their best regular issues, so forget that rationalization. "White Room" and "Crossroads" are headed toward Zephood but not there yet, "Tales of Brave Ulysses" was idiocy ahead of its time, "Spoonful" probably spawned 10cc's name, and "I Feel Free" 's been transformed into a Renault commercial and covered by a former Germ married to a prominent Republican. The remainder is overreverent to a distant past I never cared much about to begin with (if other prominent Republicans see said past differently, and they do, that only proves my point), and in this archival format, with its produce-department packaging, the rock's stripped of time and place and continuity, and all that's left is songs-as-vegetables and their present cultural meanings, which mostly suck. I know "Badge," "Sunshine of Your Love," and the godawful "Born Under a Bad Sign" primarily from the couple seconds' worth of each I've heard on "classic rock" outlets prior to

switching back to the disco station, and I still don't know whether it's "till my sea's all dried up" or "my *seed's.*" The counterculture trucks on.

425. HADES
Resisting Success Torrid, 1987

Five one-time burnouts-of-the-month from Bergen County's teen utopia first stall their Rush-and-Rudimentary-Peni-rooted nimbleness like molasses in January, then they bowl you over with it. Their "Widow's Mite" 45 initially hit me as a dimwitted Judas Priest/*Jesus Christ Superstar* mix (if they wanted to "resist success," I figured, they were sure going about it in the right way!), and it's no help that one guy's T-shirt advertises a toe-the-line punk troupe, that "Masque of the Red Death" has three parts and words from Edgar Allan Poe, that the ubiquitous solos never leave the driveway. But none of that matters, not when Alan Tecchio's convincing you with his cat-o'-nine-tails castrato that his throat's getting trampled by golf shoes, not when the trebly components keep exploding out of the rumbly ones, evoking some night-noise that rises up from your toes, through your lungs, only to be muffled into your pillow. The follow-up, *If at First You Don't Succeed* (an admission?), has silly titles like "Tears of Orpheus" and "Aftermath of Betrayal—The Tragedy of Hamlet," plus confused comments on the evils of diplomatic immunity, plus one anti-fruits-of-FDR number where Hades tell some "burden to society" to "Get a job! Get a job! Get a job!" just like the Silhouettes or Joe Friday or somebody. But this one's got the tilted sound all those bands recording for SST would give up their Hummel collections for.

426. KILLING JOKE
What's This For Editions EG, 1981

The funkless "groove" doesn't "go" anywhere (it just *is*), but these artsy Eeyores really did get a meritorious rump-bump going beneath all their echoplex churn.

More mechano/ethno/disco if less songfully resolute than their debut, best when the Europrance passes over and the pulses start rolling two or more at a time, as wallpaper goes their last decent LP's at least decorative. Drummer Paul Ferguson's the unsung star, and "Tension" starts exactly like the Knack's "My Sharona." The mostly illegible Weltanschauung is your usual end-is-near Weltschmerz, so it's shallower idea-wise than it thinks it is, but maybe that's where its humanness (and maybe even its rock 'n' roll) comes from. Nonetheless, after a time: Zzzzzzzzz.

427. WHITE ZOMBIE
Psycho-Head Blowout Silent Explosion EP, 1987

Berserk Medusa-with-rattlesnakes rock with jungle-rumble timekeeping that turns Black Sabbath in-side out and six-string switcheroos that drag you screaming through the ultratwisted offal-encrusted

sewer pipes of Gotham City's black-and-white under-world, plus post-Ginsberg/post-catechism-upbringing linguistics pouring like Morton Salt from Rob Straker's expando-hoarse epiglottis: No meaning anywhere. Raw gradual-flux deepgrooves form multilayered rhythmatrix nonintermittence, pattern-repetitive to a near mechanistic degree, with self-deconstructing adverse-percussive stun-variations packed so solid they lurch harder than most funk swings. Riff-protein

clogs every last cranny, and Straker mumbles his deranged streams of pretension through saliva, so fortunately you can't understand him. On the follow-up he learned to enunciate just as his band ran out of bile to vent, and they "made up" for passion-loss by grossing us more, boosting amps and "chops," racing faster, sucking pumice. Time after that they hired Bill Laswell, whose presence frequently tends to be the kiss of death.

428. GORE
Mean Man's Dream Red Rhino, 1988

This clodhopper has words, but nobody sings 'em. That's right: In Holland (where these three power-pukers hail from), the disc allegedly comes with the traditional "lyric sheet" enclosed, but no lyrics. There's words on the paper, but not on the vinyl. Hence, little Dutch kiddies can take time out from sticking their fingers in dikes and play the record in their rooms and sing along without being obstructed by some pesky vocalist with a big mouth—sort of like Mr. Micro-phone, only cheaper. The band plays like Magilla Gorillas: knuckle-dragged Sab-riffs lurching around the cage and sustained like one paw's grasping the tire-swing, drums rolling around the zoo like runaway meatballs. The movers enter your apartment and rearrange all the furniture in a real rhythmic way, drunk potatoheads who don't diet enough dance a jig on your roof, toilets back up at Our Lady Queen of the Rafflebook Church after the building's been raided by machete-wielding albino pig-worshipers en route to a grocery store that advertised "California-grown garden-fresh canker sores, 44 cents a bunch" this morning, and eventually the savages get arrested for holding hostages without a license and removing shopping carts from the supermarket premises. The bass and guitar are real heavy, so make sure your stereo's well supported. And if you feel like curling up in an easy chair with Veblen's *Theory of the Leisure Class,* don't worry about losing out on any exceptional nuances or anything. 'Cause there aren't any!

429. STEPPENWOLF

Steppenwolf Dunhill, 1968

So here's the big mystery: Did these easy riders actually *read* Burroughs (like, carry a tattered copy cross-country in their backpack) to find that "heavy metal" line, or was it just a coincidence of nature, or what? (Steely Dan and Soft Machine I've got no doubts about, but when it comes to Steppenwolf, I'm from Missouri.) Anyhow, what they debuted with was a couple molten dodderchord rhumbas of attempted but fortunately unsuccessful preboogie barrelhouse purism glazed in the nauseatingly translucent film that forms on the butt-ends of Spam loaves, plus too much sub-Doors (i.e, sub-sub—Tom Jones) doper-schmaltz. John Kay's got far too much generically "deep" ecology at his disposal, not one of his five five-minute ostriches has enough sand storm to it, and his roots-moves ("Berry Rides Again," where he steals Chuck Berry lyrics all the way through, plus Willie Dixon's "Hootchie Kootchie Man") primarily convince me he's white. And though I appreciate cocksucking and goddamns and post-Donovan banana-peels and pre-Mayfield pushermen as much as the next guy whose idea of "biking" is a Schwinn without training wheels, I gotta confess that only one of the three big Fox-Mike hits really makes me wanna take the world in a love embrace.

430. AC/DC

For Those About to Rock We Salute You
Atlantic, 1981

Mutt Lange helped 'em embezzle synth-doodles from *Who's Next* and execute some convoluted drama that'd show speedthrashers the way, thus providing these 'roos with their most "progressive" wax ever (a contradiction by definition but what the hey), not to mention a multiplatinum chart-topper. My grayboy ears enjoy getting slapped by "Let's Get It Up" 's feral staggerstep rap and "Evil Walks" 's "Werewolves of London" riff, but the "concept" is something

more perverted: "Let's Get It Up," "Put the Finger on You," "Inject the Venom," "Snowballed," "Night of the Long Knives," a two-wheeled cannon on the cover. The appendage they "salute" with ain't above the waist, get it?

431. PAGANS

Buried Alive Treehouse, 1986; rec. 1977–79

From the street where nobody lives, dead-end America, northern Ohio, here's four or five superbly snotty torpedos that feel punk the way Dion and the Belmonts feel punk, plus twelve or thirteen additional Brit-accented ripoffs you can dispose of at your leisure. Side Two's got wildman drumming in the middle, the exquisite "Boy Can I Dance Good" has psychological problems plus vocalwreck and guitarwreck from Pere Ubu's Crocus Behemoth. (If every song here danced as good as "Boy Can I Dance Good," I'd call this the best album in the world.) Bobby Darin and the Stones and the Nightcrawlers and especially the Who get gobbled up and splattered in chartreuse tones upon your shiny new penny loafers, and in the compact handful of coveted singles, bomb-shelter-dwellers with untuned strings smash hardballs stamped "boredom" and "emptiness" and "shit called love" through your windows. Very heterosexual, big fucking deal.

432. DIVINYLS

Desperate Chrysalis, 1983

Christina Amphlett comes from the Marianne Faithfull Maneater School of Look-What-They've-Done-to-My-Voice-Ma, and she pouts a lot. You never mind having her around, but you end up respecting her more than you actually wanna hear her. The riffs, middling-catchy mutable-to-professional scuzzfuzz stuff, are way too saturated with soy to sink your battleship; Christina's personality ought to, but it's not as raunchy as her sagging nylons suggest it oughta be. She's more Lene Lovich than Joan Jett. She puts "Elsie" and "Boys in Town" over, and the Easybeats cover is a good loyal Aussie stroke, but mostly she masks her vulnerability too much, and quirkiness ain't quite the word for it. She hiccups, retches, leaps and jumps, pretends she's Ray Davies, lets her breath drift up a foot from her head so her tongue can shoot out like a frog's and nab it. The chantoozie-pyrotechnics are endearing sometimes, but more often way too precious. After a while, she gets to you, and not in the way she intends to.

433. BROWNSVILLE STATION
Say Yeah! Big Tree, 1973

The selection of nonoriginals—"Question of Temperature," "Sweet Jane," "Barefootin'" (a discordant Jesus and Mary Chain ancestor), Hoyt Axton, Terry Knight, Jimmy Cliff—ain't a heckuva lot more auspicious than Mötley Crüe's, truth be told, and how these legendary missionary-position garage-gum survivalists trump up the guitars and delinquence ain't much more spectacular than what Mötley do with Brownsville Station songs. Only two cuts get Lutz/Koda credit, and Cub Koda's more famous as a record collector than as a singer or a guitarer, which *never* bodes well. And since these blues-harping spuds' entire image relies on the idea that they'd be just as happy as a softball outfield, uneventfullness is a given, and it's easy to wonder why they bother. But they named an album *School Punks* at a time when being punks wasn't something one was proud of unless one came from Detroit (which Brownsville did), and like *Reckless* and *American Fool* in the eighties they didn't use their roots as "roots," and there lies their meager charm. "Smokin' in the Boys Room," which my buddy Mike Murphy useta segue into Steve Miller's "The Joker" up in *his* floor-number-two room back in North Potomac Green back in *our* weekend-dopester don't-get-caught days, ain't Mötley. Having never heard "Getting Better" by the Beatles, I always thought Cub was groaning "Teacher doncha kill me, *up* with your rules," as if he was pretending rules were *good*. But he wasn't.

434. CIRCLE JERKS
Group Sex Frontier EP, 1981

Back in that one brief moment many years ago when LA HC actually seemed to some gullible souls (like yours truly) as if it might amount to something someday (which of course it never did, unless Guns N' Roses count), four fulminating fuckups laid groundwork that would soon occupy the lives of a million Circle Jerk imitators, including the Circle Jerks themselves (who should've topped this off by finding honest adult jobs instead). The songs don't all sound the same, and there's fourteen of 'em in thirteen minutes, and Paul Westerberg filched an idea from the personal-ad one ("Group Sex") in "Lovelines." You can sing along: Rich people suck, gay people suck, my job at Burger King sucks, to spray-paint or not to spray-paint, to skate or not to skate, maybe I'll shoot myself or maybe I'll just raid the refrigerator. These are protests against military-industrial tyranny from tiny suburban toddlers, lying on stomachs and pounding fists and feets against the linoleum 'cause mom won't give 'em no more root beer. They don't know shit about shit. That's what makes 'em bearable.

435. BETTY DAVIS
They Say I'm Different Just Sunshine, 1974

Damn few good heavy metal albums by black women, that's what I say. The first Nona Hendryx LP just couldn't cut it, sorry. So this is my token, sort of: Convict me of Affirmative Action and lock me up. Or don't. Because this platter would deserve a spot in this book even if Betty Davis looked as pale and ugly as the dweebs in Iron Maiden, which she doesn't. And I don't say that just 'cause she married Miles Davis and dated Jimi Hendrix a few times either. Guitars come from Buddy Miles and two other guys, and they are lethal and plentiful indeed. Decent songs, unfortunately, *aren't*, though the ode to T-Bone Walker and Bo Diddley is appreciated, and there's no way to resist "He Was a Big Freak," where Betty shrieks from the toenails up about whipping her beau with a turquoise chain. Very kinky stuff, kinky as Betty's much-picked 'fro (plus those blue platform boots and that psychotronic sci-fi getup place her on the mid-seventies martian-funk vanguard, out there with La-belle and Boney M!). She don't sing too hot (real scraggly and world-worn, like tobacco's in her cheek, yet ultimately kinda pedestrian), so her blues, especially, tend to drag. But between the wah-wahs and congas she does manage to carve a niche in this world for her big-mama brand of individualist sugarcane feminism. And her groove's usually funky enough to get by.

436. LITA FORD
Stiletto RCA, 1990

A grown woman entertaining young boys who just sprouted their first pubic hairs last week, Lita plays the Big Blond Bombshell so bodaciously that Madonna oughta sign up for lessons, and if you don't suppose she sees humor in said situation, you're wrong. In the dumbest song on *Stiletto*, her best set since leaving the Runaways behind, she drools so long over some lothario's "big gun" that you worry she's doing her gender grievous harm, but then she turns the tables: "Got my tongue in my cheek, makin' noise for a livin'." So it's only a joke. And sure enough, what comes next is her remake of "Only Women Bleed," the most feminist power-ballad prototype on the books, and not even the overly "significant" song choice can keep her guitar tapestries from spilling blood. Otherwise, this disc is further evidence that pop-metal was the first musical genre to figure out how to turn the CD-age studio into an aesthetic advantage: There's all sortsa fetching hi-tek whooshes and wobbles and giggles and boinks that increase the fun-quotient simply by being so incidental and amusement park–like. It's an idea initiated by Def Leppard on *Hysteria*, which Lita obviously studied in detail: Lep-based "Pour Some Sugar on Me," their Aeroqueen-grooved riff-rap, on "Sugar Sugar," the first 45 Joe Elliot ever bought; Lita's "Cherry Red," which sounds just *like*

"Sugar On Me," harks back to "Cherry Bomb," the first 45 the Runaways ever made.

I wish Lita didn't insist on passing herself off as some heavy metal Isis, and her critique of LA's gangsta life-style suggests she went to see *Colors* but caught *West Side Story* by mistake. But Mike Chapman invests other chants (especially "Dedication") with his glam-bop Midas touch, and the one *Stiletto* slice *guaranteed* to leave a few scars is the big schmaltzy slow one. "Lisa," in the tradition of Precious Metal's "Emily," Shakin' Street's "Susie Wong," and such perverse hard-rock restroom-door-sign-switchers as Joan Jett's "Crimson and Clover" and Suzi Quatro's "I Wanna Be Your Man," is a love song to a woman from another woman. The press release claimed that Lita dedicated it to her mom, but pubescent boys don't get press releases, and vicious rumors surely littered the schoolyards like flies. Wouldn't surprise me a bit to find out that's how Lita wanted it. Always keep 'em guessing: best policy I know.

437. RIOT
The Privilege of Power CBS Associated, 1990

With Grandmixer D.St. manning turntables that no previous metal band had thought to acknowledge as a musical instrument, Riot's seventh songbatch is the most blatant attempt so far to forge a hard-rock equivalent of such post-hip-hop dance collages as M/A/R/R/S's "Pump Up the Volume" and De La Soul's *3 Feet High and Rising*. Precedents include Black Sabbath's *Sabotage*, Def Leppard's *Hysteria*, and Queensrÿche's *Operation: Mindcrime*, but not since quick-cut pioneer William Burroughs invented the phrase "heavy metal" has anyone made such a point of suggesting why the two disciplines might be meant for each other. Still, Riot's experiment ain't half-near successful: Mark Reale's slop-the-hogs ax-sludge and Tony Moore's helium-inhalation screech repeatedly make way for Japanese clarinets and "Radar Love" crescendos and Tiananmen Square newscasts and opera arias, but said particles almost never coalesce into hooks, much less beats.

In addition to D.St., who's probably most famous for his scratch-gymnastics on Herbie Hancock's "Rockit," guests include the Tower of Power horns and harmolodic guitar god James "Blood" Ulmer. We're supposed to get off on the hodgepodge alone, but avant-garde composers have been using pastiche-techniques as art statements for years, and if Riot are more vulgar, they also don't have as much to say. *The Privilege of Power* is ostensibly a concept disc about "the media controlling people's attention," and though a few songs split the difference between thrash and radio-metal anthemically enough, the chorus shrieks mostly tend toward your usual "metal soldiers marching through the night" wearing "black leather and glittering steel." The remake of Al Dimeola's "Racing with the Devil on a Spanish Highway" bores for seven long minutes, and I'll never trust an album that divides itself into an "Act One" and an "Act Two."

"Killer" 's documentary fragment about fragmentation grenades is spookily self-reflexive, and when producer Steve Loeb opens "Runaway" with movie dialogue telling a sleepy "John Doe" he's "the hope of the world," it's a deadpan slap at HM's populist delusions. If the surrounding pretension wasn't so hard to take, this record might've marked a smarter future for a sickly genre.

438. VOX POP
. . . .
The Band, the Myth, the Volume Goldar
EP, 1982

Starring Jeff Dahl (who's played in the Angry Samoans, invented the term "speedmetal" in Powertrip, and written liner notes for Blue Cheer), this semilegendary California grunge-placenta combo loaded their corpuses with drugs and girls' makeup and demolished Grand Funk and Runaways and Faust songs on stage when nobody else would, and here they cut horrific multidirectional farts that alternate between Ted Falconi–type busy-signals (if you play 'em at 33) and Leigh Stevens–type burning bushes (if you play 'em at 45). The nihilismo slogans ("Work! Sleep! Wake up, then eat!") squeeze somewhere between the Mekons'

"32 Weeks" and the Godfathers' "Birth, School, Work, Death"; the only thing that resembles a rock 'n' roll song ("Become a Pagan," not near as r'n'r as either side of 1980's "Cab Driver"/"Just Like Your Mom" 45) has a vocal round highly reminiscent of "Row, Row, Row Your Boat." (See also: Grand Funk's "Ups and Downs.") "Procession" 's Sonic Youth protoplasm builds to a Detroit climax, and the "C Side" lands you inside an eternal closed groove you'll be too tired to notice. The outer jacket proudly displays male member Don Bolles's male member. It's small.

439. Repo Man
. . . .
MCA/San Andreas, 1984

Executive-produced by the tall Monkee with the cap and featuring a greasy performance by Harry Dean Stanton, the videotape's worth renting if you get the chance, and the soundtrack could be worse. Iggy does his geezer-period shtick like usual only with more mouth-graffiti (chickens on hooks, teen dinosaurs, ashtray-heads, microscope jokes) and more power-chords, plus Watusi-beats courtesy an ex-Blondie. Black Flag do their most memorable dunce-anthem ("TV Party"); Suicidal Tendencies do their only memorable dunce-anthem ("Institutionalized"), a raplet which, despite commentary to the contrary, is neither the best song ever written about moms and dads (something by the Coasters or Cheap Trick is, probably) nor the worst song ever written about anything (something else by Suicidal Tendencies is, probably). Fear and the Circle Jerks offer respective ideas on improving the national economy, the latter make their hokey hick-move before contemplating their hokier speedmetal one. The Plugz make their hokey barrio-move a few times before transforming once and for all into arena-brownnosers called Cruzados who everybody would've ignored if they'd come from Fort Wayne instead of East LA, overmilked standup-comedy nobodies salute Pablo Picasso (via Jonathan Richman) and blaxploitation seatbelts. Come 1999 or so, who knows how unhinged this'll sound? Or how average: Time wounds all heels.

440. DREAM SYNDICATE
Days of Wine and Roses Ruby, 1982

The first of LA's (and the world's) countless paint-by-numbers scavengers of the velvet undergroove, these marshmallows whined and chimed Lou Reed references into overtasteful feedback that mostly just lies lifeless on the loft's floor, but acts up some (in "Halloween," "Then She Remembers," "That's What You Always Say") when the sick gerbil of an anti-rhythm starts putting its exercise wheel to use. Karl Precoda's fuzz (no world-wonder, but it revs on Side Two) beats Steve Wynn's bored inflections (as much Robyn Hitchcock as Lou) no contest, and the only wisp-poetry that sinks in through the moodzak has 'em suddenly brainstorming that certain TV shows are (gasp!) fiction. But the title's a Jack Lemmon movie, and in '82 it was nice to hear that somebody beloved by seedy characters who say "daddy-o" was covering "Don't Fear the Reaper" and "Ballad of Dwight Fry" (later Bryan Adams's "Cuts Like a Knife" even!) live. Prime attraction, I bet: The smooth transitions between high-volume white-heat-mode and low-volume Nico-mode were unobtrusive during collegiate listeners' homework sessions.

441. RIOT
Fire Down Below Elektra, 1981

With a title nicked from Bob Seger's *Night Moves,* this is '71-style dynamo-rhythm phoenix-from-the-ashes squawk ten years after the fact, a living fossil to rival the tuatara or coelacanth or even Minnie Minoso—five wicked eastern-seaboard fugitives thirsty for tequila shoot bullets straight from their chestbelts. There's a baby harp seal on the cover, but the guitars are completely fuzzy, in fact it's THE KIND OF SOUND THAT CLUBS HARP SEALS OVER THE HEAD. And good thing too: As any youngster knows, the *mere existence* of these animals is detrimental to the Canadian economy, seeing how DANGEROUS COD WORMS, which serve as parasites upon codfish, thus endangering the nation's way-lucrative cod-fishing industry, reproduce inside the seals' bodies. The fishermen need their fishing wages to survive, and the blood lost can't compare to that shed in nineteenth-century Chicago packing houses, and anyhow seals aren't an endangered species like pit-footed bandicoots or blunt-nosed leopard lizards, and nobody'd think twice if they weren't anthropomorphized as being so darn "adorable," and if they weren't killed *somehow* there'd be overpopulation, and don't believe a word of this 'cause I have no idea what I'm talking about, okay?

442. Deep Six
C/Z, 1985

A half-dozen disher-outers of what oughta be known everywhere by now as "Bigfoot Rock" (an overacted punkmetal-recontextualized blues-mutation specific to the Pacific Northwest) who draw on Sabbath (for density) and the Stooges (for beat) and 'Smith (for structure and screams), and though most make you forget vegetarians and bearded women and Rajneesh-worshipers and log-cabined survivalist psychos for a couple minutes, none make you forget Paul Revere and the Raiders. Green River mourn love's snafus over a slightly modified (or not) swamp-thump; the Melvins eat pit bulls and spit out the pits, and thus serve as the concrete proof of hominid survival anthropologists have long craved; King Crimson fans Skin Yard squirt melancholic muck-monologues mannered enough to gag a maggot farm; Soundgarden buttress their lowdown hoedown with a Bon-hamesque foundation. The U-Men and Malfunkshun get lost in the scuffle. More Harry than Hendersons, it all runs together, but it documents a moment and predicts future predictability. By 1988, watching the third-generation Sasquatches in Blood Circus or Mudhoney or Tad was already more like seeing a picture of music than seeing the real thing. Using arty artlessness and pretentious primitivism as protective barriers between musicians and audience, howling with a frigid glibness that pretended their not-totally-unfounded cynicism about the relationship between music and emotion is its own justification, their sounds communicated nothing, save perhaps that somebody in the band had an okay record collection once.

443. PRIMAL SCREAM
Volume One Mercenary, 1987

No doubt 'cause its amateurish loam suggests I'm dog-paddling through the tarpits of La Brea, I really enjoy this zero-pretension glop when I'm in another room. But when I get close I notice how half-formed the rhythms and melodies are, so inevitably something's lost in the translation. Nonetheless, this is one of the few "speedmetal" recs I know of that retains even a pinch of the primal boogiefied thump that made HM such a cathartic Epsom-bath in the olden days. Steve Alliano's megaton drum-pudding, an unceasing tumble that primarily reminds me of the wonderful Irish sport street bowling, allows Rob Graham to shout out blinded-by-the-light socio-political anxieties like Paul Bunyan while Keith Alexander wanks big as Babe the Blue Ox. "Last Breath" throws down some backward-Sab crater-funk, Side Two's chock-full of Voivod's patented flying-saucer-flattening-the-cornfield feel, and my favorite song concerns one Mr. McCreedy, who's apparently teed off at the kids playing handball against his garage door, or maybe I heard it wrong. Don't think there's a Volume Two yet, but assuming this trio of bandwagon-jumpin' mud-flappers learn to play their instruments by then, it'll stink.

444. IRON BUTTERFLY
Heavy Atlantic, 1968

Glad I'm not the otorhinolaryngologist of that serious tinnitus case on the cover, where the Butterflies enkindle their iron into this Easter Island–sized ear-totem. But *Heavy* likely ain't as loud as *Heavy Funk,* their never-released (and maybe never recorded) collaboration with Funkadelic that's likely festering to

this day in some crack-house basement somewhere in the bowels of Detroit's Cass Corridor. Here, these Cali missing links distill your average extra-sensory-percepted organ-and-ax drugstuff. They low stentorianly in the style of their oft-tourmate James Morrison, not exactly fleet-footed and for shorter spans than you'd expect (no half hours like "In-A-Gadda-Da-Vida," thank you very much). "Gentle as It May Seem" 's an insouciant little roundabout rockola not far from the MC5's *Back in the USA*, complete with a Jan and Dean reference and a couple absurd interruptions where somebody stops the proceedings and interjects "C'mere, woman!"; "So-Lo" 's not the drumoff you'd predict, but "Iron Butterfly Theme" comes close; "Stamped Ideas" aims its protest brick at "people made of plastic in a mold." "You Can't Win" says you might not wanna get a haircut and go stick napalm onto VC, but "He'll lock you up and in your head he'll pound it." "He" being "the Man," who's everywhere you look, gol-darn it.

445. SOUNDGARDEN
Screaming Life SubPop EP, 1987

This muscle-of-hate seventies revisionism really ain't so bad if you compare it to these Seattlites' way-overpraised ensuing output: The *Fopp* EP leads with a smartly hard (or hardly smart, hard to tell) Ohio-

Players-as-Zep cover, but supposed lovegoat Chris Cornell's got zilch on the Players' Sugar Bonner; the *Ultramega OK* LP has deadassed art-noise about deadassed people, or something in the neighborhood. This first try leaves footprints as big as a small boy's in the snow, putting forth monstrously concentric riff-grooves that might've fit okay on *Houses of the Holy* or *Physical Graffiti*: "Entering"'s like Bobby Plant rapping to some Rick-Rubined Bonzo-beat, and "Hunted Down" and "Nothing to Say" (both mixed more devastatingly on a rare 45 you'll never find) are Zep-bottomed jawbreakers filled with Iommiesque gunk. There's *Odyssey*-and-*Iliad*-style travelogue yeomanism from here till Kingdom Come, and since Soundgarden's not entirely averse to resounding twang or lush acoustica, they fare better than most weight lifters. But this is a cowardly performance-art copout anyhow, disgustingly one-dimensional dicksize-insecurity, and Cornell can't reach high notes. Within a year, the shtick made the New Kids on the Block seem interesting by comparison.

446. TED NUGENT
. . . .
Double Live Gonzo Epic, 1978

In a sense, it blunders bigtime like any concert twofer. Even back when the loinclothed one used to truly chow down on bow-and-arrow-bagged Bullwinkles without removing the antlers, he was hopeless over three or four minutes at a time, and here "Stormtroopin'," "Stranglehold," and "Motor City Madhouse" each stretch past eight, and "Hibernation"'s music-school drivel keeps "going" for fourteen of the little fuckers. Still, you don't know the man till you's heard him rap, and here he does, yielding a *comedy* concert twofer, not unlike Lou Reed's from the same year. And if no antic's quite as outlandish as Lou slagging rock-crits by name, a few come close, like the one about Murder City being a healthy place to live and how Ted's guitar's from there and it'll castrate rhinoceri at sixty paces. And then there's that strawman-shoot about people who wanna get mellow getting the fuck out, which always raises one unavoidable question: IF THEY WANTED TO GET MELLOW, THEY WOULDN'T'VE COME TO A TED NUGENT CONCERT, WOULD THEY? Usually the Flavor Flav of the seventies jabbers his mumblejumble too fast for ya to figure out what his deal is, but a few stick-to-the-roof-of-yer-cabin riffs kinda make up for it, especially in "Baby Please Don't Go" and "Motor City Madhouse" and "Great White Buffalo" (Nuge's Obligatory HM Injun-Condescension; Ted, o'course, digs Tonto and company 'cause they *killed* all them woolly bullies). Damn near across the board, the dangerous parts were recorded in *Texas*. Go figure.

Photograph by Naomi Petersen

447. GONE
. . . .
Gone 2—But Never Too Gone SST, 1986

On which Black Flag fretboardmeister Greg Ginn uncovers the theoretical missing link between Black Sabbath's "Supernaut" and Miles Davis's *On the Corner*, an all-instrumental thunderjazz hybrid so wide you can't get around it—bassosaurus-counterboogie semi-beefed by prickly distortion-hugeness, over tempo-dynamic bongobeat, with all three variables returning to given coordinates at predetermined intervals. Ginn's axstorm galvanizes toward nuclear winter, incorporating splintered time-shifts, subtle solo-spacing, on-the-what jams amid the raveups. His tool wails like a street drill, a six-shooter, a baby babirusa, a helicopter with a split personality, the Indy Time Trials, and with Andrew Weiss and Simeon Caine making half-Latinoid whoopie behind him, he finally has legs to stand on. Now if only one of the three displayed a smidgen of soul, this sucker'd be good to go.

448. THIN LIZZY
Johnny the Fox Mercury, 1976

Scott Gorham's Brian Robertson's concise crunch weaves through the beat like in a funk band, and a callow Bono probably jotted down the passing comments about potato famines and immigration into his shamrocked diary. There's characters and everything, so maybe this is supposed to be a rock opera—a working-class-mythos fugitive-kid-shooting-drugstore-attendant saga, this is just one more twist on life's eternal Johnny B. Goode/Johnny Too Bad/Johnny Rotten/Johnny Ryall motif. None of which is any reason you oughta waste your time (the pro-verbial "penetration-of-human-condition" ain't near Mellencamp or even Iron City Houserockers or probably even Billy Falcon), but the incredible "Johnny the Fox Meets Jimmy the Weed" might be: With jam-master drum-hoodoo introducing prescient talk of how "around the bay they got some crazy dee-jay send you straight into heaven," talk of places only black men (like the singer) can hang out, this could be the elusive rock-rap link between Hendrix and Run-D.M.C. Elsewhere, the drawl in "Borderline" 's got a Neil Young *After the Gold Rush* feel, "Boogie Woogie Dance" and "Massacre" are scrappy-enough Zepfunk, "Rocky" could be Kiss or Alice Cooper, "Fool's Gold" rips "Sweet Jane," and "Don't Believe a Word" 's got the sort of paradoxical wordplay Phil Lynott might've learned from old Smokey Robinson singles. A lot of stuff, but it's somehow too diffuse to add up to the story it works so hard to be—in the end, it's just a lot of stuff.

449. PRONG
Primitive Organs Mr. Bear EP, 1987

This gruesome NYC crewsome (with ex-Damage Mike Kirkland on bass and mouth, ex-Swan Ted Parsons on skins) spoons out a furious nerve-center-aimed quasi-intellectual anchor-thrash with nimble leads and solos skittering off like varicose veins, a thrusty steak-knife-blade slash-spume that frequently brings to mind chicken legs (raw) with bones sticking out. Swirling bass lines emerge like cobras from the hairline form-changes that embellish the noise-basket, and in a strange way the jazzistics actually seem kinda catchy, which is to say you can halfway hum 'em when you next decide to spin 'em, maybe three years later. Which is a long time, which is 'cause too much of the time if you're not paying close attention (and why should you?), the whole schmear grinds away not unlike rote middle-of-the-roadkill metalcore (Kirkland grumbles so's you can't make out the lyrics). In the long run, though, creative strategies do lift Prong above the pack of slack hacks. And golly, if you stick around long enough for the closing cut, you even get to hear 'em "stretch out"!

450. ANTHRAX
I'm the Man Island EP, 1987

"Censored Radio," "Def Uncensored," and "Extremely Ill Uncensored Live" versions of one dingbatty thrash-rap Beastie/Kinison imitation/parody demonstrate how far these supposedly "fun" panderers will go to get their quasipolitical quasithrash accepted by a nonspeedmetal crowd, and that places 'em far ahead of one pack and far behind another. Obnoxiously overrated, devoid of character and crunch, they probably scored a point or two higher on their SATs than most heavycore morons. So they brag that their feet smell, that they wipe each other's butts with each other's faces, and that they "like to be different, not cliché," which I guess just means they don't have the horse sense to sell their old Iron Maiden albums or

change out of their Bermudas when the temperature drops. They improve the title cut of one of the lamer Sab-with-Ozzy LPs (Oz's operatics trounce Joey Belladonna's, but Anthrax add some "Sweet Leaf" at the end, a paradox since they're antidrug like Nancy Reagan); they squander five minutes on a thing called "Caught in a Mosh," but "mosh" ain't in my dictionary. (I'm told it's something like slamdancing.) Their second-best thrash-rap, "I Am the Law," repeatedly mentions Judge Dredd, so maybe it's an homage to Jamaican ska-toaster Prince Buster. You gotta be quicker on the draw than this to make a joke out of something that's already a joke, catch my meaning?

451. THE PROLETARIAT
Indifference Homestead, 1986

Laurel Bowman, who is either a man or a woman, sings anthems in the rain, so high-pitched and high-strung they jet past Geddy Lee, toward Art Bears/Slapp Happy cabaret chanteuse Dagmar Krause: "Homeland" starts loud 'n' fast, gets even louder as it slows down, and has Bowman stretching the two-syllable title to eight syllables at one point and to twenty-one seconds at another; "The Guns Are Winning" builds soaring U2-gone-heavycore axlines to an orgasm that goes "The guns! The GUNS! Are winning! Are WINNING! Again! The guns are winning again! Again! AGAIN! AGAIN! AGAAAIINN!!!" then makes way for "No Real Hope," or rather (first) "No Real Hope/Prelude." Original Proletariat throat

Richard Brown's dozen turns at bat aren't quite so extreme and Frank Michael's fed-back-atop-its-own-residue buzz ain't as jagged as it was on these Beantowners' '83 debut, the denouncements of "cheap visions of the flesh" are perturbingly prudish, and the war-kills-work-dehumanizes-rich-rule-poor-starve-nobody-cares-everybody-dies polemic lacks insight and compassion. But the stuff's seemingly contradictory status as punk rock made inspirational by virtue of its pomp-rock grandiosity still puts it over, and in its own way, I think it's a trip.

452. SCIENTISTS
Blood Red River Au Go Go Australian import EP, 1983

Formed as powerpoppers in Perth in 1981, these pretenders eventually transferred to Sydney and incorporated more frantic rhythms and more somber shades of the blues, and before too long they'd theoretically discarded most compositional restraint. Cleaning up an act this trashy defeats the purpose, like draining muckwater from a swamp to save the minnows, and that's exactly what happened on such later discs as *Atom Bomb Baby* and *Weird Love*, but here Kim Salmon hides his mannered beat-degeneration mewling under unwashed blankets of crisscrossing barrage that dive-bombs until it melts like the wings of Icarus. With endlessly mutating skincrawl feedback and sloppy-when-audible howlation consorting with an unsteady beat that headbutts hornily as a mouflon ram in rut, amelodic sizzlers like "Burnout" and "Spin" split the difference between the Stooges' "Dirt" and Hendrix's "Fire." Still, though Salmon's fine yelping like Harmonica Frank or wheezing like Hasil Adkins or shrieking like Suicide's Alan Vega, his crooning's even more maudlin than Iggy's or Nick Cave's (two apparent influences), and the levity-lacking backwoods/backdoor–man myths he dredges up would be old hat even if they weren't so unspecific. So though this earfood's got its portion of meat, the Scientists never once threaten to break free in entirely their own way.

453. CACTUS

'Ot 'n' Sweaty Atco, 1972

Of particular note is how much "Bad Stuff," the first track on the studio side, sounds like both "Cosmic Slop" by Funkadelic and "Bambi" by Prince (which is to

say Cactus wanted it to sound like "Purple Haze" by Hendrix). It's followed by ready-for-AA croons and Latin-mass organ and a boogie named for the mazurka, a polkalike Polish dance where your foot slides twice instead of just once. Live in Mexico, Peter French, who wants very much to look like Jim Morrison, begs to backstroke in your ocean girl oowee-baby whilst Werner Fritzchings introduces "Roll Over Beethoven" riffs to the Wide World of Onanism and Duane Hitchings bangs too damn much electric piano. Live side's noisier, surprise surprise.

454. LAUGHING HYENAS

Merrygoround Touch and Go EP, 1987

Signficantly more earthquaking than this, if you can locate 'em, are a few scattered previnyl cassettes that for some reason I pegged upon initial exposure as a "natural" follow-up/extension to the Stooges' *Funhouse,* real convenient seeing how these hellhounds

Photograph by Marty Perez

washed their paws in the same Washtenaw County water basin. Live, they moved as messily as rusted-out Barracudas coming to life on the freeway's edge, and words were irrelevant to the effect, 'cause you couldn't hear 'em: While guitarist Larissa Strickland (yeah, a *girl*) spewed a baneful sore that chafed like the real-life blues, bassist Kevin Strickland (no relation to Larissa—it's a trick question!) and tubster Jim Kimball banged out the most sporogenous beat to bang its way from between the Great Lakes since Iggy went solo. John Brannon should've varied his primal therapy more, but you got used to it. On *Merrygoround,* the dirges start to sound far more like Doorsish art-rock than rock 'n' roll, and the nailed-down heartbeat and soul-stabbing Episcopalian-minister's-kids fear-of-sin stanzas are some salvation but not enough. Which ain't to imply that you won't need to scrub your walls afterward.

455. VERTICAL SLIT

Under the Blood Red Lava Lamp Old Age cassette, 1986

Over a decade-and-a-half span, Buckeye Tim Sheppard made scores of experimental recordings, most of which he distributed to a few buddies. Formats ranged from unamplified ambience to free-form industriousness, but on this live souvenir of his "best"-known trio, early-seventies Europrog provincialism collides with early-seventies rustbelt cellar-crunge (or maybe it's a merger of Dust and MX-80 Sound, both of whom have LPs entitled *Hard Attack*!), adding up to a moss of pedal-mass not unlike Hearthan-period

Pere Ubu, though not even fractionally as uplifting or even intelligible. The skewed drama-club recitation is even furrier than the broadside-of-a-barn-door *sturm und clang*. (Even.) The top snakes, the bottom bumps, Joy Division's "I Remember Nothing" gets atomized, and glorious surface noise assures the avant-garde credentials. Incidental drugginess gets stirred in with a spoon called Memorex, and though not a thing goes anywhere, it doesn't-go-anywhere in a *real talented way*.

456. THE BYRDS
(Untitled) Columbia, 1970

More than one Iron Age metalcrew (particularly BÖC, if my memory serves me), claimed they were aping the Byrds not the blues, which makes sense: This was, after all, the first truly self-consciously unsmiling art-rock band to coldly emphasize, for no discernible musical end except perhaps to simulate technology, the symphonically machinelike sound qua sound and technique qua technique and form qua form (and cosmic sci-fi) that would before too long become (unfortunately) unquestioned HM staples. This hotlick-boogie-predatin' double-half-live job, from the period after which they pretended to be everycowboys singing sad sad songs (gratuitous Poison allusion) (gratuitous admission of gratuitous Poison allusion) oughta be proof for headbangers-in-doubt. Only Roger McGuin's left from before, and there's lotsa ace-or-not Bob Dylan and Gram Parsons and Lowell George tunes that aren't exactly Nazarethed or anything, but "Love on the Bayou" and "Hungry Planet" and maybe "So You Want to Be a Rock 'n' Roll Star" and the quasi-Hindu "We'll Come Back Home" do a scuzzy riff-rumble. Most relevantly, Side Two's filled to the brim with the egg-noodly (and of course eventually wearisome) sixteen-minute-plus "Eight Miles High," with gradually expanding goo-circles sprayed skitzily and with minimal vocal accompaniment till the "jazzoid" end-jam; it might well've inspired not only Hüsker Dü's '84 crit-hit cover version, but also HD's almost-side-long "Dreams Re-

occurring" from the same year. As for *(Untitled)*'s title, it's a contradiction, right?

457. THE FLESHEATERS
Greatest Hits SST, 1987; rec. 1980–83

Chris Desjardins's poesy has been tagged "genius" by more fluent men of letters than I, but the few images I can ferret out fly straight over my head, so maybe I'm just not very bright. Timber wolves, graveyards, dirt roads, pool halls: They've all been done before, too many times, right? I thought so. So if you're gonna gamble your shekels on any of the Flesheaters' waxings, and by no means whatsoever should it be construed that I'm insinuating that you oughta, it'd better be this one. The comp's got some handy angles that sink in over time plus a couple mire-reminiscent guitar lines (the one in "Hard Road to Follow" is identical to the one in Dire Straits' "Money for Nothing"!), but Desjardins sings real simpy-like, with all these bogus (or "real," doesn't matter) beatnik Jimbo Morrison nonrhymes that he'd like us to believe make him some evil headless hearseman or whatnot. Unlike Donna Summer or whomever, he's got not a thing he needs to get off his chest, so he ends up doing a dippy approximation of what Elvira's hairdresser might sound like. These LA moviegoers put a jigger or two of BÖC's "Hot Rails to Hell" in "The Wedding Dice," but most of the remaining blues-dementia just makes me switch over to Bon Jovi, who at least have a sense of humor. Then again, you're not me, are you?

458. FEEDTIME
Shovel Rough Trade, 1988

Nothing histrionic on this stern slab of ale-bellied Aussie hermit-slide sludge, and maybe that's what's wrong. There's no pickup to speak of, and some glitz or at least a good kick in the funny bone couldn't hurt; in retrospect, U2's accidental plagiarism of "Gun 'Em Down"'s lustless Diddleythump in "Desire" seems entirely appropriate. A dime-store Angus, guitarist

Rick (no last name, like Pelé!) picks his vector-shaped boogie riffs and nonchalantly digs 'em deeper and deeper into the soil. His pals don't wanna impress you, just document the outrage they feel when they're walking the streets, so they snarl what's in their heads, no big deal: escape, domestic turmoil, what happens when you stop praying, what happens when kids stay out late, parties without central heating, motorbikes. They worry about pregnant moms and bearded derelicts, and you don't know why seeing such strangers out the bus window bothers 'em, you only know it does. The itchy squalor piles so high in "Gun 'Em Down" that you never figure out whether the runaway the cracked voice keeps bellowing about is the killer or the victim. The serrated edges of the fracas grate as if the musicians are ignoring each other, which makes for a blunt and bumpy ride through the junkyard, and at first I trusted every last tirade. Maybe I still do, but trust ain't the same as excitement, and mainly I'm bored rigid.

459. SONIC YOUTH
Confusion Is Sex Neutral, 1983

They always called themselves a rock 'n' roll band, but even in their garage days they came off more like what Manhattan No-Wave-spawned cyberspace hippies figured a r'n'r band *ought* to be. You can tell they're not happy people—they do their *The Stooges* parody ("I Wanna Be Your Dog") the same year Sisters of Mercy do theirs ("1969")—but you can't tell why, though apparently marital squabbles and teenage heck have something to do with it. Appropriately released on an art label, with a lyric by one Swan and a cover photo by another one, the laid-backish gothic grindclang and gutter erotica sound as if they're recorded inside a cavern, and the subdued vocals try so hard to disturb you can only laugh, especially when Kim Gordon imitates the devil. In "The World Looks Red" and "Confusion Is Next" in the middle of Side Two, the futurism effects and nonsense about gravity and the world postanarchy and roly-poly fish-eyes are funnier than you'd expect. But confusion's always been much more than sex, and that's always been one of Sonic Youth's problems.

460. KING CRIMSON
In the Court of the Crimson King Atlantic, 1969

A history of sixties rock: On March 6, 1959, a month and three days after The Day The Music Died, Jerry Lieber and Mike Stoller gathered up four violins and a cello and the Drifters and recorded "There Goes My Baby," which begat Phil Spector, which begat *Pet Sounds*, which begat *Sgt. Pepper's Lonely Hearts Club Band*, which begat *Days of Future Passed*, which begat this shit, which killed everything. But so what, it was already dead. Greg Lake's singing in "21st-Century

Schizoid Man," one of the best jazz compositions about neurosurgeons and napalm-rape that Robert Fripp's ever kicked the dog around the room on, sounds like the album cover looks. The album cover, which predates such mouth-as-cave sleeves as Possessed's *Beyond the Gates* and Fates Warning's *Awaken the Guardian*, has this big red crinkled face, and you can look down his throat and see his tonsils and look up his nose and see his adenoids, and you feel like a doctor. My six-year-old son thinks it's real neat. The Frippertonic one merely dances a sprightly ballet across the remaining faerie-grounds, but we're entertained by purple pipers and evergreen gardeners and pattern jugglers and dancing puppets in the nine-and-a-half-minute title-encyclopedia (170 seconds shorter than the longest track, 187 seconds longer than the shortest one), and they make the emerald-gleaming jesters and weeping unicorns and purple fog in *National Lampoon's* "Art Rock Suite" seem like no joke. Which is some sort of accomplishment, probably.

461. LIVING COLOÜR

Vivid Epic, 1988

Though avant-guitar god Vernon Reid's rarely as note-slashingly nuclear as he was on Ronald Shannon Jackson's early LPs, it's still neat to hear his voodoo-chile forest-fire in so commercial a context. When, in "Funny Vibe," Public Enemy's Chuck D and Flavor Flav pay back what they've owed Vern since his "Sophisticated Bitch" solo on *Yo! Bum Rush the Show*, he splatters all over 'em (about time *somebody* did). And the momentum really kicks in when Reid and bassist Muzz Skillings go progresso, sculpting multitudinous heavyweight McLaughlin/Metallica changes into surge-hooks that keep lifting us up and heaving us into the mud. But when these bloods ain't syncopating their powergroove feedback toward the moon, their funk's never stretched or twisted, no curves get thrown. Once the rhythm section finds a pocket, nobody can figure out what to do with it, so they're confined to it, and the cleaned-up studiofication of the innards (drums, for starters) makes the mohawked choppiness sag even more.

"I Want to Know" is innocuous matching-shirt-and-socks postpowerpop, in "Glamour Boys" Hollywood star Corey Glover brags that he's plenty more "fierce" than disco-goers even as his backup's slicked into the Urban Camp Radio realm by the cameoing production of noted glam-boy Mick Jagger, and the chatty taped-over-airwave adverts do no good whatsoever. Instead of gnashing Reid-rage re Goetz/Howard Beach, we get vague "politics" à la your typically astute indie-thrash mob: Substance beats style, wishy-washiness sucks, firebombs are not the most humane sort of eviction notices, like that.

Oddly enough, Living Coloür fare best when they dig into larger-than-life Anglo-Saxon psych/Zen antipoetry semioticizing, such as in the Glover-penned "Middle Man," philosophy-wise very Geddy Lee, and in the stoner-type introspection of "Broken Hearts," a gushingly gorgeous acoustic-to-electric ballad with graceful folk-fluttering over Def Jam beats. Glover, who unlike most hard-rock vocalizers can do more than just shout, but who's generally too unragged not to be overwhelmed in an ax-happy sphere, actually lets out some credible blood-curdle shrieks in the massive "Desperate People," the metaphysical was-not-was-ness of which has the anxiously displaced feel of seminal soul-metal like Love's "Seven and Seven Is" and the Chambers Brothers' "Time Has Come Today." And given their solipsist propensities, this foursome picked the perfect coverable in David Byrne's "Memories Can't Wait": Reid wails creepier than anywhere, and that "party in my mind" line comes out bubbling like Dr. Funkenstein himself. It makes chicken soup (the kind that "eats like a meal"!) out of chicken poop. But as for the other stuff and whatever this band's done since, stop kidding yourself, okay?

462. **SCRATCH ACID**

Scratch Acid Rabid Cat EP, 1984

This black goop has a mind of its own. It surrounds you, engulfs you, knocks you prone, violates you, forces you to stew in it and accept its stench and finally admit that you and it are one and the same. But really you're not. The punk-rock Zep of "Communication Breakdown" and "Immigrant Song" sideswipes Motörhead and the Pop Group, mauled bones and tendons and organs fly everywhere, and when somebody tries to piece the confusion back together the particulars are all too shuffled and the victims come back to life as Japanese movie reptiles with unmatched soundtracks and toe jam and they stomp all over your head. Or rather, they tap-dance, with pretty violin and cello and piano arrangements. But the feet are great big dogs, and David Yow's old-man-of-the-woods yowl curls around your earlobes and sends your hammers careening into your anvils, and it hurts. At first. The eight mind-boggles range from the demiclassical haunted-house epic "Owner's Lament" to the self-punishing cluttered-house metaphor "Mess," and they're full of tribal beats, Arab axes, shrieks and wheezes and coughs and cackles, and they surge toward you like a four-by-four car-crushing mud-slinging monster machine. But when you're left unscathed, you realize it was only a dream. By then, the thrill's gone.

463. **ELECTRIC PEACE**

Medieval Mosquito Barred, 1987

Former punk-rock unknowns transfer into a scheme of things where they reconstruct the nasty fray metal made back in the Nixon/Ford era, not merely by namby-pambily copping a lick here and there to scratch the surface, but by diving in jackknife-style and making a big splash. I only heard this pancake 'cause I was on the Restless Records mailing list and some guy in the band's a janitor there or something, so they distributed it for him as a favor, even though

they were too stupid to sign his band. A friend of mine compares Electric Peace to Deep Purple around the time of *Machine Head/Fireball*, but to me they're real tough to pinpoint—no direct ripoffs I can identify, just monster lo-fi riff/groove tendencies, switch-hit arrangements, no paucity of distortorama hooks, an extrahistrionic bassist who yowls that you shouldn't be nervous 'cause it's natural, just like drilling for oil. Since they're scavengers-for-scavenging's-sake they're as insignificant as camp can be, but what sets 'em apart from the scavenger hordes is their swirliness-of-keyboards, their thickness-of-riff, their buffoonishness-of-lyric, and their propensities for both incidentally expressionist noize (à la Blue Cheer or the MC5) and uncalculated rhythmic swing (à la Richard Wagner or James Brown). They're bound to be a collector's item someday if you're into that sort of thing (and who *ain't* into getting rich?) so purchase copies for all your close relatives—sure beats savings bonds!

464. **DIAMONDHEAD**

Behold the Beginning Metal Blade, 1987; rec. 1980–81

Metallica's already covered two of these supposedly sinful songs (the first one and the last one, and maybe another one on some non-LP B-side by now, who cares) on this collection by these more-famous-by-the-minute practitioners of so-called "New Wave of British Heavy Metal." Lars Oilrig (Metallica's drummer) gonzoed out the liner notes, and what's inside (I'm told) is remixes of early eighties numbers Lars claims were chewier the first time around when I wasn't paying attention. A couple tracks do sound kinda flat, I suppose, but only "Waited Too Long" is anything like overripe. The music's modularly repetitive hip-swung bassplay logistics with a vocaler who hoots out his hog-callin' "sooey"s like some fried-food-shunning Plant/Osbourne hybrid; the long songs have too many save-the-whales cosmos-breaks, so the short ones are best. Best of all, and also loudest though not fastest, is "Shoot Out the Lights," which has a bizarre rhythmical and lyrical similarity to another tune released in England in 1980—Joy Division's "Interzone." They both groove precisely the same almost (s'posed to be based on some ancient Limey soul standard called "Keep On Keepin' On" or something, so go ask the Queen if you're really curious), and both mention "a friend of mine." I detect a plot.

465. ALICE COOPER
Pretties for You Straight, 1969

At this point, the Mr. Dressup routine is so raw it's almost amusing (they don't even have good taste in skirts yet), so I can endure a minute or two of the Euroclassy love-is-blue schmaltz-sendups and studio-goofing blood rites. In "Living" and "B.B. on Mars," Glen Buxton and Mike Bruce get tumultuously hairy in an Amboy Prunes sort of way, "Red Rover, Red Rover" has all these freedom-skronk sax-honks and slide-runs slowing and speeding the tape, and I betcha Tony Iommi liked the grungebuilds in "Fields of Regret" and "Reflected," the latter a nascent version of "Elected" with good weasely pedal-pumping. The titles are like time travel ("Titanic Overture," "10 Minutes Before the Worm," "Swing Low, Sweet Cheerio," "No Longer Umpire," "Earwigs to Eternity"), but the five decompositions that last longer than 180 seconds revert to Doorsish jamnation, and a few of the shorter ones are prissy post-*Pepper* pretension. A minestrone of empty gestures, it's a conversation piece at best.

466. ATOMIC ROOSTER
In Hearing of Atomic Rooster Elektra, 1971

Liner notes aren't as awesomely awful as Pat Salvo's on '72's *Made in England* ("In 1968, the year of potent herbs, powerless flowers and Anglomania, several lunatic crews of British musicians stormed the portals of America . . ."), and despite the honorable piano-bombast in, no kidding, "A Spoonful of Bromide Helps

the Pulse Rate Go Down," I'd actually get more out of this one if it were *more* operatic. But John Cann's guitaring here's much less timid than Steve Bolton's turned out to be, and at least they ain't got Engelbert Humperdinck's "canbasher" (as Salvo calls Ric Parnell!). The organist is Vincent Crane, formerly of the firebreathing Crazy World of Arthur Brown, and Paul Hammond's supposedly got the world's largest drumkit, but that's only 'cause Manowar hasn't been born yet. The structures are uptight and outasite like Keith Emerson doing the funky Broadway in Dyke and the Blazers' orchestra pit, and though the mystical riffs do get kinda jazzbo, ya play it at 45 and everything's hunky-dory.

467. BOOMERANG
Boomerang RCA, 1971

No inscriptions on the truly astounding front cover, just this aboriginal cannibal chucking his 'rang toward your ring-dang-doo, but Michael Cuscuna's backnote, which pegs early seventies grunge's "return to the roots of loud, jumping music" as an explicit "reaction to the complexity and eclecticism of progressive rock" is documented *proof* of a theory I've had for years. Ha! The guitarist is a seventeen-year-old with a Latin surname, the Semitic-surnamed organist useta be in Vanilla Fudge ("but the complex arrangements and psychedelic effects that characterized the Fudge and that era are now part of our formative past"!), the drummer is apparently Italian, and the bassist's last name is Casmir so don't ask me about that one. So *Boomerang* contains no aborigines, but it does contain some pelvis-pulverizing riffs (in "Juke It," "The Peddler," the ridiculously sexist "Cynthia Fever") and sandpaper surfaces ("Hard Times"). And also some majorly gimptitious "string orchestration" (in "Brother's Comin' Home"), which shoots holes in my hypothesis, but what the fuck.

468. JIMI HENDRIX

Band of Gypsys Capitol, 1970

It's plugged as his "funk" move, where he finally comes to terms with James and Sly (you know—his *race*). But he'd already done that (in "Fire," "Purple Haze," "Crosstown Traffic"), and though "Message of Love"'s Popeye quotes come close, despite a no-honkies-allowed membership that even Bobby Seale would've approved of, this is art-funk at best, brain-dead "improvisatory" addict-muzak at worst. Buddy Miles is an overinflated balloon who wouldn't hit his full stride till the California Raisin Advisory Board rediscovered him, and the chop-demonstrations on Side Two last way too long and go way too slow; "Machine Gun" reportedly pertains to Viet Nam, and I'll grant that it features some heady onomatopoeizing (hey, Jimi could wank his weenie with the *best* of 'em, no argument there!), but if I had to fight a war myself I'd draft the Commodores version, I think.

469. MÖTÖRHOME

Double Live . . . Bozo! Soso cassette, 1989

College boys swelled up by foolish pride overdose on ironic umlauts, hire Ted Nugent and Paul Stanley as master-baiters of ceremonies, flush commodes, half-remember seventies paradiddles, and keep losing track of their groove. You might not get the joke, so it's no great loss one way or another if you keel over without having heard auteurish amnesia like "The Bulge" ("a love song," natch) and the Dizzy Gillespie cover and the Village People ripoff about YMCA swimming lessons, but the shaggy-dog sagas are a horse-latitude of a different color. "Undertow"'s all manly maritime metaphors: Noted jazz critic Mike Rubin drops his anchor and starts to submerge, tries not to rock the boat and sees if the relationship will float. Or, okay, maybe that one's not so hot after all, but how 'bout "Stallion Road," Leviticus-scale wanted-poster-child pathfinder-metal worthy of Jimmy Page *and* Gordon Lightfoot: "Faithful mount, trusty steed/A friend in harness is a friend indeed/Out of the frying pan and into the skillet/There is no food unless you kill it. . . . Water, birth, the planet earth, the careless seed is sown/Beyond the Valley of the Octagon, where real men roll their own." Dudley Do-right lives.

470. LOCK UP

Something Bitchin' This Way Comes Geffen, 1990

After Living Coloür and Faith No More broke through, oodles of callow Caucasians tried to incorporate the herks and jerks they mistook for "funk" into post-*Paranoid* crunge, and inevitably the outcome was laughable. While Lock Up isn't necessarily the exception that proves the rule (bass-popping's dead on its feet, singing gets lost in the shuffle, ubiquitous rapping can't hold a candle to Warrant's occasional same), at least they make some commendable diversions from the crooked and narrow. These are primarily the work of Tom Morello's guitar, which seems fond of dainty little offhand semiblues/orchestric squigs but can get positively ossified when it wants to. The songs too often come off as chants supporting good riffs, though that might just be 'cause Brian Grillo mans the mike with a Michael Stipe (or maybe late Eric Clapton?) fan's fear of projection. There's momentary indications (e.g., something about heading straight home soon as the movie's over) that real thinking might be going on—"Half Man, Half Beast" even aims for a statement midway between "Welcome to the Jungle" and the Dictators' "Science Gone too Far," albeit without the wit of either. Vince Ostertag works Cuban-style percussion extras into "24 Hour Man," a boogie about working all day not fucking all day, and in "Kiss 17 Goodbye," about graduating high school feeling like a number, Grillo seizes a piece of Paul Westerberg's "Sixteen Blue" empathy. So there's no lack of potentially smart stuff going on here—the band just seems a wee bit bashful about it all.

471. KING'S X
Out of the Silent Planet Megaforce, 1988

As the eighties ended, an optimist or two posed the idea that snooty time-signatures might mark the future of guitar music (which probably *has* no future), and usually it was easy to scoff, but these Edwardian Texans had a born-again black guy with a mohawk up front, so in their case it was only natural to investigate. Usually, said investigation wasn't worth the bother—if the person you live with once upon a time had high school classmates who listened to too much Styx, he or she could be expected to ask you, "What the hell is that shit anyway?" I mean, the opening salvo is called "In the New Age," gimme a break. Yet somehow said salvo's Sab-crunch and dainty choruses and overall intenseness of trying-real-hard-to-say-something-important manage to add up to a certain non–New Age *je ne sais quoi,* and what comes next but a nice ode-to-summer after the manner of Zep's "Dancing Days." Another tune borrows its title ("Shot of Love") from Dylan's Christ period, and a few more suggest that these skeezixes consider themselves soldiers following in the footsteps of Their Father Who Art in Heaven, and those of us who aren't (or anyhow, those of us who stand in the way of those who *are*) will get our comeuppance in the long run. So what this debut mainly (more or less) amounts to is just another comic book good-vs.-evil parable, not exactly *rare* in the annals of metallurgy. But I'll cut it some slack for, I dunno, not being real *ugly* about it.

472. SLAYER
Reign in Blood Def Jam, 1986

Since bassist Tom Araya shrieks out ritualistic Marvel Comics descriptions of a hell you're not even satisfied (as you are with Roky Erickson, say) he himself believes in, his band's misanthropic strangulation and asphyxiation sneers come across as just one more bullshit occult cop-out. Even when Slayer get smart and use Auschwitz or the bubonic plague or Salem as evidence that Down Under is where we are *right now,* they never give any indication of why such a state of affairs would anger them into cranking out such agonizing slashology. None of which makes too terribly much difference when the murk-caged, petulant crud on this Rick Rubin–produced platter is bludgeoning its way through the backward Satanism and thunderstorm kabooms and out your speakers. When you're thirsting for heat from below, how words sound matters more than what they say, and when Araya spits out hardened-artery consonants in lines like "tighten the tourniquet around your neck," it can sound pretty chilling.

With neither songs nor grooves oriented around a traditionally recurring hook/riff framework, Slayer is (or *was,* for a couple years, until their blur turned into just one more hackneyed hard-rock cliché) as pure a clatter as any band that's ever called itself metal has produced; unfortunately, "purity" 's got nothing to do with why real people listen to music. *RIB* does swing, sort of, but unlike Aerosmith (whose Steve Tyler helped inspire Araya's throaty operatics), Slayer's got too much mega-complicated chord-and-tempo-transforming distortion to be "funky." There's no commercial concessions at all, and First Amendment threats being what they've been these last few years, it's not hard to figure why CBS refused to release *Reign in Blood,* and why Warner Bros. barely promoted the thing: In 1986, any LP whose cover had a devil-goat being carted around on a throne amidst naked decapitated bodies hanging upside-down above a firepit full of floating heads was treading on seriously flimsy ice. Yet Slayer signaled a rock-exploitation future not only louder and more tasteless than Tipper Gore could ever imagine, but also stupider and more predictable. This is the best album they will ever make, and it's harmless.

473. HEAD OVER HEELS
Head over Heels Capitol, 1971

As transmogrified/petrified bar-boogie goes, this mushmouthed mushroomism from (I think) Cleveland could be worse, but what makes it most notable is its rumored personnel intersection with the Human Beinz, who set the *Guinness* world record for double-negatives with "Nobody But Me" in the mid-sixties and who should by no means be confused with "Human Be-ins," which didn't happen till a couple years later, in San Francisco. Following the dense battering of Junior (of Foreigner fame) Walker's "Roadrunner," we get a shameful half-hour's worth of folkified cardiac arrests, including a Plant-impersonating "Red Rooster" and an item called "Children of the Mist" with cave dwellers and fog in it. Eventually in "Question" and "In My Woman" some pumping Ron Asheton chug and Tito Puente timbale (not at the same time, which would've been *real* interesting) halfway kick the thing into gear. Then there's more dilapidated porch-punk.

474. SWANS
· · · · · · · · · · · · · · · · · · · ·
Time Is Money (Bastard) . . . a Screw . . .
PVC cassette, 1986

On their even duller early records, these Gotham grouches generally played cavernous slow-fi theater-slop, all dragging and weighted through the floor-boards. They play the same stuff here, but they consolidate it with pinball-lizard emulator beats, double-tracked vocals, fake-horn charts, pianos and cellos and oboes, even this melancholy babe named Jarboe who quivers sorta like Kate Bush in mid-yawn. Select moments bounce and boom like boxing kangaroos (or at least like "We Will Rock You" by Queen), but the side effect is that you can finally decipher M. Gira's self-pitying basso-profundo denunciations, moaned more or less like Lurch on "The Addams Family": Sex is flesh is money is time is work is degradation is power is sex, nothing we didn't already know. Rape your immediate supervisor, "irony" like that. The limbo-dance number that went "as low as I can go, I will go there" didn't come till later, but the two "disco" EPs united here constitute the band's liveliest product by far—the only time they threatened to get your fat buttocks off the potty. Still,

Photograph by Wim v.d. Hulst © 1989

you're not supposed to enjoy this music; it's supposed to be "good for you," like liver. Not exactly my idea of a wild time, bucko.

475. BLACKFOOT
· · · · · · · · · · · · · · · · · · · ·
Tomcattin' Atco, 1980

Fronted for some two decades by bluegrass master Shorty Medlocke's singing/guitaring grandson Rick and seasoned in the same Jacksonville barbelt that produced Lynyrd Skynyrd, Blackfoot always played the chest-hair-thumping stars 'n' bars game with too much middlebrow professionalism to approach either Skynyrd's heroic hellraze-flair or Black Oak Arkansas's snuff-dip chutzpah, but they deserve a couple heart-and-loyalty points for staying so stubbornly southern for so long—Rick was still the same frazzled-longhair-in-leather come '87 when the Cult were diminishing said pose to a parody. Here, despite periodically pointless solos, speedboogie slaughter like "Warped," "Streetfighter," and "Gimme Gimme Gimme" works for the most part as pure banal bottleneck brawn, unassuming garbage lifted from the dustbin of routine by its slobbering lack of fashion sense. In his rangy hard-guy groan, Rick asks his "good-god mama" what's wrong with her face, then pledges to mess up the face of whatever man messes with her. The cover's got a panther with his eyeballs extracted, and Gramps guests on "Fox Chase," but you can rest assured this here ain't no animal-lib lisp.

476. ANGUS
Track of Doom Restless/Medusa, 1987

They take their name from either the first name of one of the great bookbag-wearers of our time or from the last name of early seventies recorder-grunge combo Bull Angus, and their title (called *Crack of Doom* on the sleeve's hypesticker, by the way, but *Crack of Doom* was actually an LP Restless/Medusa released *later* that month by D. C. Lacroix!) may well be a reference to Sab's "Hand of Doom" with a speck of race-music train-mythology tossed in for the "track" part. Crass cover too: Two centaurs with lotsa muscles and real ugly mugs, carrying a head on a stick. And the singer, Edgar Lois, appears to be something of a transvestite, but he also appears to weigh a ton—the Divine or Sylvester of metal, I tell you. Plus, though the music ain't about to jump on no speed-wagon, it's also by no means slow, which is to say it's more Budgie-fast than Slayer-fast; doesn't sacrifice brawn for the sake of briskness, but it doesn't dilly dally either.

The guitar player blows, but the rhythm section's one o' those push 'em back, push 'em back, push 'em wa-a-a-ay back machines that tackles everything that moves. And Edgar-baby's got one o' those operatic vibratos that they just don't make anymore—he can reach high notes without sounding as if his Levi's for Gals are too tight, he can hold notes till next week, and of course (being from Holland) he's guttural. Most gear tune of all, "The Gates," has this "Hey! Hey! Hey!" chant like in "Macho Man" by the Village People or "Steppin' Out" by Paul Revere and the Raiders, and ACTUALLY APPEARS TO BE ABOUT A BOY AND A GIRL WHO LIKE EACH OTHER, a pretty unknown topic in indie-metal circles, to say the least. I could do without the CSNY-type acoustic introspection that kicks off Side Two, and the ballads and instrumentals are as boring as all heavy metal ballads and instrumen-

tals, but this is far from the worst album I've heard in my lifetime—I wouldn't *buy* it if I were you, but if you do, make sure the bass is all the way up and the treble all the way down when you play it. Trash like this always sounds *better* that way!

477. SLAYER
Hell Awaits Metal Blade, 1985

It's a put-on, I gather. Dave Lombardo's trouser-pressing drums start slower than Jeff Hanneman's rhythm-rivets, your balance control gets a workout, and riffs that lasted five seconds on the Stooges' *Raw Power* hang around for five minutes. Tom Araya crams in as many multisyllabic incantations as'll fit, sounds as if he's speaking Latin sometimes, and when he shuts up and lets the matted mayhem reverberate on its own you're almost ready to want to believe these Cali dream dates have met Moloch up close and personal. Homicidally ignoramoid upside-down-crucifix corked-anus pudwank, some kinda mono-functional camp-meeting onslaught with words you're not allowed to hear so they must be irrelevant, that's all obvious. All I wanna know is: Why?

478. MOLLY HATCHET
Flirtin' with Disaster Epic, 1979

Molly, not a member of the band, useta behead people in Salem in the 1800s; the band, though they always desecrated their dust-protectors with Vikings as if they were Iron Maiden, are your typically fast and fat and funky po-man's Skynyrds from Jacksonville. Joe Brown drawls Bobby Womack's "It's All Over Now" juicier than Dr. John (w/Dirty Dozen Brass Band) or John Anderson, the jukejoint-ivory danceability incorporates loose-as-a-caboose western swing, Dave Hlubek and Steve Holland riff bull's-eyes like the sharpshooters they likely are. A whole LP's more than anybody short of an unreconstructed Dixie denthead ought to admit to liking, but "Flirtin' with Disaster" itself's one sweaty swamp-siren, breeding punk-rock turmoil more fervently than any new-wave Top 40 Joe Jackson or Herman Brood or the Police or Bram Tchaikovsky attained in '79, no bout adoubt it.

479. POWER TOOLS
Strange Meeting Antilles/New Directions, 1987

Three cool cats of the jazzistic variety (harmolodic can-honcho Ronald Shannon Jackson, ECM ax-employee Bill Frisell, punkfunk bassosaur Melvin Gibbs) get their respective rocks off on okra-influenced beatspuzz like what would happen if six was nine, but as often as not the freedom-now's just too sweet for its own good. They're not exactly afraid to get their hands dirty, they just don't do it much, and they've got two left feet. Which is to say that though their power-trio power-lunch has some unfurlingly maniacal ripchord jam-squawk (especially "Wolf in Sheep's Clothing," "Unscientific American," "Blame & Shame," "The President's Nap"), "Wadmalow Island" and "A Song Is Not Enough" and "When We Go" are primed for radio stations that call themselves "The Wave," and the rest is shot through with the savorless substance scribes at *Down Beat* euphemistically refer to as "nuance"—too much overmanicured counter-point, a *lameduck* president's nap. I blame Frisell.

480. RUSH
Rush Mercury, 1974

These snowdogs' one true "rock" record, produced all by their lonesome with no help from welfare handouts or Neil Peart (that's John Rutsey on drums), has some wing-heeled Snuffle-upagus riffola not hor-ribly far from certain '71–'73 Zepalikes. Geddy hasn't quite developed his, er, "voice," so mainly he just apes Robert Plant, fairly persuasively I suppose but it's just not the same. He also *tries to sing the blues,* which suggests that perhaps his Ayn Randian, er, "philoso-phy" hasn't quite developed yet, either—like, what is he, a GUILTY WHITE LIBERAL or something?? Shame on him! And the Lichtenstein-style low-art packaging would in no way impress Allan Bloom, and what the hell's this "Working Man" rubbish (besides their most Metallica-like thingamajig ever, I mean)? Didn't Sir Ged quack through his oversized adenoids once that Bruce the Boss don't speak for the Maple Leaf fans in *his* igloo? (Or was that Neil? Hard to keep track, they all smell the same from here!) Mere woo-pitching *love songs,* with titles stolen from Glen Miller, no less... Take off!! And does that blotch on Geddy's forehead mean he's a Hindu, or has he just been munchin' too many Yukon Cornelius Choco-bars, or what? Hose-heads no less than fountainheads, Rush are enigmatic enough to make Atlas shrug.

481. THE ROCKETS
Live Capitol, 1984

Motortown journeyhacks skippered by Mitch Ry-der's buddies Jim McCarty and Johnny "Bee" Badan-jek, they hit really big where I'm from and not so big everywhere else, just like Seger/Nuge/MC5 years before. Flaunting sax and soul-girls and borrow-ing Berrychuck walkduck riffs, sly (if old-fashioned) enough to name an earlier LP *No Ballads,* they were made for bars, though probably not ones where you'd find me. But pub-metal slops hogs live, and that's just what the Rockets do beneath this cheesy K-Tel cover-artlessness, providing a reductionist armpit-fart kick especially in McCarty's self-depre-cating stenchification of Fleetwood Mac's "Oh Well." The other cover's Lou Reed's "Sally Can't Dance," a tasteful choice if arguably too fucking late (they should've done "Disco Inferno" instead), and the primarily googoomucky lovehurt originals feature such romantic rock myth songmatter as record machines and radios and cruisin' Woodward on Friday night lookin' for action or maybe crack, I'm not sure. The best stuff's saved for the end, 'long about when Dave Gilbert complains that he's getting "a little tired o' singin' all by myself," but truth be told most Detroit-rock's as crummy as rock from anywhere else. Anything to avoid the Ford line, y'know?

482. FREE
Fire and Water A&M, 1970

This is, perhaps, the ensemble responsible for slowing everything hard and bluesful down to the trudge that stopped the world so rock 'n' roll could get off, and by any reasonable standard this is the most auspicious LP they made. It goes: leaden boogie about two primitive elements, short drum solo, macho moan advancing toward bitter yearn for freedom, overearnest memory-of-youth-gone-by moan that evokes this and that, short piano solo, derivative lament about an unfortunate young white man with long hair who is unhappily burdened with the ballast of whatever experience he has been persuaded to refer to as a "heavy load" though he never gets real specific about it or anything, okay paranoid taunt at highfalutin mucky-muck of big-cheesedom, attempt at heartfelt done-somebody-wrong song sung by cretin with an aorta made of alfalfa, lecherous lava-eater of a worldwide Top 10 smasheroonie with a riff that shakes you all night long like a funky cold medina. When I was a very small lad, I used to eat my vegetables first so I'd be able to savor the yummy stuff in peace at meal's end. Oftentimes, it was cold by then.

483. GRAND FUNK RAILROAD
Live Album Capitol, 1970

Ostensibly one of the most "authentic" (ho hum) live-doubles ever constructed (there's no "technical assistance," so I guess amps and recording equipment don't count, and you're s'posed to play all hour-plus-twenty nonstop "without interruption," which had to be difficult in the pre-CD age but mayhaps that fabled prole-community-in-*Solidarnosc!* GFR built up all just went out and bought a second turntable for the occasion), but really what we got here is, like, a Political Document of the *real* "Silent" (har har) Majority, i.e., all those scorched young mechanic-trainees and busboys ('cept this was before any had

jobs, see) who were one day gonna steal the world out from under their rabble-rousing older siblings (so conscientious rock critics had to pretend to enjoy the music, which was humorous for a while) but hereupon were content to just sit on their duffs and swallow reds and observe Mark Farner wail and whine, and real soon thereafter they changed their minds and decided to just sit back and pretend it never happened. For the record: My favorite number, "Inside Looking Out," which features nickel bags, outwears its welcome nine minutes before it ends. Grand Funk's "Paranoid" is considerably slower than Black Sabbath's, their "Heartbreaker" is considerably slower than Dionne Warwick's, "Into the Sun" lasts a whole side but *isn't* the longest song, "T.U.N.C." is ".C.U.N.T" spelled into a mirror. Several linguistic quirks are self-consciously sequestered from underground Aframerican crime culterculture. Most altruistic admonition: "Brothers and sisters, there are people out there who look just like your brother. But they're *not!*"

484. HEAD OF DAVID
LP Blast First UK import, 1986

Four innocent-looking outland-Brit scooter-grebos debut with an amped-up doomsday that flexes its baby biceps like the Swans meet "Space Truckin'," taking preglam Killing Joke's metalblat hybrid a few steps further into the alleged abyss. In the process,

they burglarize the MC5 ("five seconds of decision . . ."), borrow half-baked snuff fantasies from the
Sonics of Youth (titles: "Joyride Burning X," "Shadow
Hills of California"), pickpocket Rema Rema or maybe
Boomerang (African headhunter poster inside), and
update Suicide ("Rocket USA" done post-Challenger
as imploding sludge: "gonna crash, you die"). This is
quasinihilist smegma not exactly wrung free of pre-
tention, but too guileless and unsmoothed to let it get
in the way—Pitch it to the suburbs, stuff it into the
mainstream, and platinum should've come easy.
'Course, by the time HOD made their followup in '88,
they'd befriended postmortem producer-at-large
Steve Albini. They named it *Dustbowl*, and in honor
of either the title or that summer's impending Great
American Drought, he dehydrated 'em.

485. 1994
• • • • • • • • • • • • • • • • • • • •
1994 A&M, 1978

If it were ten years later, or if a man were singing, you
could completely ignore it—Karen Lawrence is constantly in pain again and on her knees again and all
that, and usually she couldn't buy a personality if she
wanted one. But as little women with big hearts tend
to do, she belts 'em out like tomorrow never comes,
more hostile than Kat Arthur in Legal Weapon even,
and with the Iggy riffs in "Radio Zone" boxing Elvis
Costello's tympanic membranes and the "Sweet Jane"
leads in "Once Again" arching around an "Immigrant
Song" bass line, the combination's potent enough.
Steve Schiff's fretboard holds its own even during the
flapdoodle, and both sides end with messages to girls
with unusual names based in Romance languages, neat
'cause you know this ain't no pickup ploy (or maybe
it is, in which case it's even neater). Too bad about the
martyrdom.

486. THE EDGAR WINTER GROUP
• • • • • • • • • • • • • • • • • • •
They Only Come Out at Night Epic, 1972

R*eal* white boys singing the blues, that's what Edgar
and his Beaumont brother Johnny were, and here the
lead albino has hot red lipstick, a gold cheek-ring, a
diamond dookie-rope, blue eyeliner, lotsa yellow hair,
and pink nipples. That's on the front; on the back he's
got clothes on, and Dan Hartman's silk shirt lets you
know who's the real dandy of the bunch, which
perhaps explains why nothing here rocks as hard as
"Instant Replay," Dan's '79 bubbledisco hit. We're
talking competent midtempo overglorified under-
wrecked meals on wheels, with Ronnie Montrose and
Rick Derringer and tasteful piano/calypso snoozing
and a song called "Round & Round" that's not as good
as Aerosmith's or Ratt's or New Order's. We're also
talking the moderately useful "Free Ride," not to be
confused with "Slow Ride" by Foghat (though I did for
about fifteen years anyway), and the very useful
"Frankenstein," not to be confused with "Godzilla" by
Blue Öyster Cult (or "Frankenstein" by the New York
Dolls). The "Frankenstein" here's as fierce as its title
and lots speedier. Its horns are corny, and in the
background Edgar plays basketball with baby pigs.

487. ANGEL CITY
Face to Face Epic, 1980

These new-wave-era Aussie AC/DC clonelets have a curtly crunchy riff/shout/riff snotblues base, but they could live without Doc Meeson's cosmopolitan erudiction, not to mention his powerpap leanings. Doc's worldview transports Bon Scott's proledom into some moneyed literary-man realm, a total incongruity but an intriguing idea nonetheless; his barefooted flag-wavers play Snakes & Ladders and his smelly-footed postcard salesmen get locked up, fine. But when he balances whiskey and rolling dice with "*vis-a-vis ou vois*" and Renoir (even Big Brother), he can't help but let his cat outta his bag: He's not the guttersnipe he wishes he was. His cough's developed barely a third of the way toward Bonville and at least half of the way toward Peter Garrettville, and his French feels more natural than his street talk, and I wonder if the Chris Bailey on bass is the same as the guy in the Saints, who in more ways than one come from the same place. Probably not, but it's a small world, ain't it?

Photograph by Alen Macweeney © 1989

488. BLACK SABBATH
Sabbath Bloody Sabbath Warner Bros., 1974

Genesis made a less anemic album that year, but you'll be excused if you have trouble telling 'em apart: Geezer on Mellotron, Iommi on bagpipes and flute, "Rick [Fucking] Wakeman appears courtesy of A&M Records," and say howdy-do to all Ozzy's architects and acrobats. It's a meandering drag, with yucky packaging and title cut that show Ozzy sinking into the gory devil-flick gratuitousness of his self-parodic adulthood. The deathbed on the cover is AIDS before its time, and the most appropriate title, "Fluff," is reasonably amiable as harpsichord instrumentals go; "National Acrobat" 's murk makes for a scarier (and therefore stupider, but who cares) "prolife" discourse than Graham Parker's "You Can't Be Too Strong" if not King's X's "Legal Kill" if not the Sex Pistols' "Bodies"; and "Killing Yourself to Live" evolves into a formidable chunk of lard. But mainly the damsel-in-distress gruel-poesy deserves blame for Europe and Saxon and W.A.S.P. and Judas Maiden and Ronnie James Dokken, and there's things in life a person just cannot forgive.

489. ARGENT
All Together Now Epic, 1972

Their eponymous debut's allegedly more "Zombiesque," but as long as you've got a copy of *Odessey and Oracle*, why worry? Rod Argent "is a perfectionist. His writing can take months, searching for the right word," the liner notes inform us. "He loves to own beautiful things, but as so often happens with Geminis, he has two sides to his character." Though Rod's on orchestral organ here just as he was in "Time of the Season," the situation's not so much creepy anymore as just confusing: Roadies, agents, press officers, wives, under-assistant West Coast promo men, and some mysteriously grinning fatso named "Fred" (Flintstone?) get their pictures on the jacket, and if Chris White (ex-Zombies bassist) helped write five of the seven songs, how come he's not in the band? Russ Ballard's tunes aim for Junior Walker and come out like a malfunctioning lint-remover, "I Am the Dance of Ages" contains a generous helping of bad weather, and I'm still waiting for Cerrone's disco version of "Pure Love," which has four mystical movements ("Fantasia," "Prelude," "Pure Love," "Finale"). "Hold Your Head Up" is highly inspirational for impressionable youngsters who've got nothing better to do than sit around listening to Argent albums, a category that obviously sometimes includes me.

490. DEF LEPPARD
. . . .
On Through the Night Mercury, 1980

One way or another, you can theoretically trace all eighties metal ("pop" *and* "speed") back to the metal here. Pubescently punktious teenagers weaned on AC/DC, Mott, T. Rex, and who knows what else (Joe Elliot wears a *Never Mind the Bollocks* T-shirt sometimes), the Leps forefronted Anglometal's so-called "new wave" as boys girls could want. They did ultragenerically unbent singalong anthem-rock ravers, with no mascara and not too much mastery of chops, almost as if it never occurred to 'em there was another way. The first line in the first song's perhaps purloined from Ian Hunter's "Once Bitten Twice Shy," an invisible classic revived nine years later by Great White, and the band would never overdrive again like

they do in "It Could Be You," "Rocks Off," and "Wasted," but there's no color, no voice. The ones called "Overture" and "Sorrow Is a Woman" inevitably drift toward Nod on fancydan featherbeds, and by the time "When the Walls Come Tumbling Down" pushes its simpy save-the-ozone bedtime story aside for its freon sub-Zep chuckachucka, thus finally suggesting an ounce of ambition beyond the mere doing-of-it, the mediocre mythmash damn near comes as a relief.

491. VANILLA FUDGE
. . . .
Vanilla Fudge Atco, 1967

Legendarily psychodelphian Long Island boggerdowners, the Fudge are included here for primarily historical/hysterical interest, just like everybody else except more so. "You Keep Me Hanging On," their biggest bang, is to the Supremes (and Kim Wilde) what Grand Funk's "The Locomotion" is to Little Eva (and Kylie Minogue), which is to say slower. *Lots* slower—they really sound *trapped* by that woman, y'know? The opener and closer are Beatles covers (but what *wasn't* in those days?), the second cut's from the Impressions so what, the third's from the Zombies so what. The fourth's from Sonny Bono, which makes me smile, but Sinatra's rendition makes me smile wider. (Average song length, cover versions: 5:40. Average song length, originals: 0:22. Honest.) The musician named Timmy has the yippiest threads and Buddy Holly–est glasses, but Vinnie's more likely to be adopted by the Mafia. Shadow Morton produced, but his Shangri-Las productions are noisier. I got my copy for a quarter.

492. XAVION
. . . .
Burning Hot Asylum, 1984

Two years after "Beat It," at the high-water mark of potential rock-funk integration, six gutsy African-Americans happy to be in Memphis's middle class and determined to stay there make a real explicit metal-move, the kind Shalamar tried in "Dead Giveaway" and Kool and the Gang tried in "Misled," embellishing every studio-slicked Hall and Oates melody with some curt sort of dime-a-dozen AOR solo. It's not a bad cash-in at all: Not only is the bassist twitchier than in your average metal assemblage and the guitarist raunchier than in your average funk assemblage, but Dexter Haygood can actually *sing*, a rare HM distinction for sure. Until the inevitable heart-gush sets in, a few songs spritz straightaway into your fists and feets alike, "Self-Built Hell" with tricky electrobeats and laid-back raps and "Burning Hot" with "Super Freak" bass-slaps plus lusty sing-splat direct from Prince's "Party Up." Southern Caucasoid Greekboys usually let members of Xavion's racial stock on the bandstand while the rest of the Animal House remains off limits, so I'm dying to know whether that thanks to "die-hard fans in fraternities and sororities" means white ones or black ones. Betcha I can guess why Xavion didn't put their own picture on the front cover though.

493. PUSSY GALORE
. . . .
Sugarshit Sharp Caroline EP, 1988

Like Mötley Crüe, these life-sucks-like-Hoover swindlers play loud "blues"-based rock, pretend to revolt by pretending to be revolting, wear weird clothes, do

Photograph by Michael Lavine

sacrilegious renditions of songs we should've forgotten a long time ago, have no extraordinary sense of rhythm but manage to pull an okay riff out of the hat now and then, and unite like-minded folks whose

expectations they refuse to challenge. The Mötleys sell more records, but the Pussies (who usually sound like the Standells playing *Metal Machine Music* but getting all the notes wrong) get better reviews. It's supposed to be quite avant-garde how they make their records real murky and leave all the mistakes in, but maybe you gotta live in Manhattan to understand that sort of thing. Anyhow, this strikes me as their least conceptual disc (i.e., fewer cusswords that just might offend your mom if she's a nun!), and it's the only one where the guitar noise ever serves any sort of expressive purpose, so I'm sure they won't mind me saying it's their best. (Gotta pay my respects somehow.) It's still pretty pathetic, especially Side Two, which has some okay *titles* ("Adolescent Wet Dream," "Sweet Little Hi-Fi") but sinks for the nitpickable reason that there's no music on it. (Okay—I like how everything stops and the quasi-inebriated vokist says "one riff" then everything starts back up again. Big deal.) Side One's their cover of Einstürzende Neubauten's Teutonic crap-rap radiator-bang. "Yü Gung," complete with unclodlike beat boosting "Don't Believe the Hype" and "It Takes Two" samples through a blur that almost leaves the ground—never realized the words were "feed my ego" before, and with these prima donnas that line means a lot.

494. MISS DAISY
. . . .
Pizza Connection GWR, 1989

This greaseball power trio from Italy indirectly snubbed their nation's far superior late-eighties synth-disco subculture (starring Fun Fun, Alexander Robotnik, Vivien Vee, et cetera) in order to pass themselves off as Sergio Leone fans à la ZZ Top circa *El Loco* or Mötörhead circa *Ace of Spades*. Which was fine, because their grunge was thick and their dynamic sensibilities were sensible and their names were real long hilarious Italian ones nobody could pronounce and they tended to wear things like crucifixes and coke spoons around their necks and their lyrics bypassed enunciation in favor of annunciation (as in Luke I., chapter 26, verse 38). Best of all, *Pizza*

Connection came out right around the time *Do the Right Thing* was making putrid anti-pizzeria sentiments aggravatingly popular, and the album cover's got a green-white-and-red Italian flag on it, which can perhaps be construed as a rebuttal to Public Enemy's 1988 demand that everybody commence counting down to armageddon and getting the green-black-and-red in. So in PE's "Burn Hollywood Burn" in 1990, Flavor Flav referred to a 1989 movie called *Driving Miss Daisy* as "bullshit." You'd have to be pretty naive to pass off such a taunt as a mere coincidence, and I'm sure we can expect the controversy to continue unabated for years on end.

495. MONTROSE

Montrose Warner Bros., 1973

Obviously the main claim to fame is the singer, one Samuel Hagar, the airborne-rangin'/Iran-bombin' voice-of-reactionary-America who o'course confounded Van Halen toward the Land of Commonplaceness an unlucky thirteen years hence. His slimeball whine's as aggravating early on as it'd ever end up being, but in "Bad Motor Scooter," "Space Station #5" (complete with swell cybernetic blips), "Rock Candy," and the redone flipside of Elvis's "I Don't Care If the Sun Don't Shine" (look it up), pretty much the whole thing in fact, his ensemble (guitared, natch, by ensemble namesake Ronnie, who once strummed on Van Morrison LPs nobody ever heard) torches the communal farm, real fast-like. "I just quit my job making toothpicks outa logs" makes for more poetic peevishness than not driving fifty-five any day. But Sammy's still Sammy.

496. RADIO BIRDMAN

Radios Appear Trafalgar Australian import, 1977

A bland supper-club exercise in Stooge-worship that once struck some suckers (e.g., me!) as snaggle-toothed, this overpraised piece of merchandise stars Michigan med student/Army pilot Deniz Tek, who transplanted himself to Sydney and commenced stealing a band name from a line in one song ("1970") off the Stooges' *Funhouse* and covering another song ("T.V. Eye") from the same LP. But if his surf-gonzo was "rooted" anywhere other than in "Hawaii Five-O," it was rooted in *Raw Power* and the MC5's *Back in the USA*, which is to say in the more regimented end of the Mo City/A-Squared continuum. And though Birdman aimed for faithfulness to said maelstrom, it's a gross understatement to complain that their emaciated sound and pianistically Doorsish lounge-lizardry (in "Man with Golden Helmet" and "Love Kills," especially) only regimented it more. The primary attraction, a scant one indeed amid all this smarm, is such Detroit specificity as the title "Murder City Nights" and the passing references to Woodward Avenue and Metro Airport. But mainly Birdman do for Iggy what Rush do for Zep, and they're not half as humorous about it.

497. HUMBLE PIE

Rockin' the Fillmore A&M, 1971

Seven songs on four sides, which is six more than Jethro Tull fit on *Thick as a Brick*, I guess, but it's still proof that not only could knuckleheads like the ones here get away with anything and everything in the seventies, but that P. T. Barnum was right. For Side Two's twenty-four minutes of Dr. John's "Walk on Gilded Splinters" and Side Three's sixteen minutes of Muddy Waters's "Rollin' Stone," mainly what happens is the shrimp on guitar (Steve Marriot, mostly) plays a lick then the shrimp on the mike (Steve Marriot, mostly, since Peter Frampton was apparently busy feathering his hair and polishing his vocoder for his new calling as the Jon Bon Jovi of the seventies) yells a couple words then the shrimp on guitar plays the same lick again then the shrimp on the mike yells a couple more words and the licks get bigger and the words get repeated like Van Morrison having a conniption fit and this keeps happening for a while until the guitar overtakes everything and thousands of people stand up to strut like ptarmigans and maybe heave some Roman candles at each other, but don't ask me 'cause I've never lasted all the way through either song. Sides One and Four have a Willie Dixon song, a Ray Charles song, an Ashford and Simpson song ("I Don't Need No Doctor"—a hit), and more, mostly aimlessly flabby, but "Hallelujah (I Love Her So)" romps through the quicksand, and as the Dixon opens, Reverend Steve's hoping the people behind the glass plate are ready. I bet they're not.

Photograph by Sheree Levin

498. RASZEBRAE
. . . .
Cheap Happiness or Lofty Suffering
Unseen Hand, 1985

Four postfeminist LA gals reimagine Rough Trade '79 as a heavy metal label, but Ingrid Baumgart's feedback only makes the antitunes more formless and unfollowable, and the numb way Debbie Patino declaims her "existentialist" bluebook graffiti has no emotional connection whatsoever to what she's singing. B-movie star Janet Hudson and bike-demolition pro Katie Childe do a nervous Beefheart herky-jerk underneath, so as late-eighties subterranean sounds qua sounds go it's not unfun, but nothing's done with it, and the couple cuts that might've made decent singles ("To Be Excessive," especially) get lost amid the monochromatic odes to Hendrix and Jean-Paul Sartre and

pre-INXS suicide blondes. If punk did so darn much for female rock 'n' rollers, how come "Youth Song" 's a feebler "Immigrant Song" cop than Heart's?

499. STATUS QUO
. . . .
Hello! A&M, 1973

Ubiquitously unknowing and dependably fraternal, Status Quo's good-natured protogrebo workhorses have been tallying UK hits since time immemorial, and they'll probably continue to do so till the international date line disappears beneath its meridian. The hits will always sound exactly the same as the songs on this album, as they always have, except back in the sixties when the group powered flowers into mellifluousness like "Pictures of Matchstick Men" (their one *U.S.* smash, albeit as "*the* Status Quo," and an uncle to both Bon Jovi's "I'll Be There for You" and the Fall's "How I Wrote 'Elastic Man' "). Though *Hello!*'s libretto reads "it's so long since I sang songs for you," what Francis Rossi really sings is "it's so long since I sang something new," and when you flip the disc over, "And It's Better Now" examines the same theme. "Roll Over Lay Down" opens the LP four-wheel-driving the Dead's "Truckin' " like nobody short of the Pop-O-Pies, and once that's over the guitar's nothing, the singer's nothing, nothing's nothing. We get Creedence-boogie, ZZ-boogie, Stones-boogie, long-boggie, short-boogie, pump-boogie, plod-boogie, boogie-woogie, and cheese-boogie-with-ketchup-and-onions.

500. DEATH ANGEL
The Ultra-Violence Enigma, 1987

All the hepper since the drummer's fourteen and still has baby fat and every last little sleepy-eyed haircut-needer in the quintet's both an adolescent and a Filipino-or-something ethnic and each other's cousin, there's more finesseful aggression here than in any Mahavishnu/Rush–style zigzag foisted upon the gullible mosh-masses this side of the Metallicoids—trancelike at times, but other parts make your tooth enamel ache, sorta like Moe telling Larry and Curly to "wake up and go to sleep." The singer's the prez of his student body (and not even underachieving "gifted student" Deb Gibson ever pulled that one off), and though his son-of-Geddy squawkola and asinine raping-of-virgins-deep-in-the-lair poetix are tough for a graying geezer like me to deal with, there's plenty of high-concept maestro-flash instro-passages ('specially in the title opus, which lasts till adulthood), and nobody can claim these tykes don't have time to improve. Me, I got 320-some votes on my no-Twinkie-price-hike platform back in '77, but lost out to the usual bitching-for-the-sake-of-bitching of Don Weingust, a flute-playing fan of the Grammy-winning heavy metal band Jethro Tull. I'll never live it down, but you can consider this revenge.

THE *100* BEST HEAVY METAL SINGLES NOT AVAILABLE ON ANY OF THE *500* BEST HM ALBUMS

1. THE BOB SEGER SYSTEM · *"2+2=?"* Capitol, 1967

2. THE TRASHMEN · *"Surfin' Bird"* Garret, 1963

3. JEFFERSON AIRPLANE · *"White Rabbit"* RCA, 1967

4. RUN-D.M.C. · *"Rock Box"* Profile 12-inch, 1984

5. THE KNACK · *"My Sharona"* Capitol, 1979

6. ELTON JOHN · *"Saturday Night's Alright for Fighting"* MCA, 1973

7. IAN HUNTER · *"Once Bitten Twice Shy"* Columbia, 1975

8. RAMONES · *"Bonzo Goes to Bitburg"* Beggars Banquet UK import, 1985

9. 13TH FLOOR ELEVATORS · *"Fire Engine"* IA, 1966

10. THE MOVE · *"Do Ya"* United Artists, 1972

11. BON JOVI · *"I'll Be There for You"* Mercury, 1989

12. MICHAEL JACKSON · *"Beat It"* Epic, 1983

13. FUNKADELIC · *One Nation Under a Groove Special EP Side 3 and Side 4* Warner Bros. 7-inch EP, 1978

14. JEFFERSON AIRPLANE · *"Somebody to Love"* RCA, 1967

15. CRASS · *"Sheep Farming in the Falklands"* Crass UK import, 1983

16. JOURNEY · *"Don't Stop Believin'"* Columbia, 1981

17. DINOSAUR · *"Repulsion"* Homestead, 1986

18. CHARLIE DANIELS BAND · *"Everytime I See Him"* Epic, 1983

19. BRYAN ADAMS · *"Cuts Like a Knife"* A&M, 1983

20. KISS · *"Detroit Rock City"/"Beth"* Casablanca, 1976

21. CICCONE YOUTH · *"Into the Groovy"* New Alliance, 1986

22. DEAD BOYS · *"Sonic Reducer"/"Down in Flames"* Sire, 1977

23. GRAND FUNK RAILROAD · *"We're an American Band"* Capitol, 1973

24. CINDERELLA · *"Coming Home"* Mercury, 1989

25. **CYBOTRON** · *"Eden"* Fantasy 12-inch, 1986

26. **MICHAEL JACKSON** · *"Dirty Diana"* Epic, 1988

27. **PUBLIC ENEMY** · *"She Watch Channel Zero?!"* Def Jam, 1988

28. **BUZZCOCKS** · *"Harmony in My Head"/"Something's Gone Wrong Again"* United Artists UK import, 1979

29. **CHEETAH CHROME MOTHERFUCKERS** · *Furious Party* Belfagor Italian import 7-inch EP, 1986

30. **THE BABYS** · *"Midnight Rendezvous"* Chrysalis, 1980

31. **LITA FORD** · *"Kiss Me Deadly"* RCA, 1988

32. **BOMBERS** · *"Don't Stop the Music"* West End 12-inch, 1979

33. **SUGARLOAF** · *"Don't Call Us, We'll Call You"* Claridge, 1975

34. **T. REX** · *"Jeepster"/"Get It On (Bang a Gong)"* Cube UK import, c. 1985; rec. 1971

35. **SLAUGHTER** · *"Up All Night"* Chrysalis, 1990

36. **THE CELIBATE RIFLES** · *"Sometimes (I Wouldn't Live Here If You Payed Me)"* Hot Australian import, 1984

37. **FREE** · *"Wishing Well"* Island, 1973

38. **ALICE COOPER** · *"Only Women Bleed"* Atlantic, 1975

39. **RAM JAM** · *"Black Betty"* Epic, 1977

40. **MINOR THREAT** · *In My Eyes* Dischord 7-inch EP, 1981

41. **X** · *"White Girl"* Slash, 1981

42. **ALICE COOPER** · *"I Never Cry"* Warner Bros., 1976

43. **AGE OF CHANCE** · *"Bible of the Beats"* Riot Bible UK import, 1986

44. **THE SWEET** · *"Blockbuster"* Bell, 1973

45. **DEEP PURPLE** · *"Hush"* Tetragrammaton, 1968

46. **GANG OF FOUR** · *"Love Like Anthrax"* Fast Product UK import, 1978

47. **RATT** · *"Round and Round"* Atlantic, 1984

48. **DAN REED NETWORK** · *"Get to You (Spanish)"/"Get to You (Dub)"/"Ritual (Dido Slam)"* Mercury 12-inch, 1988

49. **WARRANT** · *"Cherry Pie"* Columbia, 1990

50. **SKID ROW** · *"I Remember You"* Atlantic, 1990

51. **FASTER PUSSYCAT** · *"House of Pain"* Elektra, 1990

52. **RASPBERRIES** · *"Go All the Way"* Capitol, 1972

53. **VOM** · *Live at Surf City* White Noise 7-inch EP, 1978

54. **THE STATUS QUO** · *"Pictures of Matchstick Men"* Cadet Concept, 1968

55. **BLUE ÖYSTER CULT** · *"Burnin' for You"* Columbia, 1981

56. **HONOR ROLE** · *"Twist"*/*"Lives of the Saints No. 135 (Naked Wife)"* Homestead, 1988

57. **CHEECH AND CHONG FEATURING ALICE BOWIE** · *"Earache My Eye"* Warner Bros., 1974

58. **NEIL YOUNG** · *"Rockin' in the Free World"* Reprise, 1989

59. **QUEEN** · *"Fat Bottomed Girls"*/*"Bicycle Race"* Elektra, 1978

60. **MADONNA** · *"Act of Contrition"* Sire, 1989

61. **JOE WALSH** · *"Rocky Mountain Way"* Dunhill, 1973

62. **WHITE LION** · *"When the Children Cry"* Atlantic, 1988

63. **MICK FARREN AND THE DEVIANTS** · *Screwed Up* Stiff UK import 7-inch EP, 1977

64. **HÜSKER DÜ** · *"Eight Miles High"* SST, 1984

65. **LOVERBOY** · *"Working for the Weekend"* Columbia, 1982

66. **VAN HALEN** · *"Why Can't This Be Love"* Warner Bros., 1986

67. **PARLIAMENT** · *"Red Hot Mama"* Invictus, 1970

68. **HEART** · *"Never"* Capitol, 1985

69. **WARREN ZEVON** · *"Boom Boom Mancini"* Virgin 12-inch, 1987

70. **AEROSMITH** · *"Janie's Got a Gun"* Geffen, 1989

71. **STEELY DAN** · *"Black Friday"* ABC, 1975

72. **WARRANT** · *"Heaven"* Columbia, 1989

73. **BAD COMPANY** · *"Movin' On"* Swan Song, 1975

74. **IRON BUTTERFLY** · *"In-A-Gadda-Da-Vida"* Atco, 1968

75. **THE DOORS** · *"Hello, I Love You"* Elektra, 1968

76. **SPINAL TAP** · *"Christmas with the Devil"* Enigma, 1984

77. **FANNY** · *"Charity Ball"* Reprise, 1971

78. **BLACKFOOT** · *"Train, Train"* Atco, 1979

79. **U2** · *"Bullet the Blue Sky"* Island, 1987

80. **ROKY ERICKSON** · *"Bermuda"* Virgin, 1977

81. **TRIO** · *"Bum Bum"* Mercury German import, 1982

82. **RICK DERRINGER** · *"Rock 'n Roll Hootchie-Coo"* Blue Sky, 1973

83. **BANG TANGO** · *"Someone Like You"* MCA/Mechanic, 1989

84. JESUS AND MARY CHAIN ·
"Upside Down" Creation UK import, 1985

85. STEVIE STILETTO AND THE SWITCHBLADES · *It's a Bogus Life*
Razor 7-inch EP, 1985

86. THE GUESS WHO · *"American Woman"* RCA, 1970

87. JANET JACKSON · *"Black Cat"*
A&M, 1990

88. CELTIC FROST · *"Return to the Eve (Party Mix)"* Combat/Noise 12-inch, 1986

89. SONIC'S RENDEZVOUS BAND · *"City Slang"* Orchide, 1978

90. LAST SACRIFICE ·
"Suspended"/"Acid Rain Dance" Valis, 1986

91. TESLA · *"Love Song"* Geffen, 1989

92. JANITORS · *"Good to Be the King"* In Tape UK import, 1986

93. VOX POP · *"Cab Driver"* Bad Trip, 1980

94. CRABBY APPLETON · *"Go Back"*
Elektra, 1970

95. LIGHTNIN' ROD AND JIMI HENDRIX · *"Doriella Du Fontaine"* Celluloid 12-inch, 1984; rec. c. 1969

96. JUDAS PRIEST · *"Living After Midnight"* Columbia, 1980

97. JO JO GUNNE · *"Run Run Run"*
Asylum, 1972

98. THE OBSESSED · *"Sodden Jackal"/"Iron & Stone"/"Indestroy"* Invictus, 1983

99. WENDY O. AND LEMMY ·
"Stand by Your Man" Bronze UK import, 1982

100. LONE RAGER · *"Metal Rap"*
Megaforce 12-inch, 1984

25 REASONS DISCO-METAL FUSION ~~IS~~ WAS INEVITABLE IN THE '90s

. . . .

1. **A**xl Rose, a real good dancer, has been known to hang out with George Michael.

2. **G**uns N' Roses and White Lion, who've both ended albums with polyrhythmic whatchamacallits ("Rocket Queen" and "Cry For Freedom") have members who allegedly used to play in disco bands. Not that they'll admit it in public.

3. **R**ock City Angels end *Young Man's Blues* with a 12-inch dance remix of "Beyond Babylon."

4. **J**unkyard (whose Chris Gates once covered Kool and the Gang's "Hollywood Swinging" with the Big Boys) ends *Junkyard* with "Hands Off," stealing the same Lynyrd Skynyrd licks that Latin hip-hop thrush Sa-Fire steals in "Thinking of You."

5. **A**lbum-ending cuts predict the future. Always have, always will.

6. **D**isco icon Stacey Q, who occasionally entertains indie metalcore singers on her tour bus, has been known to wear Motörhead and Sex Pistols shirts on stage.

7. **G**uns N' Roses and the Cult have spawned serveral "promising" new "boogie" bands (Junkyard, Rock City Angels, Johnny Crash, Circus of Power, Royal Court of China, Salty Dog, Dangerous Toys, Company of Wolves, D.A.D., Black Crowes, Law and Order). Significant boogie landmarks of the seventies include "Get Up And Boogie," "Boogie Oogie Oogie," "I'm Your Boogie Man," "Jungle Boogie" (already remade by 24-7 Spyz!), "Boogie Fever," "Boogie Shoes," "Chains" by Bionic Boogie, and, of course, "Boogie Flap" by Disco Tex and His Sex-O-Lettes.

8. **B**oogie Man Harry Casey, the mad scientist behind K.C. and the Sunshine Band, was reincarnated in 1989 as Dino, incorporating Free-like riffs in a hit single that says "that's the way it has to be 'cause that's the way I like it" instead of "that's the way uh huh uh huh I like it uh huh uh huh."

9. **V**illage People, "Sleazy" (1979): "I like my music loud and mean/I'll rock until I bust my jeans/'Cause I'm sleazy."

10. **T**he congas and Burundi drums on the 1989 Virgin Records videotape *Glam Rock* link glam to disco, as do the clothes.

11. **T**he video of the Beastie Boys' "Hey Ladies" features polyester evening wear, a "Ballroom Blitz" sample, and a Foghat eight-track, revealing the revisionist-history glam/metal/disco connection only months after Def Leppard canonized the Sweet, et al., in the video for "Rocket," a song that somebody remixed for clubs with reams of acid-house-style echo.

12. **R**ap-absorbing metal acts such as Def Lep, Lita Ford, Warrant, Anthrax, Metal Church, Faith No More (who do a song called "Arabian Disco" and who aren't averse to hosting vogueing contests during their live sets), and Faster Pussycat will accidentally absorb the disco recently reabsorbed by rap acts such as L'Trimm, Rob Base, and the Jungle Brothers.

13. **I**n 1978, Kiss went Top 15 with the mirror-ballish "I Was Made for Lovin' You," as did Ace Frehley with his cover of Hello's "New York Groove," which sounds curiously like Bohannon's "Disco Stomp." Rick James's most metal moment is called "Love Gun," same as Kiss's seventh album.

14. "**C**hildren of the Grave" by Black Sabbath has exactly the same rhythm as "Call Me" by Blondie. (So do "Dum Dum" by the Butthole Surfers and "Let the

Day Begin" by the Call, not to mention Karen Kamon's "Manhunt"—you know, from the *Flashdance* soundtrack.)

15. Celtic Frost, who use plenty of "def" beats on *Into the Pandemonium* and cover two seventies glam-rock tunes on *Vanity/Nemesis,* worship Prince even to the extent of covering "Erotic City" live and trying to dress like him on the back of *Cold Lake.* And Sylvester, the glam-disco diva who probably inspired Prince's "Baby I'm a Star" and whose 1973 cocksuck-rock hors d'oeuvre "Down on Your Knees" may be twenty years ahead of its time, was a Poison fan (said so on his deathbed). And Celtic Frost's Tom Warrior wants to do a solo LP someday that sounds like Poison's debut album!

16. Here's how Miami mambo-rockers Bandera look: A wild scraggly-haired soul sister who dresses in fruit stripes or hides her nude naughty bits behind palm fronds, a savagely nonsmiling stiletto-featured barrio guitarist in studded leather, and an aging *salsero* pianist in freshly pressed zoot suit resembling Bun E. Carlos welcoming you aboard Fantasy Island. Peacock rock, sort of.

17. Vernon Reid, whose Living Colour once toured with Anthrax, has predicted a thrash/house-music merger. As long as somebody other than Living Colour tries it, it'll be great.

18. The Chambers Brothers invented acid-house with their feedback-drenched 1967 number-11 hit "Time Has Come Today," and Chicago house architect Marshall Jefferson says he's been strongly influenced by Sabbath and Zep.

19. Bubblesalsa producers, like power-ballad producers, make the sound full-bodied and sumptuous, make it *shout.*

20. In "For Amusement Only," on his amazing 1979 album *The Syncophonic Orchestra Featuring Alirol and Jacquet,* Alec Costandinos fuses nineteenth-century-classical Eurodisco with early-Lucifer's-Friend-type prog-grunge. And he ain't dainty about it.

21. Disco-metal already? See: Led Zep's "Fool in the Rain," Teena Marie's *Emerald City* and "Lovergirl," Billy Squier's "The Stroke," Stacey Q's "Hard Machine" and "Insecurity," Madonna's "Burning Up," Kix's "Sex," Stacy Lattisaw's "I'm Down for You," Trust's "Palace," Tantra's "Top Shot," Cerrone's "Rocket in the Pocket," Cheap Trick's "You're All Talk," Bombers' "Don't Stop the Music," Cybotron's "Eden," Jimmy Castor Bunch's *Phase Two* and "The Return of Leroy," Precious Metal's "Mr. Big Stuff," Apollo Smile's "Thunder Box," Andrew Ridgeley's "Mexico," Dan Reed Network's "Ritual (Dido Slam)," the Beastie Boys' "A Year and a Day," Hot Chocolate's "Disco Queen" and "Heaven Is in the Back Seat of My Cadillac," David Bowie's "Stay," Les Rita Mitsouko's "Someone to Love," Pat Benatar's "Invincible," ZZ Top's "Legs," and a couple songs each on *Sheila and B. Devotion* and Foxy's *Party Boys.*

22. Or for that matter, why not the first few Santana albums, "Sympathy for the Devil," Deep Purple's "Hush," Spencer Davis Group's "I'm a Man," and maybe even "Jump into the Fire" by Nilsson? (Afro-Carib counterrhythms are important.)

23. Van Halen's "Dance the Night Away," obviously, and "Dancing in the Streets." "Push Comes to Shove" too. And their "Hot for Teacher" video (the glitzy dance-routine part.)

24. At the release party for their 1990 album *Pornograffitti,* a bash attended by members of Skid Row, Poison, White Lion, Warrant, the Jet Boys, Whitesnake, Blue Murder, Great White, the Bullet Boys, Sacred Reich, XYZ, Silent Rage, and Bang Tango, Extreme covered Wild Cherry's "Play That Funky Music White Boy," which topped the charts for three weeks in 1976.

25. Has anybody come up with any better ideas?

THE NIPPLE-RINGS GO ON FOREVER
BUT THE RIFFS REMAIN THE SAME:
INTRODUCTION TO THE '90s UPDATE

The main thing you can say about "heavy metal" in the '90s (the first eight years anyway—I'm writing this toward the end of 1997) is that it was everywhere and nowhere; that is, everybody wanted to *sound* metal (or at least have guitars loud enough), but almost nobody wanted to admit it. The decade didn't kick off that way, exactly—in the beginning, Firehouse, Mr. Big, Extreme, and the Scorpions were still hitting with power ballads. But the bottom had already started to fall out way back between Poison's "Fallen Angel" and "Every Rose Has Its Thorn" videos in late 1988, when they traded in their mascara, magenta guitars, and bubblegum hooks for body hair, Harley shirts, and health-food blues. And in a lot of ways, the albums Warrant, Skid Row, and Faster Pussycat released in 1989 were haircut metal's final commercial gasp—before long, thrash and grunge had scared all three bands into turning nasty and dissonant, overcompensating for their unjustified early girly-rock reputation by crossing over into muscleman brutality.

By the summer of 1991 (before Nirvana came along, word-historical types should note), MTV-type shagmetal bands were experiencing a gigantic crisis of confidence. Platinum poodlehairs like Poison and Cinderella (whose new concept involved hippie-era white blues and *Exile on Main Street* muffle-mouthing) started making blatant bids for the respect of the non-MTV cognoscenti—a dubious distinction for a genre that thrives on upsetting parents and rock critics, rather than begging their approval. Squeeze-played between B-boys on the left and born-again art-rockers like King's X on the right, longtime hair-hacks suddenly started worrying about "integrity," of all things, which gave them a big, fat inferiority complex. What would they do to catch up? Where would *you* turn?

You could unplug your guitars (Tesla), adopt cellos and Elvis Costello affectations (Enuff Z'Nuff), collage art-noise into trumped-up dark shadows (Faster Pussycat), pop your bass (White Trash), combine chunky electrofunk with adult-contemporary ballads (Bon Jovi, Def Leppard), practice your emotional dynamics (Great White), cover Tom Waits (Bulletboys), dig out Dad's power tools and Cat Stevens singles (Mr. Big), bury your head in purist '70s quicksand (Junkyard), counter your dirty-old-man mind with sitar instrumentals and airwave static (Blackeyed Susan), lose your angelically earnest wedding songs in paradiddle puddles (White Lion), underproduce your bullheaded redneck slop until your liver ruptures (Dangerous Toys, Jackyl). Or you could even pretend that four-minute Max Factor sleaze might still matter in this land, which is what L.A.'s Tuff did on their 1991 debut *What*

Comes Around Goes Around—they knew their utopia was being pulled out from under them, but at least they were stubborn enough to be sarcastic about it: "Hippies turned to punkers and rockers turned to glam, everyone's a poseur now unless they like to slam." Kind of sounded like an appeal to liberty and justice for all.

Likewise, up-all-night pop-metal insomniacs Slaughter did okay on 1992's *The Wild Life* by continuing to pump up weekend-celebration shoutalongs with pomp-gone-glam melodrama and antsy falsetto choruses that helped suburban girls break free of their seventh-grade grind: "You'll feel like an animal that's been uncaged." (A time-proven rock 'n' roll notion—as soon as three o'clock rolls around, you finally lay your burdens down. School's out for summer.) But more often, just like how in the late '60s the rise of FM radio had conned perfectly good AM garage bands into turning "progressive," '90s Nerf-metal bands had to adjust to the fact that all the little girls loved Eddie Vedder more than them. Local H, a refreshingly haircut-sounding, artificial-grunge duo, even wrote a song about the quandary in 1996: "If I was Eddie Vedder, would you like me any better?"

By 1995, hairfarm hasbeens Warrant, Quiet Riot, Kix, and Slaughter were releasing albums on tiny indie record labels you never heard of, which made them Obscure Indie Artists now, so it was every rock critic's responsibility to pay attention to them instead of Commercialized Major Label Pabulum like P. J. Harvey, but most critics shirked their duties. Not such a bad idea, to tell the truth: the old pop-metal bands almost all wound up with more tuneful singing than guitars, and their ballads devolved into Collective Soul/Candlebox-type, grunge-Jovi things, not *real* heartbreaks like Warrant's old "I Saw Red."

Meanwhile, older geezers from the distant '70s and '80s just kept making more mediocre albums. Motörhead started sounding a bit too much like sped-up Iron Maiden and not enough like sped-up Chuck Berry. Aerosmith made unctuously hammy horn-goo and impossible-to-tell-apart slow jams where nothing sounded at stake, then they signed zillion-dollar contracts and stuck their boring songs into passionate videos about purse-snatching car-crashing window-smashing middle-fingered bungee-jumping problem children. Vince Neil made solo albums where he never sang about racing Indy Lights dragsters or ending anybody's life in alcohol-fueled traffic accidents, and then rejoined dumb studs Mötley Crüe, who'd slowly progressed toward incorporating funk rhythm and pop harmonies, an improvement over shouting at the devil, but what wouldn't have been?

And of course there was still Metallica, who, early in the decade, abandoned the quasi-Wagner drama that had initially made their music semi-interesting, and then actually got better when they abandoned metal pureness for boogiefied '70s hard rock and short haircuts on their 1996 album *Load*. At least they weren't so bloated anymore, and their junk-bonder I-told-you-so "King Nothing" was as close as they'll ever come to "Like A Rolling Stone." Basically, they were tolerable when the guitars were playing or when Jim Hetfield tried to sing, but I couldn't stand when he'd just sit around growling his head off.

The smartest aging veterans, I guess, just threw food at the wall, and if it stuck, fine. And if it didn't stick, well, that was fine, too. Voices-for-the-ages Robert Plant and John Lydon made ambitiously ignorable albums that tried to sound, by turns, Teutonic, Middle Eastern, jangling, funky, and loud. David Lee Roth did more white-Negro shoot-your-mouth-off shoot-'em-ups about the local mini-mall; Queen demonstrated that, unlike most fortyish rock relics, they were still too frivolously insincere to settle for the "well-earned wisdom of middle age." Then their singer died tragically of a sexually transmitted disease.

Supposedly Uriah Heep even released a great comeback record called *Sea of Light* in 1995, but I never heard it. I did see Rush in concert in 1996, though, and it occurred to me that their sound had basically started at Led Zeppelin, then got rid of all of Zep's sex and blues, so only boys would like it. And it also occurred to me that the whole concept of a celibate Zep was really an outlandish idea. But anyway, the best thing I heard at the show was two guys coming up the aisle during intermission. Guy #1: "They started out to play '2112' and I thought they were gonna play the whole thing but then they *didn't*." Guy #2: "Yeah—It was like a *wet dream* or something." I'm not sure if I heard him quite right. Maybe he meant he woke up before he reached the good part, like I always do.

Which isn't to say I haven't slept through a lot lately. I admit it: more than any decade before, the '90s produced lots of heavy metal *I never heard*. Or wanted to, for that matter—keeping up with the whole genre would've been painful, pointless, and probably impossible, so naturally I gravitated toward those loud-guitar styles that struck me as most rewarding. I'm sure I'll be discovering decent '90s albums I never knew about until I die. But for the most part, considering black metal, death metal, thrash metal, sheet metal, shit metal, industrial metal, viking metal, grindcore, rapplecore, and whatnot, there sure do seem to be lotsa creeps out there who feel they can impress me merely by how unmusical they can make themselves sound. It's hard to imagine a more deluded reason for being.

If you're inclined to disagree, or if you're still hung up on metal's so-called "real" stuff and you want a comprehensive overview of it (and thankfully of lots of stuff that isn't so "real" as well), I adamantly recommend you obtain a copy of Martin Popoff's indispensable *The Collector's Guide to Heavy Metal* (available from Box 62034, Burlington, Ontario, L7R 4K2, Canada), which quite wittily reviews an unwieldy 3700 albums—including everything Judas Priest, Iron Maiden, and Paradise Lost ever recorded. His favorite new '90s bands, which I have no opinion of whatsoever, are Tea Party, Spiritual Beggars, Doctor Butcher, Meshuggah, Rocket from the Crypt, Sentenced, Clutch, Dearly Beheaded, and Mourning Sign; maybe they're all wonderful. I'm interested in hearing Anacrusis, the Wildhearts, Mekong Delta, and My Dying Bride someday, too. You never know.

What I *do* know is that—from Florida's keys to the frozen tundras of Scandinavia—unlistenable Satan-worshipping metal jokers have never stopped multiplying like cockroaches. Chances are, they'll still be around long after the rest of the human species is extinct. The most popular such coteries, Sepultura from Brazil and Pantera from Texas (or possibly Florida, who cares—someplace in the South), also rank (with Iron Maiden!) as two of the lousiest excuses for popular music I've ever been exposed to, so I can only imagine what *unpopular* ones sound like. It was hard for me to figure out what purpose all these bands could serve in the '90s. After fifteen years of thrash and grunge fusing punk and metal til we all threw up on each other, there wasn't a void to fill like there used to be. Noise attacks had become merely conventional. And music calling itself metal had long lost its humongously thudding and churning Led Zeppelin sense of rhythm, so for the most part these kinda bands weren't exactly born to rock. If they tried hard enough (which the northern European bands the Gathering and Tiamat actually did!), they might have made it as Muzak.

The British sub-subgenre calling itself "grindcore" had real possibilities, I thought at first, seeing how Napalm Death, Cannibal Corpse, and the like seemed composed of pre-med students addicted to the elongated terminology of emergency surgery and to a sound vaguely reminiscent of old screechpunks Die Kreuzen or Void doing brain abortions with electric coat hangers. There was even a band called Lawnmower Death who briefly turned grindcore inside out by making its speedfudge-gnarled violence *cute,* with chicken clucks, kazoo farts, Kim Wilde covers, and titles like "Sharp Fucka Blades of Hades/March of the Mods" and one called "Satan's Trampoline" that suddenly transforms into "Don't You Want Me" by the Human League. But otherwise the Spinal-Tapness I hoped for was nowhere to be detected; now that the grunge-style tumult was finally being taken seriously by people (rock critics, for intance) with intellectual delusions, stupidity usually just wound up seeming stupid after all. In other words, one big thing metal lost in the '90s was an ability to be *made fun of*—I used to try to be amused, but now I'm disgusted.

It's hard to believe that anybody found most of this stuff engaging, that it surprised them or made them laugh. By 1991 young lions like Corrosion of Conformity and Prong (and Die Kreuzen too) were acting like they wanted to be *jazz* combos, plying us with amorphous outpourings of whatever came into their hearts, all Texture and Sound and voices-that-work-as-instruments, daringly creative gutwrench heaving Molotov cocktails at song structure whilst venting pint upon pint of Very

Important Pain before the economy collapses or a runaway asteroid collides with the U.N. building or mom comes home and shoos them off to bed. Sonic Youth guitar whizzbanger Thurston Moore (who'd once named "Expressway to Yr Skull" after a lame Buddy Miles album) went even further, consorting with real live jazz cats, and plotting his own obsolescence as if it wasn't already a foregone conclusion. Sliming out fusion-rooted sludge with tummyache vocals, clogging up your kitchen with dirges, letting their twang sprout from shifting peatbogs of drum-muck, these beatniks concentrated coldheartedly on manly musicianship and composition to the detriment of anything compelling—like humanity, or hooks, or hair.

Everybody wanted to be a performance artist, everybody had a concept: Celebrity Skin made opera-glam with arch-rock changes that sounded bad, but wore lizard costumes and Kabuki outfits so you knew the badness was intentional; Primus immersed their white trash yarns in oinking basswank and nasal-congested auctioneer barking and "zany sound effects" (but now and then managed decent old-timey square-dance wobbles and loony cartoony videos despite themselves); Living Coloür had supposedly "intriguing" (in a "jazz" way) time changes, but reduced soul classics to guilt-rock turds; thrash clowns Green Jello scored on MTV with a remake of "Three Little Pigs"; nuke-rockers Celtic Frost covered old Roxy Music and David Bowie songs; Faith No More and Fishbone wore pajamas like Roxy Music had never sung about in "Pyjarama" (but Johnnie Fingers did used to wear in the Boomtown Rats); bland virtuosos Galactic Cowboys stuck unserious titles on thick-as-a-brick, twelve-minute pomp compositions; I Napoleon made Canadian-lumberjack sissy-boom-bah, suggesting too much time spent without earmuffs in the land of ice and snow.

The more popular that the more pretentious streams of post-punk metal becaame with the youth of America, the harder they were to tolerate. Helmet dressed like white working-class rap fans and made Big Black guitar clamor, but were proof that whatever personality quirk inspired people to be exciting singers in the '90s conflicted irrevocably with whatever personality quirk inspired people to be exciting guitar players, because it was real hard to find bands with both. Molasses-in-January torture-rockers Tool set drill-sergeant hollers and Gumby-in-Hell claymation videos to a yawning-chasm lack of structure: instead of concrete songs beginning and ending, volume knobs simply opened and closed, engulfing you like a sperm whale's mouth. And swaggering operatic-gutbust lunkhead Danzig was an even bigger chore to hear, howling about werewolves and how tormented he thought his soul was—though his MTV smash "Mother" was at least catchy enough to catch me off guard with its helpful advice about how my mom shouldn't let her babies grow up to be cowboys who hang around dangerous people like Marilyn Manson.

Marilyn Manson combined industrial-dance deathbed whispering with death-metal barfs and horror movie bullshit with Jesus bullshit, so like Black Sabbath in 1970 people naturally assumed they hosted decapitation rituals in their catacombs. Their drums could pound glammily on occasion, but their lyrics tended toward your usual dorky decadence slogans: "Abortions in my eye," "I am the god of fuck," "Time for cake and sodomy," "I wasn't born with enough middle fingers." So of course one day in 1996 my then-eleven-year-old son Linus (a Green Day/Presidents of the United States fan) came home from school and said he'd now decided Marilyn Manson and rap-thrashers Korn and Rage Against the Machine are cool, too, which I suppose was inevitable, but it still convinced me that peer pressure really sucks. Some Australian group who Linus claimed sounded like No Doubt played in his school auditorium that year, but I guess one reason his peers dig Korn and Manson is 'cause they *don't* sound like the kinda bands who'd play a school auditorium.

I've never had the energy or patience to check out Korn myself, so I let my buddy Sara Sherr do it instead. First she taste-tested one of their CDs: "The only thing I remotely liked about it is that the singer would sing like the Tasmanian Devil and sometimes the guitarist for about three seconds would sound like some Steve Albini tight-ass rock band, but then they would sound like Primus and then Rage Against the Machine without the politics—only cuss words. Twelve-year-old boys would like it." Next she saw them live: "Lead singer in glittery sweat suit, dreads, rest of band in various states of bag-wear. When they were going full-bore, Rage style, I got caught up in the moment of the thing, I admit. The crowd below was a sea of hormone-overflowing bodies. Security guards' flashlights were like lighthouses. It was weird and striking and scary. Korn had four moves, basically: loud, fast, hard like Rage/Primus with Tasmanian singing, then quieter, grungier, slower, with Alice in Chains singing, primordial Pink Floyd underwater slime, and then three-second searing Albini bursts. No hooks to be found. No 'songs.' There were anthems, though. There's a song called 'Faget,' which is their version of Rage's 'fuck you I won't do what you tell me to.' It's just something incendiary and offensive and adolescent repeated over and over again. Well, guess what the chorus is: 'Faget, all my life what am I.' But the ironic thing (Alanis would be proud) is that it's supposed to be about the singer's tormented high school years. And I wondered if the audience felt like the tormented or the tormentor when they were shouting that—or maybe they just wanted to say a bad word."

Droopy-boxer-shorted, middle-American paleface teenagers didn't care how clumsy their racial crossover was, as long as it was earsplitting and in their face. The Korn/Rage/311 genre was a culmination of post-Beastie, body-fluid-swapping that had been going on full-bore between metal and hard rap since the beginning of the decade. In 1991 bands like Mordred and Riot were already chopping up their guitar chaos with the abrupt editing technology they'd picked up from '80s dance music;

Mordred even had a hip-hop-style turntable jockey who mixed in Funkadelic/Thin Lizzy/James Brown snippets, police sirens, and stereo demonstration records whilst doubling on proggy keyboards.

"By 1991," I wrote in *Stairway to Hell*'s first edition (in "Afterthoughts," the only section I've deleted in the edition in your hands), "such Eurogoth gangs as KMFDM, Bloodstar, Pankow, Treponem Pal, and Young Gods had begun to mix death disco into post-hardcore metal, salvaging a necessarily impersonal sound via black-hole echo architecture and Arnold Schwarzenegger imitations, sometimes using samplers instead of guitars." I went on to predict that "before the nineties are half over" this subgenre would go mainstream. "A total dronathon of nuclear Sabbath sludge, huskified gutter-guttural accents, and beatboxes riveting like staple guns set on automatic—horrible music for a gullible world, how can it go wrong?" Well basically, how it went wrong is that the bands who finally made the sound famous (Ministry, White Zombie, Nine Inch Nails, Marilyn Manson, Gravity Kills) were horrible in more ways than I'd ever envisioned them being.

Frankly, most music that got classified under the "industrial" rubric seemed useful for one thing, if that: on cold days, if you were feeling under the weather, you could let its cold roar surround you like a sleeping bag. It helped to be brain-dead on antihistamines with no desire to be challenged or otherwise made to think (because then you'd just realize how *dumb* it was); personality (i.e., any concrete evidence of actual *Homo Sapiens*) would just get in the way of the lull. Too rigid for dancing, too emaciated for catharsis, too metronomically restrained for mere interesting background sound, industrial in the '80s had struck me as useless in a very piddly way—the province of elevator musicians (Front 242) and vivisection candidates (Skinny Puppy) who pretended to conjure a "grim mood," primarily by draining all the life and surprise from synthesized European disco.

Nineties industrial metal bands were at least wackier and more raucous. Treponem Pal gave French-accented absurdist advice to "bruzzers and seesters" and raunchily remade "Radioactivity" by Kraftwerk and "Funkytown" by Lipps Inc. Pankow grunted and beeped and honked phlegmy profanities about alcohol, scatology, and fascist dictators in inebriated Italian unison. Although not nearly as smile-inducing, at least later hypes like Marilyn Manson and Psychotica do an engaging kind of fast, high, hoarse, wicked-witch rapping now and then. (Manson's catchiest track is the new wavey cyborg-pop concoction "Wormboy," by the way; Psychotica's is "Starfucker Love.") Lately, Manson and Trent Reznor have even been drooling their share of cabaret-serenade panty-soaked ballads full of hushy come-ons like "You are the one I want and what I want is so unreal."

Said music isn't nearly loose enough to be the disco-metal fusion I'd proclaimed inevitable in *Stairway to Hell*'s first edition. But in 1997, Prodigy, who catapulted from England's rave scene to the top of the American charts, actually did justice to disco-metal. 1997 also saw metal acts collaborating (rather ineptly) with techno acts on the soundtrack to *Spawn*, not to mention a rave-punk scam calling itself "digital hardcore" emerging from Germany. Ninety-five percent of it was just generic slampit horsedookie with technoid beatboxes stuck underneath, making the music slightly angular, albeit still useless from a rhythm perspective—like a less imaginative Big Black without the songs, or like the fast moments on one of those early '90s Ministry CDs I'd rid myself of a few years earlier. No *Sprockets*-type introductions, not even any sleazy German accents! I mean, the nerve . . .

I can't deny that "Deutschland Must Die" from digital hardcore frontrunners Atari Teenage Riot was a hilarious *song title*, though. And they also had one excellent single, "Sick To Death," where the girl's voice reminded me more of Poly Styrene (of the great late '70s British sax-punkers X-Ray Spex) than any riot grrrl ever had. Riot grrrls, in case you're lucky enough to have forgotten, were femme-led hardcore bands like Bikini Kill and Bratmobile who lived in the northwest corridor, Magic-Markered SLUT on their tummies, and yelled out editorial doggerel about YOU! DO! HAVE! RIGHTS! (and occasional trailer-trash truths about oral sex traded for rollercoaster rides on the carnival midway when grownups' backs are turned) over stock school-of-Sabbath riffage. For the most part they sounded uncannily similar to Old Skull, who were three nine-year-old boys from Wisconsin acting their age by yowling about shooting pizza delivery men in the head.

"Hardcore" had meant less than it wanted to in the early '80s, and even less ten years later. It even had its own old boys' network—graybeards like Dag Nasty and Bad Religion who'd never stopped hibernating in sweaty clubs with their high school buddies. No matter how little money they made, how unruly their slampits got, or how much their music was "just a hobby," their guitar-pop purism and pantywaist platitudinizing made them as predictable as pros—and maybe as skilled. Bad Religion's small 1995 hit "21st Century Digital Boy" was a good *mainstream* rock record, closer to Styx than to Black Flag. Still, by the early '90s, how anybody would've cared much about a *punk* rock record was a good question to ask your clergyman, even if there *were* still a couple of bands out in the sticks (mostly Ohio: Sister Ray, Thomas Jefferson Slave Apartments, the hardcore-nitwits-disguised-as garage-rockers New Bomb Turks) trying to turn fucking up, being fucked over, and saying "fuck you" into a celebration. The first real punk bands to finally wind up on MTV were nothing to get excited about—Social Distortion's organic rectangle-rock could've afforded more additives, and although L7 griped about always being billed as an "all-woman guitar band," for quite a while they had trouble coming up with anything more distinctive than their gender for anybody to write about. (Eventually, they started including one track per album with either glittery Burundi drums or vocals and guitars partaking in that funny old new wave trick of sounding like robots—which was considerate of them.)

Early in the decade, people with a social and financial stake in such things claimed bands like North Carolina's Superchunk as evidence of a resurgent indie-label American rock scene, even despite said bands' damnably familiar sonic attributes: flat mumbling that aimed to show how desperate it was by shooting upward into a whine as verses ended, above thick guitar scuzz and rhythm sections that could most charitably be described as well-mannered. The sound could be rather anthemic, as anybody who had ever bought a Squirrel Bait, Soul Asylum, Dinosaur Jr., or for that matter Dag Nasty or Bad Religion record already knew well. An earnestly swooping kind of worm's-eye-view-of-woe loser-next-door metalpop, Hüsker Dü had more or less originated the style on *Metal Circus* in 1983, so by Superchunk's (and then Nirvana's) 1990–91 heyday there was not much remotely "new" about it; art-metal pioneer Frank Kogan once descibed Nirvana as "a remarkable synthesis of Hüsker Dü type music with Bob Mould type vocals." (Bob being Hüsker Dü's singer, get it?) Funny thing is, when Nerf-grungers like Better Than Ezra and Dog's Eye View scored with the sound in 1996, old Superchunk and Nirvana fans cried "how unoriginal!" just like I had when Superchunk and Nirvana first came out.

And to this day you *still* get new band after new band who sound like third-rate Hüsker Dü (or Hü-ever). A&M Records has been tossing them at dartboards nonstop ever since kicking themselves silly after dropping future Claire Danes cronies Soul Asylum from the label an album too early (after 1990's *And the Horse They Rode in On*): Dishwalla, Jackopierce, Hollowbodies (whose publicity bio I wrote—am I a whore or what?), Lustre (theorized by Robert Christgau to consist mainly of ambitious Collective Soul and Better Than Ezra roadies!), Figdish, Orbit, the Gin Blossoms (if they count). Names on a page.

I had first used the word "grunge" to describe the Ramones' *Too Tough to Die* in *The Village Voice* in 1984; in 1987, reviewing Skin Yard, I wrote the following in *Creem Metal:* "Sometime in the not-so-distant future, you're gonna switch on MTV and hear all this hype about how the not-so-distant future of hard rock lies in the Northwest." Boy, what a prophet! As was Tom Carson in the *Voice* in 1988, when he foresaw the indie sludge of Seattle and Manhattan eventually "settling down to being, if not rock and roll as anybody knew it, then some bizarre sort of terminal postrock blues." Within half a decade, alumni of Pussy Galore and Mudhoney were literally starting up blues bands, fleeing the present by turning their music's always-implicit nostalgia into its main gimmick. These weren't arty guys after all; they were *roots* rockers, making noises already done livelier eons ago by poor people in '30s Mississippi or awful boogie-plod hacks in '70s hockey arenas. At least those oldtimers talked in full sentences and didn't constantly insist on being "frantic" and "deranged," honking boring free-jazz saxophones everywhere.

Meanwhile, Paul Bunyanesque boondock-bred longhairs (Screaming Trees, Tad, Pearl Jam, Soundgarden) kept raining from towns in the *Twin Peaks* neck of the woods determined to reclaim late-'60s acid rock, washing away the rain with their black-hole suns and opting for whatever wanderlust can be had from manly downtrodden Sasquatch howls and big roaring wah-wah excavating the wild frontier. For most of them, naturally, resuscitating Vietnam-era rock was their most profound idea, and they used it up quick.

Both the groovy grunge ghoulies of greater Seattle and more explicit early '70s reconstructionists of the Monster Magnet/Masters of Reality/Raging Slab stripe helped answer a prescient question polka fan John Wojtowicz had raised in 1986 in the fanzine *Why Music Sucks* (inspired by the Golden Palominos' '70s arena-rock revivalism): "What do you think the music of the early '90s will be like when *everyone* is trying to sound like that ALL OVER AGAIN?" Basically, Seattle seemed to subscribe to the fallacy that if you fill up the whole room with bullshit, it's not bullshit anymore. Pearl Jam didn't really play hard rock at all hardly (more like a fattened version of folkish college-radio jangle— "loud mush," women's tennis fan Chris Cook dubbed it), but they had a real even flow and now and then (in "Jeremy," say) managed to hit on epic blowhard emotion from the rise and fall of their guitars. Wittgenstein fan Frank Kogan even swore that Eddie Vedder bellows like David Clayton-Thomas used to in Blood, Sweat & Tears. Me, I still have trouble telling Pearl Jam, Temple of the Dog, and Alice in Chains (who have goatees, I think) apart.

Eventually bands from everywhere else on earth stole Seattle's sound. After one of my brother-in-law's Thursday-night poker games in 1994, the twenty-somethings whose house it was played Pearl Jam's first album repeatedly until everybody got tired of it, so they put on the debut album by San Diego's Stone Temple Pilots instead and everybody was happy again—funny, seeing how (at the time) both ensembles sounded exactly the same. Said similarity is something rock critics held against the Pilots, since it meant they weren't "original," which once again made no sense because I'd never noticed Pearl Jam (or anybody else from Seattle) being huge musical innovators in the first place. Fact is, most every caroming hard rock hit and Pearl-Jam-brand mood saga STP put on MTV was more or less likable—even the *Unplugged* ones, where they borrowed the old man from Arrested Development's rocking chair. Before long they were even taking my advice and trading in their piety for hooks, clothes, and dance steps. By their surprisingly glammy "Big Bang Baby" in 1996, to quote male music critic Jane Dark in his fanzine *Sugar High*, needle-crazy Scott

Weiland and crew were making a good "argument for heroin: never has a band so benefited from not being able to remember what it sounded like twenty minutes ago."

Not all bandwagon grunge felt so carbonated, of course. Despite a certain statuesqueness to their guitar sound, British pretenders Bush *beat around* the bush too much and could be windbaggy as all hell—their singer had nice cheekbones, but always sounded like he was trying too hard to take a dump. Like their fellow sensitivity addicts Live (dorks from York, Pennsylvania, led by awk-ward-dancing baldhead Right Said Ed Kowalczyk), Silverchair (cute Australian teens enamored of dreary undertows of rainy-afternoon darkness), and Seven Mary Three (sluggish clods from Orlando who inherited Foghat's facial hair), Bush never made me want to jump around. '70s-church-base-ment-folk-mass seminarians Collective Soul from Georgia were only marginally better, breaking from their sacred weekend-youth-retreat, this-little-light-of-mine-I'm-gonna-let-it-shine campfire harmonies for maybe one propulsive-enough claustrophobia-twister per album.

In 1996 somebody insisted in the rock critic forum of America On-Line's Velvet Rope music industry billboard that "grunge departed from the standard reliance on I, IV, and V," news for sure to chord-illiterate me, and thus suggesting that all I'd needed to do to appreciate all those tedious plodding Seattle CDs from the past few years was to dig out my pocket calculator—about time somebody explained this stuff! But anyway, just to contradict myself, the truth is, I *like* grunge nowa-days, now that it's finally learned to speed up (how come nobody ever bothered to point out that almost all of Nirvana's hits were *ballads*???) and bounce around a bit and use comprehensible words and . . . well, just plain SELL OUT, maybe. I was never a huge Nirvana fan, but now I'm in love with bands who *sound* like Nirvana. Local H, Ruth Ruth, Everclear, Sponge (Detroit drag-queens who for a single or two came off like a grunge Psychedelic Furs), Stone Temple Pilots (do Weezer count?), plus I forget their name but I vaguely recall some other Nirvana-sounding big-bang babies doing a great song about "come on over and shoot the shit, I love you so much you make me sick." 1996 was easily the best year for grunge ever! I really believe that, and if you love rock 'n' roll (or maybe if you hate "innovative guitar chords," hell if I know) you believe it, too. Likewise, I'm convinced that alternative-rock's increased ability to score pop hits in the last couple years has *improved* guitar rock—indie-level-on-up—not made it worse. So the elusive alternative to alternative is . . . alternative! Whaddaya know!

And now that "alternative" and "big hair" people finally tended to be the same, punk could start catching up with the rest of the world, too! The punk audience I cared about in the mid-'90s wasn't the little one going to smelly clubs to argue about whether bands sell out when they make hit vid-eos; it was the big one that goes to middle school, who never heard of punk before, but who bought Green Day and Offspring CDs because, on MTV, fast songs about kids having fights and going nuts sound like real life. Linus (my oldest offspring; he was eleven in 1996, remember) even asked me if the Offspring were "early alternative." The Offspring, D Generation, Rancid, Green Day ("lower-lower-middle-class white-boy rock," Metal Mike Saunders of the Angry Samoans called them, like 1970 Grand Funk), and Veruca Salt (whose alleged American thighs didn't supply enough AC/DC to their rhythm or riffs, but who were okay once you decoded "Seether" as being about a private part) had a peacock's sense of color; this was the re-*glamming* of punk. And it was embraced by normal suburban stripmall rats, junior-college jocks, and princesses running with the boss sounds (as seminal glam punk Billy Idol used to say).

Basically, "alternative music" put hard rock back on the radio. And increasingly, "alternative" in the '90s just meant kids who'd cut their teeth on hardcore punk, college radio, hip-hop, or industrial dance drones crossing over to metal by accident. Had Nirvana, Pearl Jam, Stone Temple Pilots, Smashing Pumpkins, the Red Hot Chili Peppers, Nine Inch Nails, Alice in Chains, Rage Against the Machine, the Offspring, Soundgarden, Urge Overkill, Weezer, Sponge, Bush, Silverchair, Collective Soul, and so on, come out fifteen or twenty years earlier, they would all have been thought of as nothing *but* heavy metal. By 1996 alternative purists were stupidly grumbling about the big summer outdoor music fest Lollapalooza (which had actually been addicted to loud guitars ever since Perry Farrell of Jane's Addiction first founded it) "turning into" a testosterone-stoned Metalpalooza, when really it felt way more like '70s-palooza. Out there in the mud and sunburn scorch of the Kansas City tour-opening show I saw, Metallica/Soundgarden/Screaming Trees wound up dangerously close to Grand Funk/Uriah Heep/Mountain. And they didn't draw the nasty leathered metal-beast horde that worrywarts feared, either—the audience was just your average corn-fed Midwestern 15-to-25 post-AOR crowd, with hardly anybody half as scary-looking as Metallica's road crew. Overall fashion sense was more "alternative" than "metal." And in the end Soundgarden and Metallica both emitted an arena-worthy churn, as huge as all outdoors, and a sea of young people surfed their guitar waves accordingly.

All of which is to point out, without patting myself on the backbone or anything, that *Stairway to Hell* was somewhat "ahead of its time" in anticipating what the loud-guitar audience would gravitate toward in the first few years after the tome's initial publication. The first edition came out in early 1991, a good half-year or so before "Smells Like Teen Spirit." I'm actually kind of proud (like, why the fuck haven't any labels offered me an A&R job yet??) of the roster of bands in it who were virtually unknown undergrounders at the time, yet eventually became well-known MTV and rock radio (or at least *Billboard* chart) fixtures (some of them even household names in certain households) not long after, to wit: Bad Religion, Butthole Surfers, Dinosaur (who changed their name to Dinosaur Jr.), Flaming Lips, Green River (who changed theirs to Pearl Jam), Meat Puppets, Prong, Pussy Galore (who renamed themselves the Jon Spencer Blues Explosion), Lock Up (renamed Rage Against the Machine), Scratch Acid (renamed Jesus Lizard), Soundgarden, the Vibrators (who changed their name to Green Day—okay, I lied about that one), and White Zombie. My wife used to own a Butthole Surfers T-shirt, and I was kind of self-conscious walking around with her when she had it on. But now that people know who the Butthole Surfers are, and wouldn't think it refers to hemorrhoid suppositories, I think wearing it might be fun. I doubt I'll wear a shirt saying "I'm a Clit Girl" very soon, though. . . . Also, I was driving Linus's junior-high carpool to school late in 1996, when two bright-eyed eleven-year-old girls in the backseat started singing along to the Butthole Surfers song "Pepper" on the radio, and they knew all the words. I thought it might be the end of the world.

So learn from the past and don't start complaining about any perceived lack of metal and overabundance of obscurity in the hundred albums I've added for the '90s, okay? Most everything in the book up to this page is already outdated (especially the preceding appendices on metal singles and disco-metal fusion, which I kept intact simply to preserve the impure integrity of the book's original edition). Lots between here and the end of the book might be just as outdated within a couple months, or at least whenever a Stone Temple Pilots greatest hits album comes out (especially if it includes "Big Bang Baby," "Tumble in the Rough," "Unglued," and "Sex Type Thing," as opposed to too much of the ponderous Pearl-Jamness that drags down their regular albums). My '90s list has way more music from Mexico (and the rest of the Spanish-speaking world) and northern Ohio than Seattle because those were the places that were still doing something *refreshing* and *alive* with loud distorted guitars, whether said metal alloys were reflected chartwise or not. Green River's *Dry As a Bone*, Soundgarden's *Screaming Life*, and the *Deep Six* compilation were already included in the *original* edition, and heck if I'm gonna be redundant, you know?

I also naturally (for the same reason) left out the three 1990 albums (by Love/Hate, Electric Angels, and Extreme—the first two of which I still like, the third of which I can't imagine how I ever tolerated) that *did* squeak their way into the first edition—which I already disagree with a lot, in case you haven't put two and two together. It's pointless for me to go into detail about why. Let's just say I think I overrated and underrated lots of stuff and left plenty of stuff out and included plenty I shouldn't have.

If I had the energy (and if some nice publisher was paying me enough) to give the book the overhaul it really deserves, I'd write about all the pre-'90s LPs that I fell in love with since *Stairway*'s publication. Or maybe adding them would screw up what made the original text so original (or whatever), who knows, but it won't hurt to list them (and this is only the tip of the iceberg, by the way): AC/DC's *Dirty Deeds Done Dirt Cheap*, the Brains' *The Brains*, Cheap Trick's *All Shook Up*, Cinderella's *Long Cold Winter*, Alice Cooper's *Flush the Fashion*, Count Five's *Psychotic Reaction*, Crack the Sky's *Crack the Sky*, Faster Pussycat's *Wake Me When It's Over*, Foreigner's *Foreigner* and *Head Games*, Girlschool's *Hit and Run* and *Screaming Blue Murder*, Golden Earring's *Moontan*, Heartbreakers' *L.A.M.F.*, Holy Cows' *We Never Heard of You Either*, Hounds' *Puttin' on the Dog*, James Gang's *Rides Again*, Jefferson Airplane's *Surrealistic Pillow* and *2400 Fulton Street*, Joan Jett's *Bad Reputation* and *Up Your Alley*, Frank Kogan/Red Dark Sweet/The Pillowmakers' *Stars Vomit Coffee Shop*, Loverboy's *Get Lucky* and *Loverboy*, Nazareth's *Razamanaz*, the Nomads' *Outburst*, Pull My Daisy's *Pull My Daisy*, REO Speedwagon's *Hi Infidelity*, Santana's *Abraxas*, Skatt Bros.' *Strange Spirits,* Skid Row's *Skid Row*, Slade's *Keep Your Hands Off My Power Supply* and *You Boys Make Big Noize*, Starz' *Violation*, Streetheart's *Under Heaven Over Hell*, the Tubes' *The Tubes*, Warrant's *Dirty Rotten Filthy Stinking Rich*, and every Hanoi Rocks and Babe Ruth LP I've ever tracked down.

What I *did* include in my '90s countdown, on the other hand, were a drawerful of CDs that came out in the '90s (thanks to the old-stuff-reissued-or-even-issued-for-the-first-time-on-CD craze) even though they contained music actually recorded fifteen or thirty years earlier. Just like with the first edition, I want to expose future generations to the best loud-guitar rock available, fleeting fashionability be damned. On the other hand, there are several '90s acts not generally associated with metal (Rancid, Thomas Jefferson Slave Apartments, Sleater-Kinney, Weezer, Caifanes, Prodigy, the Offspring, Aterciopelados, Gillette, Santa Sabina, Mocket, Cornershop, Local H, and so on) who I'm an admirer of more than one album by, but for whom I decided to limit myself to just one representative album striking me as their *most* metal (or maybe simply their easiest to write about, decide for yourself). I used the same *Stairway* rule of thumb as before: at least half of the tracks on every album I included had to *sound* metal to me. But I also tried really hard to avoid work, and I hope the update reads that way. The only apology I can offer is to anybody wagering money I'd rank *Middle of Nowhere* by teen power trio Hanson at number 66.6.

THE *100* BEST HEAVY METAL ALBUMS OF THE *'90s*

1. RANCID

Let's Go Epitaph, 1994

I included oi! albums in the original version of *Stairway to Hell* but excluded Clash albums, so *Let's Go* makes the cut this time and its more Clash-reggae followup . . . *And Out Come the Wolves* doesn't, even though the latter may well be my favorite rock album so far this decade. (Really, I'm just copping out—I like *Wolves* so much that I'm scared I'd sound like an ostentatious creep writing about it! And the band's self-titled 1993 debut on the other hand comes off a bit too slamdancey, with only three tunes I care about: "Rats in the Hallway," "Detroit," "Hyena.") Formaldehyde-mohawked Oaklanders whose loutish pumping-of-fists can be traced back to '60s ska and '70s glam, Rancid's lyric sheets read like police blotters of lost young urban lives, with as many restless girl characters as fugitive boys, as much loneliness as aggression, as much greyhound riding as heroin injecting (and even steak eating assuming "Tenderloin" gets its virile diet from "Stranglehold" by Ted Nugent the same way it gets its virile hooks from "Stranglehold" by UK Subs). I'm told the band's words are autobiographical, but I don't hear them that way at all; mainly, they're about boys fighting with parents or getting stood up by girls, so they decide to run away to California or explode like time bombs or get stoned or flirt with new girls or roll the dice of their life—in other words, they're about the same thing that great rock 'n' roll has *always* been about. In fact, you could almost dismiss Rancid as a Stray Cats version of punk if their metalbilly greaser-jig of a rhythm didn't have such a brutally natural forward bounce to it. Ragged and kissed in doobie-dub echo, absolutely enthusiastic even when it's ready to give out, their harmonizing has an uncanny sense of where to put exclamation marks—now and then it almost even threatens to overflow into the Jimmy Dean *Oklahoma!*-ism of early Springsteen. But without risking such romantic ruin, *Let's Go* could never pack 23 sloganlike titles full of such anthemlike power, peaking with vengeful St. Mary on the lam packing her loaded .44, into its loaded 44 minutes.

2. CAIFANES

El Silencio RCA Latin, 1992

In 1987, this quintet rewrote Mexico's rock record book by selling half-a-million copies of "La Negra Tomassa," a partly parodic, somewhat waltzlike electrified cumbia version of a traditional Cuban salsa (called "Bilongo" in its less-emotionally-sung if better-to-dance-to Eddie Palmieri version). By their third album, Caifanes were opening with a speedZepped blitzkrieg called "Metamorfeame," then flowing through Salvation Army funeral honking, stuttering chamber group guitar figures, rumbling ocean rhythms surging and bellowing like sea elephants. There's a spaghetti-western sense of space learned off old prog-metal records, but Alejandro Marcovich—whose bluesless-toned solo in "El Communicador" just plain ravishes—grew up on Argentine folk music. Acoustic gloom builds toward belted-out jubilation, Police-like Caribbean-rhythm dexterities shift into slashing and scraping wah-wah parts, and onetime-goth-girlie-hairstyled pretty boy Saul Hernandez sings like if Robert Plant had grown up absorbing romantic bolero croons from his sister's old José José records. Saul's always gliding into Algerian-rai-worthy falsetto "aaaah" notes which come off absolutely melodramatic without sounding stilted, maybe on account of how he rolls so many r's and l's. In fact his voice is so soft and swishy and squishy, it makes me wish he had a vagina so I wouldn't feel so queer swooning over him.

3. BABE RUTH

Grand Slam: The Best Of EMI/Harvest
Canada import, 1994; rec. 1972-1975

Janita Haan is Calamity Jane with a voice of a voice and one of the funkiest laughs I've heard (check her masterpiece "The Mexican"), a big mama whiskey voice in a small woman's body. Babe Ruth is her stagecoach, and it's the kind of stagecoach obsessed with Sam Houston and Davy Crockett and the Alamo and late '60s Italian movies about Clint Eastwood taming the West by killing for profit (*two* covers of Ennio Morricone themes!). But it's also a symphonic post-Zep extended-beyond-six-minutes mellotron-metal kind of stagecoach with the London Symphony Orchestra lending a gorgeous hand sometimes and flugel horns years before Chuck Mangione made them famous. And I'll be damned if it's not *also* the kind of stagecoach that has more fluid Latin percussion to it than Santana or even War: congas, timbales, cowbells, castanets, soul basslines. Not to mention "ass Afro perc," whatever that is— for all I know it has something to do with the lowdown superfly pimp guy dueting as Janita rap-rhymes "want my seed" with "have some weed" in "Doctor Love" years before Kiss made *him* (the Doc) famous; said assman bassman shows up too in the next song "Gimme Some Leg," wherein Janita seems to get raped at the end. "Black Dog," folk-droning made funkier then louder then scarier Nazareth-style, opens with bells-tolling-for-thee then spins into a hellhound-on-your-trail fable warning of an evil nocturnal canine with knife-sharp canines and no awareness of sin. "Wells Fargo" is an epic where armed sheriffs head overland to the Rio Grande as shots ring from above; "Hombre de la Guitarra" is instrumental salsa with party voices; "Joker" is sixteen-ton funk about playing poker; "Jack O'Lantern" is a compact little shin-kick about "scaring all the ladies to death in your new blue jeans," "Dancer" is one of the only tracks that you *couldn't* dance to.

4. PRODIGY

The Fat of the Land Maverick/Warner Bros., 1997

Oi!-lectronica up your arse: After a couple listens I decided that rather than the mannered pretension it initially struck me as, the vocal in their pre-album hit "Firestarter" is basically just hard funny lagered-up Cockney hey-hey-hey ranting about instigating trouble, arson, pyromania. Reminds me of Killing Joke, only way more sprightly and boingy. And Prodigy in general are like '80s electro-rappers Mantronix playing heavy metal, marrying the loose loopiness of the former to the noisy bite of the latter. Inside the CD cover we get meaningless political slogans and a clowny looking cartoon of a band; outside, a sideways but colorful sand crab. And the music itself is crablike too, clawing and grabbing its way through a zillion permutations: loud guitars via the Breeders and spy movies and L7 (who have never kicked as hard as the "Fuel My Fire"—sounds more like "kill my pride"—remake here), plink-plink beats, classical spareness, and middle eastern prettiness. Undulating rant voices inspired by John Lydon and Mark E. Smith and Saudi Arabia help demonstrate the inability (thanks to drugs?) of techno-rave artists to express complete thoughts, but at least Prodigy try: "Psychosomatic addict obscene!" "Open up your head to the shellshock!" "This is dangerous!!" Knowing it's really not is half the fun.

5. NAZARETH

Greatest Hits A&M, 1996; rec. 1973-1980

Unlike AC/DC and Black Sabbath, whose artistic reputations underwent severe revision as post-punk increasingly accepted their riffs, Nazareth actually fared worse in 1992's update of *The Rolling Stone Album Guide* than in the book's 1979 original edition, which had already dismissed them outright as "dogfood." Me, I still wanna be their dog—kicking with as much swing, humor, and beauty as any hard rockers ever, they were the first band whose sound Guns N' Roses reminded me of. This retrospective is where to start discovering why—"Razamanaz" sets soul rhythms to punk tempos; "Holiday" spoofs decadent stardom from the inside; "Woke Up This Morning" is a hilarious and furious wobble-stomper with spooky downhome-via-psychedelic guitar zoom and lyrics about arson and pets shot in the head; "Shanghai'd in Shanghai"'s gospel-murked drug-bust puns break open midway for a sample-like snippet of "Satisfaction." And just like their (sadly omitted) covers of Woody Guthrie's "Vigilante Man" and Bob Dylan's "The Ballad of Hollis Brown," Tim Rose's "Morning Dew" is a folk-identified homicide documentary re-booted by Nazareth not out of reverence but 'cause its words make destroying passersby sound cool and its ominous drone-repetition provides an optimum opportunity to pound louder and louder on your brain as your wife's screams stab you like the dirty driving rain since love is just a lie, made to make you blue. So now she's messing with a son of a bitch.

6. SUBLIME
. . . .
Sublime MCA/Gasoline Alley, 1996

Lots of their lines make me wince—dumbest (even stupider than when their dead guy pronounces "don't start a rye-ott" in his offensively minstreled fake-Jah accent) has gotta be the one about "we've got a brand new dance, it's called we've got to overcome." But thanks in part to inspiration by lōc-ed out gangstas of the L.B.C. who haven't got half their melodic sense, Sublime are expertly detailed memoirists of euphoric coastal coming-of-age regardless—bills to pay, shit under shoes, stinky Van(s), mom on pot and dad on crack, alarm clocks and arm needles, sand in your bedsheet, informers finking on your herb, white rioters in L.A., gun barrels stuck down Sancho's throat, brown-eyed twelve-year old Mexican Lolitas with budding bosoms and nicotine habits and five horny brothers and a drunk-ass dad who puts them on the street turning tricks, and more stuff about owning a dog than any album I've ever heard. What with those olde English letters tattooed to their broad jocklike barebacks, these guys *look* metal, but their sound has as many hip-hop and hippie proclivities as hardcore and Hendrix ones. And though Jamaican music itself almost never throbs with this kind of aggression, there are reggae tendencies out the wazoo as well: deep slam-your-body-down-and-wind-eet-all-around (as the Spice Girls would say) basslines, erotically minded Latin dancehall toasting, undulating nasal falsetto whines, Linton Kwesi Johnson samples, guitar strings surfing the Sahara like the Grateful Dead at the Pyramids. Sublime ride their surprisingly unconstricted groove without falling off, and they're fluent in Spanish—this is how the Minutemen (another L.A. trio with an economy-sized dead guy) should've sounded. And though Brad Nowell didn't always "play guitar like a motherfucking riot," he did it often enough. And what a warm soulful heart he had.

7. HOLE
. . . .
Live Through This Geffen, 1994

They could no doubt benefit from Axl Rose's (or Grace Slick's or Stevie Nicks's) rhythm section, and it's no great shakes how their riffs thrum somewhere between early X and early Sonic Youth, but there's no denying the intensity of their frontperson's physical gift. Courtney Love's nag-rock therapy screaming is a shtick, but she drawls like a son of a bitch and wails almost as well and makes her transitions sound natural. And let's face it, if morning sickness, breastfeeding, and bib spittle can't justify screaming, what can? And if her ex-spouse wrote all the words, why are they so much more consistently coherent than the ones on his own records? She can't look you in the eye because she fakes it so real she's beyond fake and wants the most cake and wants you to take everything and gets what she wants then never wants it again because she only loves to see things break and she told you from the start how things would end and all her embryonic friends wake up alone and walk and talk and fuck the same. She made her bed, she'll lie in it, and she'll throw her dirty dishes in the crib. (Marilyn French, *The Women's Room*, 1977: "'I hate discussions of feminism that end up with who does the dishes,' she said. So do I. But at the end, there are always the damned dishes.") She's obsessed with dismemberment and uses too damn much makeup. And she enshrines all the Jennifers whose bodies I've ever wondered about, especially the one whose ex-spouse used to use hers as a punching bag.

8. SUZI QUATRO

The Wild One: Classic Quatro Razor & Tie/Koch, 1996; rec. 1972-1980

Watching Suzi Q. on *Happy Days* when I was sixteen permanently shaped my tastes in both fast music and fast tomboys—like her fellow Detroiters the MC5 and Brownsville Station, she was a wild thing who dressed up jukebox-guitar Ubangi-stomp hooks from Marlon Brando's *The Wild One* era in motormetal thunder from Steppenwolf's "Born to be Wild" era. In 1974's "Primitive Love," primitively electronified bam-bam beats and safari synths collided under male and female voices trading off pants (both kinds probably) and chants about rough sex and jungle fever; years later, Cuban bubble-conga expatriates the Miami Sound Machine put their heaviest guitars ever into a song with the same title. Suzi makes for a sexier glycerin queen than Gavin Rossdale of Bush anyday: she dances like disco Janis Joplin in "Your Mama Won't Like Me" (about dressing like a brazen slut), dedicates "Keep a Knockin'" to "all you 16-year-old girls out there," anticipates Alanis Morissette's jealous bit-off-his-dipstick rampage in "Lipstick" while grooving like a cross between the Contours and Mouse and the Traps (i.e., Dylan rap over a "Gloria" riff). And her "Tear Me Apart" (later rockabillied by country kitty Tanya Tucker!) tears me apart.

9. THE ELECTRIC EELS

God Says Fuck You, Homestead, 1991; rec. 1975

Sipping from a Cleveland repertoire-and-musician pool shared with the Styrenes and Mirrors, wearing rat traps and revving up lawnmowers on stage, infamous for slow-dancing together at blue-collar bars in their offtime until natives got restless, and not half as "inept" as legend pretends, the Eels just plain wreck the place, a spastically squealed warp-speed splitterysplat of bent Beefheart beats and angstful Alice Cooper snot staying miraculously tuneful while dislodging contents during shipment from every acute angle available. They only played six gigs in their lifespan, and though friends and enemies had been taping me their old 45s and rehearsal outtakes for years, at first I never quite "got" it; even this definitive retrospective took a few years to challenge my skepticism about the band's somewhat performance-arty nature. But once it did, hot-damn: the two axes really are totally amazing—piling drones, dirt, ringing riffs, repetition, and feedback that Miles Davis might've liked. There are all these New York Dolls and "Land of 1000 Dances" allusions, hooty backup hooks, depression that links Sergio Leone to the Swans, offkey clarinet parts that almost fit. And best of all there's "Jaguar Ride," which takes less than two minutes to explain something evil and exciting that happened in a car late last night.

10. GUNS N' ROSES

The Spaghetti Incident? Geffen, 1993

I don't listen to this as cover songs, really; I listen to it more as Axl's personality, and maybe mine. And I listen for his high notes in the New York Dolls song, and for Slash's funniest guitar parts ever. The end of "Since I Don't Have You" mimics the opening of "Into the Groovey" by Ciccone Youth, then (give or take a dorky version of Peter Laughner's great "Ain't It Fun") the album is flawless through the end of

"Hair of the Dog" (featuring Slash's funny "Day Trip-per" quotes). The Fear and Misfits tantrums and bassist-recited Johnny Thunders ballad are wastes of (fortunately not a lot of) space, and Joan Jett's *Flashback* from the same year maybe had a more fun "Black Leather." But the band's greatest cut since 1987 is "Down on the Farm," originally done by oi! punters UK Subs, and Axled oddly enough not in his high screech, but in a fake London accent drunk with Johnny Rotten's humor and bile. It starts out squeaky and tense, then starts to kick walls open. . . . Did Slash ever listen to no-wave bands? He sure comes up with crazy noises sometimes. (And my kids love the sheep baaa-ing at the end.) More about being stuck in the suburbs than literally in an asylum, the song's as useful as *Appetite* to blast at neighbors when I've got intense cabin fever, just like a vegetable down here on the farm.

11. DÉDÉ TRAKÉ

Dédé Traké Select Quebec import, 1992

French-toasting Ramones fans in the great Plastic Bertrand tradition, Polo and Dragnet and their fellow Montrealcoholics slow down "Blitzkrieg Bop" just slightly so I can finally make out the words (they're about riding in a car!), and I understand other songs, too: "Good Time" (gang of boys working for the wild Quebec weekend), "Big Brodeur" (apparently about a big bully, since somebody keeps shouting "Pinochet!"), "Faux Pas" (who *doesn't* know what that means?). The nasal kid crooning "Good Time" struck me as a *oui-oui* bit flat, twee and EMF-like at first, but he's balanced by a tough ruffian who Falco-raps in a drastic beret-banger accent. All four Dédé Trakés bark like fraternity dogs and whistle like marching soldiers and oi! like skinheads and mow-mow-mow like mau maus (or Trashmen) and grunt "yeah!" and "hungh!" (not to mention "hey ho let's go!") for punctuation. Dragnet's guitar grinds into curtly bonered Troggs-via-Zep solos, so the music feels chunky and punky. But sugary vocal backup and tricked-up

electro-bop percolation and "Bad Bad Leroy Brown and "Sea Cruise" hooks keep it light on its feet, and party growls and trashy organ and harmonica keep you on your tippytoes.

12. KIX

Hot Wire EastWest, 1991

They've got golden voices and hearts of steel, and they rock you on and on til the break of dawn, using rhyming tongues as harmony and percussion at the same time. Like a mid-'60s garage combo or a mid-'70s disco troupe, Kix take their gags for granted as part of a *whole*, part of *music*. You want encyclopedic postmodernism? This album's got four-second textual/textural testicle remembrances of "Leader of the Pack," "Double Shot (Of My Baby's Love)," "Liar Liar," "Sex Machine," "Whole Lotta Rosie," "Whole Lotta Love," "Pump Up the Jam," "Rainy Day Women #12 & 35," "La-La Means I Love You," "Terraplane Blues," "Lady Bump," "The Chipmunk Song," and more! "Same Jane" alone mixes "Authority Song" licks, "My Michelle" choruses, and "Gudbuy T'Jane" harmonies into a best-man dilemma straight out of the altared state of Nick Lowe's "I Knew the Bride" (i.e., wedding rock, see also Chuck Berry's "You Never Can Tell," Young MC's "Bust A Move," the Fools' "Dressed in White," Stanley Holloway's "Get Me to the Church on Time" from *My Fair Lady*), except this time she's wearing a three-piece suit. And to top it all off, you get Burundied bleacher chants, revving-up dragsters, fake Australian accents, sandbox whistling contests, disco hi-hats, metal machine Muzak, vocodered cyborgs, and a buzzy housefly on the studio wall.

13. Youth Gone Wild: Heavy Metal Hits of the '80s, Vol. 3

Rhino, 1996; rec. 1981-1989

Big concept here is the many imaginative ways '80s bands took off from Led Zep's off-kilter '70s rhythmic motion. So in order of literal Zepitude, here goes: Whitesnake's six-minute magnum octopus working up a gargantuamodal sweat that progresses from *Led Zeppelin* electric boogie through *In Through the Out Door* eclectic boogaloo with no levee left unbroken in between as unctuous middle-aged fart David Coverdale ekes out Plant-like stutters and howls; Kingdom Come imbibing "Kashmir"'s occult Eastern swing; Fastway mixing syncopation-metal changes with a ZZ Top riff; Raging Slab's clumsily operatic sludge parody anticipating Soundgarden; Bang Tango's reach exceeding grasp as it careens and shrieks toward impossibly high pitches; Love/Hate stopping and starting and eating some girl scout's cookies; D.A.D. propelling bad-breath kisses through romantic surfboard chords; Cinderella driving Janis wails all night and pitting glitter hooks against Delta grime and fast-talkin' mamas against fast-talkin' jerks; Britny Fox trying to be the naughty schoolgirls they're lusting over; Bulletboys harmonizing and keyboarding their lecherous stomp so it's light as a shadow; Dangerous Toys doing the same with a song about the fun of being scared; Helix shouting like Ratt into Raspberries riffs; White Lion making wuss-metal quiver. Best menu items—"Gypsy Road," "Girlschool," "Sleeping My Day Away," "Someone Like You"—just plain cook; the worst aren't too far behind.

14. PETER LAUGHNER & FRIENDS

Take the Guitar Player for a Ride
Tim Kerr 1994; rec. 1973-1977

Easily excited, at the party though not invited, teaching naiveté to kids reared on TV, moving suicidal Richard away from windows but buying a gun to take care of number one, getting so high he just can't cum then reaching the brink so he just can't wink, getting tangled up in red (hair—not his own), learning harmonica blues from old English dudes, writing about Lou Reed records and days-long binges for *Creem*, Cleveland punk prophet Peter Laughner lived his stinking life as if he knew he'd wind up a myth. This four-sided vinyl document, lovingly if semi-sloppily assembled seventeen years after his death at 24, split as evenly as *Rust Never Sleeps* between dog-killing electric chaos and infinitely sad acoustic mercy, is Peter's testament. He covers Brian Eno, Richard Thompson, Bob Dylan twice, and Robert Johnson; he lets MC5 intros give way to Stooges riffs that he obsesses into Velvet Underground trances; he sings about tragic poets so I want to feel like Baudelaire though I've never read a word by the guy; he sings about lowlifes dressing up in women's clothes and hanging around in bars like Monty Python's lumberjacks. Pirouetting Rudies, Puerto Ricans with hyperactive glands, all-night-escapading girls on the D Train, nervous backstreet leather Cinderellas, never-been-kissed eunuchs—pretty much everybody Bruce Springsteen was afraid to be homoerotic about at the time. And the post-folk guitar-hum homilies, climbing and gelling with a Coltrane kind of majesty, are as lyrical as the lyrics. If anybody broke glass as gracefully and cruelly as Peter says Sylvia Plath did, it was himself.

15. TIAMAT

Wildhoney Century Media, 1994

Distantly filtering guttural imitations of Lurch and the Grinch so they're more spooky than kooky, Johan Edlund's v's-pronounced-as-w's Leather Nun accent and lush Viking melodies somehow lend his ungodly Euro-affectations a godlike soothing warmth. Blatant Nordic precedents might be the late '80s use of campy Marilyn Monroe homages, art-disco propulsion, and duets with French opera divas by Swiss nuke-rockers Celtic Frost and Bloodstar, but Edlund claims his music's truest inspiration is bouts of insomnia; past midnight with a thunderstorm raging outside, I don't doubt him. By *Wildhoney*, their fourth album, Tiamat had added enough atmospheric/symphonic colors to their palette to about-face their original church-arson fracas into the most uplifting depression on earth. In "Gaia," Edlund flaunts sicko references to golden showers ("when nature calls we all shall drown"—okay maybe not) and spiders and snakes. But that's not what it takes to love me, and he seems to realize this like no mosher before; his morose melodies persevere, until finally a "pocket-sized (black hole?) sun" lights the end of his CD's tunnel. Lovelorn but a gentleman, he offers us his bed and says he'll sleep on the floor, then a few songs later, wonders if we dreamt about him. His worst nightmares come from being alone.

16. THE LONDON SUEDE

Coming Up Nude/Columbia, 1997

Lately I like my Limey lads sounding totally flamey, flouncy, florid, and fairying-cross-the-Mersey, or not at all, and Brett Anderson fits the bill. On the cover, he reclines shirtlessly on his back on a mattress (guess that's the "coming up" part); in "Starcrazy," alluding to the Stones' starfucker ode "Star Star," he croons about a metal groupie's '80s spent on *her* back. He's obsessed now with the mystery girls who've been glam's great subject and fashion role model ever since New York Dolls days, "stoned in a lonely town," escaping "nowhere places" for an urban jungle of sex and drug and drag and runways and runaways. In "Lazy," "here they come with their makeup on"; "Beautiful Ones" offers almost-country-jingled almost-rapped almost-nonsense about rave-heads shaking meat to the beat and bits to the hits, getting into gangs and fads and bands when they're playing hard. "Trash," closer to the Roxy Music glamtune of the same name than the Dolls one, flaunts tacky taste, talking trash about white trash and embracing their bracelets. Over rollerskatable Burundi bumping, new axeboy Richard Oakes turns

Suede's sound like their lyrics sharper and crunchier than ever. And as for ballads (prettiest of which gets its mood from Lou Reed's *Trainspotting* beaut "Perfect Day"), they're both fey and far between.

17. THE SHADOWS OF KNIGHT

Dark Sides: The Best Of Rhino, 1994; rec. 1966-1970

Five brutally horny bowl-haircut R&B brats from suburban Chicago, featuring at least one semipro baseball player and allegedly a statutory rapist or two, the Shadows of Knight may look like farmers, but they're lovers. Even when *not* spelling out girls' names, they *sound* like they're going to. Drooling about G-L-O-R-I-A coming around about midnight, you can only guess whether there's an aluminum bat in their pants or they're just happy to see her. They started off with Muddy Waters and Willie Dixon covers and Bo Diddley beats and Link Wray rumbles, then got heavier, darker, more complex. By 1967 they were imitating Dylan ("Willie Jean"), the Byrds ("The Behemoth"—heavy title or what?), and the Yardbirds ("Someone Like Me"—cosmic tomb-rock verging on '60s Bob Seger). After everybody but frenzied-scream-of-abandon expert Jim Sohns quit, a team of pinch-hitters hooked up with bubblegum blowers Kasenetz-Katz, resulting in studio-built concoctions like "Shake"'s almost Latinly mambofied Mitch Ryder-grade handclap-soul proto-disco. Vocals headed toward fire-alarm territory, and by 1970, James Gang riffs got stolen. But the Shadows were still funniest early on, seeking advice of a gypsy woman because their baby just called them "a big dumbbell," and promising to forget their wife if you promised to love them in their backyard and basement and kitchen sink and the clink.

18. VOIVOD
The Outer Limits MCA, 1993

An advance-tape of this album first arrived in my mailbox on the very same day that Cornell University astronomer James Cordes reported the following discovery in *Nature* magazine: our Milky Way's fastest-known star, a million-year-old, radio-wave-emitting, supernova-descended pulsar, had somehow burned a 500-mile path—shaped remarkably like a guitar—through space, and was now located near the tip of the neck of the "guitar nebula." No doubt this is the sort of coinky-dink that'd get the sci-fried chaos- theorists in Voivod doing handstands. Anyway, at first *The Outer Limits* struck me as tolerable only in its acceleration mode, but eventually I found myself sucked in by dark melody. "Le Pont Noir"'s Joy Division imitation nods to separatist French Quebeckers, the cover of Pink Floyd's "The Nile Song" walks more Egyptianly than the Necros' version, "Jack Luminous" switches gears for seventeen minutes, and the CD comes with a free far-out pair of 3D glasses. Still, just like "Panorama" on its predecessor *Angel Rat*, my pick cut is the shortest, quickest, most plainspokenly punk: "Wrong Way Street," where you lose house keys and watch cars burn and people fight in the alley as the guitar gently gnarls out a pile of lawnmower squiggles. "I went outside to get a life," the singer worries, "but everything was closed up tight." Happens to me whenever I go out to get dish soap!

19. KIX
Show Bu$ine$$ CMC, 1994

These guys should be Beavis and Butthead's favorite band—two songs each with "bomb" and "fire" in the titles, and their lyrics are always blowing up things, especially girls. "I'm Bombed" is an actual *disco* Stones rip, albeit with the Zombies' erotic bassline from "Time of the Season"; "Fireboy" is a siren-guitar hybrid of the 13th Floor Elevators' "Fire Engine" with the New York Dolls' "Subway Train," complete with whistle-blowing "Working on the Railroad" quotes. "She Loves Me Not" has entombed Blue Öyster Cult guitars lightened by Steve Whiteman slipping into his trusty nasal-slimeball whine when he loses his valentine to some stud; "Book to Hypnotise" crosses "Book of Love" and "Love Potion #9" with Coasters bassman comedy and a surprise dub part; "Ball Baby" opens with *Some Girls* doo-doo-doos then molds its shouts into Dirty Water," then "Bathroom Wall" by Faster Pussycat, then "Lola" by way of AC/DC's likewise-transvestited "She's Got Balls." Disc ends with a lovelorn piano-and-viola possessive-monogamy doo-wop, bashful as the Fleetwoods. Kix ain't that afraid to be peculiar, and their nonstop hooks have the advantage of being produced and composed by a rhythm section member, bassist Donnie Purnell. They remember the crash-bang-boom; why did everybody else forget?

20. THE BUSINESS
Loud, Proud and Oi! Dojo 1996; rec. 1981-1989

Squeezed by Margaret Thatcher into a proletariat dole corner they saw no choice but to defend, the scalp-shaven oi! lads of early '80s Britain still managed to make their claustrophobia sound jolly. Unboundedly good-natured no matter how many skulls their fans split open with lager bottles, U.K. horde the Business played male-bonding rock that wobbled like a soused row in a pub. Their 1981 debut single "Harry May" is all uproarious call-and-response, and the gang's bang picks up whenever they loosen it toward Slade's ska-quaffing music-hall metal. Their lyrics can be as hard to decipher as the most Cockney (or Scottish or whatever—do I look like a linguist?) chatter in the movie *Trainspotting*, but slogans pogo out at you—"We're always on the wrong side of whatever side there was," Mick Fitz's high harsh fist of a voice proclaims in "Coventry," a riot anthem with an urgency and euphony worthy of the early

Clash. "Saturday's Heroes" praises back-alley hoodlums bashing car windows after a soccer match; "Drinking n Driving" isn't anti-. If you ask me, how these baldies are constantly kicking the shit out of cops, fox hunters, and weekend poseur punks is conclusive proof that they *enjoy* always being on the wrong side. Somehow, though, their amiability helps put their misplaced kick-the-dog aggression over.

21. Youth Gone Wild: Heavy Metal Hits Of The '80s, Vol. 1

Rhino, 1996; rec. 1981-1986

Top-secret influence on an unexpected portion of this leather-and-studs-flaunting retrospective is the ale-bellied hooliganism of Slade, and not just because the CD ends with Quiet Riot likably mangling "Cum On Feel the Noize." I detect more than a pinch of Noddyness in Twisted Sister, Ratt, Poison, Scorpions, and Judas Priest; in fact, the latter two sound so surprisingly musical that I might even consider listening to an *entire album* by one of them someday! Priest boot out an opportunistic anti-PMRC hubbub not lacking in hilarity (all your screaming about turning music down will make him deaf, Rob Halford jokes), and English-as-second-language flunkers the Scorps happily never explain how exactly a hurricane rocks or what "give her inches and feed her well" means. Of the more bombastic tracks, Accept's alternative lifestyle feels fearlessly unhealthy especially when Gothic bath-house chants spurt into their backdoor, Rainbow flirt with *Flashdance* pop, Krokus start out dramatically then fall down, Dio's butt-ugly mythology just comes off painful and bloated, and W.A.S.P.'s ode to drinking yourself sightless has some early-ZZ chunkiness and closing-time-yelling-at-bartenders to counter its codpiece histrionics. I still generally prefer the more streamlined stuff, though—Poison's fake-showoff guitar solo, Ratt's lyrics that critics call "sexist" seeing as how they're about having sex, Y&T's sunny California volleyballing. And there's still nothing better than Motörhead's "Ace of Spades" to blast out

your window if a stereo across the street is keeping you awake late at night.

22. CHICO SCIENCE & NAÇÃO ZUMBI
Da Lama Ao Caos SDI, 1995

In the video for their Macarena-metal stomp "A Cidade," Nação Zumbi's three percussionists pound away ferociously on portable drums strapped around their necks so they can dance up and down the beach like the other five musicians, not to mention thirty or so small children and sideways sand crabs. Singer Chico Science, who would lose his life in an automobile not long after releasing a testosterone-tropical trip-hop followup called *Afrociberdelia* in late 1996, is bare-chested and rubber-lipped and has plaid pants on. As rhythmically advanced as any loud rock ever, *Da Lama Ao Caos* begins beyond where the Fall left off on their densely double-drummed Hex *Enduction Hour* in 1982 (bitter rants, repetitious riffs), even sampling Mark E. Smith's voice once. "Samba Makossa" mixes swirling Manu Dibango horns and chants with rain-forest bird chatter; "Risoflora" has the jaguar-lair funk of Jorge Ben's 1976 *Africa Brasil* in its warmly expansive crooning and congas. Yet this is *rock*, on the *warpath*: Lucio Maia's guitar builds from Soweto/Saudi beauty toward thick James Blood Ulmer blues, "Shaft" wah-wah, Zep brontosaur chords, Slayer genocide. Synthesizers sneak out, and snippets of old ethnic voices. Chico spits his kinetic Portuguese raps like a red-hot rudeboy, and I flap my body parts all over the room.

23. DIE TOTEN HOSEN
Learning English, Lesson One Atlantic, 1994

These dummkopfs made a rap video with Fab Five Freddy once where they rocked my Amadeus by blackfacing themselves as bone-banging Hottentots. Their earlier Aryan import LPs feature *Clockwork Orange* shlock-operatics *über alles*, but also sport their share of guttural disco-metal midway between the Stooges and Falco, plus a few oompahs turning *biergarten* honking and yelling into punk rockabilly with a handclap camaraderie worthy of my favorite *Slade Alive* notes: "Pier-end entertainment brought up to date . . . will undoubtedly cause an outbreak of 'Boot Dancing.'" Hosen's 1983 debut *Opel Gang* was all pickled-lout vowels and sweet new wave surf riffs, and *Learning English* is almost all remakes of melodic '70s-rock-hack-disguised-as-punk classics, with actual legendary faux-punk has-beens helping out. The Vibrators/Eddie and the Hot Rods/U.K. Subs/Adverts setlist works *wunderbar* from a K-Tel perspective; I'd never heard the pretty smalltown-summer nostalgia of the Boys' "Brickfield Nights" before, and ditto ace obscurities from the Lurkers, Lurkers spinoff act Pinpoint, and senior-citizen Cockney fugitive-train-robber Ronald Biggs. Just like on GnR's *Spaghetti Incident*, the dullest cut is a Johnny Thunders ballad. And though, given the band's nation of origin, doing "Blitzkrieg Bop" kind of begs the Adolph question, I'm pretty sure Die Dead Trousers prefer bratwursts to swastikas.

24. JOHNNY THUNDERS & THE HEARTBREAKERS
. . . .
Live at Max's Kansas City '79
R.O.I.R., 1996; rec. 1978-1979

Dangerous and glamorous Doll that he was, Johnny Thunders showed you more busted glass than any girl ever seen—in his guitar noise, his lyrics, his life. Eventually he self-destructed, a shame since it turned him into just one more exploitable martyr story. Me, I couldn't care less about his heroin habit except to the extent that it helped him put over killer songs about selling his soul to the pawnshop. His overpraised ballads always missed the joyful hooks of his rockers, so the 16:1 fast-slow ratio on *Live At Max's* beats all his later live solo sets no contest. Especially

with ex-Doll Jerry Nolan drumming (as he does on the CD's five cuts not already released in '79), the Heartbreakers rank among the most powerful early-Stones-clone boogiepunks ever, cranking the R&B dance beat of *In Too Much Too Soon* into muscle metal. On *Max's*, more than on their muddily mixed but still hotter 1977 debut *L.A.M.F.*, the band sounds slightly stoned, stunting reflexes and maybe making for too much proto-Replacements lackadaisicalness. Thunders's between-song standup routine is a trip, though: "At least you're noisy tonight. You shoulda seen the kids we played for last night. I thought they were all fooking *writuhs* or somethin'."

25. TIAMAT
. . . .
A Deeper Kind of Slumber Century Media, 1997

"Atlantis as a Lover" starts with spare Philip Glass swirling, then Johan Edlund's sunken drunken wail bubbles up from underwater; subsequent tracks drag middle-eastern sitardelic throat-gargling through deep blue dub caverns, or conjure some futuristic fallout-shelter-shattering war with Ian Curtis narrating D-Day play-by-play. Given the film dialogue hidden intricately inside and birds-and-bees hallows-and-gallows sound effects exploding all over, I won't deny that headphones or a bong might help. But I've sure never heard such emotional generosity from Pink Floyd. Moaning concentric hooks about getting kicked outside and swallowing poison for food, Tiamat pull off an imprisoned vigilance, a stately sense of struggle. "The Desolate One" surges with the slow-and-low inevitability of Talking Heads' "The Overload," or like some eternal moonlit arctic dog-sled trek. Closing *A Deeper Kind of Slumber* with its title track, morphine in his eyes and sand in his veins, drawing out ritualistic keyboard notes and the words "sollllllitude" and "dyyyyying" (or "Diiiiiane"?) into funeral incantations, the singer is a siren beckoning us to meet him on "the other side." The mood dates back through millenia, or at least to the Doors: my mind knows it's pompous hogwash, but my heart wants to break on through.

26. EVERCLEAR
So Much for the Afterglow Capitol, 1997

Dig that post-coitally depressed CD title. "Amphetamine" is about a girl "perfect in that fucked up way that all the magazines seem to want to glorify these days," fleeing a bad marriage. Next song, a record store clerk runs off to Frisco and meets a girl musician who dances topless for cash at night. "I Will Buy You A New Life" is the male half of a splitup couple's phone conversation; at CD's end, a guy lashes back at his ex's holiday letter about her excellent new joblife and lovelife. The ornate lounge-revival string and tabernacle choir stylings get too ambitious now and then for their own good, but these maturing grungers maintain sonic momentum, varying their Nirvana chords with island lilts, a Zep-riffed instrumental, bagpipey Irish Spring guitars, Appalachian fiddles, Vox-organed new wave "Louie Louie" pouncing. Art Alexakis offers butterfly kisses not only to his daughter (in "Sunflowers"), but to the generous *Sesame Street* idea that a family might be any unit that helps you through. A delinquent dad and nervous-brokedown mom get one song each, and in inevitable "Cat's in the Cradle" tradition, their son now has a kid. Determined to be a fatherly conscience to his genre like Coolio is to his, Art is mostly just saying that we've all gotta face responsibility someday, and it's harder than you think.

27. NIGHT RANGER
Neverland Legacy/Columbia, 1997

Very impressive how these underrated (even by me) '80s AOR simps waited until No Doubt's and Green Day's new wave nostalgia era to make their 1978-style new wave move. The Prince Charming fantasy title track is regally rolling rock with a gleeful poser-punk nasality to it; "Slap Like Being Born" and "My Elusive Mind" indulge in the bop and badinage of *Some Girls* Stones or *This Year's Model* Elvis Costello—in the latter, Jack Blades slamdances on landmines, hangs from chandeliers, and chases Mona from Arizona down "that rusty road to Zion," thematically outdoing Billy Joel's "You May Be Right" the way he once outdid "Only the Good Die Young" with "Sister Christian." "New York Time" starts with Oriental ping-ponging, turns into stop-and-go pump-it-up "freak show/disco/limousines/crime rate" list-making aurally illustrating its lyrics' late-for-work traffic jam. "Anything For You" slips into and out of creepy Alice Cooper-circa-*Killer* acidtrip diction, cackling at you while the chorus plays straight man. "Sunday Morning," about a single guy fucking a married woman, attains a more contemplative morning-after mood recalling similar Sabbath-forenoon fornication-recovery hangovers by the Velvet Underground, Kris Kristofferson, and Chemical Brothers (with Beth Orton), with even a periodic Arabic tremor to it. Elsewhere: immaculately lush Styx-mush harmonies, hack-metal guitar solos, powerpop melodies, Pablo Cruise congas, *Sgt. Pepper*'s strings, and manly drawls, slickly recorded in no-static-at-all '80s FM fashion. Three lyrics prominently feature telephones, inevitably ones that aren't ringing. And even the slight ballad surplus only underscores the extent to which these ladies' men *think* like women—I wonder if they employ consultants.

28. *Terminal Drive*
Geffen promo cassette, 1996; rec. 1972-1982

Lake Erie beachcombers Pere Ubu created a twisted rhythm, but you could twist to it. Antisocial misfit kids stuck at home with bad complexions and oversized pants, they absorbed warped wit and sci-fi sound effects from late-night nuclear-war movies, giving their scary hooks an outrageous sense of humor that sounded spontaneous even when it wasn't. *Terminal Drive* (sadly sold in stores only as one-fifth of

Ubu's *Datapanik in Year Zero* box) is loaded with fascinating holy-grail tracks by ensembles on the northern Ohio Pere-iphery, including both pre-Ubu legends (Mirrors, etc.) and obscure '80s spinoff acts (Neptune's Car, etc.) who managed to make Captain Beefheart's herky-jerkiness palatable by not grunting so ugly. Tom Herman's 1972 "Steve Canyon Blues" is a comic book anti-war noisefolk epic with electronic effects bridging "Whole Lotta Love" and the year 3000; Pressler-Morgan's squeaky 1979 "You're Gonna Watch Me" is a pinnacle of paranoia; David Thomas's 1981 "Atom Mind" is a post-Devo physics-class rewrite of Lee Dorsey's "Working in the Coal Mine." And in general, Ubu's suicide ride culminates what Dylan and the Yardbirds (or maybe Seeds, whose "Pushin' Too Hard" gets pushed *real* hard here) started, escalating droning pulses toward surf rock from an alternate universe (alias Cleveland) where water catches on fire. Sort of like "Wipe Out" trying to wipe *you* out.

29. URGE OVERKILL
. . . .
Saturation Geffen, 1993

At first I figured Urge Overkill's rookie album in the big leagues had the same relationship to '70s rock that the movie *Dazed and Confused* had to '70s high school—crafty if punchlineless nostalgia for poor saps who missed the real thing. But eventually I heeded these snazzy fashionplates' album-opening advice to come around to their way of thinking, because how else were we gonna get along? The superbly burger-riffed "Sister Havana" would've deserved '70s car radio airplay easy, as might the track that sounds like Boston with "Miss You" backup vocals, the one that opens like a Grand Funk epic about a ship captain, the Thin Lizzy imitation, the two buckling speed-tempoed new wave hard rockers, maybe even the *All My Children* and *Beverly Hills 90210* and (brief and untitled) *Mary Tyler Moore* tributes. "Back On Me" is a bit Replacements-flimsy; as usual, UO's deep macho vocals clash less with their leisure suits than their wispy wimpy vocals do. But mostly *Saturation* turns life into one hip bachelor pad where you stalk celebs and wait on hold for Erika Kane, you chase women born under tequila sunrises and miss the aroma of their fur bottles and forget that saving them won't save you, you feel delicate Nabakov compassion for high school dropouts over dinky beatbox beats, and you fall for lesbians whose starsign is Vagitarrius and who blow you smoke until your love sets them straight.

30. Best of '80s Metal, Volume Two: Bang Your Head
. . . .
Priority, 1997; rec. 1983-1989

In the most bracing number here, blonde bombshell Lita Ford gets in a fight at a Saturday dance instead of getting laid, borrows money from dad, then winds up late at her job. Her company on this set, though, is mostly boys singing *about* bombshells, and doin' it well: L.A. Guns' gal overdoses on violin strings and folk strums; Winger's is a nubile nymphomaniac who mysteriously shows up at their door; Night Ranger's is a Christian sister "motorin'" (not "Motörhead" as I at first heard it) through the city at night in search of Mr. Right while mama worries at home. Great White pump some groupie's gas tank full by reviving an old Ian Hunter rap about hands crossing her state line; Whitesnake drift tritely down lonely roads, leaving a wife back at home perhaps. And boogie squeals from Cinderella and convoluted harmonies from Enuff Z'Nuff (only group here *overrated* by critics) might concern girls too, if I ever paid attention to their lyrics. Which leaves a pair of unintentionally ridiculous flirtations with Europop: Dio exercising pipes and exorcising demon rainbows around a ticklish Italodisco hook, and Europe top-gunning from Sweden toward Venus in a fashion not far from Opus's Austrian 1986 disco opus "Live is Life" (at least in the sense that Iron Curtain faux-fascists Laibach covered both songs)—but hey, seeing as how it's called "The Final Countdown," shouldn't it be at the *end* of this album?

31. NOIR DESIR
Du Ciment sous les Plaines Barclay
France import, 1990

On their more Ministry-like later album *Tostaky*, these froggies do a song called "Ici Paris," one of the catchiest "Teen Spirit" ripoffs I've heard. On this one, by way of comparison, Noir Desir live up to the album title, which if I'm not mistaken translates to *Throw Cement in Your Pants*. The back cover has a face carved out of stone, which is how the music sounds, too: sculpted, noble, carvern-bound. Bertrand Cantat's belting is a real howl, with all the screwy romantique vocal flourishes his language allows. He hollers maybe four songs in my language too, takes his initial melody from "House of the Rising Sun" then does hopped-up vagabond "c'mon leetle seeesterrr" Leather Nun drama atop. In one song he insists "I am not seeely" over and over, and he's dead wrong. He beckons us to "follow the western grid," hymnalizes hesitant "hoe-zah-nah"s over tense twangrunge, emotes Bonostyle (if there was anything remotely interesting about Bono's emoting) over a Motörhead stampede. "Holy Economic War" has bard harmonies dancing a metalbilly frug; "Le Zen Emoi" has Killing Joke tribalbeats slowing beneath sighing moans; "Hoo Doo" is a whistling 43-second Three Johns rant. "Hungh! hungh!" chain-gang grunts build into pagan mountaintop marches; xylophones and harmonicas and clarinets drop by; voices imitate guitars which imitate the wind which crashes Mom's perfume cabinet to the floor.

32. ¡Reconquista!: The Latin Rock Invasion

Zyanya/Rhino, 1997; rec. 1991–1995

The wooly-bullyiest dance parties guitar-rock has thrown in the '90s have been sung not in English or Ebonics or even Seattle-espresso-shop Esperanto, but in Spanish, and the *loco*-in-the-*cabeza* Afro-Latin polysyncopations here prove it. Argentine libertines Los Fabulosos Cadillacs mangle Caribbean counter-rhythms and mambo horns toward an audaciousness approaching how Led Zeppelin blew up the blues— "El Matador" is both a ceremonial gallows-pole death march and a delirious *fiesta*, opening with stampedes of militaristic rain-forest drumming that give way to mournful esophagus-undulations jetting back and forth between Kingston and Cairo; their "V Centenario" transforms a *West Side Story* parody into triple-timed reggae. Otherwise, Mexican new wavers dominate: Caifanes flirting with lounge jazz, Fobia with toybox metal-rap, Cuca with Van Halen riffs. La Castañeda and Tijuana No build atheistic nightmare rituals into stately symphonic pomp; Maldita Vecindad blend jumping-bean ska with waltz parts and dark dub spaces; token riot-*senorrrita* Rita Guerrero of Santa Sabina operaticizes like a dominatrix Grace Slick. And Mano Negra, French carousers chanting in Spanish, subject their intoxicating mesh of tropical beats and ragamuffin toasts to hallucinatory trip-hop echo effects, hunting for the point immediately before catchiness collapses into chaos.

33. GILLETTE
On the Attack Zoo/S.O.S., 1995

British sociologist Simon Frith once wrote that the Beastie Boys weren't white kids acting black so much as little boys dirtying up girls' jump rope rhymes. If so, Gillette recaptures the rhymes for the "no-boys-allowed" tree fort, and swipes *Licensed to Ill*'s old headbanging crunch to boot—"Pay Back" kicks it like "Fight for Your Right (to Party)" with Van Halen chords. This twenty-year-old suburban Chicago Latina raps raspy and rude, like Joan Jett as a varsity cheerleader. She also provides her own laugh track, a whole bunch of *different* laughs. She deals hackneyed insults about your dad tying porkchops "around your neck just to get the dog to play witcha" (dig that gum-cracking diction!), yet she sounds absolutely *proud* of the lame disses she pretends she's just now invented. Even when threatening to lapse into feminist tedium, she stays rowdy. Maybe she wouldn't hate males so much if she didn't insist on six-foot brutes with ten-inch penises and backwards White Sox caps snowing her into believing they can satisfy her all night long. But in "Bad Boys," said illiterate bullies respond glam-style to her mating calls like drunk hockey fans shouting along to Gary Glitter, and though her mama warns her they're hoods, Gillette figures they're just misunderstood. So that's why she falls for the leader of the pack.

34. WEEZER
Pinkerton Geffen, 1996

Ready to explode any minute now, as repressed and combustible as the early Elvis Costello, Weezer call themselves "the epitome of Public Enemy" in the whitest voices on earth. Rivers Cuomo screws his muscles so tight his body shakes, then it starts unraveling like his sweater coming undone. He's running down the road trying to loosen his load, seven women on his mind, one for each day of the week—four they wanna own him, two they wanna stone him, one says she's a lesbian. Girlfriends walk all over him; the drugs (or jocks?) they do scare him real good. Relationships get too serious or not serious enough ("so I better keep wackin'"), and every time he pins down what he wants it slips away. *Pinkerton*'s title and most of its obsessions come from *Madame Butterfly*; those half-Japanese girls will do it to you every time. The music is dense, bottomless. Imagine a Warrant with higher SAT scores, or a Pavement unafraid to rock: off-key heartbreak harmonies going *way* too far overboard, xylophonic dinkiness turning thunderously loud, odd operatic twists, Nerf-metal raveups mastered amid dungeonmaster's guides and Quiet Riot posters in an empty grey garage. Back in the safety zone, where geeks can't get hurt.

35. BLACK TRAIN JACK
You're Not Alone Roadrunner, 1994

Shoot, I took illegible notes while driving my car, so how 'bout I just transcribe 'em as is then let *you* piece 'em together? Here we go: B-3 More metal Soundgnden stuff Noel Metalca rffs Pery Farrl falsetto his voice gets lost umpire in the pubs hard male consenting rare plod/chug pre-Ixnay on Hombre esp. B-1 as Sandi Pygmy Anglo thru Alarm/New Model Army as much as Clash anthemic lines come out fast and furious Big Country "Not Alone" little friends "what the hell get on down" pilgramages chrge toward shoes (distorted, sort of) Later underachiever "I've never done my best so I don't know how that feels" block-lettered words "I guess I've seen it all" Play your music in the sun heart of gold tried not to let you get to me "The Reason" Bad Company size blues-sludge Side 2 upswime guitars ring & chime maybe we'll win the lottery clear vocals Television but louder no less anthemic or catchy for refusal to annunciate Duded up for Friday nights, starting fights? rentng Annie Hall at local video store taking subway to work everyday in a hurry "The Struggle" Rancid kiddie-metal twee-metal (about a fan??) w/ Poguesy vocals panflute? fastest: "Back Up" (and turn around)—almost Ramones slows down call those h/c bomb changing Cinderella & BTO then go! go! go! like Kix Clash uplift they'll get you through seeming to have tempo switches and c + response pompodous of Love Maurice space cowboy his 2nd best song pickers, grinners, simmers. really love your peaches.

36. THOMAS JEFFERSON SLAVE APARTMENTS
Bait And Switch Onion/American, 1995

At first I thought the bait-and-switch part was how the first six songs were good and the second six useless, but then I found stuff I liked about the second six, too—even the one I initially dismissed as an annoying hardcore tantrum has a point to it, namely that we should bomb Cleveland's Rock and Roll Hall of Fame before Kurt Cobain's shotgun gets inducted. Columbus's Ron House screams like his body's contorting itself all over the room and his hands are covering up his microphone, nasal squeaks and Iggyfied yelps and screwily metal-buzzed guitar-gangliation ringlets boosting his rhythm and momentum and helping him turn corners. His hyperactive autistic-kid gargle mushing out like Elmer Fudd and/or various Jonathan-Richman-bred bedwetters (Gordon Gano, Daniel Johnston, Jad Fair), he cheats on his wife in a crosstown bar, picks fights with the world, tries to figure out whether some girl's stuck-up or just shy, and plans to die like his dad. TJSA's version of the vast-wasteland-mouthed Ohio classic "Cyclotron" has intentionally cruddy sound as if they learned the song off a twentieth-generation descendant of a cassette recorded over the pay phone down the hall from the Electric Eels' soundcheck stage. Its words (about amyl nitrate, pasty faces, and preferring war to sex) seem to be dogpaddling through a spittoon.

37. ATERCIOPELADOS
Con el Corazon en la Mano
BMG/Culebra, 1994

Three Colombian boys and one Colombian girl who variously wear blue lipstick, dog collars, leopard-skin shirts, anti-fascist T-shirts with bloody swastikas, or no shirts at all (but black electrical tape over the singer's nipples), Aterciopelados have an extremely long and hard-to-pronounce name, I'm sure you'd agree. On *Con el Corazon en la Mano*, slams-under-two-minutes-long outnumber ballads four to two, but even the speedgnarl has a comely complexity—Breeders-ish, maybe, except instead of whispering like your feeble-minded niece, Andrea Echeverri raves on full-bodily like a well-adjusted grown woman. Her midtempo music rocks my bodyline even further, jarring open sambafied tropicality with telegraphed new-wave-via-Nirvana guitar-

crank hooks. "La Cuchilla" turns a Tejano border two-step nasty, and "La Sirena" switches from an itchy Link-Wray-in-Africa twitch into a punk polka with bandito exclamations. (On the *grupo*'s 1995 followup *El Dorado*, they downplayed the punk and upplayed the polka, and possibly *improved*.) In "Para Mi Solito," Echeverri maneuvers into a spoken rap, then starts to chant a lengthy lusty waist-winding mantra about "Yo la tengo, Yo la tengo, Yo la tengo!"—Caribbean shortstop lingo for "I got it!," as any Luis Aparicio (or Ira Kaplan) fan could translate. Or maybe it's an answer parody of the Mexican Maserati accents in "Wango Tango" by Ted Nugent.

38. VOIVOD
Angel Rat Mechanic, 1991

On Voivod's ProSet Music Card (No. 244 out of 260), bassist Blacky has on a *Confusion is Sex* T-shirt, but though these brainy Quebeckers originally suggested said old Sonic Youth LP covered by AC/DC on the soundset of *Aliens*, this platter here is closer to R.E.M.—a surprisingly shambly college-radio move. Few other thrash mutants have ever come close to the gorgeous ethereality of "Clouds in My House" or "Freedom," but then again, R.E.M. have never rocked with half the propulsion of "Twin Dummy" or "The Outcast" or "Panorama." Lickety-split and non-retro and alive, drawing on everything from sea chanteys to shortwave static, *Angel Rat*'s cybergarage fairy tales twist and turn nonstop, but their average track length is still kept to an unbloated 3:32. Matter-of-fact through-his-nose, frontman Snake keeps trying to get poetic, singing "requiems" about waiting for a girlfriend's letter or a solar eclipse, wondering if bats are angels or rats. He puns on his band's groove by rhyming "assembly line" with "daily grind," forgets how to smile, frets about falling skies and oceans filled with Desert Storm oil, but never once resorts to doom or gloom—it's the end of the world as Voivod know it, and he feels fine.

39. Cleveland . . . So Much To Answer For

Cle 1996; rec. 1975-1996

In and around Cleveland, garage then glitter then punk then indie somehow managed to flow into each other with no delusion that "revolutions" were at stake, so new bands felt no need to selectively forget what made old ones great. Groups constantly covered each others' songs, and this is one of the few places on earth that remembers the Velvet Underground were something more dangerous than a New Age chamber-strum group—they had a rhythm section, for crissakes! Even today, the Velvets' hard jangle is a blatant influence on Cruel Cruel Moon, who inherit their boy-girl harmonies and wallopy twang by way of two earlier Ohio units, namely Human Switchboard and Death of Samantha. Inspired by the stay-sick/turn-blue antics of late-nite boob-tube B-movie host Ghoulardi, bands were frequently founded as "art projects for troublemakers," in the fuck-'em-if-they-can't take-a-joke/humor-in-a-jocular-vein sense. Ugly Beauty, who would actually improve by doing three actual songs on Cle magazine's otherwise-kinda-iffy Cleveland Squawks! sampler a year later, end . . . So Much To Answer For with a twelve-minute/55-part suite about running on empty through summer at the beach; otherwise, even more than Cle's nearly-as-recommended Big! Wave comp from a year earlier, this two-CD set proves conclusively how northern Ohio united repetition and sarcasm into a sad destructive buzz.

40. EVERCLEAR

Sparkle and Fade Capitol, 1995

Art Alexakis is a guy my age (mid-'30s) sharing a two-story house outside of Portland, Oregon with his wife and daughter. He sounds like a decade ago he should've been reciting plain old melodic Petty/Mellencamp parables. But now it's the '90s, so he dresses "alternative" and adds Nirvana powerchords, even though the first and last songs on Sparkle and Fade still both analyze life in a "small town." He's a reformed junkie fronting a trio named for pure grain alcohol, so self-destruction figures prominently in his writing, yet what most makes him refreshing is his addiction to picket-fence normality and his restless obsession with the hungry and hollow place inside where good things die and lovers lose the power to make each other laugh. Backed by '90s rock's most Eagles-soaring sway and uplift this side of Garth Brooks, Art files reports on suburban marriage, parenthood, adultery, divorce, and how breathing fire looks bad on a resumé so we better get ready for the real world—dangerously grownup topics for alt.rock. "Santa Monica" and "Summerland" deal expressly, almost every other track tangentially, with escaping to begin a brand new life in a new place—west of here beside the ocean, if at all possible.

41. RAMONES

Mondo Bizarro Radioactive, 1992

Rock 'n' roll made old men out of them and made it easy to scoff "fast crazy three-chord two-minute alienation, so what?," but they learned to play and Joey learned to sing, and their dozenth studio collection wound up ranking among their most listenable ever. Even the gratuitous censorship-is-bad protest is commendably catchy, and elsewise acid-warped-funhouse-mirror cover art encloses Byrds beauty ("I Won't Let It Happen"), Doors duskiness ("Take It As It Comes" and the Billy Idol/Sisters of Mercy-black brooder "Poison Heart"), Beach Boys suntan oil ("Touring," originally done doowop as "Doreen is Never Boring" in 1982 by the Mystics), and three lyrics about being in a rock 'n' roll band. Emotionally, the Ramones rarely felt more punk, at least in the '60s sense: anxiety keeps them happy, trouble helps them cope, nothing's right til it's all wrong. They fight you and screw your girlfriend, they shoot arrows at the sun, they run away from crackpipe cabbies and headcase Heidis and a fatal attraction who stays on their tails through the poetically paranoid "Tomorrow She Goes Away," their name tattooed to the back of her brain (as Faster Pussycat would say). When she's gone, they can get on with the rest of their lives.

42. LOCAL H
As Good As Dead Island, 1996

Two hicky bubblegrunge boys, one white, one black; guitar played through bass amp. Goofy psychedelic opening cut, then equal parts (1) pretty post-Warrant tearjerkers, including one with a kazoo solo worthy of "Smells Like Nirvana" by Weird Al Yankovic, and (2) pretty post-Offspring yellalongs, including one where the singer gets revenge on all the crass badass hi-fivin' steroid fucks who picked on him back in Zion, Illinois by telling them "you've got no taste in music and you really love our band" and dissing their hair and stonewashed jeans still unchanged since 1983—funny, since the first time I saw Local H live, almost every girl in the stadium had big Jersey/NE Philly hair and every boy had a rectangular body and a hockey jersey. Brian Krakows of rock obsessed with how things (mainly with chicks) used to be better and other one-horse-town secrets, Scott and Joe don't need more friends and just don't get it and keep it copacetic and learn to accept it and know they're so pathetic yet come up with more memorable lines and melodies per square inch than Kurt Cobain ever did regardless, with a buoyancy no other grunge (give or take Stone Temple Pilots in a few scattered tracks) can match. (P. S.: Their 1995 debut *Hamfisted* isn't at all—especially its minute-long ballad about falling for a riot grrrl.)

43. LA DERECHA
La Derecha BMG/Culebra, 1994

Until I checked my atlas just now, I never realized that Colombia is both just an isthmus away from Mexico and a hop, skip, and a Cuba from Florida. Still, said geography might explain why my two favorite Colombian hard rock bands of all time (La Derecha and Aterciopelados) both use off-kilter guitars that straddle psychedelic playfulness and Latin-folk loveliness after the manner of my favorite Mexican band, Caifanes, but whereas Mexican *rock en español* is increasingly hot among Latino kids in California, Florida kids are said to opt for fine Colombian. Anyway, La Derecha are average-looking Bogota boys who dabble in Clash-style dub, but are more fun pushing their basslines and wah-wahs toward 1975 disco, or imagining how War or Santana would sound covering Falco's "Der Kommissar" ("Ay, Qué Dolor") or U2's John Bonham homage, "Bullet the Blue Sky" ("Sin Catalogor"—no Bono jetfighter sermon in it, thank God). They feel wobbly and rural and warm, almost like one of those pine-cone frat outfits where you can't figure out which one is the Blowfish and which ones are Hootie. But when Derecha show off their chops, the jam actually jells, maybe because they come by their salsa pianos and Tropic of Capricorn counterpercussion and flamenco tapestries naturally, and put savageness on top.

44. SANTA SABINA
Simbolos RCA Latin, 1994

Simbolos is twisted post-prog gloom, concocted by alleged fans of existentialism and magic mushrooms. But even Santa Sabina's doziest Goth seems somehow *giddy*, with all kinds of cheesily telegraphed New-Orleans-jazz-via-Roxy-Music new wave keyboard-woogie tweaks and skittery space-station statics. The rhythm section shifts gears on a *dinero*, from classical to Transylvanian industrial to Bonham-stomping to '80s AOR to electrotropical samba to full-bore disco, and producer Adrian Belew (from King Crimson) gets more loud improvisatory angularity out of Pablo Valero's overdriven Cult-riffed *guitarra* than producer Alejandro Marcovich (from Caifanes) did on these cross-genderal Mexicans' equally *bueno* if more keyboard-oriented 1992 debut (which nonetheless did contain their most wacked-out metalpunk blitz in "Partido en Tres"). Guerrero wears a cape resembling bat wings but opens throat and heart with a womanfleshly voluption (to match her fishnetted figure) that Anglo vampirettes like Nina Hagen and Siouxsie Sioux never managed—she likes to rap, take Yoko-like gargling solos, and build proto-orgasmic gasps into miniature operas. The last track, "Insomnio," opens with ticking alarm clocks predating Faithless's 1997 Gothic dancefloor hit "Insomnia" if not Green Day's Insomnia. Reminds me of how once back in college a mate of mine spoofed the Fifth Dimension's "(Last Night) I Didn't Get to Sleep at All": "Last night, I didn't get to beat it off," har har.

45. YOUNG CANADIANS

No Escape Zulu Canada, 1995; rec. 1979-1980

Canadian Content devotees consider Steve Martin lookalike Art Bergmann an auteur on the level of Lou Reed, if not Kim Mitchell I suppose. In the early '80s, his beery spitball-rock trio helped make Vancouver the hemisphere's most endearingly suburban-wimpy punk municipality this side of Bloomington, Indiana (home of the Gizmos, Panics, and Jetsons); largely by virtue of its more grime-fuzzy partly-Bob-Rock production, *No Escape* feels more metal than even-more-recommended (and equally lovingly packaged) concurrent Zulu best-ofs by fellow 'couver garagers the Modernettes and Pointed Sticks. Shiny highlights include "Hullabaloo Girls" (skintight-clad chicks danced the wah-watusi to jungle drums on TV in 1963 but now everybody dances in discos like G. I. Joe); "Last Tango (Femme Fatale)" (melody from Blondie, subtitle from the Velvets, lyrics about treacherous women); "I Hate Music" (and chords, melodies, and the beat, but he learns to love the charts); "Hawaii" (hula-pogo about vacationing like the rich do, in fucking Miami, Las Vegas, and Tahiti too, with little Cuban refugees); "Data Redux" (tick-tocky spy-

treason romance); "Well Well Well" (guy walks over great unwashed on way to central interior job at bank with Chinese teller); "Fuck Your Society" (angry protest against girl in tight sweater); "Just a Loser" ("so go get lost"). And then there's the live-in-concert parts, where Art instructs drunk Canucks to throw their Molson's cans at each other, not at him.

46. Those Were Different Times

Scat, 1997; rec. 1973-1976

The Styrenes, least compelling of the three incestuously obscure '70s Cleveland bands documented on this collection of stage/studio/cellar outtakes, talk twinkletoed of petticoats and pleasure boats, with spans of electroblipping atmosphere-woosh and guitars emitting jazz-horn bleats, and zigzagging staccato time changes being epic without being egotistic. The Mirrors' repetitiously-strummed frown-melodies and cheesy Farfisy organ curlicues and deadpan wimp-whimpering about girls up the road putting on a show display an ease that entirely sucks me in; they played Velvet-Underground-style chamber-folk, they've since admitted, just *because* it was easy. And if the Electric Eels' "Stucco" feels stuck in place and their "Now" like inedible MC5-brand new-thing-jazz honkscreech, their "Safety Week"'s claustrophobic collision of gray Cadillacs coming through bawler Dave E.'s window til he can't stand (it?) anymore (so he's lying on the floor) will eternally pack a rude-ass wallop. And their infamous hate-language-and-response dirges "You Crummy Fags" ("I'd blow your head off for a dollar") and "Spin Age Blasters" ("pull the trigger on the niggers"), inspired at least in the latter case, Eel/Mirror/Styrene Paul Marotta has insisted, by "racist bullshit literature" at the American Nazi Party HQ at Lorain & 110th in Cleveland, are absolute antisocial provocation as a life force whether you approve or not.

47. THE OFFSPRING

Ixnay on the Hombre Columbia, 1997

A proud corporate sellout gratifyingly unstraitjacketed by slamdance, the fourth album by these platinum punkoids may well omit their two best songs and biggest hits ("Come Out and Play" and "Self Esteem," both available on 1994's less consistent *Smash*, which maybe I should be including in this book but I never listen to it all the way through and I've written about it so much in other books that I have nothing interesting to say about it anymore) (and they also do a really fun drunk-driving song called "D.U.I." on 1997's *I Know What You Did Last Summer* soundtrack, which maybe I *also* should be including since it's also got Kula Shaker conga-rocking Deep Purple's "Hush" and Type O Negative Quaaluding Seals and Crofts' "Summer Breeze" and Toad the Wet Sprocket covering the Beatles harder than L7 cover B.Ö.C., or then again maybe I shouldn't since its best track is actually a phone-sexy Hooverphonic trip-hop thing that's got nothing to do with metal and neither do the bands imitating U2 and Oasis plus the Korn track really reeks—see, you think it's *easy* to figure out what counts as a metal album, don't you, but it's really not at all, so there!), but it ("it" meaning *Ixnay*, remember *Ixnay*?) is nonetheless barbecued in chunky chucka-chucka and healthy disposition suggesting Van Halen's late '70s California more than Black Flag's same. "Gone Away" and "Amazed" communicate grunge-type pessimism with an almost-glammishly voice-sky-diving clarity and gravity, but mostly *Ixnay*'s heart comes from less serious semi-novelties: "Me And My Old Lady," wherein a sex-revelling Dexter Holland Ph.D. (of microbiology!) airplanes into pinched Perry Farrell falsettos around Sahara surf guitars; "Mota," a cheeba ode with forceful barrio shouts; basically, any tracks where Dr. Holland's high boyish register keeps fox-on-the-run beats light on their feet and where gang harmonies turn his words anthemic. "Don't Pick It Up"—about why you shouldn't pick up transvestites, dog turds, or stupid and contagious diseases—starts out with an *a cappella ba-baa-BAA* out of "At the Hop," then evolves into a ska rhythm around which Holland resurrects Johnny Rotten's slimy snarl from "Problems." And in "Way Down the Line," parents pass drunken abuse and teenage pregnancy down to their kids, and the cycle repeats generation after generation. It's what-comes-around-goes-around determinism chasing a Stones-guitar bounce, with a freebie reggae break at the end. Maybe Dexter should get his next Ph.D. in sociology.

48. THE DANDY WARHOLS

Come Down Capitol, 1997

They're from Portland but want to look like decadent Lower East Side hipsters from the Velvet Underground era; one has his hair sliced into an Andy Warhol shag (hence their name), and a couple resemble beatniks. Their best moments are punch-drunky actual songs with ballsy garage riffs and '60s organs underneath, managing to sound grounded and stoned (at the same time) as deep Arthur-Lee-like vocals quaver about how girls and boys better beware of each other and how if the guy finds his way to "Minnesoter" he plans to rock some girl like a doctor and jack off when her shirt's off; in fact in the inner sleeve are a couple pictures of the one female band member with *her* shirt off, and I can empathize. The hit, about how heroin's not so trendy anymore, aims for sarcasm and achieves radio-ready preciousness. Another cut sounds like an electro-wah-wah version of "Legs" by ZZ Top, and another namedrops Kim Deal. But half of the disc is seemingly endless spirals of swirl and clank, post-Kraut fuzz-loop tapestries wobbling back and forth while dreamy mumblers repeat and repeat "I love you" mantras into a vagueness that's boringly pleasant in the background as it swells into noisy sleepyhead head-music sculptures where feedback drones on and on, like Sonic Youth whenever their words are done, or Spaceman 3 or My Bloody Valentine. Except Dandy Warhols break into song and a rocking beat more often.

49. THE NOMADS

R&R (Raw and Rare) Estrus, 1996; rec. 1983–1987

Non-Leather Nun/Tiamat-accented Swedes who've been known to cover Blue Öyster Cult and Motör-head and wear Die Kreuzen T-shirts, the Nomads simply beat the trousers off of all other '80s/'90s neo-garagers, no matter what hopped-up wa-hey criteria you apply. Basically, I'd recommend every Nomads album I own, in the following order: (1) *Outburst* (2) *R&R* (3) *All Wrecked Up* (4) *Hardware* (5) *Sonically Speaking*. On *R&R*, ten songs barely adding up to 25 minutes and released on vinyl as a ten-inch so you can call it an EP if you'd rather, they interpret the Cramps (about a rocket), Count Five (about a bus), Chuck Berry (about a train—whose passengers are "a Mötley Crüe"!), Screaming Lord Sutch, and, well, "ESP" is credited to Taylor/May, but I don't *think* Queen did it. Big transportation-mode theme, you'll notice; plus "Nitroglycerine Shrieks" (credited to Vahlberg/Östlund like most Nomads originals) has a beat out of "Train Kept a Rollin'" (about another train!), which beat isn't lost even amidst Butthole Surfers bong detonation effects. So *drug* trips enable outta-this-world psychosis here as well, though the twelve-point-program platform of "I Can't Use the Stuff I Used to Use" is more along the lines of how you used to shake 'em down but now you stop to think about your dignity. Which dignity the Nomads joyously ignore, from the go-go stripper's tits on their cover on down.

50. D.A.D.

Riskin' It All Warner Bros., 1992

Danes putting over deliriously good-natured early-AC/DC grooves in a Bon Scott slaver amenable to Elvisbilly yelps and deejay-like airwave monologues,

Disneyland After Dark reach across the pond for a warped Western shitkick motif (their longhorn-steer logo belongs on a saloon wall), then flavor it with two punchlines per half-minute. Their guitars love Duane Eddy/Link Wray twang and ethereal tapestries, their rhythm is prone to disco breaks and swing-jazz shuffle, and if the song where they refuse to cut their hair snails a bit, the title cut has enough caffeine in it to implode. Obsessed with television and money, they've just got too many witty words to quote, epistemological (nothing real except the money they make—even though they print it themselves!), paranoid (when they're alone they tie their heads to the TV and unplug the phone), culinary (milk in the fridge turning to cheese, "each of us is a can of tomato"!?), ethical (right and wrong weren't so confusing back when Walt Disney taught them politeness on mom's knee), self-effacing (check watch on wrist then punch self in face with fist—a Dylan quote!), navel (press bellybutton to escape). Visa card bills lead them to wonder how come if they're so smart they're not rich, but to be this verbose and clever in a language foreign to one you were born to, you've gotta have an IQ around 300, I promise. If D.A.D. had a penny for their thoughts, they'd be millionaires.

51. LA CASTAÑEDA

Servicios Generrles II BMG Latin, 1993

A sequel whose predecessor was a demo tape, performed by a migrant-labor-truck's worth of Mexican artfucks who on the dead-tree-embellished inside cover wear animal masks and martial-arts makeup and brandish skulls-on-sticks like a run-for-the-border answer to Gwar, *Servicios Generrles II* is some powerfully heathen new brand of peyote-and-tequila death-hallucination metal. Said grunt-thump gets its bearable lightness of being from heavyhanded dirge pianos, reverberating funeral-mass recitations, washes of stormy weather seeping through your dungeon door; in "Lafiebredenorma," Castañeda even counter their elegant glottal graveyard plod with violin violence out of "Le Freak" by Chic. Most of the more overdriven of their stampedes get back-loaded toward disc's end, where tribalist Killing Joke tom-toms escalate in the direction of disco expansiveness, tension-ridden thrash, and full-on Afro-Latin carnival syncopation that makes Sepultura's Brazilian-grindcore collaborations with Amazon drum warriors sound like mental patients throwing up with a *National Geographic* special on in the background by comparison. Saxes squawk out metal chords as guitars play James Brown horn charts, and one-named Salvador's deep, harsh, impatient Jim Morrison melodrama is never once less than serious, groaning its stentorian basso-profundo anguish into the sunless ice-age evening like some forlorn wooly rhino who just saw his first hunter and knows the writing's on the cavewall.

52. BANG TANGO
Dancin' On Coals Mechanic/MCA, 1991

Shimmying *Vogue* coverboy Joe LeSté gushes lonesome and lush and hiccups blissful and hyperactive about darkness and horniness and fear and food, diving toward pretty and ugly places his apparent forebears Ian Astbury and Billy Idol were afraid of, engaging heartstrings. These crucifix-clad San Fernando Valley guys work saxes, strings, soul sisters, harmonicas, acoustics, electro-erotic Eurodisco pulsations, and textures learned from blues and funk and radio ballads into a teen-bop redefinition of '70s Zep/Sab virtuoso metal; or if you prefer, they recreate British Goth kitsch as the excitingest kind of rock 'n' roll, linking hard rock's brute force and singing-that's-more-than-just-moaning to Goth's moody beauty, up-to-date studio silliness, and midnight-blue mausoleum lust, finding common denominators in the two genres' shared senses of clamor, glamour, and How To Pick Up Girls. So "Dressed Up Vamp," composed in homage to LeSté's near-namesake Vampire LeStat from Anne Rice novels, emotionally reminds me of "Looking for a Kiss" by the New York

Dolls. "My Saltine" is a delirious garage quickie, "Big Line" gets licks from Shocking Blue's "Venus," and the Sam the Sham "blrlrlrlrlrlrowww" at the beginning of "Cactus Juice" is Bang Tango's answer to *Wango* Tango," by Ted Nugent. Two minutes into the slinky slow one "Emotions in Gear," LeSté lets loose with "oh my gah-ahd, I'm so a-lah-hive"—rejoicing like he's getting all his ecstasy from just *living*.

53. MONKS
Black Monk Time Infinite Zero/American, 1997; rec. 1965-1967

Anti-atomic-bomb U.S. Army artillery soldiers on leave from the Geinhausen base outside Frankfurt and playing for pfennigs in gasthauses, the Monks wore all black and shaved square-shaped bald spots on their noggins to resemble wax statues. They originally considered the names Molten Lead and Heavy Shoes (how metal can you get?!!), then commenced chanting crazed beat-poetry monologues about "people cry! people die for you! people kill! people will for you!" and "it's beat time! it's hop time! it's Monk time!" Inspired by the imaginary prehistoric funk of Mesopotamia to ineptly abuse all instruments as rhythm, their bizarre repetition and ability to be good in theory but somewhat tedious to listen to much surely influenced (less rocking) later Kraut-kuntry native sons of the Faust/Can/Amon Düül school—keys traverse down the scale and back to transmit "sarcasm," a banjo adds jigginess (most pronounced in the Holy Modally Rounded "Love Can Tame the Wild"), "Blast Off!" zooms like a rocket, and stripped-down ultraprimal hate stomps (one even called "I Hate You") gradually louden Yardbirds fuzz into assault-with-deadly-handgrenade distortion. Lyrics anticipate everything from "Pussy Galore coming down and we like it" to Springsteen's brother at Khe Sanh fighting off the Viet Cong. But Gary Burger edits his vocab into idiot-savantness so as not to confuse Germans, and makes a point of burning out his certifiably insane tonsils *before* impaling you with the mikestand.

54. MANSUN
Attack of the Grey Lantern Epic, 1997

Not to be confused with Marilyn Manson or Hanson or Beck Hansen or Jeff Beck, Mansun are well-hyped British arena fakes whose five UK Top 40 hits in twelve months and blonde jumpsuited blitz-kid looks reminded England's stupid music press of Duran Duran; singer Paul Draper gets likened also to Bowie and Cobain (even though where those two merely knew the man who sold the world, "Mansun's Only Love Song" claims the whole blooming "center of the universe is up for sale"!) Their sound takes off from early Suede: metallic guitar swirls and mincy expandavowel vocals, and once their CD finally kicks in halfway through there's enough pickup to make me stand and salute. Its most memorable tracks start and end with shimmering electro-orchestral studio effects—shuffled "I Am the Walrus" babbling, Queen/Sparks/Supertramp synth/string/singtweeness embellishments, modern-major-general cadence-call na-na-nas, all flouncing about and swooping toward crescendos. Still, I wish Mansun had less Anglophile-asskissing "whimsy," less "Cups and Cakes"-by-Spiñal-Tap (as my pal Chris Cook calls it) music-hall shtick, and more to say about how "his lipstick's running, his dress is stolen, he's got high heels on, and his flock don't care." To justify their glam, they need to take a few more walks on the wild side.

55. URGE OVERKILL
Stay Tuned 1988-1991: The Urge Overkill Story Touch And Go promo EP, 1993; rec. 1988-1991

Heading out in their Americruiser on a westbound (of course) highway, rolling into your room to set a bad example and your town to help you party down, all life's roads leading them nowhere, this trio of Chicago martini-metal dandies make fun of '70s AOR riffully and tunefully enough to pass (a la BÖC, Pink Fairies, Death of Samantha) for both satire and the item itself. I may well be the only living human who actually slandered Urge's obscure 1986 *Strange I . . . EP* in two major publications upon release; dumbly branded them white supremacist homophobes since a member or two had once baited "faggots" with Steve Albini in Run Nigger Run. But despite sporadic grime-concealment of hardguy-radio-announcer vocal acuity, this publicly unavailable eight-track (though not in the '70s sense) mini-compilation eventually won me over: songs about "kids" and cars and bottles of booze (bottles of fur weren't til later) and the drummer's birthday; another that gets its title from Robert Redford's *The Candidate* and theme from Alice Cooper's "Elected" and guitars from Neil Young; another about a fake street gang with Head East keyboard cheese. These dapper dans milk classic American band myths to the hilt, and in "Ticket to LA" they sip *Stairway to Hell*'s tastiest Beaujolais this side of Teena Marie.

56. SISTER RAY
To Spite My Face Resonance, 1990

Band picture on back cover: one hairy-headed metal Aryan with a bloody viking's hatchet, two Italian brothers one with a mustache beneath his nose and the other with *his* nose chopped off and a meat cleaver in front of him, plus a fourth guy pictured only on the table in his official flag-in-the-background Air Force photo. Sister Ray are working class family men and art students from outside Youngstown, Ohio (a.k.a. the best place to get a hotel room overnight if you're driving from Philly to Detroit in two days), and attitudinally at least, theirs is one of the best if not only legitimate piss-off-and-die/you-always-bring-me-down/I'm-my-only-friend/fist-through-a-wall punk rock albums of the '90s. Three songs (of seventeen) under two minutes, only three over three, no political protests except maybe the minimum wage and age-of-unmajority ones and the dark-as-Pere-Ubu one about violence on the screen; more typical is the great put-your-money-where-your-mouth-is one where some brat's self-immolation gets thrown back in his all-talk-no-action face, or the ones somehow straightforwardly rather than sensationalistically pondering (sub)standard pre-grunge-pigfuck topics: death, rotting, old coots with guns. Despite the band's name, there's no discernible Velvet Underground influence, except maybe via the Stooges and Peter Laughner. "Alone With My Thoughts" ends with sax squealing, the speedracered cuts rival Motörhead or the Angry Samoans in terms of compacting catchy creativity into a small space, and the structures turn more ambitious (but not difficult) on Side Two. The drawling is assured and all-out yet completely melodic; the guitars have moments of pure sanctity, but serve more often as wacked-out buzzsaw-spew heart attack machines. Sister Ray's early singles crossed Pink Fairies with ('60s) Pink Floyd and struck me as damnably "normal" at the time, and I slagged them in print to an extent that I swear I remember the band insulting me by name on some live cassette. Whatever they called me, I deserved it.

57. SUPERGRASS
. . . .
I Should Coco Capitol, 1995

Thanks to its glitter connections, plenty of '70s punk's boy singers had high girlie voices: 999's Nick Cash, the Only Ones' Peter Perrett, the Adverts' T.V. Smith. But by the '80s, rock falsettos were more the province of angelic pomp-chirp choirs like Asia and Journey. Hardcore punk bullies decided all sissified squealing was off limits. These days, Melvins-reared grunge goats just bellow and croak, which makes me all the more thankful for Gaz Coombes of Supergrass, who easily ranks with the most twee-tonsiled punks ever. To boot, between pummeling metal chords and playful studio embellishments, S-grass's 1995 debut *I Should Coco* (apparently named, not unlike Thurston and Kim Moore's first kid, after my six-year-old-that-year

daughter Coco) kicks harder than most any "Britpop" this decade. The words are almost all about boys leaving home, never to return: heading underground, down where the downboys go. The band's three teenagers do what "we're not supposed to." They discover oral sex ("She's So Loose"), get busted for weed (the fuzztoned blitzkrieg "Caught by the Fuzz"), and do their best to meet people who seem "strange"—an adjective Coombes sneaks into at least four different lyrics, screwing his hiccups silly-high, Bee Gees/Sparks/Lou Christie high. Sweet (Frankie) Valli high.

58. GREEN DAY
. . . .
Dookie Reprise, 1994

Billie Joe's problem is that he too often expects his words will do all the work for him. He knows all about burning out and burning bridges and burning holes in your stomach on the newfound downbound shittown streets of life, but his voice pretends most brinks of self-destruction are nothing to get excited about. The only song here he sings with loads of passion is "Basket Case"—especially the part where he confesses "I think I'm cracking up" as if he'd already begun to crack. "When I Come Around"'s Skynyrd-skinned bubble-boogie shuffle eventually started associating itself in my cerebrum with divorced moms of my kids' friends who regularly depended on me to be a babysitter and confidant but who I secretly had silly crushes on, but Billie doesn't put over the less catchy couch-potato lack of motivation in "Longview"'s lyrics nearly as clearly as Alice Cooper had with similar hits in days of old. And the album doesn't really rev into higher gear until the Who-guitar-symphony jam at the end of its third track, and "punk rock" had been a dead bore for more than a decade, and Green Day still had too much young-adult woe-is-me, not enough teenaged louie-louie. So it took me a year to note the hotshit AOR-anthemic paradiddle interludes in songs like "Chump," "In the End," and "Welcome to Paradise."

Eventually, though, I decided what I should've figured all along: like most fake punks, these brats are best when they stop worrying about integrity and just get *physical*.

59. THE GATHERING

Mandylion Century Media, 1995

"**R**eal" metal—the leaden non-haircut sludge variety—has overweighted itself into vomitous life-hating bloat ever since the Iron Maiden Age. Since the mid-'80s, as it's evolved into even "realer" thrash and deathmetal and grindcore, the genre's Cookie Monster mouths have only cannibalized more corpses and mangled more *Grey's Anatomy* jargon. So I gave up hope years ago, never expecting any Central European Wicca covens to give me second thoughts. Meticulous, cinematic, and clear, this femme-led Holland (no dyke jokes!) quintet's production is paradoxically credited to Waldemar Sorychta, from ex-Slayer-dude Dave Lombardo's indigestible current outfit Grip Inc. Yet by 1995, what infrequent carnivorous chord progressions and puking cave-grunts still remained simply worked as supplementary seasoning. The Gathering throb through six-minute-long black forests of bluster atop an Alps-threatening thumpmarch, twists and turns mirroring terrain patterns on old Roger Dean album covers (even though *Mandylion*'s graphics run more toward Aztec hieroglyphics); credit Amsterdam's hash industry if you want. In "Strange Machines," her time-travel imaginings possibly inspired by *Back to the Future*, Dutch treat Anneke van Giersbergen shouts out not only to Cleopatra, Gershwin, and Beethoven, but to Chaka Khan—hey, I don't mind overblown pretension a bit if you're *soulful* about it.

60. URINALS

Negative Capability . . . Check It Out! Amphetamine Reptile, 1997; rec. 1978-1982

Urinals in the sense of Marcel Duchamp's (or R. Mutt's?) 1917 porcelain restroom masterpiece "Fountain" ("the only works of art America has given us are her plumbing and her bridges"), considered by Courtney Love's first ex-husband Falling James "perhaps the greatest L.A. band of all time" (though how could a Courtney ex forget Fleetwood Mac?), these two UCLA film students and one philosophy major recording in various dormitory TV lounges and cafeterias released three seven-inch 45s in their lifespan and their debut album twenty-odd years later, passing off primitively half-finished bam-bam no-fi garage-noise miniatures as songs which they gave such poetic names as "I'm White and Middle Class" and "Sex" and "Ack Ack Ack" (their best, about Johnny who might be a girl taking his gun and shooting you down "like this") and "Scholastic Aptitude" and "She's a Drone" (a proto-oi! bee for insect incense with "I" in their "I'm a Bug"?) and "Salmonella" and "You Piss Me Off" and "Don't Make Me Kill Again" and "Male Masturbation," 31 in all. Cover the Yardbirds, 13th Floor Elevators, and Soft Machine (don't ask me which song that is) and Hanna/Barbera (via *The Jetsons*—and featuring a trombone!), too, and maybe the Barrett and Nolte in the writing credits are Syd and Nick, and their jagged guitar melodies (which are oddly numerous) seem largely based on "Radar Eyes" by late '60s idiot-savants-cum-figments-of-Lester-Bangs's-imagination the Godz. And they yodel, sort of.

61. SEGURIDAD SOCIAL

Un Beso y Una Flor WEA Latina, 1995

They look like mean, musclebound, dockworking pirates, with Schlitz-like bull tattoos and rugged vests and leather boots and wind-beaten scowls. They come from Spain, and on the best parts of this greatest-hits anthology, they incorporate salsa-style syncopation as loosely and unclinically as any hard rockers ever. "Quiero Tener Tu Presencia" vamps African guitar lines into an intense Afro-Caribbean call and response; "Ay Tenochtitlan" opens with a "somebody scream!" scream like in some early Sugarhill Records disco-rap, then builds bongos and bullfight bolero toward a tremendously exuberant mesh of melody and dance-floor rhythm. José Manuel Casan has a baritone that convincingly pulls off both wine-and-roses seduction and safety-pinned spite, so even cuts that start off sober, like the eight-minute "El Viajero," have a way of turning into full-on surprise parties when you're not looking. But mostly this is unabashed toughguy rock, complete with dramatic mood shifts and big spurts of secret-agent-man-in-garageland guitar motion. AOR-hating alternative types are forewarned, though, that the harmonica solos and dit-dit-dit stutters in "Solo Tu" are straight out of "The Heart of Rock & Roll" by Huey Lewis and the News—these crazy foreigners, they don't care what we think.

62. THE QUEERS

Don't Back Down Lookout, 1996

The Queers' band name is ironic. Earlier records lightly bashed "gayboys," and they still bang out plenty of bullyboy anthems, total heteropunk—they're quite talented at yelling "fuck you" and "motherfucker," and they rip off Japanese wrestler words in the chorus to "I'm OK, You're Fucked." "Brush Your Teeth" is sung to sound like "Brush Your Tit," and my son Linus and his friend Stephen (both twelve years old) laugh at "No Tit" more than I'd hope (they never heard the phrase "flat as a board" before!). Three titles contain the word "girl," "Janelle Janelle" is sweet empathy for a lonely *Welcome to the Dollhouse*-type Weinerdog, and "I Can't Get Over You" has an actual person-without-penis (flat-as-a-bored Lisa Marr of Cub) helping sing. Formula is

high New Hampshire harmonies over loud fast leather-jacketed chords, with a taste for secretly vulnerable pre-*Pet Sounds* punky/peachy Beach Boys stand-your-ground machismo. Said singsong can feel fairly insignificant; who needs another Ramones clone? But then you notice an entire song about men washing dishes (not just one line like in "Bad Boy" by Ray Parker Jr.), how liberated of them! Surfing through Palmolive: *there's* a water sport I can relate to.

63. NIRVANA

In Utero DGC, 1993

Still have no clue as to why this is considered such a great album, but it's not bad—a bunch of sloppily-constructed curios, for the most part, wrapped in art obsessed with innards and hieroglyphics (my favorite: tapir mother-and-child reunion, upper-left-hand corner, back). The two hits and two best tracks by far are also the two where Scott Litt's "remixing" corrects Steve Albini's pretentious musicality-sublimated-to-convolutedly-squeezed-out-skronk production. Albini murders the dark Fairport Convention melody of "Pennyroyal Tea" by feeling compelled to make it ugly; "Tourette's" is just generic Bad Brains shriekcore poop about underpants; "Scentless Apprentice" is a decent riff with no song attached. "Milk It"'s staccato yelling-for-no-reason (à *la* P. J. Harvey in "Dress") and "Radio Friendly Unit Shifter"'s flat mumbling (à *la* Steve Albini in Big Black) somehow manage to be more compelling—the wild-animal-roar of a solo Kurt tears off toward the end of the latter helps. "Rape Me," about being used and left to suffer, starts like a hillbilly "Teen Spirit." "Dumb" sounds bored or stoned—hangover music, downtrodden. Two of the more pastoral tracks feature cellos. And though I'll never give a fuck about angel hair, baby's breath, or aqua seafoam shame, the two hits do have their share of memorable lines about relationship stuff—drawn into her magnet, locked inside for weeks, in debt to her advice, got a new complaint, everyone's gay, everything's his fault, he's married. Buried.

64. HEROES DEL SILENCIO

. . . .

Avalancha El Dorado, 1995

Bob Ezrin (Kiss, Alice Cooper) produced these Spaniards in L.A., and on the sleeve they thank Roxy Music guitarist Phil Manzanera (playing the Dr. Livingstone role Adrian Belew plays with Caifanes). They've got a grey serious sound to go with the grey serious band photo on their CD cover, everybody scowling through wrinkled skin, though at least the drummer wears new wave swim goggles. Patient and dirgeful, all songs (save the minute-long album intro) over four minutes and two over six, *Avalancha* is a towering architectural wonder made tional by excitedly over-the-top über-mannered gondola-crooning, deep-throaty gargle-drama climbing heights yet never sounding strained. "Iberia Sumergida" and "Dias de Borrasca" are nearly Sabbath-like in their Army-of-Hannibal's-pachyderms ramalam, howling more airily than any Trouble or Saint Vitus quicksander. "Parasiempre" is more Zeppelinesque, not so much an avalanche as a Pegasus stampede of flying hoarse tracheas. Saxes and dubbish AOR synths get torqued into ominous splendor; bluesish riffs circle the encampment, flowing into sweeping weepy rhapsodies of woe and sustain with tones maybe reminiscent of Edge in U2 if he was starring in a violent western movie. Lost somewhere inside, beneath all the sculpted black forests of reverb, kids with holes in their mittens shiver through their teeth and gargoyles mask themselves backwards.

65. GUNS N' ROSES

. . . .

Use Your Illusion I Geffen, 1991

Basically the fraternal *Blues Your Delusion* twins meant GnR giving up glitter disco noble savage night-

school for roots archivism and avant-garde "experimentation." The second cuts on both sets ("Dust N' Bones" here, "14 Years" there) sound exactly the same, but there aren't enough heart-tug hooks anymore, or sometimes ("Coma," "Dead Horse") for less than fifty percent of a song. Show-off instrumental passages try hard to serve as ends in themselves, instead of embellishing a good beat; the new drummer's a "metal" clod, so don't try dancing to him. Instead of showing us how reckless-crazy he is, Axl too often settles for *telling* us ("give the other fella hell," he says), and I don't always believe him anymore. There are parts that might be really impressive if you read the lyric sheet, but they feel cold out the speakers. On the other hand, the ornate tension of Slash's squealing guitar-squall climax *does* halfway justify "November Rain"'s elongated length, adding up to cool corny Catholic mix of death and prayer, melodically at certain moments reminding my son Linus (six at the time) of "Up Where We Belong" by Joe Cocker and Jennifer Warnes. Which he heard an instrumental version of while watching *The Simpsons*.

66. SUEDE

. . . .

Suede Nude/Columbia, 1993

Bernard Butler's atmospheric guitar wash congealed into thick screeching raunch, but he too rarely played riffs as hooks. And like most transvestite vocals, Brett Anderson's struck me as wrongly affected at first, grating maybe because they're not really *rock*, their style meant instead to hark back to days of lounge lizardry and martinis shaken not stirred. Yet eventually I started getting off on how his Sparks-sniveling spoiled-schoolboy whine mannerisms echo into heaven, spinning into high sunshiney pirouettes with a little bouquet hidden behind their back until he hitches his pitch higher still and blushingly hands the pretty posies to you, then bang!—"will su-huh-hum wuh-hun give me a guh-hun." Even the glam-miest American bands are scared to sound so emasculate. Critics made a big deal about how Brett's ambiguous lyrics supposedly revolved around same-sex encounters, causing everybody to wonder if he was gay even though he'd slept with Elastica's singer, but if it takes being gay to sleep with her, what the heck, count me in. The cover has a pair of bodyhairless naked short-haired young people of indeterminate gender passionately kissing, thus creeping out my brother-in-law Marvin, who dug the Raspberries-like trouble chords in "Metal Mickey" regardless. Maybe he shoulda just imagined 'em as two chicks.

67. STABBING WESTWARD
Wither Blister Burn & Peel Columbia, 1996

Living in Philadelphia the autumn this came out, Stabbing Westward struck me as Dokken fans pretending to be Nine Inch Nails, the worst of both worlds. But their album shows them more like a cross between Bang Tango and Depeche Mode: they zoom their drum machines *and* forward-rumble them. The lyrics are antsy girlfriend-problem material, straightforwardly free of idiotic Trent Reznor/Marilyn Manson affectations—in "I Don't Believe," Christopher Hall even kicks himself for being a stupid and naive fuckup. He's better off singing in his high ragged blues-based register than sapping momentum with constipated-breath whispering, and most of his undead vocalizing frontloads itself into the first three tracks, as do the band's most charged Zepbeats—"Shame," which asks "how can I exist without you" but sounds more like either "how can I have sex . . ." or "how can I obsess. . . ," is a genuine whopper. Later on "Falls Apart" has a land-of-ice-and-snow rhythm curving into Killing Joke knots over fast electroprocessing, and the hop-hippity "So Wrong" sounds like Hall is rapping "so rope" instead (as in the Beasties: "I'm so rope they call me Mr. Roper"). Moments most in need of Rolaids come in the sex-raver "Inside You," smarmed up with seduc-

tion routines worthy of Jodeci. Stabbing Westward may well be the first metal act ever to pledge to a lady that they'll "confide" in her. How '90s.

68. P. J. HARVEY
Dry Island, 1992

When much-ballyhooed dame Polly Harvey is good she's very very good, just like the women she sings about, and when she's bad she's horrid. Frank Kogan compares her wailing to "Chrissie Hynde having a cow," but her first (and only half-decent) album rocks harder than *Learning to Crawl* (even *Radio Ethiopia*) nonetheless. I'm impressed by the hefty blues-density of the guitar bwaangliations, and Polly's band and mouth have a sense of rhythm Courtney Love (say) doesn't. Her best songs are without fail her shortest ones, though: "Dress" (about staging the feminine show and shaking her fruit true—though it's *gross* how she smears on lipstick I must say); "O Stella" (post-Dylan-rapped lesbian compliments, catchy rumbling riff, "leh-zhur" pronounced the Gang of Four way); "Sheila Na-Gig" (childbearing hips, ruby red lips, alluding to *South Pacific* wash-man-out-of-hair stuff like John Cougar used to); "Joe" (fast early Police skeedle-weedling with Jimmy Page shockeroos). Yet most every time the tempos slow down and the guitars bid adieu, *Dry* devolves into cabaret kitsch; there's something restricted in Harvey's crooning that guarantees she'll come off phonus-balonus whenever she pretends to slip into a trance, and her theatricality is overbearing method acting, and the off-key Stravinsky strings here don't make up for the stale cocktails over there. As for the lady digging water metaphors, big deal—so does Eddie Money. The walking basslines in "Water" must be dedicated to Jesus, since it's about walking on it, right? But at least *Dry* (no H_2O!) beats her later royal scams, where she alternated hissing about little fishies in dead-in-the-water whispers with letting Little Stevie Albini switch production knobs meaninglessly between ugly noise and uninhabited silence at random points having nada at all to do with the rest of the music.

69. RUTH RUTH
Laughing Gallery American, 1996

New York Nirvanabees Ruth Ruth exude a franticness harking back to the less-surly/better-groomed end of mid-'60s sockhop-nobodies- shooting-for-frathouse-stardom garage rock. Too fast for grunge, too pretty for hardcore, yet loud enough for both, at best they're a dance combo, powered by handclaps, na-na-na-na's, hokey-pokey instructions, hyper bass motion, drumbeats echoing Iggy Pop's "Lust for Life" or the Cars. "Uptight" earns its title, wound up and wired like *This Year's Model* Elvis Costello; "Mission Idiot" turns into John Cougar whenever Chris Kennedy's voice speeds up. But the music's most blatant antecedent is the Who. Two songs strip down "Baba O'Reilly" hooks, and "Pervert" rewrites "5:15"—our narrator waits behind a lady he doesn't know at 5:00 each day, "blowing my mind on the rush-hour train" (as in "out of my brain on the 5:15"), then heads home to masturbate. Kennedy is constantly recalling childhood traumas—getting chased after school's out by fourth-grade lynch mobs for his faggot haircut, for instance. He throws away 45s that remind him of one girlfriend, yearns over another for her leather jacket, and murders a prom queen who dumps him because he can't get it up. A love-spurned sadsack overrun with antisocial neuroses, he's never in with the in crowd. But in his modern-rock-radio nugget "Uninvited," he crashes the cool kids' party anyway.

70. SLEATER-KINNEY
Call the Doctor Chainsaw, 1996

Always flinched at these riot cuties' silly protest about how some "they" wants to socialize and sterilize you, which naturally never spells out who this "they" is, but why quibble? Like Courtney Love with thankfully less volatile a temper, Corin Tucker is most everything her indie foremothers (and forefathers) were scared to be; her huge unwinding delivery catches in squeaks and snarls and feral cries of "fire!" in a crowded moshpit. So her Portland triad of post-lib lesbian role models comes off reliably impish and alive and kicking, and attacking beauty myths like Naomi Wolf doesn't prevent them from ranking with rock's most easy-on-the-eyes ensembles ever. When Corin frets that good things never want to stay, I want to pin their pictures to my door so they'll invite me back after the show to wrestle on their bedroom floor. Their distinctive-if-slightly-samey racket sets the Raincoats' unschooled post-punk femme-folk to butcher beaver-cleaver guitar clang, but on an earlier CD they covered "More Than a Feeling." On 1997's more uneven *Dig Me Out* they added a B-52s bassline and dum-ditty-dum little-baby hook or two, but *Call the Doctor*'s where Corin stakes her claim as queen of rock, asking to be your Thurston Moore—as if the king of indie monotones ever belted with half her balls. I mean ovaries.

71. WARRANT
Cherry Pie Columbia, 1990

"I Saw Red" is Nerf-metal's all-time most chilling cheated-on betrayal ballad, and maybe if Veruca Salt or Joan Jett covered the rural-rapped front-porch-swinging title track its virgin fetish wouldn't bug blue-nose spoilsports so much. There's a sweet ode to a lonesome woman living down the hotel hallway from you, a thrash-tempoed speedo with words you ignore, a new-wavish big-beat boogie ("Love in Stereo") about a *ménage à trois* (deadpan line: "I never had two women before, but I'm an open-minded person"). And the rest of *Cherry Pie* is surprisingly Southern, from Blackfoot train-blues remake to Johnny Paycheck outlaw sequel (with Elton John melody but so what) "You're the Only Hell Your Mama Ever Raised" to (especially) "Uncle Tom's Cabin," Tom 'n' Huck bodies-in-the-wishing-well American folklore easily deserving of its own Greil Marcus *Mystery Train* chapter (and preceded by Segovia guitar tapestries straight out of Heart's "Crazy on You," and boasting one of the most poignant TV-movie-style MTV videos ever this side of Skid Row's "18 and Life"). Tying it all together is Jani Lane's rich drawl, taking Paul Rodgers's big burly cumbersome ball of overturned sod and (at least as ably as the voices in Foreigner, Loverboy, or Urge Overkill) shaping it into something honeyed and popwise.

72. WILDSIDE
Under the Influence Capitol, 1992

Like Axl Rose in 1987, Drew Hannah screeches about facing the meanness and viciousness wherever you wind up escaping to, in a high haggard Janis vibrato above soul bass, rhythm guitar, and drumroll hootchiecoo; his band likewise swipes *Appetite for Destruction*'s coiling intros, swaying summer-breeze-gush slowdowns, abrupt shifts into psychedelic breaks, and interludes (pantaludes?) where people pant a lot. They could probably afford to chuck the ballads, especially the whiney suspicion-blues "How Many Lies." But their album still deals out as many loaded guns and thorned roses as either *Use Your Illusion*. Paraphrasing the McCoys' "Hang on Sloopy" and David Bowie's *Aladdin Sane* and Axl's homesick-for-green-grass "so far away" bawl from "Paradise City" in song titles, they shriek operatically about bad girls picking up all kinds of strangers if the price is right, about abused girls taking blame for adult sins, about playing along with the grownups who think you're menacing though you know you're not, about having sex way past curfew. In "Lad in Sin," Hannah swears if you get too close he'll get under your skin, and you'll feel his reign of terror. He's been told he's rotten, so now he's shooting up the world, and what keeps his cruelty real is his vulnerability—"Look up here, is it pain or fear, can you see it burn in my eyes?" You've been hurting him, so he wants to kill you.

73. SERGIO ARAU LA VENGANZA DE MOCTEZUMA
Mi Frida Sufrida SDI, 1994

Forefathers of Mexico's current rock wave were the comedic '80s "guacamole rock" troupe La H. H. Botellita De Jerez, whose 1994 comeback album *Forjando Patria* was a borderline candidate for this book, though in the end I decided it wasn't metal quite often enough. (Best parts feature pirate yo-ho-hos chanted over Hendrix riffs and Indian bhangra hey-hey-heys and "Hooked on a Feeling" ooga-chuckas over Speedy Gonzales ska; they also shoot guns and meow like cats, and my favorite band member is the one dressed in a priest's collar, choking a rubber chicken.) Anyway, Botellita were originally led by one Sergio Arau, an editorial cartoonist and government illustrator who has also directed films about slum life and illegal immigrants in L.A. The name of his '90s band translates to "Montezuma's Revenge," and on *Mi Frida Sufrida* they sound like ranchero hands crossing over to heavy rock—fairly standard on the more traditional ballads despite high lonesome cowboy hiccups, but downright idiosyncratic when they cloak hat-dance accordions with gigantic powerchords chomped from Led Zeppelin, the Yardbirds, and "Hocus Pocus" by Focus. "Dame Posada Catrina" is either "Taps" or "Reveille" (I never took bugle lessons in the Army) tapped out on hard guitar, with jaunty Tex-Mex bouncing underneath. Inside his CD sleeve, Arau wears both a matador's cape and a gas mask.

74. NIRVANA
Nevermind DGC, 1991

Actually, I don't have a copy handy right now, but I can assume you're at least partially familiar with this one, right? It's got the "no I don't have a gun" song, the "I'm the one who likes all the pretty songs" song, some others I forget. For years I've had this running argument with my friend Chris about "Come as You Are"—I swear it's a ballad; he says it's fast. On the radio, if I listen close, I could maybe admit midtempo, but to me it still *feels* dirgey and draggy. Nirvana's biggest "innovation," if they had one, was adding Hüsker/Replacements-style comeliness to Seattle's sound, which before them had been a nastier Stooge/Sabbath-style sludge beast, not far from stuff Flipper (whose T-shirt Kurt Cobain wears inside *In Utero*'s sleeve) had been grinding out since 1982, only with less heart. I don't particularly care for the *grain* of Cobain's voice, his sore-throat hoarseness; I do like his drawl, though. And it *is* fun to lose and to pretend. An allergy-shot nurse told me once that she always figured "Smells Like Teen Spirit" (a hit when she was seventeen) had something to do with "lots of different kinds of kids"—albinos, mulattos, and so on, though she couldn't figure out how mosquitoes got in there. My wife heard Kurt saying "they only love you 'cause you're famous." First time *I* heard the song, I thought "Die Kreuzen," or maybe "Squirrelchuck Asylum," only with the a huger sound thanks to "Wild Thing" parts, but big deal—still felt like loud folk rock, and if this band was so great, how come no kids wore "Nuke Nirvana" T-shirts? I dug those anarchy cheerleaders, though, and that its volume got up the dander of radio programmers. Yet even when I decided its lyrics were "Louie Louie," I still cringed at its bogus use of the editorial "we." Denial denial how would I know oh whatever nevermind a little goof I'd always been Amen.

75. MARIA FATAL
Maria Fatal Aztlan, 1995

COVER PHOTO: incredibly erotic, with a lovely androgynous Latina bound by wrists above her head and with bare brown breasts emblazoned with a flower and iguana painted on in bright colors. PERSONNEL: six California Chicanos who beat (excellent though less metal) units like King Chango and Pastilla to the title of the first important *rock en español* band from U.S. TEMPOS: half fast, half slow. VOCALS: heart-aflame Saul (of Caifanes) Hernandez-style scaling-of-volcanotops, building through six minutes of gradually increasing intensity in "Pórtate Mal," sometimes chanting ritualistically or jazzily mirroring rung bell notes or repeating lines into roundelay-like overlapment. RHYTHMS: range from (without drawing lines around) ska two-steps to funk to twisted hatdances to tribalism more natural than industrial thrash bands will ever give you (or me). GUITARS: tease with film-noirish spy themes then get chased by horns, bang machine gun targets like Metallica, bluesify into gutsily bruising ZZ-raunch or evocatively cruising Clapton-weep. KEYBOARDS: tastefully classical to overblownedly prog. EMBELLISHMENTS: rocket and gong sounds, airplanes hovering overhead then igniting in distance because burning airlines give you so much more as Brian Eno (who the break in "Las Aves" reminds me of) would say, sax solo peeled off to finish last song. FOLLOWUP ALBUM: didn't cut it.

76. CINDERELLA
Still Climbing Mercury, 1994

On *Heartbreak Station* in 1990, these Philly mall-shriekers retreated into blues nostalgia, tossing out the scarves, mascara, and light-socket perms that had landed them on MTV in the late '80s. But *Still Climbing* put Cinderella back on Gipsy Road, spinning emotional wheels, scaling life's ladder even as shitty advice from smiling faces telling lies wound up as stones in their passway. Tom Keifer's hairspray-scarred throat plunges down when the world's toppling around him, flies up when his bottle of hurricane gets him high as a kite. His falsetto pushes like Janis and soars like Robert Plant, and his axe chimes, climbs, circles, claws, clangs; zinewriter Frank Kogan once likened Keifer's explorations to the band Television, "if (Tom) Verlaine could have sung and his rhythm section could have rocked." A warm piano ballad about finding hope in a world gone mad is preceded by "Freewheelin'," wildass punk rock wherein Keifer pretends all his work is "overrated," spitting fast funky sass at his crumbling dreams. His grooves open wide with a tuneful soul that grunge slobs and lo-fi snobs will never know, so he's got plenty to be pissed about. Mainly, he wants his MTV back: "They can't take the city from the boys looking pretty."

77. COBRA VERDE

Egomania (Love Songs) Scat 1997; rec. 1995-1997.

On earlier outings, former Death of Samantha "glitter punk" John Petkovic's '90s "avant glam" band sounded too intense and obtuse and grumbly, too close to their fellow Ohioans Afghan Whigs in other words, though the Roxy Music blues-sculpture guitars still made more sense than any anorexic quietude by eventual Cobra-Verde-absorbers Guided By Voices. But now the singles compilation *Egomania* is Petkovic's solidest set of songs since 1988. In real life, his job entails covering horse races for the *Cleveland Plain Dealer*, so whatever journalism urge you detect in the chorus that goes "give me a story I can sell" might not just be your imagination. The older he gets, the prissier and prettier and more *Ziggy Stardust*-ed his croons get—C.V.'s pinnacle moment, oddly omitted, was a 1995 45 called "One Step Away from Myself," which sounded like early '70s hard rock Bowie covering Stone Temple Pilots' "Sex Type Thing" with a cheapo antique analog synth line waffling through. The band still growls and plods at times, and "Blood on the Moon" is at least John's third "blood" title. But Verde's redo of "Underpants" by old Cle-wavers the Easter Monkeys has a fruitily looming bounce, their "Never My Love" (via '60s pop hacks the Association) turns shlock otherworldly, and everywhere falsetto-pitch vocal swish and fancy-nancy pipe-organ drama perverts hetero-riffed cock-rock until it's kinky and pink.

78. GIRLS AGAINST BOYS

House of GVSB Touch and Go, 1996

On the scene like sexy cash machines but ranting slogans more evocative than explicit ("I love it when they turn the flame on . . . you can blow it all in one crazy shot"), Girls Against Boys seem hardboiled in a sinister something-up-their-sleeve sense, and wicked handsome to boot—that they dress dapper for female fans who love their necks, even excelling at that fashion chicks dig so much where bangs fall in front of foreheads, makes them far more colorful than indie pop's prudish old ascetic monk aesthetic. And where Jon Spencer's snazzy hair and suits contradict his music's pathetic fear of being musical, these strapping young specimens (from NYC via DC), whose mailboxes may well match Spencer's for perfume residue, at least counter their skunk-gunk with vocal hooks sometimes. This is their most consistently fabulous record, despite (or because of) fleeting flirtations with sampled technotronics and industrial percussion clank and inhale/exhale production and Eurogothpop stained glass sheen. Words about mambos, too, but what GVSB still mainly add up to is just a better-than-most Fall tribute band—spasmodically declaimed live-wire shouts over choppy (louder-than-Fall) riffbuzz overload; forced trance rhythm made dense by two bassists in place of peak-period (c. 1982) Fall's two drummers.

79. THE PIXIES

Death to the Pixies 4AD/Elektra, 1997; rec. 1987-1991

They were apparently too lazy to write coherent lyrics, and some of Black Francis's vocal affectations are more irritating than others—best thing you can say about his asinine monster-screech is that he sets it to better music than Pantera. But more than indie stars that came directly before (Hüsker Dü) or after (Pavement) them, the Pixies did manage an early-Cars-era sort of new wave bounce that can pack a bit of bang when the guitars on top are walking the line between surf music and Ted Nugent. Nirvana learned a thing or two from both the riffs and loud/quiet mix on this here best-of, which showcases infrequent moments of rockabilly, reggae, robotic-ness, backwoods blues shtick, simulated sex, Spanish, and country as well, though (by the way) country's *real* black Francis at the time was African-American smoothie *Cleve* Francis, a moonlighting cardiologist who hit the C&W charts with, no shit, "You Do My Heart Good." And Black Francis seems even more damnably minor compared to, say, Pere Ubu's David Thomas, who his physique and mental condition re-mind me of. His songs are mainly frivolous cannabis cartoons in the worthy tradition of Steve Miller, Wings, and T. Rex, only not as good. "Here Comes Your Man," basically a Velvet Underground/Beach Boys pastiche, gets more sweetness out of its box-cars than R.E.M. or Joe Ely ever did; "Hangwire"'s chorus crosses Die Kreuzen's "Live Wire" with the Stones' "Hang Fire" though its verses are more Devo. I also love the one about marijuana if you got some gouge away, but I can't stand the one where the monkey gets his head bonked then goes to heaven. On the live disc apparently included to drive *Death to the Pixies'* price up and artistic value down, Francis attempts more stupid tongue tricks, and girly-girl Kim Deal duets with him more. Easy to see how what passed for a generation found these guys fun; hard to figure why anybody found them important.

80. CORNERSHOP
. . . .
Hold On It Hurts Merge, 1993

Outside of Ohio at least, nobody lately has done more with Velvet Underground repetitive ragga-trance basslines than these Punjabi sons of Delmore Schwartz. They beef up their foreign-exchange-stu-dent bovine-worship beats into feedback raveups out of "Sister Ray" and Jimi Hendrix; "Tera Mera Pyar" is even a remarkable facsimile of the Velvets' bloody yarn "The Gift." They're a bit eager to curry our fla-vor with aimless eclecticism, though—open with a

song named after a teenybop star, do one called "Born Disco, Died Heavy Metal," do preacher-sam-pling *My Life in the Bush of Ghosts* malarkey, and end with a number plinked out on toy organ followed by a Mekons-style counterfeit Dave Dudley trucker par-ody about corned beef hash. They also often tend to damage their own melodies by intentionally muf-fling and distancing vocals, and their English-language singing always sounds blanky (and Beckly) unemo-tional compared to their yoga-guru singing, and for Indians they're sure awful British, quoting "Heaven Knows I'm Miserable Now" by the Smiths and I bet the *Daily Mail*, whining about "racist, sexist, homo-phobic" something or other. There's too much "fight the powers that be," too little "Summer Fun in a Beat-up Datsun," but the band eventually figured that out on their own. *Hold On* is more protesty and also more metal-noisy and less pointless-breakdance-beat-instrumental-oriented than Cornershop's later albums, but also not nearly as beautiful and thus not half as good. Even here, it's the idyllic sitar sides that stand out, jammies like "Kalluri's Radio" and "Coun-teraction"—the latter of which interrupts its Hinduis-tic chanting with gunshots.

81. GUNS N' ROSES
. . . .
Use Your Illusion II Geffen, 1991

"**G**et in the Ring" is one of the few songs on either *Illusion* that rocks *at all*, not to mention the only time Axl's hate hits paydirt; even its embarrassing parts are aimed at rock critics, always a fun target. The "seen that movie too" amid "You Could Be Mine"'s bitch-slap rappin' and slap-rap bitchin' and metal-disco machinations is a *Goodbye Yellow Brick Road* rip, as are piano parts elsewhere. The Celtic Frosty sex-grunt "My World" is intriguing just because it's so in-ane. In "Shotgun Blues" Axl walks the line but somebody keeps moving it; in "Pretty Tied Up" an aging rock band becomes a joke; "Breakdown" and "Estranged" have heart-startle turnarounds. And of the countless foolish reasons why I convinced myself

"Civil War" foretold the Gulf War, a few almost still make sense: (1) Its *Cool Hand Luke* sample (which makes for a perfect voicemail message: "what we've got here is a failure to communicate, some men you *just can't reach*") could be Bush addressing the nation about Hussein. (2) There's stuff about never falling for Vietnam but now having genocidal blood on your hands. (3) We're fighting over the "promised land" (think Bible, not Berry/Springsteen). (4) From Iraq's perspective, it really *was* a civil war.

82. THE AFGHAN WHIGS
. . . .
Honky's Ladder Mute UK import EP, 1996

Cincinnati throbbers Afghan Whigs put some neurosis back into sex, a good thing since by the mid-'90s so many bald penis-lookalikes like R. Kelly and Aaron Hall were always on TV slurping about sex like they're *comfortable* with it. Also, the drummer and bassist try soul-music stuff (which unfortunately comes out more like Gang of Four stuff), giving the band's not-unchunky mood-jangle forward motion as long as the singer stays in his wound-up and wounded Jim Morrison mode. In their intense-enough 1994 MTV hit "Gentleman," Greg Dulli said indecision was his enemy. But too many of his vocals sound indecisive and hushed anyway, and too many of his lyrics are inarticulate going-to-hell-for-sins nonsense. On *Honky's Ladder*, the title track has a constipated got-you-where-I-want-you-motherfucker push to it, "Blame, Etc." gets its chorus melody from "Have You Never Been Mellow" by Olivia Newton-John, and Dulli's overmannered suffering-romantic reading of "If I Only Had a Heart" rocks less than when the Tin Woodsman did it. But his "Creep" almost works—doesn't quite capture the Georgia grits-and-gravy of TLC's original, but it's less disjointed, and Dulli's codeined vocal sounds less detached than TLC's hoarse red-haired chick (who always thinks she's being so sultry) did. Plus, the cheating lyric does fairly flesh out Dulli's sullenly obsessive slime-ball-sex-object shtick.

83. MOCKET
. . . .
Bionic Parts Punk in My Vitamins EP, 1996

Two boys and one girl from Olympia, Washington, Mocket's voices and guitars turn nervous squalls and squiggles and squoogles sounding like Voivod starting up car engines into tough little cyborg rhythms. Multiply this by retro futurism out of quaint old nuclear synthesizers plus toolbox-untuned Sonic Youth guitar racket and you better stand back, but even the Theremin breaks happen within the structural context of nicely concise songs: the CD runs just 21:41, which divided by eleven averages out to under two minutes per track. Instruments stop and start in sudden sproings, choppiness more the main point than chops; the sputtering harks back to provincial dance-this-mess-around keyboard post-punk of the early '80s, when skinny white guys with skinnier ties were turning funkbeats Japanese at tempos enabling numerous new kinds of nerd-motion. Matt Steinke's physics-grad monotone inevitably gets upstaged by the autistic arm-flailing girlsqueak-through-her-nose of charmer Audrey Marrs, who plays bass and beatbox, and whose "go! go! go!" cheerleading punctuates Steinke's silly spurts about (are-we-not)-(six-million-dollar)-men manning mean machines: recharging batteries, radio-free shortwave static inside our ears.

84. SOUNDGARDEN
. . . .
A-Sides A&M, 1997; rec. 1986-1996

I probably have the strangest relationship to Soundgarden of anybody on the planet, since the only music I'm familiar with by them is (1) their *really* early Sub Pop 45-and-EP junk that only absolutely devout record collectors know (which I heard since I actually used to review it in my "Selectric Funeral" column in *Creem Metal* in the mid-'80s; future millionaire Bruce Pavitt used to send me test pressings with notes attached, which if I'd saved I might be a millionaire myself), and (2) their much-later MTV hits that every teenage girl in America knows. Nothing in between, because I'd stopped paying attention. (I've had similar experiences with techno music, White Zombie, the Butthole Surfers, lots of stuff.) Anyway, this best-of CD just came in the mail to me the day before I gotta turn the book into the publisher (hence this entry is gonna be way too fucking long, but I'm on deadline, so edit it down yourself, okay?), and what I like on it is "Black Hole Sun" (only time Soundgarden sound like a garden, Frank Kogan says—and I say said garden *does* seem to exist on a humid summer day when the sun's only now coming out to wash away the rain); "Ty Cobb" (their fastest, not about .400 batting averages and you can tell it's supposed to be hardcore punk because the words are "go ahead and fuck you all" crap, though it sounds more like an imitation of one of those old virtuoso-rhythmed/high-pitch-speed-toasted "Dead End Job"/"Landlord"/"Fall Out" early Police *fake*-punk B-sides not unlike the Bad Brains' "Pay to Cum" or the Beastie Boys' "Sabotage" were except more square-dance-fiddled); "Spoonman" (you know they wack that spoon-player upside his fool head if he tries that spoon shit on the band bus, same thing my bro-in-law Marvin used to say about the human beat box fatso in the Fat Boys, but outside of his spoon-jazz solo this really does sound like it could've been a hard rock hit in the early '70s, and *not* just because it's about Indians); "Rusty Cage" (where their Zep-roiling actually manages Zep's *energy* for once and their words actually add up to something approaching emotion, since despite all his rage Chris Cornell's still just a rat in a cage); "Pretty Noose" (doomy Joy Division I-heard-the-noose-today-oh-boy melody since Chris don't like what we got him hangin' from); "Burden in My Hand" (worth two by Bush, thanks to those "Bohemian Rhapsody" laments about just having murdered somebody); "Outshined" (prettified Sabbath-trudge about "looking California but feeling Minnesota, oh yeah"); "Blow Up the Outside World" (explosive title plus late-Beatle melody worthy of, uh, Stone Temple Pilots). On other days, Soundgarden expand and contract their Zep rhythms fairly proficiently, but they trudge too much (especially in "Fell On Black Days," a truly overrated blues bore), and

they've got almost none of Zep's senses of humor or un-imitative magnificence. Phallus-proud Chris mentions his "snake" in three different songs, and how that makes him any less retarded than when his band's most obvious Zeppelin-tribute-band predecessors named themselves Whitesnake kind of eludes my comprehension. Early on, especially, the songwriting is full of filibustering baloney, and the playing (especially in "Jesus Christ Pose") is limited to coldly impressive precision that I can't relate to nearly as much as, say (still speaking of gardens) Savage Garden (most metal song: "Break Me Shake Me"). And I might not be alone: when I saw Soundgaren second-headline behind Metallica at Lollapalooza in 1996, I swear I didn't see a fan in a Soundgarden T-shirt all day (Rancid and AC/DC and even Sid Vicious shirts were more popular), suggesting they may well simply be one of those background-for-day-to-day-activities crews that nobody actually *cares* about—a soundgardentrack, you might say.

85. ARTIFICIAL JOY CLUB
Melt Crunchy/Interscope, 1997

At first called Sal's Birdland, whose CD went "double plywood" according to singer Sal, Ottawa's Artificial Joy Club share Canadian-content overemoting proclivities with Alanis Morissette, Jane Child, even Celine Dion, except with guitars frequently as loud as their mouths. They brag about getting feet stuck in bionic orifices in "I Say," which sounds like if Alanis did "Smells Like Teen Spirit." Sort of Sheryl Crow on a sugar high, Sal's as addicted to popular tabloid urban folklore culture as to her own verbosely vacuous wordplaying diarrhea, which she tries her best not to pretend is anything else. She imagines getting "porked" by Martians and wed to rednecks, tells us Capricorn's her starsign, awaits her publisher's clearing house check. *Melt* might just be the buzzword-per-minute champ of '90s rock: chatlines, tongue V-chips, lesbian porn, badda bing badda boom, cheeky monkeys, Brady Bunch lunches, Forest

Gump, "attitude," shut up shut up, she's giving up. It's hard not to sneak peeks at the lyric sheet. One song starts "rah rah rah," the next one "blah blah blah." The modern-rock hit "Sick & Beautiful" opens with a mangled Smashing Pumpkins quote about ashtrays, then Sal begs you to light her up and butt her. "Spaceman" is a strummy *Ziggy Stardust* tribute, and the finale is a waltz about a drunken Vietvet next door and his drunken wife who swap 911 calls now instead of body fluids. The sound is a swoopy but stocky blat with funky wah-wahs turning grunge as the generally-definable beat turns disco; Sal's dippy gulps and yelps now and then get lost in the throb. But she's no shrinking violet—inside the sleeve, she's even pissing into a urinal.

86. GREEN DAY
. . . .
Insomnia Reprise, 1995

Too often this financially failed followup to the megaplatinum *Dookie* leaves me twiddling thumbs between climaxes—"Jaded"'s just speed-for-speed's-sake hardcorps pandering, and you could chop off the first and last few songs and not lose much. The momentum picks up a pinch with the Stooges groove of "Geek Stink Breath," but that doesn't stop the song from being the band's most ignorable MTV hit ever. So *Insomnia* doesn't really start cranking until track *six*, the totally wound-up and spring-loaded "Bab's Uvula Who?," where Billie Joe gobs about his knack for fucking everything up. Still seems, though, that this onetime silly-love-song addict could do worse than place a *moratorium* on slamdance slogans like "fucked up" (and "bored" and "self-destruction"), and he's too quick to assume that ascendant chorus phrases will save him from his teeter-totter verse mumbling. But now and then, they do: the bus-stop breakup ditty "Stuart and the Ave" is bouncy girl-problem angst, and the Glenn Branca-conducting-"Pinball Wizard" foreplay opening up "Panic Song" is positively prog by Green Day standards. "Brain Stew" is an even more metal departure, lowdown-

slow, with a clompy robot-gunk riff waiting for the break of day and feeling like it ought to sleep and sitting cross-legged on the floor like it's 25 or 6 to 4. Half-zonked but unstoppable—an appropriately bloodshot insomnia sound.

87. MISSION OF BURMA
. . . .
Signals, Calls, and Marches Rykodisc, 1997; rec. 1980-1981

Ivy League looking nurd-rock pioneers from Boston in neurotically normal clothes (like I wear myself—no wonder critics loved them so much) trying to appear intense on the inner sleeve while the rest of their inner sleeve lists all the words from their lyrics in alphabetical order (longest being "perpendicular" and "Elysian") and their draft-table-designed outer sleeve revels in comforting mathematical precision (in the great geometry-punk tradition of Wire), Mission of Burma were almost certainly victims of overprotective toilet training practices. In their truly intense "That's When I Reach For My Revolver," they complain about how mom and dad taught them boundaries and the virtues of restraint and they used to have heroes but that's all behind them now so watch out for stray bullets. Their almost-as-intense "Academy Fight Song" is some herky beef jerky, possibly about fencing contests in prep school hallways. "All World Cowboy Romance" is loud Muzak washing you from all angles, and "Max Ernst" is named after a German anarchist decal-frottage artist from the outset of the century. The rhythm is a rigid rumble, scritching sub-Gang-of-Four one-step-forward-two-steps-back march-funk at best. And the vocals are psycho-killer semaphore signals, a Morse-Code missing link between *Talking Heads '77* and "Cannonball" by the Breeders, willing to project but not willing to have a personality. Give or take guitarist Roger Miller, who curdles and convulses and whooshes his tremolo towards snipers in the university belltower, the whole band sounds rather afraid to let go.

88. THE GATHERING
. . . .
Nighttime Birds Century Media, 1997

I've long figured that Metallica would be better if they'd just stick to *pretty* parts; they've never been as transcendent as the doomed opening of their early teen-suicide epic "Fade to Black." Nordic clans Tiamat and the Gathering are what could have happened if, instead of collapsing into a Satanic wrestling match, "Fade to Black"'s arrangement had just kept getting more resplendent instead: synth, flute, pianos, wind-chimes, tambourines, female voices, Latin mass yodel-ing between "Ave Maria" and "Hocus Pocus," wooden shoes, you name it. The wigwam tom-tommed title track of *Nighttime Birds* has fanciful words about noc-turnal migration, but the big deal is the singing. Cute-as-a-bug Anneke van Giersbergen, hair shorter than any of the Dutchboys' in her band, was hired at 21 in 1994 to write and soar, so now the Gathering get played on Netherlands pop radio and draw death-metal's most female audience ever. Goth crowds dig her too, but Anneke's magnificent every-word-a-high-quivering-crescendo rafter-shaking, entirely devoid of passive-aggressive ice-queen frigidness, is more in the decades-latent double-duchess tradition of goddess-on-mountaintop Mariska "Venus" Veres of Shocking Blue. *Maybe* with smidgens of Janita Haan (Babe Ruth), Sonja Kristina (Curved Air), and Anisette (of Danish '70s Greil Marcus *Stranded* discography ob-scuros Savage Rose) tossed in.

89. D GENERATION
. . . .
D Generation Chrysalis/EMI, 1994

These New York mascara-abusers are only as itchy-scratchy as the fake Guns N' Roses party band in the first episode of *My So-Called Life*, but I don't mind: they also have hair like Rayanne, the sluttiest girl on the show! Their songs concern being trapped in the city, selling drugs, agreeing with Claire Danes that cafe-terias are the embarrassment capitol of the world like a prison movie (well sort of), and making out with someone curiously resembling Ricky, the bisexual boy on *My So-Called Life* who frequents girls' restrooms. The latter topic shows up in "Frankie," which has Bo Diddley drums and is one of four truly *fast* numbers; too much of the slower stuff veers toward sappy Soul Asylum slop, though "Vampire Nation" is a bass-elastic brooder about being a lunatic street person. "Degen-erated" ("Johnny don't care about the world as long as he can fuck his girl and prove that he's a man") is a fu-riously cheerful Hanoi Rocks/Ramones pastiche with furiously pissed *a cappella* wah-wah solos; another song has an extended "Surfin' Bird" "ooma-mow" break. On their 1996 followup, rerecording a few songs and pretending to write some new ones for a different label, they came off like a damn college radio band.

90. THE ZEROS
. . . .
4-3-2-1 . . . Zeros Restless, 1991

They start out by introducing themselves one-by-one, so I will too: Sammy Serious looks sensitive and has a ricepaper fetish, Joe Normal reads the *National Enquirer* and uses baby's teething rings as shoulder epaulets, Danny Dangerous carries around dynamite and dresses like a mâitre' d', and Mr. Insane wears a straightjacket and uses his drumstick as a bone in his hair. They all wear hi-hi-hi-top tennis shoes going up to their knees topped by a rainbow of colors topped by lion manes sprouting like grape cotton candy, and they all serve as missing links between Poison and Green Day. Very suburban, very Hollywood, very simple, their toons are unthreatening and undeep and unconcerned with impressing you enough to de-serve their own Saturday morning TV show. A cou-ple are just cheers or chants or countdowns; the rest are speedy miniature powerchord powerpop blasts plus a ballad or three, cleanly produced, with swishily pretty but raggedy harmonies worthy of Redd Kross. All about girls, needless to say—sticky sweeties chewing gum and meeting Zeros for coffee and missing curfew and taking Zeros home to meet

Mom; death rock babes who fall for Zeros when what Zeros really want is rich chicks, but love's not fair. My favorite is the bittersweet outcast plaint "Society"—about a young lady who doesn't mind that Zeros have big noses and untied laces and big purple hair they don't comb.

91. TED NUGENT

Spirit of the Wild Atlantic, 1995

Damn near half of these twelve songs spell out why the buck stops at his bow and arrow, overkill even by Tedly's deadly standards. The seven-minute mammal-murdering expedition "Fred Bear" mixes Who keyboards with James Gang guitars for some epic trailblazer tragedy, then "Primitive Man" climaxes with naked guys drumming on tree stumps. The big statement comes when Ted aims the speedy snot-and-response "Kiss My Ass," his snappiest and funniest shout in years (equates letting a dog hump his shin with animal rights!), at leftie straw persons like Janet Reno, the U.N., President "Billary," and (my personal favorite) Courtney Love. The only other track that overturns police cars like classic '70s Nuge is the semi-overlong roadkill-riffed street-riot reaction "Just Do It Like This." But *Spirit* is still extroversion with a big beat—"I Shoot Back" is an Amboy-acid-axed take on "There Was a Time" by James Brown as Michael Douglas might've sung it in *Falling Down*, and "Lovejacker's barefoot-and-boppy beach-soul and "Hot or Cold"'s shattered Stones cloning are more evidence that being a horny old geezer of 46 just means Ted was paying attention way back when frat-party rock used to *dance*. Like he says, "everybody sucks, but I suck less." If you can't stand the heat, get out of his firing sector.

92. THE SMASHING PUMPKINS

Bullet With Butterfly Wings Virgin promo cassette EP, 1996

Their first few MTV songs always used to hit me like amorphous pissant hissy fits; whenever Billy Corgan's inflection disappeared into the woodwork like some susurrating cadaver, I wanted to inflict bodily harm on the maroon. But by 1996 I was starting to get off on his artificiality—from the distance of a party at the other end of the block, his clothespinned-nostrils falsetto occasionally even reminds me of Axl Rose, the *king* of despite-all-my-rage-I-am-still-just-a-rat-in-a-cage. Intoxicated by madness, I fell in love with his sadness for a month or two, so while no way will I ever make it through any of his two-disc monstrosities (cool kids never have the time), I will admit to enjoying most of his big hits: "Butterfly with Butterfly Wings," "Butter With Bulletfly Wings," "Pumpkin With Smashed Wings," "Dead Keyboard Player I Never Heard of Before With Angel Wings," "Rat With Butterfly Wings," "Rat With Zero Wings," "Rat With 1979 Wings" (two songs with numbers in the title!), "The One Where They Toilet-Paper Trees and Terrorize Convenience Stores," "The One Where Moon Aliens Get Whacked Upside the Head by Umbrellas," the loud ones, the pretty ones, you name it (and you and I should meet) . . . well, anyway, hardly any of said smasheroos actually show up on this tape (which stupidly is commercially available only as one-fifth of a tedious box set); what you mostly get instead are a handful of likable remakes of old new wave classics by Missing Persons and the Cars and Blondie and, most notably, Alice Cooper. Whose "Clones" suggests that Billy Corgan may well be the only android on earth who agrees with me that Alice's 1980 skinny-tie/short-hair bandwagon jump *Flush the Fashion* is still his best album since 1971.

93. FLUFFY

Black Eye The Enclave, 1996

Avoiding the grating tantrums riot grrrls love so much, bopping as catchily as Elastica at their rare best and as hard and fast as P. J. Harvey at hers, mostly what this all-female Brit foursome's crass reduction of supposedly classic noise does is weed out the boring parts. Their guitars aren't terribly different from a zillion riot grrroups dating back to Frightwig feminizing Flipper riffs in mid-'80s San Francisco: a loud, repetitive clang, hardcore slowed down or sludge-metal speeded up, seasoned slightly by surf and Hendrix, quick enough to kick without being too hasty to be tasty. But the snotty richness and sexy hoarseness of Amanda Rootes's battery-acid-bedraggled growl doesn't cartoon itself into a creature feature; in her high register she snarls sarcasm like Johnny Rotten, and in "Too Famous" she captures the torrid thump and brazen buffoonery Kim McAuliffe perfected back in England's all-time greatest femme-rock band Girlschool. Fluffy's best song, "Deny Everything"—advice about how you gain nothing from admitting to your mate you've been fooling around elsewhere—is oddly available only on their earlier *Five Live* EP. But the longplayer still brims with recognizable slices of human life. In "Technicolor Yawn" ("Bed of Vomit" on the EP), Rootes even wakes up in puke. Let's hope it was her own.

94. JET CIRCUS

Step On It Word/Epic, 1990

First I got suspicious about how Jet Circus are a metal "band" with just two people in it. Then I noticed their CD starts with a rapped "Victory Dance" mixing big bad blooze-squeal scats with cutiepie astrobilly beats, plus they cover "Be Bop A Lu La," so I figured they must be Sigue Sigue Sputnik rejects cashing in their hot licks on one last journeydude fling. Then I heard one of 'em (Ez Gomer, I hope) yowl in yeasty gutturals not very unlike Leather Nun, so I checked the notes and found out, sho'nuff, Jet Circus are *Swedish*. Then somebody 'splained me how Word isn't Epic's Swede subsidiary but rather a *Christian* label, after which I noticed how on the cover one of 'em's stepping on a skull (guess that's the "it"). I haven't the slightest what this has to do with Christianity, and ditto for Terry Haw's Sir-Lord-Baltimore-via-Iron-Maiden fork-scraping-blackboard shriek-drama. I suppose applesauce about "blood of Jesus Christ" *is* blatant once you read the lyric sheet and find out it's there, but put-ons like the part where the Steppenwolfish grime stops and somebody says "excuse me, you know God *loves* bass guitar" are more up this duo's alleyway. The only critic they're out to dazzle is their chosen diety, so as long as they get their message out they're free to treat religion like just another excuse to throw mudpies.

95. THEE HYDROGEN TERRORS

Terror, Diplomacy & Public Relations Load, 1997

Rhode Islanders who put out their homemade record themselves, Thee Terrors churn out a curmudgeonous rant-punk that crosses the Fall (especially in "Radio Saturn vs. Hackamore Brick," rhyming with "the walls of my library are three feet thick" and partly named for an obscure 1970 Velvet Underground tribute band known only by Greil Marcus) with the Butthole Surfers singing about brown heroin ("Mexico") with Pere Ubu (Crocus Behemoth falsetto before "Superstar" reverts into a screaming mess) with the Contortions (tensely twined rhythms all over and "Whiskey Terror"'s no wave free jazz sax solo) with too many late '80s post-hardcore dorks I've long happily forgotten. When I saw them live, *Stairway to Hell* fan Guy Benoit stood sideways to sing and pulled his mike chord into the men's room and shut the door. Here, he chronicles the routineness of life, pays homage to Henry Mancini and Andy Warhol in his titles, names another "Sissy

Bar" (about a bike part or a homosexual drinking establishment?), plays characters much older than himself, and ends with an incongruously polite and lengthy PBS-documentary-like list of liner note explanations. There's less than 25 minutes of actual "songs." But two tracks, one of which starts with a snippet of salsa, are inept mixmaster screwing around (courtesy one "DJ Hono") that in Prodigy's Era you can almost get away with counting as "music."

96. THE UPPER CRUST
. . . .
Let Them Eat Rock Upstart, 1995

These brash Boston bluebloods (Lord Bendover, Lord Rockingham, The Duc d'Istortion, The Marquis de Rocque, Jackie Kickassis) wear Louis XIV wigs, powdered faces and royal robes, and they pretend to be rich. It's a totally singleminded gag, but at least partly because said tycoons do rhythm and melody and double-entendres like AC/DC hasn't since Bon Scott died, their jokes manage to be songs first, parodies second. Like, "Let Them Eat Rock" is ostensibly AC/DC's "Let There Be Rock" as done by Marie Antoinette (hence the guillotinest French Revolution anthem since Mel Brooks's '82 rap "It's Good to be the King," if not Queen's "Killer Queen"), but actually it protests the Peculiar Plight of Poor People, sickly pale ones sorting through trash behind your favorite posh eatery: "They're thin as a rail, I don't know what in the hell they want." Likewise, the brisk blues "Friend of a Friend of the Working Class" exhibits an empathy for the masses that makes workclothes-wearing mogul Bruce Springsteen sound like Spinal Tap: "Your lot is a hard one, or so I have heard." Other themes include locating good help, Little Lord Fauntleroy's transvestite tendencies, and what the Crust's Boston ancestors the J. Geils Band once called "First I Look at the Purse." "Little Rickshaw Boy." which spoilsports might call racist, frames itself between a Vapors "Turning Japanese" start and a coda where rapid guitars mimic koto music. My only real complaint is that the disc omits the Crust's earlier demo-tape tune "Badminton"—I miss hearing them say "shuttlecock."

97. KIK TRACEE
. . . .
No Rules RCA, 1991

Like Bang Tango and Slaughter, Kik Tracee turn postZep prog changes into mucky Top 40 hooks, letting quiet rusticness and loud tech merge into a wicked flow. Stephen Shareaux whipcracks boisterously like Axl, nose clogged and mouth full and wailing postSupremes asides: "and there ain't nothin' you can do about it." Hidden in the pantry with your cupcakes, his "Mrs. Robinson" remake ranks with the cutest GnR parodies ever. Too much of the rest is gratuitously noisy elephant stomp changing tempos and wanking off, but there's a psychedelic nuggetness to the silly lyrical pretensions and odd production touches. "Trash City" is a police-sirened "Welcome to the Jungle" facsimile; "Tangerine Man" marries the Byrds' "Tambourine Man" with Zeppelin's "Tangerine"; "Generation Express" stutters like "My Generation" and turns mechanical claps into a train clickity clack; "Hard Time" rocks hard about how easy-looking girls make boys feel hard; "Soul Shaker" puts Enigma monk-howls above clodhop Cult funk (sneaky since its title comes from "Love Removal Machine"), succeeding as soul music if only in the Collective Soul/"Soul Stripper" (by AC/DC) sense. Climax is the transcendent way "Big Western Sky" drives Kik Tracee's shooting-star car into California, right back where they started from.

98. THE YOUNG GODS
. . . .
The Young Gods Wax Trax, 1990; rec. 1987

Zurich's singing/drumming/guitar-riff-sampling power trio the Young Gods wear a shitlike substance on their bare chests (it's supposed to look "primeval"), and they sound like shit, too. That's what I like about them. It's robot shit, chewed-up concrete (as in *musique*), wildly dense and lumpy. Rhythm section ain't shit (drummer needs lambada lessons), but hey, nobody's perfect. They use samplers not to quote memories but (in theory) as sound machines per se; on record, there's no way to be sure the landmine feedback and lightning bolt beauty are Memorex— you'd need headphones to identify *any* of the undigested bows, buttons, horn charts, and moody melodies lost deep in their stool. Immersed in urban sewage, Franz Treichler's mad harsh bistro gutturals fall emotionally flat; his most moving moment is a Gary Glitter cover. Still, these oily Schoenberg-fixated wackos take fiery-esophagus Eurodrama so far overboard it's hard not to be amused. What makes them grade-A threepenny-slopera Swiss cheese isn't their intense romantic souls or newfangled instrumentation, but rather just that their paint job is so collosally congealed: to paraphrase Robert Christgau, their samplers sound like guitars that sound like synths that sound like cement mixers. As does their singer, but with a funny accent.

99. WHITE TRASH
¿Si O Si, Que? Elektra, 1994

They really try to *look* white trash. Album cover suggests they can dress snazzy in a midwestern prom date kinda way (white bucks, sky blue rental, fuzzy blue dice in their Lincoln Continental) when they want but more often wear Marvin the Martian or "Titties 'n Beer" T-shirts and smoke cigars and swig tequila. The guy in the Army jacket looks like Sean Penn. Their 1991 debut sunk into stiff mojo-minstrel funk (even a track titled "Good God," gawd) after its Axl-attempt first track, but White Trash 1994 is damn near a whole different ensemble, with brass section now thankfully stifled. Their metalfunk still might be a bit too much bassline, not enough everything else, but this time they're yanking painfully high vocal pitches through more transformations than you can tally, à la Love/Hate back in 1990. Opening cut once again is a

decent GnR rip, squeals stretching out "I don't give a daaaaaamn"s. "Got to Get Away" is noisy garagey escape-punk and "Señorita" says he'll leave her in the morning as well, but despite creative punctuation the bottle doesn't quite kick in til its final few ounces. "Come Tuesday" gives good uplift to plaints about being in love with a TV character; "21 Club" aims for disco; "Find Me Somebody" applies Sabbath rumbles and Zep shocks to comedy rhyming "comb your hair" with "kiss your derriere."

100. BOREDOMS
Soul Discharge Shimmy-Disc EP, 1990

On their LP cover, these Kabukiesque Japanese slapstickers wear K-Mart disco tank tops and Raiders sweatshirts and Devo goggles, and the "singer" (named Eye Y, I think—the sleeve credits him with "AAAHG") skydives and does *Heil Hitler* salutes like a Teenage Mutant Ninja Ramone. "TV Scorpion" opens by gunkifying Madonna the way Black Sabbath's "Children of the Grave" would've gunkified Blondie's "Call Me" if "Call Me" had come first instead of the other way around, then some stuttering-Martian scat-chatting hysteria evolves into potbellied pig squeals. "Sun, Gun, Run" commences with mystical Yes-notes beneath barking dogs and laughing hyenas on top, then turns into pure freejazzcore war-whoop anarchy where mental patients grunt as if kicked in the gut; "52 Boredom" hangs Godzilla-poop powerwah and geisha squeaks on the tail of "52 Girls" by the B-52s. Of course, by the '90s, the only thing more clichéd than a noise record or a bricolage record was a record that was both, even if it happened to be the most "extreme" (or "inaccessible," or how 'bout just "repulsively fucked-up") rock 'n' roll ever attempted. Plus, I still think it's possible I mighta been supposed to play the thing at 45 instead of 33.

ACKNOWLEDGMENTS

Countless people have helped me formulate the ideas I espouse in these pages, and there's no way I can list all of them, but a few deserve to get real mad if they don't see their names in print. At the top of the list have to be Robert Christgau, who started me writing at New York's *Village Voice* while I was still in the Army in Germany, no easy task, and Doug Simmons, his heir to the *Voice* music editor throne, who kept track of my many displacements since and managed to publish me once in a while anyway. Other editors who've earned specific plugs are Eric Weisbard at the *Voice*; Milo Miles, ex- of *The Boston Phoenix*, John Payne of *LA Weekly*; Nathan Brackett of *Rolling Stone*; and Dave Di-Martino, John Kordosh, and Bill Holdship, all at *CREEM*, whose greatness lasted much longer than many illiterates will ever admit. Certain entries herein are reprinted (generally in drastically altered form) from the above publications, and from *BAM* and *Spin* and *The First Rock & Roll Confidential Report* and *Buzz* and *Request* and a fanzine or two as well, and in more than one case more than a word came from the editor's head, not mine.

Christgau's Record Guide played a major role in inspiring both this book's form and its content, and if you don't own a copy, you should probably trade *Stairway to Hell* to somebody who's got doubles. Other texts that've taught me more than this one will ever teach you include Greil Marcus's *Stranded* and *Mystery Train*, Lester Bangs's *Psychotic Reactions and Carburetor Dung*, Richard Meltzer's *The Aesthetics of Rock*, Simon Frith's *Sound Effects: Youth, Leisure, and the Politics of Rock 'n' Roll* and *Music for Pleasure*, Dave Marsh's *Fortunate Son* and *Rolling Stone Record Guide*, and several essays in *The Rolling Stone Illustrated History of Rock & Roll*. Additional literary assistance on the musical tip came from, among other sources, *The Harmony Illustrated Encyclopedia of Rock* by Mike Clifford, *Rock from the Beginning* by Nik Cohn, *Hammer of the Gods* by Stephen Davis, *The Noise* by Robert Duncan, *The Sound of the City* by Charlie Gillett, *The New Trouser Press Record Guide* by Ira Robbins, *After the Ball* by Ian Whitcomb, and *Rock of Ages: The Rolling Stone History of Rock & Roll* by Ed Ward, Geoffrey Stokes, and Ken Tucker. Robbins is owed special thanks for answering some annoying questions over the phone about how to go about writing a book.

George Smith mailed me an immeasurably helpful three-page shopping list of obscure metal albums recommended for inclusion, a few of which I actually tracked down (usually at Wazoo Records in Ann Arbor, which as often as not didn't charge me for 'em); George also taped me a pile of good out-of-print stuff, and I hope not all of the punk rock I've included is too arty for him. Other loans and tapes came from Mike Rubin, Doug Sheppard, Chris Stigliano, Metal Mike Saunders, Michael

Freedberg, Laura Morgan, and Rob Michaels, the last of whom worked up some gigantic phone bills from law school straightening out various contradictions and confusions in those truths I deem self-evident. Jack Thompson, Chris Cook, Richard C. Walls, Richard Riegel, Phil Dellio, Robert Sheffield, Lisa Lacour, Arsenio Orteza, John Petkovic, Molly Priesmeyer, Sara Sherr, and Don Allred have all permanently altered my thinking about this band's strengths or that one's liabilities. The list goes on, but I want to make special note of Frank Kogan, whose off-the-left-field-wall elucidations inside and outside of his periodic *Why Music Sucks* pamphlet (a.k.a. *Why Mucous Slacks,* a.k.a. *Why Mildred Skis,* you get the idea) have damn near flip-flopped my sensibilities over these past few years.

I want to thank Michael Pietsch and Kathy Belden, this book's editors, for trusting my proposal, then helping me pull it off. I want to thank my mom, Margaret M. Eddy, without whom I would've spent my childhood in an orphanage somewhere. And I guess I better thank the bands who made the records, without whom I'd likely be slaving away as a cub reporter for some sleazy suburban weekly. In the immortal words of Jim Bouton, I'm glad you didn't take it personally—there's no stupidity or pretension I accuse anybody of in this volume that I'm not guilty of at some time or another myself. Read closely, and you'll be able to tear my thesis all to hell. If you can find it, that is.

ALBUM TITLE INDEX

INDEX TO THE *100* BEST HEAVY METAL ALBUMS OF THE *'90s*

· ·

The following pages list the 100 best album titles of the '90s, alphabetically by performer or group name; numbers in parentheses denote each title's position in the 100 entries. (See pages 275-284, for the index to the 500 best heavy metal albums in the universe.)

Other titles of interest

**THE ACCIDENTAL
EVOLUTION OF
ROCK'N'ROLL**
**A Misguided Tour Through
Popular Music**
Chuck Eddy
430 pp., 101 illus.
80713741-6 $15.95

THE AESTHETICS OF ROCK
Richard Meltzer
New introd. by Greil Marcus
360 pp., 14 illus.
80287-2 $11.95

ANTI-ROCK
The Opposition to Rock'n'Roll
Linda Martin and Kerry Segrave
382 pp.
80502-2 $14.95

ARE YOU EXPERIENCED?
**The Inside Story of the
Jimi Hendrix Experience**
Noel Redding and Carol Appleby
258 pp., 28 photos
80681-9 $14.95

**BOB DYLAN: THE EARLY
YEARS**
A Retrospective
Edited by Craig McGregor
New preface by Nat Hentoff
424 pp., 15 illus.
80416-6 $13.95

THE BOWIE COMPANION
Edited by Elizabeth Thomson and
David Gutman
304 pp., 15 illus.
80707-6 $14.95

CHRISTGAU'S RECORD GUIDE
The '80s
Robert Christgau
525 pp.
80582-0 $17.95

COUNTRY
The Twisted Roots of Rock 'n' Roll
Nick Tosches
New preface and appendix
290 pp., 54 illus.
80713-0 $13.95

**THE DA CAPO COMPANION
TO 20th-CENTURY
POPULAR MUSIC**
Phil Hardy and Dave Laing
1,168 pp.
80640-1 $29.50

THE DARK STUFF
**Selected Writings on Rock Music,
1972–1995**
Nick Kent
Foreword by Iggy Pop
365 pp.
80646-0 $14.95

ERIC CLAPTON
Lost in the Blues
Updated Edition
Harry Shapiro
256 pp., 50 photos
80480-8 $14.95

GIANTS OF ROCK MUSIC
Edited by Pauline Rivelli
and Robert Levin
125 pp., 24 photos
80148-5 $7.95

**THE HENDRIX
EXPERIENCE**
Mitch Mitchell and John Platt
176 pp., 201 illus.
(including 71 in color)
80818-8 $24.95

HEROES AND VILLAINS
The True Story of the Beach Boys
Steven Gaines
432 pp., 66 photos
80647-9 $14.95

**IT CRAWLED FROM
THE SOUTH**
An R.E.M. Companion
Fully Revised and Updated
Marcus Gray
560 pp., 48 photos
80751-3 $17.95

KEITH RICHARDS
The Biography
Victor Bockris
416 pp., 26 illus.
80815-3 $15.95

**THE LIFE AND TIMES OF
LITTLE RICHARD**
Updated Edition
Charles White
337 pp., 70 photos
80552-9 $13.95

NO COMMERCIAL POTENTIAL
The Saga of Frank Zappa
Updated Edition
David Walley
240 pp., 28 photos
80710-6 $13.95

NOWHERE TO RUN
The Story of Soul Music
Gerri Hirshey
416 pp., 26 photos
80581-2 $14.95

PIECE OF MY HEART
A Portrait of Janis Joplin
David Dalton
287 pp., 91 illus.
80446-8 $14.95

PINK FLOYD
**through the eyes of . . . the band,
its fans, friends and foes**
Edited by Bruno MacDonald
400 pp., 32 photos
80780-7 $14.95

ROCK ALBUMS OF THE 70s
A Critical Guide
Robert Christgau
480 pp.
80409-3 $16.95

SOUL MUSIC A-Z
Revised Edition
Hugh Gregory
390 pp., 48 photos
80643-6 $17.95

THE SOUND OF THE CITY
The Rise of Rock and Roll
Newly illustrated and expanded
Charlie Gillett
604 pp., 64 pp. of illus.
80683-5 $16.95

STRANDED
Rock and Roll for a Desert Island
Edited and with a new preface
by Greil Marcus
New foreword
by Robert Christgau
320 pp.
80682-7 $14.95

TRANSFORMER
The Lou Reed Story
Victor Bockris
464 pp., 32 photos
80752-1 $15.95

Available at your bookstore

OR ORDER DIRECTLY FROM

DA CAPO PRESS, INC.

1-800-321-0050